MONASTIC STUDIES

THE CONTINUITY OF TRADITION

Edited by

JUDITH LOADES

HEADSTART HISTORY

1990

HEADSTART HISTORY 1990
P.O. BOX 1
BANGOR
GWYNEDD LL57 1SB

ISBN 1 873041 00 4

Set by MARGOT LONG
Printed by COPYCAT, BANGOR
Bound by THOMAS LOUGHLIN, LIVERPOOL

CONTENTS

EDITOR'S PREFACE

The papers in this volume were read at the MONASTIC STUDIES conference which was held at University College of North Wales, Bangor in September 1989. I was honoured that invitations to give the main papers were so readily accepted by Professor Christopher Holdsworth (University of Exeter), Professor John Bossy (University of York) and Dom Aidan Bellenger (Monk of Downside). Others responded to my call for papers and this provided a wealth of scholarship on many aspects of the history and development of religious orders from their foundation until the twentieth century. In that context the robed presence of those in orders and the final words of Dom Aidan's talk was a reminder that they not only thrive but play an important role in our time.

This volume is a record of that conference. Some papers are missing either because they were not submitted, or, as is the case with Caroline Brett, Graham Loud, Dom Alberic Stacpoole and Marilyn Dunn, they had arranged for the papers to be published elsewhere. Both Jean Dunbabin and Frank Johnston had expected to be at the conference but were unable to attend at the last moment so their papers were read by Graham Loud and myself.

My interest in monasticism and medieval manuscripts began over twenty five years ago when I worked in the Codrington Library at All Souls College, Oxford, during the librarianship of Professor Ernest Jacob. The nature of my work, the fact that the library retained its own manuscript collection, and sheer proximity to the Bodleian meant that I was fortunate enough to know Dr Richard Hunt, Mr Neil Ker, Dr Beryl Smalley and the then holder of the Chichele Chair, Professor Richard Southern. Through them I learned to appreciate the exquisite beauty of such volumes as the Amesbury Psalter and the way of life which produced it.

It was a pleasure to bring together so many scholars of monasticism and my thanks go to them for making it so memorable. But there are other acknowledgements to record. I am grateful to the Duke of Beaufort and the National Library of Wales for allowing me to reproduce the maps in David Williams' article and to Tom Pollock of COPYCAT, Bangor for producing the design and artwork for the cover and for all other drawings and diagrams. On a personal note I must thank my husband, David Loades, Professor of History at University College of North Wales, Bangor. The production of this volume has meant that domestic chores have moved even farther down the line of priorities. In addition, any flat surface in the house which was not covered with his proofs was swiftly covered with mine. I offer him thanks and apologies.

MONASTIC STUDIES could not have been produced without the technical knowledge and skills of Margot Long. She has been a good friend for more years than either of us care to remember and she has been sorely tried these last few months. I am grateful to her and to Jane Roberts and Peter Biggs in Oxford. This is the first of the HEADSTART CONFERENCE volumes and my ignorance of all aspects of publishing were all too apparent to the staff of COPYCAT, Bangor. I must therefore record my thanks to Chris Gibbs and Kim Francis who have survived with great courtesy every problem with which they have been presented, and who have resolved every crisis. I owe them and all the staff a debt which goes beyond financial reward. I also record my thanks to Fiona Pinder who has helped me in the office so that I can be free to supervise publication. Hard work comes easily to me since application and tenacity of purpose was learned many years ago from my first husband, Dr Peter Atkins, Chemistry Fellow at Lincoln College, Oxford. I thank him for that important example.

In December 1970 Richard Hunt promised my newly—born daughter, Juliet, that as soon as she could read he would show her Duke Humfrey's Library so that she could be put on the right track for what really mattered. He carried out that promise when she was two and a half. I offer her a copy of this book as a reminder of the day she played with the gate at the Arts End and then, clutching the great man's hand, they set off on their tour. It must have worked since she is now reading history at University College, Swansea with a clear predilection for all things medieval.

I end by thanking those who support my work in any way for it is only with the encouragement and constructive criticism of those who participate in the various activities and publications I organise, that I can produce anything of value to the profession and the subject.

Judith Loades
Bangor, July 1990

EARLY EGYPTIAN MONASTICISM AND THE CHURCH

Graham Gould

The Egyptian Desert Fathers of the fourth and fifth centuries were the first Christians to articulate a specifically monastic version of the Christian way of life. This essay will consider some recent contributions to our understanding of the origins of monasticism in fourth century Egypt and particularly of its relations to the Church and Christian community as a whole.[1] An influential theory about early monasticism has seen it as a movement of protest against the secularisation of the Church, a rejection of the state–supported Christianity of the era of Constantine, and an attempt to return to the values of primitive Christianity and the 'hard sayings' of Jesus on poverty and renunciation.[2] The studies whose conclusions are to be discussed here will shed some light on the likely accuracy of this assessment, but they themselves start from different standpoints. They represent two important developments in the study of early monasticism: the increased availability of new evidence (in the form of published papyri) for the situation of the Church and monasticism in Egyptian society, and a renewed willingness to question the purpose and historical value of early monastic sources such as the *Life of Antony*[3] and the various lives of Pachomius.[4]

In an article published in 1977, E.A. Judge drew attention to a recent addition to a collection of papyrus documents, including several legal submissions and various business records, belonging to one Aurelius Isidore of Karanis and dating from between A.D. 267 and 324.[5] The new text, probably datable to 6 June 324, is Isidore's account of a physical assault upon him by two of his neighbours following a dispute. Pamounis and Harpalos attacked him with a club after he had stopped their cow grazing on his land, 'and if I had not obtained help from Antony, a deacon, and Isaac, a monk, who were passing by, they would quickly have finished me off all together'.[6] This comment is the earliest datable use in any source, literary or documentary, of the word μοναχος with the meaning 'monk'.

As Judge points out,[7] this document alone would have been sufficient to disprove the once popular theory that the rise of monasticism should be dated to the latter half of the fourth century and not, as the *Life of Antony* claims, to the last quarter of the third.[8] But its significance lies not in the bare reference to a monk but in the fact that this occurs in the context of a secular document belonging to an archive in which no other clear references to Christianity are preserved. In Judge's view this shows that by 324 the monk is a 'recognised figure in society',[9] that monasticism is a 'public institution'[10] whose members, designated by μοναχος or the equivalent term αποτακτικος, 'renouncer' enjoy 'a publicly recognised station in life of an occupational kind'.[11]

Judge goes on to argue that the use of these terms marks the emergence into public awareness of the male asceticism which had been traditional in the Church at least since the second century, and that what requires explanation in the early fourth century is not the presence of such asceticism but how its practitioners came to acquire a new social status and name[12]. He assembles the papyrological evidence for the existence of ascetic individuals or groups of 'brothers' during the late third and early fourth centuries, including those where the term αποτακτικος designates variously a scribe, a landholder, and parties to legal arrangements concerning property.[13]

Judge's reconstruction of the early history of monasticism on the basis of this evidence is not without its problems. His suggestion that the term μοναχσζ was first used for Christian ascetics in response to 'a feature that caught the popular eye (the "solitary" life–style, or a detail of dress?)' has not found favour,[14] though this does not affect the validity of the evidence he cites for the practice of asceticism in fourth century Egypt. More problematic is his attempt to define clearly the different *kinds* of ascetic whom we find in the evidence. He believes that the απστακτικσζ is a distinct 'urban category of monk', 'living still within his village, and participating actively in its civil and church affairs',[15] whose existence is recognised by writers such as Egeria, Jerome (who condemns them strongly) and the author of the *Historia Monachorum in Aegypto*.[16] He thinks that this church–based movement can be distinguished from the asceticism of Antony and that the total withdrawal from the community of figures like Antony 'must have seemed a kind of censure on' the απστακτικσί.[17] The problems with this reconstruction are as follows. First, Jerome's sharp contrast between the three forms of monk, anchorite, cenobite and (in Judge's view) απστακτικσζ is clearly both too schematic and too prejudiced to be taken at face value, and is not in fact supported by the *Historia Monachorum*, a text which unlike Jerome's letter) was written on the basis of direct knowledge of Egyptian conditions, and which does not regard monks who were found in the desert and those who lived in or near towns and villages as in any sense belonging to different classes.[18]

Second, the fact that the word μοναχσζ was applied both to figures such as Isaac of Karanis (who in Judge's view is a model απστακτικσζ, living in his village and closely involved with the life of the Church and community) and to anchorites such as Antony does not in fact suggest that in the eyes of contemporaries their asceticism belonged to different traditions.[19] Judge argues that Isaac and other early monks from the papyri prove that Athanasius was accurate in using the term μοναχσζ to refer to Antony in the period after his emergence from solitude in *c*.305 — 'the point at which the practice [of asceticism] became the centre of public excitement and began to constitute a social movement'.[20] This argument would be invalid if the two forms of asceticism were distinct and Antony was representative of a tradition of total withdrawal from the community.

Third, the papyrological evidence itself supplies no real support for the distinction. Two fourth century monks whose correspondence has been preserved, Apa Johannes and Apa Paphnutius, are considered by Judge as examples of the απστακτικσζ and anchorite respectively.[21] Johannes seems to be a member of a community of brothers and is involved in the legal affairs of his correspondents or clients. Paphnutius, detached from community affairs, is the true anchorite. But this contrast is overdrawn. Johannes is twice referred to as an anchorite, which proves that this term too belonged to both alleged kinds of monks. Paphnutius too has brothers dwelling with him and is involved in business affairs of some kind.[22] He may be more isolated from the worldly affairs in which Johannes is involved, but he is not demonstrably a different sort of monk.

Fourth, and most important, Judge makes little use of the evidence of the *Life of Antony* itself, despite his frequent contrasts between the anchorite monasticism represented by Antony and the type represented by Isaac. The *Life* provides a clear picture of Antony's origins in the ascetic tradition of his day. Following his decision to dispose of his possessions and follow an ascetic life he continued to live near his own home, 'for monasteries were not yet common in

Egypt, and no monk knew anything of the far desert: each who wished to pay attention to his way of life lived alone and practised asceticism not far from his own village'.[23] Antony proceeded to learn the ascetic life and virtues from some of these men before making his own radical move, departure into more complete solitude first by hiding himself in a tomb and then in the desert.[24] Here surely is an account of the pre—monastic forms of asceticism, local to the village or community, which can be confirmed from Judge's presentation of the evidence from the papyri. There is no need to see Antony's asceticism as differing from that of the common ascetic tradition of the Egyptial Church as represented by his teachers. Before his withdrawal to the desert he (and presumably they) was no solitary but continued to be involved with and respected and loved by the villagers as a 'friend of God'.[25] His position was perhaps not dissimilar from that of Johannes or Paphnutius. A remarkable letter addressed to Paphnutius by Valeria may illustrate something of what was meant when Antony was described as a friend of God: 'I believe that through your prayers I will receive healing, for through ascetics and devotees revelations are made known'.[26] What distinguishes Antony is his move to the desert, seen by the *Life* as a natural consequence of his desire to serve God further in asceticism and personal conflict with demonic temptations.[27] There is no reason to think that his move marks a *rejection* of his 'roots' in the older ascetic tradition, or that it marks in itself a rejection of the Church as a whole as subject to secularisation or dilution of its ideals. The papyrological evidence for fourth century asceticism supplies, in other words, some support for the *Life of Antony's* picture of the emergence of monasticism as a natural outgrowth from a Christian community which was already disposed to admire the ascetic life.[28]

These general observations on the papyrological evidence for fourth century asceticism and its agreement with the account found in the *Life of Antony* form a necessary preliminary to a more specific (although in this context, necessarily selective) discussion of the relations between monasticism and the wider Christian community as they are presented in the lives of Antony and Pachomius. This is a subject profoundly affected, as was indicated above, by new questions about the historical value of these sources raised in recent work. For Michael Williams it is a mistake to regard the *Life of Antony* as a historical source at all.[29] It must be read against the background of the many images of Antony which we may assume to have been current in the fourth century, including those which presented him as a gnostic visionary or a charismatic figure isolated from ordinary society and dependent for the development of his religious ideals not on scripture, tradition and practical reflection on his ascetic experience but on personal revelations of esoteric spiritual wisdom. In reaction against this picture Athanasius diverted attention from Antony's possession of an unpredictable and anti—hierarchical charisma by drawing him back into the normal society of other monks and laity to whom he acts as a healer and spiritual guide.[30]

Williams' account does not seem particularly plausible. Timothy Barnes has argued that the Greek Text of the *Life* is a transcription of a Coptic original which may have been written by a close disciple of Antony:[31] if this is so, then generalised attacks on the historicity of the *Life* becomes more difficult to justify. But the specific problem of Antony's relation to other monks and lay people is one on which our previous discussion sheds some light. Antony is portrayed in the later chapters of the *Life* as a 'physician to all Egypt',[32] willingly accepting the duties of a healer and teacher.[33] If, as Williams' suggest, the historical Antony began his career as a figure isolated from society, dependent on personal vision rather than the inheritor of an established ascetic tradition, then it would indeed be necessary to question the plausibility of regarding him as having become, in later life, a thoroughly 'domestic' and approachable figure,[34] very much attached to the Church's ministry and orthodox teachings.[35] But on the other hand, a figure whose own asceticism *was* the product of a tradition which was an established part of Church life and whose practitioners regarded themselves as the helpers and guides of the lay community (as did Johannes and Paphnutius), and whose withdrawal to the desert was not motivated by a rejection of the Church, might well regard an active ministry of the type which the mature Antony is reported to have exercised as the natural fulfillment of his own vocation, and not as necessarily incompatible with his own quest for ascetic perfection. Antony's yearning for contemplation and the inner life did drive him to free himself from company where possible and to regret the disturbance caused by petitioners and questioners.[36] But this regret is only relative. The relationships in which his ministry involves him are clearly, in the view of the *Life*, an integral part of his self–understanding. In helping to situate the *early* chapters of the *Life of Antony* in their historical context therefore, the papyrological evidence assembled by Judge not only confirms their picture of the ascetic tradition which Antony inherited, but also helps to show how the overall portrayal of Antony in the *Life* can be regarded as coherent and convincing.

Williams believes that the fact that the *Life of Antony* includes many features which could be interpreted as anti–gnostic indicates that Athanasius felt the need to counter a gnostic 'image' of Antony. It may be questioned whether this is a likely account of the *Life's* composition – why should Athanasius have tried to redeem so apparently unpromising a figure for orthodox at all? – or whether it actually tallies with the facts: is it really convincing to suggest that a work crammed with accounts of Antony's supernatural experiences should have been written with the express purpose of countering a picture of Antony as even more of a visionary?[37] Precise evidence is entirely lacking to support Williams' own purely hypothetical image of Antony; so there is nothing to compel us to believe that Athanasius' work should be seen as a polemical and fundamentally unhistorical response to a gnostic threat to orthodox Christianity. Williams suggests that Antony's vision of a demonic impersonation of providence ($\pi\varrho\acute{o}\nu o\iota\alpha$) should be seen as a rejection (by Athanasius) of the gnostic use of this concept[39]. But the *Life* continually identifies the work of divine providence in the life of Antony and attributes teaching on providence to him.[39] If Williams' theory of the anti–gnostic purpose of the *Life* was correct, we might expect Athanasius to show more caution in using what could be interpreted as a gnostic idea (but could equally well be perfectly orthodox).

Recent work has also raised the question of the relationship of early monasticism to gnosticism with respect to the lives of Pachomius. These situate the Pachomian monastic community firmly in the context of the Christian community as a whole. The Bohairic life stresses Pachomius' decision to give us his charitable service in the local Christian community to become a monk; but when he found his monastery at Tabennesi he initiates good relations with Christians in the surrounding countryside by building a church in a local village when it becomes necessary, and bringing his own community to worship there with the villagers.[40] An unnamed bishop opposed Pachomius' attempt to found a monastery in his diocese.[41] But this incident must be balanced against the encouragement offered to him by another bishop, Arius, who is described as an ascetic – probably a Christian belonging to the older ascetic tradition revealed by the papyri.[42] When Pachomius appeared before a synod at Latopolis in 345, the year before his death, to answer questions which had been raised concerning his gift of insight ($\tau\grave{o}$ $\delta\iota o\varrho\alpha\tau\iota\kappa\acute{o}\nu$ $\alpha\upsilon\tau\grave{o}\nu$ $\lambda\acute{e}\gamma\epsilon\iota\nu$: his abiity to perceive the state of the soul of others), he was able to appeal to the bishops present as fellow monks and themselves members of his community.[43]   There was certainly opposition to Pachomius therefore, but no inherent tension between monasticism and episcopate; rather, the case of the 'ascetic' bishop proves that the hierarchy itself was able to take on board the ascetic ideals existing in Egyptian Christianity, while the synod of Latopolis proves that by this date the elevation of monks to the episcopate was already well under way.   There is external evidence for the historicity of the Greek life's reference to the two bishops, Philo and Mouis.[44]

The new questions raised about the relationship of Pachomian monasticism to the Church stem not from any direct attempt to undermine this evidence but from a specific discovery: the corpus of Coptic gnostic writings found at Nag Hammadi, and the possibility that it was compiled and used in the nearby Pachomian monastery at Chenoboskion.   The evidence for this lies in the fact that the bindings of several of the Nag Hammadi codices were strengthened with scrap papyrus which included letters and other documents which appear to have come from the Pachomian monastery.[45]   Whether or not this is so may still be considered an open question,[46] but assuming that it is the case that the Nag Hammadi codices were used by the Pachomians, what effect does this have on our understanding of the relationship of the monastery to the Church?

An extreme solution would be to regard the fact as evidence that the Pachomian community was in origin a sectarian gnostic movement, consciously separated from the wider Church.   This idea could be correlated with the view that Coptic Christianity was almost exclusively gnostic in origin, and that orthodoxy did not begin to predominate in upper Egypt until a comparatively late date, perhaps not even until the activities of Athanasius brought the monasteries increasingly under control from the time of his first visit to the Pachomian community in 329.[47]   Recent work however has not supported the clear—cut distinctions between an orthodox, Greek—speaking Christianity in Alexandria and an essentially gnostic or heterodox version outside the city.[48] There is a closer connection between the culture of the two areas that was once thought, and the evidence of papyri from the second and third centuries does not suggest that gnosticism predominated in the country areas or that gnostics were necessarily the first to use Coptic for preaching and writing.[49]   There is no need to assume that the Nag Hammadi discoveries are evidence for a sectarian gnostic context for early Pachomian monasticism:[50] they may represent a relatively isolated outbreak of enthusiasm for gnostic spirituality in a generally orthodox context.

Charles Hedrick, for example, suggests that enthusiasm for visions led the Pachomian monks to collect the markedly visionary Nag Hammadi texta and to use them until forced to dispose of them following the publication in 367 of Athanasius' thirty—ninth festal letter, directed against the use of apocryphal books.[51]   His detection of 'gnostic proclivities' in the Pachomian texts has not however found favour: again we must bear in mind that visionary experiences were part of the common currency of monastic spirituality and by no means an indication of specifically gnostic ideas.[52]

The Pachomian monks need not therefore even have perceived that the Nag Hammadi texts were, in their doctrinal teaching, radically opposed to orthodox Christian ideas, for there is no need to think that they were themselves particularly acute theologians; they may not, as James Goehring suggests,[53] even have regarded the distinction between orthodoxy and heresy as one to be drawn over narrowly doctrinal issues.   It would be possible for a community to support

Athanasius while still using the Nag Hammadi texts for spiritual enlightenment.[54] Despite this Goehring argues that relations between the community and the hierarchy were looser in the earlier years, when Pachomius himself was leader of the community, than they subsequently became under his successor Theodore.[55] In dealing with Athanasius' visits to the community in 329 and 363, for example, he writes that, 'It is no accident that whereas Pachomius hid from Athanasius to avoid ordination ... Theodore ... marched out with the leaders of the community to greet him'.[56] The implication that Pachomius' support for Athanasius was qualified or hesitant, is misleading. In both lives Pachomius does go out to meet Athanasius. He hides only when the question of his ordination is raised by the bishop of the diocese, who is present, and his refusal to be ordained does not itself imply a rejection of Athanasius or of the hierarchy and priesthood in general.[57] The contrast with Theodore's behaviour is much less stark than Goehring represents, and the evidence for a significant change in the relations of the Pachomian community with the hierarchy consequently uncertain.

It is thus not clear either that the possession of the Nag Hammadi texts by the Pachomian community proves that they were in any way consciously gnostic, or that the community's relations with the hierarchy and local church were ever weak (Goehring does not challenge the historical value of the other evidence for good relations, some of which has been noted). There seems to be no good reason not to accept the account of the community's possession of apocryphal texts given in the Bohairic life and in another document;[59] this explicitly claims that the community used such texts without being fully aware of their heterodox character, and pledged to abandon them when instructed to do so by Athanasius.

It has not been possible to do full justice to all the arguments put forward by the different contributions cited in this essay, whether for or against the idea that good relations existed between early monasticism and the Church. A good deal more work is needed before we are in a position to understand fully the historical context and precise evidential value of the lives of Antony and Pachomius. It *may* be true 'that the "orthodoxy" of the movement portrayed in the sources can no longer be accepted as an accurate representation of the facts'[59] — that in this respect the lives bear the mark of the characteristic doctrinal concerns of Athanasius. But even in respect of the relations of early monasticism with Alexandria, the absence of positive evidence for bad relations must be emphasised. And this does not affect the main argument sketched in outline here: that the evidence of the lives for good relations at a *local* level — village churches and local bishops like the 'ascetic' Arius and the judges at Latopolis — between monasticism and the Church is substantial and cannot easily be dismissed. It cannot therefore be proved that early monks were actually dominated by gnosticising concerns;[60] nor is it any longer possible to suggest that upper Egyptian Christianity as a whole was exclusively heterodox. By supplying additional evidence for the origins of monasticism in an existing ascetic tradition with an accepted place in the local Church, and thus providing a check on the reliability of the literary texts, the evidence of the papyri has made an important contribution to our understanding on early monasticism.

NOTES

1.   It is therefore a response to the work of others rather than a piece of original research in its own right: hence the general title. I hope to document some of the suggestions made here more fully in future work.

2. See recently R.A. Greer, *Broken Lights and Mended Lives : Theology and Common Life in the Early Church* (Pennsylvania and London, 1986), pp 162–66. Particular importance is attributed to a literal interpretation of Jesus' teaching on poverty by W.H.C. Frend, 'The Monks and the Survival of the East Roman Empire in the Fifth Century', *Past and Present* No. 54 (1972), pp 10–11; 'Athanasius as an Egyptial Christian Leader in the Fourth Century'. *New College Bulletin* (Edinburgh) 8 (1974), pp 26–27; 'Town and Countryside in Early Christianity', *The Church in Town and Countryside*, ed., Derek Baker, *Studies in Church History* 16 (Oxford, 1979), pp 27–28; 'Early Christianity and Society: A Jewish Legacy in the pre–Constantinian Era', *Harvard Theological Review* 76 (1983), pp 68–69. Frend links this element in early monasticism to a response to economic hardship and social oppression in Egyptian peasant society. For a criticism of these established views see R.M. Price in his introduction to *A History of the Monks of Syria by Theodore of Cyrrhus* (Kalamazoo, 1985), pp xxiii–xxvii.

3. *PG* 26, pp 835–976; to be cited as *VA* followed by chapter number.

4. The lives used here are the *First Greek Life* (G1), ed., F. Halkin, *Sancti Pachomii vitae Graecae, Subsidia Hagiographica* 19 (Brussels, 1932), pp 1–97, and the *Bohairic Life* (Bo), ed., L. Th. Lefort, *Sancti Pachomii vita bohairice scripta, CSCO* 89 (Louvain, 1925). These two texts are available in English in *Pachomian Koinonia*, tr. Armand Veilleux, 3 vols (Kalamazoo, 1980–82), volume one. References are by chapter number.

5. E.A. Judge, 'The Earliest Use of Monachos for "Monk" (P. Coll. Youtie 77) and the Origins of Monasticism', *Jahrbuch für Antike und Christentum* 20 (1977), pp 77–89; see also his 'Fourth Century Monasticism in the Papyri', in *Proceedings of the XVIth International Conference of Papyrology*, eds., R.S. Bagnall, G.M. Browne, A.E. Hanson, and L. Koenen (Chico, CA, 1981), pp 613–620. For Isidore see A.E.R. Boak and H.C. Youtie, *The Archive of Aurelius Isidorus* (Ann Arbor, 1960).

6. 'The Earliest Use of Monachos for "Monk"', p 73, text 11.13–16 (my translation).

7. *Ibid.*, p 75.

8. The view of one of the earliest critical works on the history of monasticism, H. Weingarten, *Der Ursprung des Mönchtums in nach–constantinishcen Zeitalter* (Gotha, 1877). For a discussion (rejecting the theory) see Archibald Robertson in *St Athanasius: Select Works and Letters, The Nicene and Post–Nicene Fathers*, second series, volume 4, pp 188–191.

9. 'The Earliest Use of Monachos for "Monk"', p 72.

10. *Ibid.*, p 75.

11. 'Fourth Century Monasticism in the Papyri', p 616.

12. 'The Earliest Use of Monachos for "Monk"', pp 76–77, 85–86; 'Fourth Century Monasticism in the Papyri', p 615.

13. 'The Earliest Use of Monachos for "Monk"', pp 80–83; 'Fourth Century Monasticism in the Papyri', pp 616–619.

14. 'The Earliest Use of Monachos for "Monk"', pp 88, 86, rejected (with due caution) by F.E. Morard, 'Encore Quelques Réflexions sur Monachos', *Vigiliae Christianae* 34 (1980), pp 395–401.

15. 'The Earliest Use of Monachos for "Monk"', pp 89, 79.

16. *Ibid.*, pp 78–80.

17. *Ibid.*, pp 88, 85.

18. See Jerome, Letter 22.34, *CSEL* 54, ed. I. Hilberg (Vienna and Leipzig,

910), pp 196–197 and *Historia Monachorum in Aegypto*, ed., J. Festugière, *Subsidia Hagiographica* 34 (Brussels, 1961), prologue 10 and 5.1–4 (Judge refers to the Latin version by Rufinus of Aquileia, but there can be no doubt that the Greek text is the original).

19.   'The Earliest Use of Monachos for "Monk"', p 85.
20.   *Ibid.*, p 77; cf. 'Fourth Century Monasticism in the Papyri', pp 613–614. The reference to Antony's emergence is to *VA* 14–15.
21.   'The Earliest Use of Monachos for "Monk"', pp 83, 88–89. For Johannes and Paphnutius see respectively B.R. Rees, *Papyri from Hermopolis and other Documents of the Byzantine Period* (London, 1964), numbers 7–10 (pp 12–20) and H.I. Bell, *Jews and Christians in Egypt* (London, 1924), numbers 1923–1929 (pp 100–120).
22.   John as anchorite: documents 7 and 10 (of the four only 7 *clearly* involves him in the secular affairs of another person). Paphnutius involved in business of some sort: documents 1923, 1924 and 1925 (referring to brothers dwelling with him).
23.   *VA* 3.
24.   *VA* 3–4 for his ascetic teachers; 11–13 for his move to the desert.
25   *VA* 4.
26.   Document 1926 (text 11.8–11, my translation).
27.   *VA* 11.
28.   For a different series of papyri referring to ascetics in the context of Church life see E. Wipszycka, 'Les confréries dans la view religieuse de l'Égypte chrétienne', *Proceedings of the Twelfth International Congress of Papyrology*, ed. D.H. Samuel (Toronto, 1970), pp 511–525. But the evidence is on a whole much later than that collected by Judge.
29.   M.A. Williams, 'The Life of Antony and the Domestication of Charismatic Wisdom' in *Charisma and Sacred Biography*, Journal of the American Academy of Religion Thematic Studies 48.3–4 (1982), ed., M.A. Williams, pp 23–45.
30.   *Ibid.*, pp 30–34, 38–40.
31.   T.D Barnes, 'Angel of Light or Mystic Initiate? The Problem of the *Life of Antony*', *JTS* 37 (1986), pp 353–368.
32.   *VA* 87.
33.   For various aspects of Antony's ministry to other monks see *VA* 14–15 (the first formation of ascetic communities in imitation of him), 44–45, 48, 54–5; for lay people see 56–64, 72–80, 84–87.
34.   *VA* 67.
35.   *VA* 67–70.
36.   His continuing desire for solitude is stressed in 49–50 and 84–85 – neatly framing the sections on his ministry.
37.   *VA* 66 is particularly emphatic that Antony *is* directly inspired and taught by God.
38.   *VA* 40; Williams, pp 32–33.
39.   See *VA* 8, 19, 32, 49, 74, 78, 89.
40.   Bo 9, G1 27, 29, Bo 25. See G.E. Gould, 'Pachoios of Tabennesi and the Foundation of an Independent Monastic Community' in *Voluntary Religion*, eds., W.J. Sheils and Diana Wood, *Studies in Church History* 23 (Oxford, 1986), pp 21–24. M.S. Burrows, 'On the Visibility of God in the Holy Man. A Reconsideration of the Role of the Apa in the Pachomian *Vitae*'. *Vigiliae Christianae* 41 (1987), pp 11–33 stresses the extension of Pachomius' ministry and influence to the community in general and not just to the monastery, as does Philip Rousseau, *Pachoius: the Making of a Community in Fourth Century Egypt* (Berkeley, 1985), p 161.
41.   Bo 58, cited by Frederick Wisse, 'Gnosticism and Early Monasticism in

Egypt', in *Gnosis: Festschrift fur Hans Jonas*, ed., Barbara Aland (Göttingen, 1978), p 434 as evidence of the fear of bishops for autonomous ascetic communities.

42. G1 81; Bo 54.

43. G1 112.

44. D.J. Chitty, *The Desert a Citty* (Oxford, 1966), p 41, n. 57.

45. J.W.B. Barns, 'Greek and Coptic Papyri from the Covers of the Nag Hammadi Codices: a Preliminary Report', *Essays on the Nag Hammadi Texts in Honour of Pahor Labib*, ed., Martin Krause (Leiden, 1975), pp 9–18.

46. As by A. Veilleux, 'Monasticism and Gnosis in Egypt', the *Roots of Egyptian Christianity*, eds., B. Pierson and J.E. Goehring (Philadelphia, 1986), pp 271–306. H. Chadwick, 'The Domestication of Gnosis', in *The Rediscovery of Gnosticism I*, ed., Bentley Layton, suppl. *Numen* 41 (Leiden, 1981), pp 3–16 accepts the connexion, as does the most thorough discussion, G. Scholten, 'Die Nag Hammadi Texte als Buchbesitz der Pachomianer', *Jahrbuch fur Antike und Christentum* 31 (1988), pp 144–72.

47. G1 30, Bo 28. Wisse, 'Gnosticism and Early Monasticism in Egypt', p 433, refers to Athanasius' 'high–handed methods' of bringing monasticism under his control.

48. See Rousseau, *Pachomius*, pp 18–22.

49. C.H. Roberts, *Manuscript, Society and Belief in Early Christian Egypt* (Oxford, 1979), pp 1–6, 51–54, 60–73; D.J. Kyrtatas, *The Social Structure of the Early Christian Communities* (London and New York, 1987), pp 155, 172–3.

50. Accepted even by Wisse, 'Gnosticism and Early Monasticism in Egypt', pp 438–40, who thinks that the Pachomian communities were not actually sectarian but provided a point of re–entry for for heterodox ascetics into the Church.

51. C.W. Hedrick, 'Gnostic Proclivities in the Greek *Life of Pachomius* and the *Sitz im Leben* of the Nag Hammadi Library', *Novum Testamentum* 22 (1980), pp 78–94. For the festal letter see *St Athanasius: Select Works and Letters*, pp 551–2.

52. G.G. Stroumsa, 'Ascèse et Gnose: aux origines de la spiritualité monastique', *Revue Thomiste* 81 (1981), pp 557–73 esp. pp 558–9; Schlten, 'Die Nag Hammadi Texte', p 165 is also unconvinced, and (pp 167–171) thinks the alleged evidence for gnostic connexions in inadequate.

53. J.E. Goehring, 'New Frontiers in Pachomian Studies', in *The Roots of Egyptian Christianity*, pp 246–247.

54. *Ibid.* pp. 247, 252.

55. His use of Max Weber's theory of the 'routinisation of charisma' to describe changes in the community's organisation and relations with the hierarchy is too complex to discuss here.

56. 'New Frontiers in Pachomian Studies', p 245. For the visit of 363 see G1 143–144 and Bo 200–203.

57. For Pachomius' attitude to ordination see Gould, 'Pachomios of Tabennesi', p 21.

58. Bo 189 and a fragment of a Sahidic life (S6); for a French translation of this see *Les Vies Coptes de Saint Pach'me*, tr. L. Th. Lefort (Louvain, 1943), p 334.

59. Goehring, 'New Frontiers in Pachomian Studies', p 246. Rousseau, *Pachomius*, 19 does not however think that the orthodoxy of Pachomius is 'merely a gloss imposed by later compilers'.

60.   Stroumsa, 'Ascèse et Gnose', p 572, comments that a clear distinction
      between orthodox asceticism and gnosticism is precisely the latter's *lack* of
      concern with the wider 'social' implications of its existence.

THE DISTINCTIVENESS OF PALESTINIAN MONASTICISM
450 – 550 AD

John Binns

The century following the Council of Chalcedon (451) was a period of dramatic growth in the monasteries of the stretch of desert to the east of Jerusalem. This was a growth not only in the number of monasteries, the population of the monks and the prestige of the institution — although it was all that — but also of a style of the monastic life which showed itself in the self–consciousness of the monks and their relationships with the society around them. Like the dramatic but quickly passing flowering of the Palestinian desert after the spring rains, the flowering of the Palestinian monastic life was short–lived. But although short–lived, the monasteries of this period had a lasting significance for the history of the Church.

The main witness to this process is Cyril of Scythopolis. Cyril was a native of Galilee and a monk of Palestine. He lived from about 525 to about 560.[1] In this short life he wrote the Lives of seven of the great monastic leaders of his day. The Lives were written after careful research and contain a wealth of chronological, topographical and historical information. They have been recognised by scholars as invaluable historical sources.[2] Of these Lives the two fullest and most significant are those of Euthymius and Sabas.

Euthymius was Armenian by birth. He was born in 376, came to Jerusalem in 405 and died in 473. Sabas was a Cappadocian, born in 439, came to Jerusalem in 456 and died in 532.[3] The careers of these two saints spanned over 125 years. The extent to which the monastic life developed is shown by a comparison of these two men. The following two episodes from their Lives shows the contrast.

The year is 459 and Euthymius is established as an abbot of stature. The newly consecrated Patriarch of Jerusalem, Anasthasius, who had been surprised on a previous visit by Euthymius' prophecy that he would become Patriarch, came to pay a complimentary visit. He sent word of his impending arrival. In somewhat rhetorical fashion the saint replied:

> The constant enjoyment of your paternal solicitude, most venerable father, is a source of delight to me. However, although the previous occasion of playing host to you in no way inconvenienced me, it is now the case that the coming of your blessedness would overstrain my weakness. I therefore entreat your holiness not to trouble yourself to visit my mediocrity. If you decide to come, I shall receive you with joy. And If I receive you I shall have to receive every visitor and shall no longer be able to stay in this place.[4]

The Patriarch cancelled his visit, this response would have received the sympathy and approval of the early ascetics. The Egyptian Father, Arsenius, made a similar statement to the Patriarch of Alexandria; and, since Euthymius claimed to have modelled his way of life on that of Arsenius, it is clear that the Saying of Arsenius lies behind that of Euthymius.[5] Both men agreed. Solitude must be protected at all costs and little benefit can be expected from hob–nobbing with senior ecclesiastics.

So Euthymius occupied his monastery on the beautiful plain of the Sahel close to the Jerusalem to Jericho highway perhaps a couple of hours walk away from the centre of the Holy City, yet he is never recorded as visiting the capital after his initial pilgrimage in 405 nor as making any journey outside his monastery except to travel deeper into the desert during Lent.[6] Here again the early monks would have approved. Antony, for example, made only two brief visits to Alexandria, one in an attempt to achieve martyrdom and the other in order to defend the beleaguered Nicene faith, Pachomius never went to the capital, although some of his monks occasionally took a boat downstream to Alexandria.[7]

Our second episode took place fifty seven years later. The year is 516 and again a new Patriarch is taking up his office. The Patriarch is a certain John and he has been chosen because he was prepared to bow to pressure from the Monophysite Emperor Anastasius to anathematise the Council of Chalcedon. Sabas was a convinced Chalcedonian and was among those who persuaded John to defect to their side. A summons went out throughout the desert and 10,000 monks poured into the capital. St Stephen's Basilica was large enough to hold this multitude and there they gathered, with the Imperial officials and the Emperor's nephew Hypatius present. The new Patriarch ascended the pulpit, flanked by Sabas and Theodosius, the other leading monk, and then ensued one of those extraordinary mass demonstrations which took place in the early church. The congregation kept shouting 'Anathematise the heretics and confirm the Council'. Then, 'the three with one voice anathematised Nestorius, Eutyches, Soterichus and everyone who did not accept the Council'. At this, the Imperial official retired to the safety of Caesarea and the Emperor's nephew hastily gave substantial gifts of cash to the churches and monasteries.[8]

The picture is a powerful and striking one. The Patriarch is located firmly between the two saints — he speaks with one voice with them — the Imperial officials accept their decision. It shows a monastic institution fully integrated into the church and playing an active role in political life. The leaders of the monks seem as much at home in the world of ecclesiastical politics as they are in the solitude of the desert.

The events at St Stephens do not seem to be an isolated and uncharacteristic intervention into an alien world. The fact that the gathering of the monks of the desert at St Stephens took place at all suggests that not only were the leaders at home in the city but also that the communication lines between the City and the Desert were sufficiently well developed to enable this huge crowd — because clearly it was huge, even if Cyril's figure of 10,000 is an exaggeration — to be marshalled at short notice. Sabas' connections with the Patriarch continued. Later in the Life, he is asked to participate in two delegations from the Patriarch to the Emperor, along with a number of other monks.[9] While in Constantinople, Sabas is a regular visitor in the Palaces and stays for the winter. One of the company, Leontius of Byzantium, stayed behind in the Imperial capital to represent the interests of his colleagues back in the desert. The connection between Desert and Emperor developed after the death of Sabas when the Origenist conflict was in full swing. Palestinian monks became regular visitors. As well as Leontius of Byzantium (almost certainly to be identified with the author of several philosophical and theological works),[10] both Theodore Askidas of the New Laura and Domitian of the monastery of Martyrius were at home in the Imperial Court and were promoted to prestigious posts within the church. The Chalcedonians, Gelasius and Conon, attempted to follow their example but lacked the necessary connections to make the most of their diplomatic mission.[11]

The Palestinian monks have changed since the time of Euthymius. They have entered into the mainstream of ecclesiastical and political life. The monks' perception of their role has changed. No more is it expected that a monk should limit his experience to his community set apart living a retired life in a deserted place, receiving visitors with a show of reluctance and a touch of guilt. The monk has a central and an active part to play in the life of a Christian society.

This development was made possible by the geography of Palestine. The desert in which the monks lived was small in size and varied in vegetation. Those who have visited Jerusalem are familiar with the spectacular drive to the Dead Sea. In a car journey of half an hour and twelve miles, the road drops about 3,000 feet. The olive groves of the Judaean hills are quickly left behind, and give way to a stretch of arid grazing land where Bedouin camps nestle in the folds of the hills. Then the landscape empties further, vegetation becomes increasingly sparse and even herds of Bedouin goats disappear from the horizon. Finally the cliffs descend to the salt flats on the shores of the Dead Sea with their strange geological formations and African plants and animals. The extent of this change is shown vividly by the rainfall. In the hills round Jerusalem about 500 mm. of rain falls in the year — similar to the rainfall in London, except that it falls almost entirely between the months of October and March. on the shores of the Dead Sea, the average precipitation is well under 100 mm. per year.

In this environment the monks could easily find an empty, inaccessible and rocky ravine ideally suited to the solitary life; water would run most of the year along the bottom of the valley, and the dry, non—absorbent soil ensured that such rain as fell would not soak into the ground but could be collected in reservoirs and cisterns. The collection of plants formed a valuable ascetic labour and could supplement the ascetic diet. Markets for home—made baskets and ropes could be found in the towns and villages a short mule—ride away. And the desert stretched south in the Negev for endless miles, an invitation to the advanced ascetic seeking an austere Lenten retreat. All this was available within ten miles of the City of Jerusalem. It was the dramatic contrast between Desert and City, in close proximity yet sharply delineated by geographic factors, which made the Palestinian desert an inviting terrain for the prospective monk.[12] The way of life of the monks was shaped by their environment, or, more accurately, by their two different environments — the City of Jerusalem and the Desert which was so close to it.

Jerusalem — the Holy City — dominated the consciousness of the monk from the start. The monks of the Palestinian desert had a double vocation. They were both pilgrims and monks. Sabas, for example, was a young monk in Cappadocia. He was, we are told, 'seized by the God—pleasing desire to discover the Holy City and to lead a life of silence in the desert round it'.[13] Euthymius, similarly, came to Jerusalem, and, after he had first venerated the Holy Places, he settled at the monastery of Pharan, and Cyril makes a point of recording the shortness of the distance between the monastery and the city — 'six miles'.[14] In other parts of his writing, Cyril uses an interesting phase — 'to withdraw to the Holy City' (ἐἰ τὴν ἁγίαν πόλιν ἀναχϖρῆσαι).[15] Here the word withdraw is used to describe a process of moving, not to a place of solitude, but to a city. In many cases, including those of Euthymius and Sabas, the withdrawal was from a non—urban environment to an urban environment, a strange reversal of the normal monastic progression, although of course both found their way back to a monastery before long.

Euthymius and Sabas were both monks before they left their homeland to travel to Jerusalem. Cyril clearly felt that this was the correct procedure, for he took care to ensure that he made his monastic renunciation before he left his city of Scythopolis to go to the City. He does not describe himself as entering a monastery at this stage and his renunciation is clearly made in order that he might make this great pilgrimage as a monk.[16] The call to live in silence at Jerusalem comes as a stage of monastic vocation which properly follows after the call to become a monk. Many monks once arrived remained in the City. We hear of many monasteries in Jerusalem. The monastic communities presided over by Melania and Gerontius on the Mount of Olives were especially well-known in the early fifth century and were involved in the Origenist controversy which broke out in Egypt in 400. Many monks were attracted to the area around the Tower of David on Mount Sion and were living in a disordered and undisciplined manner. The first action of the new Patriarch Elias, according to Cyril, was to build a monastery near the episcopal palace and to bring together the 'ascetics of the Holy Church of the Resurrection who had been scattered in the district around the Tower of David' and he assigned to each of them a comfortable cell.[17] The Church of the Resurrection was the centre of the pilgrimage business and it may be that the Patriarch felt that the presence of this random collection of ascetics was bad for tourism. Under the leadership of Euthymius, Sabas and others the focus of the monastic life moved out of the City to the desert to the East. A sign of this shift of emphasis is given by Cyril's list of the names of the archimandrites, a title which in Palestine was given to the recognised leaders of the monastic population. The early archimandrites, Passarion, Gerontius and Elpidius, were residents of Jerusalem. The next famous name is that of Marcianus, whose monastery was at Bethlehem, not in Jerusalem itself, but not far away and another pilgrimage centre. After his death in 492, the leadership passed to Sabas and Theodosius, of the desert monasteries, and no future archimandrite lived in the City.[18]

The monks who went to Jerusalem did not, as monks in Egypt or Syria, withdraw into the desert, but to a particular desert, the desert of Jerusalem. The withdrawal process thus becomes more complex. City and Desert are both essential to his choice of dwelling. The City challenges the traditional categories of monastic vocation.

The City is the place of salvation. In it the Christian faith is discovered with an immediacy and a directness not encountered elsewhere. Justin Martyr's exuberant certainty is familiar. 'If anyone wants proof for the birth of Jesus Christ, let him go to Bethlehem and see for himself both the cave in which he was born and the manger in which he was laid'.[19] A more measured statement is provided by the letter which Sabas and Theodosius addressed to the Emperor appealing for his support.

In the Mother of Churches, Sion, the great mystery of piety for the salvation of the world was manifested and accomplished, and then, beginning from Jerusalem, through the divine and evangelical preaching, the light of truth was raised to the ends of the world. Through the victorious and venerable cross and life-giving resurrection, we, the inhabitants of the Holy Land have all received the true and not illusory confession and faith, ... the holy City of God, Jerusalem, the eye and luminary of the whole world whose inhabitants touch as it were with their own hands the truth each day through the venerable places in which were wrought the mystery of the Incarnation.[20]

The formal expression of the significance of Jerusalem had its counterpart in popular devotion. Shortly after the death of Sabas, in the mid–fifth century, a pilgrim from Piacenza wrote his impressions of his visit.

> In the place where the Lord's body was laid, at its head has been placed a bronze lamp. It burns there day and night, and we took a blessing from it and then put it back .. [this would have been a small quantity of oil placed in an ampulla especially sold for the purpose] ... earth is brought to the tomb and put inside and those who go in take some as a blessing.

And at the Sepulchre itself

> they offer oil to be blessed in little flasks. When the mouth of one of these little flasks touches the wood of the Cross, the oil instantly bubbles over, and unless it is closed very quickly, it spills out.[21]

These testimonies express something of what Jerusalem meant to the monk. The power of salvation was present in a real and *tangible* form. Those who live in Jerusalem, and the desert was part of Jerusalem, live within touching distance of God.

The diplomatic activity of Sabas is given in a prominent part in the later stages of Cyril's narrative of the saint's Life. The motive force for this unusual monastic occupation was the need to protect the Holy City. Sabas' first visit to Constantinople was made at the height of the Monophysite controversy, in 511, when Patriarch Elias was under pressure from the Emperor Anastasius to give his support to the Monophysites. The Patriarch turned to Sabas. He 'summoned him and besought him to go with them [some monastic superiors] and strive with all his might to protect the mother of Churches from disturbance since the Emperor Anastasius was attempting to overthrow and overturn the whole state of the churches in Palestine'.[22] The second visit was during the reign of Justinian, in 530, and on this occasion the need was for a remission of taxes to pay for the repair of the damage and destruction caused by the Samasitan Revolt in Palestine, especially the re–building of churches.[23] The monks commanded respect in the Imperial capital. Anastasius, although sympathetic to the Monophysite cause, was, according to Cyril, a 'lover of monks' and greeted Sabas with reverence, and was quick to respond to the requests made by the old man.[24] The Patriarch's instinct that the monks were the right people to take on delicate political missions in a hostile environment was fully justified.

The monks could offer protection to the City in other ways too. A perennial problem to the dwellers in the Judaean hills on the margins of the deserts was drought. A serious drought took place between 516 and 521. After five years of little rain the shortage of water had reached a critical level, and the forthcoming Feast of the Dedication of the Church of the Resurrection would be attracting huge numbers of visitors to Jerusalem. The Patriarch employed workmen who dug down 200 feet in the more humid areas of the City in the hope of finding water, but with no success. In desperation the Patriarch turned to Sabas, and the old man eventually agreed to pray for rain. During the night the wind changed. 'There was thunder and lightning and the rain cascaded down, so that before dawn the conduits were filled to the brim and torrents poured from all sides'. Even the tools of the Patriarch's workmen were washed away and the mounds raised during the search for water were swept away in the torrents. The account concludes: 'The cisterns of the Holy City were filled to the brim and the

Feast of the Dedication was celebrated with joy and gladness'.[25] The story is set in the context of the institution of pilgrimage and shows how the saint was called on to assist in the arrangements being made for the care and welcome of the pilgrims. It is also a statement of power. The power of the Patriarch with his money and labour force is contrasted with that of the holy man who stands alone before God in prayer. The reader is left in no doubt where the true power lies.

The image of the holy man as a figure of power was presented in the classic paper of Peter Brown, 'The Rise and Function of the Holy Man in Late Antiquity'.[26] The power available through the holy man is shown by the miracle stories.

> These miracle stories are of the sort that assume that the holy man is there to play a role in society based on his power. Furthermore, just as the miracle demonstrates a hidden, intangible nucleus of power, so the miracle story is often no more than a pointer to the many more occasions on which the holy man has already used his position in society.[27]

Brown analyses the function played by the holy man in a society which was fluid and insecure. His authority could be used by villagers in a variety of ways to make sure that their lives ran smoothly, or at least that major catastrophies could be mitigated. He could help to resolve conflicts between villagers, protect them against overbearing officials, offer help in less tangible ways. He offered security and support in the insecure world of the villages. His ability to provide mediation and patronage arose from his position as an outsider, as a stranger. His ascetic struggles are described by Brown as 'a long drawn—out, solemn ritual of dissociation – of becoming the total stranger'.[28] Brown's perceptive observations have changed the way we have come to look at the holy men of the Byzantine world. It is sufficient here to note how the presence of Jerusalem has provided a new setting for the exercise of these monastic responsibilities. Brown's holy men were villagers, living in the mountains of Syria, and their concerns were those presented to them by their clients, the anxieties and hardships of rural life. The ascetics of Jerusalem belonged to their City, and the problems which confronted them were on a larger scale. Sabas had to intervene in a conflict with the Emperor, not one of his tax officials. He had to respond to a drought affecting the whole city, not to say the provision of water to an isolated community. (Although as abbot his monks brought to him these problems too. Other of his miracles describe the finding of a spring for a newly founded monastery, a curse on the flocks of some shepherds who were interfering with the access of monks to their cisterns).[29] The role that Cyril presents his monks playing in society does not differ from that described by Brown. But it is a different society that benefitted from the power of the Palestinian holy men. Different demands, different clients, different tasks, all led to a different place in society and a different perception of the proper role for a monk. He has become institutionalised, and works within the context of ecclesiastical, political and social life. The holy man is placed within urban society, as an essential part of it.

The need to represent Jerusalem effectively led Sabas to become a visitor to the very heart of the Byzantine Empire – the City of Constantinople. Once there he presented the needs of the people of the City to the Emperor. To the Emperor Justinian, for example, he asked for a tax remission to rebuild after the Samaritan Revolt, but also a new hospital in the city for the care of sick pilgrims, money to complete a magnificent new church dedicated to the Mother of God and fortification in the desert to protect the monasteries against barbarian tribes.

To these, he added a further request: that the Emperor may 'extirpate the Arian heresy, together with those of Nestorius and Origen, and free the city and the church of God from the bane of these heresies'.[30] The mention of the *city* before the *church* is, surely, not only because Sabas is especially concerned about the place where he lives. The letter he composed with Theodosius referred to above describes Jerusalem as the place where the faith originated and from where it went out through the preaching of the apostles to illuminate the whole world. In the removal of heresy, the same divinely ordered progression takes place. First, Jerusalem is purified, and then the true Catholic Faith can be imparted to the world. But, if the Holy Places are in the hands of heretics, the future orthodoxy of the church rests on shaky foundations. A monk of Jerusalem had a clear responsibility to play his part in the elimination of heresy.

Triumph over heretics is a central theme of Cyril's writings. For Euthymius, the enemy is Monophysitism. For Sabas, it is Origenism. The course of the conflict follows a similar pattern. In both cases heretics have striking success and form the majority party in the desert or the monastery; the saint reacts to their presence through the tactic of flight rather than argument or struggle; an orthodox group builds up around him; final victory against the heretics is achieved only after the saints' death, and, it is implied, as a result of the power of the saints' intercession.[31] It is not surprising that in a history which describes the century beginning with the Council of Chalcedon in 451 and ending with the Second Council of Constantinople in 553 the theme of orthodoxy and heresy should be so prominent.

In his treatment of the theme of the overthrow of heresy, Cyril has little interest in the doctrinal debates which divided the parties. The sections which summarise the points at issue in the conflicts are few in number. A diatribe on the evils of Origenism by the aged Abba Cyriac is reported, as are the views of Euthymius on Trinitarian theology and Christology, which are given in two passages which rely greatly on quotation from works of Theodoret and Justinian.[32] But these sections read as though they are intrusions into a work which is intended to be primarily historical and Cyril seems to lack confidence in his handling of these themes.

Instead he emphasises the scandal to the church caused by division. The title Monophysite, for example, is seldom used. Cyril prefers to call these heretics Aposchists, or those cut off from the church. When he describes the Reunion of the Aposchists of Marcianus' party, the process used is the Biblical method of drawing lots, after which, when the choice falls on the side of the Chalcedonians, they go to Jerusalem where 'they were received by the Archbishop, who celebrated a public festival with the whole mass of monks and citizens; there were great festivities in the squares of Jerusalem in joy at the Reunion'.[33] Cyril does not tell us what another historian, Zachariah of Mitylene, recounts — how this reconciliation was the result of a bout of bargaining on the doctrinal issues with hefty concessions on the part of the Patriarch to avoid offending Monophysite sensitivities.[34] The scandal, in Cyril's view, was not heresy by schism. The solution was not through theological debate, but through receiving communion from the Patriarch.

The reason for this approach is to be found partly in the composition of the monastic population. Since the monks were recruited from the pilgrims who arrived at Jerusalem they came from many provinces and even from outside the Empire. The list of Euthymius' first disciples is indication of this international quality — they came from Cappadocia, Armenia, Sinai, and one out of the twelve came from Galilee.[35] As the Lives proceed Cyril often records the country of origin of the characters he describes showing the wide geographical range of the monks' origins. This internationalism prevented a distinct doctrinal position from developing in the monasteries of Palestine, as happened, for example, with the monasteries of Egypt with their aggressively Monophysite traditions.[36] The presence of a variety of doctrinal standpoints in the monasteries made the monks accept the necessity of doctrinal pluralism within their communities.

They did not have to look far to discover an alternative basis for unity. The truth was present in the Holy Places of the Holy City. The Patriarch presided over the Church which celebrated the Liturgy in those places. Those who were in communion with him were in communion with the truth. The combination of an international community with a strong focus of unity did not eliminate all conflict — the struggles described by Cyril prevent the possibility of drawing that conclusion — but they did provide a means of achieving a resolution to the conflict. Again, the presence of Jerusalem has challenged and transformed the categories of thought of the monks.

In the course of the century following the Council of Chalcedon the monasticism of the Palestinian desert developed from a style of life characterised by withdrawal to solitude and away from contact with either the institutional church or the political state to an alternative style of life characterised by involvement. This recognition of the necessity for involvement led the monk into new and unexpected places far from the lonely and barren wilderness. This change in the nature of their life was forced on them by the unavoidable fact of the presence of the City of Jerusalem. It made the option of withdrawal ultimately impossible. Although the monk might occupy a wilderness as terrifying, barren and demon–filled as any in the ancient world, it remained a desert close to the walls of a city, and a city of unavoidable significance for the Christian. The City was part of the monks experience and its existence and its needs could not be ignored.

The monk was obliged to accept a role within society and to work out his vocation within it. If the church was worldly and influenced by political pressures, then the monk could no longer ignore it, refuse ordination and retire. He was part of the church and had to accept responsibility for its welfare. If the Emperor was pursuing unacceptable policies, then action was demanded.

A contradiction was inherent in Palestinian monasticism. The monks were called to both withdrawal and involvement. This led to tension and conflict, as Cyril so vividly describes. It also led to new perceptions about the nature of monastic life which were hammered out in the hard realities of desert life in the communities of Jerusalem. It is a contradiction proper to a way of life which follows a God who lived rooted in the tensions and divisions of first century Palestine. It is a contradiction forced on the monks and a contradiction which led them in new and creative directions.

Finally, a caution and a regret. The caution is against the assumption that a new and revolutionary approach to the monastic life was pioneered and perfected in Palestine. The writing of Cyril makes it clear that bitter conflicts divided the monastic population, which led on occasions to violence and death on the streets of Jerusalem.[37] The work of later authors, notably John Moschus, paints a picture of life in the Palestinian monasteries which differs little from the life elsewhere.[38] The argument of this paper is that there were also new approaches being tried and new solutions to old problems provoked in the monks by their responsibilities towards the City of Jerusalem. These opened out new perspectives in the thoughts of the monks.

And the regret. The approach to monastic life, church life and political life being developed in Palestine had much to give to the church. It was not to be. On the Eastern frontier, invading forces were building up. In the sixth century attacks were launched. Jerusalem fell to the Persians in 614 and then, after peace was made between Rome and Persia, to the Arabs in 638. Strategius, a monk of Sabas' monastery, recorded in flat, prosaic tones the scene after the Persian invasion. Seven found dead on the altar of St George's Church outside the City, 28 in the Hall of the Governors', 275 in cisterns, 2,270 before the gates of Holy Sion, and so on. The total number of dead was 38,877 or 66,509, depending on which version is read.[39] Along with the Christian population, something else died that day — the monastic ideal of the Palestinian desert created with care, faith and persistence by the monks about whom Cyril wrote.

NOTES

1. These dates are deduced from autobiographical passages in the writings of Cyril. See E. Schwartz, *Kyrillos von Skythopolis*, Texte und Untersuchungen 49/2 (Leipzig, 1939), pp 71.11–20; 164.20–24; 180.9; 222.10–14; 224.9.
2. For example, E. Stein, *Histoire du Bas–Empire*, Vol. 2 (Paris, Brussels 1949) p 699.
3. Cyril gives two alternative dates for the death of Sabas, 531 and 532. 532 is the correct date. For the evidence see the discussion in E. Stein, 'Cyrille de Scyhopolis, à propos de la nouvelle édition de ses oeuvres', *Analecta Bollandiana* 62 (1944) pp 169–186 (pp 171–180).
4. Schwartz, *Kyrillos*, p 52.10–17.
5. *Apophthegmata Patrum* Arsenius 8.
6. After the winter rains, water and edible plants are more abundant in the Judaean desert. This gave rise to the common custom among the monks of travelling deeper into the desert during Lent. For example, Schwartz, *Kyrillos*, pp 56.19–57.11.
7. *Life of Antony*, 46; p 69. *Life of Pachomius*, First Bohairic Life, 89; 107.
8. Schwartz, *Kyrillos*, pp 151.7–152.12.
9. Schwartz, *Kyrillos*, pp 139.20–147.9; 173.12–179.14.
10. A full discussion of Leontius of Byzantium, and the identification of Cyril's Leontius with the author, is David B. Evans, *Leontius of Byzantium, an Origenist Christology*, Dumbarton Oaks Studies 13 (Washington, 1970).
11. Schwartz, *Kyrillos*, 194.13–195.6; 198.5–9. Although Conon was ultimately successful, 198–22–25.
12. The life style of the monks is reconstructed, from archaeological evidence by Y. Hirschfeld, 'The Judaean Desert Monasteries in the Byzantine Period; their Development and organisation in the light of Archaeological Research' (dissertation, Hebrew University of Jerusalem 1987). The bulk of this work is to be published by the Yale University Press.
13. Schwartz, *Kyrillos*, p 90–7–8.
14. Schwartz, *Kyrillos*, p 14.3–11.
15. Schwartz, *Kyrillos*, p 224.2. Compare 204.3–4.
16. Schwartz, *Kyrillos*, p 71.11–20.
17. Schwartz, *Kyrillos*, p 116.4–8.
18. For a list of archimandrites, see A–J. Festugière. *Les Moines d'Orient*, (Paris, 1961–1963) Vol 3/2, p 149.

19.   R. Brownrigg, *Come, See the Place* (London, 1985) p 108.
20.   Schwartz, *Kyrillos*, pp 152.21–157.23.
21.   Antoninus Placentinus, *Itinerarium*, 18, 20.
22.   Schwartz, *Kyrillos*, p 139.21–27.
23.   Schwartz, *Kyrillos*, pp 173.6–9; 175.7–11.
24.   Schwartz, *Kyrillos*, p 142.20.
25.   Schwartz, *Kyrillos*, pp 167.25–169.24.
26.   P.R.L. Brown, 'The Rise and Function of the Holy Man in Late Antiquity', *Journal of Roman Studies* 61 (1971) pp 80–101.
27.   Brown, 'Rise and Function', p 87.
28.   Brown, 'Rise and Function', p 91.
29.   Schwartz, *Kyrillos*, pp 101.9–19; 160.14–161.2.
30.   Schwartz, *Kyrillos*, pp 175.3–176.2.
31.   This process by which the heresies were overthrown provides a structure to the *Lives of Euthymius and Sabas*.
32.   Schwartz, *Kyrillos*, pp 39.18–41.3; 42.16–44.4; 229.31–231.19. For the dependence of these passages on Theodoret and Justinian, see B. Flusin, *Miracle et histoire dans l'oeuvre de Cyrille de Scythopolis* (Paris, 1983) pp 74–83.
33.   Schwartz, *Kyrillos*, pp 66.18–67.20.
34.   The two accounts are analysed by Schwartz, *Kyrillos*, pp 366–370.
35.   Schwartz, *Kyrillos*, pp 25.17–26.14.
36.   See W.H.C. Frend, *The Rise of the Monophysite Movement* (Cambridge, 1972).
37.   Schwartz, *Kyrillos*, pp 193.19–194.12.
38.   John Moschus produced a collection of anecdotes under the title of the *Spiritual Meadow*, or *Leimonarion*.
39.   Stratagius, *The Capture of Jerusalem*, p 23.

MONKS AND LITURGIES: THE INFLUENCE OF THE MONASTERIES ON THE DEVELOPMENT OF THE MEDIEVAL LITURGY

Martin Dudley

Central to the life of the medieval monastery was the celebration of the liturgy. This is true whether we are concerned with Saint—Riquier under Abbot Angilbert, Cluny under Odo, Hugh or Peter the Venerable, the Clairvaux of St Bernard, or the Grande Chartreuse of St Bruno. The monastery is always a liturgical community, whether liturgy takes pride of place, as at Cluny, or shares a relative equality with silent contemplation or manual labour. Liturgy involves particular skills and requires special equipment. It is more than a written text. If we are studying liturgy, we are studying the performed text, those who perform it, and the norms that govern the performance. Monks were involved in all aspects of the liturgical venture: the study of ancient texts, the writing of new ones, the building of churches, the making of books, vestments, vessels, bread and wine for sanctuary and altar, and the solemn performance of the Church's liturgy, of the Mass, the Office and the other rites that mark the religious life. But the needs of the monastic liturgist are rather different from those who serve other forms of liturgical community, and the dissimilarities must not be overlooked in any such study. This paper is, of necessity, a limited and somewhat superficial survey of the main areas of monastic liturgical development and innovation — the editing and compilation of texts, *laus perennis*, ritual, the private Mass, and the contribution of Benedictine poets and theologians. Any consideration of the Office, though essential to a complete picture, is here omitted because of the complexity of the question.[1]

My starting point is the beginning of the Benedictine centuries. It is a convenient point because the rise of Benedictine monasticism as the normative form of cenobitic life parallels the spread of the liturgical rite of the City of Rome as the normative rite. It has been estimated that in the realms of the Carolingians some 420 monasteries were constructed or reconstructed in the period 768 to 855.[2] We may safely say that the architecture of this period was essentially monastic and we may equally safely affirm that the liturgy was also firmly in monastic hands. The Carolingian monarchs set out to reform a Church which had fallen into a sad state of corruption, disorganisation and ignorance[3]. Their tools for this purpose included monasticism and the Roman liturgy. Hence the parallel developments. The monasteries performed a vital stabilising political and cultural role. There was a general desire for sacred places and for elaborate liturgy. The Carolingian basilica — the abbey churches of Saint—Denis, Aniane, Centula, Hersfeld and Fulda, for example — were enormous reliquaries open to all comers. They served both monks and pilgrims, sheltering the bodies of the saints and attracting the devotion of the faithful.[4] The so—called Gallican Liturgy, already decadent, had been abolished by Pepin the Short in 954. Initially the Roman liturgy had spread in the Frankish Kingdoms because of the initiative of individuals rather than because of official action. The Popes contented themselves with sending copies of their liturgical books without troubling themselves as to the use which might be made of them,[5] and what emerged was a composite liturgy which eventually returned — triumphant — to Rome. In fact, the essential elements of the missal and even of the office had been settled before the Carolingian monastic revival, but it was during the great monastic centuries, the ninth to the twelfth, that the minor texts were established: formulas for benedictions of the lessons, absolutions, etc., which enriched the primary texts.[6]

THE SACRAMENTARIES

The development of the Romano--Frankish liturgy and the role played in that development by the monasteries may be illustrated by the history of the Sacramentary. The Sacramentary is the presider's book. It contains all that he needs for the Mass and other liturgical functions. It does not contain the lections or the parts sung by the *schola*. The oldest form of Sacramentary is that which we term the 'Old Gelasian' and it dates, in its original form, from the seventh century. It exists today, in the Vàtican Library, in a single manuscript copied at the nunnery of Chelles, near Paris, about 750. The liturgy contained therein is that used in Rome in the seventh and early eighth centuries. The Roman prototype left Rome before 715 and came, perhaps by monastic hands, to Gaul. In common with other sacramentaries it contains certain specifically monastic formulae.

Another class of sacramentary is termed 'Frankish Gelasian' or 'Eighth Century Gelasian'. This family has, in Bernard Moreton's words, 'a certain Benedictine flavour'[7] stemming from a now lost original, the Sacramentary of Flavigny, named after the Benedictine Abbey in Burgundy founded by Pepin III. These sacramentaries provide a mass in honour of St Benedict the Abbot on 11 July, stemming perhaps from the translation of his relics to Fleury—sur—Loire. The Sacramentary of Gellone, the only primitive recension of the original Sacramentary of Flavigny, qualifies Benedict as *venerabilis pater*, *gregis pastor*, *decus monachorum*, and his name concludes the list of Latin Fathers in the *communicantes* of the Canon. Clearly a part of the book's supplement, a sort of pontifical, came from a monastic customary and contains an impressive number of entries suitable to monastic use. It is reasonable to say that it was compiled by monks, used as much material as possible from the old Roman books already circulating in the Frankish kingdom, and that it met the needs of Frankish churches and more especially monasteries. The editors of the Gelonnensis claim that it was assembled by a team of Benedictine monks, around 760–770.

In addition to the old and new versions of the Gelasian Sacramentary, another type of Roman mass book circulated widely north of the Alps. This we call 'Gregorian', though it was probably redacted not under Gregory the Great but under Honorius I (625–638). The Gregorian exists in thirty five or so ninth—century manuscripts. The version that interests us is the 'Hadrianum', the papal book sent by Pope Hadrian I to Charlemagne towards the end of the eighth—century. This Roman text was rather disappointing to the Carolingian liturgists. It was a papal mass book and as such did not correspond to the presbyteral sacramentaries with which they were already familiar. Yet it had come as a gift from the Pope. It was to be handled both respectfully and critically. In the provision of a Supplement to the Hadrianum we have a clear example of monastic liturgical activity. Against the conclusion of Bishop, Lietzmann and Bourque, that the supplement *Hucusque* was compiled by Alcuin, Dom Jean Deshusses has demonstrated that the compiler was the monastic founder and reformer Benedict of Aniane.[8]

Born around the middle of the eighth century, Benedict was a faithful servant first of Pepin and then of Charlemagne. He then decided to become a monk.[9] Drawn to an extreme asceticism, he led a life which included all kinds of mortifications, fasts, prayers, vigils and silence. Ardo, his biographer, tells us that he abandoned the Rule of St Benedict as one meant for beginners and weaklings and he preferred the oriental rules, particularly those of Pachomius and Basil. In 779 or 780, he founded a monastery at Aniane where, again, eastern austerity prevailed. But by 787, Benedict had become convinced that eastern practices were too difficult for the majority of his monks, and so he turned back to the Benedictine Rule and, with a complete change of liturgical outlook, gave up wooden and glass chalices and cheap vestments without silk and built a new church noted for the splendour of its columns, altars, lights, costly vestments and silver vessels. He introduced the full Benedictine life in his abbey. A student of the Rule, he strove to reform the whole of contemporary monasticism and this made him a naturally ally of Charlemagne and Louis the Pious and a companion in the reforming work of Alcuin, Adalhard of Corbie, Paul the Deacon, and others who made the Carolingian renaissance possible. As Abbot of Aniane, Louis made him superior of all the Benedictine houses in Aquitaine. Then Louis moved him closer to Aachen, the imperial capital by making him abbot of Marmoutier in Alsace and finally, between 815 and 816, abbot of the new model abbey of Inde, six miles from the imperial palace. Benedict seems to have totally abandoned his desire for liturgical simplicity and developed instead a passion for elaborate and minutely regulated ceremonies. Sixteen canons of the *capitulare monasticum* of 817, enacted by a synod at Aachen, deal with the office alone. Opinions vary on the value of the reforms of Benedict of Aniane, and it is no part of this paper to pass judgments, but rather to observe his liturgical contribution. He may have bequeathed to later medieval monasticism, an undeniable ritualism, but more importantly he gave a real shape to the bold liturgical programme required by Charlemagne:

> Correct carefully the Psalms, the notations, the songs, the calendar, the grammar in each monastery ... and the catholic books. Because often some desire to pray to God properly, but they pray badly because of the incorrect books ... If there is need of writing the Gospel, Psalter and Missal, let men of mature age do the writing with all diligence.[10]

We should not therefore be surprised that he produced for his abbeys, around 810–815, a thoroughly up–to–date sacramentary with a copious, useful and even necessary series of appendices: a carefully corrected Hadrianum with the Supplement *Hucusque*.[11] The Supplement draws chiefly but not exclusively on the Frankish Gelasian Sacramentary and consists mainly of Sunday and votive masses. Benedict filled a space left in the Rule of St Benedict of Nursia. That space is the area of eucharistic theology and practice. The silence of the Rule allows for strong and creative leadership in the area by abbots and this is what Benedict of Aniane provided.[12]

THE PROCESS OF REFORM

The resources of the monasteries made them the ideal vehicle for the spread of the Romano–Frankish liturgy. Not only did they provide the context for liturgical celebration, but they also provided hospitality. It was primarily by staying at another abbey that monks became acquainted with liturgical developments, experienced them in practice and transmitted them. The monasteries could also produce copies of the texts. When we read the provenance of the manuscripts which preserve Benedict's Supplement, we find there a catalogue of the major monastic scriptoria. There are copies made at Marmoutier, St Amand, Corbie, St Alban's, Mainz, as well as Reichenau (on Lake Constance) and at neighbouring St Gall. A further sacramentary, that which is now in the Museo Nazionale at Trent and which belonged to the ecclesiastical province of Salzburg, illustrates the influence of individual abbots. The Sacramentary of Trent was copied as early as 825–830 from a Salzburg exemplar. From 785–821, the bishop, and then archbishop of Salzburg, was Arno, monk and then Abbot of St Amand, one of the leading churchmen in the Carolingian reform and a close friend both of Alcuin and of Benedict. He had also been to Rome on a number of diplomatic missions and was presumably acquainted with the Roman liturgy. Alcuin, Benedict and Arno almost certainly shared their liturgical experiences, the texts they acquired, and the texts they wrote. The frequent travels of these abbots and the ability of their scriptoria to produce new copies of texts were major factors in the creation of the Romano–Frankish and Romano–Germanic liturgical heritage of the Middle Ages. It would have taken a month or six weeks to copy an average sacramentary. Those who regularly copied liturgical books, like the eleventh century monk Ottloh of St Emmeran, who produced 19 missals, 3 evangeliaries, 2 lectionaries, 2 works of Saint Augustine, one psalter and four office books for Matins, were, we must suppose, a little faster. At Reichenau, Regimbert, who died in 846, had copied 42 manuscripts. And his scriptorium had such a reputation that on 22 April 998, Pope Gregory V demanded that it copy a sacramentary every year for the pope's own use, and this requirement lasted for at least a century.[13] The warnings about copying were very necessary. Benedict warned that the Hadrianum was marred by a variety of scribal errors and even the restored text could be 'corrupted once again by the carelessness of copyists'.[14] Frequently the errors were not noticed because the Latin of the clergy was of too poor a standard to notice that it didn't make sense.

LAUS PERENNIS

Dom Philibert Schmitz dismisses the idea of the *laus perennis* in a short paragraph. Some monasteries, like Remiremont and Luxeuil, adopted it, but it was rare and the practice did not last. One gains the impression that it was not quite Benedictine.[15] Yet one early medieval church stands out above all others as a much imitated model. This was the monastery of Centula or Saint–Riquier, near Abbeville, which was rebuilt in the decade after 790 by Abbot Angilbert, a friend and perhaps nephew of Charlemagne. The new church, of a 'remarkably novel and monumental character'[16] was dedicated to the Saviour and All Saints, but the chief altar was related to the tomb of St Riquier, an ascetic who died in 645. The Centula was built, in Braunfels's words, because of a demand for almost sumptuous religious pomp.

There were three churches: that of St Riquier, another of St Benedict, the third of the Blessed Virgin Mary. They were linked by the cloister extended to make a processional way (it being about 600 feet from St Riquier to the Lady Chapel and about 400 from St Benedict's to the other two). Abbot Angilbert was firmly committed to *laus perennis*. The three hundred or so monks were divided into three choirs, plus thirty boys each, who sang as an angel choir from a galley in the westwork. Angilbert had prescribed what was to be sung where and when, in the main church, in the ancillary churches, and in procession. The most important feature of the church — Conant calls it a historical landmark — was the 'westwork' or entrance element.

> At the base there was a vaulted outer vestibule which contained the
> tomb of Angilbert and a remarkable painted stucco relief of the
> Nativity on a gold mosaic ground ... Beyond this there was an inner
> vestibule which served as narthex or antechurch — in effect a low,
> shadowed western transept with its vault carried on a forest of piers
> and columns. It contained a font and an altar.
> The vaults of this whole section of the church served as a platform

for a chapel of the Saviour in the form of a tall spire—like central
altar space, cut off from the main nave by an arched screen and
surrounded on three sides by aisles and galleries ... at St Riquier the
entrance element was an entire vertical church, with vestibule,
subsidiary altar and font below, and a chief altar, dedicated to the
Saviour, at the platform level.[17]

Professor Stephen Nichols observes that the design of the tower—church was
intentionally linked to the Church of the Holy Sepulchre in Jerusalem and its
liturgy, especially at Easter, with a cast of some fifteen hundred, involved a
complex symbolism. It was a living tableau, a ritual expression of the Paschal
victory.[18] Centula in all its magnificence was never outdone. Its true
contribution to medieval religion is to be found in drama rather than in liturgy as
such, but it remained an inspiration.[19]

LITURGY AT CLUNY

The mantle of Angilbert fell in part, at least, on the monks of Cluny. The
task of the medieval monk was that of 'keeping before the world the mystery of
Pentecost, in showing mankind what the Church essentially is: the holiness of
God communicated to men'.[20] Monks were to become, as far as human frailty
allowed, dwellers in paradise.

> The silence and peace of eternity must begin for them here and now;
> they must live as the angels, joining with them in the eternal praise
> of God; each one by asceticism sharing in the depths of his heart in
> the mystery of Christ.[21]

From this spiritual foundation we can the better understand the reason for
Cluny's elaborate celebration of the liturgy, an elaboration not, of course, unique
to the Cluniac family. Though Cluny shared many eucharistically—centred
devotions with other monasteries, our main sources for Cluniac life, Ulrich and
Bernard, both of whom wrote in the second part of the eleventh century, refer to
the training of priest—novices in a way that implies there was something special
in Cluny's devotion. Leclerq again:

> It was a worship and an asceticism. All that the monk had to do
> was to adhere to the inexhaustible marvels that the Church spread
> out before the eyes of his faith, throughout the Christian year. A
> ceremonial whose etiquette was regulated in its least details made it
> possible to carry out, so to speak, a delicate technique, the service at
> the court of the King of Kings. It called for sustained effort and
> perpetual self—abnegation from each one, always, and at all times.[22]

The most characteristic aspect of Cluny's culture was anticipated eschatology.
The Cluniac vision embraced heaven and earth with an emphasis on continuity
between the Church in glory and the Church committed to the Apostle Peter,
hence the adherence to Peter's successor and the city of the Apostles. The
monastery was situated at the theological point where earth opens directly onto
heaven and 'already the splendour of the heavenly Jerusalem was bathing Cluny
in a spiritual luminosity'.[23] Cluny was a community of praise, of constant
prayer, an imitation of the eternal uninterruptedness of the heavenly liturgy.

> Take away this vision, and the transparent luminosity of Cluny
> turns opaque, the institutional structure becomes an insupportable

weight, and the marvellously choreographed liturgy degenerates into ritualism.[24]

Cluny was the most obvious flowering of this heavily liturgical monasticism but not its originator. It was the heritage of Benedict of Aniane. The Abbey of Baume, from which Berno came to find Cluny and of which Odo was a monk [admitted by Berno in 909], followed the practice of Aniane. But it received this practice by way of St Martin at Autun and St Savin in the diocese of Poitiers.[25] Lackner believes that Cluny was also influenced both by Celtic monasticism and by the liturgy and monastic practices of the Eastern Church. The latter came not just in the form of specific rituals and ceremonies but in the 'minutely detailed regulation of the monk's life and the emphasis on the representative, the splendid, the sacral element'.[26]

Schillebeeckx calls the priest of this period the ritualist and it has been said that the most characteristic feature of Cluny's life was ritualism.[27] Yet, as Hallinger says, the ritualism of Cluny never excluded an aliturgical approach. There are the first traces of individualistic affective devotion. Odo, despite his profound reverence for liturgical workshop, prefers private prayer. The whole liturgical endeavour would be simply foolish piety were there no interior life. Hallinger continues:

> The attitude of early Cluny towards ritualism was more broadminded than people are inclined to admit. It allowed for both objective and subjective elements, embracing as it did not only the liturgy but also an inward spirituality completely stripped of ritual expression.[28]

Thus, according to Hilpisch, 'not *decor*, but *affectus*, inner piety, became the watchword of the new piety' which received its stirring from the liturgy; for behind all the grandiose pageantry there was really 'simple adoration'.[29] Giles Constable has shown that the view of Cluny's liturgy as overburdened with accretions derives from Edward Bishop, who said that it presented 'an exalted model of faddy and fussy ritualism'.[30] This attitude to Cluny is based on the contemporary taste for liturgical simplicity and on an out–dated view of the distinctive character of Cluny, a view rebutted by Leclerq. Constable's judgment is important:

> To say that the Cluniac liturgy was long is an historically ascertainable statement, but to say that it was too long is a value judgment based on personal liturgical preferences, which should have no influence on the study of liturgical history.[31]

Whilst it can be shown, Constable says, that the psalmody and ceremonies at Cluny in the eleventh century were much longer than the Rule required, there was no evidence that by contemporary standards they were too long. As we well know, and as Dom Paul Tirot's sources testify, Cluny was almost universally admired, and its liturgy and customs spread widely. They were on the whole well suited to the devotional needs and ideals of monks at the time.

The monastic life at Cluny was, therefore, primarily devoted to a form of *laus perennis*, albeit more subtle than that of Centula. A high degree of ritual skill as required by the principal participants, and all the monks frequently took up a supporting role in the liturgy, wearing albs and maniples, going in procession, chanting, etc. The liturgy required a substantial cast. The provisions in the customaries prescribe exactly what is to be worn and done throughout the year. The Cluniac monk, to be truly a monk, is involved in incessant prayer, public or private.

Cluny's overflowing liturgical life gave birth to new festivals and to hymns and prayers and praises of every kind to the Saviour and his Mother. But with regard to the Mass Cluny, contrary to frequently expressed opinion, was a follower of fashion and not a leader.[32] The rite used at Cluny seems to have been rooted in the *Ordo Romanus Primus* and other of the Roman *ordines*. Certain Gallican, ad perhaps oriental, elaborations had been added: the *Suscipe Sancte Trinitas*, *Orate pro me*, and some additional chants were of Gallican origin; incensings, kissings of the altar, the particular form of the offertory and peace processions and the multiplicity of ablutions were either of Gallican or oriental origin. The tendency to liberality in candles, vestments and ornaments was unroman, but a marked simplicity, especially in the chant, was characteristic of both Rome and Cluny. The controlling influence of Odo's spirituality was significant in limiting the development of ever greater solemnity. He refused to enhance the splendour of the liturgy and reduced, or at least did not increase, the frequency and number of solemn celebrations of the Mass. He objected to ostentatious singing and personally would have been content with a glass chalice for the wine and a wicker basket for the eucharistic bread. Odo insists that it is the interior life alone which can ensure the validity of liturgical worship.[33]

Theodore Klauser[34] reminds us that chaotic conditions prevailed in Rome from the end of the ninth century and that 'the clergy of Rome and the Roman people lost all interest in the liturgical life of the Church'. Thus such life was maintained he credits to some of the new Roman monasteries founded by Cluny in the tenth century, monasteries already immersed in Cluny's liturgical spirituality. Though Klauser and Jungmann hold to the thesis that these Cluniac monasteries carried the Frankish rite to Rome and disseminated Frankish liturgical texts, Hunt, following an unpublished work of Dom Bernard Bignon of Saint—Wandrille, holds that Cluny itself maintained a purer Roman form. St Hugh, as against St Odo, favoured greater solemnisation but this tendency existed elsewhere as well. Hunt therefore concludes that there was little, if any, liturgical innovation at Cluny. Tirot, who also used Dom Bignon's work, argues for a quite specific originality in monastic liturgy and a common root in it for Cluny, Cîteaux and Chartreuse. Further scholarly research will be required before the matter can be decided.

THE PRIVATE MASS

A private Mass so—called, *missa privata* [considered as synonymous with *missa lecta* and *missa solitaria*], may be defined as one with no congregation, just priest and server, in which the priest assumes the liturgical functions of other ministers, *schola*, and congregation. However, Jungmann says that it is one that involves privacy of intention on the part of the celebrant rather than simplicity of ritual;[35] this interpretation is challenged by Van Dijk and Walker.[36] Häussling argues[37] that the use of the term 'private' in the sense of 'solitary' as used by Nussbaum, betrays a post—Tridentine understanding of the term. 'Private' in the early Middle Ages did not refer to something done alone but more than likely something 'privated' or deprived of the elaborate or special.[38]. So what did 'private' mean?[39] *Privatus* means privation, lack and together with its derivatives takes on various meanings suggestive of the familial and nonfestive. In the Rule of St Benedict, privatis diebus means non—holy days and *dies privatus* is used to mean a weekday, rather than a Sunday, throughout the

Middle ages. 'Private' related also the domestic, hidden, secret, and reserved. In the feudal age it refers also to those acts, individuals and objects that are not public or subject to public authority; they belong to a different sphere. Might not this understanding of private have something to do with the parallel meaning of 'familia', the household? So, the Hanc igitur: '... servitutis nostrae sed et cunctae familiae tuae, ...'. Also the 'household' references to the servants of God 'famulorum famularumque'. Duby[40] points to the development of family and privacy. 'The res familiaris was clearly a cornerstone of family life, where family here refers to a community distinct from the community of all the people, defined by its natural meeting place, or perhaps I should say its natural place of confinement, the house.' This is related to the monastic family with the abbot as pater familias. And the parish churches became, in the feudal era, 'the seeds around which small closed societies of parishioners crystallized'. Was it then social change that influenced liturgical change?

Vogel's excursus on the 'private' Mass, which was revised and updated by the translators, suggests seven important, yet not exhaustive, factors in the emergence of this reduced form of the solemn Mass:

1.   The attempt to replicate the liturgy of the Roman basilicas and shrines with their manifold eucharistic celebrations in the local church[es] of an episcopal city or monastery; this is central to Häussling's theory;

2.   the establishment of daily Mass in cathedrals and monasteries and then several daily coventual and non–conventual Masses including the *missa matutinalis*, *missa maior* and others, as well as the need to create more and more priest–monks; this seems to be, at least in part, Vogel's own view;

3.   the understanding of the Mass as an *opus bonum* to be offered frequently in intercession, or as an act of subjective piety; this is essential to Nussbaum's theory;

4.   the *redemptiones paenitentiales*, which advised the sayings of impressive numbers of Masses [as commuted penances] which could only be accomplished if many monks and canons were henceforth ordained;

5.   increasing devotion to the Blessed Virgin and to the faithful departed with the growing custom of having at least one Mass per day *de Beata* and *de requie* in communities;

6.   the endowment of more and more chantries in cathedrals and monasteries [and much later even parishes] and the resulting need for more priests;

7.   the stipend system itself which encouraged even slovenly priests to celebrate daily for the Mass–penny.[41]

No single factor stands alone, and there are other factors besides these. With them stands the fundamental question: which came first, the increased number of Masses or the increased number of priests?

Nausbaum, who is very frequently cited with approval, e.g. by Vogel, Schillebeeckx, and Klauser, set out to show the origin of the private Mass in the monasteries, where the monks are said to have begun votive Masses and Masses for the dead. This accords with ninth century evidence, but private Masses are mentioned earlier and more recent research suggests other origins. Angelus Häussling not only disagrees with this argument but also regards Nussbaum's views as historically incorrect. He argues that the celebration of several conventual Masses and permission for daily private Masses was not due only to subjective eucharistic piety but was also part of an effort to replicate in the monasteries the solemn liturgy as it was celebrated in Rome. The monks of Rome sought to make their abbeys an image of the city with its many churches: the stational Mass was represented by the community celebration, and the Masses in the 'titles' by those celebrated in monastery chapels.[42] 'Just as there were various daily celebrations in Rome at the numerous titular churches and sanctuaries, so it was thought desirable to have many daily eucharistic celebrations in each monastery in order that the liturgy might be as solemn as possible, and this required a great number of priests'. Nussbaum, following Jungmann perhaps, argues, on the contrary, that subjective piety was the primary reason for multiplying Masses in monasteries.[43]

The starting point for this argument is the emergence of the votive mass.[44] Van Dijk and Walker argue that it was the approval given to the ordination of monks, by the Roman Synod under Boniface IV in 610, that increased both the overall number of priests and the number of Masses, and Jungmann agrees that it seems to have marked the turning point. Thus 'the faithful spurred on by this liturgical revolution, sought more and more Masses for their varying needs (*vota*) and, in their turn, gave it pastoral significance'.[45] This is evidenced by the provision of votive Masses in the Sacramentries. The Old Galesian Sacramentary, the composition of whose Roman ancestor is dated by Vogel between 628 and 715, contains some 60 Masses for various occasions: for travellers, in time of trial, for seasonable weather, for monasteries, for weddings, in time of war, for rulers and judges, for the sick and dying, for the blessing of homes. Apart from the Masses of the Temporal Cycle with additional ceremonies [Christmas, first week of Lent, , Ember Days, Holy week and the Paschal Triduum, Ascension, Pentecost, etc.], it also has 66 feasts in the Sanctoral Cycle together with other Masses. The provision for both votive Masses and the Sanctoral increases and the tenth century Sacramentary of Fulda has one hundred and eighty votive Mass formularies.

Van Engen suggests a date sometime in the eighth century for monasticism ceasing to be a lay movement, so that by the time of Rupert of Deutz [c. 1075–1129/39], most of his fellow monks were priests and a daily Mass was expected of all devout Benedictine monks, but not of Cistercians or Carthusians among whom it was an extraordinary privilege even in the twelfth century for anyone to say mass daily.[46] The regulations for Cluny in the eleventh century [Rupert's house was Cluniac] allowed daily celebration by priests, either before Prime or in the interval before and after Terce and also after None. It was also possible to get permission, though not on a regular basis, to say Mass whilst the Solemn Mass was in progress.[47] Most said Mass privately, and it was for monk–priests that Rupert wrote his book *De divinis officiis*.

POETS AND THEOLOGIANS

The theological writing of the monastic theologians was frequently liturgical in character even when not explicitly a commentary on liturgical texts. They also wrote liturgical texts themselves, amplifying, adapting and replacing existing texts. Notker and Stammerer [Notker Balbulus], monk of St Gall [c. 840–912], was a real poet. His work was inspired, he tells us in the preface to his collected sequences, by the arrival in 860 or 862 of a monk from Jumièges bearing an antiphonary in which each note of the Alleluia corresponded to a syllable.[48] This was a mnemonic device for preserving melodies. Notker developed and perfected the technique. His first sequence was *Laudes Deo concinat orbis* [Let the world sing praises to God]; his second *Psallat ecclesia* [Let the Church sing]. Many other texts are claimed as authentically monastic. Rabanus Maurus [776 to 784–856] is credited with the *Veni, Creator Spiritus*. Peter Damian [1007–1072], prior of the Benedictine hermitage of Fonte Avella, was a Gregorian reformer and a poet. His works included *Crux mundi benedictio* for Holy Cross Day and *Paule, doctor egregie* for the Conversion of St Paul. Hermann the Lame, monk of Reichenau [1013–54], usually receives the credit, though on insufficient evidence, for the *Salve Regina* and the *Alma Redemptoris Mater*. Leclerq points to monastic poetry as 'the common fund of the universal liturgy' which arose in monastic milieus and expressing the aspirations of monks everywhere.[49]

Rabanus Maurus had been educated at Fulda and then at Tours under Alcuin. He returned to Fulda as master of the monastery school and became abbot in 822. In 847, having resigned his abbacy five years earlier after some political difficulties, he became Archbishop of Mainz. His promotion of the evangelization of Germany led him to seek a higher standard of theological education for monks and clerics, and he wrote *De clericorum institutione*, a kind of pastoral and liturgical manual. It is divided into three books, of which the first deals with ecclesiastical persons, sacerdotal vestments, and the sacraments, and the second with public prayer, the canonical hours, religious practices, and the liturgical year.[50]

Rabanus Maurus' pupil Walafrid Strabo [*c.* 808–849] had been educated at Reichenau and then later at Fulda. Elected Abbot of Reichenau in 838, he was caught up in Carolingian dynastic politics and exiled to Speyer, though restored to his abbey in 842. His treatise *Liber de Exordiis et Incrementis quarundam in Observationibis Ecclesiasticis Rerum* is a fascinating handbook on matters of liturgical and archaeological interest. It deals with churches, altars, sacred vessels, and with the principal liturgical rites.[51]

Heiric of Auxerre [841–876/7] forms a link between the teaching of the Carolingian schools and the later Middle Ages. At Auxerre he taught the philosopher Remigius of Auxerre who wrote a liturgical treatise *Explicatio missae*, which was incorporated into the *De Divinis Officiis* of Pseudo–Alcuin.[52]

Later monastic liturgists of note include Abbot Berno of Reichenau [died 1048], the canonist Bernold of Constance [died 1100], Odon of Tournai [died 1113] and his confrere and contemporary Rupert of Deutz [1075–1129/30] , and the Benedictine cardinals of the Gregorian reform, Humbert of Silva Candida, monk of Moyenmoutier, and the hermit Peter Damian.

CONCLUSION

As we have seen, the Benedictines influenced the content of the Roman liturgy during the early Middle Ages and provided certain standards by which it was judged. From the ninth to the twelfth century the monastic liturgy grew richer and it developed to the point where it could easily account for the entire day. So lengthy and burdensome had it become that the monks, we are told, stumbled through because of weariness and drowsiness. In the words of Van Dijk, sheer liturgical exhaustion had drained the strength of the monasteries. The reordered priorities of the Cistercian life inevitably affected the liturgy. To

clear the day for   long spells of work not only were many accretions of the office
and elaborations of chant and ceremonial removed but the second Mass was
dropped.   The single conventual Mass could now be celebrated early in the
morning, though on festal days at Cîteaux the 'liturgical tradition of the
monastic centuries' was retained and there were two conventual Masses.
Inevitably, the Cluniac Rupert of Deutz found fault with the Cistercians who,
under the pretext of labour to be done, took advantage of Benedict's silence and
abstained from daily celebration of private Masses.[53]

Not only was strong criticism levelled at the burden of liturgy, the
monastic life was also ridiculed.   There were attempts at reform, notably by
Peter the Venerable, whose inheritance as Abbot of Cluny was an overloaded
timetable and a greatly increased number of monks, 300–400 rather than the
60–80 of the mid–eleventh century.   Following the twelfth century's marked
tendency to prune the liturgy, in both the old and new orders, Peter made some
fairly minor alterations.   The conservative backlash was immediate, even though
his concern, as a true successor of Odo, was that the liturgy, however long,
should be understandable.   What was surprising was that Benedict's monks did
not really seem to have the will or method of restoring the liturgical balance.
Overstrained theories of monasticism bore their fruit in extreme laxity of
practice; and good men, distressed at this divergence, could imagine no better
remedy than to screw the theory one peg higher.   If the monastic life survived the
crisis of the late eleventh and early twelfth centuries with an impressive show of
vitality both in new foundations and in the reform of older communities, that
vitality was not given liturgical expression.   The unexpected liturgical
renaissance of the thirteenth century seems to have come from the papal court,
the Franciscans and the Dominicans.   The papal chaplains, the curia and the
Friars had other duties to perform.   Their prayers were shorter and unadorned.
Their chant was simpler as well.   Van Dijk and Walker cogently argue that the
Gothic mind, now emergent, broke everything.   It broke the calmness of the
Crolingian script; it broke the walls of its churches for more light and colour; it
broke their roofs for more space and sound; it broke the monument where liturgy
was preserved as a monastic monopoly.[54]

NOTES

1.   On monastic liturgy in general, see   Dom Brukhard Neunhauser,
        'Monastische Liturgie', *Ecclesia Orans*.I, (1984), pp 153–73, Pontificio
        Instituto Liturgico, Rome.   On the Office, see Paul F Bradshaw, 'Daily
        Prayer in the Early Church', Alcuin Club/SPCK, (London, 1983).
        pp 124–49; J.D. Crichton, 'The Office in the West: The Early Middle
        Ages', in *The Study of Liturgy*, eds., Cheslyn Jones *et al.*, SPCK,
        (London, 1980), pp 369–77; William Storey, 'The Liturgy of the Hours:
        Cathedral versus Monastery', in *Christians at Prayer*, ed., John Gallen,
        University of Notre Dame Press, (Notre Dame, 1977), pp 61–82; Adalbert
        de Vogüé, 'The Rule of Saint Benedict: A Doctrinal and Spiritual
        Commentary', *Cistercian Studies Series 54*, Cistercian Publications,
        (Kalamazoo 1983), pp 127–72.
2.   Carol Heitz, 'L'architecture carolingiene', (Paris, 1980), p 6.
3.   L. Duchesne, 'Christian Worship', SPCK, (London, 1923), p 103.
4.   Henri Focillon, 'The Art of the West: I Romanesque', Phaidon, 3rd
        edition, (Oxford, 1980), p 68.
5.   Duchesne, *op cit.*, p 104.
6.   Jean Leclerq, 'The love of learning and the desire for God', Fordham
        University Press, (New York, 1961), p 238.

7. Cyrille Vogel, 'Medieval Liturgy: An Introduction to the Sources', The Pastoral Press, (Washington DC, 1986), p 73.
8. H. Deshusses, 'Le Supplément au Sacramentaire grégorien: Alcuin ou S. Benoît d'Aniane?' *Archiv für Liturgiewissenschaft*, 9 (1965), pp 48–71.
9. Bede K. Lackner, 'The Eleventh Century Background of Cîteaux', *Cistercian Studies Series 8*, Cistercian Publications (Washington DC, 1972), pp 4–7.
10. Josef Semmler makes the claim about ritualism in *Leikon für Theologie und Kirche*, 2nd edition, Herder (Freiburg, 1958), volume 2, col. 179. See Lackner *op. cit*, p 38, for Latin text.
11. Vogel, *op. cit*, p 86.
12. Kevin Seasoltz, 'Monastery and Eucharist: Some American Observations', in *The Continuing Quest for God*, ed., William Skudlarek, The Liturgical Press (Collegeville, 1982), p 229.
13. Vogel, *op. cit.*, p 104.
14. Vogel, *op. cit.*, 87f. Benedict quotes Jerome: 'There is no point in correcting a book if copyists will not preserve accurately what has been corrected'.
15. Philibert Schmitz, 'Histoire de l'Ordre de Saint–Benoît', 2nd edition, (Maredsous, 1949), vol, 2, p 341.
16. K.J. Conant, 'Carolingian and Romanesque Architecture 800–1200', Penguin, Harmondsworth, 2nd integrated edition (rev) (1987), pp 41–60; Wolgang Braunfels, 'Monasteries of Western Europe', Thames and Hudson (London, 1972), pp 31–3.
17. Conant, *op. cit.*, 41f.
18. Stephen G. Nichos, Jr., 'Romanesque Signs: Early Medieval Narrative and Iconography', Yale University Press (London, 1983), pp 107–110.
19. Among the many studies of the liturgical origin of drama, see Grace Frank, 'The Medieval French Drama', Oxford University Press (London, 1954).
20. Jean Leclerq, 'The Spirituality of the Middle Ages', Burns & Oates (London, 1968), p 107.
21. Leclerq, *ibid.*
22. Leclerq, *ibid.*
23. Chrysogonus Waddell, 'The Reform of the Liturgy from a Renaissance Perspective', in R.L. Benson and G. Constable, *Renaissance and Renewal in the Twelfth Century*, Clarendon (Oxford, 1982), paperback (ed. used) 1985, p 102.
24. Waddell, p 103
25. Paul Tirot, 'Un <Ordo Missae> monastique: Cluny, Cîteaux. La Chartreuse , C.L.V., (Rome, 1981), p 14.
26. Lackner, *op. cit.*, p 60.
27. Edward Schillenbeeckx, 'The Church with a Human Face', SCM, (London, 1985), pp 161–63.
28. Kassius Halinger, 'The Spiritual Life of Cluny in the Early Days', in *Cluniac Monasticism*, ed., N. Hunt, p 46.
29. Cited in Lackner, *op. cit.*, p 61 and n. 70.
30. Edmund Bishop, 'Liturgica historica', (Oxford, 1918), p 269.
31. Giles Constable, 'The Monastic Policy of Peter the Venerable', in *Pierre Abelard – Pierre Le Vénérable*, Éditions du Centre National de la Recherche Scientifique (Paris, 1975), p 127.
32. Noreen Hunt, 'Cluny under Saint Hugh 1049–1109' (London, 1967), pp 112–114 and 208–210.
33. Hallinger, *op. cit.*, pp 44–46.

34. Theodor Klauser, 'A Short History of the Western Liturgy', Oxford University Press, 2nd edition (Oxford, 1979), p 75f.

35. Joseph Jungmann, 'The Mass of the Roman Rite', Benziger (New York, 1950), volume I, p 215f.

36. S.J.P. Van Dijk and J.H. Walker, 'The Origins of the Modern Roman Liturgy', Darton, Longman & Todd (London, 1960), p 47f.

37. Mönchskonvent und Eucharistiefeier, Liturgiewissenschaftliche Quellen und Forschungen 58, (Münster, 1972), p 246, n. 336.

38. Vogel, *op cit.*,p 157. On p 207, n 56, it is recorded that in the Early MA the actual term 'missa privatae' occurs only once: Walafrid Strabo *De exordiis et incrementis rerum ecclesiasticarum*, cap 26; MGH. Capitularia 2, p 506 line 26. The *Revised Medieval Latin Word–List* has no use of *missa privata* before 1400!

39. Georges Duby, 'A History of Private Life II: Revelations of the Medieval World', Harvard University Press, (London, 1988), pp 6–8.

40. Duby, *op. cit.*, p 7.

41. Vogel, *op. cit.*, p 156.

42. Robert Cabié, 'The Church at Prayer: Volume II – The Eucharist', Geoffrey Chapman (London, 1986), p 137, n.29.

43. Jungmann, *op. cit.*, volume I, pp 216–17.

44. The expression *missa votiva* occurs for the first time in Letter 3 of Eugene of Toledo, d. 657, *PL* 87:412.

45. Van Dijk and Walker, *op. cit.*, p 48.

46. Van Engen, 'Rupert of Deutz', University of California Press, (Berkeley, 1983).

47. Jungmann, 'The Mass of the Roman Rite', volume I, p 225, n. 86. Hunt, p. 108, with reference to Ulrich's consuetudinary.

48. Though there are some problems with his story; see Richard H. Hoppin 'Medieval Musics', Norton (New York, 1978), pp 155–6.

49. Leclerq, 'Love of Learning', p 237.

50. *PL* cvii, c. 293–420; cxii, c. 1165–1192; critical edition by A. Knoepfler, *Rabani Mauri de institutione clericorum* (Munich, 1901).

51. *PL*, cxiv, 919–966; critical edition by A. Knoepfler, (Munich, 1890 and 1899)

52. Chap. 40; *PL* ci, 1246–1271.

53. Super quaedam capitula Regulae divi Benedicti abbatis, libri III, *PL* clxx, 511; cited by Lackner p 19.

54. Van Dijk and Walker, *op. cit.*, p 26.

THE SPIRITUALITY AND MIRACLES OF ST RADEGUNDE

Joan M. Petersen

A few people are aware the the chapel of Jesus College, Cambridge, is dedicated to the Blessed Virgin Mary, St John and St Radegunde, but in general, little is known in these islands about this last saint. As she was of Germanic origin and lived most of her life in what is now France, where the fourteen—hundredth anniversary of her death was celebrated in 1987, this is not altogether surprising.

The sources for her history are the writings of Gregory of Tours and the poems and *vita* of Venantius Fortunatus, together with a second *vita*, written by the nun Baudonivia, who had been her personal servant from an early age.[1] It is to these two last items that we chiefly owe our knowledge of her spirituality and miracles.

The *Vita I*a of Fortunatus was written between the death of Radegunde in 587 and his own death in 609. Baudonivia's life was written between 609 and 614.[2] Both lives, though based on personal recollections, suffer from the limitations of medieval hagiography. As they were written to edify what was probably a largely monastic audience rather than to promote historical truth, the authors pay little attention to the chronological order of events and to dating, they make abundant use of *topoi*,[3] and they attribute to their subject deeds and personal characteristics that earlier writers have already attributed to other holy persons. The *Vita II*a has indeed not always received the appreciation that it deserves, perhaps because Baudonivia applies to Radegunde descriptive passages lifted from the *Vita* of St Caesarius of Arles (by Cyprian of Toulon and others) and from other *vitae* by Venantius Fortunatus.[4]

The story of Radegunde's life falls into four periods: her childhood and adolescence at the royal residence at Athies—sur—Somme; her married life with King Chlothar I; her life as deacon and penitent at her country estate at Saix in the region of Poitou; and her life as a religious at Poitiers.

The *Vita I*a covers the first three periods; Fortunatus tells us that his purpose is to bring before a wider audience details that have hitherto been known only to an inner circle.[5] Consequently he omits all reference to public events, such as the arrival of the relic of the True Cross at Poitiers, which would have been familiar to his hearers, but supplies information about Radegunde's early life, which he must have obtained from her personally, and about her miracles. Baudonivia expressly states that she is not inserting in the *Vita II*a any information already supplied by Fortunatus.[6] In spite of its linguistic and literary shortcomings, her *Vita* has a warmth and vividness, which the *Vita I*a lacks.

From the *Vita I*a and the poem *de excidio Thuringiae* (at one time believed to be spurious, but now generally accepted as the work of Fortunatus, based on material supplied by Radegunde), we gather that Radegunde was born *c.* 520, and that she and her brother were brought to the kingdom of the Franks as captives after the Frankish invasion of Thuringia.[7] Radegunde was assigned to the King by lot as booty and was brought up in the company of other children (probably the fruit of Chlothar's previous unions) at the royal residence at

Athies–sur–Somme[8] in preparation for marriage with him when she was old enough. As well as the usual feminine skills, she was taught to read and write. Her games and pastimes are significant for the future. She liked to look after the younger children and to organize little services and church processions for them. She used to tell the children that it was her ambition to become a martyr.[9]

When she reached marriageable age, probably eighteen or nineteen, the King, after one unsuccessful attempt when she slipped away from him by night, legally married her at Soissons.[10] For some years she led what must have been a difficult and frustrating double life. Unlike many of the holy persons described in medieval hagiographies, she appears to have consummated her marriage, but she had no children[11]. Outwardly she appeared as the queen, arrayed in gorgeous robes and adorned with jewels, but in private she practised the most painful fasts, austerities and penances. She organized the palace as a hospital and reception centre for the poor, whom she tended with her own hands. She enjoyed entertaining holy men, particularly bishops.[12] The King is reported to have said that he had married not a queen but a nun.[13] How long this double life continued we do not know, but the final break with her husband probably took place in 555, on the death of her brother, whom she suspected that the King had murdered.[14] At any rate, apparently with the King's consent ('directa a rege') she made her way to Noyon, where she begged the bishop, Medard, to clothe her as a religious. At first he demurred, on the grounds that her husband was still living, but so importunate was she that he finally made her a deacon.[15] Much controversy surrounds this question, but the reason for this step appears to be that the diaconate was open to married people, provided that the couple consented to separate.[16]

Radegunde now settled on her estate at Saix, which had been given her by her husband, probably as her bridal *Morgengabe*.[17] There she drew up a register of poor people and continued her charitable work among the sick and poor on a methodical basis.[18] She also inflicted still greater fasts and penances upon herself. Probably she was now living as a penitent,[19] as will be explained later. How long this life of service and penitence lasted we do not know, but it seems likely that the dissolution of the marriage was brought about by Germanus, bishop of Paris, after Chlothar had made two unsuccessful attempts to persuade Radegunde to come back to him.[20] We may surmise that once the marriage was terminated, Radegunde was able to assume the status of a religious. Gregory of Tours uses the phrase 'mutata veste',[21] but he does not say when this occurred or make it clear whether he is referring to her becoming a deacon or later taking the veil. At any rate, Chlothar furnished a sum of money, perhaps as a final settlement, to enable Radegunde to fund the monastery at Poitiers, which contained about two hundred sisters and which was her home for the rest of her days;[22] her life there was solaced by the friendship of Venantius Fortunatus, a wandering Italian poet, who came to rest at Poitiers and ultimately became its bishop in *c.* 590, but saddened by an unhappy relationship with Maroveus, the bishop of the diocese, and by the rebellious conduct of some of the sisters, which came to a head after her death. It is to Baudonivia and to Gregory of Tours that we owe the details of her last years and of her death and funeral in 587.[23]

RADEGUNDE'S SPIRITUALITY

As Jean Leclercq has pointed out in a recent article, it is to the *Vita II*[a], to which we owe our knowledge of Radegunde's spirituality,[24] though in my opinion, the outward manifestations of it, described by Fortunatus, and the tone of Radegunde's letter to all the bishops,[25] reproduced by Gregory of Tours, afford us some clues as to its basis.

We know that Radegunde was much preoccupied with the question of martyrdom, even as a child.[26]   Martyrdom had so long been presented to Christians as the highest good that even after the Peace of the Church, children and adults alike sought after it, and various substitutes had to be devised for it. One of these — indeed the most important of them — was the monastic life itself. Fortunatus says of Radegunde, 'Quid autem sanctissima ieunii, obsequii, humilitatis, caritatis, laboris et cruciatus ferventer indepta sit, si quis cuncta percurreret, ipsam praedicaret tam confessorem quam martyram',[27] obviously regarding her severe fasting, particularly during Lent, and her penances as the equivalent of martyrdom. Not only did she wear a hair–shirt, but she also lay on a bed of ashes covered by a hair–cloth. During Lent she bound three broad iron circlets round her neck and arms and implanted chains round her body. She also burned her body with a heated metal plate, shaped like a cross.[28]   'Animus armatur ad poenam', says Fortunatus of these terrible tortures, 'tractans quia non essent persecutionis tempora a se ut fieret martyra'.[29] This may well be the explanation offered to Fortunatus by Radegunde herself, but there may also have been a more immediate cause for her self–inflicted sufferings. Michel Rouche has put forward an ingenious hypothesis.[30]   Owing to her sense of guilt for her brother's death, because she had persuaded him to remain in Gaul and not to join their cousin Amalafrid in Constantinople, and her failure to keep a secret, youthful vow to remain celibate, she had to live for some time as a penitent at her home at Saix. For one in such a position her strict dietary regime would have been normal. The practice of wearing iron circlets was a penance of Germanic origin, appropriate to parricides and to those who had murdered their own relatives.[31] There are certain difficulties about this theory, which we need not go into here, but on the whole, it offers a likely explanation.

From the letter published by Gregory of Tours we can infer something of Radegunde's deep devotion to the Church as one, holy, catholic and apostolic, and of her conviction of the unity of all Christians by their baptism. The letter is addressed not to the bishop of the diocese alone, but to all the bishops and to the whole Christian people.[32] A monastery such as hers, she believes, can only succeed if it is understood by 'the physicians and shepherds of the flock' and gains their support. She believes in the Church as an hierarchical structure and describes its bishops as 'my masters and my apostolic fathers'.[33] This being so, we can understand how intensely distressing it must have been for her to be at variance with her diocesan and to lack his spiritual guidance. It was probably this sense of being without direction that lay behind her decision to adopt the Rule of St Caesarius of Arles for nuns for her community.[34] The chronology of Radegunde's early years at Poitiers presents many difficulties, but it seems probable that the Rule was adopted at some time in the mid– or late 550s, when she foresaw that with about two hundred women in the community, many of whom were of aristocratic origin and autocratic in their outlook, trouble lay ahead. The existence of a firm and tested Rule would be of great assistance in maintaining discipline. The adoption of the Rule and the journey of Radegunde and the abbess to Arles to consult with the abbess Lilliola there are undoubtedly two separate events. The journey must have taken place in c. 570, after Radegunde had made several attempts to establish a better relationship with the Bishop. The purpose of the visit was to obtain counsel and moral support as to how to proceed and no doubt, to discuss the difficulties that had arisen, with someone outside their situation.[35]

From what Baudonivia tells us, it seems that the Rule of Arles was the framework of Radegunde's daily prayer life. No doubt it had undergone some modification, since it was drawn up for a different set of women in a different set of buildings; for example, the Rule provides for a communal dormitory for the sisters, whereas we know that at Poitiers there were private cells, at any rate for Radegunde, the abbess and some sisters, who were living as solitaries.[36] On the other hand, the basic essentials, such as the strict rule of enclosure and the liturgical practices, were probably similar.[37] The Rule of Arles was based on the Rule of Lérins and included monastic practices derived from Pachomius, Cassian, the Rule of the Fathers, and Augustine. Radegunde would therefore be continuing in a very ancient tradition.[38] The Rule of Arles provided for the recital of eighteen psalms during the night–office, six psalms during each of the day–offices, and Scripture readings during the vigils.[39] Such a programme would afford Radegunde many opportunities for reflective prayer; from what Baudonivia tells us, she appears to have been a contemplative and a mystic. Her prayer was continuous, particularly at night. 'Semper in corde et ore cursum decantans, intra arcana cordis sui secrete iugis laus Dei personabat'. Even when unwell or in the state between consciousness and sleep, she used to chant the psalms in spirit with the saints. We are told that the praise of God was so often on her lips that she would summon Eodegunde, the portress of the monastery, by calling out, 'Alleluis!' instead of her name.[40] On one occasions she was so much intent on the spiritual world that she failed to hear noisy, secular singing going on outside the monastery.[41]

As St Teresa of Avila was to do later, she combined intense practicality with the life of a visionary and mystic. Baudonivia affords us glimpses of two of her visions. During the first year of her time at Saix she had a vision of a ship shaped like a man, which appears to represent the Church as the Body of Christ. His message was, 'Modo in genu sedes, adhuc in pectore meo sedem habebis'. This appears to signify that she was still at the beginning of her spiritual development, but would ultimately reach the profoundest depths of spiritual experience. The second vision occurred a year before her death, in 586. She saw both the place prepared for her in the next world and the Master, to whom she had committed herself with so much devotion. He appeared in the guise of a richly dressed young man, who called her the first jewel in his diadem.[43] This vision is in the classic tradition. There were to be many women mystics, among them St Gertrude of Helfta, St Catherine of Siena and St Teresa of Avila, who would see a vision of Christ as their heavenly Bridegroom. In both cases, Radegunde confided the contents of her visions only to faithful friends, who were asked not to divulge them during her lifetime.[44]

Radegunde's prayers for peace are an outstanding example of her gift for intercessory prayer. She was always anxious for the peace and salvation of her country and was capable of playing a political role; when as a religious, she observed the coming of bitterness and strife, presumably the outbreak of the revolt of Chramn and Childebert against Chlothar I in 561, she wrote to the rulers concerned, begging them to make peace with one another.[45] When through her intervention, peace was restored, her devotion to God, we are told, became more intense.[46] Another manifestation of this gift was her practice of praying for her persecutors and urging others to do the same.[47] At night she used to pray for the safety of the monastery, making the sign of the cross.[48] According to Baudonivia, she was 'ialla, quae dolores omnium in se sola transtulit', which seems to me to be a description of a true intercessor.[49]

Another important aspect of Radegunde's spiritual life is her talent for pastoral care and spiritual direction. We are told that her reason for appointing an abbess, substituting the abbess' power for her own and handing over to her her possessions, was that she wanted to feel free to follow in the footsteps of Christ;[50] doubtless she also wanted to have the same kind of freedom to help others. For some years, probably from 569 to 587, when the Bishop of Poitiers did not visit the monastery, there seems to have been no one available to give spiritual direction or instruction to the community. For most of his time Fortunatus was still a layman, who acted as Radegunde's secretary and liaison officer with the outside world. There was, in fact, no one who corresponded to Caesarius in relation to Caesaria at Arles. We know from Baudonivia that Radegunde applied herself daily to prayer, study and preaching[51] and from Fortunatus that she had some knowledge of the writings of the Fathers.[52] We may also surmise that she expounded the Scriptures from her own experience. She was the teacher as well as the loving mother of her community. If any sister plucked up courage to ask her questions about the Scripture readings, she would give an explanation 'with holy and dutiful care and with motherly affection', but if she believed that a sister's failure to understand was due to her not paying full attention to what was being read, she would speak to her severely.

Radegunde's personal spiritual nourishment was probably derived from outside contacts. We know that from her early married days, she enjoyed the company of holy men and liked to consult hermits,[54] and we gather from Baudonivia that she was in the habit of receiving holy men at the monastery, in the *salutatorium* or parlour. From them she used to 'pluck little flowers from which to display the fruit of good works to herself and her followers'.[55] She was always ready to learn from others.[56] Underlying her prayers and her good works was so deep a spirit of humility that she used to say that anyone who had the care of souls ought to have a strong fear of universal praise.[57] This same deep humility also manifested itself in her daily activities. She was content to perform the lowliest domestic tasks, such as clearing out the latrines, oiling and cleaning the sisters' shoes, chopping wood and scouring the kitchen 'till it shone'.[58] It is difficult for us to grasp how revolutionary it was for any free—born lady at the time to do such things, let alone a royal princess.

The cult of the relics of the saints played an important part in the spiritual life of Radegunde. This cult had come into existence in the Gallic Church in the late fourth century, when Ambrose gave Victricius, bishop of Rouen, the relics of no less than thirteen saints, with which to dedicate Rouen Cathedral in 396. In his sermon on that occasion, which he afterwards expanded into the treatise *de laude sanctorum*, Victricius told the people that in the form of relics, part of the heavenly host had visited Rouen, so that even in this life, its citizens would henceforward live in its company.[59] Radegunde's devotion followed similar lines. She had begun to collect relics at Athies; when at Saix, she acquired relics of St Andrew and other saints, and once she was installed at Poitiers, gifts arrived from all over the known world, including a finger of St Mammas from Jerusalem.[60] Radegunde venerated the relics in the belief that, through them, she was linked with the saints in continuous meditation and that she was singing the hymns and psalms in their company. Baudonivia tells us that since Radegunde, through concentration of mind and spirit and through fervent prayer, beheld the Lord in contemplation, she would have asked him to descend from heaven and live on earth in visible form, had that been possible.[61] As it was, she was led to seek a physical relic of his cross, in fact to be for the West what Helena had been for the East. In spite of her years of seclusion, she had not forgotten royal protocol; through the agency of King Sigebert she had a request to the Emperor Justin II for a relic of the True Cross, which was granted in 567/8[62].

Owing to the hostility of Maroveus, a bishop of Poitiers, which has already been mentioned, there was some difficulty over an appropriate reception for the precious fragment.[63] We do not know the reason for this hostility; we can only conjecture that Maroveus, on the one hand, was afraid that Radegunde was trying to establish the monastery as a 'peculiar', independent of episcopal jurisdiction, for which papal provision had been made for the women's community at Arles,[64] and on the other, that he was angry at the request for the relic being made through King Sigebert and jealous lest the monastery might become a more popular and lucrative place of pilgrimage than his cathedral, which lacked a focus of devotion comparable to the tomb of St Martin at Tours. At any rate the relic was eventually brought from Tours, where it had been temporarily lodged at the men's monastery (also founded by Radegunde), to Bishop Euphronius, with much ceremony and amid scenes of great rejoicing. Venantius Fortunatus wrote the famous processional hymns *Vexilla regis* and *Pange, lingua, gloriosi* in honour of the occasion.[65] The relic remains to this day in the guardianship of the Benedictine sisters of the Abbaye de sainte Croix de Poitiers, who are the direct spiritual descendants, in an unbroken line, of Radegunde and her community.[66]

RADEGUNDE'S MIRACLES

It is not my purpose either to discuss whether the miracles reported by Fortunatus and Baudonivia in fact occurred, or except in three obvious instances, to attempt to rationalize them. Rather, it is my intention to try to see how far they conform to hagiographical practices and whether there are literary precedents for any of them, which might be known to our two authors.

For the modern reader, the accounts of the good works and spirituality furnished by Fortunatus and Baudonivia are sufficient evidence for her personal holiness, but to the medieval mind, the performance of miracles was of greater validity as proof of holiness than mere descriptions of good works and prayer. The holy person was expected to display ability to perform 'apostolic works'.[67] These included miracles such as giving sight to the blind, casting out devils, increasing a substance in short supply, and above all, raising the dead. Other qualifications for holiness included the ability to break the chains and fetters of prisoners and to control birds and animals. The miracles could be performed by holy persons while still living or from their tombs after death. Broadly speaking, in Eastern Christendom miracles were performed by living holy persons, whereas in the West they occurred after death. What is interesting is that Fortunatus follows the Eastern tradition in his miracle–stories, but Baudonivia, for the most part, describes miracles, which occurred after the death of Radegunde, following the tradition of Western writers. Though Fortunatus had only a slight knowledge of Greek, he had doubtless heard stories of Eastern holy men in his student days at Ravenna, and both he and Baudonivia must have had access to various Latin works, such as the *Vita S. Martini* and *Dialogues of Sulpicius Severus*, the Latin subject–collection of the *Apophthegmata patrum*, the *Vita S. Caesarii Arelatensis* of Cyprian of Toulon and others, the *Dialogues* of Gregory the Great and some of the writings of Gregory of Tours, notably the *Vita patrum*, where Western holy men are portrayed as miracle–workers.

Fortunatus records eighteen miracles performed either by Radegunde or through her agency. She restored the sight of Bella, the daughter of a nobleman, by signing her eyes with the cross, and healed three demoniacs by means of physical contact.[68] In a fourth case, that of a woman called Leubila, the demon came out while Radegunde prayed.[69] On two occasions, Radegunde made use of leaves: in one, she healed a blister by first making the sign of the cross over it and then covering it with a leaf, proffered by her assistant;[70] in the other, a blade of wormwood, which she used to keep on her breast to refresh herself, was laid on the eye of one of the sisters, whereupon the blood and pain departed and 'a pure light sprang from the green herb'.[71]   Material objects, such as Radegunde's hair–cloth,[72] or the touch of her own hands were also efficacious, but in one of the latter cases, one wonders whether it was not the diet of fruit, rather than the fact that it was proffered to the patient by Radegunde, which brought about the cure.[73] In the same way, it may have been the commonsense treatment of giving a patient, who suffered from spells of extreme heat and extreme cold, a good, hot bath that caused her to recover, rather than a miracle.[74] It is also possible that Radegunde brought a little girl (presumably one of the children entrusted to the sisters for education) back to life by means of a long spell of mouth–to–mouth resuscitation, rather than by miraculous means. After working on the lifeless body for more than seven hours, Radegunde, we are told, rose from prayer and the child from death.[75] After all, this means of reviving apparently dead persons seems to have been known in Old Testament times.[76]

The miracles described by Fortunatus belong almost entirely to the third and fourth periods of Radegunde's life, when she was either at Saix or at Poitiers. The one exception, when she was still married to the King and staying at Athies, was when the chains of some prisoners, for whom she felt compassion, broke while she was saying her office at night.[77]

Floreius, a fisherman who worked for the community, was saved from death by shipwreck, through invoking Radegunde by name, a common type of miracle.[78] Two other stories relate to candles: in both cases, the patient recovers completely when the candle has burned itself out. In one of these cases this must have taken some time, since the candle was the patient's own height.[79]

Of a different genre is the story of Radegunde's appearance to Domnolenus, a tax official, at the time of her own death, when she was asked to build a church to house the relics of St Martin, and to free seven men, whom he had imprisoned.[80]

Finally, there are two miracle–stories, which appear to have been inserted both to provide light relief and to illustrate Radegunde's power over nature. One is a trivial story of a bat, which fell to the ground dead, when it attempted to bite through a thread, which had been spun by Radegunde's own hands.[81] The other concerns a bay–tree, which Radegunde had ordered to be transferred to her cell 'for her delight'. It refused at first to take root, but at her intercession, it came completely to life.[82]

There are biblical or hagiographical precedents for the great majority of all these stories, which can be found in Latin works, to which Fortunatus would have access. An example of sight being restored through the blind person being signed with the cross by a holy man is to be found in the *Dialogues* of Gregory the Great, when Bishop Fortunatus healed a blind man by this means and by prayer.[83] There are at least six parallel examples in the works of Gregory of Tours. One of the healers was a holy woman called Monegunde.[84]

Paulinus of Milan in his life of St Ambrose cites a number of cases where Ambrose drove out demons by the laying–on–of–hands, remarking on one occasion that as Ambrose failed to mention it in his own works, it is not his business to comment on the reason for this![85] Sulpicius Severus supplies one

example in his *Dialogues* and one in his *Vita S. Martini* of hands or fingers used
in exorcisms.[86] There is a close parallel between Martin giving an afflicted cook
a finger to bite and Radegunde treading on the neck of a woman suffering from
demonic possession: in both cases the demon came out through the bowels.[87]
Caesarius of Arles also carried out personal exorcisms, and Gregory of Tours cites
three examples in the *Vita patrum*, where the exorcist, like Martin in the case of
the cook, puts his fingers in the patient's mouth.[88]

The holy woman Monegunde may have been Fortunatus's inspiration for
the two stories of Radegunde's use of plants for healing. Sometimes she used to
spit on vegetables or leaves from apple–trees, and it was her practice to apply
leaves to wounds.[89]

There are many precedents for the use of textiles, which had been in
contact with a holy person, as a means of healing. Particularly efficacious were
small fragments of Martin's cloak or hair–shirt; Caesarius's scarlet cloak, when
applied to a Goth wounded by a lance; a patch cut from Caesarius's chest
protector, which cured a lady called Agretia of a haemorrhage; and his
horse–cloth, contact with which enabled a paralytic to walk.[90]   Thus
Radegunde's hair–cloth was not unique.

The ultimate inspiration for many of the miracle–stores about the raising
of the dead is the Elijah–Elisha sequence in 1 and 2 Kings. Fortunatus describes
Radegunde's resuscitation of the little girl as 'more beati Martini tempore
praesenti antiqui norma miraculi'.   Sulpicius Severus describes two such
miracles: the resuscitation of a death catechumen and the restoration to life of a
house–slave of a man called Lupicinus. In both cases Martin cleared the room, as
Jesus did in the case of Jairus's daughter as a Radegunde was to do, and lay upon
the corpse, as Elijah and Elisha had done. There are similar stories in other
writers, but these two must surely be what Fortunatus had in mind.[91]

Stories of the breaking of chains and fetters abound. Their origin is, of
course, the story of St Peter in Acts 12. Suffice it to say here that according to
Gregory of Tours, numerous broken chains and fetters were to be found on the
tomb of Nicetius, bishop of Lyons, whose powers in this respect were renowned.[92]

Gregory of Tours tells two stories of Martin coming to the rescue, when
his name is invoked by travellers during storms. A further story of this type is
told by Sulpicius Severus of an Egyptian in danger of drowning during a storm in
the Tyrrhenian sea.[93]

Stories of the appearance of saints to individuals in dreams are quite
common. Gregory of Tours consecrated a former store–room as an oratory at the
request of Martin, who appeared to him in a dream.[94] Gregory the Great, in
Dialogue IV, reported four visions of saints, who appeared to persons at the point
of death, but so far, the only example of a saint appearing at the point of his or
her own death, as Radegunde has done to Domnnolenus, that I can find is that of
St John the Almsgiver, which occurs in the Greek life by Leontius.[95]

The story of the apparently dead tree may be linked with two stories told
by Gregory of Tours about the power of Sulpicius Severus to revive moribund
trees and plants.[96]

The eight miracle–stories related by Baudonivia fall into the categories of
miracles, which can appropriately be performed by a holy man or woman. With

two exceptions the miracles are reported as having been performed by Radegunde after her death. The first exception is the miraculous increase of a substance, a story very common in hagiography, the archetype of which is the story of Elijah and the window's cruse of oil. According to Baudonivia, there was a barrel of wine at the monastery, which never became empty. Incidentally Gregory of Tours relates a similar miracle involving Radegunde, whereby there was always an overflowing supply of oil in a lamp in the monastery chapel.[97] The other exception is a story told to illustrate Radegunde's power over living creatures. She is reported to have silenced a night–bird, presumably an owl, which created a disturbance by hooting in a tree in the middle of the monastery.[98]

Only three patients in Baudonivia's stories of healing are mentioned by name: they are all people, who received healing through invocation of the saint's name, though one of them also lay on her hair–cloth.[99] In one of these cases, that of Vinoberga, a servant who after Radegunde's death, presumed to sit in her stall, there is an element of punishment, such as is common in the writings of Gregory of Tours.[100] There is one miracle relating to a candle, but the rest are generalized descriptions of healings at Radegunde's bier or tomb.[101]

Apart from the miracle relating to the candle, there are precedents for all these stories. Accounts of miraculous increases of wine or oil are found in the *Dialogues* of both Sulpicius Severus and Gregory the Great,[102] and there are numerous stories of the power of the holy man or woman over birds and animals in late antique and early medieval literature.[103] There were healings at the bier of Severinus and at the openings of the tombs of Gervase and Protase at Milan. Indeed healings at biers and tombs are a commonplace of Western hagiography.[104]

This investigation has shown that the accounts of Radegunde's miracles are typical of the work of late antique and early medieval hagiographers and do not add anything useful to our knowledge of her life and character, though they provide a useful source for the background of daily life at the monastery. We have seen that in many instances, the basic stories are traditional and have been taken over from the fourth century onwards and given a literary dress. Since a number of the stories are common to both Eastern and Western Christendom, we may postulate the existence of a corpus of material, which was common to the whole of the Mediterranean area and which in the late sixth and early seventh centuries, was making its way to Northern European through the mediation of writers, such as Sulpicius Severus, Gregory the Great, Gregory of Tours and Venantius Fortunatus.

As has already been stated, the two lives, which we have been considering afford us sufficient evidence of the holiness and spirituality of Radegunde, without the addition of their authors' accounts of her possible miracles. They have also shown us something of her administrative and pastoral ability, in which she foreshadows the great abbesses of the later Middle Ages and the foundresses of religious congregations of later times.

NOTES

1.   For references to Radegunde by Gregory of Tours, see *Liber in gloria confessorum* [hereafter LGC] p 104, in *Monumenta Germaniae historica : scriptores rerum Merovingicarum* [hereafter MGH SSRM] 1(ii), ed., B. Krusch (Hannover, 1885, anastatic reprs., 1969), 364–366; *Liber in gloria martyrum* [hereafter LGM] 5, *ibid.*, 39–41; *Libri historiarum* [hereafter

LH] 3.4, in MGH SSRM 1(i), ed., B. Krusch and W. Levison (Hannover, 1951); 7, 105; 6.29, 295–297; 34, 304–305. 7.36, 357–358; 9.3, 415; 39, 460–475; 10.15–18, 501–509. For Baudonivia as Radegunde's personal servant, see Baudonivia, *Vita S. Radegundis, liber ii* [hereafter *Vita* II^a] prol., in MGH SSRM 3, ed., B. Krusch (Hannover, 1896), p 337. Her connection with Radegunde may have begun at Saix, but more probably at Saix.

2. The latest possible date for *Vita* II^a must be 614, prior to the death of Queen Brunhild, who died in that year, but who is represented in *Vita* II^a 116, p 389, as being still alive.

3. e.g., Venantius Fortunatus, *Vita S. Radegundis, liber i* [hereafter *Vita* I^a] 2, MGH SSRM 3, p 365: 'in quantum altitudo saeculi tangit regio de gramine orta, celsa licet origine multo celsior actione'.

4. Cyprian of Toulon *et al.*, *Vita S. Caesarii Arelatensis, libri ii* [hereafter *Vit. S. Caes. Arelat.*], ed., B. Krusch, in MGH SSRM 3, pp 48–501; Venantius Fortunatus, *Vita S. Hilarii Pictavensis*, in *Monumenta Germaniae historica: auctores antiquissimi* [hereafter MGH AA] 4(ii), ed., B. Krusch (Berlin, 1885), pp 1–7; *Vita S. Marcelli, ibid.*, pp 49–54.

5. *Vita* I^a 1. p 365.

6. *Vita* II^a prol. p 378.

7. Gregory of Tours, LH 3.7, p 105; Venantius Fortunatus, *Vita* I^a 2, p 273 *de excidio Thuringiae*, ed., F. Leon, MGH AA 4(i), *Carm. App.* 1, pp 271–275; *Carm* 8.1, pp 21–24, 179.

8. The matrimonial affairs of Chlothar I are somewhat confused, but from the evidence available, it appears that his partners were: (1) Ingunde; (2) Aregunde, sister of Ingunde; (3) Chunsina; (4) Guntheuc, widow of his brother Chlodomir. Ingunde and Guntheuc were probably the only official wives, the rest being concubines. As they were dead by the time that Radegunde was of marriageable age, Chlothar was free to marry her officially and she was able to receive a *Morgengabe*.

9. *Vita* I^a 2, p 365.

10. *Ibid.*, p 366.

11. *Ibid.*, 5, p 366–367.

12. *Ibid.*, 4, p 366; 8, p 367.

13. *Ibid.*, 5, p 367.

14. *Ibid.*, 12, p 368. For Radegunde's lament on the death of her brother, see *de excidio Thuringiae, Carm. App. 1*, pp 123–156, MGH 4(ii), pp 274–275.

15. *Vita* I^a 12, p 368. For discussion of Radegunde's consecration as deacon, see Sister Theresa, CSA, 'Women in the diaconate', *Distinctive Diaconate*, Study 23, fasc. 4 (April 1985), pp 110–116 (obtainable from the Community of St Andrew, 2 Tavistock Road, London W11 1BA); Michel Rouche, 'Le mariage et le célibat consacré de sainte Radegonde' in 'La riche personalité de sainte Radegonde' (conférences et homélies du xive centenaire, Poitiers, (1987) [hereafter *La riche personnalité*], Poitiers, 1988, pp 79–98.

16. See Rouche, in *La riche personnalité*, p 87.

17. *Vita* II^a 3, p 380. For an explanation of the *Morgengabe*, see Rouche in *La riche personalité*, pp 82–83.

18. *Vita* I^a 17–18, p 370.

19. e.g. *Vita* I^a 25–26, pp 372–373.

20. *Vita* II^a 4, pp 380–381; 6, p 382.

21. LH 3.7, p 105. For an interesting interpretation, see Rouche, in *La riche personalité*, pp 85–87.

22. For the number of sisters, see LGC 104, p 364.

23. *Vita* II^a 21–28, pp 392–395; LGC 104, pp 364–366.

24.   Jean Leclercq, 'La sainte Radegonde de Venance Fortunat et celle de
       Baudonivie: essai d'hagiographie comparée', in *Fructus centesimus:
       melanges offerts à Gérard J.M. Bartelink* ... ed., A.A.R. Bastiaensen *et al.*,
       (Steenbrugge, 1989), pp 207–216.
25.   LH 9.42, pp 470–474.
26.   See 9n above. For substitutes for martyrdom, see J.M. Petersen, *The
       Dialogues of Gregory the Great in their late antique cultural background*,
       Studies and Texts 69 (Toronto, 1984), p 73; F. Graus, *Volk, Herrscher und
       Heiliger im Reich der Merowinger* (Prague, 1965) pp 92–95.
27.   *Vita* Iᵃ 21, p 371.
28.   *Ibid.*, 6, pp 367; 22, 372; 25, 372–373.
29.   *Ibid.*, 26, p 373.
30.   Rouche, in *La riche personalité*, pp 85–890.
31.   See H. Platelle, 'La violence et ses remèdes en Flandre au xiᵉ siècle',
       Sacris erudiri 20 (1971), pp 101–169, esp. pp 145–146, 152.
32.   The text of the letter is found in LH 9.42, pp 470–474. Note especially
       the opening and closing sentences.
33.   LH 9.42, p 470.
34.   For the history of the adoption of the Rule of Arles, see A. de Vogüé's
       commentary to Césaire d'Arles, *Oeuvres monastiques* 1, SC 345, (Paris,
       1988) pp 443–460 [hereafter *Oeuvres monastiques* 1]; Y. Labande–
       Mailfert, 'Les débuts de sainte Croix', in *Histoire de sante Croix de
       Poitiers* [hereafter *Sainte Croix de Poitiers*], Mémoires de la Société des
       Antiquaries de l'Ouest, 4ᵉ série, t19 (Poitiers, 1986–1987), pp 41–45.
35.   If we accept that the *Epistola* of Caesaria the Younger to Radegunde
       (*Oeuvres monastiques* 1, 476/477–494/495) was written in the early days
       of the monastery at Poitiers, c. 552–557, as its wording and general tone
       suggests, we come into conflict with the statement of Gregory of Tours
       (LH 9.40, 464–465) that Radegunde and the abbess went on a journey to
       Arles as the result of the dispute with Maroveus, bishop of Poitiers,
       concerning the relic of the True Cross (567/568), and that it was after this
       visit that the Rule of Arles was accepted, in c. 570. But if the decision
       was made only at this date to adopt the Rule, why did not Radegunde and
       the abbess take the copy home with them? What would be the sense of
       the statement in the letter, 'Ego feci quod praecepistis: transmisi exempla
       de regula'. We must, I fear, accept that Gregory of Tours, though a
       serious and careful historian, sometimes makes errors of fact (cf. 62n
       below) and that on the whole, the hypothesis that the Rule was originally
       adopted early in the monastery's history, but assumed a new importance
       after the visit to Arles in c. 570, is the more tenable.
36.   For Radegunde's private cell, e.g., *Vita* Iᵃ 22, p 371; 29, p 374; 33, p 375;
       37, p 376; for the solitaries' cells, e.g. LH 6.29, pp 296–297; 9.40, p 466. It
       is generally assumed that as Radegunde had a private cell, the abbess
       must also have had one, but nowhere is this explicitly stated. For the ban
       on private cells at Arles, see Caesarius of Arles, *Regula virginum* [hereafter
       Reg. virg. p 51, in *Oeuvres monastiques* 1, 236/237–238/239.
37.   For the rule of enclosure at Arles, see *Reg. virg.* 2, in *Oeuvres monastiques*
       1, pp 180/181. The fact that the sisters were not allowed to leave the
       monastery to follow in Radegunde's funeral procession, but had to watch
       it from the turret windows (Gregory of Tours, LGC 104, p 365), shows
       that this part of the Rule of Arles was strictly observed in the monastery
       at Poitiers.
38.   For the historical origins of the Rule, see A. de Vogüé's commentary in
       Oeuvres monastiques 1, pp 45–87.

39. For these and other liturgical provisions of the Rule, see *Reg. virg.* 66, in *Oeuvres monastiques* 1, pp 252/253–256/257; for the readings at vigils, see *ibid.*, pp 68–69, 258/259–266/267.

40. *Vita* II^a 19, p 390; 8, p 383.

41. *Vita* I^a 36, pp 375–376; see also *Vit. S. Caes. Arelat.* 1.46, pp 474–475.

42. *Vita* II^a 3, p 380.

43. *Ibid.*, 20, p 391.

44. *Ibid.*, 3, p 380; 20, p 391.

45. *Ibid.*, 10, p 384. For the revolt of Chramn and Childebert, see Gregory of Tours, LH 4.13–21, pp 144–154.

46. *Vita* II^a 10, p 385.

47. *Ibid.*, 8, p 383.

48. *Ibid.*, 28, p 390.

49. *Ibid.*, 11, p 385.

50. *Ibid.*, 5, p 381.

51. *Ibid.*, 8, p 383; 17, p 390.

52. *Carm.*, 8.1, pp 53–61, MGH AA 4(i), pp 179–180. Radegunde may have read portions of the authors mentioned in *florilegia*, but as the three Greek authors in the list were partly available in Latin translations (even by the end of the fourth century, there were at least two Latin versions of Athanasius's life of Antony in circulation), it is possible that she was able to study the texts.

53. *Vita* II^a 9, p 384.

54. *Vita* I^a 6, p 367; 8,p 367; 13, p 369; 18, p 370; *Vita* II^a 4, p 381; 9, p 384.

55. *Vita* II^a 9, p 384.

56. *Ibid.*, p 383.

57. *Ibid.*, 14, pp 386–387.

58. *Vita* I^a 23–24, p 372.

59. *de laude sanctorum* 3, PL 20 p 445; see also E.W. Kemp, *Canonisation and authority in the early Church*, 1948, pp 4–5.

60. *Vita* II^a 13. p 386. St Mamma is probably identical with St Mamas or Mammes, who according to Basil (*Hom.* 23, PG 31 589) and Gregory of Nazianzus (*in ix dominicam*, Or. 44, PG 36 620), was a shepherd of Caesarea in Cappadocia. He is said to have suffered persecution and martyrdom (c. 275). According to Eastern Christian tradition, he was stoned to death in the reign of the Emperor Aurelian, but the Roman martyrolgy informs us that 'he underwent a prolonged persecution from youth to old age'. A number of legends have become attached to him, but in reality, little is known about him.

61. *Vita* II^a 16, pp 387–388.

62. *Ibid.*, pp 388–389; Gregory of Tours, LH 9.40, pp 464–465; LGM 5, pp 39–40. Gregory of Tours differs from Baudonivia in placing Radegunde's search for relics of the martyrs *after* the arrival of the relic of the True Cross. He appears to have confused two separate expeditions made to the Near East by the priest Reovalis. The first, mentioned by Baudonivia (*Vita* II^a 14, pp 386–387), was for the purpose of collecting the relic of St Mammas; the second occurred rather later, probably c. 570, when Radegunde sent 'missos suos, supradictum presbytrum cum asliis', to the Emperor in Constantinople to convey her thanks for the relic and to give him a simple present. For Helena's invention of the True Cross, see Socrates, *Hist. trip.* 2.18, CSEL 71, rev. ed. 1952, pp 114–115.

63. LH 9.40, pp 464–465; *Vita* II^a 16, p 388. These passages give the impression that Maroveus was not at first ill–disposed towards the reception of the relic, but was worked upon by some of the inhabitants of Poiters.

64.   For the permissin to establish a 'peculiar', see Hormisdas, *Epistola* 2, in
      Oeuvres monastiques 1, pp 354/355.
65.   LH 9.40, p 464; *Vita II*ᵃ 16, pp 388–389. For the hymns by Venantius
      Fortunatus, see *Carm.* 3.3 (Pange, lingua, gloriosi), MGH AA 4(i), 28; 6
      (Vexilla regis), *ibid.*, 34, which are familiar to English–speaking
      Christians in the nineteenth–century translations by J.M. Neale (*Hymns
      Ancient and Modern*, Standard edn, 96, 97; *English Hymnal* 94, 95, 96;
      New English Hymnal 78, 79, 517).
66.   For an interesting accunt of this community, now established at La
      Cossonnière, Saint–Benoît–sur–Quinçay, near Poitiers, see *Sante Croix de
      Poiters.* The Rule of St Benedict was probably adopted at the time of the
      reforms of Benedict of Aniane, c. 817.
67.   See Matt. 10.1; Luke 9.1–2; Cassian, *Collationes* 1.9, ed., M. Petschenig;
      CSEL 13(2), (Vienna, 1886), p 16.
68.   *Vita I*ᵃ 27, p 373; 28, p 373; 30, p 374; 33, p 374.
69.   *Ibid.*, 28, p 373.
70.   *Ibid.*, 20, p 371.
71.   *Ibid.*, 34, p 375.
72.   As above.
73.   *Ibid.*, 20, p 371.
74.   *Ibid.*, 29, p 373–374.
75.   *Ibid.*, 37. p 376.
76.   e.g., 2 Kings 4.34.
77.   *Vita I*ᵃ 11, p 368.
78.   *Ibid.*, 31, p 374.
79.   *Ibid.*, 20, p 371; 32, p 374.
80.   *Ibid.*, 38, p 376.
81.   *Ibid.*, 30, p 374.
82.   *Ibid.*, 22, pp 374–375.
83.   Gregory the Great, *Dialogues* 1.10 [hereafter G.Dial.], *Les Dialogues de
      Gregoire le Grand*, ed. A. de Vogué, 1–3, SC 251, pp 260, 265, (Paris,
      1978–1980), t2, 92/93–94/95.
84.   Gregory of Tours, *Liber de virtutibus S. Iuliani* [hereafter VSJ] 22, MGH
      SSRM 1(ii), p 51; LH 2.3, p 42; 6.6, p 251; *Vita patrum* [hereafter VP]
      5(1), MGH SSRM 1(ii), p 678; ;15(3), p 722; 19, p 738.
85.   Paulinus of Milan, *Vita S. Ambrosii* [hereafter Vit. S. Ambros] p 28, ed.,
      A.A.R. Bastiaensen, Vite di santi 3, (Milan, 1975), pp 90/91.
86.   Sulpicius Severus, *Dialogues* [hereafter SSDial] 2(3), p 15, Sulpicius
      Severus, *Opera*, ed., C. Halm, CSEL 1, (Vienna, 1866), p 213; *Vita S.
      Martini* [hereafter SSVM] 17, Sulpice Sévère, *La view de saint Martin*, ed.
      J. Fontaine, SC 133–135, (Paris, 1967–1969), t1, 288/289–290/291.
87.   As above; *Vita I*ᵃ 30, p 374.
88.   *Vit. S. Caes. Arelat.* 2.2, p 484; 4, p 485; Gregory of Tours, VP 2(1),
      p 219; 4(4), p 226; 9(2), p 254.
89.   *Ibid.*, 9(3), p.289; LGC 24, p 243.
90.   SSVM 18.3, t1, 292/293; SSDial 2(3).9, p 207; *Vit. S. Caes. Arelat.* 2.12,
      p 488; 9, p 487; 13, p 489.
91.   *Vita I*ᵃ 37, p 376; cf. SSVM 7, t1, 268/269; 8, *ibid.*, 270/271; 1 Kings
      17.21; 2 Kings 4.34–35; Matt. 9, esp. v25. For similar stories, see *Vit. S.
      Caes. Arelat.* 1.39–40, p 472; 2.2–4, pp 484–485; GDial 1.2, t2,
      26/27–30/31; 2.32, 226/227–228/229.
92.   Gregory of Tours, VP 8.6, p 247. For similar stories, see e.g., *Liber de
      virtutibus S. Martini* [hereafter VSM] 1.23, MGH SSKM3, p 600; *ibid.*, 36,
      p 605; *ibid.*, 4.16, p 654.

93.   VSM 1.2, p 588; 9, pp 593–594; SSDial 2(3).14, p 212. The Egyptian was
       not yet a Christian.

94.   LGC 20, p 759; GDial 4.12–14, t3, 48/49–58/59.

95.   Leontius of Naples, *Vita S. Iohannis Eleemosynarii* p 46, ed., H. Gelzer,
       Freiburg i/Br and Leipzig, 1903, pp 260–261. No Latin version of this life
       appears to have been available at this time, but possibly this was a story
       common in the Mediterranean area in the late sixth century.

96.   Gregory of Tours, LGC 49–60, pp 327–328.

97.   *Vita* IIᵃ 10, p 384; Gregory of Tours LGM 6, p 40.

98.   *Vita* IIᵃ 19, pp 390–391.

99.   *Vita* IIᵃ 11 (Mammezo), p 385; 12 (Vinoberga), p 385; 15 (Leo, who also
       lay on Radegunde's hair–cloth), p 387.

100.   Numerous stories relate to people, who suffer physical punishment, such as
       contraction of their limbs, for e.g., working on Sundays, until the power of
       the holy man or woman is invoked; e.g., VSM 3.7, pp 183–184.

101.   *Vita* IIᵃ 24, p 393; 25, p 394; 27, p 394; 28, pp 394–395.

102.   e.g., SSDial 2(3). 13, pp 200–201; GDial 19, t2, pp 55–56 (the closest
       parallel among several examples). This is a *topos*.

103.   The power of the holy man or woman over living creatures is a *topos* of
       hagiography. Other examples contemporary with Radegunde or a little
       later, are Columbanus (Jonas, *Vita Columbani abbatis* ... 1.17, MGH
       SSRM 4, p 83) and Brigid of Kildare (Cogitosus, *Vita*, PL 72, pp 782–783.

104.   For further examples, see Gregory of Tours, VSM 2.3, p 160; 6, p 161;
       13, p 163; Eugippius, *Vita S. Severini* 46, ed., R. Noll, (Berlin, 1963),
       114/115; *Vit. S. Ambros.* 14, 70/71.

WHAT WAS AN EARLY ANGLO–SAXON MONASTERY?

Sarah Foot

No writer from the early Anglo–Saxon period defined precisely what a *monasterium* (in Old English a *mynster*) was, but the canons of the 747 council of *Clofesho* did specify how the inmates of such an institution ought to conduct themselves. *Monasteria* were to be, as their name implied, virtuous dwellings of stillness, and of those who quietly laboured for the Lord; they were not to be refuges for those indulging in boisterous arts, but habitations of prayer, reading and the praise of God, of sober and continent living and psalmody.[1] The majority of descriptions of religious houses or of the monastic life found in early English texts are, however, exceedingly vague and do little to clarify the nature of early English monasticism. *Monasterium*, *coenobium*, and the Old English *mynster* were in fact used synonymously, and very imprecisely, to denote a wide variety of types of establishment by the writers of early Anglo–Saxon historical and hagiographical texts as well as by those who drafted charters and secular and ecclesiastical legislation.

It is possible that by the early eighth century communal religious houses had become such an ordinary part of the ecclesiastical structure, and presumably also of the local landscape, that it could safely be assumed that anyone, lay or cleric, would understand what sorts of institution these words signified, thus obviating the necessity for further clarification. During the tenth century, however, the protagonists in the Benedictine reform of religious houses which reached its apogee in King Edgar's reign (A.D. 959–975) not only stated very precisely what a reformed *monasterium* should be like, but also defined the character of English religious houses in a past golden age before the depredations of vikings or of 'rapacious strangers' had reduced them to the parlous state of decay believed to pertain in *ca* 960.[2] The assumption underlying these accounts was that the earliest Anglo–Saxon religious houses, those founded under the inspiration of the first Roman mission, had all pursued the same life as that adopted by Augustine at Canterbury on Pope Gregory's recommendation, and that this was in essence if not in fact equivalent to life under the Rule of St Benedict.[3]

While modern historians have dismissed the tenth–century monks' criticisms of the unreformed houses as hyperbole, and have rejected the reformers' assertion that early English houses were exclusively Benedictine, the farther–reaching influences of this tenth–century literature have not so readily been appreciated.[4] Not only has reforming rhetoric affected historical perceptions of the reform itself, but it has also, more importantly, influenced our understanding of the condition of religious institutions in the centuries that preceded the revival. It is necessary to set aside the unrepresentative picture presented by later monastic commentators and to view the early Anglo–Saxon Church more objectively, according to contemporary standards.

To this end, I present here some of the conclusions about the nature of early Anglo–Saxon religious houses which may be drawn from the sources written in England before the end of King Alfred's reign; by demonstrating how minsters were perceived in the period before *ca* 900 it is possible to come closer to understanding what such establishments were really like.[5] I concentrate on three issues which illustrate the functions minsters were apparently designed to fulfil:

the motives inspiring the founders of houses and their benefactors; the composition of monastic communities and the ideals which motivated individuals to adopt the religious life; and the activities pursued by religious within and without the cloister.   In order to retain as much freedom as possible from traditional images of early English monasticism, I have chosen to adopt a neutral terminology for the religious life and to avoid the rather loaded word 'monastery' which has previously been used by most historians to translate *monasterium*, *coenobium*, and *mynster*. I shall use instead the single word 'minster' to denote all houses, without intending to convey anything more than that each such institution supported a community of those nominally following a religious life.[6]

One of the difficulties in attempting to re–evaluate the early evidence lies in the nature of the sources themselves. While the saints' lives may incidentally provide a good deal of information about the activities of their subjects, many such incidents served only to demonstrate the individual's adherence to accepted patterns of saintly behaviour. Equally the canons of church councils reveal much about the ideals of monasticism as perceived by the episcopal draftsmen of such literature, but little of the monks' own perceptions of such issues. An undue proportion of the available evidence also relates to the histories of the larger, richer houses; small, impoverished, non–royal houses are much less frequently described. However, the most grave difficulty lies in the fact that for the earliest period of Anglo–Saxon Christian history the historian is dependent to a large extent on the writings of Bede, which tend to reflect his own idealistic, and arguably unrepresentative, opinion of the practice of monasticism, derived from his own experiences at Jarrow. It also appears, because of the paramount importance Bede placed on church unity and conformity of religious behaviour, that he may deliberately have presented a standardized version of the monastic practices of different houses as part of his overall aim of demonstrating England's common ecclesiastical heritage. Thus, the *Historia ecclesiastica* may reveal rather what Bede thought a minster ought to be, and little of what houses other than Wearmouth and Jarrow were truly like.[7] If this were true it would serve to reinforce our opinion of the unreliability of the tenth–century reformers' version of events, since theirs is heavily reliant on a selective reading of Bede.[8]

In attempting to get closer towards a definition of what a minster was, it seems appropriate to begin by considering how and why such an institution might have been founded. The acquisition of sufficient land to support a community collectively (ideally obtained in the form of a grant made in perpetuity) would seem to have been a prerequisite for the creation of a new minster; both narrative and documentary sources from the early Anglo–Saxon period seem to equate the process of founding minsters with the granting of lands for their sustenance. Bede described how Benedict Biscop obtained seventy hides from King Ecgfrith with which to found his minster at Wearmouth,[9] and Alcuin told how a certain Wilgils was given 'in perpetual gift a number of small landed properties ... for the purpose of building a church to God' on the Humber estuary where he had previously lived as a solitary.[10] Similarly, many charters record the granting of lands for the purpose of founding minsters to layman as well as to those who had already taken the habit.[11]   Churches were not, however, all uniformly well–endowed and many of the early grants of which record survives were relatively modest; Hild's first community on the north side of the Wear, for example, was established on only one hide of land.[12]   There are also a few references in the sources to those who were unable, through lack of land or other resources, to found houses; this may, for instance, have been the reason why the monk Trimma could not build a minster at Hatfield Chase where King Edwin had first been buried.[13]

There were, however, substantial economic advantages in holding land designated for the service of God, for it was freed from all secular obligations, other than the building of bridges and fortresses and the provision of military service.[14] Even though such privileges were not necessarily inviolable (Boniface protested to Archbishop Cuthbert in 747 that English monks were being wrongfully forced to participate in royal building programmes),[15] Bede demonstrated in his letter to Bishop Ecgberht of York that the existence of these financial benefits might offer considerable incentives to the fraudulent to pretend to establish minsters on their own estates, while in fact continuing to live within them in a basically secular fashion with their wives and children.[16] It is, however, all too easy to dwell unduly on the iniquities of those who founded minsters for personal gain, forgetting that the majority of new foundations must reflect rather the devotional zeal of their first inmates and benefactors.

From the outset Anglo–Saxon monasticism incorporated elements of both the active and the devotional life, and there is no evidence that early Anglo–Saxon religious saw this as in any way incongruous. It is thus extremely hard to say whether a minster was created to fulfil an active pastoral role or to satisfy the contemplative zeal of an individual or family. The first houses in most areas were mission stations, housing groups of religious who combined a life of some corporate devotion with the work of converting the local populace; such communities continued to assume responsibility for the spiritual welfare of these people beyond their initial nominal conversion. Thereafter, some houses might deliberately have been positioned near a centre of population with the intention of carrying the teaching and sacraments of the faith to the laity as were Cedd's churches in Essex (such as Bradwell),[17] or as is hinted in the admittedly dubious foundation charter for Breedon–on–the–Hill in Leicestershire.[18] Others may have been created primarily as places devoted to the contemplative life, in fulfilment of the devotional piety of a family or individual, as it would appear were the minsters at Wearmouth and Jarrow founded by Benedict Biscop.[19] But even a minster originally established without the needs of the laity in mind like Wilgils' Northumbrian cell could find itself attracting the populace to visit or even settle in its vicinity, and so become obliged to provide for their spiritual welfare.[20]

Hagiographers naturally had a good deal to say about the pious motives which inspired their subjects to adopt the religious life, although their remarks are not necessarily to be taken literally and may often reveal more of their own than of their subjects' views on such matters. A number of future saints apparently chose religion in childhood or early youth, or were consigned to the cloister by parents ready to enjoy salvation vicariously. These included Bede himself,[21] Eata, later abbot of Melrose,[22] and Boniface.[23] Some monastics came to an understanding of the emptiness of worldly pursuits only after experiencing these directly; Guthlac and Eosterwine had both been soldiers before they renounced the world and laid down their arms to become soldiers of Christ.[24] Many also came to the minsters in widowhood, or as a means of escaping from uncongenial marriages; entry to the religious life was recognized in several texts as grounds for dissolving a marriage.[25]

It is also possible that minsters may to some extent have been considered suitable refuges for the otherwise unemployable, and not just surplus daughters who could be much more cheaply wedded to Christ than to man, but the mentally and physically less able. Such individuals were by early medieval standards unsuited to sanctity (unless they could be cured by a miracle), and were denied elevation to the priesthood by canon law,[26] so it is unlikely that the contemporary sources would comment on their presence within religious communities. However, since many minsters played a prominent part in the care of the sick, and some of them (such as Ely and Dacre) included men described as doctors,[27] it may plausibly be argued that such communities did take responsibility for those unsuited by age or infirmity to life in the world. Wilfrid first entered the minster at Lindisfarne in order to accompany one of the king's former companions, a certain Cudda, who decided to leave the world because he had developed a paralytic infirmity,[28] and at least one of the nuns at Barking was seriously disabled.[29] Special arrangements were made in the latter house and elsewhere (at Whitby for example) for the care of the infirm and the sick.[30]

It is now generally accepted that no one monastic rule which now survives was used exclusively to regulate the customs of any single religious house in England at any time before the monastic reforms of Edgar's reign imposed the Rule of St Benedict on all religious houses. Although various rules, including those written by Benedict and Columbanus, were known in England in the early period, no one, not even Bede, seems to have expected that all minsters would follow identical rules. The various ecclesiastical synods in the eighth and early ninth centuries instructed only that minsters be governed regularly, and did not attempt to direct what sort of rule was to be followed.[31]

Instead, the inhabitants of early minsters seem to have devised their own systems on the basis of pre-existing rules with which their first leaders were familiar, adapted to conform with their individual ideas and to suit local circumstances. Groups of houses may have followed similar sets of customs and more than one 'rule' may have governed the activities of one establishment. For example, at Wearmouth and Jarrow a composite set of regulations was devised and written down for future reference, and this was used in conjunction with the Rule of St Benedict and a privilege from Pope Agatho obtained by Benedict Biscop to order the way of life in these houses.[32] At Lindisfarne, Cuthbert arranged and composed a rule of life which was apparently observed thereafter 'along with the Rule of St Benedict'.[33]

Entry to the religious life may have been marked by the formal taking of vows, marking the postulant's acceptance of the discipline of the house; this presumably involved a promise of obedience to the community and its head, the renunciation of personal property, and some commitment to remain within the monastic life permanently. The council of Hertford in 672/3 directed that monks were not to wander from place to place but were to 'remain under that obedience which they promised at the time of their profession'.[34] But, although this might suggest that the concept of stability was recognized at this period, it seems that a number of clergy, monks, and indeed nuns refused to remain within their parent houses and caused a good deal of concern to the ecclesiastical establishment.[35] On the other hand, the maintenance of regular pastoral ministry to the laity was incompatible with complete enclosure, and the personal histories of various individuals demonstrate that some monastic populations could at times be quite fluid.

Descriptions of the daily activities of the members of religious communities are frequently to be found quite incidentally included in narrative accounts in saints' lives of miracles or other significant events which took place within minsters or on their estates. Such texts naturally stress incidents in their subjects' lives deemed to demonstrate their sanctity and distinguish the saints from their less exalted companions, but the mundane details of daily life are more likely to be ignored as irrelevant. Consequently only a partial picture of a monastic day can be assembled, and even that must be pieced together from a variety of sources of different date relating to diverse geographical areas; only the anonymous Life of Ceolfrith, Bede's *Historia abbatum* and Æthelwulf's poem *De abbatibus* provide anything approaching a comprehensive picture of the activities pursued within individual minsters. However, certain pursuits appear to have been common to a number of houses and by examining these, it may be possible to define more closely the features which characterized the minster.

A minster's liturgical obligations seem to have provided a framework for its inmates' daily lives. Stories in saints' lives are often placed in context by being described as occurring after 'the psalmody of the third hour',[36] or 'when the accustomed time of nightly prayer arrived'.[37] It is not easy, before the tenth century, to establish a timetable for the monastic offices from the literary evidence, but it does seem that most houses engaged in some form of corporate devotional activity more than once in the day, and that these offices were based on a mixture of psalmody, reading from Scripture, and intercession. At Jarrow, at least, the offices which began and ended the day were apparently considered the most important.[38] Many communities also held a service in the middle of the night, for which the majority of their number would be woken, perhaps by a bell or other signal.[39] Other offices, possibly including a mass,[40] may have taken place during the day, but there is insufficient evidence to be certain how many such services there may have been. It was stipulated at the reforming council of *Clofesho* in 747 that 'the seven canonical hours of prayer by day and night be diligently observed, by singing proper psalms and canticles' according to the Roman model, but there is only one other reference to a seven–fold office, in a letter from the East Anglian king, Ælfwald, to Boniface, datable to 747x749.[41] Several texts do, however, give the impression that there was a recognised sequence of offices at appointed hours,[42] even if most references to these are very imprecise.

Presumably attendance at the office was compulsory; Bede at least told of a recalcitrant monk who refused to 'go to the church with the brothers to sing psalms and pray and listen to the word of life', and implied that he encountered his unpleasant end as a direct consequence of this.[43] However, there were circumstances in which certain individuals might be excused from this requirement.[44] The liturgical obligations of those who were engaged in activities outside the confines of their parent house, whether in ministering to their lay neighbours or attending to estate business are unclear. Perhaps those working in distant parts of the estate stopped whatever they were doing to say the office in the fields; they may even have continued to work while singing psalms and praying.[45]

Manual labour would certainly seem to have played a part in the lives of some early Anglo–Saxon religious, but it is far from clear whether all the inmates of minsters engaged in arduous physical work. Eosterwine, although of noble birth, was reputed to have taken his fair share in a variety of types of agricultural and domestic labour, and to have assisted with iron–working at Wearmouth;[46] Cuthbert also apparently considered physical endeavour to be important, working with his hands even when he was praying at night.[47] He was said to have ensured that he himself was not so abstinent in food that he should become unfit for necessary labour.[48] Other monks and nuns may, however, have interpreted the concept of labour more liberally and engaged only in the lighter agricultural tasks, such as weeding or fruit–picking, while the heavier work was performed by the communities' slaves and tenants. Labour undertaken for the good of the community collectively also encompassed a number of domestic activities, including the preparation of food and the weaving of clothes and ecclesiastical vestments as well as, in some houses, the manufacture of liturgical vessels and ornaments,[49] glass–making, and sculpture. It is, however, quite probable that many noble–born religious shared the attitude of the nun Leoba, who although reputed to have worked with her hands, 'for she had learnt that he who will not work should not eat', in actuality 'spent more time in reading and listening to Sacred Scripture than she gave to manual labour'.[50]

A good deal of the monastic day in many houses must have been devoted to intellectual pursuits, ranging from the learning of literate skills, through the private reading of Scripture and exegesis, to more advanced theological study and the composition of original literary works. Various texts singled out reading as an appropriate activity for religious,[51] and specified minsters' responsibilities in educating particularly the young in their care (who might include children of the laity destined for secular careers, as well as child oblates).[52] The level of study obviously varied considerably from house to house, and this was one of the grounds on which a particularly outstanding individual might gain permission to leave his first minster. Boniface, for example, was allowed to leave Exeter because of its lack of suitable teachers and go to Nursling,[53] and Aldhelm moved from Malmesbury to study with Hadrian at Canterbury.[54] While some religious were engaged in their own studies, or in copying texts for their libraries or to send to other communities,[55] others may have been involved in copying books or charters and other documents on behalf of lay people.[56] Such intellectual endeavour would keep these individuals apart from those labouring in the fields.

Except in the most austere houses some part of each day was presumably spent in relative idleness and relaxation, but not surprisingly the sort of literature on which I have been dependent thus far is not particularly informative on this subject. Adomnan's vision of the iniquities perpetrated at Coldingham is quite revealing, giving a picture of a house devoted to feasting, drinking, gossip and 'other delights' the saint was too coy to mention.[57] The women were said to spend their time weaving elaborate garments with which to adorn themselves.[58] Further possible monastic pursuits are indicated from the directive of the council of *Clofesho* of 747 that minsters were not to be filled with poets, harpists, musicians, and buffoons, and that solemn religious festivals were not to be celebrated with games, horse–racing, and feasting.[59] Similarly, Alcuin accused the boys being educated at Wearmouth of hare–coursing and fox–hunting.[60] If one were to interpret Alcuin's letters literally, one might think that English monks did nothing (other than dressing up in finery) besides drink and feast: the letters contain innumerable references to immoderate eating and excessive drinking. Other texts also refer to the undue consumption of alcohol in early Anglo–Saxon minsters; Guthlac was mocked by the other brothers at Repton for his refusal to drink beer, of which English monks seem to have been inordinately fond.[61] Indeed the reputation of the English abroad was already tarnished in the eighth century; Boniface reported that English monks were notorious throughout Europe for their drunken behaviour.[62]

Many communities apparently engaged in a variety of activities for the benefit of their lay neighbours, some of which took their members away from the confines of the minster. All religious houses were deemed to have a paramount intercessory role, being expected to pray and say masses for the souls of their king and his people in general, as well as petitioning for particular individuals.[63] The minster itself acted as a focus for the laity, the community providing a model of devout behaviour for its neighbours, and the church a visible symbol of their faith. Many of the local inhabitants must have attended at least at major feasts to receive the sacraments, if not every Sunday as Bede and the canon lawyers thought they should.[64]

A number of ecclesiastics travelled away from their minster to preach to the laity, such as the visiting priests who came to Boniface's father's house,[65] or Cuthbert, who undertook lengthy perambulations throughout his diocese, travelling purposely to preach to specific groups,[66] as well as to administer baptism.[67] Bede laid great stress on the importance of preaching and on the role of minsters in this work; he did not envisage that this labour should be restricted entirely to those in clerical orders, or even exclusively to men.[68] Its importance was also stressed by Boniface and by Alcuin.[69]

There has been much debate between historians as to whether distinctions should be drawn at this period between houses with an active pastoral role and those devoted exclusively to contemplation.[70] If parochial ministry is defined in purely sacramental terms, it is clear that its exercise in the early Anglo–Saxon period was restricted to a few establishments comprising sufficient numbers of priests able and willing to perform such functions. If, however, the *cura animarum* is understood to encompass a broader range of pastoral activities, including preaching, teaching, the care of the sick, the giving of alms and the reception of visitors, then there is nothing in theory against the presumption that most if not all houses were partly involved in some of these activities, although the nature of the source material is such that they are unlikely to be mentioned in relation to the activities of each community.[71]

It is in fact clear that early Anglo–Saxon monasticism was characterized by its diversity of practice. The only conclusion to be drawn is that an early Anglo–Saxon minster housed a congregation of people who had decided that they wanted to live communally apart from the rest of the world, nominally devoting their lives to the service of God. Beyond this insistence on shared separation it is impossible to reconstruct any single model to which all houses even in one part of one kingdom conformed, let alone to define a structure applicable to the whole country.

The strictest of houses may have been organized on lines similar to those set out in the early monastic rules used elsewhere in the western Church; these would have been notable for their communal poverty, regular corporate worship and individual devotion. Such a way of life would not have been incompatible with the provision of some sacramental and other pastoral services to the laity. Many other establishments seem, however, to have been less rigidly structured, and may have shared more characteristics of the secular noble life; these houses maintained more frequent and informal contacts with their lay neighbours.

A minster was therefore whatever its occupants wanted it to be. This was often not what bishops or leading ecclesiastics like Bede, Boniface, or Alcuin thought it ought to be.

NOTES

1.   Council of *Clofesho*, A.D. 747, c. 20, eds., A.W. Haddan & W. Stubbs, *Council and Ecclesiastical Documents Relating to Great Britain and Ireland*, 3 vols (Oxford, 1869–78), [hereafter Haddan & Stubbs], III.362–376, at 369.   Compare the similar sentiments attributed to St Cuthbert : Bede, *Vita Sancti Cuthberti*, c. 22, ed., B. Colgrave, *Two Lives of Saint Cuthbert* (Cambridge, 1940), [hereafter Bede, *Vita Cuthberti*], at 228–230.

2.   Æthelwold, 'Old English account of King Edgar's establishment of minsters' eds., D. Whitelock, C.N.L. Brooke, M. Brett, *Councils and Synods with other Documents Relating to the English Church: I 871–1204*, 2 vols, part I, 871–1066 (Oxford, 1981), [hereafter Æthelwold, 'Old English Account'], I.142–154, at 146–147.

3.   *Ibid.*, 145.

4.   See, however, P. Wormald, 'Æthelwold and his continental counterparts: Contact, comparison, contrast', in ed., B. Yorke, *Bishop Æthelwold: his Career and Influence* (Woodbridge, 1988), [hereafter Wormald, 'Æthelwold'], 13–42, at 39–41; and A. Gransden, 'Traditionalism and continuity in the last century of Anglo–Saxon monasticism', *Journal of Ecclesiastical History*, 40 (1989), 159–207.

5.   The arguments sketched here are presented fully in my doctoral thesis: 'Anglo–Saxon minsters A.D. 597–*ca* 900: the religious life in England before the Benedictine Reform' (unpublished PhD thesis, University of Cambridge, 1990), [hereafter Foot, 'Anglo–Saxon minsters'].

6.   See further my forthcoming article: 'Anglo–Saxon minsters: a review of terminology', in eds., J. Blair & R. Sharpe, *Pastoral Care Before the Parish* (London, 1991).

7.   My reasons for reaching this conclusion are set out in full in the first chapter of my thesis, 'Anglo–Saxon minsters'.

8.   Wormald, 'Æthelwold', 38–41.

9.   Bede. *Historia abbatum*, c. 4. ed., C. Plummer, *Venerabilis Baedae Opera Historica*, 2 vols (Oxford, 1896), [hereafter Plummer], I.364–387, at 367–368.

10.   Alcuin, *Vita S. Willibrordi*, c. 1, ed., W. Levison, *MGH SRG* VII.81–141, [hereafter Alcuin, *Vita Willibrordi*], at 116.

11.   For example, P.H. Sawyer, *Anglo–Saxon Charters* (London, 1968), [hereafter Sawyer], no. 84 (A.D. 718 for ?727); no. 235 (A.D. 688 for 685x687).

12.   Bede, *Historia ecclesiastica*, IV.23, eds., B. Colgrave & R.A.B. Mynors, *Bede's Ecclesiastical History of the English People* (Oxford, 1969), [hereafter Bede, *Historia ecclesiastica*], at 406.

13.   Anon,. *Liber beati Gregorii papae*, c. 19, ed., B. Colgrave, *The Earliest Life of Gregory the Great* (Lawrence, Kansas, 1968), at 104.

14.   Nicholas Brooks, 'The development of military obligations in eighth– and ninth–century England', in eds., P. Clemoes & K. Hughes, *England Before the Conquest* (Cambridge, 1971), 68–84.

15.   Boniface, *Epistola* no. 78, ed., M. Tangl, *Die Briefe des heiligen Bonifatius und Lullus*, MGH Epistolae selectae (Berlin, 1916), [hereafter Boniface, *Epistolae*], 161–171, at 171.

16.   Bede, *Epistola ad Ecgbertum*, c. 12, ed., Plummer, I.405–423, at 415–416.

17.   Bede, *Historia ecclesiastica*, III.22, at 282–284.

18.   Sawyer, no. 1803 (A.D. 675x692); F.M. Stenton, 'Medeshamstede and its colonies', in eds., J.G. Edwards *et al.*, *Historical Essays in Honour of James Tait* (Manchester, 1933), 313–326, at 316–318.

19.   Bede, *Historia abbatum*, cc. 4, 7, at 367–368, 370–371.
20.   Alcuin, *Vita Willibrordi*, c. 1, at 116.
21.   Bede, *Historia ecclesiastica*, V.24, at 566.
22.   *Ibid.*, III.26, at 308.
23.   Willibald, *Vita S. Bonifatii*, c. 2, ed., R. Rau, *Briefe des Bonifatius, Willibalds Leben des Bonifatius* (Darmstadt, 1968). [hereafter Willibald, *Vita Bonifatii*], 454–524, at 460.
24.   Felix, *Vita S. Guthlaci*, cc. 18–19, ed., B. Colgrave, *Felix's Life of Saint Guthlac* (Cambridge, 1956), [hereafter, Felix, *Vita Guthlaci*] at 80–82; Bede, *Historia abbatum*, c. 8, at 371.
25.   Aldhelm, prose *De virginitate*, §xix, ed., R. Ehwald, *Aldhelmi Opera, MGH Auctores Antiquissimi* XV (Berlin, 1919), [hereafter Ehwald, *Aldhelmi Opera*], 226–323, at 249; Theodore, Penitential, II.xii.8, 11, 13, ed., P.W. Finsterwalder, *Die Canones Theodori Cantuariensis und ihre Uberlieferungsformen* (Weimar, 1929), 285–334, at 327–328.
26.   Ecgberht, *Dialogi*, responsio 15, Haddan & Stubbs, III.403–413, at 410.
27.   Bede, *Historia ecclesiastica*, IV.19, IV.32, at 394, 448.
28.   Stephan, *Vita S. Wilfridi*, c. 2, ed., B. Colgrave, *The Life of Bishop Wilfrid by Eddius Stephanus* (Cambridge, 1927), at 6.
29.   Bede, *Historia ecclesiastica*, IV.9, at 360.
30.   *Ibid.*, IV.24, at 418.
31.   Council of *Clofesho*, A.D. 747, c. 4, at 364; council of *Clofesho*, A.D. 803, Haddan & Stubbs, III.541–548, at 546.
32.   Bede, *Historia abbatum*, cc. 6, 22, at 369, 375.
33.   Anon, *Vita S. Cuthberti*, III.1, ed. Colgrave, *Two Lives*, 60–138, at 94–96.
34.   Bede, *Historia ecclesiastica*, IV.5, c. 5, at 350.
35.   Compare council of *Clofesho*, A.D. 747, c. 29, at 374–375; legatine council, A.D. 786. c. 6. ed., D. Dümmler. *MGH Epistolae* IV.19–29, at 22; and Boniface, *Epistola* no. 14, at 25.
36.   Bede, *Historia abbatum*, c. 18, at 382.
37.   Bede, *Vita Cuthberti*, c. 39, at 284.
38.   See anon, *Vita Ceolfridi*, c.14, at 393.
39.   Bede, *Vita Cuthberti*, c. 45, at 300; Bede, *Historia ecclesiastica*, IV.23, at 412.
40.   For the celebration of a conventual mass on Sundays compare council of *Clofesho*, A.D. 747, c. 14, at 367; Bede *Vita Cuthberti*, c. 44, at 296. For individual daily celebration see Æthelwulf, *De abbatibus*, c. 18, ed., A. Campbell, *Æthelwulf De Abbatibus* (Oxford, 1967), [hereafter Æthelwulf, *De abbatibus*], lines 562–566, at 45; Bede, *Historia ecclesiastica*, IV.22, at 402–404.
41.   Boniface, *Epistola* no. 81, at 181–182, at 181.
42.   Compare Aldhelm, *Carmen ecclesiasticum* III, lines 44–5, Ehwald, *Aldhelmi Opera*, 14–18, at 16; Æthelwulf, *De abbatibus* c. 15, line 495, at 41; Bede, *Historia abbatum*, c. 12, at 376.
43.   Bede, *Historia ecclesiastica*, V.14, at 502–504.
44.   See Bede, *Vita Cuthberti*, c. 40, at 286.
45.   See George Ovitt, 'Manual labour and early medieval monasticism', *Viator*, 17 (1986), 1–18.
46.   Bede, *Historia abbatum*, c. 8, at 371–372.
47.   Bede, *Vita Cuthberti*, c. 16, at 210.
48.   *Ibid.*, c. 6, at 174.
49.   For references to smiths within minsters see Æthelwulf, *De abbatibus*, c. 10, at 25–6; Bede, *Historia ecclesiastica*, V.14, at 502.
50.   Rudolf, *Vita Leoba*, c. 7, ed., G. Waitz, *MGH Scriptores* XV.I, 118–131, at 125.

51.   Compare council of *Clofesho*, A.D. 747,. c. 7, at 364–365; Boniface, *Epistola* no. 30, at 54; Alcuin, *Epistola* no. 31, at 73.

52.   *Ibid.*, and compare Bede's account of the education provided at Barking: *Historia ecclesiastica*, IV.8–9, at 358–360.

53.   Willibald, *Vita Bonifatii*, c. 2, at 464–466.

54.   Aldhelm, *Epistola* no. 2, Ehwald, *Aldhelmi Opera*, at 475–478.

55.   Boniface requested various houses to copy manuscripts for his own use abroad; compare *Epistolae* nos. 30, 34–35, 75–76, at 54, 58–60, 158–159.

56.   See for example Sawyer, no. 1429 (A.D. 736x737), and further Foot, 'Anglo–Saxon minsters', 294–302.

57.   Bede, *Historia ecclesiastica*, IV.25, at 424–426.

58.   *Ibid.*

59.   Council of *Clofesho*, A.D. 747, cc. 20, 16, at 369, 368.

60.   Alcuin, *Epistola* no. 19, at 55; compare *ibid.*, no. 114, at 168.

61.   Felix, *Vita Guthlaci*, cc. 20–21, at 84.

62.   Boniface, *Epistola* no. 78, at 170–171.

63.   See council of *Clofesho*, A.D. 747, cc. 10, 27, at 366, 373.

64.   *Ibid.*, c. 14, at 367; Bede, *Epistola ad Ecgberhtum*, c. 15, at 419.

65.   Willibald, *Vita Bonifatii*, c. 1, at 462.

66.   Bede, *Vita Cuthberti*, c. 12, at 196; compare Bede, *Historia ecclesiastica*, IV.27, at 432–434.

67.   Anon, *Vita Cuthberti*, II.5–6, at 86.

68.   Alan Thacker, 'Bede's ideal of reform' in eds., P. Wormald, D. Bullough, R. Collins, *Ideal and Reality in Frankish and Anglo–Saxon Society* (Oxford, 1983), 130–155, at 130.

69.   Boniface, *Epistola* no. 78, at 166; Alcuin, *Epistolae* nos. 31, 129, at 72–73, 191–192.

70.   Eric Cambridge, 'The early Church in County Durham: a reassessment', *Journal of the British Archaeological Association*, 137 (1984), 65–85.

71.   See further Foot, 'Anglo–Saxon minsters', chapter 7.

MAPPING CISTERCIAN LANDS
WITH ESPECIAL REFERENCE TO WALES

David H. Williams

The publication of my *Atlas of Cistercian Lands in Wales*[1] represents the sum total of information obtained from a wide variety of sources. Perhaps the first means of recognising former Cistercian estates is the occurrence of the term 'grange', i.e. a farming establishment, on large–scale maps. It was not an exclusively monastic nor indeed entirely Cistercian term — the Premonstratensians of Talley Abbey numbered 'granges' amongst their farming units,[2] but in the Middle Ages it was a term more associated with the Cistercian Order than with any other, and was in itself indicative of the idealistic early contrast between the directly worked economy of the white monks as opposed to the manorial structure associated with the Benedictines. If one is aware of the presence of former Cistercian lands in a particular area, and a place named 'grange' is located there, in most instances it is the location of the medieval monastic farm. The Ordnance Survey maps frequently reveal the term over and over again in the neighbourhood of what were Cistercian abbeys. In the case of Tintern — Rogerstone Grange, Trellech Grange, Woolaston Grange, Upper Grange, Lower Grange, all occur on such maps within a relatively small area of SE Gwent. Even Cardiff has its Grangetown reflecting Margam's medieval Moor Grant. A note of caution must however be sounded, for some farms or country houses have only been named 'grange' in relatively modern times. A classic example lies in one of my parishes where today stands a substantial house known as Pool Quay Grange, not far from the site of medieval Strata Marcella Abbey. The house however was not a grange of that monastery. Indeed it was built only in 1873 to be the vicarage for the newly designated parish of Pool Quay. When the house was sold in 1959, it being the policy of the Church in Wales not to permit such former parsonages to be termed the 'Old Vicarage', the new owner styled it a 'grange' — possibly quite unaware of the earlier Cistercian ownership of the immediate area. There are other such instances.

The second means of identifying former Cistercian granges is to consult the few medieval surveys of ecclesiastic lands. The first of real assistance was the *Taxatio Ecclesiastica* compiled on the authority of Pope Nicholas IV about 1291 A.D. as a basis for assessing clerical income for taxation purposes.[3] It has its drawbacks, inasmuch as that it omits certain properties which it is clear from other sources were owned at that date by the monastery in question. It makes, for example, no mention of Tintern Abbey's valuable manor at Woolaston (Glos.) nor of Aberconwy Abbey's largest grange of Nanhwynan (Gwynedd). Such cases apart though, the *Taxatio* gives useful lists of the properties of all the Welsh Cistercian houses at that period. One difficulty remains: not all those granges it records can be identified with certainty today, and not least because of the problem occasioned by orthography. In the case of Llantarnam Abbey the *Taxatio* gives Pelren (for the correct form of Pwl–pan Grange), Mayster (for Maes–tir Grange), Torald (for Dorallt Grange), Russok (for Rhyswg Grange) and Cadlonet (for Cil–onydd Grange). Four of its grange names (Conesiding, Crip, Kynemot and Makenel) are quite unrecognisable on the Ordnance maps of today.[4]

A more comprehensive survey in some respects was the *Valor Ecclesiasticus* of 1535 compiled following the statute which gave all first fruits and tenths to the Crown.[5] Following close on its heels are the still more detailed *Ministers Accounts*, itemising all the monastic lands whilst they were in the king's hands between the Suppression (1537–40) and their date of sale or demise.[6] The place–names the latter surveys contain – often down to the holdings of individual tenants – allow quite accurate maps of individual Cistercian granges to be made. A good example is Strata Florida Abbey's grange of Blenaeron where tithe–map evidence as well as a charter from the Lord Rhys showing the use of rivers as natural boundaries,[7] allow the exact extent of this grange to be plotted. Taken together these sources demonstrate that the grange lay between the river Aeron to the west and the river Camddwr on the east, with Hant Hirfain forming the extreme north–western limit, the Tawelen the south–western boundary, whilst Nant Tyn–y–swydd and the river Teifi marked the south–eastern perimeter. In instances such as Blaenaeron, some farm names occur on modern maps which do not appear in medieval documentation. This does not mean that such land was not Cistercian, rather that sub–division and the evolution of new holdings has occurred in post–monastic days.   At Blaenaeron, sometime prior to 1596 the 600 acre farm of Esgair Berfedd–ganol (*NGR: 666653*) was divided between the three sons of Lewis David Wynn – one of the resulting 200 acre holdings being termed Bron y Capel (*NGR: 662649*).[8] Similar evidence exists of the partitioning, prior to 1564, of Aberconwy Abbey's estate of Tiryrabad.[9]

These late medieval surveys, and later accounts, indicate amalgamation by the Cistercians of their smaller granges into larger more easily administered units, perhaps from the early fourteenth century on – as the number of labouring *conversi* dwindled, and an increasing tenantry took their place. The charter of the Lord Rhys names Castell Flemish (*NGR: 654632*) as a grange of Strata Florida.[10]   By the suppression it was but a small element in the large area encompassed by Blaen–aeron Grange, where the tithe–map reveals a 'mynachty' place–name (*NGR: 636628*) – the 'Mynachty Blaenaeron' of the post–dissolution accounts,[11] and very probably a separate entity in earlier days. In the case of Whitland Abbey the grange termed Castell Cosan by the Suppression was in fact an amalgamation of at least three granges listed as individual units in the 1291 *Taxatio*: Cilgryman Grange (*NGR: 234252*), Nantweirglodd Grange (*NGR: 231322*), and the apparently detached Blaenpedran Grange (*NGR: 266323*).[12] Several former granges of Llantarnam Abbey came to comprise its later manor of Wentsland and Bryngwyn.[13]

A more precise indicator of the extent of Cistercian lands came with the compilation of tithe apportionment maps subsequent to the Tithe Act of 1836.[14] The Cistercians had a 'hidden benefit' in that the Lateran Council of 1215 confirmed their exemption from paying tithe on land newly brought into cultivation – whether acquired before or after the Council, as well as on land acquired before that date and till cultivated by the monks.[15] This privilege of tithe–exemption was jealously guarded, and passed at the Suppression to the later secular owners of Cistercian lands. Consequently, where the tithe maps indicate that certain lands were free from any payment, and where from other sources we know that these lands were formerly in Cistercian ownership, the bounds of former granges can be delineated with great accuracy. Cornwy Llys Grange (formerly of Aberconwy Abbey) comprehended 600 tithe–free acres. Tirymynach township (formerly of Strata Marcella Abbey) 649 tithe–free acres, and so on.[16] In all these instances, care should be taken to peruse the tithe maps of the adjoining parishes, for whilst very often granges were delimited by a parish boundary, in several cases they straddled two or more such parish limits. The grange of Hafodwen (which the monks of Strata Florida **are** alleged to have appropriated from the nuns of Llanllyr) extended into three parishes: Llanfihangel Ystrad, Betws Bledrws, and Llanfihangel Pont Steffan.[17]

An additional aid to delimiting lands of the white monks came in 1338–40 when the bishop of St David's, on account of the 'manifest poverty' of Strata Florida and Whitland Abbeys, granted those monasteries one–third of the greater tithes from lands they owned but not of their appropriation, and which lay in parishes where the patron was the bishop himself or in those parishes pertaining to the collegiate churches of Abergwili and Llanddewi Brefi.[18] The right to thee 'tryanes' also persisted in new hands after the Suppression, and are reflected in tithe apportionments, thus further unmasking the extent of Cistercian lands in Dyfed. Tithe maps, or the lack of them, also can indicate substantial areas which, because of their former Cistercian custody, evolved as lands completely exempt from any diocesan rights and persisting into modern times as extra–parochial areas. A large stretch of the Caldicot Levels, Greenmoor — once pertaining to Tintern Abbey to have had this status at the time the local tithe maps were compiled.[19] There are several other instances in Wales.

Tithe maps and the accompanying apportionments render yet another valuable service. They reveal place names such as 'grange' and 'mynachty' which have been lost on the more modern Ordnance Survey maps. A good example is Whitland Abbey's Blaenpedran Grange (*Fig. 1*). A glance at the Ordnance Survey map shows us the source of the Pedran and, therefore, the rough location of the grange — for 'blaen' refers to the head of the valley, but the 'grange' is not named nor precisely indicated. A study of the tithe map,[20] however, shows clearly the former place names of Cae'r Mynach and Clynmynach, now replaced by Blaengilfach–isaf and –uchaf, and thus fix the grange–nucleus more exactly. In the same way, estate plans play a significant role in showing details long lost. The survey by John Aram in 1763 of the Duke of Beaufort's Manor of Porthcaseg[21] depicts on one folio Tintern Abbey's former Rogerstone Grange (*Fig 2*). This plan shows clearly St John's Well (now the site of Chepstow Waterworks) and St John's Mead (field 16) leading to the supposition that the grange chapel was dedicated to St John. Roger's 'ton' or manor was only granted to Tintern in 1219 by the Earl of Pembroke,[22] and the likelihood is that it was already a developed and valuable property with its own church. The plan also reveals the site of the grange fish–pond, the mill (demolished only in recent years) and its leats, as well as a former sheep–cot.

To these basic aids for mapping can be added the evidence of early charters, and the confirmations of them sought for various reasons in later years. Thus, among the foundation grants to Tintern Abbey (1133) was 'Merthyr Gerain';[23] Earl Gilbert of Pembroke's confirmation lists 'Merthyr Gerain, with the church' (*c.* 1140)[24]. and a century later, Gilbert Marshall expanded yet further: 'Nertgtr Gerain, with the church and the wood'.[25] Most Cistercian houses prepared edited collections of their charters in cartularies — such as the 'register books' which survived the dissolution at Neth and Strata Florida, but are now lost.[26] Were these volumes extant for Welsh Cistercian monasteries they would be invaluable, but alas they are not! After the suppression much litigation ensued between parties claiming lands or rights formerly monastic, or finding their possessions challenged and attacked.[27] In these proceedings also a significant amount of helpful material is to be found. Taken together, the several sources listed in this brief chapter enabled us to present a more or less accurate and comprehensive portrayal of the extent of Cistercian lands in Wales.

FIG 1   **BLAENPEDRAN GRANGE, DYFED**

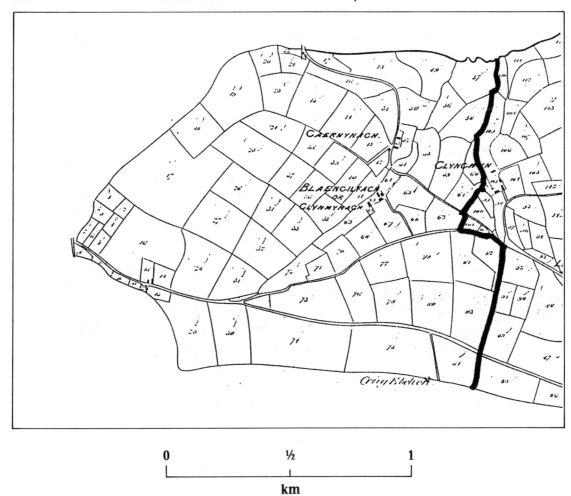

0   ½   1

km

**From the West Clirhedyn Parish tithe-map: Reproduced by
permission of the National Library of Wales**

FIG 2

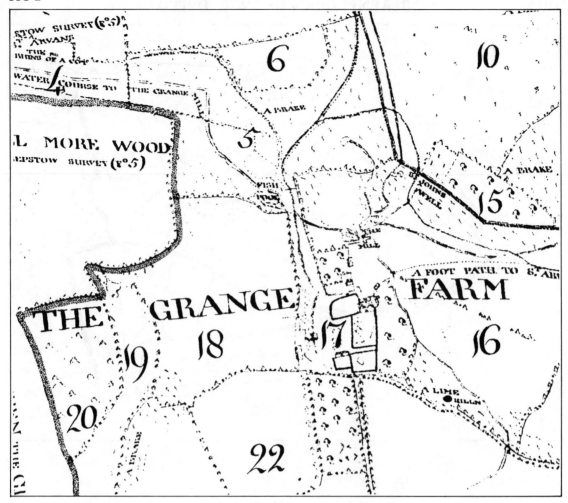

Rogerstone Grange, Gwent: NLW, Badminton Estate Plans, Vol. 2 (1763):
Field 16 is St. John's Mead

NOTES

1.   University of Wales Press, Cardiff, 1980.
2.   F.G. Cowley, *The Monastic Order in South Wales, 1066–1349* (Cardiff, 1977) p 67.
3.   Record Commission, London, 1802.
4.   *Ibid.*, pp 281b, 284b–285.
5.   Record Commission, London, 1810–34; Vol IV contains the material for the Welsh dioceses.
6.   The relevant class at the Pubic Record Office (Chancery Lane) is *SC* 6 (Hen VIII).
7.   S.W. Williams, *The Cistercian Abbey of Strata Florida* (London, 1889) Appx. xi–xii.
8.   E.G. Jones, *Exchequer Proceedings Concerning Wales* (Cardiff, 1939) p 93.
9.   National Library of Wales, *Cernioge MS* 64.
10.   Williams (1889) Appx. xi.
11.   National Library of Wales, *Cwrtmawr NS* 873D, f. 33.
12.   *Taxatio* 282. Castell Cosan also comprehended the 'cwrt' near Dyffryn Tawe (*NGR: 206253*).
13.   David H. Williams, *The Welsh Cistercians* (Caldey Island, 1984) II, p 224.
14.   R. Ian Jack, *Medieval Wales* (London, 1972) p 223.
15.   Williams (1984) II, pp 240–241.
16.   *Ibid.*, p 241.
17.   *Atlas* 58 (No. 147).
18.   Cowley (1977) 186; Williams (1889) Appx. l–liv.
19.   NGR: c. 395587.
20.   For the parish of (West) Cilrhedin, Pembrokeshire.
21.   National Library of Wales (Map Room) Badminton 2; prior permission to consult is necessary from the Estate Office, Badminton, Avon.
22.   *Calendar of Charter Rolls* (Rolls Ser.) III, 1307/104.
23.   *Ibid.*, pp 88.
24.   *Ibid.*, p 97.
25.   *Ibid.*, p 98.
26.   Williams (1984) II, p 197.
27.   See, for example, E.A. Lewis and J.C. Davies, *Records of the Court of Augmentations Relating to Wales* (Cardiff, 1954); E.A. Lewis, *Early Chancery Proceedings Concerning Wales* (Cardiff, 1937); E.G. Jones, *Exchequer Proceedings Concerning Wales* (Cardiff, 1939); T.I. Jeffreys Jones, *Exchequer Proceedings Concerning Wales* (Cardiff, 195).

MONASTICISM IN CHESHIRE 1092–1300
A TALE OF MEDIOCRITY

Anne Frances Dawtry

In the centre of the city of Chester and dominating the landscape for miles around stands the cathedral church of Christ and the Blessed Virgin Mary. Renamed shortly after the dissolution of the monasteries when Chester was chosen as the seat of one of six new bishoprics,[1] the cathedral occupies the site and buildings of the former Benedictine monastery of St Werburgh, founded in 1092[2] and now approaching its nine hundredth anniversary. At the time of the Dissolution, the lands and spiritualities of St Werburgh's were worth a little over £1000[3] per annum. This figure compares favourably with the value of other Cheshire monasteries such as the Cistercian abbeys of Vale Royal and Combermere, valued at £518 and £225 respectively and the Augustinian abbey at Norton worth £180 a year.[4] Yet in terms of national wealth St Werburgh's was only amongst the second rank of Benedictine houses. This is not simply a sixteenth century phenomenon. Throughout the Middle Ages the historian of monasticism in Cheshire is faced with a saga of continual difficulties. Several of the monastic houses founded in the county during the twelfth and thirteenth centuries floundered within a few years of their foundation whilst those monasteries which did survive were often poorly endowed and lacking in important patrons. This paper seeks to examine how and why this situation occurred. In order to place the fortunes of the Cheshire monasteries in perspective comparisons will from time to time be drawn between Cheshire houses and those in neighbouring counties particularly in Lancashire and Yorkshire.

Monasticism arrived late in Cheshire. Whilst in Yorkshire and Northumberland monasteries such as Lindisfarne, Jarrow, Wearmouth and Whitby were springing up as early as the seventh century,[5] Cheshire played no part in the golden age of Celtic monasticism. The nearest Celtic monastery to Chester was at Bangor and is y Coed or Bangor on Dee and its monks, numbering some two thousand according to Bede, were slaughtered after the Battle of Chester in 615.[6] The nearest nunnery to Cheshire was at Hanbury in Staffordshire, reputedly founded by Werburgh herself.[7] It is possible that a monastic establishment may have been attempted at Chester in the pre–Conquest period since the Domesday Book takes note of a *monasterium* here but nothing more is known of this foundation and since it is recorded as waste both in 1066 and 1086,[8] it had almost certainly been deserted well before the Norman Conquest, possibly in the eighth or ninth centuries when so many other northern monasteries fell foul of the Vikings or declined as a result of secular interference.[9] The largest pre–Conquest ecclesiastical foundation in Cheshire was the church of St Werburgh built in 907 by Aethelflaeda, Lady of the Mercians, in order to house the bones of St Werburgh herself which had been brought from Hanbury. Yet at this time St Werburgh's was not a monastery but rather a collegiate church served by a community of secular canons.[1]. After the Norman Conquest an attempt was quickly made to reintroduce monasticism to the north. The revival began in the north east with the foundation of the Benedictine abbey of Selby in 1069. This was quickly followed by the establishment of other major Benedictine houses at Whitby (1075), Durham (1083) and St Mary's, York (*c.* 1086). These houses set in motion the impetus for a far reaching monastic revival in the north east which was to gather even greater speed in the twelfth century after the arrival of the Cistercians and Augustinian Canons.[1]. By 1215, in Yorkshire alone, there were eight major Cistercian abbeys[12], eleven houses of Augustinian Canons,[13] and three houses of Premonstratensian Canons[14] as well as several small priories of Benedictine monks[15] and twenty seven nunneries[16] all of which were to survive until the dissolution.

In Cheshire progress was much slower. The first monastic foundation in the county was not made until 1092 when Hugh Lupus, the first Norman Earl of Chester, replaced the secular canons serving the collegiate church of St Werburgh with Benedictine monks. The late date of Chester's foundation may have resulted from the difficulties experienced by the earl in obtaining help in the establishment of his monastery, Hugh had requested aid and personnel from the Norman abbey of Bec, but Anselm of Laon, who was abbot at this time, refused to come personally or to send any monks in order to help Hugh set up his abbey. According to Eadmer it was only when Anselm thought that Earl Hugh might be dying that he relaxed his former intransigent attitude and granted the necessary assistance for the foundation of the monastery.[17]

Nearly two decades now elapsed before the foundation of any further monasteries in Cheshire. In 1115, however, William, Constable of Chester, set up a house for Augustinian Canons at Runcorn near his castle of Halton. The canons were to serve the constable's chapel in Halton castle and look after pilgrims and travellers crossing the ford over the Mersey. Situated as it was so close to the river the original priory soon became the victim of frequent flooding. As a result William's son, another William, gave to the monks a new site on higher ground at Norton in 1134.[18]

In the same year as the transfer to Norton was taking place in the north of the county, a Savignac abbey was being founded in the north, at Combermere on the Shropshire border by a certain William Malbanc.[19] Combermere soon became a Cistercian house when, in 1147, the Savignac order merged with the Cistercians.[20] The establishment of Combermere was closely followed by the foundation of a Benedictine nunnery situated within the city of Chester. Established in 1140 by Hugh son of Oliver on a site near the castle on the south western perimeter of the town, this nunnery appears to have had some links, at least initially, with the nunnery of St Mary's, Clerkenwell in London.[21] During the late twelfth century further monastic foundations were made in Cheshire at Poulton (1158) and Stanow (1172),[22] both Cistercian dependencies at Birkenhead (1185),[23] a Benedictine priory and at Warburton where the Premonstratensians established themselves in 1190.[24] Shortly after the beginning of the thirteenth century a further Augustinian priory was founded at Mobberley in 1204.[25] Thus by the early thirteenth century Cheshire could boast some nine religious houses.

Yet these figures are deceptive. No less than four of Cheshire's nine monastic foundations, namely the Cistercian dependencies of Poulton and Stanlow, the Premonstratensian priory of Warburton and the Augustinian priory of Mobberley were to disappear within a century of their foundation. At Warburton the community seems never even to have become fully established. The priory was founded in 1190 by a certain Adam de Dutton as a dependency of the abbey of Cockersands in Lancashire. The monks of Cockersands, however, seem to have regarded the gift with less than enthusiasm and after Adam de Dutton's death in 1215 the abbey sold Warburton back to his heirs.[26] Poulton disappeared because of its geographical position on the Welsh borders. From the time of its foundation in 1158 the monastery was constantly harried by Welsh raiders until in 1214 it was finally decided to move the monks away from their

border site to a new abbey at Dieulacres in Staffordshire.[27]   The monks of
Stanlow also suffered because their priory was founded on an unsuitable site.
Situated as it was on an island in the middle of the River Mersey, the priory and
its buildings were frequently subjected to serious flooding until in 1296 the monks
were offered alternative accommodation at Whalley in Lancashire.[28]   The
Augustinian prior of Mobberley, on the other hand, failed because the monks
were not able to secure an adequate endowment.   The founder, Patrick de
Mobberley only granted the monks the site on which the priory was built for the
duration of his own lifetime.   After his death in 1228 his heirs refused to renew
the lease and the monks were deprived of the site.   They were thus made
homeless and had to look for alternative accommodation which they found at
Rocester in Staffordshire.[29]

Such tales of misfortune are not uncommon amongst small religious
houses.   Yet when Cheshire was deprived of no less than four of its monasteries
during the course of the thirteenth century this left the county with only four
houses of monks at Chester, Birkenhead, Combermere and Norton and one house
of nuns also at Chester.   Moreover the foundation of new religious houses was in
Cheshire, as elsewhere, virtually over by 1215.   In compensation for the four
monasteries of which it was deprived during the course of the thirteenth century,
Cheshire received only one new major monastic foundation, namely the
Cistercian abbey of Vale Royal founded by Edward I in 1277 and several small
friaries.   At the time of its foundation Vale Royal showed great promise.   The
house was intended for one hundred monks and was so named 'that no other
monastery should be more royal in its wealth and honour'.   Yet again the
promise was never fulfilled.   Shortly after 1281 a dispute arose between Edward I
and the monks, the endowments of the abbey ceased to grow and the building
programme ground to a halt.[30]

To look at the figures in another way.   By 1214, with nine monasteries in
the county, Cheshire with an area of 1032 square miles had an average of one
religious house every 114 square miles.   In comparison with other neighbouring
counties this figure was already low.   By the same date there were already in
Yorkshire eight Cistercian abbeys, eleven house of Augustinian canons, and three
houses of Premonstratensian canons as well as eight small Benedictine and
Gilbertine priories and twenty seven nunneries.   Admittedly Yorkshire was and is
a much larger county than Cheshire, covering an area of no less than 60899
square miles.   Yet if, for purposes of comparison with Cheshire, we divide
Yorkshire up into its various constituent Ridings, the picture remains no less
impressive, at least in the North and East Ridings.   By 1214 the North Riding
had an average of one monastery every 82 square miles and the East Riding one
every 106 square miles.   Only in the West Riding does the average fall below that
of Cheshire with one religious house every 133 square miles.   Yet whilst the
Yorkshire figures remained stable throughout the thirteenth century, the
Cheshire averages fell dramatically.   By 1300 there were only six religious houses
in the county, that is one religious house every 172 square miles, a very poor
average only matched by Lancashire with one monastery every 208 square
miles.[31]

It is not only in terms of numbers of houses but also in terms of wealth of
endowments that the Cheshire monasteries fared far worse than their
counterparts in other parts of the north and Midlands.   With the exception of St
Werburgh's, Chester and Combermere the monastic houses of Cheshire seem to
have been very poorly endowed during the twelfth century.   In contrast to the
Augustinian house of Nostell in Yorkshire[32] which within thirty years of its

foundation possessed land in sixty four vills in thirteen counties, its sister priory of Norton in Cheshire acquired very little land in the first half century after its foundation. The landed endowment of the canons seems to have consisted of no more than one or two bovates of land in various vills in north–east Cheshire together with occasional parcels of land in more distant counties. The canons therefore relied almost entirely upon profits from the tithes and churches which they had been granted by their founder, William fitz Nigel and by his subtenants.[33] Such reliance upon profits from tithes and churches was not unusual for a house of Augustinian canons since the majority of the patrons of the order were not members of the aristocracy but men of a lower social status, royal or baronial officials, who could ill afford to part with large acreages of land but who had in their gift large numbers of churches and tithes, which in the reforming climate of the twelfth century they could not retain without severe ecclesiastical censure.[34] Yet what is unusual about the churches acquired by Norton is the distance of most of them from the priory. Some of these churches were situated as far away as Nottinghamshire, Lincolnshire and Oxfordshire and must have proved extremely difficult to exploit successfully.[35] Bridlington Priory, in the East Riding of Yorkshire, which was founded by a cousin of William fitz Nigel in 1113,[36] also relied quite considerably upon profits from the churches and tithes which it possessed. Yet Bridlington's churches were nearly all situated within a fairly close radius of the house[37] and were therefore much easier to control than Norton's scattered properties. The endowment of Norton only really seems to have increased in the fourteenth century when the priory became a fashionable burial place amongst the local gentry.[38] As a result the number of canons was increased from thirteen to twenty six and the house was also granted abbatial status.[39]

The monks of the Benedictine prior of Birkenhead were also poorly endowed during the twelfth and thirteenth centuries. The only substantial grant which the monks ever received was the bequest made by their founder, Hamon de Massey who, in addition to granting the monks the site of the priory, also endowed them with two churches and land in five vills on the Wirral peninsula.[40] Other gifts to the priory were small and of little value and this is also true of Poulton's endowments during the twelfth century. The properties given to the priory never consisted of more than a few bovates of land given by small landowners of a low social status, subtenants whose gifts needed to be confirmed by their overlord. Thus the gifts given to the priory by Joel and Urian sons of Rannulf de Hules in the late twelfth century were confirmed in the court of their lord, Madoc son of Griffin, Lord of Bromfield who was himself to found the Welsh Cistercian Abbey of Valle Crucis, near Llangollen a few years later.[41]

The abbeys of Combermere and St Werburgh's Chester fared rather better. From its founder, William Malbanc, Combermere received the gift of four vills in Staffordshire and a quarter of the two of Nantwich together with its saltpans.[42] The abbey also enjoyed the patronage of Robert de Ferrers, Earl of Derby, who before 1138 granted to the monks at Combermere land at Ashbourne in Derbyshire.[43] The abbey of St Werburgh's, Chester, received from its founder, Hugh Lupus, Earl of Chester, twenty seven hides of land which had belonged to the secular canons who had served the shrine during the pre–Conquest period,[44] two manors in Anglesey, the manor of Irby on the Wirral and five hides of land at Weston on Trent.[45] Yet neither abbey ever became particularly wealthy since endowments to both houses declined dramatically after the death of their respective founders. Hugh Lupus's successor as Earl of Chester, Richard I (1101–20) granted to the monks of Chester only a mill at the Bache, some two miles outside the city and one or two tenements within Chester itself.[46] Earl

Hugh II (1154—81) granted to the monks of St Werburgh's only one church, that of Prestbury, and a yearly rent of 12d from some properties in Chester,[47] whilst Ranulf III (1187—1232) granted only the church of Chipping Campden in faraway Gloucestershire.[48] Combermere too remained relatively poor. As late as 1291 the abbey was only valued at £90 a year, a striking contrast to the Cistercian abbeys of Fountains and Rievaulx, whose annual income was calculated at £356 and £241 respectively.[49]

The history of monasticism in Cheshire during the twelfth and thirteenth century therefore is one of constant setbacks and unfulfilled promise. By 1300 four monastic houses had disappeared from the county. Of those which did survive few had adequate endowments whilst even the two largest houses in the county, the Cistercian Abbey of Combermere and the Benedictine monastery of St Werburgh in Chester experienced difficulties in maintaining a steady flow of endowments from the middle of the twelfth century onwards.

Yet why did the Cheshire monasteries experience so many serious difficulties? The problems experienced at Mobberley, Poulton, Runcorn and Stanlow are undoubtedly attributable to the carelessness of the founder, either in the initial choice of site, or in the failure to ensure that the monastery's endowment would survive his death. Such reasons do not, however, explain why the abbeys of Combermere and St Werburgh's, Chester and the priories of Norton and Birkenhead were so poorly endowed, at least relatively speaking, during the twelfth and thirteenth centuries. The answer to this problem seems to lie instead in an examination of political organization of Cheshire under its earl.

One of the chief features of the post—Conquest revival of monasticism in Yorkshire is the extent of royal interest shown in the establishment and development of monasticism within the county. William I actively encouraged the development of Selby Abbey by granting to the monks, in 1069, the site on which the founder, Benedict of Auxerre had already illegally established himself. He further supported the monks of Selby through the granting of land in a number of other nearby vills.[50] William I was also responsible for granting to Stephen and the other refugees from Whitby land at Lastingham where they established themselves for a short while before moving to York.[51] Bridlington Friory was founded *ex praecepto et consensus Regis Henrici*[52] whilst Henry I was also a generous patron of Nostell.[53] Finally Henry II was supportive to both the abbeys of Jervaulx and Roche.[54] Such gifts did not stem merely from royal piety. Monasticism in England had a long tradition of loyalty to the king expressed most forcibly in the prayers for the royal household in the *Regularis Concordia.*[55] The Norman kings, therefore, were not slow to patronize the religious houses of Yorkshire in order to foster a spirit of cooperation between the king and the church in an area which was, politically, difficult to control. In turn this royal patronage was of substantial importance in the establishment and further development of monasticism in Yorkshire. Once the Norman kings had shown an interest in the re—establishment of a monastic presence there the baronage were not slow to follow suit. At Bridlington, for example, the royal lead was followed by Earl William de Warenne, Anschetil de Bulmer, Picot de Percy and Hugh de Laval.[56]

In Cheshire, on the other hand, the king played virtually no part in the establishment and endowment of monasticism during the twelfth century. Royal patronage seems to have been confined to the occasional confirmation of property and privileges as in the charter addressed by Henry II to Norton in 1155.[57] It was only in 1277 that royal concern for the establishment of monasticism in the

CHESHIRE RELIGIOUS HOUSES

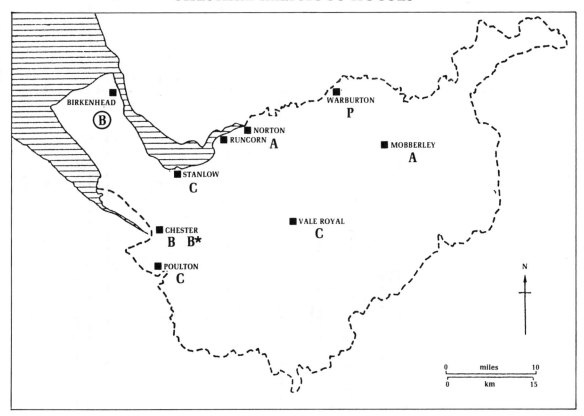

```
                            KEY

           A  -  Augustinian Priory
           B  -  Benedictine Abbey
          Ⓑ  -  Benedictine Priory
           B* -  Benedictine Nunnery
           C  -  Cistercian Abbey
           P  -  Premonstratensian Priory
```

Anne F. Dawtry

NUMBER OF MONASTIC HOUSES IN CHESHIRE 1092-1300

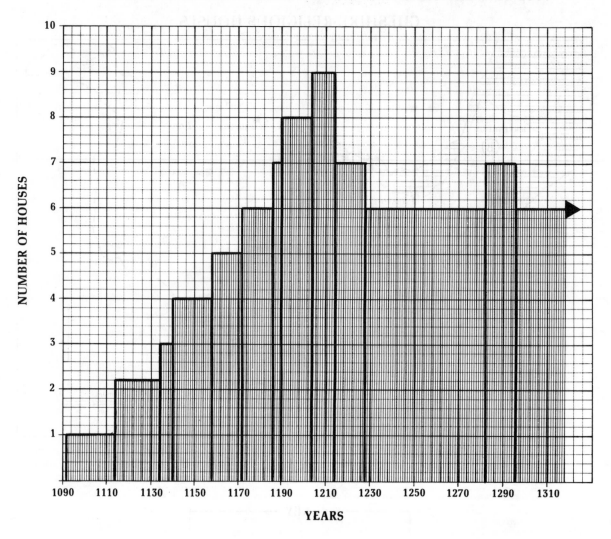

TABLE RELATING TO DENSITY OF MONASTIC HOUSES IN NORTHERN AND WESTERN ENGLAND IN 1215

County	Area of County (in square miles)	Number of monasteries	Density of monasteries
Cheshire	1032	7	1 to 147 sq. miles
Lancashire	1875	9	1 to 208 sq. miles
Shropshire	1347	12	1 to 112 sq. miles
Staffordshire	1153	15	1 to 77 sq. miles
Yorkshire, E.R.	1172	11	1 to 106 sq. miles
Yorkshire, W.R.	2789	21	1 to 133 sq. miles
Yorkshire, N.R.	2128	26	1 to 82 sq. miles

county was shown by the monarch when Edward I founded the Cistercian Abbey of Vale Royal in Delamere Forest. Edward's initial endowment was for a house of one hundred monks and the abbey was named Vale Royal, not only because it was founded by the king but also in order to show that 'no other monastery shall be more royal in its wealth and honour'. Yet even here royal interest was to be short lived. After an argument with the monks Edward withdrew his support and the abbey received no further endowments from the crown.[58]

The lack of royal involvement in the development of monasticism in Cheshire may have been due at least in part to the fact that the Norman kings had less pressing political problems in Cheshire than in Yorkshire. Cheshire had never formed part of the independent Viking kingdom in the north but had instead maintained relatively close links with the Anglo–Saxon kings during the pre–Conquest era. In the early tenth century Cheshire had been firmly controlled by Aethelflaeda, Lady of the Mercians, who was sister to Edward the Elder[59] whilst in the eleventh century the county had been competently managed for Cnut by Earl Leofric.[60]

Yet the lack of royal involvement in the patronage of monasticism within Cheshire was also partly the result of the extraordinarily powerful position of the earl within the county. Although the palatinate of Chester did not come into being until 1301 the Norman earls were virtually autonomous in many respects. The earldom seems, for example, to have been fiscally independent from the rest of the country since, throughout the twelfth century there is little mention of Cheshire in the Pipe Rolls.[61] The earl also exercised many judicial rights which were normally reserved to the crown and Earl Ranulf III even issued his own version of the Magna Carta in which he refused to acknowledge some of the promises made by King John at Runnymede.[62] Indeed, except during the minority of Earl Rannulf III (1181–7), the Norman kings seem to have interested themselves little in the affairs of the earldom. It thus fell to the earl rather than to the king to encourage and nurture the development of monasticism within Cheshire.

Where such encouragement was forthcoming monasticism flourished, not only as a result of the benefactions made by the earls themselves but also because of the encouragement which the earl's support gave to other potential benefactors. Thus the endowments made by the first Earl, Hugh Lupus, to St Werburgh's Chester were emulated by his subtenants who made a number of generous donations of their own to the house.[53] The importance of the earls support can also be seen in the case of the Cistercian abbey of Combermere. Hugh Malbanc, the founder was anxious that Earl Rannulf II (1129–53) should be regarded as the official founder and protector of the house,[64] and the earl's interest does appear to have been beneficial to the abbey. Combermere, although never rich was able to expand at a much steadier rate than most other religious houses in the county.

Yet at times the earls could be far from active in their patronage and encouragement of monasticism both inside the county and out. The grants made by Earls Richard I, Ranulf II, Hugh II and Ranulf III to the abbey of St Werburgh's, Chester, were small[65] as were their gifts to the Benedictine nunnery in Chester. Moreover, Warburton and Norton received no gifts at all from the earls, the latter surprisingly since the priory was founded by William fitz Nigel, an important official in the service of the earl. Outside the county too their gifts lacked generosity. The gifts of Hugh Lupus and Ranulf I to St Evroul were small[66] as were those made to Leicestershire and Lincolnshire monasteries by

Ranulf II and by Lucy the widow of Ranulf I.[67] Furthermore the Earls of
Chester could, on occasions, be actively hostile to a particular religious house.
Earl Richard, who quarrelled with the monks of Chester over the ownership of
the manor of Saighton, threatened to 'alter and change the foundations of the
said abbey to another religion', presumably implying that he would expel the
Benedictine monks and replace them with those of another order.[68] The same
earl also kept the abbacy of St Werburgh's vacant from 1116 when the troubles
over the manor of Saighton started until the time of his death at the sinking of
the White Ship in 1120. Earl Ranulf II, too, confessed on his deathbed that he
had done great harm to St Werburgh's during his lifetime, and died
excommunicate, although he attempted to make reparation by granting to the
monks two manors in his will.[68]

Such occasions of active hostility towards the monasteries were admittedly
rare, but the general lack of interest which the earls showed towards the
establishment and further development of monasticism in the county tended to
have an adverse effect on its future development. Without the positive lead of
king or earl few members of the aristocracy were prepared to be generous towards
the religious houses of Cheshire. Thus by reason of the political organization of
the county and the disposition of the earls the religious houses of Cheshire largely
missed out on what was, elsewhere, a century of general wealth and expansion
and unfolds for us instead a tale of mediocrity

NOTES

1.   D. Knowles, *The Regligious Orders in England* (Cambridge, 1961), 3 vols.,
      3, p 358. The other abbeys chosen to be cathedrals were Bristol,
      Gloucester, Peterborough, Oxford and Westminster. Of these
      Westminster was only to retain its episcopal status for a decade.
2.   R.V.H. Burne, *The Monks of Chester* (London, 1962), p 1.
3.   D. Knowles, R.N. Hadcock, *Medieval Religious Houses in England and
      Wales* (London, 1953), p 62 [henceforward M.R.H.E.W.].
4.   Other Cheshire values in the *Valor Ecclesiasticus* are as follows: St James'
      Priory, Birkenhead — £90 and St Mary's Nunnery, Chester — £66.
5.   D. Knowles, *The Monastic Orders in England 940–1216* (Cambridge,
      1963), pp 165–6.
6.   Bede, *Ecclesiastical History* Book II, Chapter 2, ed., L. Shirley Price;
      Bede, *A History of the English Church and People* (Penguin, 1979), pp
      102–3.
7.   J. Tait, *The Chartulary or Register of the Abbey of St Werburgh, Chester*
      (Chetham Society 79, 1920), pp vii–xiv.
8.   Domesday Book, f. 263a.
9.   R. Fleming, 'Monastic land and England's defence in the Viking age'
      E.H.R. 100 (1985), pp 247–65; G.W.O. Addleshaw, *The Parochial
      Structure of the Church in North Britain* (Bothwick Pamphlet 43, 1973),
      p 24.
10.   F.T. Wainwright, *North–west Mercia 871–924*, (Transactions of the Hist.
      Soc. of Lancs. and Ches. 94, (1942), pp 3–55, p 19.
11.   For Selby, see R.B. Dobon, 'The First Norman Abbey in England'
      Ampleforth Journal 74 (1969), pp 161–76; for Whitby and St Mary's
      York, see L.G.D. Baker, 'The Desert in the North', *Northern History* 5
      (1970), pp 1–11.
12.   Fountains (1132), Rievaulx (1132), Byland (1135), Roche (1147),
      Kirkshall (1147), Sawley (1148), Jervaulx (1150), Meaux (1151).

13.   Bridlington (1113), Nostell (1114), Guisborough (1119), Kirkham (1122), Drax (1130), Warter (1132), North Ferriby (1140), Newborough (1150), Marton (1150), Healaux Park (1186), Bolton (1194).

14.   Easby (1151), Coverham (1196), Egglestone (1198).

15.   Middlesborough (1120–30), Richmond (1146), Monkbretton (1153).

16.   For a list of these nunneries see *M.R.H.E.W.*, pp 209–33.

17.   Eadmer, *Vita Anselmi*, Rolls Series 81 (1884), p 359.

18.   J. Tait, 'The Foundation Charter of Runcorn (later Norton Priory)', *Chetham Society Miscellany*, N.S. 3 (1939), p 3; W. Beaumont, *A History of the Castle of Halton and Abbey or Priory of Norton* (Warrington, 1879), pp 148–9.

19.   Ed., R.L. Ritchie, *Annales Cestriensis* (Record Society of Lancashire and Cheshire 14), p 21.

20.   The unification of the two orders took place on 7th September 1147; A. Manriques, *Annales Cisterciensis* (1642–52), 4 vols, 1, p 104.

21.   W.F. Irvine, 'Notes on the History of St Mary's Nunnery, Chester' *Journal of the Cheshire Archaeological and Antiquarian Society* 13. pp 67–109, p 71.

22.   V.C.H. *Cheshire* 3, p 152.

23.   G. Barraclough, 'Facsimiles of Early Cheshire Charters' *Record Society of Lancashire and Cheshire* (1957), p 44.

24.   *Cockersand Cartulary* (Chetham Society 1st Series 43), pp 735–6 [henceforward *Cockersand Cartulary*].

25.   The priory is mentioned in a letter of Innocent III in 1204; ed., C.R. Cheney, *The Letters of Innocent III* (Oxford, 1967) no. 542.

26.   *Cockersand Cartulary* pp 738–9.   The advowson of the chapel of Warburton was finally sold to Geoffrey de Dutton in 1271; *ibid.*, pp 739–40.

27.   M.J.C. Fisher, 'Dieulacres Abbey' *Unpublished University of Keele M.A. Thesis* (1967), pp 16–18.

28.   *Whalley Coucher Book* (Chetham Society 1st Series, 10, pp 1–5).

29.   Tanner, *Notitia Monastica*.

30.   *Calendar of Charter Rolls 1257–1300*, p 215.

31.   See Appendix below.

32.   T.N. Burrows, 'The Estates and Benefactors of Nostell and Bridlington Priories with special reference to the Twelfth and Thirteenth Centuries'. *Unpublished University of Western Australia Ph.D. Thesis* (1979).

33.   Tait, 'Foundation of Runcorn', pp 12–13, 18–21.

34.   For a discussion of these problems see M. Chibnall, 'Monks and Pastoral Work in the Twelfth Century', *J.E.H.*, 18 (1967), pp 165–72 and G. Constable, 'Monastic Possession of Tithes and Spiritualia in the Age of Reform', *II Monachesimo e la Riforma Ecclesiastica 1049–1122* (Milan, 1971), pp 304–35, p 304.

35.   These included the churches of Radcliffe on Soar in Nottinghamshire, Burton in Lindsey (Lincolnshire) and Pirton (Oxon); Beaumont pp 148–9.

36.   Burrows, 'Nostell and Bridlington', p 40.

37.   *Ibid.*, p 41.

38.   P. Green, 'Excavations at Norton Priory' *Current Archaeology* (Jan., 1980), p 346.

39.   J.P. Green, 'The Elevation of Norton Priory, Cheshire to the Status of Mitred Abbey', *Transactions of the Historical Society of Lancashire and Cheshire* (1979), pp 78–113.

40.   J. Ormerod, *History of Cheshire* (London, 1813–16), 3 vols, 2, p 458. This land was at Claughton, Moreton, Tranmere, Higher Bedington and Saughall.

41. Ormerod 2, p 865.

42. W. Dugdale, R. Dodsworth, *Monasticon Anglicanum* 5, pp 323–4.

43. *Calendar of Charter Rolls 1126–57*, p 428.

44. *Cartulary of Chester* 1, pp. xix–xx, ed., G. Barraclough, *The Charters of the Anglo Norman Earls of Chester* (Record Society of Lancs. and Cheshire 1988), pp 2–7 [henceforward Barraclough, *Charters*].

45. *Ibid.*, p 17.

46. *Ibid.*, pp 40–43.

47. Barraclough, 'Early Cheshire Charters', p 22; Barraclough, *Charters*, pp 146–7.

48. *Cartulary of Chester*, 2, p 338.

49. *The Clerical Taxation of Pope Nicholas IV.*

50. Ed., J.T. Fowler, *The Coucher Book of Selby Abbey* (1893–5), 2 vols, 1, p (14)–(15); 2, p 11.

51. *Cart. Whit.*, 1, pp xxxvi.

52. *EYC* 2, no. 1135.

53. *EYC* 3, no. 1428; see also W.E. Wightmann 'Henry I and the Foundation of Nostell Priory', *Yorks. Arch. Journal* 41 (1966), pp 57–60.

54. For Jervaulx see *EYC* 5, no 374; for Roche see B.D. Hill, *The Cistercian Monasteries and their English Patrons in the Twelfth Century* (University of Illinois, Urbana, 1968), p 72.

55. Ed., T. Symons, *The Regularis Concordia* (London, 1953), pp xxii–xlvi. Prayers for the royal family are prescribed throughout the *Regularis Concordia*; *Ibid.*, pp 5, 13–14, 21,22, 28.

56. Wightmann, p 58.

57. Beaumont, pp 148–9.

58. *Calendar of Charter Rolls 1257–1300*, p 215.

59. J.D. Bullock, *Pre–Conquest Cheshire 386–1066* (Chester, 1972), p 54.

60. *Ibid.*, pp 56–7.

61. The earldom only appears on the Pipe Roll during the minorities of Hugh II (1154) and Rannulf III (1181–7) when in the charge of a royal keeper; VCH Cheshire 2, p 4.

62. G. Barraclough, 'Some Charters of the Earls of Chester' *Medieval Miscellany for D.M. Stenton*, Pipe Roll Society New Series 36, p 4.

63. *Cartulary of Chester*, pp 18–20.

64. B.L. Cotton, MS Faustiana, B VIII, fol. 25r.

65. Irvine, p 96.

66. Barraclough, *Charters*, pp 1–2, 10, 20.

67. *Ibid.*, pp 66–7, 105–6, 27–8. These included the gifts of a church at Barrow on Soar and a chapel at Quorndon to be abbey of St Mary du Pré, Leicester, the gift of one bovate of land at Woodsthorpe to the monks of Belvoir and the grant of certain tithes to the monks of Spalding.

68. *Cartulary of Chester*, pp xxv–xxvi; *Life of St Werburghe of Chester* (Early English Text Society 87, pp 182–3).

69. *Cartulary of Chester*, pp 231–3; Barraclough, *Charters*, pp 138–9.

WILLIAM I'S RELATIONS WITH CLUNY FURTHER CONSIDERED

H.E.J. Cowdrey

William the Conqueror's dealings as king of England with the abbey of Cluny and with its abbot, Hugh of Semur (1049–1109), constitutes a minor, but puzzling, detail of the events of his reign. There were three known occasions of contact between them. In order of probable importance though not necessarily of occurrence, William first sought from Hugh the dispatch of a group of professed Cluniac monks — six or twelve in number according to different sources — to advise and assist him with the reform of the church in England; but he encountered Hugh's firm refusal. Secondly, William sought and, in this case, received from Abbot Hugh the benefit of spiritual confraternity with his abbey; in return, William and Queen Matilda sent to Cluny generous gifts of ecclesiastic vestments. Thirdly, Abbot Hugh is on record as having met the king during a visit to Normandy. The principal evidence for these contacts is to be found in two sources, one considerably and the other very much later than the events that they record. One is a collection of material apparently made at Cluny after 1121 by an unknown Cluniac monk, which is usually referred to as Anonymous II.[1] It drew heavily upon earlier Lives of Abbot Hugh by Gilo of Tusculum, Hildebert of Lavardin, and Reynald of Vézelay; it also utilized other material, mostly written. The other is the longer, and forged, foundation charter of the Cluniac priory of St Pancras at Lewes. Sir Charles Clay established that, as it stands, its date of composition is almost certainly later than 1201 and that it was possibly drawn up and sealed fictitiously as late as 1397 x 1417.[2] However, it clearly includes older material of historical value, perhaps derived from a foundation narrative.

The most recent substantial discussion of William I's relations with Cluny is a paper published in 1981 by Professor Frank Barlow.[3] In it, his most important suggestion is that the communications between the king and the abbot of Cluny about the dispatch of Cluniac monks should probably not be dated, as by recent commentators, to the very early years of the Conqueror's reign;[4] a date in the second half of it is more likely. The historical record preserved in the forged Lewes foundation charter provides a likely context during Abbot Hugh's visit to Normandy for which it is the principal source. Barlow's hypothesis is that Hugh came to Normandy at some time between 1078 and 1080 to confer with the king 'on some unknown business'. This visit was, according to the charter, the occasion of discussions about Lewes between Hugh and its founder, William of Warenne, later earl of Surrey. In 1076 William and his wife Gundrada had decided upon its foundation when they were diverted to Cluny while on a journey to Rome. The king was involved because Abbot Hugh insisted upon his written consent, but even so the foundation had run into difficulties which had involved the retention of the first prior, Lanzo, at Cluny for a whole year. William of Warenne was minded to transfer the church of St Pancras to the abbey of Marmoutier. But matters were resolved when Abbot Hugh's visit to King William in Normandy gave William of Warenne a chance to discuss matters with Hugh in person. Barlow concludes: 'The problems of Lewis could easily have led to a consideration [by the king and the abbot] of what part Cluny could play in the English, and possible Norman, Church at large or in the Conqueror's St Martin *de Bello* [Battle Abbey] in particular. In these circumstances the king's request for six or twelve monks ... may have been little more than an uncalculated response to the impression that the saint made on him at their meeting'.[5] As for Hugh's grant of confraternity to William, Barlow concludes from Anonymous II that it was probably made while the intermediary, Warmund, abbot of Bourg–Dieu, Déols (dioc. Bourges) from *c.* 1074 and archbishop of Vienne from 1076, thereafter holding both offices, was abbot but not yet archbishop, that is, in 1075 or 1076.[6]

It is not the purpose of this paper to exclude Barlow's conclusions, which stand as a possible resolution of the problem so far as the scanty and unsatisfactory evidence allows. But further light may be shed on William's relations with Cluny if they are set in a fuller context than Barlow provides, especially from the Cluniac side. This context will first be outlined, and then the problem will be reconsidered in its light.

In part, the context is set in Normandy itself. It is well known that, especially through the reforming activity of William of Volpiano, abbot of Fécamp (1001–33), Cluny had an appreciable to indirect impact upon Norman monasticism during the first half of the eleventh century.[7] Less often noticed are the direct dealings between Cluny and the duchy that, according to Orderic Vitalis, took place in the ten years or so before the Norman conquest of England with regard to his monastery of Saint–Evroult, founded just before 1050 in the far south of the diocese of Lisieux. These dealings must have been ambivalent in their effects, encouraging Duke William to look to Cluny as a source of monastic reform but warning Abbot Hugh to caution in his response. The encouragement to Duke William was that Robert of Gandmenil, abbot from 1059 to 1061, had, as a young man, received permission from Abbot Thierry (1050–7) to visit Cluny. When he had spent some time there, Abbot Hugh allowed him to bring back a distinguished monk of Cluny named Bernfrid, who later became bishop of an unknown see; Robert for some time retained Bernfrid a Saint–Evroult with honour, so that he could instruct its monks in the customs of the Cluniacs.[8] Abbot Hugh thus demonstrated his willingness to allow one of his monks who was of the calibre to be a bishop to travel as far as Normandy in order to instruct a favoured monastery in Cluniac monastic ways. The warning to Abbot Hugh came soon afterwards, when the future Abbot Mainer (1066–89), who had entered Saint–Evroult under Abbot Robert, received advice and leave from Abbot Osbern (1061–6) to go to Cluny. According to Orderic, Mainer went in a state of terror and shame because of Saint–Evroult's misfortunes since Abbot Robert had withdrawn to Italy and Duke William has intruded Osbern in his place, with the result that Osbern was excommunicated by authority of Pope Nicholas II. At Cluny, Mainer was a model subject of Abbot Hugh for a year during which he 'fervently learnt to undergo the discipline of the cluniacs'. Osbern recalled him to become prior of Saint–Evroult only when Pope Alexander II had regularized the situation there.[9] Abbot Hugh must have learnt from Mainer about the spiritual and physical perils that might befall monks in the domains of William of Normandy.[10]

There is a wider context, too, in Cluny's every–increasing willingness to answer the favour of reforming kings by sending monks to establish monasteries in their lands, to advise about ecclesiastical affairs, and possibly to serve as abbots and bishops. Although it was only under Abbot Hugh than Cluniac monks at all frequently became bishops,[11] Cluny began to assist well–disposed kings under his predecessor Odilo (994–1048). In Germany, the Emperor Henry II upon a visit to Cluny in 1022 gave it gifts including a jewel–studded golden crown and received confraternity; with Henry's support, Bishop Meinwerk of Paderborn successfully asked Odilo and his community for thirteen monks to establish a monastery at Abdinghof.[12] Odilo also had dealings with King Sancho II el Mayor of Navarre (1000–35).[13] A number of spanish monks came to Cluny and learned its Customs, which they took back to Spain; *c.* 1021 one of their number, Paternus, became for a time abbot of the principal Aragonese monastery of San Juan de la Peña.[14]   Abbot Odio's letters refer to Sancho's admission to Cluny's confraternity and to his gifts, as well as to Odilo's wish to maintain contacts with his sons and successors.[15]   By 1053 at latest, the train of events had begun by which the strongest of Sancho's sons, King Ferdinand I of León and Castile, came to pay an annual *cemsis* or tribute to Cluny.   The attestation of a charter by a 'Frater Galindus clunia(ce)nsis' suggests that by 1053 Abbot Hugh was employing one of his monks, evidently of Spanish origin, as a legate in León.[16]

It was under Ferdinand's son and successor, Alphonso VI (1065–1109), that Cluny's relations with the kingdom of León–Castile became extremely close. In the troubled circumstances of his accession, Alphonso believed that he owed his escape from captivity by his brother to the intercessions of the Cluniacs.   In 1077 he doubled his father's *census* to Cluny and in 1090 confirmed it in perpetuity;   Abbot Hugh granted him exceptional liturgical commemorations. He reign saw the establishment by himself and by his nobility of a number of Cluniac houses which were subject to Cluny and which followed its Customs; they included San Isidoro de las Dueñas (1073), San Salvador de Bilafreda (1975), San Zoile de Carrión (1076), San Juan Battista de los Eremitas (1077), Santa Maria de Nájera (1079), and San Coloma de Burgos (uncertain).[17]   From the mid–1070s it became usual for Alphonso to have at his court at least one Cluniac monk who advised him on ecclesiastical matters; such monks were often themselves promoted to high ecclesiastical office as abbots or bishops.[18]   A critically important figure was the monk Robert, well established in Spain by 1077, who was Alphonso's intimate counsellor at court until, probably in 1080, he became abbot of Sahagún.   He played a central part in the crisis that arose in 1080 between Pope Gregory VII and King Alphonso, attracting the pope's extremest censure.[19]   His successor at Sahagún was, however, another Cluniac monk, Bernard of Sédirac, who in 1086 became archbishop of the new reconquered city of Toledo.[20]

For the present inquiry, the most significant document to survive from these events in Spain is the letter of 1077 that Alphonso VI addressed to Abbot Hugh in connection with his doubling of his father's *census*.[21]   It was full of praise for the monk Robert, who was the king's constant counsellor and who had urged him to increase the *census*.   To Alphonso, it said, he was the most excellent and dear of monks, and to Hugh he was a close a most faithful *confrater*; Alphonso thanked Hugh fulsomely for sending to his kingdom and for his particular benefit this portion of his monastic flock.   He earnestly besought him that Robert, whom he held supreme and most dear in all his affairs, might stay with him throughout his life and help him by words and deeds.   'For you assuredly know how all the advice that he gives is of benefit to you.   Consider me', the king pleaded, 'and for no cause whatever cease to allow his permanent residence in our lands'. Alphonso's main plea, however, was that Hugh would increase his bounty by sending some more of his monastic family (*aliquos tue sanctissime religionis domesticos*) for their common benefit in a place – by *locum* Alphonso seems to mean his whole kingdom rather than a particular locality in it – which was both Alphonso's and Hugh's because Hugh had begun to water it from his most holy fountain of Cluny.   He at once stipulated his own side of the bargain, which was to double the *census* and so provide wheat for the sustenance of the community at Cluny.   It will be noticed that Alphonso wished to keep Robert with him as a familiar counsellor, as he did for the next three years;   it is not stated that further monks who might come were destined for high ecclesiastical office as

abbots or bishops, or even for settlement in existing or new monasteries. He
made a general request on behalf of his kingdom; it was possible, but not stated,
that any or all of the monks who came might, like Robert, eventually receive
ecclesiastical office. It is not known that Hugh sent more monks from Cluny in
response to this letter.[22]

To return to the background in Normandy, Germany, and Spain, to King
William I and Cluny: Alphonso's request of 1077 for the dispatch of more Cluniac
monks may help to elucidate William's very similar request in Anonymous II.
William's request has usually be understood thus,[23] hereafter interpretation A:
wishing worthily to make appointments to (*ordinare*) the sees and abbeys of
England, King William sent a letter to Abbot Hugh asking him to send six of his
monks, by whose counsel he might carry out his duty in this matter of making
appointments (*de ecclesiis ordinandis*), and when he had made them (the six
monks) rules (of churches), that is, abbots and bishops, he might be confident
about the care and ruling of their flocks.[24]   But, by analogy with Alfonso's
request, this passage is patient of another translation, hereafter interpretation B:
wishing in a general sense fittingly to set in order (*ordinare*) the sees and abbeys
of England, King William sent a letter to Abbot Hugh asking him to send six of
his monks, by whose counsel he might carry out his duty of setting churches in
order (*de ecclesiis ordinandis*), and then, when rulers (not necessarily the six) had
been appointed for the churches, he might be confident about the care and ruling
of their (the churches?) flocks. According to interpretation A, the six Cluniacs
were destined themselves to become abbots and bishops; according to
interpretation B, this was not necessarily so: as in Spain, so in England they
would be royal counsellors who might or might not eventually become prelates.

Interpretation B has three powerful arguments in its favour. First, it
understands the verb *ordinare* in the sense of 'set of order', rather than 'ordain
to ecclesiastical office', that it twice bears in Abbot Hugh's reply as excerpted by
Anonymous II: Hugh at once seized upon William's good intention, according to
interpretation B, of in general setting in order (*ordinare*) the people with whom
God had entrusted him in the way of salvation; and he referred to his need of
monks for places that he himself must set in order (*loca a me ordinanda*).[25]
Secondly, however, if William's proposal to make payment for the monks is left
for later discussion, Abbot Hugh's letter continued in exclusively monastic terms,
of his responsibility for monks who had been professed to him and who in
England would not be subject to any obedience or discipline. Hugh's objection
that the monks would fear no chapter in a land where there was no Cluniac house
to relieve or to constrain them, would lose force if they became bishops or abbots,
or lived in a settled community; it was natural if they were to serve at large as
long—term counsellors at the king's court.[26] Thirdly, at no time in his reign did
William greatly favour monk—bishops but preferred royal clerks and chaplains,
while all save two of his new abbots came from Normandy or Maine. In this
light, too, interpretation B makes the better sense.[27]

Historians read Abbot Hugh's reply to William, which Anonymous II cites
verbatim,[27] very differently, some finding it angry, scornful, and rude, but others
seeing only a forceful statement of Cluny's general policy blended with implicit
pastoral advice. Unquestionably it can be read in several ways according to the
reader's presuppositions, but there is a strong case or a relatively mild
interpretation. Hugh addressed the king respectfully and cordially *domine rex,
karissime domine*), and without irony described himself as his friend (*amicus*).
He began by genuinely applauding William's request in so far as it proceeded
from his good intention in seeking the salvation of the English people, and he

concluded by inviting the king to ask some other favour and to bear patiently with his refusal since it would be incompatible with a friend's salvation to do otherwise. In the body of the letter, Hugh took up William's offer to reimburse Cluny for the loss of personnel and their spiritual and temporal services by an annual payment of a hundred pounds of silver for each monk. The bargain that William proposed calls for careful assessment. In all respects save a crucial one, it is reminiscent of the exchanges made or proposed with the Emperor Henry II's support in respect of Abdinhof, and in King Alphonso VI's letter of 1077. Such exchanges should probably be considered against the background of the gift—exchange of a diplomatic, not commercial nature that for centuries had been part and parcel of relations between great men and institutions, lay and ecclesiastical.[28] Accordingly, Anonymous II commented that William's proposal was advanced 'on the grounds of friendship and amity' (*sub titulo amicitiae et gratiae*).[29] The novel and shocking element in it was William's brash commercialism in putting a price upon each monk sent; this, according to the Anonymous, was what made the arrangement unacceptable to Hugh: 'He who wished to become a buyer (*emptor*) could not do so, because he did not find a seller (*venditor*) of monks'.[30] It was the diversion from the familiar conventions of aristocratic gift—exchange to the novel and brash language of the market—place at which the abbot bridled. The king's proposal also approached dangerously near to simony, although an express comment that Abbot Hugh refused the king 'because his petition was for a sale and seemed simoniacal' had to await the twelfth—century draftsman of the chapter—heading to Anonymous II.[31] This may express a later understanding of simony, for which William was not notorious during his lifetime. In any case, Abbot Hugh did not develop his objection in terms of resistance to the king's simony, but of his own obligation as abbot to safeguard the welfare of those who were, and would continue to be, his monastic subjects. Especially if interpretation B of Anonymous II's introduction to the letter is preferred, the king's stake in the matter was limited — the dispatch of six monastic counsellors, not the filling of as many major ecclesiastical offices. Hugh's letter bears the aspect of a forceful exposition of his own position in face of a royal proposal that ran counter to accepted diplomatic rules as between kings and churchmen, rather than of a personal and ill—mannered rejection of royal generosity. Anonymous II credibly recorded that William at first was extremely upset at being denied a request that he backed up with so generous a gift, but that, on reflection, he took Hugh's point and admired him the more for his integrity as abbot. This suggests that the letter caused no lasting trauma.[32]

Although it is scanty and the result of several decades of Cluniac tradition, Anonymous II's account of William's request for monks and Hugh's answer may well be judged to have the ring of basic reliability. If two interpretations of its account of William's request are possible, interpretation B has a remarkably close parallel in Alphonso's request of 1077. The Anonymous gives an intelligible account of Hugh's reaction, and it cites his letter in reply at length. The next question to arise is how this version compares in subject matter (the problem of date will come later) with that in the longer version of the Lewes foundation charter.[33]

Massive substantial differences between the two accounts leap to the eye. According to Anonymous II, the king and the abbot were at a distance and exchanged formal letters; in the charter, the king raised the matter in a conversation that William of Warenne overheard when all three were together in Normandy during the abbot's visit. For the Anonymous, William's request was sent at the beginning of his reign in England; the charter locates it in the course of negotiations about Lewes during the later 1070s. In the Anonymous Will requested six monks, but in the charter twelve. If the Anonymous is open to different readings about how they were to be used, the charter is unequivocal: William would make all twelve of them bishops and abbots in the land of his inheritance that God had given him — that is, in England. In the Anonymous, the story is told at length and it its own right. The charter introduces it as an aside by which William of Warenne justified his fear that Prior Lanzo of Lewes might quickly receive further royal preferment: whereas for the Anonymous the king seems to have wanted the monks to counsel him about the affairs of the kingdom and perhaps to be prelates, in the charter William, in the middle of his reign, had already appointed the better candidates in England to ecclesiastical dignities and had perforce turned to Cluny![34]   Unlike the Anonymous, the charter says nothing about William's offer of payment, or abut Hugh's reply to him, or about his own reaction thereafter. In short, the contrast between the two sources is so extensive and so detailed that the historian must follow either the one or the other; it is unlikely that they can be reconciled or combined.

The concluding section of the charter in which the reference to the king's remarks to the abbot is to be found is riddled with improbabilities. Barlow has sufficiently shown that Abbot Hugh's supposed concessions to William of Warenne are almost certainly unauthentic and William's alleged reasons for seeking them therefore implausible.[35] As regards William's request to Hugh for monks, there is no confirmation of the assertion that, by 1978, William had run out of suitable candidates for ecclesiastical promotion: between 1078 and 1987 there were only seven new bishops, all save one chosen from among royal clerks and chaplains; of sixteen or so new abbots, all seem to have come from houses in William's lands. Nothing suggests that he was scraping the barrel of clerical talent.   Although the number twelve for the Cluniac monks who William allegedly requested has been widely countenanced, or even preferred to Anonymous II's six, it is manifestly excessive in view both of the slow turnover of bishops and abbots and of William's policy for replacements. The known events of the foundation of Lewes leave scant room for a period of coolness on the king's part. Not only does the longer charter not mention it, but the genuine charter, surviving as an original, appears to have been quickly followed by royal *acta* that indicate friendly relations.[36]

There is nothing to impugn the acceptability of the longer charter, based perhaps on a foundation narrative, as evidence for a visit by Abbot Hugh to King William between 1078 and 1080 during which they met in William of Warenne's presence. But it seems likely that, when the charter was long afterwards put together, it introduced into its account of the visit a reference to negotiations about sending monks that may have occurred long before. There are two possibilities. One is that, whether by direct dependence or from another source, the charter follows with modification of detail the story as in Anonymous II, presenting it according to interpretation A. Indeed, it is the first evidence to survive for such an interpretation. Alteratively, it cannot be excluded that William of Warenne overheard in 1078/80 an authentically recorded conversation between king and abbot recalling negotiations by then long past that Anonymous II correctly located in the earliest years of William's reign. With his wounds long since healed, the king now felt able to jest to his friend about his continuing problem in finding good bishops and abbots with hyperbole about how many Cluniac monks he would need nowadays.

What, then, may be concluded about the date of William the Conqueror's approach to Abbot Hugh for the dispatch of monks? Despite the fragility of the evidence in the longer Lewes foundation charter, the possibility of a date between

1078 and 1080 must be kept open because of the similarity of King Alphonso VI's request of 1077 for an unspecified number of Cluniac monks to be sent to his court as permanent counsellors. The case becomes a little stronger if it is thought that, in the light of interpretation B of Anonymous II, William indeed made a similar request. William could have heard of Alphonso's approach and have decided to follow suit; a channel of communication from Castile to England at about this time was Alphonso's negotiations with William about his possible marriage to one of the Conqueror's daughters.[37] This would sidestep a possible objection to a date in the 1060s for the Conqueror's approach to Cluny: that Alphonso, who was *au courant* with Cluniac affairs through the monk Robert and others, would scarcely have made in 1077 an approach of a kind that he knew Hugh to have rebuffed ten years or so earlier.

But Alphonso may have felt confident that his case in 1077 differed from William's in the 1060s because of the long–standing relations between Spain and Cluny and also of the magnitude and diplomatic propriety of Spanish gifts, and because of the established Cluniac monastic houses in León–Castile. And strong reasons can be advanced for preferring a date for William's request at the beginning of his reign. The much earlier source, Anonymous II, which claims to follow a written request from the king, unequivocally states that the approach took place then (*cum praefatae regionis potiri coepisset*), in the context of a general desire to do well for the English church (*volens digne episcopatus et abbatias terrae illius ordinare*);[38] only the very late and, as has been suggested, highly improbable account in the Lewes charter places it in the context of the foundation of Lewes. Moreover, however one reads the Anonymous, but especially if interpretation B is followed, it is hard to envisage the king's entertaining the idea of recruiting a group of Cluniac counsellors at a time when Lanfranc was well established as archbishop of Canterbury and as William's trusted right–hand man in ecclesiastical affairs. Lanfranc's view of Cluniac monasticism is unknown, though there is no evidence for such contact with Cluny as Anselm had while abbot of Bec.[39] But it is not likely that William would have sought the sending of six or twelve monks, especially if they were to become bishops and abbots, without consulting Lanfranc, or that Lanfranc would have been much in favour. So drastic a change in William's policy in mid–stream is barely credible, and an early approach is far more easy to envisage.

The use of the royal title in the Anonymous's account, and still more in Abbot Hugh's letter which it cites, points to date after William's coronation on Christmas day 1066 but his alleged reluctance to be crowned does not establish it:[40] Hugh may have been unaware of this reluctance. An exchange of letters soon after the battle of Hastings (14 October 1066) cannot be excluded. The way may have been prepared. Encouraged by Hugh's recent dispatch of his monk Bernfrid to Saint–Evroult, William may have begun to canvass means of ecclesiastical reform during his diplomatic preparations for the conquest of England. His envoy to Pope Alexander II may have discussed them with the pope and others like Archdeacon Hildebrand, and may even have visited Cluny during his journey.[41] But the most likely time for the exchange of letters is during William's stay in Normandy from late February to early December 1067, when the uncertainties surrounding the loyalties of Stigand of Canterbury and Aldred of York may have made him particularly anxious to strengthen his ecclesiastical entourage.[42] A date after the ecclesiastical measures of 1070 and the accession of Lanfranc to Canterbury is unlikely. If 1067 is the most likely date for William's approach, a powerful factor in Abbot Hugh's refusal may have been the warning that William's recent dealings over Abbot Osbert of Saint–Evroult provided. It may have reinforced the habitual caution that Hugh expressed in his letter. An early date for it, 1066 or more probably very soon after, cannot be proved but is very likely.

The two further occasions of known contact between King William and Abbot Hugh call for only brief comment. William's reception of spiritual confraternity is expressly referred to only in Anonymous II.[43] He is not commemorated in any of the major Cluniac Necrologies.[44] According to the Anonymous, the gift occurred when William was king of England:[45] time must be allowed for any temporary estrangement that may have occurred after Hugh refused William's request for the dispatch of monks. The *tempus ante quem* depends on how the Anonymous is read. It names as Hugh's messenger ' *dominus Warmundus*', who afterwards rose from abbot of Déos to be archbishop of Vienne.[46] The latest possible date is thus 1076, when Warmund became archbishop. The Anonymous is, however, ambiguous about whether Warmund came before or during his abbacy, that is, before or after *c.* 1074. Those who have argued for his travelling to Normandy while abbot of Déols have done so without regard to his having previously been a monk, and latterly, prior of Cluny itself.[47] The Anonymous's description of his as *dominus* (rather than *abbas*, or an equivalent), and the word 'afterwards', more naturally suggests that he travelled while still at Cluny; indeed, a mission to convey confraternity to a king would be a more likely task for a prior of Cluny than for the abbot of a distant Cluniac dependency. Thus, the most likely dates are 1073 or early 1074 – dates when William's presence in Normandy and Maine is attested.[48] The sending of rich presents by William and Matilda is also noticed in Gilo's *Life of Abbot Hugh*;[48] this time, the basis was a normal gift–exchange in the tradition of the munificence to Cluny of Henry II of Germany and the Spanish kings. Perhaps William had learnt the lesson of an earlier rebuff.

For Abbot Hugh's visit to King William in Normandy, the longer foundation charter of Lewis is the only, and very late in many respects unreliable, source. Barlow has sufficiently established that such a visit would have taken place between 1078 and 1080;[50] it is credible as perhaps drawn from the fund of older material upon which those who drew up the charter depended. That such a visit took place is fairly securely attested by Cluny's own traditions, not only as recorded by Anonymous II but also by Gilo, according to whom William 'often honoured Father Hugh with embassies, self–commendation, and gifts, which proclaimed the pledge of his life'.[51] It is reasonably certain that Abbot Hugh's visit to Normandy occurred.

The conclusions of this inquiry may be summed up as follows: (i) Probably very soon after late 1066, with 1067 as the likeliest date, though just possibly in 1078/80, William asked for, and was refused, the dispatch of six Cluniac monks for his purposes as king of England. The figure of twelve is too suspect to be seriously entertained. (ii) Probably in 1073 or 1074, but possibly in 1075 or 1076, Prior, or Abbot, Warmund brought William from Abbot Hugh the gift of spiritual confraternity with Cluny; in return, King William and Queen Matilda made rich presents to it. (iii) Between 1078 and 11080, the king and the abbot almost certainly met in Normandy when the latter paid a visit to the duchy.

NOTES

1.   *Bibliotheca Cluniacensis*, eds. M. Marrier and A. du Chesne (Paris, 1614), cols 447–62; most of the material relevant to this paper is reprinted in P. Migne *Patrologia Latina* [hereafter *PL*], clix. 923–8. For discussions of

the dates of the sources for Abbot Hugh of Cluny, se H.E.J. Cowdrey, 'Two Studies in Cluniac History, 1049–1126', *Studi Gregoriani*, xi (1978), pp 22–30; F. Barlow, 'The Canonization and Early Lives of Hugh I, Abbot of Cluny', *Analecta Bollandiana*, scviii (1980), pp 297–334, repr. *The Norman Conquest and Beyond* (London, 1983), pp 257–95. (Barlow's conclusions are debatable; I hope to consider them more fully elsewhere).

2.   The charter is printed in W. Dugdale, *Monasticon Anglicanum*, new edn. by J. Caley, H. Ellis and B. Bandinel, 6 vols. in 8 parts (London, 1817–30), v. 12–13; also in *Recueil des chartes de l'abbaye de Cluny*, eds., A. Bernard and A Bruel, Collection des documents inédits sur l'histoire de France, 6 vols. (1876–1903) [hereafter cited as Bruel with the number of the item], p 3651. For the date, see *Early Yorkshire Charters*, viii, ed. C.T. Clay, Yorkshire Archaeological Society, Record Series, Extra Series, vi: Warenne Charters (1949), pp 59–62.

3.   F. Barlow, 'William I's Relations with Cluny', *Journal of Ecclesiastical History*, xxxii (1981), pp 131–41, repr. *The Norman Conquest and Beyond*, pp 245–56. (References hereafter are to the reprint).

4.   See Barlow (as n.3), p 254, n.1. A later date was proposed in older works, e.g. *PL* clix. 927B.

5.   Barlow (as n.3), p 254.

6.   *Ibid.*, pp 247, 253.

7.   For recent summaries, see B. Golding, 'The Coming of the Cluniacs', *Proceedings of the Battle Conference on Anglo–Norman Studies, III, 1980* (Woodbridge, 1981), pp 65–77, at pp 65–6; D. Bates, *Normandy before 1066* (London/New York, 1982), pp 218–25.

8.   *The Ecclesiastical History of Orderic Vitalis*, ed., M. Chibnall, 6 vols. (Oxford, 1969–80), ii. pp 74–5.

9.   *Ibid.*, ii. pp 96–7, 107–8.

10.   *Ibid.*, ii. pp 90–115, esp. pp 94–9.

11.   J. Mehne, 'Cluniacenserbischöfe', *Fruhmittelalterliche Studien*, xi (1977), pp 241–87, esp. pp 254–63. The *Historiae Tornacenses* recorded that Gregory asked Abbot Hugh for monks whom he might duly make bishops, and that those whom he sent included the future Pope Urban II: iv. 11, *Monumenta Germaniae Historica* [hereafter *MGH*], Scriptores, xiv. pp 340–1; cf. Orderic Vitalis (as n. 8), ii. pp 298–301.

12.   *Vita Meinwerci ep. Patherbrunnensis*, cap. 28, ed. F. Tenckhoff, *MGH Scriptores rerum Germanicarum* (1921), p 32.

13.   For the complex and unresolved problems of Spanish history in the eleventh century, the following especially bear upon the subject of this paper: P. David *Etudies historiques sur la Galice et le Portugal du vi^e au xii^e siecle* (Lisbon/Paris, 1947), pp 341–439; H.E.J. Cowdrey, *The Cluniacs and the Gregorian Reform* (Oxford, 1970), pp 214–47; P. Segle, *Konigtum und Klosterreform in Spanien. Untersuchungen uber die Cluniacenserkloster in Kastilien–Leon vom Beginn des 11. bis zur Mitte des 12. Jahrhunderts* (Kallmünz, 1974); C.J. Bishko, 'Fernando I and the Origins of the Leonese–Castilian Alliance with Cluny', *Studies in Medieval Spanish Frontier History* (London, 1980), II; J.F. O'Callaghan, 'The Integration of Christian Spain into Europe: the Role of Alfonso VI of León–Castile', *Santiago, Saint–Denis, and Saint Peter. The Reception of the Roman Liturgy in Leon–Castile in 1080*, ed., B.F. Reilly (New York, 1985), pp 101–20; J. Williams, 'Cluny and Spain', *Gesta*, xxvii (1988), pp 93–101.

14.   Ralph Glaber, *Historiae*, 3.12, *Raoul Glaber, Les Cinq Livres de ses histoires*, ed. M. Prou (Paris, 1886), pp 61–2.

15. *Epp*, 2–3, *PL* cxlii. 941–2; cf. Jotsaldus, *De vita et virtutibus s. Odilonis abbatis*, 1.7, *PL* cxlii. 902B.

16. For the *census*, see Bruel, 3443, 3509, 3638; Galindus is discussed by Bishko (as n. 13), pp 24–6, who cites the unpublished charter Madrid, Academia de la Historia, Colección Velázquez, IV, leg. 4, no. 1420.

17. Bruel, 3452, 3481, 3492, 3507–8, 3540, 3582. For a survey of Alphonso's gifts, see Segl (as n. 13), pp 47–76, and for non–royal gifts, pp 128–47.

18 Listed by David (as n. 13), p 362.

19. Robert is referred to in Bruel, 3441, 3509, 3582. For the crisis, Cowdrey (as n. 13), pp 230–9.

20. For Bernard, see esp. J.F. Rivera Recio, *El Arzobispo de Toledo Don Bernardo de Cluny (1086–1124)* (Rome, 1962), esp. pp 11–17; *ibid.*, *La Iglesia de Toledo en el siglo xii (1086–1208)*, 2 vols. (Rome, 1966–76), esp. i. pp 125–34.

21. Bruel, 3441 (misdated 1070).

22. But I have not been able to check Rivera Recio's reference to P. Sandoval, *Cronica de los cinco reyes* (Pamplona, 1615), 1 ib. 18, c. 10: *El Arzobispo* (as n. 20), p 13.

23. Including by the present writer: Cowdrey (as n. 1), p 143.

24. *PL* clix. 924AB. The phrase *terrae illius* establishes that, in Anon. II's view, William's plan was restricted to England and excluded Normandy.

25. *PL* clix. 924B and D.

26. For William's bishops, see J. Le Patourel, *The Norman Empire* (Oxford, 1976), pp 35–6, 49–51; for his abbots, D. Knowles *The Monastic Order in England*, 2nd edn. (Cambridge, 1963), pp 112, 704, also Barlow (as n. 3), p 253.

27. *PL* clix. 924–925A; Cowdrey (as n. 1), pp 143–4.

28. This subject needs further investigation, but see H.E.J. Cowdrey, 'Legal Problems Raised by Agreements of Confraternity', *Memoria. Der geschichtliche Zeugniswert des liturgischen Gedenkens im Mittelalter*, eds., K. Schmid and J. Wollasch (Munich, 1984), pp 233–54, at pp 236–7.

29. *PL* clix. 924B.

30. *Ibid.*

31. Marrir and du Chesne (as n. 2), col. 453A.

32. That William would hear and reverence ecclesiastics who addressed him plainly is suggested by whatever lies behind his exchange with Guitmund, monk of la–Croix–saint–Leufroi and later bishop of Averesa, about his promotion to ecclesiastical office in England: Orderic Vitalis (as n. 8), 11, pp 270–81.

33. as n. 2.

34. '... timuimus', runs William of Warenne's supposed charter, 'ne dominus Lanzo cum redisset, cito aufereretur nobis, quia rex quos meliores inveniere potuit in dignitates ecclesiae exaltavit, et nobis audientibus requisivit ab abbate quod mitteret ei duodecim de sanctis monachis suis, et eos omnes faceret episcopos et abates in terra haereditatis suae quam ei dederat Deus', *Monasticon* (as n. 2), v. 13a.

35. (As n. 3), pp 249–50.

36. The documents are best edited by Clay (as n. 2), pp 54–7. No. 2 is the authentic foundation charter of Lewes which Clay dates *c.* 1078–82 but probably before Dec. 1081 (although Barlow points out that the *tempus a quo* could be earlier: (as n. 3), p 249, n. 14). No 3 is King William's notification to Archbishop Lanfranc of Canterbury and Bishop Odo of Bayeux that he has confirmed to the abbey of Cluny the land at Falmer (Sussex) given by William of Warenne and his wife. This act of goodwill to Cluny appears to come from, or very soon after, the date of no. 2

because (i) Falmer is mentioned in it, and (ii) the gift is said to be *sanctus Petrus de Cluniaco* rather than to St Pancras. In no. 4, which Clay dates 1081–3, William I confirms to Lewes Priory the manor of West Walton, Norfolk.

37. *Vita Simonis comitis Crespeiensis auctore Synchrono*, cap. 5, *PL* clvi. 1215DE.
38. *PL* clix. 924A.
39. As young men, Lanfranc and Abbot Hugh are likely to have met at Pope Leo IX's council of Reims in Oct. 1049. For Anselm, see *Ep.* 37, *Sancti Anselmi Cantuariensis archiepiscopi Opera*, ed. F.S. Schmitt, 6 vols. (Edinburgh, 1946–61), iii. pp 144–8. In his Customs for Christ Church, Canterbury, Lanfranc shows that he had read and used Bernard's version of Cluny's Customs: *Decreta Lanfranci monachis Cantuariensibus transmissa*, ed., D. Knowles, Corpus Consuetudinum Monasticarum, iii (Sieburg, 1967), p. xviii; but for the non–Cluniac nature of Bec's Customs up to Lanfranc's time, see *Consuetudines Beccenses*, ed., M.P. Dickson, CCM iv (Sieburg, 1967), pp. xxx–xlii. Lanfranc is most likely to have obtained Bernard's Customs after 1078 from Prior Lanzo of Lewes — another argument for a late date (1079/89) for Lanfranc's compilation: M. Gibson, *Lanfranc of Bec* (Oxford, 1978), pp 240–1.
40. Guillaume de Poitiers, *Histoire de Guillaume le Conquerant*, 2.28–9, ed., R. Foreville (Paris, 1952), pp 216–19.
41. Orderlic Vitalis (as n. 6), ii. 142–3.
42. For the archibishops' actions after the battle of Hastings, see the Anglo–Saxon Chronicle, D version, *a.* 1066; William of Poitiers, 2.38 (as n. 40), pp 242–5. William's conciliatory attitude to distant monasteries and his desire for spiritual benefits from them are exemplified in his charger of Apr. 1067 for Saint–Benoît–sur Loire: *Regesta regum Anglo–Normannorum, 1066–1154*, i: *Regesta Willelmi Conquestoris et Willelmi Rufi, 1066–1100*, ed. H.W.C. Davis (Oxford, 1913), p. 2, no. 6a.
43. *PL* clix, pp 923.
44. *Synopse der Cluniacensischen Necrologian*, ed. J. Wollasch, 2 vols (Munich, 1982).
45. The Anonymous II is not concerned with the relative chronology of events: Barlow (as n. 3), pp 248–9.
46. See above. For Warmund, see N. Huyghebaert, 'Un légat de Grégoire VII en France: Warmond de Vienne', *Revue d'histoire ecclesiastique*, xl (1944–5), 187–200, subject to Barlow's comments: (as n. 3), p 246. n. 6.
47. Bruel, 3003, 3282, 3439. For the imperfect state of knowledge about the succession of priors, see M. Chaume, 'Les grans prieurs de Cluny. Compléments et rectifications à la liste de la Gallia Christiana', *Revue Mabillon*, xxviii (1938), pp 147–52, esp. p 150.
48. *Regesta* (as n. 42), pp 18–20.
49. 2.15, ed., Cowdrey (as n. 1), pp 64–5.
50. Above, p 000.
51. Anon. II: *PL* clix. 923A; Gilo: as n. 49. Gilo's word *commendatione* should perhaps be translated 'self–commendation' as referring to William's seeking confraternity and spiritual benefits (cf *PL* clix. 923BC), rather than, more generally, 'favour'.

SAINT BERNARD : WHAT KIND OF SAINT?

Christopher Holdsworth

The analysis of someone thought to be a saint may take many forms, as the focus shifts from delineation of behaviour and writings to the recreation of people and surroundings in which the holy person lived. At the present time there are some who are attempting to apply insights gained from psychology to both fields, whereas others are using concepts drawn from anthropology and sociology. Here I do not intend to follow Jean Leclercq and put Bernard on the couch, so to say, nor to attempt to assess in one short hour, however sweet, the whole life of Bernard, but I shall, I think show some tendency towards the second approach which I have just referred to. Yet I will also be depending upon very traditional ways for the historian, scrutiny of texts. What I want to do now is to look again at certain features of the so—called *Vita Prima*, in particular at the miraculous element in it with the aim of revealing certain aspects of that work which can, I claim, tell us something important about Saint Bernard, in particular, what sort of a saint he was portrayed to be, and (here with less certainty) what sort of a man of God he thought he was.[1]

Over the last thirty years the *Vita Prima* has received a great deal of attention especially from Adriaan Bredero, a scholar from the Netherlands who puts most of us to shame by being able to publish most of his work in French or English. His study of the *Vita* which first appeared in 1960 cast a floud of light upon the way that it had been shaped and then reshaped to secure Bernard's canonisation, which it finally achieved in 1174.[2]. As a result of painstaking and close examination of manuscripts and a considerable range of printed materials he revealed the degree to which the *Vita* had been moulded to that one end, the way that its authors had used earlier materials, some of which they themselves had written, and the reworkings which were necessary when the first effort to persuade the pope to canonise Bernard foundered in 1163. He has made everyone read the *Vita* in a new light, so that one hopes very strongly that he will soon put us all further in his debt by completing his new edition of the whole text, for it is abundantly clear that Migne, who depended here upon that giant Mabillon, gives us a supremely unsatisfactory version.[3] It is interesting now to realise that Bredero's uncovering of what one might call the changing face of Bernard was taking place just at the same time as other scholars were revealing the changing shapes of another basic collection of materials for early cistercian history, namely the *Carta Caritatis*, the whole collection of documents which one may call for convenience the cistercian book of uses, and the early narrative accounts of the beginnings of the order.[4] The fundamental result of Bredero's work has been to warn the reader against taking the *Vita* at its apparent surface value, and to carry in one's spectacle case, so to say, a lens marked with a large query. Dom Jean Leclercq carried such scepticism almost to its ultimate point when, just over a decade ago, he seemed to be suggesting that the first part of the *Vita* revealed more about the mind of its author, William of Saint—Thierry, than it did about Saint Bernard.[5] Since then there has been some redressing of the balance: W. E. Goodrich, for example, has attacked au pied de la lettre Bredero's argument that William seriously distorted his main source, the *Fragmenta* written by Geoffrey of Auxerre, and although the jury is still out, he has certainly won my vote.[6]

My intention here is not to directly reopen the issues raised by Bredero, but to look at a side of the record which only marginally interested him, the miraculous element in the *Vita*. This he seems to have considered part of what he called the *commune hagiographicum*, that side of the *Vita* which was considerably influenced by the long—established norms of the holy man's life. At one or two places, in foot—notes, he listed episodes which he believed fitted this classification, but his list is fairly short, and I do not believe that he meant it to be comprehensive.[7] In addition he scarcely felt it necessary to categorise what he meant by the *commune hagiographicum* save by referring to that extremely significant book by Delehaye, *Les legenendes hagiographiques*.[8] That is of course, not surprising when one recalls the state of scholarship on saints lives over thirty years ago.   Now this particular furrow has been widened deeply, mainly by non—English speaking scholars, yet the only treatment known to me of the miraculous element in the *Vita Prima* in any language is that by Benedicta Ward.[9] Her valuable pages do not, I hope, exhaust the field, although they bring out what will be one of my themes.   But before I pass directly to the *Vita*, let me salute three other scholars writing in our own tongue whose work has proved liberating and suggestive; Peter Brown, Clare Stancliffe and Ronald Finucane. Just because the last analysed the records kept at healing shrines so thoroughly I do not intend to attempt a similar job on the healing miracles in the *Vita Prima*, but he does convince one of the extraordinary value of this kind of evidence.[10] Brown and Stancliffe, on the other hand, point us towards what I hope will prove to be valid questions, even though they have worked upon a very much earlier period.[11] I must also at this point acknowledge one of my former undergraduates, Bill Wilson, who a decade ago produced a seminar paper on Bernard's miracles which was, for me, one of the most fruitful moments in my teaching career.   I hope this paper will to some extent thank him for that extraordinary session.

Now let me remind you what, in broad terms, the *Vita Prima* is. Unlike most holy persons Bernard of Clairvaux was not the subject of a Life written by one person, but by three, William of Saint—Thierry, Ernald of Bonneval, and Geoffrey of Auxerre. Let me pause briefly with each of them.

William was one of the most significant friends that Bernard had. They met first around 1119 and influenced each other profoundly for the rest of their lives.[12] William, in some ways the subtler thinker, urged Bernard to attack that sparkling teacher Abelard, for example, whilst Bernard so impressed William by his manner of life that in time, in 1135, he left the fold of the black monks and became a cistercian. He also was convinced that the abbot of Clairvaux was a man of God, and so started to write the life of his still—living friend (rather like Eadmer and Anselm) around 1145, dying himself, however, three years later in 1148, five years before Bernard.[13] We can only speculate whether had he outlived Bernard he would have carried his story to the end and how he might have done so. But it is important to realise that he did follow a chronological plan once he had got past the early days at Clairvaux, and that although the latest miraculous episode he mentions can be placed as late as 1139/40, vast tracks of Bernard's activity before them seem to have been of no interest to him.[14] He concentrated, almost entirely, upon the saint on his home ground, at the monastery he so much loved, and besides drawing on his own rich memories, used a series of notes which Geoffrey put together for him.

Ernald, on the other hand, focussed largely upon the public Bernard, especially upon his doings during the Anacletan Schism between 1130 and 1138. Whereas it is easy to see how William came to write about Bernard it is not obvious at first sight why Ernald got drawn in. Most historians have done no more than to point out that he was a Benedictine abbot, author of a number of works on Biblical and spiritual themes, and that he seems to have been a friend of Bernard's because he received a letter from him written in his own hand during his final illness.[15]   Bredero has cast doubt upon the authenticity of that letter and gone on to suggest that Geoffrey of Auxerre deliberately referred to it writing in the last book of his part of the *Life* to explain Ernald's share in the whole enterprise.[16]   This suggestion has not met with acceptance and we can, I believe, point to a number of sides of Ernald's life which made him a natural co—operator for William and Geoffrey.[17]

Bonneval, where Ernald had become abbot by 1144, was a well—regarded monastery in the diocese of Chartres, situated about thirty kilometres south of the city.[18]   By then it had attracted a family of dependent priories, some within the diocese, some scattered more widely, and had attracted the interest of the counts of Blois, ever concerned to extend their influence by judicious patronage. Ernald was, therefore, well placed to be well—informed about two of the main people with whom Bernard was involved in the period about which he wrote, his bishop, Geoffreu of Chartres, and Theobald count of Blois, but there were at least two other significant links, one of which is revealed by the letters of his friend Arnulf of Lisieux.   These make clear that Ernald was also a good friend of a former prior of Clairvaux, Philip abbot of L'Aumône, a cistercian house in his own diocese.[19]   As well as this we know that his career as a monk began and ended at the famous monastery of Marmoutiers outside Tours, founded originally by saint Martin.   Ernald was there as late as 1138 and seems to have retired there by 1159, dying around 1162.   He was, therefore, probably there in the early 1120's when Bernard attracted a monk called Adam away from Marmoutiers to Foigny, a daughter—house of Clairvaux, and then on to Morimond, where he became involved in the harebrained scheme of abbot Arnold to set up a cistercian house in the Holy Land.[20]   To summarise, as an abbot with experience and literary skill, linked with two of the main actors in the period he was to describe, Ernald had impressive qualifications, which were increased by his connections within the order.   One may probably be right in concluding that it was just because he was not himself a cistercian that he appealed to those 'managing' Bernard's case for canonisation; he, better than a white monk, could reassure others that what Bernard had done out in the world during the Schism was commensurate with his monastic calling.   Once his name had, as it were, presented itself as a writer, it must have been fairly easy for him and Geoffrey to divide up the period untouched by William between them.

Geoffrey, unlike Ernald, as far as we know, but like William, knew Bernard well having been won by him for the cistercian life around 1140 and served as his secretary and travelling companion for the rest of his life.[21]   He wrote much more than either of the others and divided his work into three books, whereas theirs occupy one each.   Geoffrey and Ernald probably finished their parts by 1155—56 within three years of Bernard's death.[22]   The *Vita Prima* consists, therefore, of five books, the first by William, second by Ernald and last three by Geoffrey.

It should be obvious from this what an odd work it is in comparison with many saints lives.   It has three authors whose contributions do not go over the same ground, and hence they are not related together like Gospel writers for they overlap scarcely at all.   If one were to print them in parallel columns like a Gospel Harmony there would be very few places at all where they would deal with the same things. None of the miraculous elements which I want to discuss, occur in more than one of them, though when one looks at the sources that lie behind the Vita, it is obvious, as I have already said, that William used notes which had been prepared for him by Geoffrey, and that Geoffrey also drew on those notes and upon other earlier materials, whilst Ernald only drew slightly upon Geoffrey's earliest record.[23] Yet one must confess that the amalgamation of sections by three people does not make a particularly satisfactory whole for us today, and we know that at least one of those who knew Bernard well, disapproved of it.[24] Alexander III finally approved it in a revised form, but the revision was not thorough enough to turn a curate's egg into a consistent whole.[25] Presumably his doubts about Bernard's case in 1163 were not as much connected with what we find something of a curate's egg of a Life, but with other, more political, questions.[26]

When however we look within we find no less than 176 episodes which we may loosely categorise as miraculous. This is not to say that any very large number of them are explicitly termed *miraculum*, just as this is not a word used in the Vulgate version of the New Testament. What I include within the description is a range of experiences which the authors seem to have thought were largely to be attributed to God working through Bernard. These may be divided into four categories : visions, prophecies, healings, and more general unusual happenings (whilst recognising, too, that some episodes involved a combination of two categories, for example vision and healing). These episodes are spread very unevenly between the three authors, William has 38, Ernald 18 and Geoffrey 120, a distribution which does not reflect the different lengths of their parts of the *Vita*; William's book covers 40 columns in Migne, Ernald's 35, and Geoffrey's 65. One must not emphasise this discrepancy too much, since episodes can vary greatly in length; many of Geoffrey's occupy no more than a few lines, whilst some of Ernald's cover long paragraphs. One would not, however, be wrong in concluding that the miraculous element in Geoffrey is more significant than in the other two, but then it should be realised that he deliberately organised one of his three books around Bernard as a miracle worker.

If we arrange the episodes by decades using Bernard's entry into monastic life in 1113 to mark the end of the first period, something else is immediately obvious.[28] Most of William's episodes cannot be dated more firmly than between the beginning of Bernard's abbacy and the time William began to write, but of those that can, that is to say 14 out of 38, they occur fairy evenly before 1113, and in each succeeding decade. All of Ernald's episodes can be dated by decade, two between 1123 and 1132, and sixteen between 1133 and 1142. There is some overlap in time here with Geoffrey's material, who has seven episodes in these two decades, but the vast majority of Geoffrey's (81 of 120) fall in the last decade of Bernard's life, 1143 to 1153, or very soon after his death.

The explanation for Geoffrey's chronological distribution becomes more pressing when the episodes are arranged by the places where they occurred.[29] The majority of William's all take place at Clairvaux, a few very near to it, and the rest, with only one exception, in France. Ernald is again his almost complete opposite; nearly all his miracles take place in Italy, a few in France and only one at Clairvaux. Geoffrey, on the other hand, has almost 20% at Clairvaux (25), and about 8% near to the abbey (9), but about 35% in France (43), about 28% in the Empire and Denmark (39), and the rest (4) divided evenly between Spain and Italy.

To a very large extent those unevennesses of the quantity and spread over time and place arise from the fact that Geoffrey used three earlier sources, which were no use at all to William or Ernald. These were, in chronological order of composition, a letter of his own written from south–western France whilst accompanying Bernard on a preaching tour against heretics in the summer of

1145, the composite *Historia Miraculorum* put together by various authors either during, or soon after, Bernard's tour preaching the Crusade in the Empire and France between December 1146 and March 1147, and a description of Bernard's last illness and death which Geoffrey wrote for the Danish archbishop Eskill of Lund soon afterwards.[30]   Geoffrey had, therefore very full sources for the last eight years of Bernard's life and he was present at many miraculous episodes himself, unlike William, or, still more, Ernald.   Clearly we can recognise, too, that by that stage in Bernard's life the interest in collecting and writing down, at least in note form, material about the man whom so many were finding remarkable, must have been growing.   Even Bernard may have been getting more interested in this, since during these last years he seems to have often sent one of his companions back to see whether someone whom he had apparently healed en route, was really better or not.[31]   The effect of this pressure on Geoffrey must have been particularly deep, because he had, apparently, been first stimulated to collect notes when William began to write, and once it became known to him that William was never going to write a complete life (which could have been some time before William actually died) he must have kept his eye out for relevant material.   This simple analysis does not take us very far in understanding the meaning that these episodes had, either for the authors, or for Bernard. How do we get any further?

At this point the Halt Sign, *commune hagiographicum*, has to be observed before we can proceed. Of course it has to be admitted that each of our three authors must have been affected by every saint's life they had ever read in the cloister, or heard read, say in choir or refectory, and indeed by the Bible. But it does not necessarily get one very far to notice that some episodes in their books were influenced by their reading, and it is not enough to chalk up *topoi* as they appear and to write off such episodes.   After all, certain experiences are replicated by many people; for example, we know from hearing talk in our own families that many mothers develop expectations about the future destiny of the child developing in their womb; one should not dismiss all accounts of such intuitions as no more than *topoi*. They can still have something to say about the people who record them, and even about those who experienced them.   The question to bear in mind is to what degree any writer is affected by the tradition to which he is adding something new. As Stancliffe has shown so memorably in her study of Martin, there is a world of difference in someone moulding a real episode according to some standard derived from the past, and actually inventing episodes to show that the man of God is as good as any of his predecessors.[32] To put this point slightly differently, we need to look at each miraculous episode to see what it seems to be saying, and to look at the setting in which these episodes are placed. The frame as well as the picture repays examination.

Clearly in one paper it is impossible to observe this counsel of perfection, There is not time to read each episode, we have to approach them in groups, and to observe their general impact. What I intend to do is to look in turn at some of the miraculous episodes which occurred on Bernard's home ground, so to say, Clairvaux, and those which occurred when he was away from home. Let us turn first to the episodes included by William of Saint—Thierry.

In the first place we find a number of episodes whose purpose seems to have been to meet the needs of none other than Bernard himself, and one may suppose that he was their ultimate source. The first such episode occurred when he discovered that harvesting was not something for which his earlier training had fitted him, rather like Levin in Anna Karenina when he tried to scythe hay with his peasants as a gesture of solidarity.[33] Bernard retreated at first, bruised from the field, prayed, and returned back to work discovering that he had found the knack. There is no need to explain away this story, to demythlogise it, though this could I am sure be done (and here I speak as one who has worked on a farm), but we can pause a moment to realise that what it emphasised to the readers of the *Vita* was that Bernard needed to pray and that his prayers were answered. Just as he lacked confidence in the fields, so he also lacked confidence in those first days as a preacher, astounding as this now seems in view of his later success, but in this case he received reassurance through a dream.[34] Similarly during those early days he was encouraged that an easier future would come, which it was natural for him and for his contemporaries to express in terms of visions; he saw the valley full of monks, and on another occasion saw and heard monks singing at the site where the monastery was to move when their first buildings became too small.[35] In an age when medical knowledge was very primitive so that it was hard to know exactly how ill any individual was, we find Bernard being reassured about his own recovery from what seemed like a mortal condition with another three visions.[36]

A larger number of episodes concerns not so much Bernard's own growth in ability and understanding, as helping his community to believe that he could cope with his tasks as abbot. Here we should place the story in which he reassured his brother when he complained that they had no money: then he went off to pray, and almost immediately a donor arrived with just the sum of money needed.[37] An extension of this kind of reassurance is provided in the story of how, even at a time of great famine, Clairvaux was able to provide for everyone who came to it for help.[38] Just as the young monastery was vulnerable economically in its first days, so it needed recruits and confidence on this score was provided when Bernard succeeded in converting a group of knights who called into the abbey on their way to a tournament.[39] Then just as Bernard showed skill in gaining new members for the community, so he displayed insight in seeing which of those who joined would stick to the new way of life. Benedicta Ward has recognised how much the whole issue of conversion and perseverance was a significant part in later cistercian collections of miracle stories, but we can, I am sure, find it in these and other episodes in the *Vita*.[40] This is surely not surprising. In William's book there are two stories on the theme of perseverance, both interestingly enough concerning monks not at Clairvaux itself, but at daughter houses.[41] These display yet another side of Bernard's achievement, his concern for the welfare of his wider community, as does an episode in which in prophetic mode he gave a monk from Foigny visiting Clairvaux, a message to give to one of his fellows admonishing him.[42] It is not surprising, either, that two stories are concerned to reassure monks about their destiny after death.[43]

What may seem to us as rather less significant, evidence of his ability to affect nature, believed then to be a very natural sign of a holy man, comes across in another three episodes; control of rain when a letter being written outside remained dry when a sudden storm struck: control of a swarm of flies at Foigny, and recovery of a horse which ran off on a journey home.[44] Again, one could, no doubt, explain these episodes as quite unsupernatural occurrences, but they appeared to contemporaries as signs that God was indeed with him. They also, as we shall see in a minute, made him the equal of other well–known abbots.

Ernald, as I have already said, with one exception, to be mentioned soon, has no miraculous episodes at Clairvaux, about which, on the whole he says very little. Geoffrey, however, includes just the same categories of miraculous episodes as we have found in William; encouragement for Bernard, in this case about his own death, evidence of his ability to produce conversions, and of his

ability to appreciate what was going on far away from him.[45] Another episode
introduces a theme which was to proliferate in later collection, that of Bernard's
presence at Clairvaux even when absent. One night at Clairvaux, a monk saw
Bernard going round the choir urging on each individual to sing his best, but
when next day the seer challenged Bernard about it, he was told that that night
illness had kept him from choir, but that he had been there in spirit.[46] Here is a
theme which surely reflects the need of the community to be reassured that
Bernard was there, even when he so often after 1130 was not. The *Rule* clearly
expected that normally an abbot would be with his monks, but Clairvaux had
often to accept his absence as normal. Episodes which demonstrate the power of
Bernard's body and tomb soon after his death indicate nothing unusual in
comparison with other holy abbots.[47]

As I indicated earlier, I shall not discuss the quite considerable number of
healings which both William and Geoffrey recount as happenings at Clairvaux,
since the whole subject of miraculous healings has been so well treated recently
by others. But I must just draw attention to an interesting aside of Geoffrey's.
One day he says that as Bernard came out of the monastery he healed a boy
suffering from multiple handicaps, which themselves caused discussion later
among some of the monks. He adds that Bernard disliked laying hands on sick
people within the monastic enclosure, because the entry of people into the
community might disturb discipline there.[48] This concern lest Clairvaux should
become a healing shrine, came out even more strongly later at his funeral when,
according to other accounts, the abbot of Cîteaux forbade the dead holy man to
do any more miracles in public, because he was so worried by the chaotic scenes
which had occurred during the funeral.[49]

What is the total picture conveyed of Bernard in these episodes at
Clairvaux? It is of the effective leader of a new monastic community, able to
attract and keep recruits, to ensure through his dependence upon God that they
would survive physically, and to be confident that their and his shared life would
be acceptable to God. Many of the episodes have parallels in early accounts of
monastic communities, back as far, indeed, with those earliest communities in
the desert. William of Saint Thierry, indeed, more than once in his book,
explicitly made the comparison between life at Clairvaux with life in those heroic
days, but it would, I think, be hard to claim that he had deliberately 'invented'
episodes to fit that heroic pattern.[50] Without wanting to suggest that any one
set of monastic sources may have played more of an influence than any other I
would, for a moment, like to pursue a direction suggested to us, in fact, by
Bernard himself in something he once wrote at the request of William.

In the so—called *Apology*, when he turned to criticise the behaviour of
other followers or the Benedictine Rule in his day, he asked a series of rhetorical
questions beginning 'Did Macarius live like this?' and ending 'And did holy
Odo, Maiol, Odilo and Hugh who monks nowadays extol as princes and teachers,
follow this kind of life, or think that others should hold to it?'[51] This climax
reminds us of that series of outstanding abbots of Cluny about whose lives both
Bernard and William must have known. If we turn to their *Vitae* do we find any
similarities with the picture which we have just traced of Bernard at Clairvaux?
Indeed we do: let me mention two.

Maiol prayed for money to relieve the poor, and afterwards found just the
sum he needed, whereas Odo, praying on the slopes of Monte Gargano kept dry
during a storm whilst all around the ground was soaked.[52] On another occasion
in Rome he had asked a monk to make for him a copy of the Life of St Martin;

the job was interrupted by Vespers and the manuscript was left in the cloister to run the gauntlet of another storm. Upon return, the monk found that rain had penetrated to the edge of his book, but the text was dry.[53] In citing these parallels I do not wish to suggest more than the fact that it is highly likely that both Bernard and William knew of them, and may indeed have been, so to say, on the watch for similar occurrences[54]. Bernard could, indeed have modelled his own behaviour on what he had read of the lives of the great abbots of the most famous abbey of his day.

Perhaps I may also refer to a third and non–miraculous example which bears out this suggestion. Odo was known by his monks as the digger, *fossorium*, because he always kept his head down, whilst Bernard as a young monk was reputed not to have known at the end of his year as a novice whether the room in which the novices studied had a vault or not.[55] Whilst it seems to me likely that both of them were taking literally Benedict's advice that 'whether he sits, walks, or stands, his head must be bowed and his eyes cast down', Bernard may have taken the injunction the more seriously just because he knew how Odo had behaved.[56] Bernard, I suggest, may to a significant degree have lived like he believed the best Cluniacs had done, whereas for William we can recognise that something more in the comparison was involved.

In the early part of his monastic formation he belonged to a network of friends who had been deeply affected by the new monastic experiments of the age; many of them shifted from relatively well–established ways of monasticism, many of them much affected by Cluny, towards the new ways of Cîteaux.[57] William himself, as we have recalled, made such a transition, largely under the influence of his friend Bernard. Recently an American scholar has commented that his part of the *Vita Prima* is often just not a life of Bernard, but a praise of the whole order.[58] This is surely very true, and it surely fitted in with his own journey in life if he portrayed Bernard as being as effective as any of the Cluniacs on their own ground, even their own wet ground, if I may risk a joke. And beyond William's need for reassurance about the authenticity of the experience of the man he so much admired, we can recognise, too, the need of the people in the monastery which he led, and in the other monasteries which followed a similar way of life in the rapidly expanding cistercian order, for a man who would, so to say, show that their way of life had divine approval. That need becomes obvious to us when we raise that although the early cistercian narrative accounts, the two *Exordia*, speak warmly about Alberic and Stephen Harding, the second and third abbots of Cîteaux, they scarcely do more than hint at their sanctity, whereas their first abbot, Robert of Molesme could only be an enigmatic figure for them, since he reneged on the experiment he had started. All three, too, had another limitation as possible holy men to authenticate the cistercian monastic experiment: they had all spent a larger part of their time as monks following other customs.[59] In this connection it is relevant to recall that neither Alberic, nor Stephen were considered within the Order to be worthy of commemoration with liturgical feasts until the seventeenth and eighteenth centuries.[60] Cîteaux and Clairvaux needed a saint, in Bernard they found one. In the picture we get of him at Clairvaux, we see a man of God who moulded himself, and was moulded by his biographers, on old lines as well as on famous not so distant ones.

Now let us move, for the last stage of this paper, towards Bernard out in the world, and particularly as he appears in the work of Ernald of Benneval. Both Ward and Bredero refer to the fact that Ernald includes a number of exorcisms performed by Bernard during his visits to Milan in 1135.[61] Neither of them, however, cast a critical eye at these accounts, and so it is towards them, and similar episodes, that I wish now to direct our attention.

First of all it is worth realising that the devil is not entirely absent from
Clairvaux and its surroundings in any of the three authors. Ernald has an
episode when a monk is seduced by the devil to imagine that he was Christ
occurring during Innocent II's visit to the abbey in the autumn of 1131.[62] He
tells this in a very low—key way, and it is also worth remarking that Bernard
dealt with it without any fuss at all; he told everyone to pray and had the monk
shunted out of the church before anyone could grasp what was happening.
William, for his part, presents an episode involving a man living not far from the
monastery who had become paralysed and dumb through spells cast by his
adulterous wife which is much more highlighted.[63] It may not be merely a
coincidence that William calls these events *tragoedia*, for certainly Bernard's
reaction was theatrical. The bewitched man was brought into the church and led
before the altar, where Bernard took the vessel containing the Eucharist, placed
it on his head and forbade the devil to go on hurting a Christian by the power of
the Sacrament; '... in ipsius Sacramenti virtute, a laesione Christiani jubet
daemonem prohiberi'. Apparently the man was freed, but if such scenes were
often repeated within the monks' church one can understand why later Bernard
was more cautious about healing, let alone exorcism, here. Geoffrey's two devils
receive less dramatic treatment, an both are cast out without Bernard's
immediate presence but only that of something which had been in contact with
him, his stole, or which had actually been part of his body, bits of his hair and
beard.[64] In the latter case, which took place in Denmark, when the relics were
put on the chest the possessed monk he shouted out in German, 'Bernard you
are too heavy for me ...' which is a valuable indication of the origin of some of
the earliest cistercians in the north. Such 'conversations' with devils are a
feature of the Italian cures, just as is the use of the Eucharist as at Clairvaux.

When we follow Ernald into Italy, and also into South western France, we
find something much more orchestrated than the fairly short exorcisms
considered so far. Altogether he provides ten, six in Milan, one each in Pavia
and Cremona, one in Nantes and another episode a Parthenay in Poitou, which
although not strictly an exorcism presents many parallels with one.[65] The
majority of the afflicted (seven, one of whom as a girl) are women, whereas of the
three males, one was a boy. Not too much should, I think, be made of the sexual
inequality, except to suggest that it almost certainly reflects the by then
well—established view that women were much more receptive to the devil. All of
the exorcisms occurred during Bernard's attempts to reconcile Milan and other
Lombard cities, or the count of Poitou, to the cause of Innocent II from late 1134
to the summer of 1135. Ernald presents the journey to Poitou as though it
occurred after that to Italy, which has caused later historians some problems, but
we need to linger over that issue.[66] What I want to underline here is the general
impression that comes across in these ten episodes. I wish there were space to
linger over all of them for each has its peculiarities, but let us look at the
Milanese situation for a moment.

Bernard went to the city as one of a formidable party sent by the pope to
secure the agreement of its citizens to terms which their ambassadors had already
accepted at a great council in Pisa.[67] Milan had been a firm adherent of
Anacletus from the start of the Schism and had besides a long tradition of
holding aloof from any Roman bishop going back at least to the time of Ambrose,
whose memory was still very much alive. It was a proud community which had
only deserted one side for the other when the Staufen, one of whom they had
made king of Italy, came under heavy pressure to make peace with the emperor.

It would require much tact if Milan's adherence to Innocent were to be solidified, and Bernard seems to have played the role of dramaturge in achieving this end. Happily we are not, as we so often are, entirely dependent upon the *Vita Prima* for what occurred.

The Milanese chronicler Landolf, deeply imbued himself with the local tradition of independence, recorded what happened when Bernard arrived in the city.[68] The city churches were stripped of the gold and silver ornaments which Bernard was known to dislike, whilst both men and women adopted penitential garb, cutting their hair and wearing rags. Against such a setting, he goes on to record that a whole series of signs followed; water was changed to wine, devils were put to flight, the crippled walked and the sick were healed, as a result of which all the people were so moved that they became full of the love of 'the emperor Lothar and towards obedience to pope Innocent', so that whatever Bernard ordered was done. Here we have a fascinating general view of corporate redirection of allegiances achieved through abasement and the sharing in miraculous signs of a new order, the details of which Landolf does not give.

These are richly provided by Ernald with whom, too, we gain a sense that a deeper dislocation had occurred because the city had adhered to the wrong side. He held that the devil had been liberated, and the sign that he was not confined to barracks was the series of exorcisms performed by Bernard.[69] Ernald's story begins outside the city where the crowds received Bernard with a hysterical welcome, redolent of some of the arrivals generated when Martin was received into cities in Gaul, which themselves, as Peter Brown has shown us have their deliberate echoes of imperial *adventus*.[70] Bernard's first exorcism involved a woman possessed for seven years, just about the period that Milan had been out of Rome's control we may note,[71] whilst on the third day (a deliberate echo, one wonders of the resurrection?) in Ambrose's cathedral, right in the middle of the liturgy a young girl was brought up to him.[72] The third cure, on which I must focus, is told with the greatest detail, and forms the centre of Ernald's Milanese account; Zerbi has recently commented that these cures 'read' like a panel of a tryptych.[73]

The subject was an elderly lady of some distinction in the city, 'mulier grandaeva, civis Mediolanensis, et honorate quondam matrona'.[74] She was brought to Bernard in St Ambrose's church again. Her devil had been with her for some time, suffocating her and depriving her of the senses of sight and hearing as well as speech. She was so choked that her tongue protruded, like that of an elephant. Her appalling bad breath and general appearance çonvinced Bernard that hers would be a hard case, so he enjoined the huge congregation to pray, whilst the clergy and monks brought her up to him by the high altar. She struggled energetically, injuring a number of people, including Bernard whom she kicked. He was not abashed and turned to the altar to complete the prayer of consecration. Each time he made the sign of the cross on the host he looked round at her, and so as Ernald puts it, fought the devil in her with a sign. She became furious, as the devil sensed that his control over her was about to end. After the Lord's Prayer had been said, Bernard put the host on the paten of the chalice, and placed both on top of the woman's head (the same procedure which we have seen him using at Clairvaux), and then addressed the devil: 'Your judge is present, evil spirit, the supreme power is here. So resist Him if you can. He is present who suffered for our salvation ... and was taken from the body of the Virgin ...' (here I am abbreviating what amounts to a short creed) 'Leave this servant of His and never again come near her again'. The woman at this was torn with struggling Bernard then turned back to the altar, finished the action of breaking the host, and gave the peace to the people. With this gesture of reconciliation she suddenly calmed down, her tongue shrank back into her mouth, and she thanked God and fell at Bernard's feet.

The scene is high drama, where so many aspects of the individual herself and of her treatment recall the apostasy and reconciliation of the wider community of the city. Brown, again, points us towards the 'heavy judicial overtones of the process of excommunication at a shrine', 'in which the visible authority behind the human agent of exorcism could be seen pitted against the power of the demons'. Exorcism, too, he explains was a kind of public penance and forgiveness which aimed at the 'reintegration' of the individual into the community.[75] Here in Milan, of course, there is not so much a shrine, as a living man, wielding the power of the Sacrament as a kind of trial by ordeal set within the Mass. This fundamentally, was what Bernard did with the count of Poitou, who was subjected also to trial by Sacrament, collapsed physically and then was reconciled.[76]

Before we leave Bernard it may be worth drawing brief attention to another curious feature of Ernald's account of his acts in Milan, the way in which he brings a notable Cluniac, Matthew cardinal bishop of Albano into the story.[77] He is portrayed as ordering Bernard to heal a young boy one evening when they were discussing business in the cardinal's lodging, the abbot having been so preoccupied that he wanted to dismiss the boy with merely a blessing, but Matthew swung rank and made him lay his hands on the boy and heal him. Some days later, the cardinal himself fell ill, and then was cured by having a light meal served to him in the very dish which Bernard had used when they had dined together on the previous occasion. That a holy man should transfer power into something which he had touched was another commonplace, we find it, for example, attributed to Maiol of Cluny, and so Matthew was responding in a very traditional way to the power which he had to recognise, according to Ernald, when Bernard healed the boy in front of him.[78] Ernald's inclusion of the two episodes involving Matthew may mean even more if he were aware that Peter the Venerable had composed a *Life* of Matthew not long after the cardinal died in 1135.[79] Peter writes there not a word of Bernard, or indeed of any of the others who went to Milan earlier that same year, the reconciliation of the city turned entirely upon Matthew.[80] Ernald, on the other hand has quite a lot to say about Matthew, and it shows us a Bernard who outdoes a Cluniac in the world, just as William and Geoffrey present him as superior on his home turf.

But what I wish to underline now as I end is that whereas at Clairvaux Bernard is shown as a man of God in monastic mould, here in the great exorcisms of the Schism, we see him adopting another mould, that of Martin particularly, though neither he, or Ernald refer explicitly to that model.[81] It is surely also likely that both of them were aware of Ambrose and of some of the dramatic episodes of his life.[82] Elsewhere Bernard rarely exorcised, but on a number of occasions when his skills as a peacemaker were required, he healed people which, according to Ernald and Geoffrey, won doubters over to accept his authority as mediator.[83]

I do not, myself, believe that Bernard was adapting a role in the wider world which was entirely different to what he was used to in the quieter valley at Clairvaux, even though he often complained about being drawn out from his home. The devil was less active there, because, so to say, he had less of a chance in a community confident that since it adhered to a holy form of life and followed the true pope it could live more easily with its conscience. But for Bernard, I would suggest, the world remained one, it was not two separate circles, but a single arena in which the powers of evil and those of righteousness were pitted against one another. It seems to me that ever after the Schism which gave such a shock to his system, Bernard believed that the bonds which held the rightly ordered world together could only too easily be broken, so that the devil could rage and roar around. Abelard, Gilbert de a Porrée, and a number of others had the misfortune to confirm in his mind with the danger which he had recognised at Milan and in Poitou. But from another point of view those very same events showed that Bernard in a remarkable way united two strands in holiness, that of the prayerful monk with that of the heroic holy man, retired at one level from the world, but capable at times of erupting onto it with enormous power. Not everyone liked him, or thought that such a resurrection of late antique or early medieval modes was proper in the twelfth century, no wonder a pope hesitated whether to say 'well done', but it was this combination of characteristics which gave him such a wide appeal. What his own consciousness of these two *personae* which he had assumed may have done to him we can not explore now, but one may suppose that when he called himself 'a modern chimaera' he was reflecting some of the anguish which his dual role had created for him.[84] Some of those who knew him disliked the mixture, but his supporters were placed everywhere, often in high places, and there was a vocal kernel in the enormous monastic family which he had gathered. Ultimately he could not be left unrecognised, but as what? The last of the Fathers, perhaps, but certainly one of the last Holy Men of the old style.

Table I. Date of Miracles

	William	Ernald	Geoffrey
pre 1113	4		
1113–22	7		
1123–32	1	2	2
1133–42	2	16	5
1143–52			62
1153			12
post death			7
	14	18	88
not placeable			
within decade	24		32
Total	38	18	120

Table II. Place of Miracle

	William	Ernald	Geoffrey
Clairvaux	26	1	25
Near Clairvaux	2		9
France	9	3	43
Germany	1		39
Italy		14	2
Spain			2
	——	——	——
	38	18	120

NOTES

1. The *Vita Prima* [hereafter *VP.*, with Book, chapter, column] is in Migne, *Patrologia Latina* [herafter *PL*], 185, pp 225–368. This paper is no more than a sketch of what might be said, particularly about Bernard's awareness of himself, but I hope it may prove useful.

2. A.H. Bredero, *Etudes sur la ' Vita Prima' de Saint Bernard* (Rome, 1960), [hereafter Bredero, *Etudes*]. His essays 'St Bernard and the Historians' [hereafter Bredero, 'St Bernard'] and 'The Canonization of Bernard of Clairvaux' [hereafter Bredero, 'Canonization'] in ed., M.B. Pennington, *Saint Bernard of Clairvaux* (Cistercian Studies, 28, Kalamazoo, Michigan, 1977), pp 27–100 provide a summary of his book with much additional material.

3. Bredero, 'St Bernard', pp 31–32.

4. This vast enterprise still has not reached any very certain conclusions. An introduction to the literature up to 1978 is in my own 'The chronology and character of early Cistercian legislation on art and architecture' in eds. C. Norton, D. Park *Cistercian art and architecture in the British Isles* (Cambridge, 1986), pp 40–55.

5. L. Leclercq, *Nouveau visage de Bernard de Clairvaux* (Paris, 1976), pp 11–34.

6. W.E. Goodrich, 'The Reliability of the *Vita Prima Sancti Bernardi*', *Cistercian Studies*, 21 (1986), pp 213–227.

7. Bredero, *Etudes*, pp 73, 104, 142–4, 151.

8. Of which the second edition was published at Brussels in 1906.

9. B. Ward, *Miracles and the Medieval Mind* (London, 1982) [hereafter Ward, *Miracles*], pp 175–184.

10. R.C. Finucane, *Miracles and Pilgrims; Popular Beliefs in Medieval England* (London, 1977).

11. P. Brown, *The Cult of Saints* (Chicago, 1981) [hereafter Brown, *Cult*] : C. Stancliffe, *St Martin and his Hagiographer* (Oxford, 1983) [hereafter Stancliffe, *St Martin*].

12. Bredero, *Etudes*, 101 n.6 places the visit to 1117, Ceglar (in an unpublished thesis of 1971) to spring 1120 or some months earlier, cf.

M.B. Pennington, *The Last of the Fathers* (Still River, Mass., 1983), p 131. The date turns upon *VP*, I. vii. 33. col. 246, also discussed by L. Milis, 'William of Saint Thierry, his birth, his formation and his first monastic experiences' in *William, Abbot of St Thierry : A Colloquium at the Abbey of St Thierry*, trans. Jerry Carfantan (Cistercian Studies 94, Kalamazoo, Mich., 1987), p 26.

13.   Bredero, *Etudes*, pp 100–101.

14.   *VP*, I.xiv. 264, an event at Rheims which can be placed at the end of 1139/early 1140: Commision d'Histoire de l'Ordre de Cîteaux, *Bernard de Clairvaux* (Paris, 1953) [hereafter *Bernard de Clairvaux*], p 595. For his use of notes made by Geoffrey, Bredero, *Etudes*, pp 104–107; R. Lechat, '*Les Fragmenta de Vita et Miraculis S Bernardi* par Geoffroy d'Auxerre', *Analecta Bollandiana*, 50 (1932), pp 83–122.

15.   e.g. J.M. Canivez, 'Arnaud de Bonneval' in *Dictionnaire de Spiritualite*,. i, pp 888–90.

16.   Bredero, *Etudes*, pp 109–112. His attack on Bernard's ep. 310 has been rebutted by D. Farkasfalvy 'The Authenticity of Saint Bernard's Letter from his Deathbed', *Analecta Sacri Ordinis Cisterciensium*, 36 (1980) pp 263–268, and in the recent Italian edition, eds., F. Gastadelli, E. Paratore, *Opere di san Bernardo, VI/2, Lettere 211–548* (Rome, 1987) pp 310–315.

17.   *Bernard de Clairvaux*, p 699 is a good starting point, but does not comment upon the connections with the bishop of Chartres and the counts of Blois.

18.   Cf. *Dictionnaire d'Histoire et de Geographie Ecclesiastique*, IX, pp 1061–1069, *Gallia Christiana*, VIII. 1234–45 and Document no. xxxii, pp 213–213.

19.   Ed., F. Barlow, *The Letters of Arnulf of Lisieux* (Royal Historical Society, Camden Third Ser., LXI, 1939), eps. pp 11–13, 15–18, espec. p 15 'Venerabiis frater et amicus noster, Phillippus abbas ...' and footnote *a* on Ernald's career.

20.   Bernard, Ep. 5; J. Leclercq, H. Rochais, *S Bernardi Opera*, VII (Rome, 1974) [hereafter *Opera*], pp 28–29, and for the Morimond affair, L. Grill, 'Der Hl. Bernhard von Clairvaux and Morimond' in *Festschrift zum 800–Jahrgedachtnis Bernards von Clairvaux* (Vienna–Munich, 1953) pp 31–118, and Grill in *Bernard de Clairvaux*, pp 125–133.

21.   *Bernard de Clairvaux*, p 717 and refs. there: Bredero, *Etudes*, pp 116–117.

22.   The dates of composition are not very material to my argument, but I wonder whether 1155–56 is really established by Bredero *Etudes*, pp 120–121, once it is realised that Ernald did not die as early as 1156, *Etudes*, p 109.

23.   See note 14 above, and Bredero, *Etudes*, pp 113 and 126 for Ernald and Geoffrey.

24.   Namely Geoffrey bishop of Langres, former prior of Clairvaux; Bredero, *Etudes*, p 61. The source is the *Vita Secunda* by Alan of Auxerre, *PL* 185, col. 469.

25.   Ward, *Miracles*, p 177 claims that Alexander praised its construction, referring to *PL* 185, p 226. In fact this is William's preface and the pope's bulls announcing the canonisation, pp 622–25, speak merely of Bernard's 'holy and blessed life' and say nothing of the quality of the *Vita*.

26.   Bredero, 'Canonization', pp 83–86.

27.   I have not separated out multiple healings which took place at one location into discrete episodes; if I had the total would have been very much larger.

28.   See Table I.

29.   See Table II.

30.   These three sources can be conveniently found in *PL* 185, pp 410–416, 369–410, and *Scriptorium*, XIII (1959), pp 32–44. Their genesis and nature are discussed by Bredero, *Etudes*, pp 92–94, 77–92, 94–96.

31.   *VP*, IV.viii, 348–49, which is followed by four episodes in which a check is made.

32.   *St Martin*, pp 183–202, espec. 188, 'here is a crucial difference between Sulpicius fixing upon a genuine trait of Martin's and conveying this in biblical language; and, on the other hand, Sulpicius simply attributing such traits ... to Martin out of a desire to prove his resemblance to earlier Christian heroes'.

33.   *VP*, I.iv. 244.

34.   *VP*, I.vi. 244.

35.   *VP*, I.v. 242, vii. 247.

36.   *VP*, I.xii. 258 for all three visions.

37.   *VP*, I.vi. 242.

38.   *VP*, I.x. 255.

39.   *VP*, I.xi. 257.

40.   Ward *Miracles*, pp 195–196.

41.   *VP*, I.xii. 262, 263.

42.   *VP*, I.xii. 262.

43.   *VP*, I.x. 254.

44.   *VP*, I.xi. 255–56, 256, 263–64. The first of these episodes is called 'grande miraculum' by William, whereas he comments that the cursing of the files became a 'parable' among the neighbours of the monastery.

45.   *VP*, V.ii. 355; IV.iii. 330–331 and 331–332: IV.iii. 332–333.

46.   *VP*, IV.i. 323.

47.   *VP*, V.ii. 360–361, V.iii. 366.

48.   *VP*, IV.viii. 347.

49.   Ed., B. Griesser, *Exordium Magnum Cisterciense* (Rome, 1961), II.xx. 117; cf. Ward, *Miracles*, p 180.

50.   *VP*, I.vii. 247; cf. I.iii. 235 where William likens Bernard and his friends gathered at Châtillon before they entered Cîteaux to the church at Corinth.

51.   *Apologia*, IX. 23, *Opera*, III, p 100.

52.   L.M. Smith, *The Early History of the Monastery of Cluny* (Oxford, 1920), pp 78–79, quoting the Anonymous Life.

53.   John the monk, *Vita Odonis*, II.22: *PL* 2133, col. 72–73.

54.   Dr Joan Petersen has kindly pointed out to me that 'dryness' is a theme created in Gregory I's *Dialogues*, a source well–loved in cistercian circles, i.e., *Dialogues*, III.11 and 12 (ed., A. de Vogüém 3 vols. *Sources Chretiennes*, pp 251, 260, 265), vol. 2, pp 294–295, 298–299.

55.   *Vita Johannis*, ii.9, *PL* 133, col. 66: *VP*, I.iv. 238.

56.   *Regula Benedicti*, 7.64. Barbara H. Rosenwein, *Rhinoceros Bound Cluny in the Tenth Century* (Philadelphia, 1982), p 90, remarks that Odo kept his 'head bowed with such perfect literalism that he never looked up'.

57.   See Bredero's 'Guillaume de Saint–Thierry au carrefour des courants monastiques de son temps', in A.H. Bredero, *Cluny et Cîtaux au douzieme siecle* (Amsterdam and Maarssen, 1985), pp 115–141 (originally given at the Saint–Thierry Colloquium in 1979, and now translated in *William Abbot of St Thierry*, pp 113–137.

58.   R.M. Peterson, 'Anthropology and Sanctity in the *Vita Prima Bernardi*' in ed., E.R. Elder, *Noble Piety and Reformed Monasticism* (Cistercian Studies 65, Kalamazoo, Mich., 1981), pp 40–51, at 48 note 6. This is a valuable article although the author does not refer to Bredero. One may

note here what Stancliffe, *St Martin,* p 362 says of Sulpicius's portrait of Martin, 'it is drawn by a man who had been sufficiently struck by the Martin of flesh and blood to adopt his idea as his own; to break with his old way of life and follow him'.

59. There is a nice parallel here with the Northumbrian cult of Cuthbert rather than of Aidan who had 'Iona origins and loyalties'; C. Stancliffe, 'Cuthbert and the Polarity between Pastor and Solitary', in eds., G. Bonner, D. Rollason, C. Stancliffe, *St Cuthbert, His Cult and His Community* (Woodbridge, 1989), p 22.

60. L.J. Lekai, *The Cistercians : Ideals and Reality* (Kent, Ohio, 1977) p 255.

61. Ward, *Miracles,* pp 193–184; Bredero, *Etudes,* p 144 note 3 where some of the exorcisms are listed as examples of the *commune hagiographicum.*

62. *VP,* II.i. 272. For the date see *Bernard de Clairvaux,* p 583.

63. *VP,* I.x. 255.

64.. *VP,* IV.i. 325 and iv. 335–337. The latter is discussed by B.P. McGuire, *The Cistercians in Denmark* (Cistercian Studies 35, Kalamazoo, Mich., 1982), pp 52–55.

65. *VP,* II.ii. 274–275, ii. 275, iii. 276–277, iii. 277–278, iii. 280, iv. 280–281, iv. 281, iv. 281–282, vi. 287–288, vi. 289–290.

66. *Bernard de Clairvaux,* pp 587–589 for the chronology.

67. The best discussion is by P. Zerbi, 'I Rapporti di. S Bernardo de Chiaravalle con i vescovi e le diocesi d'Italia', in *Tra Milano e Cluny* (Italia Sacra, Studi e Documenti 28, Rome, 1978) [hereafter Zerbi, 'S. Bernardo'] pp 3–109. See too A. Haverkamp, *Medieval Germany 1056–1273* (Oxford, 1988), pp 138–140.

68. Landulfo de S. Paulo, *Historia Mediolanensis,* eds. L. Bethmann, P. Jaffe (*MGH, SS,* XX, Hanover 1868), pp 46–47.

69. *VP,* II.ii–iv. 273–283, espec. 275–76 for the end of the devil's freedom.

70. Brown, *Cult,* pp 98–99.

71. *VP,* II.ii. 274–275.

72. *VP,* II.ii. 275.

73. Zervi, 'S. Bernardo', p 68.

74. *VP,* II.iii. 276–277.

75. P. Brown, *Cult,* pp 108–109, 110.

76. *VP,* II.ii. 275.

77. *VP,* II.iii. 279.

78. Jotsaldus, *Vita Odilonis,* II.xvii: *PL,* 142, 930.

79. The *Vita* seems to have existed by 1139/41 when Peter the Venerable wrote to Cluny for a copy: G Constable, *The Letters of Peter the Venerable,* 2 vols. (Cambridge, Mass., 1967), ii. p 184, and pp 261–262 for the date of his *De Miraculis,* into which the *Vita* was encorporated. Ward, *Miracles,* points out that the longer work is a defence of Cluny.

80. *De Miraculis,* II.xvii, *PL* 89, 928–929. Matthew died Christmas Day 1135 so his 'cure' did not last very long; *De Miraculis,* II.xxii, col. 933–934.

81. Geoffrey does have an episode in which the crowd hail Bernard in whom God has reawakened the spirit of Martin, *VP,* VI.vii. 346–347.

82. For Bernard's interest in Ambrose and for M S Troyes p 284, formerly at Clairvaux, containing many of his works see J.B. Auberger, *L'unanimite cistercienne primitive: mythe ou realite?* (Achel, 1986), pp 217–218.

83. For Ernald see note 69 above. One may also note that he has Bernard complete a spectacular exorcism at Nantes on the way to win over the count of Poitou: *VP,* II.vi. 287–288. For Geoffrey see *VP,* IV.viii. 348, and V.i. 353–354, episodes at Langres and Metz.

84. Ep. 250.4: *Opera,* VIII, p 147. The passage has given rise to much comment, cf. Bredero, 'St. Bernard', pp 41–48.

THE *VITA STEPHANI MURETENSIS* AND THE EARLY LIFE OF STEPHEN OF MURET

Maire Wilkinson

It is hoped that a prefatory comment on the names *Muret* and *Grandmont* will obviate the confusion which might easily arise from references to Stephen of Muret, and from other references to the order founded by him as the Order of Grandmont. In 1079 Stephen established himself in the wilderness of Muret in a thickly wooded site at an altitude of about 416 metres in the miniature granite mountains, the Monts d'Ambazac, which lie to the north—east of Limoges. He never subsequently left his hermitage, and any cells founded before his death in 1125 were governed from Muret.[1] Within a short time from his death, perhaps only a few months, the mother house was re—founded in another wilderness at Grandmont, some ten kilometers to the north of Muret, at an altitude of about 567 metres, and from this site the order took its name. A separate cell continued in existence at Muret until the dissolution of the Order of Grandmont, a dissolution carried out in 1772, and thereafter, by papal mandate and with royal support consequent to the recommendation of the *Commission des Reguliers*. Both Muret and Grandmont lie within the diocese of Limoges and Grandmont is some twenty—seven kilometres distant from the episcopal city.

Further prefatory remarks are needed in order to express a debt of gratitude to Dom Jean Ecquet who, as is well—known, has acquired a pre—eminent reputation in matters Grandmontine. While the present writer must take leave to differ from him the the interpretation of a number of important issues pertaining to the order's history in the eleventh and twelfth centuries, she must say at once that deprived of the fruits of his immense erudition and labour, her own work could scarcely have proceeded. Only those who have worked with the Grandmont texts, and their subsequent historiography, can know the reality of the *silvae inextricabiles* of the former, and the often bewildering confusion of the latter. It is the nature of those texts to require a reformulation of their content bold enough to loose or to break the real or apparent *nodi indissolubiles*, but a reformulation which also refrains from the unnecessary hypotheses which the texts readily provoke. It is to Dom Becquet's undying credit to have brought an order and cohesion into our understanding of the Grandmont texts far exceeding that achieved by his predecessors. It is, however, some twenty years since the history of the Order of Grandmont was his primary concern. We know him now as the indefatigable editor of the *Revue Mabillon* and as a specialist in the history of the canonical congregations of Artige and Aureil. The present writer has indeed taken leave to offer a fresh interpretation of the texts, but she has built on what Dom Becquet has accomplished.

The account or *relatio* of the early life of Stephen of Muret in the *Vita Stephani Muretensis*, that is the account of his life before his entry into his hermitage in the wilderness of Muret, has long aroused serious misgivings among historians. The illustrious Mabillon himself found the incongruence of the alleged chronology of the *Vita* with that of other well established data deeply disquieting.[2] It is the view of the present writer that the *Vita* text is not merely flawed by factual error, but that it is chiefly a fictional form and actually fictitious, at least as far as the *relatio* of the early life is concerned. But the exceedingly complex issues involved in establishing the relationship between the extant manuscript versions of the *Vita Stephani* and that once found in the compilation *Speculum Grandimontis*, the now lost work of the Grandmont prior Gerald Ithier (1188–1197/98) are not the object of the present study, although it is hoped that a survey of these matters will be published elsewhere. Neither is the review of the densely coded text of the *Vita Stephani Muretensis* which we believe is needed and of the significance of its factual errors, possible within the present compass.

The essential *relatio* of that text, which in all its manuscript forms is the same, save in points of detail, will be referred to here as the *Vita Pseudo–Normativa* or the *Vita PN*, and its literary form will be treated as an imaginative mingling of the little knowledge of the saint's early life found in the traditions of his order with a complex series of optative topicalities, desirable probabilities, and *topoi*, that is conventional themes of hagiography, whose particular form was prompted by the papal reconstitution of the Rule of Grandmont in and after 1186 and by the Roman canonization of Stephen of Muret in 1189, an event whose eighth centenary was celebrated on 30 August of this year.

With the historical claims of the *Vita PN* set aside, and these are claims which not only allege an outline of the founder's life, but which also offer an explanation of the origins of the Order of Muret–Grandmont, it becomes possible to set other and reliable texts drawn–up within the order in their due place. These give an alterative account of Stephen of Muret's life and of the order's origins. This alternative account does not possit Stephen's imitation of an Italian religious congregation, and papal authorization of his *propositum*, the special form of his life in religion, but instead proffers an eclectic drawing upon the Rules of the Fathers, and notably upon the *Shorter Rules of Saint Basil*, and also upon the *Rule of Saint Augustine*, in pursuit of the life of perfection advocated by Christ in the so–called special counsels of the Gospel.

Teaching by dialogue with one disciple or with a group was the mode of instruction employed by Stephen of Muret. None of his teaching or instruction concerning the way of life of his followers was transferred to writing while he lived, but his spiritual teaching was later written down at the dictation of Hugh Lacerta, his beloved disciple, and of others; as the *Liber Sententiarum* and Hugh Lacerta was also largely responsible for giving a written form to the *Way of Life* which Stephen commanded his followers to observe.[3] Thus the alternative view of the founder's life and the order's origins revealed by the discountenancing of the *Vita Stephani* makes a very powerful challenge to its claims, for it is drawn from the oral traditions of an order which consisted for the most part of *illiterati* education by their founder to learn by listening, and to understand their obligation to speak truthfully.[4] It must be stressed that the model of the saint's life after his coming to Muret in the *Vita PN* is not directly under review here although some reference will be made to it.

The story of Stephen's early life in the *PN* account is set out at some length in the first chapters of the work with the author as storyteller, but so important was it to his purpose in writing the *Vita Stephani* that he placed it subsequently in the mouth of the saint himself during an alleged discourse with Cardinals Gregory and Peter Pierleoni (the future pope Innocent II and anti–pope Anacletus), who, it is said, visited Muret some days before Stephen's death.[5] Since the cardinals had asked for an explanation of the way of life of Stephen and his brethren, it was not appropriate to repeat information about his family already related in the extended account of his life, namely that he had been born in 1046 to noble parents Stephen, Viscount of Thiers in the Auvergne according to the longer version of the tale, and his wife Candida, and that having been taken by his father on a pilgrimage to the shrine of Saint Nicholas of Myra at Bari in 1058, he had fallen ill at Benevento on the return journey, and had been left in the care of his father's friend Milo, the archbishop of that city, who was also a native of the Auvergne, and who, after Stephen's providential recovery from sickness had supervised his education for twelve years.[6] But Stephen is made to explain to the cardinals that Milo of Benevento had educated him, and that from him he had learnt the Rule of his order by means of his desire to imitate certain Calabrian Brethren, a religious congregation whom Milo approved. He further explained that after Milo's death (in 1070 according to the chronology of the *Vita*), he lived in the household of a certain but unnamed Roman cardinal, and finally that he had been licensed by a Roman pontiff, also unnamed, to pursue the *propositum* or religious undertaking of the said Calabrian Brethren as a way of penance.[7] According to the longer account of the *Vita* this occurred in 1074 so that in reality Gregory VII would have been the pope in question.[8] When Stephen found a place at Muret which he judged suitable for a life of poverty and penance in 1076, he thereafter never quitted his hermitage.[9] We are told in the first part of the *Vita* that during the two intervening years he had visited many hermitages and solitary places commending to memory all that was worth imitating in the ways of canons, monks and hermits.[10]

The *Vita Stephani* with the account outlined above of the saint's early life, and, as will be argued elsewhere, with clear references to his Roman canonization as an accomplished fact, that is the *relatio PN*, is composed teleologically in great circles of ineluctable cause and effect, and its abundant purpose clauses direct the reader or listener along the right path of interpretation. On account of these things the story has a coherence which does not depend on the congruence of the factual data it alleges with any other known data.

It is possible to criticize the *relatio* of the *Vita PN* as an historical account on many grounds, but arguably on none so firm as those which offer an alternative view of the founder's life and of the origins of the Order of Muret–Grandmont. The alternative account contains a challenge the more telling in that it arose within the order itself and in its written form, some thirty years before the appearance of the first of the manuscripts of the *Vita PN*. But it must be said at once, lest expectations be raised that a new story of the early life of Stephen of Muret is about to be revealed, that the alternative account is that of an early life of which Stephen's disciples knew almost nothing, save in general terms, but general terms of such a kind as to render the *relatio PN* superfluous and wholly incongruous. The alternative account was certainly current in the 1160's, and presumably beyond. It is silent as to the claims of *relatio PN*, composed in or after 1189 and before 1198,[11] As has been said, it contains a different explanation.

Reference has already been made to the *illiterati* of the Order of Muret–Grandmont in its early days, but it is of the greatest importance to note that throughout the twelfth century, the majority of the members of the order consisted of these *viri illiterati*, laymen without the advantage of latin letters, although not without the advantages of learning by listening. By means of a Grandmont obituary, P. Derein was able to establish that even in the mother house itself during the twelfth century, before 1189, the ratio of laymen to priests was 130 to 23.[12] And he says of the evidence of the obituary:– 'Ceci confirme le caractère essentiellement laïc de l'Ordre de Grandmont a l'origine'.[13] For these laymen, and for that matter for the priests of the order until the last decades of the twelfth century, oral testimony was the chief and usual means of transmitting information and ideas, and the *Vita Stephani* of these oral traditions was in its unwritten form the oldest version of any life of the saint. In the form in which it was subsequently recorded in the texts of the order that version is referred to here as the *Vita Primitiva* or *P*, the *Vita Stephani* of the oral tradition, and the oldest *Vita* not on account of the time of composition in written form but on account of the age of its *relatio* which is found in two texts. The *Vita P* gives no warrant for the account of Stephen of Muret's early life in the later *Vita PN*. In a complex refutation it contradicts a claim that Stephen had been in deacon's orders.[14] This claim also occurs in the *Vita PN*. And it gives an account of the visit of the cardinals to Muret so much at variance with that found in *Vita PN* that it may be construed as a refutation of Stephen's speech to the cardinals explaining the Italian and papal origins of the order he founded.[15] That is to say the different account of the visit in *Vita P* refutes the substance of the story in *Vita PN*. In *Vita P* the cardinals do not ask for an explanation of the order's origin and Stephen gives none.[16] There are, as has been seen, reasons for regarding the *P* account as *a fortiori*, more reliable than that in *PN*; it is much nearer in time to the life of the subject, it is as will be seen dependent upon reputable witness, it thus follows that the explanation of Italian origins put in Stephen's mouth in *PN* should be treated as suspect. When we also see that the account in the texts of the *P* tradition of Stephen's religious formation, and of the origins of the order he founded is incompatible with that in the *PN* tradition then a choice arises of regarding the *relatio PN* as essentially fictitious on this count alone, or of supposing the near absurdity that what it alleged at the end of the twelfth century of the founder and the origins of the order was true, but was unknown to the brethren of the first generation after the founder's death, and at his most familiar friend Hugh Lacerta.

As has been indicated the *Vita Stephani* of the *P* tradition did not confront the *Vita PN*, but it did confront another *Vita Stephani* which is regraded here as the probable source of a *Vita Stephani* of a literate variety, that is one more likely to appeal to those clerics of the Order of Grandmont who were of a clericalizing disposition. The *Vita PN* is regarded as representing the second and much more complex stage of this evolution of a literate tradition. The first of a literate kind will be referred to here as the *Via Posterior*, because it was posterior to the *Vita* of the oral tradition fund in the form *P* although at least one text of the *P* tradition postdates the *Vita Posterior*. No text of the *Via Posterior* has survived, but as will be explained presently, there is at least sufficient reason to suppose that the *Vita Stephani Muretensis* preserved by the dominican, Vincent of Beauvais (c1194–c1264), in his *speculum Maius* is a paraphrase of the *Vita Posterior*.[17] The fact of the existence to us first by references in the most substantial of the texts of the *P* tradition the *Vita Hugonis Lacerta*, already referred to here, a life of that Hugh who had been the beloved disciple of Stephen of Muret.[18] Hugh entered the order in 1111 aged 40, and died in 1157.[19] In the first chapter of the *Vita Hugonis* it is recorded that a *Vita Stephani*, worded finely enough, by the dear zeal of paternal love, has been written elsewhere and is preserved in more sacred places and regarded in honour.

> ... cuius (Stephani sc.) etenim vita sermone est satis luculento, caro
> paterni amoris studio, alias scripta in sacratioribus locis pro summo
> honore habetur et conservatur.[20]

Caro paterni amoris studio leaves the question of authorship open, since paternal love may proceed from or be directed to the pastor of Grandmont who is apparently implied, and the pastor meant may be Stephen himself as recipient, or another pastor as in some sense the agent of the *Vita*, that is perhaps one under whose aegis the *Vita* was composed.   It is reasonable to construe the 'more sacred places' in which the *Vita* was kept as at least including the mother house of the order although the implication is not clear.   This assertion by William Dandina of Saint–Savin, a priest and brother of the Order of Grandmont, and author of the *Vita Hugonis* is compatible with Dom Becquet's view that the fourth prior of the order Stephen of Liciac wrote, or caused a *Vita Stephani Muretensis* to be written.[21]   His view rests in large part on the Elogium of the fourth prior found at the end of the now lost *Speculum Grandimontis* which states:—

> Et facta beati Stephani confessoris ... quae pene in oblivionem devenerant conscribi et recitari iussit.[22]

Dom Becquet has argued that the *Facta Stephani*, which as we agree, should be ascribed to the patronage of Stephen of Liciac, although not to his authorship, and which are identified here with the *Vita Posterior*, is the *Vita Stephani Muretensis* found in two shorter versions of thee closely contemporary manuscript accounts.[23]   These shorter accounts in Ms. Paris BN. Lat. 10.891, and Ms. University of Cambridge, 1222, Trinity College O.3.50, Dom Becquet believes to be the anterior to a longer version found in Ms. Limoges Séminaire 68,[24] These he regards as a form of the *Vita Stephani* sufficiently anterior to that undoubtedly put together by the prior Gerald Ithier after the canonization of 1189 which is found in the Limoges Ms, so that it constitutes a *Vita A*, a version anterior to, self–evidently shorter than, and in some senses different from that of Gerald Ithier.[25]   As it plain and as has already been indicated, these are highly complex matters and too extensive for discussion here, but it may be said in brief that it is the opinion of the present writer that the text itself of the *Vita Stephani Muretensis*, save in the form in which Vincent of Beauvais provides it, whatever rubrics or titles we may encounter with it, in all its extant manuscript versions was evidently composed after the Roman canonization of the saint in 1189, and, as has been said, that the text, in its essential form, the *relatio PN* here, is the same in all manuscript versions of the late twelfth or early thirteenth centuries.

As has been said, Vincent of Beauvais paraphrase a version of a *Vita Stephani*; 'Ex gestis eius', as he states, in his *Speculum Historiale*, the fourth volume of his *Speculum Maius*, the first recension of which appears to have been ready by about 1244.[26]   In this version every feature distinctive of the *PN* account is omitted. Instead it is merely stated that Stephen was the son of a very noble father of that name from the Auvergne, and that in childhood he was taken by his father to Benevento where he was educated for twelve years by Saint Milo, the archbishop, and where he learnt a rule of living well of which no other detail is given.   Thus Vincent gives no hint of a teleological structure in the story, and neither brethren of Calabia, nor Roman cardinal, nor papal authorization of Stephen's *propositum* appear. The constraints of a digest must be taken into account, but the phrasing used implies that he did not suppose that there were other parts of this stage of the story to be told, beyond points of detail.

> Hic filius Stephani nobilissimi viri de Arverniae partibus a patre suo in pueritia ductus est Beneventum, ubi a sancto Milone archiepiscopo 12 annis educatus regulam beni vivendi didicit. Denique discedens peragratis multis eremis et de canonicorum et monochorum et eremitarum vita, quae imitanda sunt memoriae commendans, in Aquitaniam prope Lamonicas (sic) ad montem prope nemorosum, qui Muretum dicitur ... pervenit.[27]

As may be seen, Milo has no divinely commissioned role to play in connection with the Calabrian Brethren, instead there are before us only the *Gesta* or (*Facta*) *Stephani*, the deeds of a Stephen who departed not from Rome but from Benevento (*Denique discedens ...*) in his search for religious congregations to imitate before he came to Muret. Vincent was thus abbreviating, whether in much or little is not clear, a *Vita Stephani* other than that with the early life narrative of the *PN* account, which is neither told here at the beginning nor related subsequently to the cardinals during their visit to Muret. It may thus be proposed that he was abbreviating a version of the *Vita Posterior*, or that text itself, since he was evidently writing within the tradition which was altered and expanded within the *PN relatio*, and, as will be seen, we know no other grounds that the author of the *Vita Posterior*, like Vincent, related a tale antagonistic in various respects to the *Vita Stephani* of the *P* tradition which knew nothing of Milo of Benevento and a sojourn in Italy.[28]   There are also grounds to assume that it was alleged in the *Vita Posterior* that Stephen of Muret was in deacon's orders and that the cardinals visited him at Muret in other circumstances than those recorded in the   account; and for different purposes.[29]   The diaconate appears in Vincent's account, as does, as we have seen, the cardinals' visit, set a few days before Stephen's death, with the purpose of inquiring who taught him is rule, and why he stayed in so sterile a place as Muret.[30]   In default of a manuscript text of the *Vita Posterior*, the paraphrased *Vita Stephani* given by Vincent of Beauvais appears to provide our only access to it. Where Vincent found the text he used is not known.

The text of the *Vita Hugonis*, to which we turn once more, composed before 1171 postdates, perhaps only by a little, the text of the *Vita Stephani Posterior*.[31]   But there is no doubt that the *Vita Stephani* unfolded in the *Vita Huganis* contains a more ancient account of the founder's life that is, that which is part of the *Primitiva* tradition transmitted by the oral witness of the order. Dom Martène, indeed, who first edited the *Vita Hugonis* observed that it contained a *Vita Stephani* other than that which he believed, correctly as we think, to have been composed in the late twelfth century, that is the *Vita Stephani Muretensis PN*.[32]   But Martène did not collate the two *Vita* forms, here *PN* and *P*. Fortunately William Dandina did collate the *Vita P* and the *Vita Posterior*, finding in the latter material which did not satisfy the canons of criticism he employed in writing the *Vita Hugonis* and the *Vita Stephani* which it enclosed.   And he vindicated his preference for the *Primitiva* tradition, as he carefully explains, because depending as it did on oral testimony, it was open to the tests which his own critical sense imposed.   As he says Hugh's signs of holiness, and his deeds — and through these knowledge of recitation or a written text might be learnt without reference to validity or veracity), but had been recognized by him to be true from the accounts of Hugh's most religious and truthful disciples.

> Huius vero signa omnia atque gesta non didicimus, sed pauca quae narramus, quattuor religiosissimis veracissimisque eius condiscipulis, qui per diversa tempora cum eo convesati sunt, referentibus agnovimus, domino Petr scilicet, valde reverendissimo priore nostro, qui ab oedem ad erudiendum digno cum honore susceptus, et pro simplicitatis ac humilitatis reverentia loco maximae veneratinis est habitus; Buidoni quoque de Miiaco qui ... in eorum cellulae cura tam bene docta primus successit; Bernardo etiam Bocardi, qui cum eodem ... aliquandiu familiarissime conversatus ... Hugone vero de Monte, cui ille pro iustitia ac fidelitate quam in eo repperit famiiarissimus ardentissime fui, et ab

eodem in ipso transmigratinis suae articulo pacis dominicae
osculum accepit salutare.[33]

The pastor of Grandmont, Peter Bernard (1164–1171), elected it appears on
account of his integrity and humility, Gui of Miliac, who well taught by Hugh
Lacerta succeeded him in the cure of the cell of Plagne (in Périgueux), Bernard of
Bocard and Hugh Dumont, both most familiar friends of Hugh, make an
impressive array of witnesses to the authority of a work which is conventionally
entitled the *Vita Hugonis Lacerta*, but which is also directed to establishing the
early history of the Order of Muret–Grandmont before it disappeared from view,
on account of the passage of time and changes taking place within the order. It
will be seen that Dandina had set himself the task of producing an *apologia* for
these first ways, and it is likely that the proper title of the work was *De
Antiquitate Ordinis Grandimontis*.[34] For a biography in which Hugh is the focus
of attention occupies only 10 on the whole brief chapters of the work's first 29
chapters. (There are in all 54 chapters.) Chapters 12–29 concern the conjoined
lives of Stephen and Hugh from 1111, when Hugh was admitted to the order, to
1125, the year of Stephen's death. The brethren were still few in number at the
time of Hugh's admission and the following fourteen years evidently constituted
the most significant in the order's early expansion.[35] The first brief chapter of
the work concerns only Stephen of Muret and that and its opening *Igitur domnus
Stephanus* below the title in Martene's edition of the *Vita Hugonis Lacerta* at
least suggest that something may be missing.[36] This supposition is strengthened
by Dandina's statement in chapter 29 that he does not wish to fall silent in
pursuit of his own task in trying to unravel what is in the *Vita Stephani
Posterior*. For having described Stephen's death he says:—

> Cum enim dicta et facta alias plene exarata, scripta modo ac
> luculenta declarat historia, sed si cuncta, quae in vita eius gesta
> sint scripta cum non audivimus, evolvere conaremur, a suscepto
> iam procul dubio proposito conicescimus.[37]

We shall return to Dandina's dissatisfaction with the *Vita Posterior*, but it may
be emphasized that he does not wish to turn aside from his own undertaking, for
it is not, he continues within his contrivance, nor is it his purpose to unravel
these doubtful matters:— '*quia non est nostri ingenii nostrique propositi*'.[38] And
on account of this it is necessary that from this point we begin to read of that
disciple (Hugh) whose holy life and good conversation greatly profited our
religion.

> Unde necesse est ... ut de illo discipulo, cuius vita pia, cuius
> conversatio bona nostrae plurimum proficit religioni, amodo legere
> incipiamus.[39]

And indeed the ensuing 24 chapters are devoted to the life of Hugh Lacerta, to
his said holy conversation and to the thaumaturgical powers of his prayers, but
Hugh's life is an exemplar of the first ways of the Order of Muret–Grandmont.
Hugh, we are told, engaged in faithful dialogue with his master concerning his
spiritual teaching (*sententiae*) and his rule for his congregation (*vitae mandata*):

> Fuit enim cum Domino ac magistro nostro Stephano discipulus ille
> usque ad obitum eius, audiens eum fideliter et interrogans super
> sententiis ceterisque vitae nostrae mandatis.[40]

And God's kindness it was to sustain this one elect from so many thousands to know humbly the things he had heard and in his day faithfully to reveal the same to future ages.

> ... Dei quoque benignitas electum hunc de tot milibus unum, qui et audita humiliter sciret suscipere, eademque futuris saeculis in su tempore fideliter revelare.[41]

Dandina ascribed whatever was faithfully written of the Way of Life Stephen imposed on his followers, and of his spiritual teaching, to Hugh, that is to Hugh's dictation.[42] As is frequently attested of hermits, Hugh not only attained a great age, but also retained a lucid mind, as Dandina puts it:—

> ... inter tot gratiarum insignia ... sanae stabilisque memoriae dono non mediocriter fulsit.[43]

Not surprisingly Hugh's death is related in the form of an elegy for what has become threatened by change. As was customary on such occasions many brethren had gathered to hear the old man's last homilies.

> Igitur qui convenerant interrogabant eum dicentes: 'Domine, quid times? quid sentis nostrae plus posse nocere reigioni?' 'Nova' inquit 'neora, fratresque novitios super omnia plus posse nocere timeo et sentio'.[44]

Too many new sites and too many novices strained the structures of the old ways of Muret–Grandmont, and distressed the dying Hugh.[45] And Dandina's own valediction of what he has written is also elegaic in tenor:—

> ... forsan et haec olim meminisse iuvabit'.[46]

Whether or not the *Vita Hugonis Lacera* be acephalous, it may certainly be seen as a work of considerable, if subtle rhetorical force on behalf of the *Antique Ways* of Muret–Grandmont rather than simply an encomium of Hugh Lacerta. In consequence Dandina's criticism of the *Vita Stephani Posterior*, while made in an eirenic manner, becomes the more telling. As we have seen, he feared he would fall silent in his own task if he tried to unfold in his mind all the deeds written in Stephen's *Vita* when he had not heard them.[47] The phrase *cum non audivimus* is crucial. There are things written of Stephen for which Dandina has found no orally given warrant, and in that their unravelling will deflect him from his own task it appears that they are not merely matter which is uncorroborated, rather they were also, at the best, matter which did not illumine understanding of the founder's life and the origins of the congregation which he had brought into being. From the elaborate repudiation of a claim that Stephen of Muret was in deacon's orders which appears in the *Vita Hugonis* evidently the claim had been made.[48] It would in any case be reasonable to suggest that the contention was found in the *Vita Stephani Posterior* because it is with that text that Dandina was taking issue. The re–appearance of Stephen's supposed diaconate in the *Vita PN* strengthens opinion in favour of the probable dependence of that text upon the *Vita Posterior* since Stephen's being in deacon's orders, or any orders, was not part of Muret–Grandmont's oral tradition.[49] He may have been in minor orders.

When we turn to the *Vita Stephani* of the *Primitiva* tradition we shall find that it much exceeds in reticence the conventions of hagiographical writing concerning a saint's life before he entered religion. It is usual that this section of a *Vita* will be compressed into a relatively short space, but that section of the *Vita Primitiva* is exiguous in compass. It is devoid of personal detail or incident and almost wholly directed to explaining how Stephen formulated the idea of the Order of Muret–Grandmont. All that exists now in the *Primitiva* tradition concerning Stephen of Muret's life in the world, and it must be borne in mind that there are lost works of Dandina which may have been germane, and a possibly acephalous text of the *Vita Hugonis*, is related by Dandina at the beginning of the latter work.[50] He says that according to the sure account of many it was proved and believed that Stephen was born in the Auvergne. His family was wealthy and noble, but when first he had evaded, as one evades a fire, his worldly position, the delights of dainty food, and the further blandishments of a life of ease he came with rapid foot to Muret where he dwelt as a new guest.

> ... Stephanus ... Arvernis oriundus certa plurimorum relatione comprobatur et credtur. Nam cum primum sanctus Dei generis nobilitatem, amorem rerum fluxam saeculi gloriam, escarum variam delectationem, et reliqua remissionis blandimenta, quasi quoddam vitaret incendium, quodam rapido cursu pervenit Murtum in quo ... novus hospes habitavit.[51]

When dealing subsequently with Stephen's death on 8 February 1125 Dandina says that this took place in almost the forty–sixth year of his conversion from which it follows that he came to his hermitage in 1079 and not 1076 as in the *PN* account.[52] His exact age appears to have been unknown to Dandina for there is no reference to it in the *Vita Hugonis*. It might appear from Dandina's phrasing that Stephen came in the ordinary sense from the world to Muret, but this may well not have been the case. Stephen was himself profoundly critical of contemporary monasticism and regarded the manner of life in many monasteries as merely secular.[53] And that principle which he regarded as the first principle of all monastic life *Bati pauperes spiritu* is a solvent of all social and material values.[54] According, therefore, to the understanding he taught his followers, the flight from worldly glory of which Dandina writes is consonant with flight from any state in which the rule of the Beatitudes observed in strict poverty was not the only rule. Stephen may have been a monk in the ordinary sense of that term before he became a hermit at Muret, and it will be seen subsequently that there is other evidence which makes this a reasonable supposition. But nowhere, as has been said, is it stated in the *Primitiva* tradition that he was in clerical orders. It is thus evident that even by about 1160–1170 when the *Vita Hugonis* was composed the living tradition of the Order of Muret–Grandmont was that very little was known of the personal detail of their founder's early life. This is quite consistent with the spiritual ideals which Stephen expounded. His followers were to dwell in the hermitage of the order *tamquam mortuos et abiectos a mundo*.[55] And they were to understand that their support in the life of perfection which they had chosen was not in Stephen himself, of himself, but in God.[56]

What was known and treasured by the brethren was rather Stephen's labour in establishing his order. And that for information we turn to the other text of the *Primitiva tradition*. This text, now a Prologue to the so called Rule of Stephen of Muret was drawn up in its original form during the lifetime of Hugh Lactera, and it records the words in which Stephen was wont to teach his followers, employing the dialogue, as has already been noted, a comparative study of various forms of monasticism and volumes of various rules of various fathers.[57]

Divina igitur inter colloquia quae cum eis iugiter habebat, cum

inter eos de diversis modis religionum et de diversarum secundum
diversos patres voluminibus regularum ... erba huiusmodi locustus
est.[58]

And these colloquies (in words of the kind which Stephen used, rather than the
words of one remembered discourse), were remembered in a harmonious relation
by Hugh Lacerta and by many others who saw and heard them, and were written
faithfully in the form in which they were remembered:—

Scripta sunt autem et firmiter observata, sicut a veridicis discipulis
eius, Ugone videlicet ... et aliis quampluribus visa et audita et
relatione concordi memorata sunt.[59]

But while the Prologue *Dum in heremi* cited here was drawn up in or before 1157,
it is found now with the version of the Rule of Grandmont corrected in 1186 by
Pope Urban III.[60] It was not part of the corrected Rule text, and does not
accompany all contemporary manuscript versions of the Rule. No manuscript in
which it appears is earlier than the first part of the thirteenth century.[61]

Stephen of Muret in the typical colloquy recalled in the Prologue reminds
his brethren that they are followers of the Christian religion and of the first and
chief rule, namely that of the Gospel which is the fund and beginning of all rules:—

... vos esse dicatis christianae religionis primae ac principalis
regulae, evangelii scilicet, quod omnium regularum fons est atque
principium ...[62]

And it may be noted that for Stephen the Gospel was not a text, something
written, but the living Word, the truth of Christ.[63] He continues saying that his
followers must also dare to say that they were subject to apostolic and canonical
institutes and they desired to follow the steps of the holy fathers in any way
whatsoever.

Nec non apostolicis ac canonicis institutionibus subiectos et
sanctorum patrum vestigia sequi quoquomodo cupientes dicere
audeatis.[64]

And he selects from the diverse ways which lead to Christ, as offshoots of the
Gospel, although they had been commended to writing by the holy fathers in
question, the rules of Basil, of Augustine and of Benedict:—

Regula beati Basili, Regula beati Augustini, Regula beati
Benedict.[65]

If anyone could show rationally to the brethren that their traditions were in
anything opposed to these twin pillars of the Gospel and the counsels of the holy
fathers, Stephen conceded that these must be corrected by the will of catholic
and religious teachers:—

... si in aliquo traditiones vestras evangelio contrarias, aut
sanctorum patrum monitis oppositas vobis rationabiliter
ostenderit, corrigendas esse cathlicorum et religiosorum doctorum
arbitrio, concede...[66]

And now Stephen turns to the education which led him to formulate the *Vita fratrum* of which he is speaking, the way of life of the brethren which leads since it is the way of perfection to eternal life. Those (traditions), he says, which I a sinner, albeit of little understanding have disposed, according to that which I received from apostolic teachers and deeply religious men, and what I have learnt in long bending over the Rules of the holy fathers:—

> ... quas ego peccator, licet exigui sensus secundum quod a doctoribus apostolicis et valde religiosis viris accepi, et iuxta sanctorum patrum regulas diu incumbendo didici ... disposui ...[67]

Thus there indeed seems reason to believe that Stephen had been a monk before he came to Muret, for it is otherwise difficult to suggest how he gained access to the society of religious men versed in the teachings of the early church, and to the collections of the Rules of the fathers which he had studied, and presumably continued to study after he entered his hermitage. As has been seen Stephen's religious formation of his followers was based on comparative studies in ascetica and on the Rules of the fathers.[68] And we read in the *Vita Hugonis Lacerta* that Hugh after his admission to Muret so advanced in holiness, that he was made an imitator of the habits of life of the best brethren, before he attained to the whole study of religious institutes:—

> ... priusquam omne religiosarum studium institutionum adeptus est'.[69]

In view of these indices to the importance of *ascetica* in the early history of the Order of Muret–Grandmont it is natural to ask where Stephen of Muret's studies had been conducted before 1079, but from the two texts of the *Primitiva* tradition we meet only silence in direct reply. Fortunately, however, one can turn to circumstantial evidence to suggest a likely area for the reading and copying of manuscripts of the variety in which he was interested.

Stephen's Rule text of prediction appears to have been the Rule of Saint Basil, or more correctly the *Shorter Rules of Saint Basil* as translated almost certainly by Rufinus of Aquileia before 397.[70] In his *Sentences* Stephen refers to Basil's Rules as of greater perfection than the Rule of Saint Benedict.[71] This opinion he may have taken from Benedict himself, or from Benedict of Aniane, but also from reading and reflecting upon the Shorter Rules. It appears to the present writer that Stephen had not only studied the Basilian text, but had also implemented its governmental ideas, and its requirement that its followers subsist from the fruits of their labour, as may be seen from the *Liber Sententiarum* and those parts of the so called *Rule of Stephen of Muret* which may be thought to reflect his teaching.

Our knowledge of extant copies of Basil's *Shorter Rules*, or of manuscripts cited in library catalogues, with the same manuscripts in question in some cases, suggests that prior to the twelfth century the work was relatively rare.[72] The manuscripts which antedate the twelfth century were written in many parts of Europe, but one may at least draw attention to the writings in Northern Spain in the ninth and tenth centuries of three extant texts of the Rule of Saint Basil, and further to the presence of that text in manuscripts of Rule Collections.[73] One other visigothic manuscript Rule Collection which does not contain Basil's Rule may also be noted.[74] Extant manuscript Rule Collections written before the twelfth century are few indeed there are nine according to our reckoning, and this paucity may well reflect the apparently limited influence of Benedict of Aniane's *Codex Regularum* of which only two exemplaras have survived from the period in question.[75]

The library of the mother house of Grandmont may formerly have contained the information necessary to substantiate the idea of a 'Spanish connection' in Stephen of Muret's early life, but the greater part of its contents was sold by weight to make book bindings in 1789.[76] We know something of the contents of Grandmont's medieval library from a catalogue apparently drawn up in the early fifteenth century, and the intendant of Limoges, Martial de Lépine, made a list of certain of its volumes in 1771.[77] It can only be said with certainty of the volumes listed in the catalogue that their presence in the library antedates its making, but it is worth noting that the Rule of Saint Basil was included together with the Rules of Augustine and Benedict and the Collations of Cassian.[78] Grandmont, as has been said observed its own Rule. There were also works of Spanish origin, whether in manuscripts of Spanish origin or provenance is not known. A collection of the sermons and works of Ildefonse of Toledo presumably included the Grandmont copy of the famous Gotescalc codex of his *De Virginitate B. Mariae* which Marten encountered.[79] The six other exemplars of the codex which the monk Gomes wrote at the monastery of Saint Martin of Albelda in 951 for bishop Gotescalc of Le Puy who placed it subsequently to his pilgrimage to Compostella in his cathedral library, belong in one case to the eleventh century, and in the others to the twelfth and thirteenth.[80] *The Liber Prognosticorum* of Julian of Toledo may have been in Grandmont's medieval library. It appears in Lepine's list, but it does not appear in the catalogue of the fifteenth century.[81] There were, however, present in the medieval library not only the *Etymologiae* of Isidore of Seville but also his *Libri Senteniarum* and a *Commentaria in Bibliam*, perhaps to be identified with his *De Fide Catholica*.[82] There was a copy of the *Libri Sententiarum* at Grosmont, the first English house of the order in the early thirteenth century.[83] It may reasonably be assumed that this was an exemplar of the codex at the mother house from which Grosmont had been founded at a time when books were few within the order.

As has been indicated, these Spanish works have entered the library a long time after Stephen of Muret's death, but they at least provide an economical hypothesis for the area in which he received his apparently monastic education. No area can however be excluded, for as has been said the *Primitiva* tradition is silent on the matter of where Stephen of Muret had begun the process of reading and reflection upon Rule texts and the Gospel, which he continued in his hermitage.[84]

The early life of the saint related in the *Vita Stephani Muretensis*, the *Vita PN* here, obscures the true sources of Stephen's inspiration, the Gospel and comparative *ascetica*, and this it seems, was part of the intention of it author who needed to justify to the order its recently corrected Rule, and to provide a model of the saint's early life which was more palatable than reality to those brethren, who, like Gerald Ithier himself, were set on clericalizing paths. And further, by means of Gerald Ithier's obscuring of the patristic origins of the Rule taught by Stephen, but, as we think by his choice, originally not written, an important instance of the transmission for ideas has been overlooked. As has been argued here, it is an instance of the transmission through Latin translations of early Greek ascetic ideas in the Latin West, and perhaps of early latin ascetic traditions more eclectic than those found in the Rule of Saint Benedict. It is the *Primitiva* account of the *Vita Stephani Muretensis* which reveals his formative passage of ideas.

The argument rehearsed here rests upon an attempt to establish a probable sequence of the *Vita* texts but it is not intended primarily as a textual argument. It is hoped that in place of the literary fare of the *Vita Stephani Muretensis*, which, on the very ground of its literary qualities is a most important and absorbing text, there has been provided the outline of an historical account of the saint's life.

NOTES

1.   Giry noted [*Manuel de Diplomatique*, Paris, 1894 p 116] the probability that a Lady Day calculus was employed in the diocese of Limoges during the twelfth century whereby a new year began on 26 March three months after a year reckoned from 26 December or 1 January. This practice explains a number of apparent discrepancies in chronological matters among Grandmont and other authors of the period. But the author of the *Chronica Priorum Grandimontis*, writing apparently at the turn of the century, makes plain the late ending of the year to which he refers as that of Stephen's death:— *Igitur beatus Stephanus ... anno ab incarnatione Domini centesimo vicesimo quarto pene completo ... sexto idus februarii apud Muretum locum migravit ad Christum.* [Ms. Archives Départementales de la Haute–Vienne 112, Grand Séminaire 10, p LXXI, a partial copy of the now lost *Speculum Grandimontis*.] That is, the tradition of the order was that Stephen died in 1124, but at a time in the year so numbered, 8 February, which we should call 1125. Other Grandmont texts bear this reading (see for example note 52 below). According to all versions of the *Vita Stephani* the death is placed in 1125 according to a Lady Day calculus, and thus in 1126 as we should reckon. This view does not appear to have prevailed among contemporaries or among subsequent commentators among whom Barnius [*Annales Ecclesiastici*, vol XII, Antwerp, 1609, 171ᵉ] is almost singular in having noticed the plain meaning of the text. Because the text includes a reference to a legatine Council of Chartres, known on other grounds to have been held in March 1124, in a year beginning 1 January or at Christmas, it has been assumed that Stephen's death occurred in February of that year.

2.   See *Annales Ordinis S. Benedicti, T.V.* (Paris, 1713), lib. LXIV, XXXVII, pp 65–67.

3.   For the *Liber Senteniarum* see *Scriptores Ordinis Grandimontensis* [hereafter *SS*] in *Corpus Christianorum Continuatio Medievalis, VIII* ed., Becquet, Dom Jean (Turnhout, 1968), no. I. For the *Vita Fratrum*, the way of life of the brethren in its first written form as the work of Hugh Lacerta, see his biographer William Dandina of Saint–Savin. *Vita Hugonis Lacerta*: [hereafter *VHL*] *Nam, quidquid vel de sententiis nostris, vel ceteris vitae nostrae mandatis invenitur fideliter scriptum, aut memoriae hominum commendatum, totum quidem per eum, sicut a domino Stepheno magistro nostro audivit memoriterque suscepit, creditur et revelatum et manifestum. SS*, no. V, p 204. See also Gerald Ithier, prior of Grandmont, in his *Explanatio super Librum Sententiarum*, who attributed to Hugh the *librum Regulae datum in praeceptis. SS*, no. XIG, p 436.

4.   See *Liber Sententiarum* [hereafter *Sent*], XII [2] *SS*. 16: *Sec veritas in primis difficilis est homini, postmodum in dulcedinem rediens sempiternam; mendacium atque peccatum placet primitus, et inde postmodum angustiam incidit homo perpetuam.* And XXVIII, *SS*. 21: *Ille qui veritatem loquitur, Deum deprecetur ut eam sibi tribuat dicere veraciter. Mendaciter enim eam dicit, nisi operibus teneat quod ore pronuntiat.* Both passages refer to a man who has come to conversion in

the religious life.

5. Vita Stephani XXXII *SS* pp 121–123. See Appendix A for the actual visit of the cardinals to Muret which did not take place in January 1125.

6. This paraphrase of the *Vita Stephani Muretensis* depends upon chapters I–XII of the shorter version of the text as edited by Dom Becquet. *SS* III, pp 105–112.

7. The time scale of the *Vita Stephani* depends on the assertion of the author in chapter XII (*SS*, p 112), that Stephen came to Muret in 1076 when he was 30 years old. All other dates are established from this year. It will be argued elsewhere that the description of the practices of the Calarian Brethren in the *Vita Stephani* is a description of the practices of the Order of Grandmont.

8. The longer version of the *Vita Stephani* was edited by Dom Martène in his *Veterum Scriptorum et Monumentorum Amplissima Collectio T VI*, (Paris, 1729), 1046 *sqq* [hereafter *VSMAC*].

9. See above note 7, for the importance of the date.

10. Vita Stephani, *SS* p

11. Dom Becquet regards the text of the *Vita Stephani* which he has edited in *SS* as the work of Stephen of Liciac, the fourth prior of Grandmont (1140–1164), either in that he composed it, or in that it was composed under his aegis. See: *Les Institutins de l'Ordre de Grandmont au Moyen Age* in *Revue Mabillon (RM)*, t. 42 (1952) pp 31–42, esp. p 32 and: *Les premiers écrivains de l'Ordre de Grandmont, id.*, 43 (1953), pp 120–137, esp. pp 127–130. and: *Bibliothèque des écrivains de l'Ordre de Grandmont, id.* 53 (1963), pp 59–79. p 63 no. 2: *SS* III, title page, *Monitum*.

12. Paris, Bibliothèque Nationale, Manuscript *latin* 1138, ff 2–6 (before 1189). See L'obituaire primitif de l'Ordre de Grandmont, *Bulletin de la Société Archéologique et Historique du Limousin*, 87 (1960), [hereafter *BSAHL*] pp 325–331 and p 330 for Δereine's ratio.

13. *Ibid.*, p 330.

14. See *VHL*, 49, *SS*, pp 201–204 and *Appendix B* below.

15. For the visit of the cardinals in the *relatio PN*, see above pp

16. For the conversation between Stephen of Muret and the cardinals in *VHL* see below, *Appendix A*.

17. See below.

18. See above, note 3.

19. *VHL* 11, *SS* p 171, pp 197–200; 13, *SS* p 172, 226–227; 14, *SS* p 175, 340–342; 54, *SS* pp 210–211 1867–1873.

20. *SS* p 167.

21. See above, note 11.

22. *Elogia Priorum Grandimontis*, IV, *SS*. XII, p 503.

23. Ms Paris, Bibliothèque Nationale, latin, 10.891 s.XII ex., s. XIII in., and Ms University of Cambridge 1222, Trinity College 0.3.50 s.XIII c.1220. Dom Becquet's opinions on these matters are most extensively set out in: *RM* 43 (1953), 'Les premiers écrivains de l'Ordre de Grandmont', esp. pp 125–130. He provides an analysis of the Paris manuscript in *RM* 54 (1964) 'La vie de saint Gaucher, fondateur des chanoines réguliers d'Aureil en Limousin', p 28.

24. In the Paris Ms, of the provenance of the house of Grandmont itself, the *Vita Stephani* is found on ff 1–28'; in the Trinity College Ms, it is on ff 90–95', M.R. James believed it probably of the provenance of Grosmont, d. York, an English house of the Order of Grandmont. See: *The Western Manuscripts in the Library of Trinity College Cambridge, A Descriptive Catalogue*, Vol 3, (Cambridge, 1902), p 233. In the Limoges Ms, Archives Départementales de la Haute–Vienne 449, Grand Seminair 68, s. XII ex. —

s. XIII in., and of the provenance of Grandmont itself, the Vita is on pp 3–31 and pp 50–53. The first entry in Ms Clermont–Ferrand, Bibliothèque Municipale 151 (s. XVII) is *Vita et miracula sancti Stephani confessoris secundum speculum ordinis Grandimontensis.* It has not yet been possible to consult this apparently very important copy.

25. See *RM* 43 (1953), pp 126–127.

26. See Göller, Gottfried; *Vinzenz von Beauvais O.P. (um 1194–1264) und sein Musiktraktat im Speculum Doctrinale,* in *Kolner Beitrage zur Musikforschung, Band XV,* [Goller, Vinzenz] (Regensburg, 1959) pp 30–31.

27. *Ibid.,* 1018–1020.

28. See below for the antagonism between the *Vita Primitiva* and the *Vita Posterior;* see *Appendix A* for Stephen's conversation with the cardinals according to the *P* tradition. Dom Becquet regards Vincent's edition as drawn from *Speculum Grandimontis,* perhaps by means of a liturgical reading. *RM,* 43 (1953), 'Les premiers écrivains', p 125 n.8. But those things which characterize the *PN* account are omitted. Phrasing common to Vincent and Gerald Ithier presumably proceeds from the *Vita Posterior.*

29. See below p 15 and *Appendix B;* also *Appendix A.*

30. *Speculum Maius* IV, p 1019.

31. See 31 ... *agnovimus, domino Petro scilicet, valde reverendissimo priore nostro* ... 36 *Domnus quoque Bernadus Dei gratia pastor venerabilis* ... *expertus est. SS* pp 186; 191. Peter Bernard was prior 1163–1170, and the *Vita Hugonis* appears to have been completed before his death.

32. ... *Guillelmus Dandina, cognomento de S. Savino, qui sub finem saeculi XII Hugonis de Lacerta vitam* ... *conscripsit, perplura de S Stephano scitu dignissima et hactenus parum nota, illi inserui. Obs. Praevia* in *Vita Stephani Muretensis, VSMAC* VI, 1046. In the margin to *VHL* 1 Martène noted *S. Stephani vitae compendium ibid.,* 1143.

33. *VHL* 31, *SS* pp 186–187. The passage in parentheses in the English paraphrase of this citation is the present writer's. It rests on Dandina's antithesis *didicimus – agnovimus.*

34. See Dom Becquet's opinion as to the possibility: 'Bibliothèque des écrivains de l'Ordre de Grandmont' in *RM* 53 (1963) no. 4, p 64.

35. *VHL,* 12: Eo namque tempore domnus Stephanus in disciplina sua noviter iam fratres, licet paucos, suscepera ... *SS* 172. Geoffrey of Vigeois places the beginning of the order at the turn of the eleventh to the twelfth century. *Chronicle* in Labbe, Philippe; *Novae Bibliothecae Manuscriptorum* vol. II, Rerum Aquitanicarum (Paris, 1657), p 296.

36. *VSMAC,* VI, 1143.

37. *VHL,* 29, *SS,* p 185.

38. *Ibid.*

39. *Ibid.*

40. *VHL,* 21, *SS,* p 179.

41. *Ibid.*

42. Above and note 3.

43. *VHL,* 50, *SS,* p 204.

44. *Ibid.,* 51, *SS* p 206.

45. *Nemus* was the order's term for a site. These were often thickly wooded and clearance was not originally intended.

46. *VHL,* 54, *SS.* p 210. (Virg., *Aeneid I,* 203).

47. As above.

48. See *Appendix B* for Dandina's repudiation of the claim.

49. In Dom Becquet's edition of the *Vita Stephani Muretensis*, reference to the diaconate, the only such reference in the *Vita PN*, occurs in chapter XXXIII, *SS*, p 124 ... *in ordine diaconatus ... feliciter migravit ad dominum.* In any event Gerald Ithier leaves us in no doubt that his work was in some part dependant on an earlier text. *Sub triplici etenim libello descripsimus ea que de eius (Stephani sc.) dictis vel factis audire aut videre seu legere partim potuimus.* Proeemium in *Tractatus de Disciplina et Correctine Morum* SS XIe, p 337.

50. The Grandmont historian Jean Levesque refers to works of Dandina other than the *Vita Hugonis* which had been carried off from the mother house. *Annales Ordinis Grandimontis*, (Troyes, 1662), p 185.

51. *VHL*, 1, *SS* p 167.

52. ... domni Stephani transitum omnibus scire desiderantibus, quadragesimo et sexto conversionis suae anno fere ... fuisse manifestissimum est. *VHL*, 29 *SS* p 185. It may be noted that Dandina having added here that the death occurred in 1124 states in 54 that Hugh died on 27 April 1157, thirty two years after his master. i.e. Stephen died in 1125 as we should reckon.

53. See Stephen's address to postulants: '... Aliud vero restat horribilius; centupliciter tibi melius est damnari in saeculo, quam hic ... . Tu vero pergere potes ad quodlibet monasteriorum, ubi magna invenies aedificia, cibosque delicatos suis teporibus constitutos. Illic bestias reperies terrarumque latitudinem, hic tantum crucem et paupertatem'. Talibus verbis vir bonus experiebatur si ille firmum reliquendi saeculum cor haberet. *Sent* [3–4], *SS* p 6.

54. *Ibid. Proeemium, SS* p 5. Primo siquidem sermone quem suis fecit Iesus discipulis, sicuti in evangelio reperitur, locutus est de institutione monachorum, cum diceret: 'Beati pauperes spiritu', [Matth. 5, 2] et sic denique suam incoepit regulam.

55. From the summary of the *Vita Fratrum*, Stephen's rule, *Qualiter fratres de vita sua inquirentibus respondeant.* *SS* I, p 61. It should be noted that the hermitage which Stephen intended was not merely a physical place, it was the community in grace of the brethren.

56. 'Errant, inquam, qui hoc dicunt ... quod Deus posse suum amittat quoniam Stephanus de Mureto morietur'. *VHL*, 28 *SS* p 184. But Stephen in his dying homily cited here, did not deny that God's grace was in him. 'Domine' inquiunt (fratres sc.) illi 'numquid adhuc auxiliabimini nobis?' 'Si ego possem, utique, fratres'. *Ibid, SS* p 183.

57. For Stephen's use of the dialogue see above.

58. *Prologus in Regula venerabilis viri Stephani Muretensis: Dum in heremi soitudine*, in *SS* II, p 65.

59. *Ibid.*

60. See Urban's letter *Quanto per infusionem*, 15 July 1186, Verona. (*JL* 15, 650) text in: *Thesaurus Novus Anecdotorum* vol 1 (Paris, 1717) [*TNA*] pp 627–629, ed., Martème, Dom E, and not especially at 628e: *et suprapositis nostrae correctionis capitulis* ... The corrections are found in the privilege and in the Rule text as we have it although they are not repeated verbatim in the Rule. Dom Becquet believes the present Rule text to be the work of Stephen of Liciac:– *SS* II, title page, and *RM* 43 (1953) 'Les premiers écrivains de l'Ordre de Grandmont', pp 121–137 esp. pp 133–134, and 53 (1963), Bibliothèque des Écrivains de l'Ordre de Grandmont, pp 59–79, no. 2 pp 62–63.

61. See Mss:– Paris, BN lat. 14.762 ff 205–206^v, SXIII; Milan, Biblioteca Ambrosiana, C 33 Sup. f144 SXIII; Berlin, Staatsbibliotek III (Phillips 1772) ff 1–5^c SXIII. It may have been the prologue to the *Liber Regulae*

Praeceptis which Gerald Ithier tells us that Hugh Lacerta composed. See above, note 3.

62.   *Prologus, SS* p 67.
63.   See *Sent* passim and esp. LXVII [I] *SS* p 34 '... Scriptura cordis quam tibi Deus immisit, tibi semper ostendit quid relinquere debeas vel agere; sic itaque scienter peccas ac si clericus esses'.
64.   *Prologus, SS* p 67.
65.   *Ibid., SS* p 66.
66.   *Ibid.*, p 67.
67.   *Ibid.*
68.   Above p   at n. 58.
69.   *VHL*, 15 *SS* p 175.
70.   See: *Histoire du Texte des Ascetiques de S. Basile*, in *Bibliothèque du Muséon* vol 32, Gribomont, Dom Jean, [*Ascetiques — Gribomont*], (Louvain, 1953), p 107.
71.   ... regula sancti Benedicti; est nempe magnae perfectionis, sed alia est maioris perfectionis; videlicet regula sancti Basilii. *SS* I, p 5. See above for the first place accorded to Basil's Rule by Stephen among written Rules, at n. 65.
72.   Dom Gribomont encountered twenty—two extant codices (and noted one destroyed in 1944) of Basil's *Shorter Rules* belonging to the period from the second half of the sixth century to the end of the eleventh century, or perhaps in the case of the latest of these, the beginning of the twelfth. [*Ascetiques*, pp 96—99]. Dom A. Siegmund in his *Die Überlieferung der griechischen christlichen Literatur in der lateischischen Kirkche bis zum XII Jahrhundert*, (*Abhandlungen der Bayerischen Benediktiner — Akademie, V*), (München — Pasing, 1949), pp 52—53, has published a list of 17 manuscripts attested in library catalogues anterior to the twelfth century, some of which were also encountered by Dom Gribomont [*Ascetiques*, p 100], who cites references to two other manuscripts of *R. Bas* (*ibid.*). If we allow a total of forty codices of which we have direct or indirect knowledge, these scarcely compare in significance with the numbers of codices of the *Rule of Saint Benedict* which may be assumed *a fortiori* for the same period. While this assumption conceals many complexities as to the prevalence of the text of *RB*, survivals give abundant evidence that it is valid. Rudolf Hanslik, for example, collated some 300 codices of *RB* for the critical apparatus of his first edition of the Rule against fifty to establish a text, the majority of those he used apparently antedating the twelfth century. See: '*Die Benediktinerregel im Wiener Kirchenvatercorpus*, in *Studia Anselmiana*, fasc. XLII, (Rome, 1957), pp 159—169, at p 168.
73.   Ms Madrid Escurial S. III. 32 (R. III. 25) S. IX prov. the library of the Duke of Olivarez: Ms London British Library, Additional 30,055, s X in., prov. S. Pedro de Cardeña; Ms Tours Bibliothèque Municipale 615 s. IX ex. visigothic script, prov. Marmoutier. This contains Basil's *Shorter Rules* but Mss Paris BN lat. 10,876 and 10,877 are of other monastic rules and once formed the rest of the volume of which Ms Tours Bm 615 was the first part. See Gribomont, *Ascetiques*, no. 12, p 98.
74.   Ms Escurial a.I.13. app. s.X in. prov. monastery of Bobatilla. For the date see references given by Boon, Dom A. in : *Pachomiana Latina, Bibliotheque de la Revue d'Histoire Ecclesiastique*, fasc. 7, (Louvain, 1932), p XIV.
75.   Ms Munich Staatsbibliothek Clm. 28118 s. IX in. prov. Saint Maximin of Triers; Ms Lambach 31 s. IX in prov. presumably Münsterschwarzach. Collections containing neither the *Shorter Rules*. not the *Rule of*

Pachomius have not been considered.

76. See Guibert, Louis, 'Destruction de l'Ordre et de l'Abbaye de Grandmont' [hereafter *Destruction*]. *BSAHL* 24 (1876), pp 339–340.

77. *Ibid.*, pp 45–52 for Lépine's visit and inventory but the details of manuscripts in the library appear to have been published by Guibert in the Paris edition of *Destruction* in 1877 which it has not been possible to consult C. Couderc provides these in 'Les manuscrits de l'Abbaye d Grandmont', *Bibliotheque de l'Ecole des Chartes*, 62 (1901), pp 362–373 at pp 365–366. See also pp 363–364 for the date of the catalogue and pp 369 sqq for its content. It was copied by the abbé Legros in his *Memòires sur l'histoire des abbayes du diocese de Limoges*, now Ms A.D. de la Haute–Vienne 137, Grand Seminaire, 35 bis. See also *Bibliotheques de Manuscrits Medievaux en France rèlevé des inventaires du VIIIe au XVIIIe siecle.* Editions du Centre National de la Recherche Scientifique, (1987) no. 644, p 80. It has not been possible to consult n. 645 here.

78. Ms. A.D. de la Haute–Vienne 137, Grand Seminaire 35^bi' f 51^v.

79. *Ibid.*, f. 52', *TNAI*,pp 78–79.

80. See Blanco García, Vicente: *San Ildefonso de Virginitate Beatae Mariae, Historia De Su Tradición Manuscrita, Texto Y Commentario Gramatical Y Estilistico* (Madrid, 1937) p 11 for Gomes' autograph, pp 7–8 for the *g* exemplars.

81. Couderc, *Manuscrits*, p 366.

82. Ms A.D. de la Haute–Vienne 137, f 52^v, f 53.

83. Ms Trinity College, Cambridge 0.3.50 ff 1–39^v. See above notes 23 and 24.

84. Two manuscripts of Rule collections in Beneventan script of the eleventh century have survived: Monte Cassino, the Abbey Library, 443 and 444, the latter belonging to the years 1075–1090. It has not been possible to ascertain the provenance of a third eleventh century transcription in Ms. Florence, Laurentian Library, Plut. XXIII, XXIII, ff 128–161.

APPENDIX A

The visit of the cardinals Gregory and Peter Pierleone to Muret.[1]

There is no reason to doubt that these personages visited Muret since William Dandina also gives an account of their coming.[2] He places the event at an unspecified time after the conversion of Hugh Lacerta in 1111, but evidently well before the last weeks of Stephen of Muret's life, that is January to 8 February 1125. Unlike the author of the *Vita Stephani*, Dandina does not assert that the cardinals were conducting a formal legation in the Limousin, but merely that sent by the pope from the number of the cardinals, they came to Limoges under the pressure of ecclesiastical necessity.[3] And these, he tells us were those cardinals who later contended for the papacy, that is in the schism of 1130–1138/9.[4]

There was an opportunity for such an informal mission to Limoges as Dandina implies when Calixtus II passed via Périgueux and Angouleme to Poitiers and thence, ultimately to Reims, in the great perambulation of France which he undertook after his election at Cluny on 2 February 1119.[5] The cardinal deacons Gregory of Saint Angelo and Peter Pierleone of Saint Cosmas and Saint Damian were in his suite and appear among the subscribers to his bulls from 18 June.[6] They subscribed his letter *Super cella* to Pons, abbot of Aniane, given at Toulouse on 15 July.[7] Peter Pierleone was with him at the Council of Reims, although there is no certainty that the cardinal deacon Gregory with him there was the cardinal of Saint Angelo.[8]

Although Limoges does not appear to have been included in the pope's itinerary, certain matters pertaining to the diocesan area were likely to have caused his considerable disquiet. The sole surviving bull of the anti–pope Gregory VIII (118–1121) or Burdinus as he had been, is addressed to abbot Adalbert and the monks of Saint Peter of Uzerche.[9] Baluze argued cogently that Burdinus if not a native of the Limousin, had been a monk of Uzerche before he embarked on an ecclesiastical career in Spain.[10] He emphasized, moreover the need to explain the apparently unimpetrated privilege from Burdinus to Uzerche, which had been granted very soon after his election, that is, at the time when news of the latter in the Limousin was presumably meagre. As he also pointed out, Uzerche existed in a loose dependence upon the abbey of Saint Martial of Limoges, which was by this period a Cluniac house.[11] According to the chronicle of Geoffrey of Vigeois, two abbots of Uzerche were appointed in the early twelfth century from among the monks of Saint Martial.[12] Thus the possible ramifications of the link between Burdinus, Uzerche and the abbey of Saint Martial of Limoges were doubtless most disquieting, and in need of prudent handling, for in 1119 Burdinus was still at large in Italy.[13] At the Council he held at Reims in October of the same year, Calixtus excommunicated Burdinus and his followers.[14] It may well have been the case that the 'ecclesiastical necessity' which Dandina tells us led the cardinals to Limoges was that occasioned by the affairs of the abbeys of Uzerche and Saint Martial of Limoges.

In Limoges they had heard much, as we learn, to Stephen of Muret's credit, and so decided to visit him, '... each desiring of his own volition to confer singly with Stephen'.[15] For many frequented his little dwelling at that time, since this man of God abounded in teaching of heavenly grace. When indeed the hour of colloquy required it, he began to discuss the problem of each one and what should be done (*causam singulorum et viam discutere*), seeing that they who

were of so very great rank had turned aside to such small and such humble
dwellings. And when each at Stephen's insistence explained why they had made
a détour to him, finding in him much wisdom, they soon asked the assembled
brethren to concede through themselves some little leave to each one of them of
more secret counsel, and they begged Stephen by no means to go away from
them. When these (sc. the brethren) withdrew, the pastor called Dom Hugh to
himself, and ordered him to sit by him; to the cardinals, as they sat together, the
man of God said: 'My lords, and friends, do not complain nor wonder at this, I
keep this man therefore, my good son and disciple with me, since whatever you
say to me in secret, I shall afterwards indicate in its entirety to him; you can
doubtless find in him as much counsel and goodness as in me, for he is wholly
prudent in counsel and faithful in what is assigned to him.' And indeed a most
worthy outcome followed from that colloquy, since even as they themselves
afterwards bore witness, the cardinals withdrew with clearer and wiser minds
concerning the state and manners of the Roman church than they had come.[16]

When Dandina means by *Roman ecclesia* the local church with its
apparatus of ecclesiastical government, or whether he means the entire Western
Church, there may have been a link between the conversation held and the
ramifications of the contemporary schism in the Limousin. But whatever the
content of the mentioned discourse concerning the Roman Church, and, as has
been seen, the problems of each cardinal, it is evident that according to Dandina
Stephen was neither asked about the origins of the order he had founded, nor
volunteered such information. The initiative, moreover, in the colloquy lay in
Stephen's hands and not in those of his august visitors.

Thus at the time when very little was known outside the Limousin
concerning the order of Muret—Grandmont, according to the *Primitiva* tradition,
and as we think in reality, the cardinals appear to have visited Muret for the
purpose for which men usually supposed they might disturb a solitary in his
hermitage, namely to seek his spiritual advice. They have not have come in the
summer of 1119 as suggested here, although the suggestion accords closely with
Dandina's terms of reference for their visit, but plainly the visit did not take
place at a time when Stephen of Muret's death was imminent. And the total
discordance between the accounts in the *Vita Hugonis* and the *Vita Stephani* as to
the manner, content and time of the visit provoke the conclusion that two
different stories are before us.[17] In the *Vita PN*, Gerald Ithier has taken the fact
of a simple and informal visit, already transformed as it apparently was in the
Vita Posterior into an inquiry into the origins of Stephen of Muret's way of life,
and has embroidered it with ideas suitable for the saint's Roman canonization,
and for the papal authorization of the Rule of Grandmont.[18] His further
assertion that Stephen's death was made known to the legates at the Council of
Chartres and published there by them in words which recognized his sanctity has
only its own warrant.[19] There is no reference to the Council of Chartres, and
thus none to the supposed announcement of Stephen's death there in the version
of the *Vita Stephani* preserved by Vincent of Beauvais which, as has been said,
we think at least to have been drawn from the *Vita Posterior*.

NOTES

1.   For Cardinal Peter Pierleone as, the anti—pope Anacletus, 1130—1138, see
      Stroll, Mary; *The Jewish pope: ideology and politics in the papel schism of
      1130*, Brill's Studies in Intellectual History, vol 8 (Leiden, 1987).
2.   *VHL* 17 *SS* pp 176—177.
3.   cf. *Vita Stephani XXXII* (*SS* p 121):   ... *cardinales* ... *cum a summo*

pontifice in Galliam missi legatione sua in partibus Lemoviciniae fungerentur ... and, *VHL* 17: *Eo namque tempore, flagitante ecclesiastica necessitate, ex numero cardinalium duo a summo Romanae ecclesiae pontifice missi, Gregorius videlicet et Petrus de Leo, Lemovicum venerunt.*

4.   *Qui tamen postmodum curam eiusdam (ecclesiae sc.) divisi invicem susceperunt. Ibid.*

5.   *J.L. ad ann.*

6.   See J.L. 6699; Robert Ulysse; *Bullaire du Pape Calixte II.* [hereafter *Robert Bullaire*] vol 1, no. 19, pp 25–26.

7.   J.L. 714; *Robert Bullaire*, 1, no. 35, pp 48–51.

8.   See Calixtus' letter, *Iustis votis*, to Marcherius abbot of Montierneuf, Poitiers, 31 March, 1123, the Lateran, in which he lists the cardinals present at the Council and at the judgement referred to. *Robert Bullaire*, II, no. 367, pp 143–144. Five other cardinal deacons named Gregory are known from this pontificate.

9.   *J.L.* 7178.

10. *Miscellanea Stephani Baluzii*, TI ed., Mansi, G.D., Lucca, 1761, p 138.

11. *Ibid.*

12. See P. Labbe, *Bibliothecae Manuscriptorum Novae*, II, p 296.

13. He was captured at Sutri in 1121 and subsequently imprisoned in the monastery at Cava. See *J.L. an ann.*

14. Orderic Vitalis, *Historia Ecclesiastica*, XII, ed. Le Prévost, A., vol 4, Paris, 1852, p 391.

15. *... illi autem dum de vita eius ac coversatione multa praeconia plurimorum relatu cognovissent atque probassent, ad eum visitationis gratia convenerunt, cupientes secreto iuxta voluntatem suam quisque cum eo sigillatim conferre sermonem. VHL* 17, *SS* pp 176–177.

16. *Ibid., SS* pp 177, 412–43, the present writer's translation with occasional substantives supplied for the sake of clarity.

17. See above p for the account in the *Vita Stephani*.

18. Of the cardinals' prediction, for example, in the *Vita PN*, that if Stephen perseveres until the end he will be numbered among the apostles in Heaven, Gerald has: *Voluit enim Christus Jesus ut servus suus qui a suo vicario apostolico, scilicet in exordio propositi sui bene agendi habuerat praeceptum, a viris apostolicis vicarii sui vicariis in fine suae conversationis sanctitatis haberet testimonium. SS*, p 123.

19. *Ibid.*, XXXVII, *SS* p 127. There is no reference to the announcement of Stephen's death in any of the early twelfth century sources which pertain to the Council of Chartres. For this see C.J. Hefele, trans. and ed., Leclercq, Dom H., *Histoire des Conciles* vol V pt I pp 647–648 and note *3* pp 648–651.

APPENDIX B

The 'diaconate' of Stephen of Muret

It has already been noted that Hugh Lacerta had an excellent even a prodigious memory. As beloved disciple it was he who assisted before all others at his master's death. While *in extremis* Stephen reposed for three days and nights upon Hugh's bosom.[1] Finally fortified by the *Viaticum*, and lying in his hairshirt to the last, with his eyes towards heaven and his hands upraised before the altar, on a Friday, he rendered his soul to God in the very hands of that disciple.[2] He had lived, so Dandina tells us, in great austerity in the matter of dress, as in food and drink. Clad in the same ragged dress, summer and winter, day and night; always in a metal harness, he added at night the wearing of a hairshirt to his mortifications.[3] According to the account in the *Vita PN*, and that given by Vincent of Beauvais, as has also been seen, Stephen died *in ordine diaconatus*.[4] This, so far as the present writer is aware, is the only evidence for the alleged diaconate. Dandina was unimpressed by the allegation, and he provides a most subtle refutation of it in a passage where the idea of subtlety was evidently in his mind. [He is writing of Hugh's superlative merits which could not be explained in words, nor grasped by human subtlety.]

> Itaque meritorum tanta creduntur insignia, quod non solum non praevalent explicari sermone, verum nec ipsa queunt humana comprehendi subtilitate.[5]

He relates that Hugh, soon before his own death in April 1157, paid a courtesy call to Stephen of Liciac, the fourth pastor of the order.[6] He was in the company of Guido of Miliac, his most faithful friend, and a venerable brother of the order, who had absorbed Hugh's habit of holy religion, that is his manner of life, with his instruction in which indeed he was excellently trained and nourished by him:—

> Huius igitur praedicti famuli Dei familiarissimus fuit Guido de Miliaco frater venerabilis, qui eiusdem sanctae habitum religionis admonitione suscepit, in quo etiam ab eodem apprime eruditus atque enutritus est.[7]

[If there be any doubt that *habitus* here means habit of life, it will be resolved by recalling that until the last decades of the twelfth century, a specifically religious dress was forbidden to the members of the order.[8]] And Dandina repeats that he had learnt the story of Hugh's life by the narration of Guido of Miliac, to whom Hugh was accustomed to impart the secrets of his heart in familiar discourse.[9]

On the day after the visit to Stephen of Liciac, the two companions having received his blessing, turned aside from their route to hear Mass at Muret, where the feast of the dedication of the church was being celebrated. With Prime completed, the first priest began the introit, and Hugh, as was his custom, directed his eyes toward the altar more intently and diligently than at any other time. And he saw a vision

> ... unum subito in veste levitica stolaque candida inter alios vidit, circa frequens ministerium satagentem; cui praeterea rasa erat corona et tempora, ipsaque barba. De quo etiam quisnam esset coepit admirari valde et incertus esse; sciebat enim duos clericos ibi

solummodo fore. Tunc vir Domini non longas diu sustinuit moras,
sed statim fratrem Guidonem per quem videlicet super illa
dubietate certus voluit esse, de loco suo semel bis terque diversis
adiit momentis, et quot ibi adessent clerici sollicitus requisivit; cui
ille totidem huiusmodi sermonem respondit, dicens: "Domine, ut
video, duo adsunt tantummodo" ...
... Qua de re certus, lectione libri Apocalypsis iam lecta, ad chorum
clericorum accessit ilico laetus, ubi supra pedes tamdiu mansit
erectus, donec divinum mysterium spatiose celebretur. Factum est
autem cum hora esset iam parata legendi evangelium, ecce
diaconus ille ad pronuntiandum eum una cum sacerdote venit ad
lectricem quod videlicet ipse secundum Lucam distincte incoepit,
etiam pronuntiando aperte usque ad finem complevit. De cuius
voce et habitu argumentum vir Dei sumpsit invincibile, quoniam de
quo diutissime dubius fuerat, hunc veris intersignis indubitanter
dominum Stephenum Muretensem credidit esse; talem enim eum in
vita videre solitus fuerat.[10]

As may be seen, Dandina is at pains to stress that Hugh had ample time in which
to determine the nature of his experience. During the introit there suddenly
appeared a figure in diaconal dress who ministered at the altar, and, after the
reading of the Epistle and gradual (the latter is implicit), in a mass protracted in
its manner of celebration, this visitor came to the lectern and read the Gospel of
the day at the same time as the priest who was assisting the celebrant. It is thus
most significant for his meaning that Hugh having seen the figure in the
dalmatic, alb and stole proper to a deacon, whose temples, crown and beard were
shaven, began to wonder greatly who it might be, and to be in a state of doubt,
(that is, as to whether there were a third cleric before him at all), for he knew
there to be only two clerics present. Hence, not to waste time in resolving the
matter, he went from his own place to brother Guido through whom he wished to
be made sure about that doubt, once, twice indeed three times at various
moments, and he inquired carefully how many clerics there were present. But
Guido's reply was the same each time. With his eyes he saw only two. Certain
therefore that he saw a vision (Qua de re certus ..), after the Epistle reading from
the book of the Apocalypse (21:2–5), he betook himself joyfully to the clerics'
choir (sc. the liturgical choir), where he remained standing for a long time during
the protracted celebration which has been noted. And it happened that when it
was time to read the Gospel (Luc. 19:1–10) behold our 'deacon', whom Hugh's
eyes could not identify in his clerical tonsure and diaconal dress, came with the
priest to the lectern, and began in a clear voice that passage of the Gospel
according to Luke, and he read it all, proclaiming it openly to the end.[11] From
the evidence of his voice, and his practice while on earth, Hugh grasped
irrefragably (for concerning him he had been very doubtful throughout), that by
true indications he believed this indubitably to be Dom Stephen of Muret even as
he had been accustomed to see him in life.[12] And with the service having been
completed in the usual way, the venerable father vanished from the sight of the
disciple beholding him.

Doubtless there are layers of meaning in the account which will remain
obscure to the modern eye, but there can be no doubt that at the core of the
subtlety is a refutation of the claim that Stephen of Muret was in deacon's
orders. Dandina has been seen elsewhere, this well–modulated manner of
argument attracted him; here he sets aural argument against visual evidence.
Hugh plainly sees the clerical tonsure and diaconal dress of the apparition; indeed
he verifies the fact that he is seeing a third cleric, but he is unable to construe

these things as signs of the person who is wearing them. The voice of Stephen,
however, he recognizes, as he does his habit of proclaiming the Gospel as the sole
rule of life.[13] Dandina's use of *habitus* earlier in the passage to mean way of life
has been noted. Here the antitheses of Hugh's aural and visual perceptions
preclude the meaning that Stephen is recognized by his mode of dress, for his
garments conceal his identity and prevent Hugh from knowing him. In a word
levitical dress is the wrong dress for Stephen just as his diaconal ministry at the
altar is the wrong ministry. These are rather the vestments and ministry of the
fictional deacon, (apparently out of the *Vita Posterior*). An identity of the real
and the fictional Stephen in terms of ministry occur in the proclaiming of the
Gospel, a diaconal function in the liturgy, and Stephen of Muret's vocation in
service of his flock and of those who sought his counsel. It was presumably the
analogy of Stephen's name and that of his eponym the proto–martyr who was
also one of the proto–deacons, which led to the invention of the diaconate.

Gerald Ithier incorporated a tale of a vision enjoyed by Hugh at Muret
shortly before he died in the collection of miracles he added to his *Vita Stephani
Muretensis*.[14] The story has been changed. Hugh has no difficulty in recognizing
the deacon Stephen, the purpose of whose visit is to call Hugh to his heavenly
reward. This account of the vision passed into the abbreviated and re–slanted
Vita Hugonis once found in *Speculum Grandimontis*.[15]

Further evidence of Stephen of Muret's lay status appears in the text
edited in *Speculum Grandimontensis* as *Conclusio Vitae Stephani Muretensis*.
This is plainly a re–working by Gerald Ithier of earlier texts concerning
Stephen's *conversatio*, his way of conducting himself at Muret, and the following
passage appears

> Dignum ergo est et eum religiosi imitentur et diligant, plebs colat,
> noxii timeant, quem ita divina virtus illustravit, ut sub laicali
> etiam habitu habuerit a Deo collata dona doctrinam que
> mellifluam, et Spiritu sancto conditam, desiderio Christi salitam de
> aeterna semper beatitudine sollicitam.[16]

Here *habitus* must mean 'form of dress' since a lay mode of life would mean that
in which Stephen was at liberty to marry. We know already that Stephen and
his followers dressed as laymen.[17] Dandina denied his diaconate and thus all
claim to major orders. He may have been in minor orders, that is those below
the subdiaconate which was firmly assimilated to the *clericatus* from the
mid–eleventh century onwards.[18] Indeed if he were a monk, this was almost
certainly the case, but these were 'negotiable' orders permitting the assumption
of a lay state.[19] There is reliable evidence, as has been seen, that Stephen of
Muret was not in deacon's orders. There is ample evidence that he lived in
religion as a layman, and that he constructed a 'lay' religious order of laymen
and clerics. This must be reviewed elsewhere.

NOTES

1. *VHL*: 27, *SS*, p 182.
2. *Ibid.*, 29, *SS*, p 185.
3. *Ibid.*, 1, *SS*, p 167.
4. *Vita Stephani*, XXXIII, *SS*, p 124. *Speculum Maius* IV, p 1019.
5. *VHL* 49, *SS*, p 201.
6. *Ibid.*, p 202.
7. *Ibid.*, p 201.

8. See the text *Qualiter fratres de vita sua inquirentibus respondeant*, in our view a summary of the unwritten rule of Stephen of Muret. (It is given by Dom Becquet as *Liber de Doctrina, Conclusio*.) Stephen says to his followers: '*A ceteris vero religiosis minime requiritur quam regulam teneant. Nam vestimentum indicat de quibusdam; isti sunt in regula sancti Augustini et ab his tenetur ordo sancti Benedicti* (*SS*, p 60). Evidently Stephen was teaching his followers how to reply to criticism of their lack of distinctive dress.

9. *VHL* 49, *SS*, p 201.

10. *Ibid.*, *SS*, p 202.

11. The mass is *Terribilis est*, for the dedication of a church or the anniversary of the same. The readings are cited from the *Missale Romanum* and these appear to accord with Dandina's indications.

12. Venerable members of the Order of Muret—Grandmont were addressed as *Domnus* or *Dominus*.

13. The repentance and salvation of Zachaeus (in Luke 19) are appropriate subject matter for an order dedicated to poverty.

14. *VSMAC* VI, pp 1085–1087.

15. See Ms A.d. de la Haute–Vienne 112, Grand Séminaire 10, pp LXX–LXXI, the *Mémoires pour l'histoire de Grandmont* of the abbe Nadaud in which he made a partial copy of *Speculum Grandimontis* finding the *Vita Brevis* in another hand among the last items following Gerald Ithier's work. See also Levesque, *Annales*, pp 66–75, who likewise transcribed the *Vita Brevis*.

16. *Conclusio Vitae* XII, *SS*, p 327. Dom Becquet has drawn attention to the similarity of certain passages to others in the *Sententiarum Liber*, *SS*, pp 322–323. It may also be noted that some of the phrasing is redolent of that of William Dandina. cf. *Conclusi* XV, *SS*, p 329[5-7] and *VHL* 30, *SS*, p 186[800-802].

17. For his repudiation of monastic and canonical dress, see above note 8.

18. See *Decreti Gratiani Prima Pars Dist. XXXII c.6, Praeter hoc* Friedberg, p 118.

19. See c.VI of the Council of Gerona, 1068, under the presidency of Cardinal Hugh Candida, *Mansi*, XIX, p 1071.

HERMITS, MONKS AND WOMEN IN TWELFTH–CENTURY FRANCE AND ENGLAND : THE EXPERIENCE OF OBAZINE AND SEMPRINGHAM

Brian Golding

The Cistercian General Chapter that met at Citeaux under the chairmanship of the abbot of the mother house in September 1147 was one of the most important ecclesiastical gatherings of the century. It was attended as was customary by all the abbots of the order (which now numbered some 300 houses) but also present were a number of other dignitaries, including the future Master of the Templars and above all, the first Cistercian pope, Eugenus III, 'not presiding by apostolic authority, but staying amongst them, as one of them, in brotherly love'. Finally, there were no less than three heads of independent religious communities, of which the most important and well–known to contemporaries was undoubtedly Serlo, abbot of Savigny in Normandy.[1] The other two men had also come a long way: one, Stephen, had travelled from Obazine in the modern department of Correze in the Bas–Limousin region of the western Massif Central, the other, Gilbert, had come from much further away, from Sampringham in the fens of south Lincolnshire. The two visitors had similar social backgrounds and educational attainments, and both were more or less reluctant leaders of religious communities they had funded. Both of them, too, had for many years been searching for the ideal rule for these communities to follow; they had taken advice from many sources and had experimented with many varieties of the religious life, and independently they had now come to the same conclusion: to pass their followers into the care of the Cistercians.

In some respects it was natural for founders of 'new monastic' persuasion to seek to affiliate with, or have their communities absorbed by, the white monks, who were, after all, by the mid–century without question the most successful, widely distributed and organised of the new groups.[2] There were already several precedents for such action; in 1119 the abbey of Cadouin, founded four years earlier by Gerald of Salles (a disciple of Robert of Arbrissel), passed to the Cistercians, and this was followed a generation later by the cession of another of Gerald's creations Grandselve, in 1145.[3] The 1147 chapter would accept the order of Savigny which possessed some thirty abbeys making it the biggest takeover yet, while other communities such as that of Dalon (which became subject to Citeaux in 1162) would join the fold later in the century.[3] These abbeys sometimes retained a degree of autonomy, though the takeover could lead to considerable hostility (as happened at the English Savigniac houses) and the new organisational arrangements were in all cases arranged on an *ad hoc* basis.[4]

However, for all that both Stephen and Gilbert had already established close ties and friendships with leading Cistercian figures the difficulties they faced in looking for Cistercian absorption were formidable. Above all, both Obazine and Sempringham contained flourishing female elements; at Obazine there were apparently some 150 nuns while the community at Sempringham was primarily organised as a nunnery and neither canons or monks were yet installed there.[5] The Cistercian attitude to women in the religious life was at best ambivalent and at worst hostile, and though by this date there were some Cistercian nuns, their position within the order was marginal and ambiguous, and there was certainly no formal recognition of their existence within the white monks' organisation.[6] It was therefore optimistic to expect that the Cistercian would accept communities of women without demur, or, if they did agree that they would do so without making substantial and significant changes to their way of life. In the event one of the petitioners, Stephen of Obazine, was successful in his request, the other was rebuffed and obliged to return to England, with the result that the Gilbertine order, though it was organised (in some ways very closely) on the Cistercian model, remained independent till its dissolution. I intend here to follow the careers and to examine the monastic programmes of the two founders, which though they bear many superficial similarities, in some important respects represent very different aspects of the twelfth—century monastic reform movement. I will concentrate upon their arrangements for the religious life of the women in their communities. Having followed the path of both men to Citeaux I will then suggest some reasons for the 'success' of one and the 'failure' of the other at Citeaux.

Stephen was born towards the end of the eleventh century in the Limousin, probably in the Correz region, of noble though not very wealthy family.[7] He was brought up at the school of the priory of Pleaux in the Cantal and was probably always intended for a clerical career. But on his father's death he assumed control of the family, and though the *Vita* stresses his charity and chastity, it is clear that he lived as a local seigneur, enjoyed hunting and good living, and had a reputation as an active *miles*. At some point, however, he decided to become a priest and from that time followed a life of asceticism, fasting, adopting the ancient custom of immersion in freezing water, and wearing a hair shirt. He also began to preach (perhaps first in his parish church) and soon acquired a reputation as a teacher. Though he does not seem to have gone on lengthy and distant preaching missions, as did so, many contemporary hermit—reformers, he certainly served as an itinerant preacher in a number of churches.[8] Already he was thinking of an eremitical life, wishing in that favourite cliché of the reforming holy men, naked and poor to follow the naked and poor Christ.[9] It is perhaps here that we can date the beginning of Stephen's long quest for the perfect way of life, a search that involved many readjustments and constant self—examination. It was also marked by frequent consultation with other religious figures, whom Stephen visited both for advice and also for validation of his own activities. So, wishing to follow the life of a hermit 'but that he might not seem to be acting rashly or without council' he visited Stephen of Mercoeur, abbot of La Chaise—Dieu (1111–46).[10] The context makes it clear that Stephen really wanted guidance on the eremitical life, and on his return he, along with a companion and fellow priest Peter, solemnly distributed their goods to the poor and 'left their native soil for exile'.[11] For ten months they stayed with a small community of hermits led by a certain Bertrand, who is probably to be identified with Bertrand de Griffeville, a Poitevin hermit who had settled in the Cantal *c* 1120.[12] Ultimately this arrangement did not work out and the two new hermits moved on, looking for a stricter life It is clear that they had not yet determined whether to continue as hermits or as monks or canons. A number of options were open to them, and it is important to stress that the dividing lines between these varieties of the religious life were far from rigid. This fluidity is confirmed by an imprecision of terminology in which hermits are frequently found described as monks and their settlements as monasteries.[13] At this stage Stephen was as ready to join a cenobitic establishment as he was to live the life of a solitary or to found his own community, and according to the *Vita* he and Peter visited all the religious places of the region looking for one where a sufficiently perfect way of life was followed. None was found.

So the two men came to Obazine, a remote but not uninhabited site near Tulle, where they made a base, living in great hardship for the first two weeks. On Easter Sunday *c* 1130 they went to the local church where barefooted they sang mass, but no one invited them home for the feast and sadly they returned to their camp. Soon, however, they began to attract visitors who brought them food, and all might have been well but for the very recent memory of a 'pseudochorita' who had set up an oratory and received many gifts just before making a moonlight flit on the eve of celebrating a solemn mass.[14]   As a consequence there was (hardly surprisingly) considerable mistrust and hostility towards the newcomers, and for a time they were left alone, living as solitaries and following ever more ascetic practices. By this time, however, they had acquired another companion, Bernard, who was to become Stephen's closest confidant.[15]   Bernard and Peter soon left to visit Limoges (in which diocese Obazine lay) where they met bishop Eustorge (1106–37), who approved their way of life and gave them permission to celebrate mass and to build a monasterium, so long as they followed in all things the customs handed down by the Fathers.[16] With this sanction Stephen moved the site of his settlement to the other side of the river Correze where he built a very small monastery, defined in the Vita as having a chapel, dormitory, refectory, kitchen, and cloister. This would suggest that Stephen already had a small group of followers who had to be housed. Certainly the Vita goes on to state that a few recruits did join the infant community and followed Stephen's guidance: but as yet no rule was formally adopted and they are revealingly said to have followed the canonical rule in the liturgy though they were eremitic in their way of life.[17]   The author of the Vita follows this with a brief excursus on the shortcomings of the regular canons, who though they sing the offices 'regulariter', happily and greedily eat well–cooked dishes, take long daily rests, and do little or no manual work. Apparently Stephen so much abhorred this practice that he decreed that all day should be spent in manual work except that time reserved for the lectio and the divine office. Though Stephen himself did not go out of the monastery to work, he was in charge of the cooking and even did the washing up. We have here, then, a small community following an extremely austere way of life of silence and fasting and following an eclectic amalgam of rules under Stephen's command.[18]

With a rapidly increasing community Stephen grew concerned. He desired solitude and was not willing to assume authority over so many. 'He had not come to this place so that a great crowd of men might collect there but to live as a solitary'.[19]   Herein is incapsulated the dilemma and tension that lay at the centre of the eremitical life. A successful hermit was, if not a contradiction in terms, at least a paradox, in that his very charisma ensured that he could not escape from the demands of followers. It was probably this tension indeed that made Stephen, like so many contemporary holy men, an awkward and disconcerting companion. He refused in any way to moderate his austerities, with the result that his followers felt obliged to imitate his example: only then did the master relax his observances for their sake. He tried to persuade his closest friend (presumably Bertrand) to accompany him to convert the Saracens even if martyrdom ensued, a course of action from which he was only dissuaded by the wise council of his friend, who argued that it was better to convert believers from their evil conduct by word and example ('Verbo et exemplo convertere') than labour in vain for those who might still not believe, or even be predestined to life.[20]   The next few years seem to have been taken up by expansion of the buildings for the growing community, while at the same time Stephen continued to feel his unworthiness as a leader. A dispute between himself and Bertrand as to which of them should be subject to the other, both wishing to take the humbler role, was only ended through the negotiation of the visiting bishop of Chartres (who had been sent to the region by Innocent II to support his party during the Anacletan schism). As canon of Chartres the bishop had already shewn himself a supporter of the reformed community at Tiron, now he decided to appoint Stephen prior.[21] This made no actual difference to the organisation at Obazine: 'no rule of another order had yet been adopted, the *instituta* of the master had the force of law and these taught nothing other than humility, obedience, discipline, and above all, continual charity'.[22]

At the same time Stephen maintained close relations with neighbouring monasteries, in particular Dalon, which was not far away in the Dordogne and had been founded as a reformed house by Gerald de Salles in 1114.[23] He frequently journeyed to these communities bearing presents and hoping for their prayers in exchange, but he also went to observe their customs which he could then adapt for his own community, acting, as the *Vita* puts it, like the bee making honey from different flowers. It should be noted in passing that the *Vita* of St Gilbert makes a similar analogy telling how Gilbert constructed his Rule from statutes plucked like so many flowers from many churches and monasteries.[24] Not surprisingly for one following an eremitical life so closely, and yet ruling over what was in effect a small independent monastery,, he maintained particularly close relations with the Carthusians. Sometime between 1132 and 1135 he made a long and arduous journey to La Chartreuse *via* Lyon.[25] When he arrived he took counsel of prior Guigo as to what religious way of life he should adopt, making it clear that though he and his brethren would gladly receive the *instituta* of any suitable order he has chosen the Carthusian way. Guigo apparently replied that the 'royal way' of the Cistercians was preferable; the number and possessions of the Carthusians were limited and were thus not suitable for Stephen's community, which was large and still increasing. He ought, therefore, to look to a cenobitic way of life that was equally suitable for large and small groups.[26] Yet how much credence should be given to this account? Did Guigo really suggest a Cistercian solution? It is true that Guigo had earlier recommended to Pons of Leras, the founder of Sylvanes, that he join the Cistercians, but we must remember that the *Vita* was written long after the successful absorption of Obazine into the Cistercian order, and also that the *Vita's* author had himself been a monk at Citeaux.[27] Certainly it was to be at least another twelve years before Stephen would make his crucial journey to Citeaux and between 1135 and 1147 much had happened at Obazine. Most importantly, if the somewhat exiguous chronology of the *Vita* is to be trusted, it was only after the La Chartreuse visit that women first settled in the community and it is unlikely that Stephen would have embarked on such a course which also involved, as we shall see, ambitious building works, if he was already determined to take Obazine into the Cistercian order. Moreover, by 1147 two more houses dependant on Obazine had been founded; this expansion, too, seems difficult to explain if Stephen had already decided to enter Citeaux.[28] When Stephen returned from La Chartreuse, rather than taking any immediate steps to follow the 'royal way' he once more expanded the abbey buildings, and constructed a new church dedicated to the Virgin 'according to Carthusian custom' for the community, and another alongside dedicated to St Peter for guests and visitors.[29] And it was shortly after this that we find the first references to women at Obazine.

'The number of lay women who were converted increased considerably'.[30] It is not clear whether this is a general statement referring to the growing role of women in the religious life everywhere, or whether it relates specifically to events at Obazine. Certainly at this time there were very few opportunities for female religious in the Limouisin. Those nunneries that did exist were small and poorly—endowed. Stephen's acceptance of women was therefore filling a definite need in the region.[31] According to the *Vita* there were 150 women in the community by 1142: if this figure is correct (and there were certainly 100 nuns at

Coyroux in the following century) then there were considerably more women at Obazine than men. Shortly after 1147 there were said to be 120 in the community at Obazine and the preponderance of women must have placed considerable strains on its economy.[32]

The appeal of the hermits to women throughout western Europe during the first half of the twelfth century is well—attested and is increasingly the subject of study.[33] Stephen was not exceptional, therefore, though he does not seem to have had any specific mission to women such as that of Robert of Arbrissel or Gilbert of Sempringham. However, in his preface to the third part of the *Vita* Stephen's biographer does write of prostitutes of noble birth who had had more lovers than any army that the richest lord could lead to war. These Stephen had brought to Christ as chaste and wholly purified: 'a greater miracle than if he had raised them to life'. This reference to the amorous lifestyle of the female recruits to Obazine may be hagiographical convention but there are clearly echoes here of Robert's Fontevraud.[34] Many of the entrants to Obazine were said to have been of high birth and the wives of noble lords, and the *Vita* shows a little of the dynamic of recruitment in a story it tells of how a local lord of great piety and justice finally entered the abbey with all his household. A procession of carts bore him, his children, wife, members of his entourage, men and women, each with their baggage, with his animals and cattle to the abbey while some of the brethren destroyed the fortifications of his house, and broke all the weapons of war. The castle thus pacified became a possession of the monastery. While the *Vita* sees such an episode as worthy of record 'because it was an *exemplum* unheard—of in our time' it is of course a commonplace event in contemporary monastic chronicles and hagiographies.[35] It is also apparent from the Obazine cartulary that a number of families did indeed enter the community *en bloc* and this could pose considerable problems of organisation : this was in many instances the catalyst for the expansion of a community's female element. A similar pattern had been seen at Molesme where Jully was established as a sister house for the female recruits, while the most famous instance of mass family recruitment is, of course, that which occurred at Cîteaux in 1112.[37] There is also an echo here of events at Fontevraud a generation earlier. In both places the quality as well as the quantity of female recruits is stressed. In the *Vita* there follows a common—place eulogy of those women who gave up their life of luxury for austerity, musk and perfumes for the smell of smoke. While the brethren were engaged in heavy work, the women prepared vegetables, washed the kitchen utensils and clothes, and cleaned the houses. None of them ever entered the dwellings of the brethren or approached them except in the presence of the prior, or with his licence, and then only for spiritual direction or in connection with their work.[38]

By 1142 there were two communities in close proximity at Obazine and Coyroux, so close that it was sometimes possible to hear the bells of one church from the other. Yet still there was no written rule for them. Just as the brethren had not yet been divided into monks and lay brethren so the sisters were not *stricto sensu* nuns. The author of the *Vita* is at pains to point out that they followed the directions of Stephen alone, whose commands were no less rigorous than any formal rule. Yet there was recognition that reliance upon one *magister* was dangerous. In particular there was the problem of what would happen on Stephen's death. A written rule would be more permanent and ensure greater stability in days to come.[39] Having decided to adopt a written code, however, the choice had to be made between the canonical and monastic paths; it was no longer sufficient for Stephen to observe canonical forms of the liturgy while following an eclectic mélange of ordinance of his own composition for the daily life of the communities. After much deliberation and after taking advice from many learned men, especially from one of Obazine's most enthusiastic ecclesiastical patrons, the bishop of Clermont, it was decided to follow a monastic rule. Since Dalon was the only nearby monastery, and good relations were already enjoyed with that house it was decided to seek teachers from there. While waiting for their arrival Stephen was received as a monk at a solemn ceremony attended by another episcopal patron, his diocesan, Gerald bishop of Limoges, who then appointed Stephen abbot of his community.[40] This was clearly a turning—point in its existence. Perhaps the most important development was the division of the brethren into two groups: the clerks were received as monks but the lay members remained lay brethren. This was a fundamental change in the community's organisation and one that was mirrored in most of the other new orders, including Sempringham.[41] Stephen next proceeded to the womens' new quarters where he ate with them in their refectory and preached a sermon in which he set out the way of life they should follow. Its essence was perpetual enclosure. They too were being fitted into a new organisational framework of much greater rigidity.[42]

The church of the nuns was divided into two inequal parts by a wall running laterally north—south. This was in accordance with the decree of the Second Lateran Council of 1139 that forbade nuns to sing in the same choir as men.[43] The eastern smaller section was entered *via* a north door by the brethren and by those detailed to celebrate the night offices and mass. In the dividing wall was set an iron grill covered with a veil on the nuns' side. Below this was a gap through which the priest would pass the eucharist. When the women communicated the priest carried the elements from the altar to the grill and the veil was drawn back for the nuns. If one of them was too weak to walk she was brought to the grill and laid out as if on a bier and so prepared to receive the *viaticum*. The monks had full responsibility for the nuns' spiritual well—being, celebrating the offices, holding chapters, hearing confessions and imposing penances and arranging the burial of the dead, but the abbot appointed a particular *sacerdos eruditus* to act as his deputy over the women. However, within the nunnery a prioress supervised all activity and as the *Vita* is at pains to point out the nuns followed exactly the same lifestyle as the monks, apart from the fact that they never left the cloister and either sang quietly or not at all though they read the hours with great devotion (which incidentally, suggests that they were literate).[44]

Strict enclosure always presented logistical problems. No nunnery could be *totally* self—sufficient, every one was to a greater or lesser extent dependent upon a male element not only for the sacraments but for heavy labour and so forth.[45] Some sort of communication was inevitable; it did however have to be carefully suprvised.[46] At Coyroux the solution was for a corridor linking the nuns' cloister to the outside world. This was enclosed by a door at either end. The key to the nuns' door was held by the prioress and though she was responsible for security, the actual passage of goods through the corridor was supervised by a portress (perhaps a lay sister). A lay brother *maturus atque probatus* styled the *procurator* or *portarius* kept the key of the outer door. He was in one sense the lay equivalent of the monk who supervised the spiritual requirements of the women. He was responsible for their exterior and temporal needs and was expected to procure these without asking anything from the laity.[47]

The arrival of the monks from Dalon was not a success. Apparently the newcomers insisted that the monks of Obazine follow the full rigour of the monastic rule from the outset and made no allowance for the fact that they were in some sense novices. This engendered much discontent and complaints were made to Stephen. Stephen is said to have calmed the rebels, but it is clear that there were major tensions that were extremely difficult to resolve.[48] We can only guess at the reasons. It hardly seems likely that the root cause was the austerity of the monastic rule. Dalon, though a house of reformed monks, does not appear to have had a great reputation for asceticism, and Stephen's own institutes were probably, as the *Vita* had earlier made clear, considerably more austere. More likely there was resentment at the introduction of new monks who, though known to Obazine, followed a different way of life. We do not know when the Dalon monks left but between 1142 and 1147 the community at Obazine continued to grow. Stephen founded two daughter houses, at Bonnaigue and Le Pestre, as well as granges (which are probably to be equated with cells in this context) nearer at hand.[49] But Stephen had still not given up the idea of ceding his foundations to another order in 1147 he left for Citeaux.

It is time now to turn to Gilbert. The opening chapters of his *Vita* include elements common in contemporary and earlier hagiographies, and care must therefore be taken in their interpretation. Thus the author stresses the nobility of Gilbert's parents. Gilbert's Norman father, Jocelin, is described as an active knight ('miles strenuus') and a wealthy ('opulentus') man with many possessions in Lincolnshire. His mother is said to have been of lesser social status and English by birth. As we have already seen, the connection between nobility and sanctity was often made by twelfth—century commentators and many of Gilbert's contemporary reformers were described in similar terms.[50] Jocelin seems in fact to have been only a member, albeit a relatively prosperous one, of the knightly class of post—Conquest Lincolnshire. Gilbert's first years were clearly a disappointment to his parents. Allegedly he had some physical deformity and was, perhaps primarily for this reason, despised within the household so that he himself related how the 'famuli' refused to eat with him. This account is used by the author of the *Vita* to stress God's grace in raising up a saint from the dust and while this portrayal of the saint as outsider is again a hagiographical commonplace, Gilbert's disability may well have been the reason why (as the *Vita* asserts) he was sent to school. The implication is that he was not fit enough to follow his father, whose eldest son he probably was, as a 'miles strenuus' and it is likely that Jocelin already intended to provide his son with one or more of his demesne churches on completion of his studies.[51]

Gilbert's first years as a student were equally inauspicious. In Lincolnshire educational options were fairly limited. Raymonde Foreville has suggested that he went either to Crowland, the only local monastic foundation of any size, or to a parish school. Another possibility is Lincoln.[52] Gilbert's presence here, though undistinguished, may have given him his first introduction to the episcopal household which he was to enter a few years later. Wherever he was first educated, it was only when firmly taken to task for his slow progress and laziness that he is said to have fled, through shame or fear, to France. This flight may be exaggerated, it is hard to see how he could have supported himself without some assistance from his family, though he is said to have been aided by modest contributions to his studies from friends. The *Vita* does not indicate where Gilbert studied, he may of course have moved from centre to centre.[53] He seems to have stayed in France for several years only returning as a *magister*.

On his return it might have been expected that Gilbert would have taken up a post in a cathedral or urban school and/or proceeded to major orders. He did neither. Instead he began to teach the children, both boys and girls, of his

neighbourhood.[54] The establishment was organised on quasi–monastic lines —
indeed, the *Vita* explicitly states that the children followed monastic discipline.
According to the *statuta monasteriorum* the boys had to keep silence except in
places where speech was authorised, and were to sleep in the same room, as in a
dormitory. The *Vita* however is at pains to point out that Gilbert still wore
costly and elegant secular dress; the saint's position was clearly an ambivalent
one within the lay world, provided as he was with an income by his father, not
yet a priest, and yet following in many respects a monastic regime. This
ambivalence was heightened when Jocelin presented his son to his two demesne
churches of Sempringham and West Torrington. It was presumably because he
himself was unable to administer the sacraments that Gilbert now employed a
chaplain, Geoffrey, to assist him in his pastoral duties at Sempringham. Here he
proceeded to the reform of the parish. He turned the people from their drinking
feasts and spectacles of what is described as a monastic life so that they became
locally famous for their devotion. In particular Gilbert seems to have insisted on
the payment of church dues and tithes, and a graphic account is given of how a
recalcitrant parishoner who kept back his tithe was punished.[55]

Sometime before 1123 Gilbert left his parish in order to serve in the
episcopal household of Robert Bloet, a bishop of Lincoln. The *Vita* suggests that
he did this because he judged it better to serve under the rule of the bishop
rather than be like those who without authority ('more acephalorum') ran hither
and thither with dissolute liberty. Again it seems as if the *Vita* may be trying to
exonerate the unpriested and theoretically irregular Gilbert from charges of
unlicenced preaching.[56] The *Vita* certainly implies by its reference to Gilbert
instructing his hearers that he did preach in his parish, but the level at which
this was practised is unknown. On Robert's death in 1123 Gilbert was retained
in the employment of his successor, Alexander 'the Magnificent'. As an
episcopal chaplain Gilbert's personal piety was noted, and the *Vita* draws
particular attention to his habit of repeating the Psalter with prostrations
whenever the name of God was mentioned, his frequent private prayer, fastings,
and self–scourgings: all, of course, part of the expected activity of a
contemporary holy man.[57]

It was at this point that the bishop prevailed on Gilbert (much against his
will) to become a priest. Alexander's intention seems to have been to make
Gilbert a penitentiary for the diocese, if this is what is meant by the *Vita*'s
statement that he wished to commit to his chaplain the keys of binding and of
loosing, and to appoint him to discover and judge the sins of all his i.e. the
bishop's people, though it may be that this merely refers to a licence to preach
within the diocese.[58] After becoming a priest Gilbert is said to have redoubled
his spiritual exercises so that he would have been thought a regular canon rather
than a secular clerk. Of his activities as a clerk we are not informed. He seldom
appears as a witness to episcopal *acta*, yet he clearly made sufficient of an
impression to be a candidate for one of the eight archdeaconries of the diocese.
Gilbert refused on the grounds that the temptation of avarice so often associated
with the office might lead him to evil.[59] It was shortly after this that Gilbert
resolved to return to Sempringham and to follow the path of poverty by selling
his goods and distributing the proceeds to the poor. It may that that his refusal
to accept office had caused offence to the bishop, certainly the offer seems to have
been a catalyst for Gilbert's later career.

The author of the *Vita*'s emphasis on Gilbert's devotion to voluntary
poverty places him firmly in the mainstream of contemporary reformers.[60] It
explicitly criticises those who believe earthly possessions convey honour when

really they bring degradation; surely a reference to those monastic reformers who saw the increase of the material prosperity of a community as an indicator of its spiritual state.[61]   Gilbert's action is paralleled not only by Stephen of Obazine but also by Norbert of Xanten who, when he resigned his prebend, sold his property and gave it to the poor.[62]   There is one significant difference, however, between the almsgiving of Gilbert and that of many of his contemporaries. Their giving seems to have been non—discriminatory; they gave to whoever asked. By contrast Gilbert is said to have chosen those poor whose poverty was rendered honourable by their fear and love of God.

All commentators are agreed that the first community at Sempringham was established in 1131. Though the *Vita*'s chronology is sometimes obscure it is possible to establish a fairly clear picture of developments.[63]   Seven girls of the village wished to leave the world for a heavenly bridegroom, i.e. this wished to live as anchoresses. Gilbert wished his goods to be used in the service of God and, we are told, originally intended these to be used for the support of a male community, but since he could not find men willing to live such austere a life as he required he made over his property for the support of the girls. This choice of women is stressed again shortly afterwards: 'he did not at first make friends for himself of men ... but called together women as his friends'. Gilbert's own account is a little different. He writes that he could not find men, and so 'I found girls, who had been frequently taught by us, and who wished, having put aside earthly cares, to devote themselves to divine service without hindrance'.[64] Yet it is clear from early charters relating to the first communities of Sempringham and Haverholme (which predate Gilbert's abortive visit to Citeaux) that the care of religious women was central in his design. The very early charter of Roger fitzGocelin (Gilbert's brother) was made to the 'handmaidens of Christ' in their poverty; the foundation charter of bishop Alexander in favour of Haverholme was similarly addressed to Christ's handmaidens, 'serving God under the care and teaching of Gilbert the priest'.[65] Two additional points can be made. The *Vita* clearly assumes that the parish girls were already prepared to dedicate themselves to religious life before Gilbert ceded his property to them, and indeed does not state that Gilbert did not intend to establish a community for women, but that he wished to use his resources for the support of a male community. Perhaps more importantly, we must remember that both Gilbert and the author of the *Vita* are often apologists: both wrote after crises and scandals had rocked the youthful order and at a time when the role of women in the monastic commonwealth as a whole was increasingly coming into question. To suggest that he was not intending to found a female community but that his hand was forced by circumstances may be a way in which both attempted to deflect criticism.

Gilbert's own account goes on to describe simply how houses and a cloister was built and how the seven girls were enclosed by bishop Alexander of Lincoln. Thereafter they would never leave and, Gilbert adds, he did not think at that time that more would be added to this small community. The *Vita* is, as we should expect, a fuller account, Gilbert is said to have provided for all their necessities, again the aid of Alexander is acknowledged, and the girls are said to have been enclosed to live a solitary life in buildings erected against the north wall of the parish church. The only way in which necessities could be passed through to them was by a single opening. These were made the responsibility of certain secular women, while Gilbert himself had the only key to the door, never unlocked except at his command and only for his entry to them, not for their exit.   Indeed, the *Vita* states that the window itself would never have been opened if humans could have lived without human things. What then was the nature of this community? It appears that it was (at least in the early 1130s) essentially eremitical rather than cenobitic. The language of both Gilbert himself and the *Vita* used to describe the seven is primarily that applicable to anchoresses. Gilbert refers to their enclosure by the bishop ('per dompnum Alexandrum ... septem inclusimus'): the role of the bishop in the enclosure of anchorites was already established by this time and was to become the norm during the thirteenth century.[66] Later he refers to them as 'inclusae Christi', a term typically applied to anchoresses. The *Vita*'s account of the girl's life, of the window, and the door whose key was held by Gilbert alone are all reminiscent of the organisation of a community of anchoresses rather than nuns. So too are the similes and metaphors used in the description. The girls are segregated from the world, pledged to eternal virginity and reserved for the heavenly bridegroom. They are said to be enclosed as 'ancillae Christi', they are exiles from their land, family, and father's house, 'imprisoned' from the world. It is also worth noting the parallel between the Sempringham community with its cells against the walls of the parish church and the home of the women of the *Ancrene Wisse* which lay under the eaves of the church.[67] These women can surely be seen as amongst those described by the author of the *Libellus de Diversis Ordinibus* as taking up Christ's yoke 'with holy men or under their guidance'.[68] Parallels can easily be found in twelfth–century England. A number of writers and clerics, of whom Anselm is only the most famous, had written for the instruction of anchoresses or had been their patrons, companions and teachers. As Dr Warren has written: 'The twelfth–century Englishwoman who desired a religious life had three choices: she could become a nun, and anchoress, or a hermitess', i.e. an unenclosed solitary. Many of these women later came under pressure to leave their isolation and enter a cenobitic community.[69]

Gilbert's asceticism owed as much to the eremitial as to the monastic tradition, and his reluctance to be clothed in the habit of a canon until persuaded in old age and with reluctance by his followers testifies to his desire to withdraw from active involvement in the cenobitic life.[70] The order certainly possessed at least one hermitage in the fens, while there was a recluse at Watton in the 1150s. These do not of course add up to a fully eremitical community but certainly reveal the influence of eremitism.[71] Ultimately Gilbert and his houses were integrated into fully–organised monastic communities, but there had clearly been tensions in that slow transition.[72] Like so many of his contemporaries the very success of the holy men and the growing needs, temporal as much as spiritual, of his followers meant a choice had to be made between flight or organisation. Gilbert chose the first alterative when he went to Citeaux; when that failed he had perforce to create an order and a rule.

The arrangement by which the community at Sempringham was looked after by lay women who passed all necessities through the window is more suggestive of an anchoress community like that of the Ancrene Wisse than a small nunnery. Yet the use of female servants brought problems of temptation to which Benedict of Aniane had long ago drawn attention.[73] The solution was the introduction of a lay sisterhood. According to Gilbert's own account this was done on the advice of the first abbot of Rievaulx (i.e. William, abbot from 1132 to 1145).[74] If this was so, then the model for these women was presumably the 'conversi' of the Cistercian. The first recruits were the original servants of the community who requested that they too be given a habit. Gilbert's response was to attempt to dissuade them by giving them a rule of the utmost austerity in order to test their vocation, and he obliged them to wait for a year before acceptance. The lay sisters are the element of Gilbert's communities about which least is known; all we are told in the *Vita* is that they had experienced great poverty and had resorted to begging, and that this experience certainly helped persuade them to join the community.[75]

The next development was the introduction of 'conversi'. Gilbert wrote how since he only had 'seculares' to look after his goods, he acquired hired labourers ('mercenarii') to whom he offered the same conditions as to the lay sisters, giving them the same habit as the Cistercian *fratres*.[76] The Vita's account is similar, telling how men were employed as *famuli* to carry out the more external and heavier tasks of the community. Like the lay sisters these were said to have been recruited from the poorest elements of rural society; some were those raised by Gilbert himself from their youth at his own expense, others were escaped serfs who had been freed in the name of religion, and others were extremely poor and beggars. These men just as their female counterparts begged Gilbert to allow them to join the community.[77]

During the 1130s the group at Sempringham must have been very similar to eremitical and semi–eremitical communities that could be found all across contemporary western Europe. It probably continued to rely for its sustenance upon the income from the two churches at which Gilbert was rector, combined with local alms and perhaps additional sums from Gilbert's patrimony. There is no evidence or surviving charter that any local lord had as yet made any landed endowment for the group's maintenance. The community at Sempringham was not yet Sempringham priory.

Between *c* 1132 and 1147 Gilbert's followers marked time. One new foundation, Haverholme, was established in 1139 but contrary to Gilbert's own account and the *Vita* there were no major expansion.[78] The story of the early flowering of the communities is given within the context of the account of Gilbert's visit to Citeaux in 1147. Gilbert wrote how the life of his nuns found approval with wealthy lords who gave him lands on which to build and how, since there were no clerks ('religiosi literati') necessary for the rule of the women and the lay brothers, he went to Citeaux in order to hand over his communities to the Cistercians' control The author of the *Vita* in more expansive style writes how wealthy and noble Englishmen brought land, estates, and many possessions and how under Gilbert's guidance they began to build many monasteries in many regions.[79] Yet there is no evidence that any substantial grants were being made at this time, and no Gilbertine foundation other than Sempringham and Haverholme can be certainly dated before *c* 1150. According to the *Vita* Gilbert was reluctant to receive these grants, and indeed rejected many, only accepting some of these benefactions because he was reluctant to oppose God's will, hinder the devotion of benefactors, or neglect the support of God's servants.[80]

The one new community to be founded during this period was Haverholme, founded by bishop Alexander at the end of 1139.[81] The 'handmaidens of Christ' of Alexander's charter were said to follow a hard and holy life, the life of the Cistercian monks as far as the weakness of their sex allowed. We do not know if this community of nuns was sent out from Sempringham because the original group there was becoming too large or whether this was an entirely new group, nor can we tell how it was ministered to, though clearly Gilbert himself could not look after Sempringham and Haverholme at the same time, even though the two communities were not many miles apart. Most interesting is the reference of the women following the Cistercian way of life.[82] While the rules followed by both the lay sisters and brethren were said to be based on Cistercian models, there is no other evidence that the nuns followed a version of the Cistercian rule at this time. The later rule of the nuns as defined by Gilbert after his return from Citeaux was Benedictine, and while this does not necessarily deny a Cistercian interpretation it is likely that the *Vita* would have specified that the nuns followed the Cistercian way of life if they had done so. It is of course possible, or even probable, that abbot William also advised Gilbert on the rule of his community, as well as suggesting a way of life for the lay sisters, but since the Cistercians at this time had no houses for women, any such rule must have had to be substantially modified for Gilbert's use. Perhaps a more likely explanation for Alexander's description is that by this time the term 'Cistercian' may have become almost generic, synonymous with any reformed monastic grouping following the Benedictine rule.

The establishment of a second house forced Gilbert to face up to the difficult problem of how to order a community primarily established for women but which necessarily also included men. The question was of course one which had always perplexed the Church and which acquired considerable urgency at the end of the eleventh and through the twelfth century.[83] The response to the problem varied considerably. One solution frequently employed was for a community of women to be linked to a small neighbouring house of monks, who would provide spiritual services and who often had a supervisory role over the women. This arrangement was that adopted, for example, at Marcigny, the early double houses of Prémontré, and at Fontevraud. At Arrouaise the communities, though constitutionally linked, seem to have been physically some way apart.[84] Proximity was dangerous; sometimes communities were moved in order that they be further away from each other. Some reformers were not so prepared to compromise. Stephen of Grandmont allegedly moved away from Gaucher of Aureil to avoid the temptation of Gaucher's female followers.[85] By contrast Gilbert was not troubled by the presence of his women followers; his flight to Citeaux seems to have been rather a flight from responsibility. Whatever the reason for it the journey to Citeaux marked a turning point in the history of the Gilbertine communities.

Though in social and education background Stephen and Gilbert were in many ways alike, they came to Citeaux by essentially different paths. Gilbert, though displaying many eremitical characteristics such as a love of poverty and an ascetic way of life, was not a hermit in the sense that Stephen was. Gilbert's life was much more stable, his vocation after his spell in the episcopal household was essentially that of the conscientious parish priest and he showed no desire to leave his parish. Stephen by contrast commenced his career as a parish priest but gave this up to lead the life of a solitary. Of all the distinctions between the two men's careers, two in particular stand out. Stephen chose the life of a hermit, he attracted followers and gradually his heritage was transformed into a monastery.[86] In the case of Gilbert the eremitical dynamic came not from the saint but from his disciples, the seven women who first wished to live as anchoresses under his care. Thus Gilbert was a director of hermits, sympathetic to the eremitical life, but never one himself. He thus stands in the conservative tradition of Anselm, Ailred and other monastic spiritual advisors of holy women, rather than that of the new radicalism exemplified by such charismatic figures as Robert of Arbrissel, Gerald of Salles or Stephen. Secondly (and in some respects this follows from the first point) Sempringham was from the start a community of religious women to which a male element was necessarily attached, rather than a group of men, who were later joined by female recruits. For all the superficial resemblances of the organisation and in the physical layout of the buildings, especially the church, there were fundamental differences between Obazine—Coyroux and Sempringham Coyroux was a dependency of Obazine, though physically separate; Sempringham was a juridical unity, and even, if it is not achronistic to use the term before the emergence of the Gilbertine order after 1147, a double house. These distinctions may well have played their part in determining the outcome of 1147.

Gilbert's own account attributes his journey to Citeaux in 1147 to the expansion of his communities and his failure to recruit *religiosi literati* to look after and rule over the women and the lay brethren and sisters. This was done in order that he might commit 'our house, the handmaidens of Christ and our brethren to their i.e. the Cistercians' rule'. However he was totally frustrated in his purpose and so, forced by necessity, he appointed Augustinian canons to undertake the care of the order.[87] His initial choice is explained by the *Vita*; he knew more about the Cistercians since they had often given him hospitality, and they were more perfect and stricter than others in their observance of the religious life.[88] Such an explanation is certainly plausible; as we have seen, abbot William had already played an important part in helping Gilbert devise regulations for his followers, and there were now Cistercian abbeys in Lincolnshire such as Louth Park or Revesby of which Gilbert must have known. The Cistercians were a good choice or a local reformer who wanted to leave the direct care of his communities to others. According to the *Vita* Gilbert was conscious of his own weakness (which may have been physical as much as spiritual; he was already in his mid–60s) and wanted to commit the group to those stronger and more capable than himself. Such a move made sense to Gilbert: it did not make equal sense to the Cistercians. Nevertheless Gilbert would seem to have made a good impression on the pope and Bernard of Clairvaux. Eugenius ordered Gilbert to continue the rule of his communities. Gilbert protested his age and general unfitness for this burden, fearing too that he would be deflected from meditation by administrative duties, as far that is a further indication of Gilbert's eremitical leanings. It would appear that Gilbert moved from Citeaux to Clairvaux. He was certainly there in October 1148, and may well have stayed with the Cistercians throughout the period from the end of the Citeaux council until the end of 1148. The author of the *Vita* stresses Gilbert's close friendship both with Bernard and with Malachi, archbishop of Armagh. This may be exaggerated. By the time the *Vita* was produced new orders were everywhere under criticism. To stress the intimacy with Bernard may have one way for the Gilbertines to deflect any criticism from themselves. Similarly Malachi's role may have been fairly minimal. He only arrived at Clairvaux for his last visit in October 1148, by the beginning of November he was dead.[89]

Apparently Stephen had for many years wanted to place his communities under the care of Citeaux.[90] This would of course accord with the account given of his journey to La Chartreuse, but as already suggested the enthusiasm for Citeaux may have been less apparent and more slowly maturing than implied in the *Vita*. Certainly Reinard, abbot of Citeaux from 1133 to 1150, is presented as one of the chief patrons of Stephen.[91] But there were problems at the 1147 chapter. Monks from Uzerche and recently come to Eugenius III to complain that their abbot had deserted them for Obazine and this inter–communal dispute could have had serious consequences for Stephen's ambitions.[92] Undoubtedly Eugenius' opinion would be critical in determining the future of the order, and it was to him, therefore, that Stephen first addressed his request. Eugenius next summoned Reinard and entrusted Stephen to him. Reinard presented him to the assembled abbots who all accepted him 'as a man of God' into the Cistercian order: 'it was his sanctity and the will of the pope that led them to take this decision'.[99] But there was of course one real difficulty to overcome; the women of Coyroux. As the *Vita* recognised, the religious life for women was acceptable but it was contrary to Cistercian custom. By accepting Obazine and Coyroux the Cistercians would for the first time be accepting formal responsibility for nuns; the two communities were closely linked juridically, one could not be disengaged from the other. An exception to the rule was made due to the influence of the pope and the abbot, but for a long time Coyroux remained the only female house incorporated *de jure* into the Cistercian order.[94] There is indeed a hint in the *Vita* that the proposal to accept Stephen was not wholly popular for reference is made to the *individia* or *molestia* felt by some because Stephen had accepted women. Once again Reinard is shown as the chief instigator of the incorporation; he gave assurance that everything contrary to the Cistercian order would be abolished gradually, since a new house could not survive rapid change. The most substantial concession was that nuns could always live in the order.[95]

After the Citeaux settlement we hear little more of the Obazine nuns in the *Vita*. Monks and *conversi* came from Citeaux to teach the Cistercian way of life and to bring Cistercian service books. Their work can have had little relevance for the women of Coyroux. There is, however, a telling reference to discontent amongst them. It would appear that shortly before Stephen's death some of the community had left on hearing a 'false rumour' that while they would be allowed to stay at Coyroux no new recruits would be admitted. Certainly there must have been concern about the future of women in the community following 1147: the concession that nuns could remain in the order was in fact ambiguous Did it just refer to the nuns who were already there or to future generations? The account of the nuns' secession is far from clear; they are said to have left with full authorisation and to have chosen to go to another Obazine house, that of La Garde—Dieu which had been founded in the diocese of Cahors after 1147 and which was ruled by abbot Gerald, who later succeeded Stephen as abbot of Obazine. It is probably that they settled at Fontmourlhes, which though a dependency of La Garde Dieu was some 40 miles away. This community had considerable autonomy and remained a house for women into the next century. The *Vita* confesses ignorance as to how the nuns left, who instigated them, and how they lived at La Garde—Dieu. The most recent historian of Obazine has suggested that what may have been the issue here was a temporary ban on recruitment imposed because of economic difficulties, which might then have been seen by some of the women as the prelude to either a total ban or the disbandment of their community. She also suggests (less plausibly) that the initiative for the move may have come from the diocesan bishop who still retained some jurisdiction over the nuns. What is certain is that all did not go well for them and that, like the prodigal son, they returned to Coyroux. The most likely reason for their difficulties was probably that their sudden influx into a new house put severe pressure on its economic base.[96]

It remains to consider why the Obazine houses were accepted in 1147 while those of Gilbert were rejected. Gilbert himself offered no explanation. In the following generation it was recorded that the pope and the Cistercian abbots said that their order were not allowed authority over others' religious life, especially that of women.[97] Yet this excuse will palpably not hold water. Obazine (and Savigny) had facilities for women, and though this may have occasioned reluctance, in their case the Cistercians overcame their scruples and absorbed both orders. Writing at the very beginning of the thirteenth century when the Gilbertine order was at the peak of is popularity, it must have been difficult for the *Vita*'s author to explain Cistercian misgivings other than by reference to their distrust of women in their houses, and he may well have been unaware that Savigny and Obazine had been accepted in 1147. Viewed from the

Cistercians' prospective, however, the 'appeal' of Gilbert was limited. Gilbert had no powerful patrons. Bishop Alexander (whose support is in any case hard to determine) had just died; William, abbot of Rivan had died two years earlier. By contrast Stephen had the active support both of the pope and the abbot of Citeaux, while Bernard seems to have supported Serlo of Savigny in his desire to bring his houses under Cistercian control. What is more Gilbert's 'rule' was inchoate; his own commitment to his followers less than certain; and there were, as yet, only two poorly–endowed communities. For all that Stephen had taken many years to determine how he was to rule his communities, by 1147 the 'order' of Obazine was well–established with Stephen no longer merely 'magister' but 'abbas' and with his followers clearly organised. By contract Gilbert still had no formal rule, all was dependent upon his will: Sempringham in 1147 was still a 'first–generation' house, rather like Obazine had been before 1142. The future of Sempringham can hardly have seemed assured in September 1147, with its less than enthusiastic leader, its lack of priests, canons or monks, and its predominant population of women. For the Cistercians to take over Gilbert's houses was a gamble, the fact that they consisted (unlike both Savigny and Obazine) *primarily* of, and for, women probably tipped the balance. It was a difficult enough task (as would shortly be seen) for two relatively flourishing and well–organised orders to be affiliated to the Cistercians, the Gilbertines posed much greater, and insurmountable, problems.

NOTES

1. J.M. Canivez, *Statuta Capitulorum Generalium Ordinis Cisterciensis* (7 vols., Louvain, 1933–41), i., pp 37–38,
2. For the expansion of the Cistercians see R.A. Donkin, 'The Growth and Distribution of the Cistercian Order in Medieval Europe', *Studia Monastica* 9 (1967), pp 167–225.
3. Grandselve is discussed by C.H. Berman, 'Mens' Houses, Womens' Houses: the Relationship between the Sexes in Twelfth–Century Monasticism' in *Medieval Studies at Minnesota 2: the Medieval Monastery*, ed.,A. MacLeish (St. Cloud, Minnesota, 1988), [hereafter Berman, 'Mens' Houses, Womens' Houses'], pp 46–47.
4. For the English opposition to the takeover of Savigny see B.D. Hill, *English Cistercian Monasteries and their Patrons in the Twelfth Century* (Urbana, 1968), pp 105–107.
5. The standard study of Obazine is B. Barrière, *L'Abbaye cistercienne d'Obazine* (Tulle, 1977) [hereafter Barrière, *Obazine*]. For Sempringham see R. Graham, S Gilbert of Sempringham and the Gilbertines (London, 1903) and the introduction to *The Book of St Gilbert*, eds., R. Foreville and G. Keir (Oxford, 1987) [hereafter *The Book of St Gilbert*]. especially xlvii–lii. I have discussed the status of the nuns in the early communities in 'The Distortion of a Dream: Transformations and Mutations of the Rule of St Gilbert', *Word and Spirit* 11 (1989), pp 60–78. The male element in the Gilbertine communities was only introduced after Gilbert's return from Citeaux in 1148.
6. There is now a considerable literature on the status of women in the Cistercian order. Particularly useful are M. Fontette, *Les Religieuses a l'age clasique du droit canon* (Paris, 1967) [hereafter Fontett, *Les Religieuses*], pp 29–41; Thompson, 'The Problem of the Cistercian Nuns in the Twelfth and Early–Thirteenth Centuries' in ed., D. Baker, *Medieval Women* (Oxford, 1978) [hereafter Thompson, 'Cistercian Nuns'], pp 227–253, and Berman, 'Mens' Houses, Womens' Houses', pp 43–52.

7. The Vita of Stephen of Obazine has been edited with a French translation
    and introduction by M. Aubrum, *Vita Stephani Obazinensis* (Institut
    d'Etudes du Massif Central, fasc. VI, Clermont Ferrand, 1970) [hereafter
    Via Stephani]. His early years are described on pp 42–44.
8. *Ibid.*, pp 44–46. He is later said to have once been priest at Pleaux (*Ibid.*,
    p 164).
9. *Ibid.*, p 46. Eremitical poverty is discussed by H. Leyser, *Hermits and the
    New Monasticism* (London, 1984) [hereafter Leyser, *Hermits*], pp 52–56.
    See also L.K. Little, *Religious Poverty and the Profit Economy in Medieval
    Europe* (London, 1978) [hereafter Little, *Religious Poverty*], pp 70–83.
10. *Vita Stephani*, p 46.
11. *Ibid.*, p 48. for hermits' companions see Leyser, *Hermits*, p 39.
12. *Vita Stephani*, p 48 and n. 22, p 49.
13. These questions are discussed by J. Becquet, 'L'Erémitisme clérical et laïc
    dans l'ouest de la France' in *L'Eremitismo in Occidente nei secoli XI e
    XII* (Miscellanea del Centro di Studi Medioevali IV, Milan, 1965), p 185;
    G. Constable, 'Eremitical Forms of Monastic Life' in *Istituzioni
    Monastiche e Istituzioni Canonicali in Occidente (1123–1215)* (Miscellanea
    del Centro di Studi Medioevali IX, Milan, 1980), pp 239–264; C.N.L.
    Brooke,''Monk and Canon: some Patterns in the Religious Life of the
    Twelfth Century' in ed., W. Shiels, *Monks, Hermits and the Ascetic
    Tradition* (Studies in Church History, 22, 1985), pp 109–129, and by C.W.
    Walker, 'The Spirituality of Regular Canons in the Twelfth Century' in
    Jesus as Mother (Berkeley and Los Angeles, 1982), especially pp 22–36.
14. *Vita Stephani*, pp 50–52.
15. *Ibid.*, p 54.
16. *Ibid.*, p 54. For the role of bishops as supporters of hermits see Leyser,
    'Hermits', p 93. The writings of the Fathers were frequently taken as
    models by eremitical groups: see e.g. Leyser, *Hermits*, pp 27–28.
17. *Vita Stephani*, p 65. See above, n. 13.
18. *Ibid.*, pp 54–56.
19. *Ibid.*, pp 58–60.
20. *Ibid.*, p 60.
21. *Ibid.*, pp 64–66.
22. *Ibid.*, p 70. The unstructured nature of most eremitical communities and
    the concomitant authority of the *magister* has been much discussed but
    see especially, L. Mills, 'L'évolution de l'érémitisme au canonicat
    régulier' in *Miscellanea del Centro di Studi Medioevali VII*, Milan, 1977
    [hereafter Milis, 'L'évolution de l'érémitisme'], pp 223–238 and Leyser,
    Hermits, pp 87–96.
23. P–R Gaussin, *L'Europe des ordres et des congrégations des Benedictins
    aux Mendiants (VI–XVI siecle)* (St Etiene, n.d.), p 87.
24. *Vita Stephani*, pp 76–78; *The Book of St Gilbert*, p 87.
25. *Vita Stephani*, pp 78–80, 25. While staying at Lyon his distrust of the
    regular canons was reinforced by their violent refusal to give him any
    hospitality. When their house burnt down that same night Stephen's
    companion and his biographer saw this as no more than their just desserts.
26. *Ibid.*, p 82.
27. For Pons of Leras and the Carthusians see Berman, 'Mens' Houses,
    Womens' Houses', p 46. The authorship of the *Vita* is discussed by M.
    Aubrun in *Vita Stephani*, pp 7–8.
28. *Vita Stephani*, p 86. The daughter houses were at Bonnaigue and Le
    Pestre (*Ibid.*, pp 106–108). See Barrière, *Obazine*, p 67 and n. 66.
29. *Vita Stephani*, pp 82–84.
30. *Ibid.*, p 88.

31. The provisions for women in the Limouisin are discussed by Barrière, *Obazine*, pp 98–100,

32. *Vita Stephani*, pp 98, 100; Barrière, *Obazine*, pp 99, 103.

33. See e.g. Leyser, *Hermits*, pp 49–51.

34. *Vita Stephani*, pp 94–96.

35. *Ibid.*, pp 86–88. The estate has been identified by Barrière as the grant of Montredon (*Obazine*, pp 123–4; 152–3).

37. Barrière, *Obazine*, pp 123–5; Thompson, 'Cistercian Nuns', pp 229–230; the events at Citeaux are described in the *Exordium Parvun* in eds., J. Bouton and J–B. van Damme *Les plus anciens textes de Citeaux* (Citeaux–Commentarii Cisterciences II, Achel, 1974), p 82. A. Bredero has shewn, however, that the earliest manuscripts of the *Vita Prima* of St Bernard date his entry to Citeaux to 1113, *Etudes sur la 'Vita Prima'* (Rome, 1960) p 59 n. 68.

38. *Vita Stephani*, pp 88–90. The arrangements made for the daily life of the nuns are discussed in more detail below.

39. *Ibid.*, p 96. The fear that a community would collapse on the death of its founder if there was no written rule was commonplace and a frequent catalyst for a more formal organisation. The canons of Sempringham were very concerned that their way of life would be threatened if Gilbert died without being formally received into the order, and used this argument to persuade him to wear a canon's habit (*The Book of St Gilbert*, pp 66–68).

40. *Vita Stephani*, p 96.

41. *Ibid.*, p 106. The 'insertion' of clerics, either monks or canons, was a frequent cause of discontent, as occurred most notoriously at Sempringham and Grandmont, where the *conversi* felt that they were being edged out of positions of authority by the newcomers.

42. *Ibid.*, pp 96–98.

43. *Ibid.*, p 98; *Historie des Conciles*, V.i. 732–3.

44. *Vita Stephani*, pp 98–100.

45. For a wide–ranging discussion of the problems involved see J.T. Schulenberg, 'Strict Active Enclosure and its Effects on the Female Monastic Experience (500–1100)' in eds., J.A. Nichols and L.T. Shank, *Medieval Religious Women, i. Distant Echoes* (Cistercian Studies 71, Kalamazoo, 1984), pp 51–86.

46. A number of expedients were employed: but it is at Coyroux and Sempringham that perhaps the most careful regulations were laid down.

47. *Vita Stephani*, p 100.

48. *Ibid.*, p 106.

49. *Ibid.*, pp 106–108.

50. *The Book of St Gilbert*, p 10; A. Murray, *Reason and Society* (Oxford, 1978), part IV, 'Nobility and Religion', pp 317–404, especially 'Nobly born saints', pp 337–341.

51. *The Book of St Gilbert*, p 12.

53. *Ibid.*, p xxiii.

53. Foreville (*Ibid.*, xviii) has suggested that he may have gone to Normandy, perhaps to the west of the duchy to Avranches or Caen but this is speculation and it is just as likely that he went to Paris. It is also possible that he studied at Laon as suggested by M.R. James, 'The Salomites', *Journal of Theological Studies* 35 (1934), pp 287–297. I am grateful to Professor Christopher Holdsworth for this suggestion.

54. *The Book of St Gilbert*, pp 14–16.

55. *Ibid.*, pp 16–20.

56. *Ibid.*, p 20. The problem of unlicenced preaching (particularly by charismatics both orthodox and heterodox) was to exercise ecclesiastical

authorities throughout the century (Leyser, *Hermits*, pp 74–77).

57. *Ibid.*, pp 20–22.
58. *Ibid.*, pp 24–26.
59. *Ibid.*, pp 28–30.
60. *Ibid.*, p 30. The fullest study of voluntary poverty in this period remains Little, *Religious Poverty*, especially part II, pp 59–96.
61. Monastic 'corruption' and its historiography are discussed in J. van Engen, 'The "Crisis of Cenobitism" Reconsidered: Benedictine Monasticism in the Years 1050–1150', *Speculum* 61 (1986), pp 269–304.
62. For Norbert see H.M. Colvin, *The White Canons in England* (Oxford, 1951), p 2. The gospel text the *Vita* author cites: 'If you wish to be perfect, go and sell all that you have, and give to the poor, and come follow me' (Matt. 19.21) is frequently associated with the twelfth–century reformers.
63. *The Book of St Gilbert*, pp 30–8.
64. *Ibid.*, p 30; W Dugdale, *Monasticon Anglicanum*, eds., J. Caley, H. Ellis and B. Bandinel (6 vols., London, 1817–30) [hereafter Dugdale, *Monasticon*], vi. pt. ii'xix (between pages 946 and 947).
65. Ed., E.M. Poynton, 'Charters relating to the Priory at Sempringham', *Genealogist*, n.s. 15 (1898–9), p 158; ed., D.M. Smith, *English Episcopal Acta I Lincoln 1067–1185* (Oxford, 1980), pp 24–25.
66. *The Book of St Gilbert*, pp 32–34; Dugdale, *Monasticon* vi.pt.ii,'xix . For the role of the bishop see A.K. Warren, *Anchorites and their Patrons in Medieval England* (Berkeley and Los Angeles, 1985) [hereafter Warren, *Anchorites*], pp 53–63.
67. *The Book of Gilbert*, p 34; Warren, *Anchorites*, pp 92–101; *The English Text of the Ancrene Riwle: Ancrene Wisse*, ed. from MS. Corpus Christi College, Cambridge 402 by J.R.R. Tolkien (Early English Text Society, original series 249, 1962), pp 75–75.
68. Eds., G. Constable and B. Smith., *Libellus de Diversis Ordinibus et Professionibus qui sunt in Aecclesia* (Oxford, 1972), p 4.
69. A.K. Warren, 'The Nun as Anchoress' in eds., J.A. Nichols and L.T. Shank, *Medieval Religious Women, i. Distant Echoes* (Cistercian Studies 71, Kalamazoo, 1984), pp 196–212.
70. *The Book of St Gilbert*, pp 66–68. See above, n. 39.
71. The Gilbertine hermitage in the Licolnshire fens provided a refuge for Becket on his flight from the Council of Northampton, eds., J.C. Robertson and J.B. Sheppard, *Materials for the History of Thomas Becket, Archbishop of Canterbury* (7 vols., Rolls Series, London, 1875–85), iii, p 324. The Watton recluse is described in ed., E.A. Bond, *Chronica Monasterii de Melsa a fundatione usque ad annum 1396*, (3 vols., Rolls Series, London, 1866–68), i. 107.
72. The difficulties encountered in the transformation of an eremitical to a cenobitical community are discussed by Milis, 'L'évolution de l'érémitisme', pp 223–238 and 'Ermites et chanoines réguliers au XII siècle', *Cahirs de Civilisation Medievale* 22 (1979), pp 39–80.
73. Warren, *Anchorites*, pp 105–109.
74. Dugdale, *Monasticon*, vi. pt ii.'xix .
75. *The Book of St Gilbert*, p 36.
76. Dugdale, *Monasticon* vi. pt ii.'xix .
77. *The Book of Gilbert*, pp 36–38.
78. It is very difficult to date with any precision the early Gilbertine priories but none (apart from Sempringham and Haverholme) seem to have been in existence before Gilbert's return from Citeaux *c* 1148.
79. *The Book of St Gilbert*, pp 38–40; Dugdale, *Monasticon*, vi.pt ii.'xix.

80. *The Book of St Gilbert*, pp 39–40.
81. The foundation charter is printed in ed., D.M. Smith, *English Episcopal Acta I Lincoln 1067–1185* (Oxford, 1980), pp 24–25.
82. 'He vitam artam, vitam sanctam, vitam scilicet monachorum Cistersensis religionis arripientes, quantum illius sexus valitudo permittit, eam tenere contendunt et tenent'. A number of English nunners, including Nun Cotham and Sinningthwaite, though not *stricto sensu* Cistercian, similarly followed Cistercian customs (Thompson, 'Cistercian Nuns', pp 242–252. See also C. Graves, 'English Cistercian Nuns in Lincolnshire' *Speculum* 54 (1979), pp 492–499.
83. Here is not the place to discuss the vexed question of 'double monasteries' but see Fontete, *Les Religieuses*, for an illuminating overview of twelfth–century developments.
84. For the nuns of Arrouaise see L. Milis, *L'Ordre des chanoines reguliers d'Arrouiase* (Ghent, 1969), i. pp 502–517. Amongst a considerable literature on Fontevraud see P.S. Gold, *The Lady and the Virgin: Image, Attitude and Experience in Twelfth–Century France* (Chicago, 1985), pp 93–115; J. Bienvenu, 'Aux origines d'un ordre religieux: Robert d'Arbrissel et la fondation de Fontevraud (1101)', *Cahiers d'Histoire* 20 (1975), pp 226–251; J. Smith, 'Procurator Mulierum' in *Medieval Women*, ed., D. Baker (Studies in Church History: Subsidia 1, Oxford, 1978), pp 175–184, and R. Niderst, *Robert d'Arbrissel et les origines de l'Ordre de Fontevrault* (Rodez, 1952). There is no full study of Marcigny, though the cartulary has been edited by J. Richard, *La cartulaire de Marcigny–sur–Loire* (Dijon, 1957) and see the same author's 'Sur l'histoire du prieure de Marcigny aux XI et XII siecles', in *Melanges d'histoire et d'archaeologie offerts a professeur Kenneth John Conant* (Macon, 1977), pp 135–40. For the nuns of Premontre see A. Erens, 'Les soeurs dans l'ordre de Premontre', *Analecta Praemonstratensis* 5 (1929) pp 5–26 and Fontette, especially pp 18–19. Particularly useful for English developments is H.M. Colvin, *The White Canons in England* (Oxford, 1951), pp 327–336.
85. Leyser, *Hermits*, p 50.
86. He thus is clearly part of the general trend amongst contemporary hermits to be absorbed into a cenobitic foundation.
87. Dugdale, *Monasticon*, vi. pt.ii 'xix; *The Book of St Gilbert*, pp 42–44.
88. *The Book of St Gilbert*, p 40. Sempringham also had links with the Cistercians via the Gant family, lords of Sempringham, since Gilbert de gant, earl of Lincoln, had founded Rufford in 1146 after lengthy negotiations with Rievaulx. I owe this reference to Professor Christopher Holdsworth.
89. The last days of Malachi are described by Bernard of Clairvaux in his Life *Patrologiae Latinae* 182, pp 1114–8.
90. *Vita Stephani*, p 110.
91. *Ibid.*, pp 110–114.
92. *Ibid.*, pp 112 and 113 n. 29.
93. *Ibid.*, p 112.
94. *Ibid.*, pp 112–114; Barrière, *Obazine*, pp 92–3, 95–6.
95. *Ibid.*, p 112.
96. *Ibid.*, p 198; Barrière, *Obazine*, pp 102–108.
97. *The Book of St Gilbert*, p 42.

FOR THE SEE OF SIMON PETER : THE CISTERCIANS AT INNOCENT III'S NEAREST FRONTIER

Brenda Bolton

From the very first moment of his election on 8 January 1198 Innocent III was acutely aware that he was successor to the Fisherman of Galilee, the Apostle Simon Peter.[1] At his consecration on 22 February, coincidentally the Feast of St Peter's Chair in Antioch, he became even more convinced of his inheritance.[2] On this day, when he became Bishop of Rome, he believed that the chair on which he sat for the ceremony was the same one which the feast day celebrated.[3] As was to be expected, tales of a vision were brought to him to consolidate these feelings. This vision, told by an aged priest and recorded in the Chapter Archives of St Peter's, reported that, while the priest slept, St Peter himself had appeared saying 'Go to Pope Innocent and tell him from me that from the day of his birth, I have loved him like a son. Now, having been promoted through all the grades of the priesthood, he has at last come to my seat'.[4] The message of this vision was crystal—clear reinforcing what Innocent himself believed. The work of the Apostle Simon Peter, whose faith Christ had prayed would not fail him and who had received the message to strengthen the brethren, was to be continued by his successor Innocent.

There was much work to be done and not withstanding his primacy of position as pope the help of others would be essential. Problems came right up to the gates of Rome itself and even arose within the City.[5] In the surrounding area, more German than Italian under Philip of Swabia and his henchmen, Markward of Anweiler, Conrad of Marlenheim and Diepoldo of Acerra, there was little interest in furthering the aims of the church.[6] The Patrimony belonged to St Peter in name alone[7] and while the Germans did not then control Campania they were still feared there more than the pope himself. In Rome the noble families, the *consortoria*, were linked and inter—linked by marriage ties and intrigue.[8] The support of a majority of these was vital to any new pope and could never be taken for granted even if the pope was, as in Innocent's case, himself a Roman. These families were notoriously fickle. The caustic comments of St Bernard remind us of this when, in his own outspoken way, he called them both irreverent and factious.[9] Neither Germans nor Romans could be counted upon to support the pope, rather the reverse. Various measures would have to be taken to bring Rome and the Patrimony more into line with what was expected of the see of Simon Peter and Innocent seems to have decided quite early on that he could best work through monastic institutions.[10] The Cistercian Order seemed to him to be particularly suitable for the tasks he had in mind. His letter to the General Chapter in September 1198 asking for Cistercian help plays on the Martha—Mary, Leah—Rachel imagery where contemplation and action were both needed.[11] He refers to himself as the helmsman in the barque of St Peter, where on storm—tossed seas the Apostle stretches out his right hand to save those in danger. Further, he promises that with St Peter, where on storm—tossed seas the Apostle stretches out his right hand to save those in danger. Further, he promises that with St Peter, their feet will be led to dry ground and there will be no danger to them of being drowned by worldly affairs.[12]

By the end of the twelfth century the Cistercians who, in St Bernard's words, were 'the restorers of lost religion'[13] had, through their remarkably strong organisation achieved much well—deserved acclaim.[14] However, the considerable donations, privileges and exemptions which had accumulated around them were contrary not only to the ascetic spirit of their founding fathers but also that that of St Benedict. Whilst the Cistercians themselves were open to criticism, the papacy too bore some responsibility for this situation.[15] Cistercians everywhere had sought and obtained a whole series of papal privileges which exempted their abbeys from local episcopal control and from paying tithes on their own lands. Such exemptions jeopardized the observance of their rule and their life of poverty at the desert margins and the order acquired instead a reputation for avarice and greed.[16] This caused Walter Map to rail and grumble that they had become the new Jews of Europe.[17] They were tempted to assert their independence not only from local bishops but also from the pope himself. But the responsibility of a pope as *abbas universalis* had become an increasingly important charge, transforming the apostolic protection of St Peter into a papal institutions expressing the exercise of the pope's jurisdiction over the whole church. This reached its highest development during the pontificate of Innocent III, expressed as it was in his confident formula of association of the pope with St Peter *sub beati Petri et nostra protectione suscipimus*.[18]

Innocent clearly admired the undoubted qualities of the Cistercians, their organisation, filiation and mutual supervision. They were ideally suited as crusade preachers and organisers and as frontier guards of the faith in those areas where the Church's writ ran weakly. Other aspects did not please him so well — as when in 1198 he was blamed for having excused the Abbot of Sambucina from the General Chapter to allow him instead to preach the Crusade in Sicily[19] — or when the mother house of Cîteaux fell into internecine quarreling in 1202 with her four daughters, La Ferté, Pontigny, Clairvaux and Morimond.[20] What was seen by Innocent as his duty to intervene when things needed to be remedied to improve the Order was seen by the Cistercians as an unwarranted intrusion into matters which only they could regulate through their institutions. Later Cistercian hagiography *c*1230 was to emphasize any resentment there may have been by indicating by just how narrow a margin Innocent had escaped going to Hell.[21] In actual fact, Innocent surrounded himself with able, intelligent and willing Cistercians, using them as legates, as commissioners of enquiry and as his confessors and chaplains. Spiritually outstanding amongst these was Brother Rainier,[22] the Andrew to Innocent's Peter.

Although Innocent enjoyed variable relations with the Order as a whole, the situation in the Patrimony closer to Rome meant that all minds, including those of the Cistercians, had to be concentrated upon the tasks in hand. The sudden death of the young German Emperor, Henry VI, in September 1197 was to present Innocent and his local Cistercian allies with a unique opportunity. Their nearest frontier was not in some far—distant place in Poland or Pomerania or even in the Baltic or Iberia. It was quite literally in those areas within the Patrimony in German hands and where ecclesiastical authority needed to be restored.[23]

Maccarrone has clearly shown how Innocent's policy towards the *Patrimonium beati Petri* was from the outset conceived in terms of reform and recovery expressed through his use of the terms *recuperatio* and papal *solicitudo*.[24] The Church, sometimes obliged to conduct political actions to restore papal territory, faced the risk that in a deteriorating situation it might be forced to resort to the same methods as those of the local lords.[25] Innocent balanced this with the need to bring peace and stability to the region. He sincerely believed that unless he could guarantee powerful overlordship, not only of Rome but of the whole Patrimony, he could not as heir to the Apostle, carry out his duty to the universal church. His justification was that the Church had received its dominion from that power given by Christ to St Peter and his successors.[26] The programme of papal government for the area was both astute and appealing. After the yoke of unbearable German oppression, that harsh military government exercised by the functionaries of Henry VI and so often experienced by the people of the Patrimony, Innocent's papal alternative offered an easy yoke and a light burden.[27] Apostolic protection and papal government in this region would be mild for laymen and monasteries alike. The pope's peace would lay stress on justice, peace and a secure road system where previously even a cardinal had been known to have been hijacked![28]

Along this road network, on the great Roman arteries going North and East, the Aurelia, the Clodia, the Cassia and the Flaminia, and the Appia and Latina running South, lay some of the sixteen or so strategically—placed and identifiable Cistercian houses of the Patrimony.[29] All seem to have been old foundations which became Cistercian later, for the most part during the pontificates of Adrian IV and Alexander III between 1154 and 1181.[30] two houses were close to Rome itself — Sant'Anastasia,[31] the present—day Tre Fontane, on the via Ostiense and S. Sebastiano[32] near the catacombs of the same name on the via Appia Antica. Guarding the Patrimony's Northern frontier were S Agostino and Montalto di Castro,[33] S Maria de Sala at Farnese near Lake Bolsena,[34] S Giusto at Tuscania[35] and S Niccolo at Tarquinia,[36] all in that area known as *Tuscia Romana*.[37] In South Etruria between the northern frontier of the Patrimony and Rome were two houses, Sant'Ella *Fallerense* at Castel Saint'Elia[38] and S Maria *Faleri* near Città Castellana,[39] both still bearing place—name evidence of Etruscan origins. Outside Viterbo near the Lago di Vico was S Martino al Cimino,[40] in many ways the most interesting monastery in the northern part of the Patrimony.

On his accession, Innocent acted to control this area. In the autumn of 1198 he had journeyed to Perugia returning by way of Todi, Amelia and Città Castellana receiving the homage and fidelity of the people of those areas.[41] He went on to intervene directly in the affairs of these Cistercian houses of *Tuscia Romana*. The Cistercian General Chapter of September 1199 recorded their own visitation of Faleria, S Giusto, S Martino, S Sebastiano, Sant'Anastasia and Sala so that reports of lax discipline could be investigated.[42] Apparently a number of monks were not living according to the Rule and few were sufficiently worthy to correct the rest. Further at Sant'Anastasia silence was not observed and women had gained access. The Chapter claimed the competence to correct or to find the means of correction, asking Innocent with humility and reverence that John, monk of Casamari should explain the monastic *conversatio*.[43] Innocent himself was clearly hinting at the possible dissolution of these monasteries divided as they were by quarrels amongst themselves.[44] This dark threat seems to have produced the required remedy. For thé rest of the pontificate the misdeeds of all Cistercian houses in the Patrimony as reported in the General Chapter were of the very slightest nature — trivial in the extreme. There was only one exception to this. The Statutes of the General Chapter in 1200 reveal something of the extent of indebtedness of S Martino, the house in that year owing twenty shillings in money of Lyon for business undertaken at the Curia.[45] In 1206 the abbot of its mother house at Saint—Sulpice in Bugey was ordered to reform its wayward daughter.[46] In the same year Innocent wrote to Abbot Peter and the monks of S Martino reminding them — lest they should be in any doubt — that they were by then in such an advanced state of poverty that scarcely three brothers could be maintained in the house.[47] Its possessions were all alienated and its debts formidable. Whilst the General Chapter seems to have taken the decision to abandon it altogether Innocent, 'wishing rather to encourage the spread of religion than to see it removed completely' from such a strategically–placed monastery, offered the vast sum of 1000 pounds to redeem its possessions and pay off the debts.[48]   To ensure its income, Innocent granted the church of S Salvatore near Orte with all its possessions.   This lavish investment in the Cistercians of S Martino *presso Viterbo* was by no means a waste of money, maintaining as it did a Cistercian house at an important frontier point.   The size of the gift, however, was not typical.   The 100 pounds in rent which he granted to the monastery of Faleria was a far more modest example of gifts by this pope to his Cistercians.[49]   Successful strategy was worth paying for. In 1207 S Martino was placed in the filiation of Pontigny and adopted as its 'special daughter'.[50]   In the case of S Martino, Innocent had not only acted as *abbas universalis*, over–ruling politely but firmly, the decision of the Cistercian General Chapter but also applied the same principle he was applying to Subiaco and Cassino; that modest corporate wealth was essential for the well–being of a monastery.[51]   Innocent had other links with Viterbo and its region.   It was a former imperial stronghold with a serious problem of heresy specifically legislated against in 1199,[52] 1205[53] and 1207.[54]   In 1207 he held is great three–day Parliament in the City, publicly receiving the homage of his vassals.[55]   He spent that summer there with the Curia,[56] returning again in 1209[57] and 1214.[58]

It was however to the south of Rome, in Campania and Marittima, that the two greatest and most important Cistercian houses were to be found in the Patrimony.   Fossanova near Priverno lay astride the via Appia[59] while Casamari near Veroli[60] guarded the approaches to the Regno by way of the via Latina and the Upper Liri Valley.   There were others but they were small by comparison: Marmosolio at Cisterna di Latina whose abbot requested affiliation to both Fossanova and Casamari in 1206;[61] Amaseno,[62] S Maria del Fiume at Ceccano[63] and S Niccolo, a cell at Albano Laziale.[64]   Innocent made his most generous gifts to the two great abbeys on his southern frontier.   He gave 100 pounds for the completion of the new church of Fossanova begun in 1187 and was present at its consecration on 19 June 1208[65] donating a further 100 pounds in annual income.[66]   He gave 200 ounces of gold *pro fabrica* for the rebuilding of Casamari together with a grange at Castrum and 100 pounds in annual rent.[67]   His donation of 100 pounds income to the house of Marmosolio at Cisterna[68] was comparable to the small–scale gifts to houses in the northern part of the Patrimony.

The threat to the Patrimony in the South came not from heresy but from the considerable and long–lasting German occupation which even prevented Innocent from making the journey to Montecassino, mother house of all the Benedictines, until the summer of 1208 in the tenth year of his pontificate.[69]   In the autumn of 1199, Casamari had been the stage for political intrigue, a spectacular banquet organised by the excommunicated adventurer Markward of Anweiler to welcome the papal legates.[70]   Three cardinals were sent by Innocent to receive his submission, amongst them Hugolino, then Cardinal–Priest of S Eustachio,[71] who outwitted the wily German after rumours were spread that the papal envoys risked capture if they dared to issue the papal mandate.[72]   After Markward's death the German threat was greatly lessened when in 1205 the brother, Rainier of Fossanova, received the submissions of Conrad of Marlenheim and Diepoldo of Acerra and played a crucial role in ensuring that their oaths were binding.[73]

In the North of the Patrimony Innocent had acted himself whereas in the South, mainly because of the German occupation he was forced to rely on others.

In this the houses of Fossanova and Casamari were of great importance. Earlier, both had played a dual role on the pope's behalf in trying to bring the kings of England and France to lasting peace or at least a truce.[74] While Stephen of Fossanova was commended to John by Innocent,[75] Gerald, abbot of Casamari,[76] entrusted with the mission to Philip Augustus, ran backwards and forwards between France and England[77] *de Francia ad Angliam et de Anglia ad Franciam discurrendo* for a whole year between 1203–4 – medieval shuttle–diplomacy. Such sensitive diplomatic negotiations required trusted men, well–informed and authoritative who could also appear neutral and impartial. That Innocent should have turned to the Cistercians of the Patrimony and especially to Fossanova and Casamari, should not surprise us. One man, Brother Rainier, probably the most significant Cistercian since St Bernard, provided the link between these two houses and the pope himself.

It is now on Rainier that our full attention must focus. The consequences of his spirituality, faith, life and work are striking and he could not but fail to set the highest example for the Cistercians of the Patrimony. His monastic vocation began at Casamari for there he was certainly an *intimus* of Joachim of Fiore.[78] He was again with Joachim in 1188 at Petralata and both were declared *fugitivi* by the General Chapter in 1192[79] although Rainier did not accompany him to La Sila.[80] In 1198 Rainier was Innocent's legate in Leon, Castile and Portugal[81] while in December of that year the Pope entrusted him with the official legation to Languedoc.[82] Here he was given power of interdict and excommunication and was instructed to preach together with Brother Guy against the Cathars. His last act of legation seems to have been in July 1199 when he returned from Languedoc suffering from ill–health.[83] He was still mentioned as legate at the General Chapter of 1199[84] and about this time became the Pope's own confessor.[85] Rainier then moved to Fossanova but nevertheless remained within the papal entourage. In June 1201 he was one of an important three–man commision set up to investigate the First and Second Orders of the Humiliati,[86] that is, the canonical *praepositi* and the *religiosio* leading a regular quasi–monastic life. In November and December 1201 he was with Innocent at Anagni and advised the pope, by his interpretation of a papal dream, on the canonisation process of Gilbert of Sempringham.[87] The author of *The Book of St Gilbert* provides valuable insight into the life of Rainier yet in so doing raises as many questions as he answers. Here Rainier is given the title of Abbot yet we do not know over which, if any house, he held this position. Already by 1201 he was renowned for his exemplary solitary life–style amongst the hills and greatly venerated, not only by the pope but also by the whole Church of Rome for his remarkable sanctity and knowledge. In truth, a holy man! Rainier interpreted the pope's dream with much confidence, in the best traditions of sacred history, and filled with the spirit of a Joseph or a Daniel, both great biblical interpreters of dreams.[88] His recommendation that Gilbert be canonised was judged by Innocent to require action without delay.

Innocent was also ready to receive Rainier's advice in regard to the Cistercian Order and to the memory of St Bernard for whom the pope had a special veneration. Rainier was eager to maintain the purity and stability of the Cistercians in the face of rash and childish behaviour. In 1202 Rainier encouraged Innocent to comply with the request of the Archbishop of Lyon to prepare a short collect in honour of St Bernard whilst he himself wrote a didactic letter[89] in 1203 to Arnald Amaury, new abbot of Cîteaux.[90] This letter,[91] rich in scriptural allusion from both Old and New Testaments, originated as an attempt to heal the divisions between Cîteaux and her four daughters over primacy. Much of the trouble, Rainier says, is that unsuitable people are entering the Order and asks that the Abbot should read a similar letter which Innocent had sent to him on this very question[92] The General Chapter of 1204 placed this item on its agenda asking the abbot of Casamari and Brother Nicholas, the pope's chaplain, to deal with the matter.[93]

Even more striking was the remarkable letter,[94] written probably between 1207 and 1209 by Hugolino who had been elevated to the Cardinal–Bishopric of Ostia in 1206 and created Legate to Germany soon after.[95] It was addressed to the abbots and brothers of Fossanova, Casamari and Salem[96] in Germany where Hugolino then was. The substance of the letter which we may analyse under three headings — eulogy, biblical symbols and stimulation to the Cistercians of the Patrimony — is arcane, full of cryptic meaning and scriptural allusion. It would, however, have been perfectly comprehensible to those to whom it was addressed and exemplifies the model whereby ideals and experience are communicated through the vehicle of a friendship with a strongly autobiographical element.[97] Hugolino was not a Cistercian but he may well have been influenced by a literary lament such as that written by St Bernard on the death of his brother.[98] This letter is surely a unique outpouring of feeling and grief and would have been the very thing Cistercians would like to hear.

Following Rainier's death Hugolino is inconsolable and hence delivers his eulogy. Practically speaking we learn that the monk Rainier had retreated to the island of Ponza off Terracina but his death is untimely to say the least.[99] Hugolino describes himself as a premature child brought to birth with his spiritual characteristics as yet unformed.[100] Why, he asks rhetorically, did Rainier abandon him 'in the womb of the world' before he had been led to the point of spiritual birth and light 'with the result that you ceased to be my father before I could be called your son'.[101] He next bewails the loss of Rainier's spiritual solace, not merely on his own account but for all men. Mauritania can say more about him than can Italy for there his miracles have 'softened the hardness of infidelity'.[102] His gift of prophecy, perhaps linked to his undoubted ability in the interpretation of miracles, his knowledge of both Old and New Testaments, his eloquence, elegance and urbanity was likened to that of Origen[103] and Didymus.[104] His anti–heretical, eremitical views may be compared to those of Hilarin,[105] Censorinus[106] and Victorinus[107] while his searching out of the real meaning of the Bible, like Gregory Nazianzus[108] and Gregory the Great,[109] meant that when, in Church, he opened his mouth 'rivers of living water seemed to flow from his inmost being'. Spain — where Rainier was legate in 1198 — knows all this well. As does Pope Innocent and even more so since it was his innocence that Rainier used to commend to the Lord with prayers and tears.[110] Described by Hugolino as an angel of the Lord, this holy man descended from time to time from the heights of contemplation wrapped in a cloud of learning and wearing the crown of spiritual knowledge on his head, at whose roar seven thunderbolts spoke uttering allegorical and moral voices. Rainier may even have possessed the ability to speak in tongues — he was frequently snatched off to the third realm of heaven in the course of delivering his words and reported arcane things which none besides himself knew how to speak. When he crossed over to the Island of Ponza so that he might be free to contemplate, kings, princes and prelates begged to be allowed to give him assistance to mitigate the rigours of such a rigid devotion. Naturally the holy man denied them this pleasure.

The Biblical imagery used in this letter is also of considerable interest. Rahel's (Rachel's) voice is heard in Roma, surely a play on Rama, that holy place,[111] and Rainier's service and devotion to the Cistercian Order is paralleled by the allusion to Jacob's service for her. Although he occasionally clung to

Leah, nevertheless he dod not part from the embrace of Rachel. Just as Leah and Rachel are juxtaposed so too are Martha and Mary as we should expect in a Cistercian context.[112] Both sisters are to wear mourning until the infidel are restored to the faith. Rainier is equated with Abisaq, the beautiful Shunamite and virgin who is used to warm the bed of the aged King David and thus keep him alive.[113] The warmth of his faith will likewise keep the Patrimony in being.

The message of the Cistercians of Fossanova and Casamari is as telling as the message of Divine Providence which refused to allow Rainier to hide his light under a bushel. The holy man's virtues cannot be described, so immeasurable are they. He represents the lasting sweetness of the word of God — the contemplation of Mary, and, always obedient, he understands Martha's struggle with the brief reward of labour. The role of the Cistercian Order is for Hugolino as beautiful and as virtuous as the young virgin Abisaq by the heat of whose love the members of a chilly and aging world now grow warm.[114] The Order's special jewel is Rainier, learned and erudite and yet possessing the popular touch. He was an inspirational communicator, clearly active in preaching to Moslems in North Africa or Spain, although this letter is the only evidence we have. In his life as a monk his personal severity was much harsher than that of the Order in general. As the text says, he expressed in himself the full rigour and glory of the Cistercian Order. His retreat to Ponza is represented not as the flight of the youthful *fugitivus* but as the search for a desert solitude, that supreme *transitus ad arctiorem vitam* by which he might enter into more intimate association with God's word.[115] The Sons of the prophets have flocked to him as if to another Elysium, desiring to gain something from his spiritual joy but he would never tolerate any mitigation of self–imposed harshness. Preferring to read rather than to sleep, to fast rather than to speak, he emulated St Jerome and produced his own spiritual writings, a collection of letters and epistles. 'Oh, where is that collection now?' begs Hugolino. 'All would benefit by reading it, adorned as these works are with the flowers of his virtues. They would be ideal preparation for putting off "the work of the flesh" and obtaining spiritual ends'. Hugolino ends by stating how rapidly and in what an unpolished form he has written this brief note in the very early hours of the morning. What he intends to do, if God so wills it, is to set down the miracles, life and merits of this quite extraordinary abbot. That he does not appear to have done so is very much our loss.

Other events were soon to require attention. The growing importance of the urban environment required a new form of mission for which the Cistercians with their concentration the desert margins were not suited.[116] Perhaps Rainier, had he lived, would have been able to change this emphasis in his role as the new Southern Bernard and as such a major spiritual force in the Patrimony of St Peter. With his untimely death this was not to be so. Rather, it was to the new mendicant friars that Innocent looked to take the gospel message to the towns. Hugolio, at first bereft, was soon to find another inspirational figure to protect and advance. Less conventional that Rainier and of at least equal spiritual significance was Francis of Assisi who has revealed to us so much more clearly than Innocent's retiring monk–confessor. Nevertheless, in the recovery of the Patrimony at this time the Cistercians had been agents of success, Rainier the inspiration and Innocent the guiding hand who, from the day of his election, had been determined to follow his predecessor Simon Peter to whom Christ had given the charge.

NOTES

1. Eds., O. Hageneder and A. Haidacher, *Die Register Innocenz' III*, Bd 1, *Pontifikatsjahr 1198–99* (Graz–Koln, 1964), [hereafter *Register* I], pp 3–5; ed., J.P. Migne, *Patrologia Latina* (Paris, 1855), *Innocentii III*; *Opera Omnia*, 4 vols [hereafter *PL*], 214, I, 1; ed., A. Potthast, *Regesta Pontificium Romanorum*, 2 vols (Berlin, 1874), [hereafter *Potthast*], I, 1.

2. *Gesta Innocentii III, PL*, xvii–ccxxviii, [hereafter *Gesta*], VII, xx; L. Duchesne, *Le Liber Pontificalis* (2 ed Paris, 1955–1957).

3. M. Maccarrone, 'La "Cathedra Sancti Petri" nel Medioevo: da Simblo a reliquia', *Rivista di Storia della Chiesa in Italia*, 39 (1985), pp 349–447; *Register* I, pp 296, 417–419; ed., A. Albani, *Collectionis Bullarum Sacrosanctae Basilicae Vaticanae* 3 vols (Rome, 1747–1754) I, *Ad Sancto Leone Magno ad Innocentium VI*, p 77.

4. *Ibid.*, pp 7980. Quod a nativitate sua, quasi filium illum dilexi et per diversos gradus promotum in mea tandem Sede constitui.

5. *Gesta*, VIII, p xxi.

6. T.C. Van Cleve, *Markward of Anweiler and the Sicilian Regency* (Princeton, 1937); M. Maccarrone, 'Innocenzo III e gli avvenimenti di Romagna del 1198', *Miscellanea Augusto Campana, Medievo e Umanesimo* (Padua, 1981), p 45, [hereafter Maccarrone, 'Gli avvenimenti'], pp 403–443.

7. For the view that a real Papal State existed before 1198 see T.F.X. Noble, *The Republic of St Peter: the birth of the Papal State 680–825* (Pennsylvania, 1984); M. Moresco, *Il Patrimonio di S Pietro: studio storico–giuridico sulla istituzione finanziarie della Santa Sede* (Turin, 1916). For the opposing view, D. Waley, *The Papal State in the Thirteen Century* (London, 1916); P. Partner, *The Lands of St Peter* (London, 1972); P. Toubert, *Les Structures du Latium Mediévale*, 2 vols (Rome, 1973); M. Laufs, *Politik und Recht bei Innocenz III* (Koln, 1980).

8. A. Luchaire, 'Innocent III et le Peuple Romain', *Revue Historique*, 81 (1903), [hereafter Luchaire, 'Innocent III et le Peuple Romain'], pp 225–277; D. Herlihy, 'Family Solidarity in Medieval Italian History', *Economy, Society and Government in Medieval Italy. Studies in Memory of Robert L. Reynolds* (Kent, Ohio, 1969); L. Halphen, *L'Administration de Rome au Moyen Age* (Paris, 1907).

9. St Bernard, *Vita Prima, auctore Ernaldo, PL* 185 (1855), 4.1, Book II, VII, pp 291–293; Luchaire, 'Innocent III et le Peuple Romain', p 226.

10. M. Maccarone, 'Primato Romano e Monasteri dal Principio del Secolo XII ad Innocenzo III'. *Istituzione Monastiche e Istituzione Canonicali in Occident (1123–1215)*, (Milan, 1980), [hereafter Maccarone, 'Primato Romano'], pp 49–132.

11. Ed., J.M. Canivez, *Statuta Capitulorum Generalium Ordinis Cisterciensis ab anno 1116 ad annum 1786*, 8 vols (Louvain, 1933–1941), I, *Ab anno 1116 ad annum 1220* (Louvain, 1933), [hereafter Canivez, I], pp 221–224. Compare C.J. Holdsworth, 'The Blessings of Work: the Cistercian view'. *Studies in Church History* 10 (Blackwell, 1973), [hereafter Holdsworth, 'Blessings of Work'], pp 59–76.

12. Canivez, I, p 223.

13. For a description of his own ascetic practices, St Bernard, *Vita Prima, PL*, pp 185, 250; J.F. Hinnebusch, *The Historia Occidentalis of Jacques de Vitry*, Spicilegium Friburgense, 17 (Fribourg, 1972), pp 112–115 on the novelty of the Cistercians.

14. C.H. Lawrence, *Medieval Monasticism*, 2nd edition, (London, 1989), pp 174–205; G. Constable, 'Renewal and Reform in Religious Life:

Concepts and Realities', in eds., R.L. Benson and G. Constable *Renaissance and Renewal in the Twelfth Century* (Cambridge, Mass. and Oxford, 1982), pp 37—67.

15. B.M. Bolton, '*Via Ascetica*: a papal quandary', *Studies in Church History*, 22 (Blackwell, 1985), [hereafter Bolton, '*Via Ascetica*'], pp 161—191; Maccarrone, 'Primato romano', pp 80—107

16. R.W. Southern, *Western Society and the Church* (Harmondsworth, 1970), pp 259—261.

17. Ed., M.R. James, Walter Map, *De Nugis Curialium: Courtiers' Trifles*, revised and translated by C.N.L. Brooke and R.A.B. Mynors (Oxford, 1983), pp 85—113, especially pp 103—113.

18. 7 July 1199. R. Fantappiè, *Le carte della prepositura di Prato, I, 1006—1200* (Florence, 1977), p 488; Maccarrone, 'Primato romano', pp 50—70, specially pp 58, 63—64.

19. Canivez, I, p 16; *Register* I, 302, pp 430—433; 508, pp 741—743; Potthast I, 335.

20. *PL* 214, 1107—1108; Potthast I, 1772.

21. Ed., J. Strange, *Caesarii Heisterbacensis Monachi Ordinis Cisterciensis Dialogus Miraculorum* 2 vols (Koln, 1851) II, pp 7—8; ed., O. Holder—Egger *Chronica Minor Auctore Minorita Erphordiensi, Monumenta Germania Historia*, Scriptores [hereafter *MGH, SS*], 24, p 196; Thomas de Cantimpre, *Vita Lutgardis Virgine*, ed., G. Henschenius, *Acta Sanctorum Bollandia*, 3 June (Antwerp, 1701), pp 245—247; Maccarrone, 'Primato romano', pp 111—112.

22. (?—d. 1207/1209). H. Grundmann, 'Zur Biographi Joachim von Flore und Rainers von Ponza', *Deutsches Archiv.*, 16 (1960), [hereafter Grundmann, 'Zur Biographie'], pp 437—546; B. Griesser, 'Rainer von Fossanva und seiner Brief an Abt Arnald von Cîteaux (1203)', *Cistercienser Cronik* 60 (1953), [hereafter Griesser, 'Rainer von Fossanova'], pp 152—167; A. Manrique, *Cisterciensium seu verius ecclesiasticorum Annalium a condito cistercio*, 4 vols (Lyon, 1649—1657), [hereafter Manrique] III, *ab anno MCLXXIV usque ad MCCXII inclusive*, pp 368—370.

23. Maccarrone, 'Gli avvenimenti', pp 437—446.

24. M. Maccarrone, *Studi su Innocenzo III, Italia Sacra*: Studi e documenti di Storia Ecclesiastica, 17 (Padau, 1972), [hereafter Maccarrone, *Studi*], pp 9—22; *Register* I, pp 126—128; *PL* 214, 76; Potthast I, 82.

25. *Gesta* XVII, xxix—xxx; Maccarrone, *Studi*, pp 10—13. Innocent used the text from Ecclesiastes 13:1, He who touches pitch shall be defiled.

26. M. Maccarrone, 'Il papa "*Vicarius Christi*": Testi e dottrina dal secolo xii al principio del xiv', *Miscellanea Pio Paschini*, Lateranum, NS, 2 vols (Rome, 1948), I, pp 427—500 and especially pp 445—459.

27. Matthew 11:30; *PL* 214, p 76; *Register* I, pp 126—128; Potthast I, 82.

28. Octavian, Cardinal—Bishop of Ostia, captured c 1192 by Conrad 'Flybrain' and held at Monte S Maria. *Gesta* IX, pp xxiv—xxv; W. Maleczek, *Papst und Kardinalskolleg von 1191 bis 1216: die Kardinale unter Celestin III and Inncenz III* (Vienna, 1984), [hereafter Maleczek, *Papst und Kardinalskolleg*], p 82; O. Hagender, W. Maleczek and A. Strnad, *Die Register Innocenz' III, Bd II, 2 Jahrgang (1199/1200)*, (Rome—Vienna, 1979), [hereinafter *Register* II], 166 (175), pp 322—323.

29. L. Janauschek, *Originum Cistercensum* I (Vienna, 1877); F. Caraffa, *Monasticon Italiae* I, Roma e Lazio (Cesena, 1981), [hereafter *Monasticon*]; M. Mastrocola, 'Il monachesimo nelli diocesi di Città Castellana, Ort e Galse fino al secolo XII', in *Miscellanea di Studio Viterbesi* (Viterbo, 1962) pp 352—419; *I Cistercensi e il Lazio*, Atti delle giornate di studio dell'Instituto di Storia dell'Arte dell'Università di

Roma, 17–21 Maggio 1977, (Rome, 1978).

30. *Monasticon*, pp 104–106.
31. *Ibid.*,179, pp 84–85. Cistercian from 1140.
32. *Ibid.*, 154, p 77. Cistercian from 1171.
33. *Ibid.*, 132, 149; *PL* 215, 703–705; Potthast I, 2198.   Cistercian in 1215–1216.
34. *Monasticon*, 101, p 141. Founded as a Cistercian house in 1189.
35. *Ibid.*, 267, pp 186–187. Cistercian from 1146.
36. Canivez I, p 243.
37. *Gesta*, XIV, p xxviii; J. Raspi Serra, *La Tuscia Romana* (Rome, 1972); A. Diviziani, 'Il patrimonio di S Pietro in Tuscia', *Bolletino dell'Instituto Storico–Artistico Orvietano*, 17 (1961); pp 3–41; J. Raspi Serra and C. Langanara Fabiono, *Economia e territorio: il Patrimonium Beati Petri nella Tuscia* (Naples, 1987).
38. *Monasticon*, 70, pp 131–132. Taken into papal protection in 1178. In 1195 the Cistercian General Chapter ordered its reform.
39. *Ibid.*, 98, p 139. Became Cistercian in 1143.
40. *Ibid.*, 299, p 195; P. Egidi, 'L'abbazia di San Martino sul Monte Cimino con documenti inediti', *Rivista di Stria Benedettina*, 1 (1906), pp 579–590; 2 (1907), pp 161–199.
41. *Gesta*, X, pp xxv–xxvi.
42. *PL* 214, 826–828, 1107–1108; Potthast I, 1772; Maccarrone, 'Primato romano', pp 112–113.
43. John of Casamari, Papal Chaplain, Bishop of Forcone, L'Aquila, (1204–1207) and of Perugia (1207–1230).
44. *Ibid.*, 243. Dominus papa pro dissolutione quarumdam abbatiarum de partibus illis, *PL* 214, 1107–1108; Potthast I, 1772.
45. Canivez I, p 260.
46. *Ibid.*, p 327.
47. *PL* 215, 1309–1312; Potthast, 2997.
48. *Gesta* CXXVI, cixii–clxiv; Potthast, 3291. For the gift of a red and gold altar frontal and 100 pounds in money of Siena, *Gesta* CXLV, ccviii, ccxxvii.
49. *Ibid.*, CXLIX, ccxxvii.
50. Canivez I, p 345.
51. Bolton, '*Via ascetica*', pp 175–180.
52. *Vergentis in senium*, 25 March 1199. *Register* II, pp 1, 3–5; *PL* 214, 537–539; Potthast, 643; W. Ullmann, 'The significance of Innocent III's decretal *Vergentis*', in *Etudes d'histoire du droit canonique dediées a Gabriel Le Bras*, 2 vols (Paris, 1965) I, pp 729–741.
53. *Cum lupi rapaces*, 16 June 1205. *PL* 215, 654–657, 673–674; Potthast, 2539.
54. *Ad eliminandum*, 23 September 1207. *PL* 215, 1226–1228; Potthast, 3187.
55. *Gesta*, CXXIV, cixii; Maccarrone, *Studi*, p 51.
56. William of Andres, *Chronicle*, MGH, SS, 24 (Hanover 1897), pp 690–773, especially p 737.
57. His second and longest stay was from mid–May to mid–September 1209. L.V. Delisle, 'Itinéraire de Innocent III dressé d'après les actes de ce pontife', *Bibliotheque de l'Ecole des Chartes*, (1957), [hereafter Deslisle, 'Itinéraire'], pp 500–534, especially p 509. Also Maccarrone, *Studi*, pp 56–57; Potthast, 3727–3802.
58. 23 June – 19 September, 1214, *Ibid.*, 4932–4938.
59. *Monasticon*, 168, p 159. Cistercian since 1125.
60. *Ibid.*, 283, pp 190–191.

61. *Ibid.*, 86, pp 135–136; Canivez, I, p 332. Cistercian since 1167.
62. *Monasticon*, 13, p 118. Unclear when this house became Cistercian.
63. *Ibid.*, 79, pp 133–134.
64. *Ibid.*, 11, p 117. ? Cistercian.
65. *PL* 215, 1435–1437; Potthast I, 3465; ed., G.H. Pertz, *Annales Ceccanenses*, MGH, SS, 19 (Hannover, 1866), pp 275–302, especially p 297. F. Farina and B. Fornari, *L'architettura cistercense e l'abbazia di Casamari* (Frosinone, 1978).
66. *Gesta*, CXLIX, ccxxvii.
67. *Ibid.*, CXLV, ccviii.
68. *Ibid.*, CXLV, ccxxvii.
69. Ed., A. Gaudenzi, *Chronica Romanorum pontificium et imperatorum ac de rebus in Apulia gestis (781–1228) auctore ignoto monacho Cisterciensi*, Società Napoletana di Sancta Patria, I Cronache, (Naples, 1888), p 34; *PL* 215, 1593–1594; Deslisle, 'Itinéraire', p 521.
70. *Gesta*, XXIII, xviii.
71. Maleczek, *Papst und Kardinalskolleg*, pp 126–133.
72. *Gesta*, XXIII, xliv.
73. *Ibid.*, XXXVIII, lxviii.
74. M. Maccarrone, 'La Papauté et Philippe Auguste: La decretale "Novit ille"', in ed., R.H. Bautier *La France de Philippe Auguste. Le temps des mutations*, (Paris, 1981), pp 378–397.
75. Maleczek, *Papst und Kardinalklleg*, pp 179–183; V.J. Koudelka, 'Notes pour servir à l'histoire de S Dominque', *Archivum Fratrum Praedicatorum*, 35 (1965), pp 5–20; *PL* 215, 182–184; eds., C.R. Cheney and W.H. Semple, *Selected Letters of Pope Innocent III concerning England*, (London–Edinburgh, 1953), pp 149–154.
76. Abbot of Casamari (1182–1209), nephew of Gerald, sixth abbot of Clairvaux.
77. *Gesta*, CXXIX, clxix–cixxi.
78. Grundmann, 'Zur Biographie', pp 437–546.
79. Canivez, I, p 154.
80. Grundmann, 'Zur Biographie', p 441.
81. *Register* II, 92, pp 132–134; *PL* 214, 78–91; Potthast, 81.
82. *Register* II, 72 (75), pp 126–134; *PL* 214, 610–615; Potthast, 716.
83. *PL* 214, 1053–1057, de infirmitate.
84. Canivez, I, p 245, coram Renerio legato Curiae Romanae.
85. Manrique, III, p 369.
86. G. Tiraboschi, *Vetera Humiliatorum Monumenta* 3 vols, (Milan, 1766–1768), I, pp 136, 140.
87. R. Foreville and G. Keir, *The Book of St Gilbert*, (Oxford, 1987), lxxx, pp 176–177.
88. *Ibid.*, lxxx. Daniel 2. pp 25–45; Genesis 41, p 1–26.f
89. *PL* 214, 1032–1033, ad instantiam dilecti filii fratis Rainieri.
90. Arnald Amaury (d. 1225), abbot of Poblet, Grandselve and Cîteaux (1202).
91. Griesser, 'Rainer von Fossanova', pp 163–166.
92. *Ibid.*, p 166. Compare *PL* 214, 1031–1034 for deserters to the Cistercian Order.
93. Canivez, I, p 304.
94. Ed., E. Windkelmann, '*Analecta Heidelbergensdia*', *Varietà*, *Archivio della Società Romana di Storia Patria*, 2 (Rome, 1879). [hereafter Winkelmann, *Varietà*], pp 363–367. I am most grateful to Professor Elizabeth A. Beckwith, University of Pennsylvania, for rendering an unedited and difficult text both accessible and elegant.

95.   Maleczek, *Papst und Kardinalskolleg*, pp 126–133. Later Pope Gregory IX (1227–1241).

96.   Eberhard, abbot of Salem (1191–1240).

97.   B.P. McGuire, 'Monastic Friendship and Toleration in twelfth–century Cistercian life', *Studies in Church History*, 22 (1985), pp 147–160.

98.   *Ibid.*, pp 155–156, note 24.

99.   Winkelmann, *Varità*, p 366.

100. *Ibid.*, p 364.

101. *Ibid.*, p 365.

102. *Ibid.*, p 365.

103. Origen of Alexandria d. 254, most prolific writer of all the Fathers of the Early Church.

104. Didymus the Blind of Alexandria d. 395. Learned theologian, dogmatist and exegete.

105. Hilarion (c 291/292–371) left the Egyptian desert to establish anachoretism in Palestine. Losing the solitude for which he craved, he retreated to Cyprus.

106. Censorinus. I can find no trace of him.

107. Victorinus, converted to Christianity 362. Rhetorician, theologian and teacher in Rome and enemy of the Arians.

108. Gregory of Nazianzus d 390. Studied at Caesarea, Alexandria and Athens and composed sermons, letters and theological orations.

109. Gregory the Great (590–604), the first monk to become pope. In spite of poor health, produced outstanding sermons and exegesis.

110. Winkelmann, *Varietà*, p 366.

11.   Jeremiah 31.15.

112. Holdsworth, 'Blessings of work', pp 64–66.

113. I Kings 1, p 1–4.

114. Winkelmann, *Varietà*, p 365.

115. M.A. Dimier, 'Saint Bernard et le droit en matiére de *Transitus*', *Revue Mabillon*, 43 (1953), pp 48–83; G. Picasso, [San Bernardo e il 'transitus' dei monache', in *Studi su S Bernardo di Chiaravalle nell'ottavo centenario della Canonizzazione* (Rome, 1975), pp 182–200.

116. L.K. Little, *Regligious Poverty and thé Profit Economy in Medieval Europe* (London, 1978), pp 146–169, 197–217.

THE ENGLISH MINORESSES AND THEIR EARLY BENEFACTORS
1281–1367[1]

Michael Hicks

The Sister Minor or Minoresses were that variety of Franciscan nuns who settled in England the later middle ages. It was in 1212 near Assisi that St Clare, the friend of St Francis, founded the first house of what were more commonly called the Poor Clares, Clarisses, or the second order of St Francis. The Sisters Minor or Minoresses were a small offshoot from the main order and lived according to the so–called Isabella rule of 1264, which was devised for the house at Langchamp established by the Blessed Isabella, sister of St Louis (King Louis IX of France). In 1281 Denise de Munchensy (d. 1304) was licensed to found two such houses in England and in 1293–4 these were duly established with nuns imported from Longchamp. Denise herself founded Waterbeach Abbey in Cambridgeshire; the other, at Aldgate in London [the Minories], was the work of Blanche Queen of Navarre (d. 1302), wife of Edward I's brother Edmund, Earl of Lancaster (d. 1295). The patronage of Waterbeach descended to Mary of St Pol, Countess of Pembroke (d. 1377), who first endowed it with the nearby manor of Denney in Waterbeach in 1336; then in 1342 she founded a third abbey at Denney; and finally, pleading the best interests of both houses, she forcibly amalgamated the two and transferred the recalcitrant nuns from Waterbeach at Denney. This process was completed in 1351. Nuns from Denny colonised the last house founded at Bruisyard in Suffolk in 1364–7 by Lionel Duke of Clarence (d. 1368), son of Edward III. This was apparently primarily for the benefit of his mother–in–law Maud of Lancaster, Countess of Ulster, a professed nun of the Augustinian priory of Campsey, who wished to transfer to a more strictly enclosed order. It replaced the chantry college she had founded within Campsey prior in 1347 and had moved to Bruisyard in 1356. There were only ever four English houses of Minoresses and never more than three at a time, although several abortive ones were planned. The Sisters Minor thus constitute on of our smallest medieval religious orders, as well as one of the latest to arrive, and were the only variety of Franciscan nuns to establish themselves in England before the Reformation.

Few the Minoresses may have been, but obscure they are not. Whilst there are still facets of their history deserving of attention, relatively little new information has come to light since 1926, the date of Claudine Bourdillon's monograph on the subject,[2] which deserves to be regarded as definitive. My purpose in this paper is not, therefore, to rewrite the history of the order in England, but to use the well–known and documented facts to illuminate that late medieval aristocratic piety of which the Minoresses were both a symptom and an expression. Why the Minoresses? What was it about the order that prompted its patrons to put so much money, effort, and personal attention into their establishment in England in preference to other cheaper, easier, and more self–evidently rewarding forms of patronage? That is the question that this paper seeks to answer.

Pace E.H. Carr,[3] we all know that late medieval people were pious. Every chantry foundation and every will testifies to the fact and reveals late medieval people putting their money where their mouths were. Such evidence, however, is highly conventional in character. It testifies principally to a conventional belief in purgatory and the efficacy of prayers for the dead. More detailed study, notably by Kathleen Wood–Legh and Clive Burgess, has identifies yet more conventions governing the nature and manner of such giving.[4]   Sometimes, admittedly, the same patterns of behaviour can be shown to have applied also in life, when they have formed only part of the total religious experience of the donors. All this tells us remarkably little about knowledge and comprehension of central Christian doctrines, of religious and moral intensity, or of the way in which religion conditioned everyday social, economic, or political conduct. To say that conventional piety was piety governing by convention is no defence to the charge that it was superficial and uncomprehending, 'insular, inert and shallow',[5] self– contained and unimportant in relations within the household, market place, or political arena. Only the unconventional, those whose patronage takes unusual forms, appear committed.[6] Can it really be that only their distinctive piety can be studied? Actually their experience sheds light on their conventional contemporaries as well, particularly when it takes forms not unique to particular individuals. The new religious orders bulk large among such minority expressions of late medieval English lay piety.

Most medieval English monasteries were already founded by 1281. Henceforth chantries are the characteristic new foundations. What lay patronage of monasticism there was — and it was diminishing — consisted mainly of extra gifts to existing houses, which raise complex technical problems for the historian of lay piety. To regard such developments as evidence of the declining appeal of the old orders overlooks the changes that such orders had undergone. It is far from clear that a new monastery would correspond to the blueprint set out in the monastic rule. The appeal of such original ideals may indeed have remained — witness the writings of Langland and continuing patronage of the Carthusians[7] — but the orders themselves were seen as having changed and indeed as having become indistinguishable.[8]   What did monasticism actually entail in late medieval England and, more important for my purpose, how did it appear to the laity? We ned to know not just what did not appeal about monasticism — there is copious evidence of that[9] — but what *did* appeal to those who *did* patronise them. The ancient original rules are little help here and it is insufficient to label as sentimental or stingy patrons who often appear to have been highly discriminating. Such problems, at present unsolved and perhaps insoluble, do not apply to new orders like the Observants, Bridgettines, Dominican nuns, or Minoresses, where one can feel reasonably confident that everyday reality still corresponded to the original rule and that it was something about this that attracted patrons in preference to other orders or forms of piety. In the case of the Minoresses, this can be supplemented by other sources, notably the papal petitions and letters. This study ceases with the fourth foundation in the belief it was only after 1367 that the order itself changed and friars lost their high reputation.

Let us start with Professor Hamilton Thompson's off quoted and celebrated observation that ultimately all medieval foundations were chantries.[10] On this basis the Minoresses do not seem the best buy. To patronise them involved an elaborate chain of decisions, conscious or unconscious, which help explain why so few such houses were founded. Why found anything when so many establishments so various in type already existed everywhere? Why create new capacity when there space in old establishments? Why found an expensive monastery rather than a cheap chantry, which yielded more masses per £ and permitted a more personalised constitution and observances. Above all, why found a nunnery, when nuns were unable to celebrate mass in person and were wholly dependent on endowments. One can appreciate Michael de la Pole's decision to substitute a house of Carthusians for his father's Minoresses 'believing that God will be served with more vigilance and devotion by them than by women'.[11] To found *anything* involved a conscious rejection of what existed and a commitment to higher expenditure, responsibility and indeed risk than benefactions of existing institutions. Monasteries belonged to fully constituted orders, whose rules and liturgies could not be tailored to founders' whims. Nunneries, above all the Minoresses, were particularly prescriptive.

There were plenty of nunneries in England by 1281 and only two more were to be founded in the rest of the middle ages, those of the Dominicanesses at Dartford (1356) and the Bridgettines at Syon (1415).[12] In practice most patrons were content with what was already available. In several respects the Minoresses offer nothing new; alternatively it might be argued that they satisfied the same needs as their older rivals. It is hardly surprising, for example, that the moving spirits behind each foundation and most subsequent benefactions were women. Nor is it unexpected that all the dedications include the Virgin,[13] since she was the model of Christian chastity that all nuns were supposed to emulate and the patron saint of countless other nunneries as well. It was also quite normal that widows as well as virgins could become nuns. Even the markedly aristocratic character inherited from Longchamp was shared by older English houses like Amesbury and Stratford.[14] If the Minoresses did not monopolise aristocratic patrons of aristocratic nuns, they nevertheless benefited from a kinship network of patrons that were exceptionally tightly knit and enduring. Bourdillon was able to include fifty out of sixty known benefactors over ten generations in a single family tree.[15] Such connections, she observed, often suffice to explain patronage of the Minoresses rather than some other order

> Interest in the Order indeed ran in families to such an extent that one has an impression of a kind of charitable entail ... In such an Order as this men [sic] could take a proprietary and personal interest; in one visit to either of the houses a patron could become acquainted with all the Sisters there; and so a touch of human feeling would add warmth and colour to the inspiration of religious piety.[16]

But such a network is the result, not the cause, of the introduction of the Sisters Minor.

Obviously the founders must have been already acquainted with the order they introduced. Hard though she tried, Bourdillon did not discover where Denise de Munchensy encountered them,[17] though it must obviously have been abroad. This was undoubtedly true of Queen Blanche, a niece of St Louis and the Blessed Isabella, whose first husband was buried in the house at Provins, capital of her county of Champagne, and who was already interested in them by 1291.[18] The countesses of Pembroke and Ulster may have come across them for the first time in England. Prior acquaintance, essential though it is, can have been only part of the answer, for it does not explain why they did not support orders already in England or introduce Poor Clares, Dominican or Augustine nuns which Queen Blanche at least knew and patronised. There must have been some characteristics that distinguished the Sisters Minor from their rivals, that prompted founders to single them out, and cause subsequent benefactors to patronise them over such a longer period of time.

The foundation of 400 houses of Franciscan nuns throughout medieval Europe obviously owed much to popular enthusiasm for the Friars Minor. This was certainly a factor in England, where several benefactors also patronised the

Franciscans. Denise de Munchensy was buried in the London Greyfriars, Edmund Earl of Lancaster helped found a friary at Preston, and Elizabeth de Clare set up another at Walsingham. Above all, Mary of St Pol, the benefactress of the London Greyfriars, who has been proposed as a member of the third order of St Francis, was accompanied by 17 Franciscans in 1324, prescribed that one should be external rector of her Cambridge college, and bound the college itself to support the Franciscan mission.[19] Such contacts must not be exaggerated, however, for it is obvious that the Minoresses came much later to England and in much smaller numbers than elsewhere. The English scarcely participated in the tremendous enthusiasm for Franciscan nuns displayed by the Italians, French, or Spaniards. Perhaps they were more acutely conscious how little the second order of St Francis had in common with the first.

The very concept of Franciscan nuns seems at first a contradiction in terms: that is, if we envisage Franciscan friars as essentially evangelist and mendicant, engaged in preaching and begging in the outside world. Like St Francis, St Clare had striven for absolute poverty and an extremely austere lifestyle, but such ideals proved impractical and by 1263–4 every house of Poor Clares and Minoresses had to be allowed corporate property. Under their rules, Bourdillon observes, Poor Clares and Sisters Minor alike

> were no more poor than any ordinary Benedictine nuns. They were bound to no further poverty than that which was involved in the universal three–fold vow of religion.

Perhaps from the start and certainly by the mid 14th century individual nuns were allowed to possess private property. In giving the London sisters pittances in 1299,[20] only six years after their arrival in England, Edward I's Queen Margaret treated them like any other monks or nuns.

If it was not evangelism, mendicancy, or poverty that distinguished these nunneries from those of other orders, there were nevertheless four important differences. First of all, a factor whose importance is difficult to assess, the Minoresses used the Franciscan liturgy.[21] Secondly, St Clare and the Blessed Isabella made elaborate provisions to keep their enclosure inviolate. Only Franciscan minsters—general and provincials, cardinals and bishops, each with strictly delimited retinues, could enter the precincts without a special papal privilege. The front door was to be placed high on the outside wall, where it could be reached only by ladder, and a revolving rota permitted communication with outsiders without the sisters being seen[22]. Liturgy and seclusion may distinguish all varieties of Franciscan nuns from other English orders, but they cannot explain the preference by English founders for the Sisters Minor rather than Poor Clares. What separates them, distinguishes the Minoresses also from all other English orders, and thus explains why they were preferred to Clarisses is the provision confined to the Isabella rule that imposed on the Friars Minor the obligation of acting as chaplains, confessors, and visitors of the nuns.[23] Another factor also of relevance in an order much patronised by married and single ladies, particularly in later years, was that the Minoresses, unlike the Poor Clares, admitted widows as well as virgins.[24]

The supervision of the Friars Minor was a special privilege that was denied by successive popes to all but Longchamp and its daughter houses. The friars considered it an onerous obligation irrelevant to their evangelical mission, sought to shrug it off, and had to be compelled to undertake it. The advantages for the patrons are obvious. Since nuns could not become priests, they could not celebrate mass, hear confession or give absolution, which normally had to be undertaken by hired chaplains, who were not highly educated or highly–trained as spiritual guides and posed moreover a constant threat to the nuns' chastity. Given the necessity for male priests within the enclosure, friars were vastly preferable. They too lived disciplined lives according to a rule, they were well–educated and highly trained in the cure cf souls, and their reputation was still excellent. Their supervision ensured – or appeared to ensure – that discipline, observance, and (perhaps above all) chastity that was expected but too seldom found in religious houses for women. It was not that the supervision of the friars directly impinged on patrons, who have left no other record of their interest in it, but that it offered guarantees for the quality of future religious and moral standards in a way denied to all other nunneries of whatever type.

This does not mean, however, that the Minoresses were otherwise indistinguishable from other orders of nuns. There are ample indications to the contrary in the papal records, all relating to the strictness of enclosure, which has already been identified as a distinctive feature of the Isabella rule. Of course all nunneries were supposed to be strictly enclosed, but in practice many outsiders, often male, had access to the precincts.[25] The nuns needed the ministrations of their chaplains, visitations by their ecclesiastical superiors, maintenance of the fabric by masons and carpenters, and the many–sided assistance of tradesmen, domestic servants, and estate officials. The nuns were obliged to offer hospitality to wayfarers, frequently ran schools, and received visitors. Their churches often doubled as parish churches and objects of pilgrimage. Nor did nuns always remain within their cloisters. Superiors, like Chaucer's prioress, had separate households, incomes, and even other residences, engaged in much worldly business, and indulged in worldly fashions and pastimes. Often other nuns attended them outside the cloister.[26] Nuns were allowed to take exercise outside the cloister and to holiday with their families. Most nuns were obedientiaries, taking responsibility for the collection of revenue and supply of goods that often required their absence from the precincts. They must have been as common a sight then as they are today. If a monk outside his cloister seemed a contradiction in terms to Chaucer (and indeed to Langland),[27] how much more true this must have been of a nun. Far from being secluded from the contamination of the world, nuns were constantly and *legitimately* exposed to lay and male society, and were denied the peaceful contemplation that ecclesiastical authorities expected of them, to often with serious moral effects. That strict enclosure was also highly valued by layfolk, especially aristocratic women, as shown by their patronage of the Sisters Minor.

Of course, no order could be completely self–contained. English houses of Minoresses do not seem to have featured the upstairs entrance, the Isabella rule made necessary allowance for bulk deliveries at the back door and for a trustworthy male porter at the front, and indulgences were secured that attracted pilgrims to all four houses.[28] That enclosure was nevertheless unusually strict is indicated by two pieces of evidence. First of all, it was because her numerous noble visitors meant that she could have no 'peace of her conscience' at Campsey Priory that the Countess of Ulster sought her transfer to Bruisyard,[29] where, by implication such visitors could not gain admission. Actually they could if they took the rather extreme, elaborate and expensive step of securing a special papal licence. It is the many such privileges that demonstrate that enclosure was a reality rather than a sham and that even V.I.P.s could not obtain access without one.

Patrons wanted admittance to the claustral precincts throughout the period of this study.   As early as 1291 Queen Blanche and her husand were licensed to enter houses of Minoresss, Dominicanesses, and Augustinian nuns, she with five or six honest matrons, he with eight companions; neither was allowed to dine or stay there overnight.   Similarly Denise de Munchensy's granddaughter Denise de Vere and her husband were licensed in 1311 to enter Waterbeach twice a year with their retinue.   Many others followed: thus in 1353 Maud Lady Lisle of Rougemont, mother of a Minoress, was allowed to enter Aldgate and Denney twice a year with two honest matrons; in 1363 Sir John Beauchamp and his wife Elizabeth, daughter/mother of another, were authorised to visit her at Denney once a year with six honest matrons, but not to eat or spend the night there; and in 1366 the Earl and Countess of Suffolk were allowed into the Minories once a year with one man and four matrons aged over 60.[30]   Apparently the papacy always conceded admission to petitioners, but it strove to restrict the frequency of visits, to curtail the numbers admitted, to restrict them to females of at least middle age, and to prevent visitors from dining or staying overnight.   That these privileges were particularly sought after emerges not just from the papal letters themselves, but from repeated applications by the same suitors anxious to extend their terms.   Pope Clement VI, for example, had allowed the Lady of Clare to enter such houses with four or five ladies, yet in 1357 she petitioned again merely to add three men and to be allowed to stay overnight there with two matrons.[31]   It took three requests in 1366 for the Countess of Arundel to secure admission for herself and four women aged only 40 for three whole days provided that they were decently dressed and did not stay overnight; she gave up seeking four whole days and nights for herself and trying the secure admission for her sons, daughters, and kinsfolk.[32]   Such specific privileges should properly be taken with others, perhaps not solely or primarily secured with the Minoresses in mind, such as those that permitted any religious to eat meat in the petitioner's presence, sometimes in their own houses.   One such dispensation explains how it was that the London Minoresses thrice dined with the Lady of Clare in her London house in the 1350s.[33]   After the period covered by this paper others forged yet closer links, perhaps as the order itself changed, a knight taking up residence in Bruisyard in 1369–1383[34] and Thomas of Woodstock breaking the party wall between the Minories and his town–house, so that he could attend the nuns' services whenever he chose.[35]   For other orders, for which such privileges were not sought, the implication is that admittance did not require papal permission and thus passed unrecorded.   Maybe some privileges to enter houses of unrecorded women without specifying the Minoresses nevertheless had them in mind.

The best known of all such cases is undoubtedly that of Mary of St Pol, Countess of Pembroke, whose exceptionally long career of piety is well–documented from the moment of her widowhood in 1324. Her close connections with the Friars Minor have already been recorded. In 1333 she was licensed to enter monasteries of religious women once a year with six matrons, which she had amended to four matrons and four knights in 1334, and in 1347 she was authorised to take eight honest persons, no sex being specified, into religious houses of both men and women. In 1342 she was licensed to serve meat to religious at her table. More specifically, and also in 1342, she was licensed to enter the abbeys of Waterbeach and Denney with eight honest women, amended at once to a permanent right to enter Denny with twelve attendants, and finally in 1364 she was licensed to enter Denney and all other houses of enclosed nuns with four honest matrons over sixty years of age and to eat and sleep there, no time–limit being stated.[36]   She seems to have availed herself fully of this permission. Archaeological investigations at Denney have revealed that part of the nave of the former Templar preceptory on the site was converted a this time into a comfortable, self–contained apartment, presumably for Mary herself, where she could stay in comfort, observe and participate in the nuns' services, without taking irrevocable vows herself. Certainly she dated several letters at Denney and was interred there in a tomb already built in the choir depicting herself in the habit of a Minoress.[37]

What can we make of all this? At one level there are obvious attractions in patronising an exclusive order that keeps everyone else out but admits oneself. Such a privilege was a fashionable status symbol carrying with it agreeable social intercourse with genteel ladies, who were often kinswomen, and it may have been one that ladies competed to obtain. Hence the repeated desire for attendance by a retinue appropriate to worldly rank and for the nuns to be allowed to eat meat in their benefactress' presence. However pious they were, noble ladies did not intend to give up their comforts or to fast just because they were visiting a nunnery. Clearly there is an element of truth in this interpretation, but it is surely unduly cynical. In particular it ignores the object of these privileges. If noble ladies sought to be allowed to enter houses of Minoresses more frequently, for longer and with more attendants, or stay overnight or for several days, surely we must presume that they had already availed themselves of the limited privileges granted so far and tha they intended to do so in the future? What they were actually seeking was not more social intercourse, but the right to participate: not just in the benefits of monastic prayers, which is a commonplace, but also in the observances themselves. Not to visit just for a few hours, but for several days and nights. They wanted to share in the sisters' worship. Presumably this offered something unobtainable outside. Perhaps it was a higher spiritual quality, the result of stricter enclosure and Franciscan supervision, but perhaps instead it was the opportunity to share in the Franciscan liturgy rather than the uses of Sarum, York or Hereford. At present we cannot tell. Whatever the attraction was, it was certainly remarkably long–lasting and that, as Bourdillon observed, argues strongly for the maintenance of high standards.[38]

Mary of St Pol lived very much like the Blessed Isabella a century earlier and Cecily Duchess of York and Lady Margaret Beaufort a hundred years later.[39] All four practised a strenuous personal piety almost monastic in character without becoming nuns. The Lady Margaret (and, indeed, Elizabeth de Clare) took a vow of chastity, one of the three monastic vows, others may have done so without being recorded, and certainly some, Denise de Munchensy[40] and Mary of St Pol among them, deliberately decided to remain single. With the exception of the Countess of Ulster, however, all of them baulked at the other two vows of poverty and obedience, preferring instead to practise their religion within their existing context of rank, command, wealth and comfort. Apart from the Blessed Isabella herself, a spinster, all those noblewomen listed were wealthy widows, as were the Countess Maud and the Countess Marshall[42] among other benefactresses. Of course late medieval dowagers are notorious for their wealth and lack of responsibilities,[43] which enabled them to indulge their piety and to emerge from the shadow of their husbands and impinge on records in their own right. Widowhood and piety alike could come early, in their twenties for Mary of St Pol and Elizabeth de Clare, and it was surely common experiences in childhood that explain the religious community of the first Duke of Lancaster and his sisters. Many of these benefactresses were still married, such as Queen Blanche and Queen Margaret, Denise de Vere, and the countesses of Arundel and Suffolk. The appeal of the order was not confined to ladies vowed to absolute chastity or preparing for death, but embraced wives in the prime of life still childbearing and still busy with worldly affairs and childbearing. Some husbands and even some other men shared their outlook whatever it was.

What is thus revealed about the piety of enthusiasts for the Minoresses? Before an answer can be given, some prior consideration must be given to the routine, everyday observances that formed the context for their occasional contacts with the sisters. Thanks to the recent work of Dr Mertes we now know that the religious life of all great noble households was highly regulated. There were often several household chaplains, daily services in the household chapel, a diet varied by church festivals and fast days, formal provisions for almsgiving and offerings, and an itinerary that frequently included monasteries and shrines.[44] The value that lords and ladies attached to their private religion is shown by the privileges they sought from their bishops and the popes. Some such favours, like the right to choose a confessor[45] or to have plenary remission of sins at the hour of death,[46] can be unfavourably interpreted as mere evasion of the need for repentance, hard penances, and of the hard pains of purgatory: as a substitute, in short, for living a good Christian life. Perhaps however they should not be, since they did not come automatically to the social elite, required expenditure both of money and time to obtain them, and indeed to implement them. They also reveal a genuine concern for sin and forgiveness, the intention to confess, make proper recompense for sins, and to take communion, and a desire to take personal responsibility for one's own salvation. Everyone's natural confessor was their parish priest, who can seldom have been in the company of his greater parishioners, can scarcely have known them, and rarely possessed either the professional training or the independence of mind of Chaucer's idealised Parson. Instead of these, recipients of indults to choose their own confessor supplied clerics who knew them and their failings, who might often be constantly in their company, who were more highly educated and better trained than many parish priests for this role, and who were often, indeed, Franciscan friars. They thus subjected themselves to a more continuous and perhaps more effective pastoral regime. Such confessors and household chaplains could often exercise considerable influence over their employers.[47] Similarly it was the desire for regular services within the household that prompted episcopal licences for private oratories and often resulted in the costly construction and adornment of substantial structures. Indults for portable altars enabled mass to be celebrated privately everywhere,[48] occasionally even during interdicts,[49] and were designed to ensure that household services should always continue and should not be interrupted by mere accidents of time or place. Sometimes a further dispensation permitted the celebration of mass before daybreak,[50] a particularly austere expression of piety, self–evidently for the benefit of the petitioner. A dispensation for religious to eat meat at one's table[51] indicates a partiality for monastic company and regular resort to it, whether in one's own household or in the monasteries themselves. Dispensations to enter enclosed houses of men and/or women,[52] obviously not targeted solely at Minoresses, reveal a desire to participate in their observances too. Most of these dispensations were secured by most of the known benefactors of the Minoresses. They reveal a domestic religion governed neither by the formalities of calendar or timetable, but an arduous and fervent regimen commencing before daybreak, centering on the mass and the confessional, involving conversation and commensalism with monks and nuns, including regular retreats to share the observances of enclosed religious, and altogether obviously *shaping* the framework for other aspects of life rather than fitting in the space left by other occupations. Did religion take priority over other activities and thus condition them?

It is this religious lifestyle that is implied by support for the Minoresses. To say this is not to imply that it was lacking from those who did not patronise them, those whose access to religious houses did not require papal dispensations, and who thus passed unrecorded.[53] No attempt has been made to assess how widespread such privileges were among the aristocracy as a whole, which would be a major task; but it is immediately obvious that such favours were shared by many others and that benefactors of the Minoresses patronised other forms of religion. Elizabeth de Clare, for example, supported not just the first and second orders of St Francis, but also founded chantries, planned to visit Santiago, patronised the Austin canons of Anglesey, the secular chapter of St Paul, and the Benedictines of Ely, and refounded a Cambridge college. Franciscan friars and sisters and another Cambridge college also enjoyed the favour of her friend Mary of St Pol, but so too did a heritage at Cripplegate, the Carthusians, and the Benedictines of Westminster and Battle.[54] Several conclusions arise from the wide spectrum of religious institutes thus patronised. Firstly we can be sure that it was not just the Minoresses among all these objects of their patronage that these wealthy benefactresses visited. They must have entered the other houses too. Secondly, it is hardly credible that it was only those of their patrons who also favoured the Minoresses who desired to enter the precincts of these other institutions and to participate in their observances. They must also have entered cathedrals, priories, hospitals, friaries etc and attended their services. We have already seen the flood of visitors to the Augustinian nunnery of Campsey that so disrupted the Countess of Ulster's observances.

What was it that caused these very different institutions all to appeal to the same minds? At present we can hardly guess at an answer. The patterns of giving were personal to each individual and were arrived at after frequent changes of mind and emphasis. Patrons were knowledgeable about and discriminating in what they chose to back. It follows that in the 14th century as in the 15th, at least at this level of society, patrons already had a clear set of preferences and tastes, which determined what they supported. It was merely their religious criteria and how they expressed them, not necessarily their knowledge and understanding, that changed over time. Evidently also the appeal of the Minoresses accounts for only part of the piety of even their most fervent adherents, who can only be fully comprehended, if then, when all their religious activities are analysed. Favour for the Minoresses was combined with other expressions of piety, in which different forms of monasticism, regulars *and* seculars, existed side by side. Those well—known rifts between regulars and seculars, parsons and friars, friars and possessioners do not seem *at this stage* to have touched these noble benefactors, who saw objects worthy of support in them all, patronised a wide rage of religious foundations, and in particular had not yet turned away from the older orders as they were later to do.

Of course the Minoresses represent a fashion that was socially restricted and short—term, to rank alongside the late medieval Carthusians, Bonhommes, triple foundations, and the cults of the Holy Name and the Five Wounds.[55] Yet they seem also to offer an insight to the religion of the contemporary nobility, which was already characterised by a highly organised non—parochial domestic piety and which eschewed the polarities current later.[56] By the late—13th and early 14th century few monasteries were being founded, perhaps because saturation point and overcapacity had genuinely been reached, but it does not follow that they had lost their appeal or importance to the aristocracy who, on this evidence, seem to have frequently visited them and attended their services. Much the same is suggested by the evidence of new foundations. If monasteries themselves had almost ceased to be founded, the vast majority of new chantries, at a time when more were being founded than in any other era, were set up in monasteries. This surely indicates personal acquaintance and trust as well as the businesslike invocation of space within and the oversight of an undying corporation. Only later, it appears, did monasticism lose its relevance and the older order cease to play an active part in the everyday religion of English aristocrats. Parochial religion, it is obvious, was already absent or unimportant to the high nobility. Was it only later, as Dr Richmond has suggested,[57] that it ceased to play a prominent part in the everyday religion of the English gentry? Perhaps the desertion of the parish church for the observances of monasteries and oratories stemmed not just from a snobbish desire for convenience and privacy, but from a search for more ordered and demanding religious observances appropriate to those of some education and pious aspirations?

NOTES

1. Research for this paper was undertaken during study leave kindly granted by King Alfred's College, Winchester in Lent term 1989.
2. A.F.C. Bourdillon, *The Order of Minoresses in England* (Manchester, 1926), [hereafter Bourdillon, *Minoresses*], pp 2, 13–14, 16, 18–23.
3. E.H. Carr, *What is History?* (2nd edn. London, 1987), p 14.
4. K.L. Wood–Legh, *Perpetual Chantries in Britain* (Cambridge, 1954); C.R. Burgess, 'Late Medieval Wills and Pious Convention: Testamentary Evidence Reconsidered' in ed., M.A. Hicks *Profit, Piety and the Profession in Later Medieval England* (Gloucester, 1990).
5. Quoted from P Heath, 'Urban Piety in the Later Middle Ages: the Evidence of Hull Wills', in ed., R.B. Dobson *The Church, Politics and Patronage in Later Medieval England* (Gloucester, 1874) [hereafter Dobson, *Church, Politics and Patronage*], p 229.
6. E.g., M.A. Hicks, 'The Piety of Margaret, Lady Hungerford (d. 1478)', *Journal of Ecclesiastical History*, 38 (1987), pp 19–38 and sources in n.2; 'Walter, Lord Hungerford (d. 1449) and his Chantry in Salisbury Cathedral', *Hatcher Review* 3.29 (1989), pp 391–99.
7. W. Langland, *Piers Plowman: The B Version*, eds., G. Kane and E.T. Donaldson, (London, 1975) [hereafter Langland, *Piers Plowman*], p 426. Were the Carthusians loyal to their original ideal or were they offering something new in the 14th century?
8. The rules of 'seint Maure', 'seint Beneit', and 'Austin' were equally disregarded by Chaucer's Monk, G. Chaucer, *Complete Works*, ed., F.N. Robinson (2nd edn. London, 1057) [hereafter *Chaucer's Works*], p 19.
9. From visitation records and satire. But can we distinguish between criticism of abuses and criticism of monasticism itself? May not those who satirise defaulting religious nevertheless approve monastic ideals? It is suggested below that support for monasticism in the 14th century was much greater than the evidence of new foundations suggests.
10. A.H. Thompson, *The English Clergy and their Organisation in the Later Middle Ages* (Oxford, 1947), p 132.
11. Bourdillon, *Minoresses*, p 26.
12. D. Knowles and R. Hadcock, *Heads of Religious Houses in England and Wales* (London, 1971) [hereafter Knowles & Hadcock], passim.
13. *Waterbeach*: the Piety of the Virgin; *Aldgate*: The Grace of St Mary and St Francis; *Denney*: St James and St Leonard [from the earlier Templar preceptory], the Virgin, and St Clare; *Bruisyard*: the Annunciation taken from the earlier chantry college. *Ibid.* pp 286–7; *Calendar of Patent Rolls 1354–8*, pp 484–5.
14. Thus Isabella of Lancaster, sister of several benefactors of the Minoresses, was prioress of Amesbury; Chaucer's genteel Prioress spoke French 'After the scole of Stratford atte Bowe', *Chaucers Works*, p 18.
15. Bourdillon, *Minoresses*, p 49.
16. *Ibid.*, pp 47, 49, & genealogical table.

17. *Ibid.*, p 14.
18. *Calendar of Papal Letters 1189–1304*, [hereafter *CPL*], p 526; Bourdillon, *Minoresses*, p 17.
19. J.R.H. Moorman, *A History of the Franciscan Order from its origins to the year 1517* (Oxford, 1968), p 406; G.E.C[okayne]. *Complete Peerage etc.*, eds. H.V. Gibbs and others, (13 vols. London, 1910–59), [hereafter *GEC*], p 422; D.N.B. sv Lancaster; Knowles & Hadcock. pp 223, 227, 228; H. Jenkinson, 'Mary de Sancto Paulo, Foundress of Pembroke College, Cambridge', *Archaeologia*, 66 (1914–15), [hereafter Jenkinson, 'Mary de Sancto Paulo'], pp 418, 420–21. Much space was devoted to St Francis in her breviary and she gave the site of Waterbeach for a new Franciscan friary, *ibid.*, p 420; *Victoria History of the County of Cambridge*, [hereafter *VCH*], iii, p 346; *CPL 1342–62*, p 285.
20. Bourdillon, *Minoresses*, pp 6, 27, 37–42, 44.
21. *Bullarium Francisanum*, ed., J.H. Saralea and others (10 vols. Rome & Quarda 1759–1908), [hereafter *BF*], ii, p 480.
22. *Ibid.*, ii. pp 482–4; Bourdillon, *Minoresses*, p 5.
23. *BF*. ii. p 41; Bourdillon, *Minoresses*, pp 8, 55–60.
24. I am indebted to Mrs Maire Wilkinson for this observation. The English Minoresses included widows from at least 1313, Bourdillon, *Minoresses*, p 88.
25. For what follows, see D.K. Coldictt, *The Hampshire Nunneries* (Chichester, 1989), esp. pp 90–3.
26. *Chaucer's Works*, p 18.
27. *Chaucer's Works*, p 19; Langland, *Piers Plowman*, p 425.
28. *CPL 1198–1304*, p 560; *1342–62*, p 68; *1362–1404*, p 49.
29. *CPL 1362–1404*, pp 37–8; *Calendar of Papal Petitions 1342–1419*, [hereafter *CPP*], p 488.
30. *CPP 1342–1419*, p 457; *CPL 1198–1304*, p 526; *1305–42*, p 82; *1342–62*, p 511; *1362–1404*, pp 31, 59. *CPP 1342–1419*, p 457, and *CPL 1362–1404*, p 31, disagree whether the Minoress was Elizabeth Beauchamp's mother or daughter ..
31. *CPL 1342–1419*, p 561.
32. *CPP 1342–1419*, pp 519, 531, 533.
33. *Ibid.*, p 102; Bourdillon, *Minoresses*, p 49 and n. 9.
34. Sir Nicholas Gernon: Bourdillon, *Minoresses*, p 67.
35. *Ibid.*, p 63n.
36. *CPL 1305–42*, pp 393, 413; *1342–62*, pp 68, 226; *CPP 1342–1419*, p 502.
37. Jenkinson, 'Mary de Sancto Paulo', pp 420, 430; P.M. Christie and J.G. Coad, 'Excavations at Denny Abbey', *Archaeological Journal*, 137 (1980), pp 138–279.
38. Bourdillon, *Minoresses*, pp 49–50.
39. W.C. Jordan, *Louix IX and the Challenge of the Crusade* (Princeton, 1979), pp 9–10; C.A.J. Armstrong, 'The Piety of Cecily Duchess of York: A Study in Late Medieval Culture', *England, France and Burgandy in the Fifteenth Century* (London, 1981), pp 135–46; M.G. Underwood 'Politics and Piety in the Household of Lady Margaret Beaufort', *Journal of Ecclesiastical History*, 38 (1987), pp 39–52; *CPL 1342–62*, p 113. The Lady Margaret's recorded piety follows the death of her first and second husbands, but antedates that of her third.
40. Denise fined to marry who she chose in 1257, remarried, but remained single c 1266–1302. *GEC* ix. pp 420–1.
41. See above p.
42. R. Archer, 'The Estates and Finances of Margaret of Brotherton, 1320–1399', *Historical Research*, 60 (1987), p 276.

43. R. Archer, 'The Problem of Late Medieval Dowagers', in ed., A.J. Pollard, *Property and Politics: Essays in Late Medieval English History*, (Gloucester, 1984), pp 15–35.

44. R.G.K.A. Mertes, 'The Household as a Religious Community', in eds., J.T. Rosenthal and C. Richmond, *People, Politics and the Community in the Later Middle Ages* (Gloucester, 1987), pp 108–37; R.G.K.A. Mertes, *The English Noble Household 1250–1600: Good Governance and Politic Rule* (Oxford, 1988), pp 139–60.

45. E.g., Countess of Ulster, Elizabeth Beauchamp, Elizabeth de Clare, *CPP 1342–1419*, p 457, 471; *1342–62*, pp 112, 179.

46. E.g., Henry Duke of Lancaster, Countess of Pembroke and Ulster, Elizabeth de Clare, Elizabeth Beauchamp, *CPP 1342–1419*, pp 69, 457; *CPL 1305–42*, pp 343, 404; *1342–62*, p 109.

47. It is worth remembering that *Le Livre des Seyntz Medecines* of Henry Duke of Lancaster was probably a penance – decidedly not an easy or light one! – imposed by a confessor, K. Fowler, *The King;'s Lieutenant: Henry of Grosmont, 1st Duke of Lancaster, 1310–61* (London, 1969), p 193.

48. E.g., Queen Blanche and Earl Edmund, countesses of Ulster and Arundel, Duke of Lancaster, Elizabeth de Clare, Elizabeth Beauchamp, and Maud de Lisle, *CP 1342–1419*, p 457; *CPL 1198–1304*, p 527; *1305–42*, pp 69, 112, 458, 511, 576.

49. E.g., Queen Isabella, Queen Blanche and Earl Edmund, Henry Duke of Lancaster, Mary of St Pol, Maud de Lisle, *CPP 1342–1419*, p 214; *CPL 1198–1304*, p 527; *1342–62*, pp 458, 511; *1362–1404*, p 57; *1305–42*, p 47. The same privilege was secured for the English houses of Minoresses, *BJ*, iv. p 386.

50. E.g., Henry Duke of Lancaster, countesses of Arundel and Pembroke, Maud de Lisle, *CPP 1342–1419*, p 2'14; *CPL 1342–62*, pp 458, 511, 560.

51. E.g., countesses of Pembroke and Ulster, Elizabeth de Clare, Henry Duke of Lancaster, *CPP 1342–1419*, pp 78, 102; *CPL 1342–62*, PP 68–9, 115, 137, 190.

52. E.g., Countess of Pembroke & Ulster, Earl & Countess of Suffolk, Henry Duke of Lancaster, Elizabeth Beauchamp, *CPL 1305–42*, p 393; *1342–62*, pp 68, 137, 607; *1363–1404*, p 59.

53. Internal accounts for most noble households and monasteries do not survive. Even when an individual's presence at a monastery is known or suspected from such accounts, e.g., by offerings or itineraries itemised in household/obedientary accounts or dating clauses, his/her attendance at services is rarely recorded.

54. *CPL 1342–62*, p 112; *CPR 1330–4*, p 477; *1343–5*, p 3; *1345–8*, p 255; *VCH Cambs*, ii. p 232; iii. pp 340–1; Jenkinson, 'Mary de Sancto Paulo', pp 418–10, 430–2.

55. For triple foundations, see M.A. Hicks, 'Prehistory, Foundation, and Re–Foundation: St Katherine's Hospital, Heytesbury, 1408–72', *Wiltshire Archaeological Magazine*, 77/78 (1984), pp 65–6; for the other cults, see R. Pfaff, *New Liturgical Feasts in Late Medieval England*, (London, 1970).

56. The shift to secular foundations had not yet happened. Thus Sir Robert Hungerford founded chantries in a parish church, secular cathedral, hospital, and houses of Trinitarian friars and Cistercian monks; his nephew William patronised Augustinian and Arrouasian canons and Bonhommes; but later Hungerfords were exclusively secular in their foundations M.A. Hicks, 'Chantries, Obits, and Almshouses: The

Hungerford Foundation 1325–1478', in eds., C. Barron and C. Harper–
Bill, *The Church in Pre–Reformation Society* (Woodbridge, 1985),
pp 123–42.

57. C. Richmond, 'Religion and the 15th–Century English Gentleman', in
Dobson, *Church, Politics, and Patronage*, pp 193–203, esp, pp 199, 203.
It is difficult to believe that any but the poorest gentlemen ever depended
on services in the parish church or participated fully in parochial life.

THE MOTIVES OF PATRONS OF THE ORDER OF ST LAZARUS IN ENGLAND IN THE TWELFTH AND THIRTEENTH CENTURIES[1]

John Walker

Any consideration of the development of a religious order, must at some point be concerned with the means by which, and the reasons why, that order was provided with lands and money by people from the outside world. However, if the means of support can be readily identified from the available source material, the motivations behind donations are not usually so obvious. Nowadays, it is generally accepted that despite the formulaic nature of most charter grants, at the heart of the vast majority of donations to ecclesiastical establishments, there lay a basic spiritual motive. Whether this came from genuine piety, guilt for past misdeeds, or a simple concern for the soul, religious feeling was clearly of paramount importance. And yet, if spiritual motivations go a long way to explaining ecclesiastical patronage in general, what factors led to a particular religious order receiving benefactions? It is the purpose of this paper to consider this question with reference to the Order of St Lazarus, one of the smaller Holy Land orders that came to England during the course of the twelfth century.

The Order of St Lazarus originated in the Holy Land in the second decade of the 12th century, following the capture of Jerusalem by the First Crusade.[2] Although its origins are obscure, it is likely that it developed from a situation whereby western knights who contracted the disease of leprosy were placed in an existing leper hospital staffed by Armenian monks, standing outside the northern walls of Jerusalem, near the gate of St Stephen. These knights included men from at least one military order, the Templars, whose rule specifically required its leprous members to enter the Order of St Lazarus.[3]

As number increased it is probable that a rudimentary organisation developed. The Rule of St Basil used by the Armenians was replaced in favour of the Rule of St Augustine, and a personnel structure developed which included a master at the head, with knights, clerics and brethren who cared for the sick. The scanty evidence at our disposal suggests that the order remained primarily concerned with hospital care (as was the case with the Hospitallers for the early part of their history), and the knights of the order seem only rarely to have become involved in large—scale military operations. Although they did take part in the Battle of Forbie in 1244 and were involved in the final siege of Acre in 1291, there is no reason to believe (as some eighteenth and nineteenth century historians have) that the order was at the forefront of the Christian fighting machine in the east.

As far as the wealth of St Lazarus goes, we know of certain possessions and rights that its members held, from a cartulary fragment of the Jerusalem house.[4] It seems that there were hospitals not only at Jerusalem, but also at Tiberius, Caesarea, Ascalon and Acre, where the headquarters of the order moved after the fall of Jerusalem in 1187, and where it remained until the loss of that city in 1291. The majority of its lands were held in the south of the kingdom around Jerusalem, Bethlehem and Hebron, but it did have some rights in the north, and outside the kingdom in Antioch and Tripoli. There is however, no evidence to suggest that it ever became as wealthy as the larger military orders, although it did attract many of the same patrons, including members of the royal family such as Fulk of Anjou, his wife Melisende, Baldwin III and Amaury I.[5] In addition nobles such as Raymond III of Tripoli and various member of the Ibelin clan patronised the order in a variety of ways.[6] However curiously enough there is no serious record of Baldwin IV, the leper king, patronising the order at all.[7]

As well as attracting the patronage of eastern Christians, numerous benefits were gained in the west. One example of this was the establishment of the order in France by Louis VII who gave them his castle at Boiny near Orlèans in c 1150.[8] Lands too were acquired in other parts of Europe including Southern Italy, the Holy Roman Empire[9] and England.

In England the order had at least thirteen houses.[10] The chief house was situated at Burton Lazars near Melton Mowbray in Leicestershire, and was probably founded by Roger I de Mowbray in c 1150. The idea is based on the first charter of the houses' cartulary,[11] which granted the order two carucates, a messuage and the site of a mill in Burton Lazars. Although this fact has never been conclusively proven, it is clear that by the fourteenth century the master of Burton Lazars regarded Roger I as the founder. Thus in a petition referring to problems with mastership disputes the opening lines speak of the founder and foundation thus, ' ... *frere Nicholo meistr' del hospitall' de Burton seint Lazare' et come le dit hospitall' estoit fondu devant temps de memore de l'ordre de seynt Lazar de Jerusalem par un Rog' de Monbray anncestr' Thom' de Monbray ore comit' de Not' et maresthall' D'engleterre* ...' .[12]

The master of Burton Lazars seems to have had some degree of authority over most of the other houses of the order (but not, as was once thought, over all the leper hospitals in England).[13] Before 1200 the order had acquired the hospitals of Tilton and Carlton, and probably also the two Norfolk houses at Choseley and Wymondhan. In the early thirteenth century Harting and Harehope were added; while the two larger houses of St Giles of Holborn and Holy Innocents at Lincoln were given to the order in 1299 and 1456 respectively. In England the functions of the order appear to have been confined to the raising of funds for the Holy Land, and the care of lepers. This function appears to have been carried out until the Dissolution, although the number of lepers in its houses was probably not very great at that time.

Although the order was widely spread over eastern England, almost all our source material is connected with the hospital at Burton Lazars and the order's lands in Leicestershire and parts of Lincolnshire. Our most important piece of source material comes in the form of the cartulary of the hospital of Burton Lazars mentioned above.[14] This was drawn up in 1404 at the command of the then master Walter de Lynton.[15] Over 400 charters deal with the order's possessions in the East Midlands, and the information therein can be supplemented by a miscellaneous collection of documents from the British Library, Public Record Office and the local record offices of Leicestershire and Lincolnshire. These include cartularies of other religious houses who had dealings with the order; various special collections of documents, (such as the petitions to chancery and exchequer contained in the Public Record Office); and a variety of individual charters making basic grants of land, not contained in the main Cartulary: This evidence is almost wholly connected with the economic and administrative side of life, and there is little evidence of internal organisation, save for a few references to mastership disputes. It tells us little therefore about hospital life, but a great deal about the order's English possessions, and more importantly for our purposes, who its patrons were.

The available evidence shows us that the grants given to the order, mainly of land and rents, were not as important as those given to the Templars and Hospitallers. However, the list of patrons does contain some of the names, including members of the Angevin royal family.[16] The order also enjoyed limited patronage from the Scottish royal house,[17] as well as noble patronage from the Earls of Derby, Leicester, and Northampton.[18] In addition they received grants from Henry de Lacy and Roger de Mowbray,[19] as well as from less well known families such as the Burdets of Newton and Lowesby in Leicestershire, and the Amundeville family in Lincolnshire.[20]

Turning aside from the history of the order and its patronage, we can now consider the more difficult problem of the motivations of its patrons. In the introduction we accepted a basic spiritual motive for ecclesiastical patronage in general. Going one step further Edward Kealey has argued that people may have been led to patronise hospitals (including the leper hospitals of the Order of St Lazarus), simply because they started to follow contemporary fashions of patronage. He notes that one of the twelfth century trends in this sphere was towards hospital patronage, following an increased interest in charity and social welfare.[21] In his book 'Medieval Medicus', he describes the dramatic rise between 1100–1154 of hospital foundations including leper hospitals. By 1100 there were only about twenty one hospitals in England, and yet by 1154 this number had risen to at least 113 (of which a third were for lepers). Kealey's argument does have some appeal, although there is a possibility that he may be describing a trend discernible from modern times, but which in the twelfth century, may have not seemed so obvious or so influential to contemporaries.

Even if people were following fashions in hospital patronage this still does not explain why people specifically chose St Lazarus. To explain this we need to consider two main types of influence. On the one hand, influences derived from the nature of the order itself, and on the other hand, influences derived from the backgrounds of the particular patrons. It will be the purpose of the rest of this paper to consider each type of influence, and to identify which was the most important in leading people to patronise the order.

Looking at the nature of the Order of St Lazarus there are two distinctive features, which combined, set it apart from other religious orders. The first is that it was a crusading order, originating in the Holy Land, and the second is that one of its main aims was the care of lepers.

A study of the backgrounds of the various patrons of the order reveals that only a very limited number were personally connected with the crusading movement. In a charter addressed to his son Robert, Nigel of Amundaville commands him to allow the brethren of St Lazarus to enjoy half a bovate of land he granted to them in free alms, '... because of the help the brethren gave to me in Outremer ...'.[22] In a similar vein, William Burden I has been described as a crusader by both Dugdale and Nichols, although the latter's reference can be discounted because it suggests that he was on crusade after the fall of Jerusalem in 1187, when in fact Pipe Roll evidence shows that he was dead by 1184.[23] Dugdale's reference (for which he unfortunately gives no specific source) seems to be rather more realistic, suggesting that he was on pilgrimage or possibly the Second Crusade in the mid twelfth century, on his return from which he founded Alvecote Priory in Warwickshire.[24]

The Mowbray family seem to have been a particularly keen crusading family with two and possibly three members being involved in the movement to one degree or another in the twelfth century. It is possible that Roger I may have made four separate journeys to the Holy Land.[25] He was involved in the Second Crusade in 1147 and made a second journey in the 1160's, during which he witnessed a charter to the order given by King Amaury I in 1164.[26] A third, but rather more doubtful journey may will have been made in 1177, shortly after the failure of the baronial rebellions of 1173–1174. He certainly made his final journey just before the Third Crusade, taking the cross in 1185, being captured by the moslems at the Battle of Hattin in July 1187, and although he was successfully ransomed by the Templars and Hospitallers, he died shortly afterwards.

Roger was not the only crusader in the family. His son Nigel I also participated in the Third Crusade, leaving England in December 1189, but unfortunately dying at Acre in 1191.[27] His eldest son William may also have been involved in this expedition, and he was certainly among Richard I's entourage in Germany, where he acted as a hostage for the king's ransom.[28]

Participation in the crusading movement could have led to these men becoming involved with, or at least aware of the activities of the military orders. Of the people we have mentioned, only Nigel de Amundeville and Robert I de Mowbray seem to have had personal contact with the order. However other patrons such as Geoffrey of Hay who also went on the Third Crusade may also have enjoyed the same contact, and we do know of examples from other countries where this was the case. Thus Louis VII's foundation at Boigny had its origins in the impression that the Order's Hospital at Jerusalem made upon the king while he was on the Second Crusade.[29]

Nevertheless it seems that it was only in a few instances that the crusading background of the order influenced its patrons. Even in charters contained in the Burton Lazars cartulary, although many of the dedications contain 'Jerusalem' in them, few mention any crusading–related motive for the actual grant.[30] If this part of the order's nature was not influential, how big a part did the second distinguishing characteristic of the order, its care of lepers, play in the motivation of its patrons?

Evidence given by the juror's of the wapentake of Graffhoe in Lincolnshire during the Quo Warrant enquiries of 1274–1275, suggests that this may have had some effect on patronage. The jurors recorded that the brethren of Burton Lazars had held one carucate of land in Carlton for eighty years, and that, '... they have that carucate of land from the gift of Elias de Amudaville along with a leprous daughter...'[31]. Aside from the possibility that this refers to an additional grant made by Elias not referred to in the cartulary, it is important because of its reference to the leprous daughter, who was also given to the order. It was quite a common practice for new entrants to leper hospitals to bring support for themselves in the nature of land or money, either from themselves or from their relatives.[32] It is probable that in the case of Elias' daughter the revenues drawn from the carucate were meant to do just that.

The cartulary of the order in Jerusalem reveals such a practice taking place in the Holy Land, when in 1248 Stephen of Salerno gave the order a rent of ten shillings so that his son Austorge should be admitted as a brother.[33] One modern commentator has argued that the patronage of the order as a whole can be seen in a similar way, in that not only did St Lazarus receive gifts when lepers entered its establishments, but also friends and relatives of the inmates continued to patronise the order long afterwards.[34] This perhaps helps to explain Elias' later grants to the order, and can once again be seen in the Jerusalem cartulary, where in 1160, Hugh Lord of Caesara is recorded as giving the order two houses in Caesarea, '... for the love of my brother Eustace, who is a brother in that house ...'.[35]   However, the cartulary of Burton Lazars contains no similar references, and while the idea appears to be as plausible as the idea that crusading connections led people to patronise the order, until further supportive material for either influence can be found, we need to look beyond the nature of the order for other motives which may have influenced its patronage.   In particular we need to look at the backgrounds of various patrons, at their family, feudal, social and geographical connections.

One of the more important influences in this section seems to have been that of family connections.   This factor has already been pointed to as an influence by such historians as Richard Mortimer,[36] and evidence from the cartulary of Burton Lazars suggests that family connections did have a substantial effect[37], whether it was in a simple confirmation of a predecessor's grant, or in additional grants of varying sizes.

Evidence from a number of families already mentioned can be used to illustrate this point. Thus members of the Burdet family descended from Robert Burdet I seem to have followed the lead of William I Burdet, who gave the order the hospital of Tilton, a carucate of land in Cold Newton and three churches at Lowesby, Galby and Haselbeech.[38] In total this forms one of the largest known grants made to the order, and it was augmented by William's son Richard, who gave another carucate of land in Great Dalby.[39] William's grandson, William III, gave the equivalent of two carucates when he assigned the order land in Cold Newton, and this and other Burdet grants were all confirmed in 1298 by William V.[40] Finally it is worth mentioning the several other Burdet family members patronised the order in a smaller way throughout the 13th century, including members of the family of Emma Burdet who may have been the daughter in law of William I Burdet.[41]

This patterning of large initial grants, followed by smaller additions by family members with a general confirmation at a later date, can be traced in the Mowbray family where Robert I provided the initial large grants in Burton Lazars,[42] his sons Nigel and Robert, and grandson William added to this original foundation grant,[43] and a thirteenth century descendant, Roger II de Mowbray made a confirmation of all the family grants to the order.[44] Although the patterning is not strictly the same, family patronage can be traced throughout the cartulary with for instance the Amundevilles in Carlton,[45] and the Belers of Eye Kettleby and Kirby Bellars.[46]

The strength of family influence can be seen at a lower level, amongst the more obscure, localised families who gave to the Order of St Lazarus in a small way.   Even when we do not know very much about them, their charters often refer to other grants made by family members. Thus we know from a charter of Hugh de Rampaine of Kirby Bellars, that his uncle Gilbert and his own father were patrons of the order in the same village.[47]   The list of small patrons contained in the cartulary can for the most part be divided into small family groupings of this sort, and even smaller groups of just father and son, as in the case of William and Gilbert de Aumary of Burton Lazars.[48]

Although in some cases the scale of donations may have faded away, the family links continued through several generations, showing a lasting connection with the original family members' chosen outlet for patronage. This is of course not restricted to the Order of St Lazarus, and for instance it is clear that the same influences were at work for the Templars.

However, family connections were not the only important influence at work. Another factor, which had little to do with the nature of the order itself, was the tie of lordship. This particular influence does not seem to have been as active at all levels of society. With the Mowbrays the connection seems to be rather tenuous. The Mowbrays were tenants in chief, and although Henry II did patronise the order this came in the 1170's by which time Roger I's original foundation charter had been made. In any case the family was not generally close to their feudal lords. Roger I and his two sons were all involved in the rebellions of 1173–1174 against Henry II,[49] and although William de Mowbray was on good terms with Richard I he was an opponent of King John in and before 1215.[50]

Nevertheless, there is evidence that other patrons were influenced by feudal ties. In the case of the Burdet tenure from the Honour of Huntingdon the problem is complicated by the complex nature of the tenure of this Honour in the 12th century, which alternated between the possession of the Scottish royal family and the Senlis family.[51] In fact members of both families patronised the order, although David earl of Huntingdon's patronage of Simon III de Senlis who held the Honour from 1174 to 1184 may have been more influential. Simon and his wife made at least two grants to the order, one of which gave the advowson of the three Lincolnshire churches of Great Hale, Heckington and Threekingham.[53] The similarity with the grant of William I is striking, although because it is difficult to accurately date his charter, it is not clear whether he made his grant before, or after that of Simon.

Feudal influences on the whole seem to have been more influential further down the feudal ladder. Thus while the Mowbays do not seem to have been much influenced by their own feudal lords, their patronage of the order seems to have been augmented by the work of their own tenants.[54] Thus if we look at the list of Mowbray tenants contained in the *carta* of 1166, we find that four people were patrons of the order, Hamon Beler, Warin Fitz Simon, Hugh II de Rampaine and Rannulf of Queniborugh.[55] To these we can add members of the families of the tenants of 1166, who held land either before or after this date. These include William I Beler who held possibly the same fee as Hamon Beler from Nigel II de Mowbray between 1224 and 1230,[56] and Herbert de Queniborough who was succeeded by his brother Rannulf before 1166.[57] In addition it is quite possible that some members of the Burdet family were tenants of the Mowbrays. Although the first record of this family holding one fee in Cold Newton comes in 1235–1236,[58] William I had made a grant there before 1184 which suggests that he had been given land there by the Mowbrays at some point after 1166, as he is not recorded in the *carta* of that year.[59]

We must however, be aware that a feudal link may not have been so influential in terms of motivation to patronage if there was no close association beyond the formal link. Feudal connections did not necessarily mean close association and involvement, and as we have shown at a higher level, tenants may not have had much in common with their feudal lords, and may not have been influenced by how their lords acted in terms of patronage. In fact to see if lordship did have any influence on patronage it is better to look beyond the basic feudal bond to more solid evidence of association, as shown by the attestations of patrons to various lord's charters.

The charters of Roger I de Mowbray provide us with a good example of an important patron whose witness lists include other patrons of the order. Thus we find that while only a possible six men who patronised the order were tenants of Roger I, at least sixteen men who witnessed his charters were patrons.[60] Of these sixteen, three were from Roger's own family. These were Nigel and Robert his sons who witnessed frequently alongside their father, and William his grandson.[61] Of the remainder Hamon and Rannulf Beler witnessed forty nine and twenty seven charters respectively,[62] while other relatively frequent attestors included Herbert of Queniborough, Mathew of Rampaine and Geoffrey of Hay.[63] This patterning whereby more patrons witnessed Mowbray charters than were Mowbray tenants can also be traced very clearly with the Templars.

Witness lists also provide us with another possible influence on patronage. This time association is not traced with the grantor of the charter, but with the other witnesses to the charter. The witness lists of the cartulary of Burton Lazars provide ample evidence of such group attestations. Thus one group of such patrons included William Aumary, John Burdet, John Fegge, William Freman, William Hasard and William Ivette. Between them they made a series of thirty two relatively small grants to the order, and as these charters show they witnessed together frequently in each other's company.[64] Where particular people appear together frequently as witnesses as in these examples, there is a very definite suggestion that they moved in the same social circles, and thus took notice of what their peers were doing, including what sort of religious houses they patronised.

Among such less important individuals one other factor is worth noting. Such people, unlike the Mowbrays who held lands in many different areas, had what may be described as limited geographical horizons. From this fact stems the idea that such people may have been influenced by their surroundings, that the best house to patronise was seen by a person as the one built closest to his own house and lands. A study of the origins of the patrons, whose names are contained in the Burton Lazars Cartulary, shows that just over forty percent of them came from an area of within four miles of the hospital, that fifty percent came from within five miles and a further twenty came from between five and ten miles of the hospital. Significantly, within the five mile radius, there was no other religious house until the early fourteenth century. Indeed eastern Leicestershire and the bordering lands of Lincolnshire and Rutland were only sparsely endowed with such institutions. In the twelfth century in that area, only three other houses were in existence, the Premonstatensian house of Croxton Kerrial founded about 1162.[65] and the Augustinian houses of Launde (founded before 1125)[66] and Owston (founded before 1161).[67] In Rutland there was an Augustinian house at Brooke (founded before 1153)[68] while in Lincolnshire the closest house was the small Templar preceptory of South Witham founded in about 1164.[69] Admittedly there was a large foundation at Leicester from 1143,[70] yet for the lesser individuals living in Burton Lazars, Melton Mowbray and Kirby Bellars and the surrounds, the most obvious choice in terms of close proximity may well have still been the leper hospital.

Having considered a number of factors which seem to have had some influence on the patronage of the order of St Lazarus we can now come to some conclusions. Firstly, and perhaps most obviously, what we have said as regards the motives for patronage of the order can to some extent be applied to all religious orders. Every order had its own identity which might or might not have appealed to prospective patron, while patrons could be influenced by the fact that their friends or relatives had entered a particular religious house. Similarly all patrons had family, feudal, social and geographical ties, to varying degrees.

A second point to make is that although we have been considering each of the various motives in isolation, it is of course the case that for most of the patrons of the order, more than one factor was taken into account. Thus Nigel and William de Mowbray may have been concerned to patronise a crusading order in the later twelfth century, not only because they were about to leave England for the Holy Land, but also because of the fact that they were related to the founder of the chief house of one such order.

Similarly, although Elias de Amundeville may have been influenced into making benefactions to the order because his daughter was in their care, his original wish to send her to the order's house in Carlton presumably had something to do with the fact that the house was founded by his grandfather. On a lower level things might be even more complex. Thus William de Aumary's decision to make grants to the order could have been influenced by knowledge that his lord, Robert de Chevercourt was a patron of the order,[71] by the awareness that many of his peers were patrons, or by the fact that he happened to live in the locality of the leper hospital.

Finally we must come to some conclusions on the question of what inspired greater patronage to the order of St Lazarus, the nature of the order, or the background of its patrons. It will already have become clear from what has been said, that the evidence suggests that it was the latter influence which had more importance. This is not to say that the nature of the order was insignificant in the minds of its patrons. Clearly important grants were inspired by such factors as the crusading connections of the order, yet for the majority of the grants, ties of family and lordship probably did more than anything to lead people to patronise the order. In the case of people lower down the social scale, ties of geography and awareness of the actions of one's peers were also important. Thus Roger de Mowbray's original foundation at Burton Lazars may well have been inspired by his recent journey on crusade to the Holy Land. However, it must be stated that after the initial crusading impulses of men like Roger had died away, it was the social ties of family and lordship, remaining consistently important to benefactors, that did more than anything to ensure a continuation of the patronage of the order which began in the mid twelfth century.

NOTES

I would particularly like to thank Dr Simone C. MacDougal for helpful comments and criticisms in connection with the preparation of this paper.

2.   A number of books have been writen abut the Order of St Lazarus. However many of them are inaccurate, particularly (although not exclusively) those published before 1900. The most modern work on the order in the Holy Land is S. Shahar, 'Des Lepreux Pas Comme Les Autres', *Révue Historique* 267 (1982), pp 19–41. Other good general studies include R. Pétiet, *Contribution a l'histoire de l'ordre de Saint–Lazare de Jérusalem en France* (Paris, 1914), [hereafter Pétiet, *L'ordre de Saint–Lazare*) and P.B. de la Grassière, *L'ordre Militaire et Hospitalier de Saint–Lazare de Jérusalem* (Paris, 1932 and 1960). An example of a work which must be treated with caution is G. de Sibert, *Histoire des Ordres Royaux, Hospitaliers Militaires de Notre Dame du Mont Carmel et de Saint Lazare de Jérusalem* (Paris, 1772) [hereafter Silbert, *Ordres Royaux*).

3.   H. de Curzon, *La Règle du Temple* (Paris, 1886), pp 239, 240.

4. A. de Marsy, 'Fragment d'un Cartulaire de l'ordre de Saint–Lazare, en Terre–Sainte', *Archives de l'orient Latin* 2 (1884), [hereafter Marsy, 'Fragment d'un Cartulaire'], pp 121–157.

5. *Ibid.*, pp 124 (Fulk), 129, 130, 135 (Melisende), 124, 128 (Baldwin III), 140, 144, 145 (Amaury I).

6. *Ibid.*, pp 147 (Raymond), 142, 150 (Ibelin family).

7. H.E. Mayer, *The Crusades* (Oxford, 1988), p 129. For a spurious story connecting Baldwin with foundations in what is modern day Switzerland, see Pétiet, *L'ordre de Saint–Lazare*, pp 144–147.

8. A. Luchaire, *Etudes sur les Actes de Louis VII* (Paris, 1885), p 208. Pétiet, *L'ordre de Saint Lazare*, p 101.

9. *Ibid.*, pp 126–147.

10. A good general account of the hospital of Burton Lazars and of the order in England can be found in *The Victoria History of the Counties of England. Leicestershire* II, pp 36–38. The most recent study on the order in this country is T. Bourne and D. Marcombe, *The Burton Lazars Cartulary: A Medieval Leicestershire Estate* (Nottingham, 1987) [hereafter Marcombe, *Burton Lazars*).

11. *British Library ms. Cotton Nero CXII* [hereafter *B.L. Cotton Nero CXII*), f. 3.

12. *Public Record Office. Petitions to Chancery and Exchequer. SC8/302/M.15081.* It is possible of course that the petition by the order to the king might simply have used Roger's name, in order to gain favour in the Royal court, because of his connection with Thomas de Mowbray, an influential man in the kingdom at the time. However, the position of Roger's charter at the front of the cartulary, and the absence of any other known charters concerned with Burton Lazars before his grant, suggests that Master Nicholas was probably reflecting not only contemporary opinions, but also historical fact.

13. J. Nichols, *The History and Antiquities of the County of Leicestershire*, six volumes, (London, 1795–1810–1811) [hereafter Nichols, *Leicestershire*), II.i, p 272.

14. See above p 4.

15. *B.L. Cotton Nero CXII*, f.3.

16. For the patronage of Henry II see L. Delisle, *Recueil des Actes de Henri II* (Paris, 1909–1927) pp 44, 118, 169, 218, and *Calendar of Charter Rolls preserved in the Public Record Office 1226–1516*, six volumes, (1903–1927) [hereafter *Charter Rolls*], IV, p 76.

17. For the patronage of King David I of Scotland see, ed., G.W.S. Barrow, *Regesta Regum Scottorum 1153–1424, The Acts of William I*, four volumes, (Edinburgh, 1971), pp 116–117.

18. For the patronage of the Earls of Derby see, *British Library ms. Harleian 3868*, f. 15, 16. For the patronage of the Earls of Leicester see *B.L. Cotton Nero CXII*, f. 110. For the patronage of the Earls of Northampton see *Ibid.*, f.4v, and *Charter Rolls* IV, p 77.

19. For Henry de Lacy see *Ibid.* For Roger I de Mowbray see *B.L. Cotton Nero CXII*, ff.3v(2), 4, 4v(2), 45.

20. For Burdet grants see below pp 13–14. For Amundeville grants see *B.L. Cotton Nero CXII*, ff. 116–118v.

21. E.J. Kealey, *Medieval Medicus* (Baltimore, 1981), pp 82–84.

22. *BL. Cotton Nero CXII*, f. 118v, '... quod fratres predicti in partibus transmarinis tantos mihi fecerunt...'.

23. Nichols, *Leicestershire*, III.i, p 337. *Pipe Rolle* 31 Henry II (1184), p 104.

24. W. Dugdale, *Monasticon Anglicanun*, new edn. eds., J Caley, H. Ellis, B. Bandinel, six volumes in eight, (London, 1846), III, p 455.

25. D. Greenway, *Charters of the Honour of Mowbray 1107–1191* (London, 1872,) [hereafter Greenway, *Mowbray Charters*), xxvi–xxxii.
26. Marsy, *Fragment d'un Cartulaire*, p 140.
27. Greenway, *Mowbray Charters*, xxxii.
28. G.E. Cockayne, *The Complete Peerage*, new edn. V. Gibbs, H.A. Doubleday, Lord Howard de Walden, ed., G.H. White, thirteen volumes in fourteen, IX, pp 373–374.
29. Pétiet, *L'ordre de Saint Lazare*, p 101.
30. For an exception to the rule see, *B.L. Cotton Nero CXII*, f. 19.
31. Ed., W. Illingworth, *Rotuli Hundredorum temp. Hen. III and Edw. I in Turr' Lond' et in curia Receptare Scaccarii Westm. asservati*, two volumes, Record Commission (1812–1818), p 284B, '.... et habuerunt illam carucatam terre de dono Elye de Mundevile cum quadam filia sua leprosa..'.
32. The statues of the Leper Hospital of St Julian near St Albans refer to this practice. See P. Richards, *The Medieval Leper and his Northern Heirs* (London, 1977). See also Marcombe, *Burton Lazars*, p 13.
33. Marsy, *Fragment d'un Cartulaire*, p 157 '...Stephanus de Salerno, dono et imperpetuum concedo, amore Dei ... et, quod filium meum Austorgium benignissime atque karitative in fratrem recipere (dignentur) ...'.
34. D. Marcombe, 'Burton Lazars and the Knights of St Lazarus', *St John Historical Society Newsletter 1986*, (*N6*).
35. Marsy, *Fragment d'un Cartulaire*, p 137, '.. et pro amore fratris mei Eustachii, qui eiusdem domus frater est..'.
36. R. Mortimer, 'Religious and Secular Motives for some English Monastic Foundations', *Studies in Church History* 15 (1978), pp 77–85, 81. For some more wide–ranging comments on the importance of the family in this period see J.C Holt, 'Feudal Society and the Family in early Medieval England: III, Patronage and Politics', *Transactions of the Royal Historical Society* 34 (1984), pp 1–25.
37. Marcombe, *Burton Lazars*, p 14.
38. *B.L. Cotton Nero CXII*, f. 98.
39. *Ibid.*, f. 40.
40. *B.L. Cotton Nero CXII* f.100. The main portion of William III's charter is only known from this confirmatory grant. However the last part of his charter is to be found immediately before the confirmation, *Ibid.* Marcomb, *Burton Lazars*, p 56, without identifying the charter as one of William III's charters, states that it begins on f.99, where the first line is erased. However this charter which is incomplete, is in fact a Papal Charter, possibly of Innocent IV. See W Holtzmann, *Papsturkunden in England*, three volumes, (Göttingen, 1952), III, p 89.
41. *Ibid.*, ff. 12, 13, 24v(2), 25(2), 25v(2), 36, 39.
42. *Ibid.*, f.3.
43. *Ibid.*, ff.3(2), 5, 45 (Nigel I); f. 42v (Robert); ff.3v, 44 (William).
44. *Ibid.*, f.4.
45. See above p 6, n.13.
46. *B.L. Cotton Nero CXII* ff.50v(2), 51, 51v(2), 109.
47. *Ibid.*, f.45v.
48. *Ibid.*, ff.13v, 16, 16v(2), 17v(2), 18, 27v.
49. Greenway, *Mowbray Charters*, xxix.
50. *Complete Peerage* IX, pp 373–374.
51. *Ibid.*, VI, pp 640–647. See also K.J. Stringer, *David Earl of Huntingdon* (Edinburgh. 1985), pp 107–108 and 126.
52. *B.L. Cotton Nero CXII* f.4v.
53. See above p 6, n 11.

54.	*B.L. Cotton Nero CXII* f.4. Roger III de Mowbray confirms the donations made to the Order, '...*ex donatione et concessione antecessorum meorum et suorum tenentium...*'.

55.	Ed., H. Hall, *The Red Book of the Exchequer*, three volumes, (Rolls Series, 1896) [hereafter *Red Book*], pp 418–421.

56.	Ed., H.C. Maxwell Lyte, *Book of Fees*, (1920–1931), three volumes, (London, 1920, 1923, 1931), [hereafter *Book of Fees*] II, p 1462.

57.	Greenway, *Mowbray Charters*, p 24.

58.	*Book of Fees*, p 519.

59.	*Red Book*, pp 418–421.

60.	Although it must be stated that often the most frequent attestors were also Roger's tenants.

61.	Greenway, *Mowbray Charters*. for Nigel I see pp 22,25, 38, 45, 48(2), 52, 53, 60, 69, 77, 80, 81, 82, 84, 85, 88, 89, 91, 106, 111, 112, 117, 119, 140, 148, 157, 166, 167, 174, 175, 183, 187, 191(2) 198, 199(2), 200, 203(2), 213, 222, 226, 229, 231, 240, 241, 249, 253. For Robert see pp 22–23, 24, 38, 45, 47, 49(2), 50, 53, 69, 81, 83. 87, 88, 89, 91, 96, 97, 98, 108, 110, 112, 143, 147, 148. 157, 166, 166–167, 184, 188, 189, 199, 200, 201, 203(2), 204, 223, 224, 234, 236, 238, 240, 247. For William see pp 148, 238.

62.	*Ibid.* For Hamon see pp 21, 22, 24, 26, 27, 31, 41, 45, 50, 64, 65, 81, 87, 90, 99, 100, 107, 108, 119, 129, 130, 135, 144–145, 148, 163, 166(2), 168, 185, 198, 199(2), 200, 203, 209, 214, 217, 222(2), 223, 224, 227, 230, 231, 234, 235, 240, 248, 253. For Rannulf see pp 29, 76, 77, 78, 119, 141, 143(2), 162, 163(2), 164, 165(2), 194, 195, 197, 198(2), 210(2), 226, 228, 230, 240, 242, 246.

63.	*Ibid.* For Herbert of Queniborough see pp 23, 33, 191, 208, 228, 242, 244, 246, 255. For Mathew of Rampaine see pp 21, 28, 29, 30, 70, 71, 128, 208, 239. For Geoffrey of Hay see pp 63, 185, 203, 214, 222.

64.	For William Aumary, see above p 15, n. 40, and for John Burdet see above p 14, n.33 For the rest see *B.L. Cotton Nero CXII* f.16 (John Fegge); ff. 12v, 14v, 19v, 20v, 21(2), 31v(2) (William Freman); ff.12, 19, 24(2), 35(2) (William Hasard); ff. 15, 22v, 30v (William Ivette).

65.	D. Knowles and R.N. Hadcock, *Medieval Religious Houses England and Wales* (London, 1971), p 187.

66.	*Ibid.*, p 163.

67.	*Ibid.*, p 169.

68.	*Ibid.*, p 150.

69.	*Ibid.*, p 297.

70.	*Ibid.*, p 163.

71.	*B.L. Cotton Nero CXII* ff. 27, 27v. He confirms William's grants, *Ibid.*, f.18v.

JACQUEMART GIÉLÉE'S *RENART LE NOUVEL*: THE IMAGE OF THE MILITARY ORDERS ON THE EVE OF THE LOSS OF ACRE

Helen Nicholson

In this paper I shall be discussing the image of two monastic orders at a crucial point in their history, as revealed by a contemporary satire.

The military order was a unique development of the monastic ideal, a response to the need of the armed forces to defend Christian pilgrims in the Latin kingdom of Jerusalem from attack by Muslim bandits.[1] Many such orders were founded for this purpose between the capture of Jerusalem by the first crusade in 1099 and the loss of the last capital of the kingdom, Acre, in 1291, but the most famous and most important were the order of the Temple of Solomon, the Hospital of St John, and the Teutonic order.

The question of their image is of great importance, for two main reasons. Firstly, the trial and abolition in the early fourteenth century of the order of the Temple has often been attributed to its unpopularity. The survival of the other military orders would therefore imply that the Temple was the most unpopular order; but this is yet to be established. Secondly, recent instigation into attitudes towards crusading during the thirteenth century have demonstrated that the crusade did not, as was previously thought, decline in popularity during this period, and that in fact crusading continued to attract support long after the loss of Acre.[2] Since the military orders, as defenders of the Holy Land, were an integral part of the crusading movement, changes in their image shed valuable light on attitudes towards crusading.

In a study of opinions and attitudes, literary sources offer a rich mind of evidence. The difficulties and dangers of using such material as historical evidence have often been discussed.[3] However, all historical evidence must be assessed according to its own restrictions, and, as an increasing number of historians are demonstrating, a study of literary sources can open hitherto undreamt–of paths for investigation.[4] In the case of *Renart le Nouvel*, the literary source both endorses the evidence of chronicles and documents and throws into relief aspects which might otherwise have been dismissed.

This particular text is of great significance in illustrating the image of the military orders. It gives a detailed and critical picture of the two most important military orders, the order of the Temple and the Hospital of St John, at a critical point in their history, that is, shortly before the loss of Acre in 1291. Four manuscripts of this text survive, all written at the end of the thirteenth or the beginning of the fourteenth century, and none of which is the original. The oldest and best quality manuscript was copied for Guy de Dampierre, count of Flanders.[5] It appears, therefore, that the poem enjoyed immediate if short–lived popularity and that the opinions it presents were endorsed by the highest nobility of Flanders and north–east France.

Jacquemart Giélée was a Flemish poet, writing, he himself informs us, in Lille in the year 1289.[6] His poem *Renart le Nouvel* is based on the popular tale of the fox, whose name means everything contrary to honour and courtesy: slyness, trickery, and unscrupulousness. Under Giélée's pen, however, the amusing satire became, while still a satire, a moralizing romance lamenting the weakness of the clergy in the face of Evil, and their failure to protect the laity from its effects.

The poem is concerned with Renart's final triumph over the last bastions of virtue. During the course of the poem, the loyalty of a knight to his king, to his friend and to his lady are all shown as being infected and destroyed by Renart. As for the clergy, Giélée depicts them as being already in Renart's grip and beyond salvation, sailing his ship of Vice, shrouded in hypocrisy in order to avoid detection, blown by the wind of sin.[7] The pope has the rudder, assisted by the cardinals, while the sailors are the clerks, priests, archbishops, bishops, deans, abbots, monks, and friars. However, after recounting Renart's triumph over the laity, Giélée returns to the clergy and describes their final downfall in detail. Renart loads them with gifts (covetousness, guile, avarice, envy and pride) and they all enter his confraternity and are permitted to wear his grey habit of hypocrisy. Then all depart to *Haut Orguel*, (Great Pride) which used to belong to Lucifer. Only the friars remain, because they are too poor to reach Great Pride. First the Dominicans and then the Franciscans ask Renart to join their order, in order to make them rich, but he refuses, giving each order one of his sons instead. Led by young Renart, the Dominicans reach Great Pride, but the Franciscans are still held back by St Francis' rule. They do, however, reach *Outrecuidier* (Big Ideas) which, Giélée informs us, is only ten leagues from Great Pride.[8]

In case, however, his readers thought that there was no one left untouched by *renardie*. Giélée goes on to deal with two groups of religious so far unmentioned. Having put his sons into religious orders, Renart decides that he, too, will make his peace with God. He declares his desire to a poor hermit; 'I wish to confess and be reconciled to God, and make amends, and enter religion.' The hermit agrees to confess him and listens while Renart first describes a life of unmitigated evil, and then demands absolution and reception into his hermitage. When, however, Renart discovers that the hermit does not (as he had thought) eat good food, drink plenty of wine and have lovely ladies with him in his cell, he declares: 'I hate such religion', and departs for home, where he is warmly welcomed by his wife and family.[9]

The eremitical life, then, remains pure, according to Giélée. Another bastion of perceived spiritual purity is, however, about to fall. Fame of Renart spreads throughout the world, until his name comes to Acre, where the Templars and Hospitallers take it up. The implication of this is that they had previously been free of it.[10]

Both orders claim Renart, and promptly go to law against each other. They nearly come to blows, but decide to take their case to the papal court.[11]

In Rome a general council is held over their case, attended by monks, abbots, kings and counts, dukes and bishops, knights, prelates, archbishops, cardinals, the patriarch of Jerusalem and Renart himself.[12] Renart gives the patriarch of Jerusalem, whom, he says, he regards as a friend, his son *Souduians* (Deceiving). The patriarch departs at once, very pleased with his acquisition.[13]

The case is then heard. So that Giélée's picture of the two orders may be better understood, rather than discuss the case piecemeal I shall give it in its entirety, in translation, and then discuss the points it raises.

At that there rose a Templar, for he well saw that he'd better do
so, and said, 'Lords, we have come here because we have brought a

plea against the Hospitallers. I will speak for us first and beg my
lord the Pope to listen well to our words. We demand Renart by
rights. For it is common knowledge that we are defenders of and
fighters for the Holy Church. We have sergeants and knights, we
must have many mercenaries and spend much gold and silver, all
to defend the Holy Church. Throughout the towns we have many
houses, estates, rents and garrisons, under many powerful lords
who often do us many great wrongs, so we have a need for someone
to maintain us and uphold our right against all, for if we do not
increase in wealth, we will have little power to sustain the Holy
Church, instead we will all have to flee and abandon the land of
Syria. The Sultan of Cairo would come over here with a fleet;
realize this, Holy Father, that our men defend the Holy Church
and Christendom against the unbelievers. Holy Father, this is
true, so you ought to come down to this, that we should have
Renart, if he wishes to enter an order. Holy Father, please ask
him.' (Lines 7549–85).

Then the pope put the question to Renart and he replied, 'I
have heard well what they said. I wish to hear the Hospitallers. I
will stay with those who need me most, according to what I hear, if
I am free to enter an order, for my wife is still alive.' The pope
replied, laughing, 'I will give you leave to enter.' 'Holy Father,
then I will take religion when I like, since I have leave to do so
from you.' (Lines 7586–98).

Then a Hospitaller arose; he was a wise man and a good
speaker; he spoke loudly and with skill. 'Lords' he said, 'both
high and low, hear our petition, and whether our request is
reasonable. The Templars are asking for Renart, to have him on
their side alone, but we ought better to have him, and for many
good reasons, for we existed before they did, from which we still
have charters. We have briefs from princes and kings, and we do
far more harm to the Saracens than the Templars do. At need we
are knights and keep up combats against the Saracens with our
swords; and in our Hospitality, which is full of charity, the
wounded and sick are cured, lifted up and put to bed; those who
would have been dead by default, who are then healthy and strong.
And I say this much to you, that if the Templars wished to help us
alright, so that they were not envious of us, we would have all
Syria, Jerusalem, and all Egypt; and Cairo would have been
subdued to Christianity a long time ago; but they are allied with
the Saracens. I say this much, that if it was not for our house, that
Christendom would perish, at least that part overseas. Without us
the Christians could hardly last six months; they would all go to
ruin. When the men of foreign lands have crossed the sea, most of
them, I am quite sure, are unwell with the effort, and if they were
not refreshed in our house they would go to perdition and a
hundred thousand would have died there who are now healthy and
strong and defend us today. Holy Father, I speak for our house, so
ask Renart, Holy Father to be master and governor of us and of our
house; you know well whether I speak reason.' (Lines 7599–7650).

At that the pope replied, 'One of you two has failed; he can
hardly divide himself in two.' Renart replied, 'A priest can serve

at two altars; I will put on both habits. My clothes will be divided
down the middle; on the right I will be dressed in the vestments of
a Hospitaller, and on the left of a Templar. On the left I will leave
my beard, on the right I will have myself shaved; I will govern
them both well.' At that there was great laughter among them;
they vested him as you have heard. In turn, the pope vested them
with him. (Lines 7651–66).

At this juncture, Fortune appears with her wheel. Renart at first refuses to get
up on to it because, he says, it will turn over and throw him down. Fortune
replies that it will not; he has thrown down Faith and Loyalty and they will
never rise again; Pride has put Humility at Fortune's feet. Renart therefore
climbs on the wheel, 'all crowned,' with Pride at his right and Guile at his left,
clad in the habit of the Templars and Hospitallers.[14]

We may assume that this picture is true, not only because satire must be
true, although exaggerated, in order to be effective, but also because it is
endorsed by other evidence. For example, in appealing to the papal court of their
claim to have Renart, Giélée's Templars and Hospitallers are behaving just as the
evidence of the papal registers for the twelfth and thirteenth centuries would lead
us to expect. Again, much as historians deny that the military orders were in a
constant state of mutual confrontation, contemporaries saw them as implacable
rivals, whose disputes did the Holy Land much harm. In almost coming to blows
over Renart, Giélée's orders are behaving exactly as they do, for example, in the
chronicle of Matthew Paris.[15]

It is worth comparing the characters given by Giélée to his Templar and
Hospitaller, for, contrary to the belief of Joshua Prawer, they are completely
different.[16] The Templar is straightforward, even simplistic, in his speech; he is
very much the simple fighting man. The Hospitaller is cleverer, a trained
speaker, able to turn at need into lawyer, doctor or soldier.[17] The Templar is
paranoid, wailing that his order is always under attack and in need of defence
from its enemies. The Hospitaller, on the other hand, is more active; he not only
promotes his own order, but seizes the initiative to attack the Templars and
accuse them of being in alliance with the Muslims. For Giélée's audience, each of
these characters would have represented their order, and therefore we may see
the differences between them as summing up the perceived differences between
the two orders.

The arguments presented by each order are also endorsed by the available
evidence.   The Templar's threat to abandon the Holy Land if help is not
forthcoming had been repeated many times in the order's history and was
obviously well known.[18] The claim that only the order of the Temple defended
the Holy Land seems to have been widely accepted, for the order always received
more prominence than the Hospital in chronicle accounts of crusade compaigns
and in romances and *chansons de geste*. Giélée, however, indicates that by 1289
the educated layman doubted it.[19]

The Hospitaller's claim that his order had existed long before that of the
Temple may be a reference to the legend that the order had been founded by
King Antiochus, in the third century B.C.,[20] but it is in any case true that the
Hospital's charters date back to the late eleventh century, while the earliest
charters for the order of the Temple date from the 1120s. The Hospitaller's
appeal to the order's dual role was also mirrored in reality; it is striking that
most of the order's references to its hospitable role appeared during periods of

military reversals. For example, in 1290 Nicholas IV had banned all unlicensed collections of alms for the Holy Land, because of abuses; in March 1291 he gave the Hospitallers permission to collect alms because they had informed him that they were not collecting for the Holy Land but for the poor and sick.[21] It must have been obvious to the order at this time two months before Acre was finally lost to the Sultan of Egypt, that hospitable work had a better public profile than the plight of the Holy Land. Certainly some donors and visitors were particularly impressed by the dual role, notably the priest John of Würzburg in 1170, who sneered that the Temple's alms were not a tenth of the Hospital's.[22]

The accusation that the military orders were themselves responsible for Christian failures in the Holy Land was an old one, first levelled against the Templars in the wake of the second crusade of 1147–8.[23] In most accounts, the Templars, and later the Templars and Hospitallers, were the Muslims' dupes,[24] but between 1209 and 1222 Otto, a monk of St Blasien, in his account of the German crusade of 1197, accused all the Palestinian Franks, including the Templars and Hospitallers, of being friendly with the Muslims.[25] Some later critics complained that the alliances of the Templars, or the Templars and Hospitallers, with the Muslims of Damascus or Cairo, were harming the Christian cause in the Holy Land.[26]

While there is no other evidence that the military orders used this accusation against each other, it appears very likely that they would have done so. Such slander was a natural counterpart of the orders' notorious quarrels. In addition, both orders were engaged, as they are in Giélée's text, in a desperate struggle for the same thing; alms. The complaints of the clergy at the third Lateran council and at subsequent local councils, as well as local disputes and the complaints of Matthew Paris, indicate that the orders were continually seeking more and more money from the west.[27] There is some evidence that the orders deliberately strove to bolster their prestige in the eyes of Christendom in order to attract alms over the heads of other monastic orders, and it seems reasonable that they should have resorted to slanders on each other in order to achieve the same end.[28] However, Giélée's account implies that both the Templar and the Hospitaller are lying, as Renart always lies when it is to his advantage to do so. This would suggest that the thinking Fleming or Frenchman did not believe that the Temple alone defended the Christian Church, that the Hospital was particularly charitable or effective in warfare, or that the Temple was alone in allying with the Muslims.

The final image of Renart is with Pride on his right and Guile on his left. Pride was, of course, the sin most commonly associated with the military orders.[29] Their reputation for guile was usually expressed in accusations of treachery, levelled at them by Europeans who wished to exonerate their own crusaders from blame for Christian defeats in the Holy Land.[30] It also appears in complaints that they were acting as the secret agents of certain monarchs, such as Henry II of England during the Becket crisis or the emperor Frederick II during his war against the papacy.[31]

Giélée does not mention the Teutonic order at all. This is not surprising. Although the order played an important military role in the Holy Land, it was not well known in Europe outside German–speaking areas, and other French and Flemish writers can be seen to have had little knowledge of it.[32]

Jacquemart Giélée, therefore, tells us little of the military orders in 1289 that cannot be told from other, traditionally more acceptable, sources: chronicles, charters and the papal registers. However, his account adds flesh and colour to the evidence contained in such sources, and he underlines the aspects of the orders which were glaringly obvious to contemporaries but which might otherwise escape our attention. Most notable of these are the fact that the orders were perceived as being constantly in dispute, although they were not, and that the image of the average Templar was as a simple knight, while the average Hospitaller was seen to be a wily individual who was neither one thing nor another, but who could defend both roles with skill. This second point throws some light on the French Templars' inability to defend themselves effectively in the face of their accusers during the trial of the order.

In the opinion of Giélée and his patrons, by 1289 the military orders were completely corrupted by *renardie*, with no redeeming features. This is surprising, for although every aspect of his criticism is endorsed by other writers, no other contemporary writer condemns these orders so completely. It may be that Giélée, or his patron, bore a personal grudge against the military orders; however, without knowing the precise identity of Giélée's patron this cannot be proven. It is unlikely that Guy de Dampierre, for example, would have sponsored an attack on the order of the Temple, as he was himself related to the master of the Temple, William de Beaujeu, and was friendly towards the order.[33] It may be that Giélée's final condemnation of the military orders combines his condemnation of clergy and laity, because these orders combined knighthood and monasticism. However, it is most likely that his particular condemnation of the military orders is a reflection on the sanctity of their place of origin, the Holy Land, the high reputation they had had in the past, their own great responsibilities, and the high hopes placed on them. Their failure to live up to these responsibilities and hopes, and the destruction of their reputation with defeats in the Holy Land, was far more significant than the failure of other monastic orders to live up to their vocations, even the friars. When Renart refused to lead the friars to Great Pride, he was saving himself for the military orders. In Giélée's poem, the surrender of the orders of the Holy Land to Renart marked the final victory of evil in the world.

NOTES

1.	A.J. Forey, 'The emergence of the Military Order in the twelfth century', *Journal of Ecclesiastical History*, 36 (1985), pp 175–195; M. Barber, 'The origins of the order of the Temple', *Studia Monastica*, 12 (1970), pp 219–240.
2.	E. Siberry, *Criticism of Crusading, 1095–1274* (Oxford, 1985); N. Housley, *The Italian Crusades. The Papal–Angevin alliance and the crusades against Christian lay powers 1254–1343* (Oxford, 1982), pp 106–110, 162–4, 252–3; S. Schein, 'The West and the Crusade. Attitudes and Attempts, 1291–1312', unpublished Ph.D. thesis, Cambridge, 1979, *passim.*
3.	E.G., D.A. Trotter, *Medieval French Literature and the Crusades, (1100–13))* (Geneva, 1987), p 249; P. Ménard quoting M.–T. Lorsin, *Les Fabliaux: contes Π rire du moyen Age* (Paris, 1983), p 46.
4.	P. Menard, *Les Fabliaux*, p 46ff; E. Siberry, *Criticism of Crusading*, pp 4–11; J. Flori, 'La notion de chevalerie dans les chansons de geste du XIIe siécle. Étude historique de vocabulaire', *Le Moyen Age*, 81 (1975), pp 211–3; J. Flori, 'Pour une histoire de la chevalerie: l'aboubement dans les romans de Chrétien de Troyes', *Romania*, 100 (1979), p 23.
5.	Jacquemart Giélée, *Renart le Nouvel*, ed., H. Roussel, Société des Anciens Textes Français (Paris, 1961), pp 7–10; C. Régnier, review of H. Roussel,

'Étude sur Renart le Nouvel du poète lillois Jacquemart Giélée', thèse principale, Lille 1956, exemplaire dactylographié, *Revue du Nord*, 41 (1959). p 117.

6.   *Renart le Nouvel*, lines 7752–7757.

7.   *Ibid.*, lines 3779–3809.

8.   *Ibid.*, lines 7199–7330.

9.   *Ibid.*, lines 7331–7432.

10. *Ibid.*, lines 7469–7473; C. Régnier, review of H. Roussel, 'Étude sur Renart le Nouvel', p 118.

11. *Ibid.*, lines 7474–7490.

12. *Ibid.*, lines 7491–7506.

13. *Ibid.*, lines 7523–7541.

14. *Ibid.*, lines 7667–7720.

15. Matthew Paris, *Chronica Majora*, ed., H.R. Luard, 7 vols., Rolls Series 57 (London, 1872–84), 4, pp 139, 256, 279, 291; 5, pp 745–6; written c 1245–1259.

16. J. Prawer, 'Military orders and crusader politics in the second half of the XIIIth century', in eds., J. Fleckenstein and M. Hellmann, *Die Geistlichen Ritterorden Europas*, (Sigmaringen, 1980), pp 227–8.

17. For example, the order of the Temple is not known to have produced any lawyers during the twelfth or thirteenth centuries, whereas the Hospital produced at least one: J. Riley Smith, *The knights of St John in Jerusalem and Cyprus, c. 1050–1310* (London, 1967), pp 272–3.

18. *Chronique d'Ernoul et de Bernard le trésorier*, ed., L. de Mas Latrie, Société de l'histoire de France (Paris, 1871), p 165 (threat made in 1187); *Die Register Innocenz' III.* ed., O. Hageneder and A. Haidacher, 4 vols. (Graz–Cologne, 1964), 3 no.247 (1199); Register of Innocent III in *Patrologia Cursus Completus: Series Latina*, ed., J.–P. Migne, 221 vols. (Paris, 1844–64) 216 cols. 54–6, year 12 no. 45 (1209); Burton annals, *Annales Monastici*, ed., H.R. Luard, 5 vols., Rolls Series 36 (London, 1864–69) 1, p 491ff. (1260); Ch. Kohler and Ch. V. Langlois, 'Lettres inédits concernant les croisades (1275–1307)', *Bibliothèque de l'école des chartes*, 52 (1891), p 55ff. (1275).

19. E.g., *Die schriften des Kölner Domscholasters, späteren Bischofs von Paderborn und Kardinalbischofs von S Sabina, Oliverus*, ed., H. Hoogeweg, (Tübingen, 1894), p 169ff; *Oeuvres complètes de Rutebuef*, ed., E. Faral and J. Basin, 2 vols (Paris, 1959–60), 1, p 508, lines 327–337; Jean Renart, *L'Escoufle: Roman d'adventure*, ed., F. Sweetser (Geneva, 1974), lines 799, 1060, 1329; 'Du bon William Longespee', in ed., A. Jubinal, *Nouveau recueil de contes, dits, fabliaux et autres pièces inédits....* 2 vols. (Paris, 1839–42), 2, pp 339–353.

20. *The Hospitallers' Riwle*, ed., K.V. Sinclair, Anglo–Norman Texts 42 (Oxford, 1984) lines 1–112.

21. J. Delaville le Rouix, *Cartulaire Général de l'ordre des Hospitaliers de St Jean de Jérusalem 1110–1310*, 4 vols. (Paris, 1894–1906), nos. 4082, 4149.

22. John of Würzburg, in Migne, PL 155, cols. 1035, 1036–7.

23. John of Salisbury, *Historia Pontificalis*, ed., M. Chibnall (Edinburgh, 1956), p 57; written 1164.

24. E.g., Roger of Howden, *Gesta Regis Henrici Secundi*, ed., W. Stubbs, 2 vols., Rolls Series 49 (London, 1868–71) 1, p 130f; Otto of St Blasien, 'Continuatio Sanblasiana', ed., G.H. Pertz, *Monumenta Germaniae Historia Scriptores* (MGHS), ed., G. H. Pertz *et al.*, 32 vols (Hanover, Weimar, Stuttgart and Cologne, 1826–1934) 20, p 327; Gervase of Canterbury, *Historical Works*, ed., W. Stubbs, 2 vols, Rolls Series 73 (London, 1879–80) 1, p 137; *Chronique d'Ernoul*, pp 12–3; Sicard of

Cremona, *Cronica*, in Migne, PL 213, cols. 511–2, note; Albert Milioli, 'Liber de teporibus et aetatibus et cronica imperatorum', ed., O. Holder–Egger, MGHS 31, pp 639–40.

25. 'Continuatio Sanblasiana', p 327.

26. The emperor Frederick II in Matthew Paris, *Chronica Majora*, 4, p 302; Robert of Artois in *ibid.*, 5, pp 149–150; Odo, bishop of Tusculanum in ed., L. d'Archery, *Spicilegium sive collectio veterum aliquot scriptorum*, 3 (Paris, 1723), p 625; cf. Delaville le Roulx, *Cartulaire*, no. 2149.

27. E.g., Delaville le Roulx, *Cartulaire*, nos. 392, 560, 2805, 3887, 4029; Matthew Paris, *Chronica Majora*, 3, p 177.

28. See chapter five of my forthcoming Ph.D. thesis, 'Images of the military orders, 1128–1291: spiritual, secular, romantic'.

29. E.G., Gerhoh of Reichersberg, 'de investigatione antichristi', ed., E. Sackur, MGH *Libelli de Lite*, 3, p 384; 'Annales Herbipolenses', ed., G.H. Pertz, MGHS 16, p 7; Guiot de Provins, 'La Bible', in *Les oeuvres de Guiot de Provins, poèt lyrique et satirique*, ed., J. Orr (Manchester, 1915), lines 1695–1788; Ramon Llull, 'Blanquerna', in *Obras Literarias*, eds., M. Batllori and M. Caldentey (Madrid, 1948), p 408, Bk 4, ch. 80, para. 7.

30. See notes 23–26 above.

31. *Recueil des historiens des Gaules et de la France*, ed., Bouquet *et al.*, new edition, ed., L. Delisle, 24 vols (Paris, 1878), 16, pp 424–6, no. 266, pp 430–2, no. 274; *Recueil des actes d'Henri II, Roi d'Angleterre et Duc de Normandie*, eds., L. Delisle and E. Berger, 3 vols. and introduction, (Paris, 1906–1927) 1, pp 407–8, no. 262; P. Sambin, *Problemi Politici attraverso lettere inedite di Innocenzo IV*, Instituto Veneto di Scienze, Lettere ed Arti Venezia, Memorie Classe di Scienze morali e lettere, 31 (Venice, 1955), p 66, no. 47.

32. E.G., Gilbert of Tournai, 'Collectio de Scandalis Ecclesiae', ed., A. Stroick, *Archivum Franciscanum Historicum*, 24 (1931), pp 56–7, para. 17 criticizes the Temple and Hospital but hardly mentions the Teutonic order; cf. Menko, *Cronicon*, ed. L. Weiland, MGHS 23, pp 555–9.

33. Delaville le Roulx, *Cartulaire*, no. 3507; M.L. Bulst–Thiele, *Sacrae Domus Militiae Templi Hierosolymitani Magistri: Untersuchungen zur Geschichte des Templerordens 1118/9–1314*, (Göttingen, 1974), pp 261, 362–3, nos. 3–4.

THE LYON DOMINICANS : A DOUBLE ACT

Jean Dunbabin

Unlike the Franciscans, the Dominicans were, from their inception, a clerical order. As each friar reached the canonical age he took the appropriate holy order, normally advancing to the priesthood with all the privileges and responsibilities of that status. There was nothing unusual in this; since the early middle ages most religious and canons had taken orders. But because the Dominicans followed an itinerant way of life, the consequences of their clericality on the rest of society were marked. Wherever they went, they preached, they heard confessions, they administered supreme unction, they buried the dead. In Languedoc where they first appeared, their services were desperately needed to combat the heretics and to reinforce a demoralized local clergy to whom they posed no threat. But elsewhere in France, where the parochial system was stronger, when a friar entered his parish each priest asked himself the question: was the Dominican intent on usurping his role, or was he merely trying to show him how to do it properly?

As is well—known, by the middle of the century the Parisian secular clergy had decided the friars were bent on usurpation; and they used all the stratagems within their power to defeat the challenge. In the end they failed. However their attempts have apparently coloured historians' assessment of the Dominicans' parochial function, leading them to concentrate so much on the conflict between the seculars and the mendicants that any element of cooperation between the two is almost forgotten.[1] I want today to suggest that circumstances in Paris were not replicated elsewhere. Although Dominicans could underline the differences between mendicants and secular clergy in order to compete successfully with parish priests, in practice they usually chose in the provinces to act as a ginger group within the clergy, promoting reform Much of the evidence used to substantiate endemic conflict between friar and parish priest comes from masters of the university of Paris, where bitter rivalry between secular and mendicant theological schools expressed itself in broad attacks on the opposition's chosen way of life. But the criticisms Paris theologians hurled at one and other drew their fire from the scholastic habit of taking any intellectual position to its logical extreme. They attacked not the men they knew but caricatures.[2] Furthermore the discipline of regular disputations in the schools allowed controversies to remain on the boil long after the cause of their instigation had been forgotten. It is therefore dangerous to ground a case for inevitable conflict on schoolmen's angry denunciations; and even more dangerous to generalize from them to the state of feeling in other parts of the country.

To see how things might work out away from the capital, let us look at Lyon. There the house of Notre Dame de Confort was founded within two years of St Dominic obtaining confirmation of his order from Pope Honorius III in 1216. As befitted an establishment in what had once been the ecclesiastical capital of Gaul, it was swiftly recognised as second dignity to St Jacques of Paris within the French province of the order.[3] Situation on the island between the Rhone and the Sâone, its church (which was consecrated in 1244 by Pope Innocent IV) rapidly became the burial ground for distinguished people, not only Dominicans like Humbert of Romans, after St Dominic the most famous Master General, but also seculars, including Henry of Susa, the great canon lawyer, referred to by his fellow scholars as Hostiensis.[4] Beside it the convent buildings expanded over the years to the point where in 1316 they could provide shelter adequate for the conclave of cardinals engaged in electing the new pope. Although the size of the community is unknown, it was obviously a large one; and more importantly for our purpose, it was the only one for many miles around.

It would be idle to deny that the inmates of Notre Dame de Confort sometimes usurped the role of the parish priest; in fact they were characterised by their energy in pastoral concerns. When the Franciscan Salimbene visited Vienne at Easter 1249, he met there the renowned Dominican Guillaume Peyraut, who had come over from Lyon to preach and hear confessions in the ancient city during the festival season. Salimbene was much impressed, not only by what Guillaume said from the pulpit, but also by his character.[5] When he asked why there was no Dominican house in Vienne, Guillaume told him of the order's preference for large convents, based only in the more populous centres, from which the brothers could travel forth into the surrounding area. This pattern was well exemplified in the career of Guillaume's Lyon contemporary, Étienne de Bourbon; he was constantly on the move, in Nevers, in Burgundy, in Forez, in the Dombes, in Savoie, preaching, hearing confessions, sorting out difficult problems for the local bishops, rooting out strange and unorthodox cults. He moved among great men, discussing affairs with the dowager duchess of Burgundy, assisting the bishop of Clermont, sharing friendship with the dauphin of Auvergne; yet at the same time he penetrated the backwoods, prying into the concerns of superstitious peasants and poor women given to black magic.[6] All doors were open to him, as they seldom were for parish priests of peasant stock. Here was a circumstance that might well give rise to jealousy among even the mildest of curates.

Étienne described his peripatetic way of life in his *Tractatus de diversis praedicabilibus*, recounting incidents from his own experience to add bulk to a collection of moral stories derived from the Christian classics. The whole he offered to any who cared to use it, as material for sermons. Étienne's awareness of the needs of other less gifted preachers than himself was echoed by Humbert de Romans. When in 1263 he retired from the Master Generalship of the order, Humbert returned to Notre Dame de Confort, of which he had once been prior, to write there his *Liber de eruditione Praedicatrum*, a hugh manual for the instruction of those who struggled to expound the word of God effectively to audiences of all sorts. As well as providing a body of model sermons and examples (some drawn from Étienne), Humbert offered his readers specific advice on composition: while sermons must make the Christian message crystal clear, they should also be embroidered with stories to enhance their appeal to the less learned. Then, because they were the only form of education most poorer listeners would enjoy, they should offer some instruction in physics, ethics or logic as they went along.[7] The combination of simplicity, colourfulness, and erudition he advocated was difficult to achieve. But his lessons gave friars a head—start in competing with bishops, let alone parish priests. There was, however, nothing to prevent the secular clergy from benefiting by his wisdom if they chose to read his book.

Because there had been very little orthodox preaching in the Lyonnais before the Dominicans arrived,[8] their activities in this sphere could not logically arouse serious objection. But more contentious was their popularity as confessors. For the obligation of annual confession, imposed on all laymen in 1215, had enhanced the parish priests' directive authority in their own communities.[9] Consequently papal privileges to the friars to hear confessions

were widely resented, in the Lyonnais as elsewhere. Even so, outside the big
cities where established convents provided a constant source of confessors, the
effects of the privileges were at best episodic. In the countryside a parishioner's
natural preference for confessing to a friar (who because he was on the move,
made a less embarrassing recipient of self–critical confidences than a priestly
neighbours) was usually ungratified. Unless a mendicant happened to pass by,
villagers were forced to make do with the local priest, no matter how
uncongenial. Besides, friars frequently confined their services only to those who,
having listened to their sermons, were moved to repent.[10] The absent missed the
opportunity. But if some who wished to resort to a friar could not, others were
apparently forced to. Treatment of the determinedly impenitent bulks so large,
both in Étienne's *Tractatus* and in Guillaume de Peyraut's *Summa de virtutibus
et vitiis*, as to suggest that parish priests sometimes kept hardened sinners for the
friars to deal with.[11] If so, the mendicant confessor with his claim to superior
technical competence may on occasion have been as welcome to his parish
counterpart as is a consultant to a conscientious general practitioner bedevilled
by a difficult case. We should not take jealousy for granted.

The friars' rights of hearing confession from the dying and burying them
within the confines of mendicant churches particularly upset the Paris secular
clergy, because these activities injured them in their pockets. But in Lyon only
men of standing, and in particular canons of the cathedral, were buried at Notre
Dame de Confort;[12] therefore while rich corporations, the cathedral itself and the
long–established abbeys, suffered deprivation, ordinary parish priests were
unaffected. And though all secular clerics stood to lose the offerings made by the
dying if a friar administered supreme unction in their place, only priests based in
the city were likely to suffer from this more than occasionally. Again the
enormous area over which the inmates of Notre Dame de Confort spread their
ministry tended to reduce tension, permitting them to present their pastoral
activities as a supplement to, rather than a substitute for, the activities of the
parish clergy. But if the Dominicans of Lyon were fortunate in the vast extent of
their territory, they reinforced this good fortune by assiduously courting local
good will. In this the cathedral chapter of the city offered them a golden
opportunity. The Fourth Lateran Council's injunction that lectures in theology
be provided in every cathedral for the education of the local clergy was not easily
satisfied in parts of France and the Low Countries, apparently because suitably
qualified secular lecturers were in short supply. Thus in 1229 the bishop of Liège
informed his chapter that he had licensed the foundation of a Dominican house,
so that the friars might instruct the clergy of his see; in 1246 the archbishop of
Reims requested Pope Innocent IV to approve a similar foundation for the same
purpose.[13] Notre Dame de Confort, established at St Dominic's command, soon
stepped into the breach in Lyon. As early as the 1220s Dominicans were giving
lectures in theology in the cathedral cloister; they continued to do so (though
perhaps not continuously) throughout the thirteenth and early fourteenth
centuries; and in 1337 the chapter set the arrangement on a sound financial
footing to ensure its survival.[14] Despite the (typical) slightness of recorded
evidence for Lyon's cathedral school,[15] some of the men who lectured there in the
thirteenth century enjoyed high international reputations: Humbert de Romans,
Hugh de St Cher, Guillaume Peyraut, and Piere de Tarentaise. Of these, only
the last–named, the future Pope Innocent V, was to earn fame as a master of
logic and speculative theology at Paris.[16] The others all of whom had had some
experience of the Paris schools, retained their more practical stamp of mind.
Leaving aside syllogisms and conjectures, they devoted their energies to writing
text books, commentaries on Holy Scripture accessible to those without
philosophical training, and introduction to Christian ethics, programmes of

education for different classes of society, and manuals for preachers. Their writings all betray an intense concern for the day—by—day problems of ordinary men and women, and especially of those ordinary men chosen to minister to others. That they found their task rewarding is implied in Guillaum Peyraut's indictment of 'those who teach at Paris, where their teaching is scarcely listened to, and do not want to teach elsewhere, where their teaching would be held dear'.[17]

Hugh de St Cher's Lyon stint was not long; but it is tempting to see it as formative in his career. His commentary on the whole of the Bible aimed to preserve the best in established Christian tradition by repackaging well—loved passages of patristic and twelfth— and early thirteenth century scholarship, and presenting them in a fashion acceptable to his contemporaries. Not for him the more scholastically—minded Paris commentaries with their emphasis on the literal sense of Scripture as illuminated by the scientific discoveries of the age.[18] Like most anthologists, novelty held no charms for Hugh. But in his preference for the great works of the past lay the downfall of his academic reputation. For, anxious to achieve far more than one man was capable of, he gathered together a team of scribes to excerpt from the texts he loved, and in the process of directing them he lost the sense of direction so necessary to a corporate activity. His commentaries sprawled, growing heavy with dead wood and with interpretational inconsistencies.[19] Nevertheless his endeavour should be judged in relation to his aim of providing the not very scholarly parish priest with a reliable and established guide to the word of God, in which he was successful. Was not this exactly appropriate to a lecturer in a cathedral school?

Important though it was, the magisterial chair at Lyon was not indispensable to the friars' educational programme. One of the earliest books known to have been written by inmates of Notre Dame de Confort was the manual of Chabert de Savoie and P(ierre?) de Rosset, which guided priests through the seven sacraments of the church. With subsequent additions from the pen of Henry of Susa, their injunctions were accepted by a synod at Sisteron some time between 1243 and 1250 as mandatory for the clergy of that diocese.[20] Equally educational but more concerned with individual consciences was Guillaume Peyraut's *Summa de virtutibus et vitiis*. In describing each vice, Peyraut set aside a section for its peculiarly clerical manifestations: thus simony, pluralism, and idle curiosity came in for sharp criticism, as did clerks assisting others in gambling and prelates overdressing to impress.[21] Occasionally the indictment was more pointed, as when Peyraut castigated cathedral chapters which recruited only from the aristocracy, as Lyon notoriously did. The defence that a cathedral lying in territory with no powerful lord to protect it must choose noble canons to do so met with the rejoinder that this was to consider only the cathedral's temporalities, not its spiritualities, which would be better served by the promotion of learned and holy men.[22] Reading Peyraut's famous work cannot have been a comfortable experience for those to whom it was immediately addressed. Yet the author was so skillful in concealing his specific barbs within a well—designed synthesis of Latin teaching (more Christian than classical)[23] on ethics, that his book rapidly became very popular throughout western Europe n account both of its lucidity and of its relevance to thirteenth—century life. By comparison with the highly technical and dry commentaries on Aristotle's *Ethics* being produced in Paris at roughly the same time,[24] Guillaume's *Summa* with its concern for the moral improvement of his own contemporaries shines out like a jewel in a dust heap.

A common characteristic of the literary work produced by Lyon

Dominicans was its reliance on excellent library resources.[25] Indeed, the urge to popularize, arising from access to many books important in the history of Christianity, was common to Hugh de St Cher, Guillaume Peyraut, Étienne de Bourbon and Humbert de Romans. Others were entitled to benefit, if only indirectly, from the wealth that was theirs. Inevitably this sense of obligation limited their search for originality. Yet Guillaume at least combined great breadth of reading with an organisational ability and the power of making incisive comments which turned his *Summa* into a piece of creative synthesis. And, judging by the number of manuscripts that survive, both his masterpiece and the commentaries of Hugh de St Cher supplied a deeply–felt need in the thirteenth century.

French religious history has suffered from the over–concentration on Paris that used to bedevil political text books. It is time to pass over the peevish verbal battles of the secular–mendicant conflict, and to look to relations in the regions. If the Lyon friar did from time to time and *faute de mieux* take over duties belonging to the parish priests, thereby causing some resentment, nevertheless their main efforts were directed to educating the clergy to a standard where they themselves would be needed no more. Seldom have men so cheerfully attempted to work themselves out of a job.

NOTES

1.   For example this is the impression given by J. Gaudemet's standard account in eds., F. Lot and R. Fawtier, *Histoire des Institutions francaises au moyen age*, t. III (Paris, 1962), pp 216–7. The secular–mendicant conflict has been of particular interest to intellectual historians in the wake of the seminal article by Y.M.–J. Congar, 'Aspects écclesiologiques de la querelle entre mediants et seculiers dans la seconde moitié du xiiie siècle et le début due xive', *Archives d'Histoire doctrinale et littéraire du Moyen Age* 28 (1961), pp 36–151.

2.   For the effect of rationalisation on the conflict, see Y. Congar, *op. cit.* Similarly the author of the commentary on the *Ethica Vetus et Nova* in Oxford, Bod. Lat. Misc. c 71, fol. 161r, proved the superiority of the secular over the religious life by deduction from the Aristotelian definition of virtue. Such arguments did not allow of compromise.

3.   Despite the fact that Lyon was outside the French realm in the thirteenth century. For a popular history of the convent, see J.D. Levesque, *Les Frères precheurs de Lyon. Notre Dame de Confort 1218–1789*, Lyon 1979.

4.   J.F. von Schulte, *Die Geschicht der Quellen und Literature des Canonischen Rechts*, (Stuttgart, 1875), t.II, p 124.

5.   A. Dondain, 'Guillaume Peyrat. Vie et oeuvres', *Archivum Fratrum Praedicaorum* 18 (1948), pp 165, 170–73.

6.   Étienne de Bourbon, *Anecodotes historiques. legendes et apologues*, ed., A. Lecoy de la Marche, (Paris, 1877), pp vii–xi.

7.   S. Tugwell, *Early Dominicans: Selected Writings*, (New York, Romsey, Toronto, 1982), provides an abbreviated translation on pp 183–384; of particular significance here are pp 251 and 373. See also E.T. Brett, *Humbert of Romans. His Life and Views of Thirteenth–century Society* (Toronto, 1984), pp 155, 175.

8.   The Waldensians, known in the Lyonnais as the Poor Men of Lyon, had attempted provide what the church did not. But their condemnation and exclusion from the city in 1180 or 1181 put an end to this; see G. Gonnett, 'Le cheminement des vaudois vers le schisme et l'héresie (1174–1218)' *Cahiers de civilisation médiévale* 19 (1976), pp 309–45.

9. The priest was expected to take the initiative in the confessional by questioning his parishioners. For an early set of model questions see the synodal decrees of Sisteron, 1243–50, clauses 31 to 39, in ed., D. Martène and U. Durand, *Thesaurus novus anecdotrum*, t. IV (Paris, 1717), ccs. 1079–98.

10. The point that it was less embarrassing to confess to a friar was made by Master Jean de Pouilly. See the response to this by Pierre de la Palud, Toulouse, Bibl. Mun 744, fol. 90r, discussed by J. Dunbabin in *The Hound of God. Pierre de la Palud and the fourteenth–century Church*. Oxford, forthcoming, chapter 3. On confession after sermons, Pierre (a Lyon–trained friar) said: 'Papal privileges given to the Preachers allow them after their sermons to hear the confessions of any members of their congregation who, after hearing the word of God, wish to confess to them. The Pope in granting this privilege supposed that many sinners would be goaded in this.' (Ms. Clermont Ferrand 46, fol. 13r).

11. Étienne de Bourbon had to deal, among others, with a recalcitrant highwayman; see *Anecdotes*, p 370. Guillaume regularly included arguments to be employed in persuading the obstinate of their sin; e.g., *Summa de virtutibus et vitiis*, (Lyon, 1585), t. II, fols. 58–60, 137–8.

12. Of course the records may be misleading; lesser men's burials would not have been noted so carefully. But ed., M.-C. Guigue, *Obituarium Lugdenensis Ecclesiae*, (Lyon, 1867), provides proof of the burial of important men in the Dominican house. On the canons buried there, see J. Beyssac, *Les Chanoines de l'Eglise de Lyon*, Lyon.

13. Brett, *Humbert of Romans*, p 13. England does not seem to have shared either the problem or the solution; N. Orme, *English schools in the Middle Ages* (London, 1973), pp 150–151.

14. J. Beyssac, *Les Lecteurs et théologaux. Nots pour servir a l'histoire de l'eglise de Lyon*, (Lyon, 1926), pp 6–10.

15. For English cathedrals the evidence is equally slight; see Orme, *English Schools*, pp 79–86.

16. M.–H. Laurent, *Le bienheureux Innocent V (Pierre de Tarentaise) et son temps*, (Vatican, 197).

17. Quoted by D.L. d'Avray, *The Preaching of the Friars. Sermons diffused from Paris before 1300*, (Oxford, 1985), p 116.

18. B. Smalley, *The Study of the Bible in the Middle Ages*, 3rd ed., (Oxford, 1983), pp 295–6.

19. R.E. Lerner, 'Poverty, preaching and eschatology in the Revelation commentaries of "Hugh of St Cher"', in eds., K. Walsh and D. Wood, *The Bible in the Medieval World*, (Oxford, 1985), p 186.

20. Eds., Martene and Durand, *Thesaurus novus anecdotorum*, t. IV, ccs. 1079–98.

21. *Summa*, II, pp 170, 188, 291, 232, 376.

22. *Ibid.*, pp 422–3.

23. Dondaine, 'Guillaume Peyraut', p 162, however overstresses the Latinity of Peyraut's sources by failing to pick up a reference to Aristotle's *Ethics* (known as the *Ethica Nova* translation) on p 19 of t.II, Lyon.

24. See for example the commentaries on the *Ethica Vetus et Nova* in Paris Nat. lat 3804A and Oxford Bod. Lat. misc. c 71, or the commentary on the *Ethica Vtus* in Paris Nat. lat. 3572.

25. Some impression of its scope can be obtained from Étienne de Bourbon, *Anecdotes*, pp xiii–xi.

ST BRIDGET OF SWEDEN AND THE ORDER OF THE HOLY SAVIOUR

Frank Johnston

St Bridget (1303–1373) was the only canonised Swedish saint and the only foundress of a religious order during the Middle Ages.[1] During her lifetime she was known principally for her Revelations which became almost the standard devotional textbook of the fifteenth century.[2] They included fiery denunciations of the morals of the age. As Gascoigne, the Oxford Chancellor, put it succinctly: 'Verba sancta et contra peccatores terribilia dixit'.[3]

Surprisingly the witnesses at her canonisation process made little reference to her work as foundress of the Order of the Saviour, but an examination of their evidence shows how her own experiences were reflected in the spirituality of the order.[4] Even as a child she received visions, which she related later in life to her confessor, of Mary as Queen of Heaven and of the Crucified Saviour which were to be the foundations of the devotional life of the Bridgettines.[5]

As the daughter and wife of provincial governors she was brought into contact with the leaders of church and state, including the king who in 1346 gave her the royal estate of Vadstena as the site of her intended monastery.[6] As the wife of an important nobleman she became familiar with the problems of managing a large household which gave her full scope for exercising the spiritual and corporal works of mercy. The turning point of her life came when her husband, Ulf, fell ill during a pilgrimage to Compostella and decided to enter the monastery of Alvastra where he died shortly afterwards in 1344. Bridget settled close to the abbey where she remained for five years.

Here the main series of her Revelations began which finally totaled more than seven hundred.[7] The authenticity of these visions was accepted by a panel of Swedish theologians and defended by her confessor, Mathias of Linköping, in a treatise known by it's incipit: *Stupor et mirabilia audita sunt in terra nostra*.[8] Among them was the text of the Rule of the Saviour 'in prima persona' since it was said to be dictated by Christ himself.[9] The saint was commanded to found a new order because the old vineyards were no longer bearing good fruit. It was to be principally for women to honour Christ's mother. In fact the details of the Rule reflect St Bridget's personal way of life without the enclosure.[10]

One of the notable features of the order was that the numbers in a monastery were prescribed by the Rule. There were to be 60 nuns with the abbess elected by the community as the head of the whole monastery, 13 priests, 4 deacons and 8 lay brothers. Naturally the Rule begins by describing the life of the nuns. Though they would be recruited from upper class families they were to wear habits of grey burrel, a rough woollen material suitable for peasants, with sheepskin lining in winter. The distinguishing feature was a linen crown worn over the veil with five flames of red cloth to recall the wounds of Christ. Details were given of the periods of silence and fasts, including bread and water on vigils of greater feasts. The morning would be spent in church chanting their special office and High Mass in honour of Our Lady. The hours were to follow those of the brethren. In England where Sheen Charterhouse stood opposite Syon on the Thames the chanting must have been almost continuous.[11] The afternoon was given up to manual work, particularly embroidery. They could receive the Eucharist every Saturday and on the greater feast days. The minimum age for profession was 18. A postulant was to spend a year's probation outside the monastery coming at intervals to have the Rule expounded and the difficulties of conventual life explained to her.[12] If the community finally accepted her the profession and clothing ceremony was conducted by the bishop who, after High Mass, handed her over to the care of the Abbess at the entrance to the enclosure.

The brethren had a similar period of probation but they had to be twenty five years old before their profession. They were to follow the fasting rules of the Augustinians. Priests and deacons were to use the breviary of the diocese. Their habit was also of grey burrel with distinguishing badges for priests, deacons and lay brothers. At their head was the Confessor General, elected by the community and confirmed by the bishop. He was in charge of the spiritual direction of the whole monastery, keeping his finger on the pulse by hearing the confessions of every member three times a year. He appointed other priests to confess those who wanted to receive the sacrament more frequently. The brethren were to preach in the vernacular on Sundays and feastdays to the sisters and visitors to the abbey church. For their studies they were allowed to have in their library as many books as were necessary, the one relaxation of the rule of poverty.[13]

Naturally the principal building in the abbey was the church, a plain but solid structure with thirteen altars for daily masses. It was arranged so that the sisters had an upper choir below the roof from which they could see the high altar. The brethren had a lower choir. In the church was a coffin and outside the door an open grave which the sisters visited after tierce to recite the De Profundis. The sisters and brethren were to be strictly separated by a high wall, the sisters' monastery lying to the south of the church whilst the 'curia' of the brethren was to the north. There were grates for the sisters to make their confessions and receive communion and a turntable wheel by which packages could be passed. There were also grates at which the community could speak to, but not see, visitors.

The abbess was in charge of all administration. In managing the economy of the abbey she worked through a procurator who probably had his offices and staff in the Outer Court. A special feature of the Bridgettine rule was the annual audit held on the eve of All Saints after which the surplus was given to the poor on All Souls' day. The rule concludes by stating that the founder of an abbey was to ensure that the diocesan bishop would act as supervisor and visitor and the local ruler as protector of the community. Finally, the Pope's permission had to be obtained for the foundation.

After Clement VI had refused to approve the new order[14] St Bridget was instructed in another revelation to go to Rome and wait there until she met the Pope and the Emperor.[15] Before leaving Sweden she had received the gift of the royal estate of Vadstena as the site of the first monastery. She arranged that her personal estate would be used for the endowment.[16] A plan for a poll tax, Our Lady's Penny, to supplement the endowment failed to materialise. The effects of the Black Death and Civil war made it impossible to collect.[17]

Whilst in Rome the saint kept in touch with her homeland through visitors including her children and journeys made by her confessor, Peter of Alvastra, to check on the progress being made at Vadstena.[18] She also sent a message to King Magnus urging him to come to Rome to obtain absolution for his grave sins and add his appeals to hers for the papal confirmation of the Rule.[19]

Either before she left Sweden or in Rome St Bridget received further visions which interpreted or adapted the rule.[20] They included details of the design of the church which was to be built of local stone. Sermons were to be simple and brief so that they could be easily understood and not bore the hearers. The strict enclosure could be relaxed for the abbess to consult with workmen and for the Confessor General on the bishop's orders. Relaxations of the Rule allowed for vegetables on bread and water fast days and baths, even for the healthy. The administration of monastic property and the distribution of alms were to be carried out by four Fratres ad Extra under the control of the abbess. Four lay sisters could be recruited for heavy kitchen work and to assist in caring for sick and elderly nuns and two additional lay brothers, again for heavy work. Finally, the abbey was to have the privilege of exposition of the Blessed Sacrament in a crystal pyx and pilgrims would be able to gain the Vincula indulgence.

Whilst awaiting the Pope's arrival the saint also received guidance about the special office to be chanted by the sisters.[21] The lessons at Matins known as the Sermo Angelicus since they were dictated by an angel developed in a weekly cycle the theme from the writings of St Irenaeus and St Bernard of Mary as the second Eve, corresponding to St Paul's conception of Christ as the second Adam,[22] an idea mentioned briefly in the hymn Ave Maris Stella — sung daily at Vespers by the saint and her 'familia' and included in the sisters' office. The lessons speak of the foreknowledge of the angels, patriarchs and prophets of Mary's role in the work of redemption, of her life of complete submission to the will of God and of her suffering during Christ's passion though she was consoled by her foreknowledge of His resurrection. The lessons concluded with an account of her sharing in the work of the Apostles, her death and Assumption. The work has been judged to be best of the Marian legends and along with the Revelations the major work of medieval Swedish literature.[23]

The lessons, originally dictated in Swedish, were translated into Latin by Peter of Skäninge who also composed the antiphons and hymns which completed the office.[24] The texts together with the Rule were sent to Sweden to be revised by St Bridget's friend, Bishop Hemming, and kept at Alvasta until the Vadstena community was formed.[25] Together they were to form the nuns in their 'imitatio Marie', the basis of St Bridget's spirituality.[26] To help the sisters to understand their office vernacular treatises were later composed by the brothers — in Swedish 'Jungfru Marias Örtegard' and in English 'The Mirror of Our Lady'.[27]

When Urban V finally reached Rome in 1368 St Bridget was able to ask for the approval of her order. It would have to be under one of the accepted rules with the Regula Salvatoris as constitutions. Though the nuns of earlier double orders, Fontevrault and the Gilbertines had the Rule of St Benedict, she chose the Rule of St Augustine which would allow greater scope for her own ideas and bring great privileges.[28] However it was not until 1370 that the pope gave a limited approval after the text had been re—cast 'in tertia persona' and with some amendments by Count Nicholas Orsino, the saint's friend and a man familiar with the ways of the Curia. Permission was given for St Bridget to establish two monasteries at Vadstena, one for nuns and one for monks.[28a] She now hoped to return to Sweden to take charge of her new foundations, but she spent her last years on a pilgrimage to the Holy Land and died in Rome in 1373 soon after her return.

After her death her daughter, St Catherine, and her 'familia' were engaged in arranging the translation of her body to Sweden where her shrine at Vadsena became a national pilgrimage centre. Alfonso of Jaen prepared an edition of the Revelation for general circulation and for use in support of the petition for her canonisation.[29]   After a short stay in Sweden supervising the work at Vadstena, St Catherine returned to Rome to persuade the Pope to issue a further bull in favour of the order without the limitations imposed by Urban V.

Progress was slow until 1378 when the Great Schism proved to be a great opportunity for the Bridgettines. The saint's followers were among the leading defenders of the validity of the election of Urban VI[30] and they were rewarded by the issue of a further bull which accepted the Order of the Holy Saviour as a double order and granted the Vincula indulgence to Vadstena and any future foundations.[31] It also raised the status of the brethren by omitted 'principally' before women.[32] St Catherine along with Peter of Skäninge returned to Sweden to take charge of the community. Unfortunately, it was not until three years after her death in 1381 that the solemn enclosure was celebrated.[33]

It soon became apparent that there were points in the Rule that needed clarification and indeed some problems that were not included at all. These were to be covered by series of Additions drawn up by Peter of Alvastra. His draft was rejected by the sisters as being too harsh especially in the matters of manual labour for aristocratic ladies,[34] but an amended version was accepted at the General Chapter of 1429.[35] They were based on the Benedictine and Cisterian rules.   They concerned such matters as the elections of the abbess and, if necessary, her dismissal and the election of the Prioress. All the nuns except the Abbess, the Prioress and the sick were to share in the kitchen work. Two searchers were to be appointed to check on breaches of the rule and a gaol provided for the recalcitrant. There were to be separate quarters for the chronic sick and snorers should be separated from their sisters.

As Sweden supported the new pope chosen by the Council of Pisa it seemed expedient to secure a further confirmation of the Rule. This resulted in 1413 in the issue of the Bull known as Mare Magnum which granted the petition and extended the privileges of the order. Brigettine houses were to be exempt from clerical taxation, the indulgences were confirmed and the Confessor General given power to hear the confessions of all penitents. In Sweden the collection of Our Lady's Penny was authorised for the support of the Vadstena community.[36]

After the Council of Constance the Brigettines seemed to have secured their position when Martin V re–issued Mare Magnum and reconfirmed the canonisation. The new pope who was interested in monastic reform spoke of his affection for the order and his hope that a community would be established in Rome.[37] However in 1422 the whole concept of double orders came under attack and they were banned, existing communities being ordered to separate. The ban did not last long.   There were widespread protests co–ordinated by Thomas Fishborn, the Confessor General of Syon who went to Rome for the purpose. The pleas of the Bridgettines were supported by petitions from the Swedish and English governments and the 'consilia' of leading Canon lawyers including Panormitanus.[38] The Emperor was also interested in saving the foundation at Lubeck.[39] This pressure resulted in the gradual relaxation of the ban as in the bull Mare Anglicanum dealing with the privileges of Syon and despite the strictures of the Council of Basle its complete removal by Eugenius IV in 1435.[40]

The mother–house, Vadstena, soon became the spiritual and intellectual centre of Sweden, a small university of the North.[41] The brothers collected a magnificent library and produced many translations of spiritual works for the use of the sisters and general circulation. In doing such work they did much to develop Swedish as a literary language.[42] The sisters' devotion to their order is possibly best shown by their decision at the Reformation to continue their conventual life in exile at Dantzig.[43]

From Vadstena other abbeys were founded in centres of St Bridget's cult such as Florence and Dantzig.[44] During the fifteenth century the order spread in centres which had supported the Roman pontiffs during the Schism especially in Scandinavia and around the Baltic.[45] Most of the foundations were made in or near important cities where wealthy families would be a source of recruits and gifts from visitors who came to hear sermons and gain indulgences.[46] Despite the long negotiations and great expense of founding a Bridgettine monastery there seems to have been 27 houses at the end of the fifteenth century.[47] Contact between the houses was kept by general chapters held at irregular intervals.[47a]

The growth of the order owed much to the interest of the Lancastrian family. Henry IV may well have come to know about St Bridget and her work during his campaigns in East Prussia.[48] He certainly supported Fitzhugh's idea of introducing the order into England first put forward as a definite plan during a visit to Vadstena in 1406.[49] Henry himself planned to convert a decayed hospital near York into a Bridgettine monastery but the scheme fell through.[50] However his children shared his enthusiasm and with more success. Philippa after her marriage to Eric of Sweden was a great benefactor of Vadstena and joined her husband and brother, Bedford, in appeals to Martin V in 1422.[51] Her younger sister, Catherine, married the Count Palatine and was the foundress of Gnadenburg.[52] Margaret, widow of the Duke of Clarence, settled near Syon so that she could benefit from the spiritual direction of Simon Winter, one of the brethren.[52a] The best known project of all was Henry V's foundation of Syon at Isleworth which soon became one of the richest yet most high respected monasteries in England. It is remarkable how bitter political opponents seem to have worked together in this enterprise. Among the early benefactors were Henry Percy, a frequent rebel against Henry IV, and Roger Walden who were translated from Canterbury for opposition to the king.[53] This interest was continued by the Yorkists. Edward IV whose mother Cecily was a student of St Bridget's writings,[54] is mentioned in the Martiloge as the second founder as he restored property 'unjustly' taken by Henry VI for his own colleges of Eton and Kings.[55] His sister, Margaret, after her marriage to the Duke of Burgundy became a great benefactor of the abbey at Gouda.[56]

Though Syon did not accept the Additions to the Rule in use at Vadstena[56] and gained independence of the mother house under the terms of the Bull Mare Anglicanum,[58] they still kept in close touch through letters and visits.[59] Again as happened at Vadstena the Syon nuns showed their devotion to their Bridgettine way of life when the abbey was suppressed for the second time by Elizabeth in 1558 by going into exile.[60]

NOTES

My special thanks are due to Mr O. Anscombe of St Deiniols Library for his generous help with my bibliographical queries and to Mrs M. Abbot for her excellent typescript from my untidy draft.

1.   Convenient short accounts of the saints are:—
          P. Debongnie in Dict. d'Histoire et de Géographie Ecclésiastiques (1938) and M. Redpath, God's Ambassadress (1947) which is based on the Acta et Processus Canonisationis Beate Birgitte, ed., I. Collin (1922–34). For

the order *cf.* M. Heimbucher, Die Orden und Kongregationen der Katolischer Kirche (1932–4) and P. Debonguie, *loc. cit.*

2. E.F. Jacob, Essays in the Conciliar Epoch (1943), p 155. For her influence in England, cf. R. Ellis, Flores ad Fabricandam Coronam in Medium Aevum (1982).

3. Lincoln College, Oxford, Ms. 117 f. 272. I owe this reference to the late Dr N.D. Hurnard.

4. *cf* R. Ellis, Syon Abbey: the Spirituality of the English Bridgettines (1984).

5. B. Klockass, Birgittas Svenska Värld (1976), p 36; A. Anderson, St Birgitta (1980), p 10.

6. T. Nyberg, Birgittinische Klostergrundungen des Mittelalters (1965), p 53; B. Klocka s Birgitta och Boûenrna (1973), p 13.

7. The first complete edition was printed at Lubeck in 1492. *cf* Ellis Flores, p 163.

8. Printed in Revelationes Celestes Bk I, ed., C.G. Undhagen (1977).

9. Sancta Birgitta, Opera Minora I, Regula Salvatoris, ed., S. Eklund (1975). The main features are summarised by Walsingham in St Alban's Chronicle (1406–20), ed., V.H. Galbraith (19 7), p 32. For other cases of rules linked with visions *cf* G. Barry, Historical Notes on the Carmelite Order (n.d.), p 73.

10. Ellis, Spirituality, p 11.

11. A.J. Collins, The Bridgettine Breviary of Syon Abbey, (1969), p vii.

12. So not entering blindly *cf* R. Whitford, The Pype of Perfection, ed., J Hogg (1979), p 41.

13. *cf* M. Bateson, Syon Monastery, library catalogue (1898).

14. Redpath, p 113.

15. Den heliga Birgittas Revelationes Extravagantes, ed., C. Hollman (1956), pp 120, 158.

16. B. Klockars, Birgittas Svenska Värld (1976), p 103.

17. Klockars, Birgittas Svenska Värld , *loc. cit.*

18. *Ibid.*

19. Revelationes Extravagantes, pp 160, 187.

20. Revelationes Extravagantes, *passin.*

21. Den heliga Birgittas Opera Minora II, Sermo Angelicus, ed., S. Eklund (1972). The text used at Syon is in A.J. Collins, the Bridgettine Breviary of Syon Abbey (1969) and an English translation in E. Graf, The Prayers and Revelations of St Bridget of Sweden (1928).

22. T. Lunden, Den heliga Birgittas och den helige Petri av Skäninge dichtverk om Jungfru Maria, in Kyrkohistorisk Årskrift (1973), p 66.

23. S. Stolpe, Birgitta (1973), p 1.

24. Lunden, *op cit.*

25. Revelationes Extravagantes, p 229.

26. T. Schmid, Birgitta och hennes Uppenbarelser (194o), p 52.

27. Jungfru Marias Örtegård, ed., R. Geete (1885); the Mirror of Our Lady, ed., J.H. Blunt (1873).

28. *cf* R.W. Souther, Western Society and the Church in the Later Middle Ages (1978), p 242; Nyberg, Klostergrundungen, p 56; Schmid, p 94.

28a. R. Steffen. Den heliga Birgittas Uppenbarelser (1909), p xxliv.

29. E. Colledge, Epistola Solitarii ad Reges; Alphonse of Pecha as the organiser of Birgittine and Urbanist Propaganda, in Medieval Studies, 1956.

30. *Ibid.*; W. Ullman, The Origins of the Great Schism (1948), pp 26, 42

31. Ellis, Spirituality, p 50; Redpath, p 54; Debongnie, *loc cit.*

32. H. Cnattingius, Studies in the Order of St Bridget of Sweden (1963), p 23.

33.   T. Nyberg, Vadstena Klosters Pionjären, in Personalisk Tidskrift (1963), p 1.
34.   F.M. Steele, The Story of the Bridgettines (1910), p 40.
35.   T. Nyberg, Dokumente und Untersuchungen zur Inneren Geschichte der Orei Birgittenklosters Bayerns (1974), p 42. Ellis, Spirituality, p 9.
36.   T. Höjer, Studier i Vadstena Klosters och Birgittin orderns Historia (1905), p 137.
37.   H. Cnattingius, p 120.
38.   Cnattingius, Studies, p 131 and W. Ullman, The Recognition of St Bridget's Rule by Martin V, Revue Benedictine, (1957).
39.   Nyberg, Klostergrundungen, p 34.
40.   Cnattingius, *loc cit.*, Redpath, p 205.
41.   Heimbucher, p 508.
42.   Heimbucher, *loc cit.*, L. Willin, The Monastery of Vadstena. Investigating the great Translation Workshop of Medieval Sweden (forthcoming).
43.   Steele, p 87.
44.   T. Lyndgren, Birgittinordens Utbredning, in Credo (1973).
45.   Cnattingius, p 149.
46.   T. Nyberg. Storia dell' Ordine di Santa Brigida, in Birgitta, Una Santa Svedese (1973).
47.   Debongni, *loc cit.*
47a   Debongnie, *loc cit.*
48.   Dantzig was a centre of her cult and the Teutonic Knights received an early copy of her Revelations; Schmid, p 11, *cf* Lincoln Cath. Ms. 114 f 16.
49.   J.R. Fletcher, The Story of the English Bridgettines, (1933), p 16.
50.   Höjer, p 252.
51.   Cnattingius, p 149.
52.   Steele, p 140; Nyberg, Klostergrundunge, p 70.
52a   *cf* G.R. Keiser, Patronage and Piety in Fifteenth Century England, Yale University Library Cazette, (1985), p 32.
53.   The list of Special Benefactors of Syon is in B.M. Add. Ms 22285.
54.   M. Noble, Some Observations on the Life of Cecily Duchess of York, Archaeologia (1800), p 7.
55.   B.M. Add. Ms. 22285, f 15.
56.   M. Van Hattum, Iets over het Birgitten Klooster te Gouda, in Niederlandsch Archief voor Kerkgeschiedenis (1943), p 259.
57.   The text of their Additions is in The Rewyll of Seynt Savioure, ed., J. Hogg, Vols 3 and 4 (1980).
58.   Höjr, p 256.
59.   M.B. Tait, The Brigittine Monastery of Syon with Special Reference to its monastic usage. (D. Phil., Oxford, 1975).
60.   Fletcher, p 43.

FIFTEENTH–CENTURY FRANCISCAN REFORM AND THE SPANISH
CONVERSOS: THE CASE OF FRAY ALONSO DE ESPINA

John Edwards

The city of Segovia, about forty–five miles north–west of Madrid, was, in the fifteenth century, a place of considerable political and economic importance. In the 1450s and 1460s, it was frequently involved in the complex and disturbed politics of the Castilian monarchy, which in some respects bore a marked resemblance to the contemporary Wars of the Roses in England. It also had a prominent Jewish community, much of which occupied a section of the walled city between the San Andrés gate and the 'Canongía', or canons' houses, beside the cathedral.[1] However, although documentary evidence is largely absent, it appears that, as elsewhere in Spain, the mid fifteenth–century Jewish population was much depleted, as a result of conversion to Christianity which took place in the decades following the pogroms of 1391. None the less, relationships between the remaining Jews and their converted ('*converso*' or 'New Christian') brethren were still, in many cases, close, here as elsewhere.[2] These links, which often included family ties, between Segovia's Jews and *conversos* were eventually to be revealed in a famous, or notorious, investigation which was carried out by the newly–founded Spanish Inquisition, with the support of the Catholic Monarchs Ferdinand and Isabella, into the religious beliefs and practices of a prominent *converso* family, the Arias Dávila. The preparatory documents for the trial of Juan Arias Dávila, bishop of Segovia, which was never completed, were largely collected and prepared between 1486 and 1491. However, much of the Segovian inquisitors' inquiry concerned the bishop's parents, Diego Arias Dávila and Elvira González, who were both by then deceased. Also involved were the bishop's nephew, Francisco Arias, *regidor*, or alderman, of Segovia, the bishop's sister, Isabel Arias, her husband, Gómez González de la Hoz, and their four sons.[3] From the surviving papers it appears that the bishop's father, Diego Arias, was a prime target of the investigation. He was *contador mayor* (chief auditor) to the previous ruler of Castile, Henry IV, and was accused by witnesses of various Jewish beliefs and practices. He was accused of Sabbath observance, of keeping dietary laws, of observing Jewish death and burial customs, of worshiping in a prayer shawl (*tallit*), of keeping the Passover and even of trying to convert non–Jewish ('Old') Christians to Judaism. He was also accused of working on Sundays and other Christian holy days, of showing disrespect for Christianity, of blasphemy and scepticism, and of defying the Inquisition.[4] However, two charges are of particular interest here. The first was that, while distributing payments from royal funds, as a Crown official, Diego refused to give money to anyone who came into his office wearing a badge which bore Jesus' name.[5] The second was that Diego conspired to secure the poisoning, by a Jewish physician, Master Xamaya, of a notable Franciscan friar, Bro. Alonso de Espina.[6] The question is how and why the attempt, in Ferdinand and Isabella's reign, to impugn the reputation of the Arias Dávila family, including the previous king's chief auditor, should have so explicitly involved the Franciscans in general and Bro. Alonso de Espina in particular.

In a sense, the accusation that Diego Arias brought about the death by poisoning of Espina is of lesser relevance, as it appears to be typical charge of the period against Jews, here transferred, as so frequently happened in fifteenth–century Spain, to *conversos*, seeing that so many Jews were baptised after 1391. Several witnesses, three of them clerics and one of these a friar, gave

evidence of the connection between Diego Arias and Espina's death. The parish
priest of La Trinidad, Antón Sánchez, claimed in 1486 to hear a friar of the
Franciscan house of San Antonio say that when Espina was found dead in Madrid
he had previously been in good health, and that Diego Arias had secured his
death because, in the reign of his master Henry IV, the Jews went about without
badges, which in Spain should have meant a red disc, and that in view of this
fact, Alonso de Espina, together with other Franciscan friars, had tried to ensure
that Christians wore badges instead, in the form, according to this witness, of a
cross, though the full facts emerge from the testimony of others.[7] The *converso*
Franciscan, Bro. Alonso Enríquez, who was later to achieve fame as an agent
provocateur in the 'ritual murder' case of the 'Holy Child of La Guardia',
which played a major part in bringing about the expulsion of Spain's Jews in
1492, named Master Xamaya as the physician responsible for carrying out Diego
Arias' wishes. According to him, Diego, and other *conversos* 'who walked about
the Court', wanted Espina dead because he preached against heresy and in
particular against the privileged treatment which many Jews were receiving in
Henry IV's Castile. He claimed that Samuel's brother–in–law, Samuel Alaf, had
said to him that the Jewish communities of the kingdom owed a great deal to
Xamaya, because he had killed so great an enemy of theirs. The friar claimed to
have heard a similar story from Juan de Amusco, a moneychanger, and from
Mosé Zaragoza, who was a leading Segovian Jew and informant of the
Inquisition.[8] The choirmaster of Segovia cathedral, Pedro Doncel, added, in
1489, that Espina fell ill while lodging in a 'boarding–house' (*aposentamiento*)
run by Dominican nuns in Madrid. According to him, Diego Arias went to visit
Espina at the convent, as did King Henry himself, but it was after an
examination, on royal orders, by Alonso García de Santa María, bishop of
Cartagena, a member of a notable *converso* family, that the friar was found dead.
'Herbs' (*yerbas*) were blamed, this being a conventional term in the period for
poison.[9]

It is unlikely that the guilt, if any, for the death of Alonso de Espina will
ever be allocated with any certainty. However, the links between Espina's
demise, *conversos* such as Diego Arias, and the wearing of badges bearing the
name of Jesus, requires further attention. According to several witnesses, a
major factor in provoking the hostility of Diego Arias and other *conversos*
towards Espina and the Franciscans was the newly–introduced custom of the
wearing of such badges by Christians and very probably in particular by 'Old
Christians', that is, those claiming not to be of Jewish origin. A public notary of
Segovia, Antonio Sanchez de Lozoya, stated that, during the period in which
Espina was preaching the desirability of an Inquisition, while this was receiving
little or no support from Henry IV, the friar urged 'all those who were Christians
to wear a "Jesus" on their hats'.[10] It has already been noted that Antón
Sánchez, the parish priest of La Trinidad, remembered the emblems as being
crosses, but the licentiate Juan de Nurena confirmed Lozoya's memory that,
during the Observant Franciscans' campaign in Segovia, 'people wore the name
of Jesus, written on paper or parchment'. He also attributed the death of Espina
to a conspiracy between Diego Arias and the Conventual Franciscans to prevent
an Inquisition in Castile and also to set back the course of the Observant reform
of the order in that kingdom.[11] The cathedral choirmaster referred to Espina and
other friars as having 'made' many people 'take the name of Jesus and wear
pieces of paper sewn on to their hats with the name "Jesus"'.[12]

The search for the special devotion to the name of Jesus, beginning with
modern liturgies and going back to the late Middle Ages, yields interesting
results. The lectionary of the Anglican Book of Common Prayer marks the

commemoration of the Name of Jesus on 7 August, the day following the Feast of the Transfiguration. The memoria does not, however, appear in the Tridentine missal and breviary, or in the modern Roman Divine Office or Anglican Alternative Service Book.[13] The old Anglican use here retains that of the late medieval Sarum missal and breviary, in which 7 August was 'the feast of the most sweet Name of Jesus', and the proper scriptural readings, collect, tract, sequence, secret and preface might also be used during the rest of the octave of the Transfiguration[14]. The Sarum use contains a collect which refers to the Name of Jesus as 'fearful and terrible to evil spirits', while the devotion as a whole appears to be based on the description of the significance of Jesus' name in Paul's epistle to the Philippians.[15] The late medieval English commemoration of the feast seems to have derived from a native tradition going back at least to the thirteenth century, though its observance was still not universal in England in the early sixteenth century despite being the most popular of the so–called 'new feasts' of the late Middle Ages.[16] However, the inclusion of the Name of Jesus in the general Western liturgical calendar originated in the career of the Franciscan saint, Bernardino of Siena. Bernardino habitually ended his sermons with the display of a painting of the Name of Jesus, in the form 'YHS', surmounted by a cross and surrounded by golden rays. The Name signified for him the revelation of God in man, and he began to use the device during a mission in Florence in 1425. Bernardino died in 1444, and was canonised as early as 1450, but his devotion to the Name of Jesus caused controversy during his lifetime and was only included in the Roman liturgy in 1530. The founder of Bernardino's order, Saint Francis himself, is said in the *Vita prima* of Thomas of Celano to have licked his lips when he said Jesus' name, but his attitude seems to have been somewhat ambiguous, as in his famous *Canticle of Brother Sun* he wrote of the Lord 'And no man is worthy to pronounce your name'. In any case, the devotion was not mentioned in the articles of Bernardino's canonisation.[17]

In its early days, the devotion to the Name of Jesus was even seen by some as heretical. Bernardino succeeded in having his symbol displayed on many houses in Siena, as well as its Palazzo Pubblico, but what the Franciscan historian Bro. Nimmo calls 'the chief sign of the reborn Franciscan spirituality' within his ministry appears, from a Latin life collected by the Bollandists, to have arisen from a battle between Bernardino and a heretical sect which originated in Lombardy. The group, led by Manfred of Vercelli, is said by contemporary sources to have preached the imminent coming of the Antichrist, specifically in 1417 or 1418, and also in favour of divorce, probably because marriage would no longer be relevant or desirable in the approaching Last Days. It was as part of Catholic efforts to defeat this sect, in which the famous Dominican missionary to the Jews in Spain, Father Vincent Ferrer, also took part, that Bernardino began to use his famous emblem. However, controversy quickly arouse over the new custom, possibly because the letters might be used in magic. In any case, Bernardino's enemies had become established in Siena, apparently with the diocesan bishop's support, in that same year a process was started in Rome to have it condemned and banned.[18] The attempt was unsuccessful, however, and the devotion spread through Catholic Europe. Although it was removed from the Roman calendar at Trent, being replaced by a memoria of Cajetano, the founder of the Theatine order, it was still a popular cult in New Castile in the later sixteenth century, according to local reports sent to Philip II's government.[19] At this stage, though, it is necessary to try to make the connection between developments in Italy and events in Segovia in the mid–fifteenth century.

Considerable complications resulted from the introduction of the

Franciscan reform of the Observance to the city, in the mid— to late fifteenth century. The original house of the order, San Francisco, was founded, outside the walled city, before 1252, and apparently included the partly—ruined church of San Benito.[20] In 1438, an attempt was made to reform San Francisco, Segovia, and bring it into the Observance, but although this eventually happened, it is not entirely clear when.[21] What is clear, though, is that a new Franciscan house was proposed, with royal support, to be dedicated to San Antonio. Bishop Moorman dates this plan to 1455, but thinks it doubtful that the house was ever established.[22] What actually seems to have happened, however, is that San Antonio did in fact come into being, but experienced a somewhat chequered career. According to the sixteenth—century Segovian historian Deigo de Colmenares, between 1455 and the time of the Árias Dávila trial, that is, the late 1480s San Antonio and the older, but now reformed, San Francisco coexisted uneasily as houses of Observant friars. Colmenares states that the rivalry led to relaxation of the rule in San Antonio, while San Francisco became more austere, perhaps to appeal to recruits of differing temperaments, and very probably in order to compete for worshippers and benefactions. As a result, in 1488 Queen Isabella, as part of the active royal policy of assisting ecclesiastical reform, and having, in 1486, obtained the appropriate bull from Innocent VIII, merged the two houses of friars into the buildings of San Francisco, and handed San Antonio over to the Second Order of Clares, the latter house thereafter to be known as San Antonio 'et Real'. The nuns also received the sum of 100,000 *maravedis* to build a new choir. The agent who carried out this move, after some difficulty and conflict, was none other than the local diocesan, Bishop Juan Arias,[23] When it is noted that his father's old enemy. Bro. Alonso de Espina, was a member of the community of San Antonio, the relevance of the development of Franciscan reform in Segovia to the fate of this *converso* family becomes clearer.

An added refinement to the story is that in 1460, the *contador* Diego Arias gave a donation and privilege to the 'pilgrim hospital' of San Antonio. This was done with power granted by Henry IV, but the hospital had in fact been under Diego Arias' patronage since the previous reign. It was on the northern edge of the Jewish quarter, and either occupied or was built on the site of a former synagogue, known as the *sinagoga vieja*. It was originally given by John II to the friars of the order of Mercy (La Merced), whose main task was to ransom Christian captives in Muslim hands and arrange their release. The royal grant was made on condition that the Mercedarians agreed to abandon certain properties in the Jewry so that the segregation (*apartamiento*) of Jews and Christians in Segovia might take place. The condition of the transfer of the synagogue to the Mercedarians was that it should be turned into a hospital, and this conversion was apparently under way in 1442. According to the 1460 document, both the *contador* and his wife were buried in San Antonio, and the first version of Bishop Juan Arias' will states that his sister Isabel was to be buried there too. The identification with Espina's convent cannot at this stage be certain, as the 1460 grant also gave money to the Mercedarians, but if it were to be shown that royal plane for San Antonio in the late 1480s involved a change of use for a house under the patronage of the Arias Dávila, the deterioration in relations between Bishop Juan and the Catholic Monarchs might be more explicable. Why Diego Arias should have patronised the house of his Observant enemies in the first place would, however, also be hard to explain, and would raise questions about the accuracy and sincerity of the witnesses already cited from the inquisitorial investigation of the Arias Dávila family. At this stage, it is not possible to resolve these questions.

In any case it has been seen that, according to various witnesses, Espina was active in Segovia, both in devotion to the Name of Jesus and in preaching on behalf of the proposal that an Inquisition should be set up in Castile to test the orthodoxy of those who had converted from Judaism during the preceding decades. It is in the latter context that Espina is best known to general historians of medieval Spain and of medieval Jews. Although the book was in fact published anonymously, he is accepted as the author of the compendium of religious and social anti–Jewish material entitled the *Fortalitium fidei* ('Fortress of the faith'). In fact, the book also contains long attacks on heretics and Muslims, as well as proposals for defeating and subjugating them, but it provides the clearest possible evidence of the friars hostility to the Jews, and hence to *conversos*, as well as the likely tensions in the 1450s and 1460s between San Antonio, Segovia, and the Arias Dávila family.[25] However, Wadding reports that Espina also published in 1452 another work, this time under his own name. It was entitled *Sermons on the excellent Name of Jesus*.[26] The story of the 'Jesus' badges here finds its context, though, interestingly, Espina appears to make no direct reference to this devotion in his advice in the *Fortalitium* on how Christianity should be preached to Jews.[27] Nonetheless, despite his subsequent fame and his apparent importance in the mid fifteenth–century controversy in Spain over the role of *conversos*, there is some confusion, both about whether or not he was a *converso* himself and about his subsequent career. There is no doubt that he was at one stage active in Segovia. In addition, it is known that he attended Juan II's favourite, the constable of Castile Don Alvaro de Luna, when he was executed in Valladolid in 1453, but after that things became less clear. Bro. Iraola believes that Espina then stayed in Valladolid, at the Real Convento de San Francisco, and survived there at least until 1491, as bishop of Trinopoli. Other sources describe him as bishop of Monopoli, Orenopoli or Termopolis. It is indeed quite possible that Espina was made a bishop *in partibus infidelium*, even though Fort suggested, in 1879, that if the friar was already well on in years when he heard Álvaro de Luna's confession, it is unlikely that he and the bishop of one of these sees were the same person.[28] Had he still been alive in the 1480s, the poisoning charge would scarcely have been credible. In any case, Fort rightly comments that Espina felt great devotion to 'the sweet name of Jesus' and that he preached 'some sermons on the matter'.[29]

This devotion indeed has one more aspect, in its original development in early fifteenth–century Italy, which is of significance for what happened in Segovia in the time of Espina and Diego Arias. Although it seems to have originated as a weapon against heresy, the devotion to the Name also became involved in the Observant Franciscans' attack on usury and especially on that carried out by Jews, together with the development, by Bernardino of Siena and others, of the pawnbanks known as *Monti di Pieta*, which were intended to put traditional money lenders out of business.[30] As Bernardino was fighting, with increasing success, to have the Name of Jesus devotion accepted by the Papacy, he was also trying to achieve action against usury. Significantly, it was Eugenius IV who, in contrast with his predecessor Martin V, eased the friar's difficulties on both counts. Pope Eugenius' bull, '*Dudum ad nostram*', promulgated in 1442 at the petition of John II's Castilian government, reaffirmed, and in some cases even strengthened, thirteen–century measures intended to minimise social contact between Christians and Jews.[31] Eugenius' successor, Nicholas V, though robust in his opposition to attempts to exclude Spanish *conversos* from Christian society, none the less reissued this bull, as did his successor Calixtus III, in 1456.[32] It is also worth noting that Bernardino consciously modelled his campaign against usury on that of the Portuguese Augustinian canon who is generally known as St Anthony of Padua (1195–1231) and to whom it is very probable that the hospital in Segovia was dedicated.[33]

The difference between conditions in these two countries was of course that in Spain, unlike Italy, the primary target of Christian opprobrium was the supposedly dubious converts from Judaism to Christianity, rather than unbaptised Jews. Between the 1440's and the 1460s, Segovia found itself at the centre of the debate about the efficacy of baptism which later spawned 'purity of blood' laws in many Spanish corporations. It is equally clear that there was a spread of the Observant reform of the Franciscan order from Italy to Spain, for example through the known contacts in Italy of Spanish reformers such as Bro. Pedro de Santoyo and Bro. Pedro de Villacreces.[34] Alonso de Esopina's commitment, both to the Observant reform, together with the devotion to the Name of Jesus, and to the Observant policy of segregating Jews and Christians, which in the Spanish, unlike the Italian, context meant casting aspersions on *conversos* too, also seems evident.[35] The paradox is that, as Colin Thompson has clearly shown in his study of the sixteenth—century Augustinian friar, Luis de León, the notion of the power of names, and in particular of divine names, had especial significance in Judaism, both before the rise of Christianity and in the Middle Ages. Abraham Abulafia, the pioneer of Spanish Kabbalah, who was born in 1240, held the view that 'Since God has created all that is, everything participates in him. He has Himself revealed his name in a series of letters' and, 'since every language is derived from the original, Hebrew, each can be approached in such a way, and Abulafia gave Greek, Latin and Italian examples too'.[36] Were Bernardino of Siena and Alonso de Espina fully aware of the significance of their devotion to the Name of Jesus?

NOTES

1.   F. Fita, 'La judería de Segovia: documentos inéditos', *Boletin de la Real Academia de la Historia*, 9 (1886), pp 270–293, 344–389; M. Asenjo González, *Segovia. La ciudad y su tierra a fines del medioevo* (Segovia, 1986), [hereafter Asenjo, *Segovia*], pp 322–324 and plan 2; E. Gutwirth, 'Social tensions within fifteenth—century Hispano—Jewish communities', unpublished Ph.D thesis (London, 1979).

2.   E. Gutwirth, 'Elementos étnicos y históricos en las relaciones judeo—conversas en Segovia', in ed., Y. Kaplan, *Jews and conversos. Studies in society and the Inquisition* (Jerusalem, 1985), pp 83–102.

3.   Ed., C. Carrete Parrondo, *Fontes Iudaeorum Regni Castellae 3, Proceso inquisitorial contra los Arias Davila seqovianos: un enfrentamiento social entre judios y conversos* (Salamanca, 1986), [hereafter *FIRC*]; J. Edwards, 'Bishop Juan Arias Dávila: "judaizer" or reformer?', in eds., D. Hook, B. Taylor, *Cultures in contact in medieval Spain: historical and literary essays presented to L.P. Harvey* (London, in press).

4.   *FIRC*, pp 19–33, 37–39, 42–54, 60–76, 78–81, 86–115, 117–120.

5.   *FIRC*, pp 33, 37–38, 72, 79–80.

6.   *FIRC*, pp 37–38, 43–44, 72, 79–80.

7.   *FIRC*, pp 37–38.

8.   *FIRC*, pp 43–44.

9.   *FIRC*, pp 79–80.

10. *FIRC*, p 33.

11. *FIRC*, p 72.

12. *FIRC*, pp 79–80.

13. *The lectionary containing the calendar etc. of the Book of Common Prayer* (London, Oxford, 1978), p 22; *Missale Romanum* (Malines, 1856), pp 462–463; John, Marquess of Bute (ed and trans), *The Roman breviary of Trent* (Edinburgh) 3, pp 799–802.

14. Ed., V. Stanley, *Sarum missal in English* (London, 1911), pp 447–452; Eds., F. Procter, C. Wordsworth, *Breviarium ad usum insignis ecclesiae Sarum* (Cambridge, 1882),pp 1, 21.

15. Proper readings in Sarum missal: Philippians 2:10–11 (office), Acts 4:8–12 (lesson), Ephesians 1:20–22 (gradual), Matthew 1:20–23 (gospel), Mark 16:17–18 (offertory), Revelation 2:17 (communion).

16. R.W. Pfaff, *New liturgical feasts in later medieval England* (Oxford, 1970), pp 62, 80, 130.

17. D. Nimmo, *Reform and division in the Franciscan order (1226–1538)* (Rome, 1987), pp 579–580; I. Origo, *The world of San Bernardino* (London, 1963), pp 117–130; S. Baring–Gould, *The lives of the saints* (London, 1897), p 5 (20 May); S.K. Cohn, Jr, *Death and property in Siena, 1205–1800. Strategies for the afterlife* (Baltimore, 1988), pp 51, 144; L. Douglas, *A history of Siena* (London, 1902), pp 183, 185; R.D. Sorrell, *St Francis and nature. Tradition and innovation in Western Christian attitudes toward the environment* (New York, 1988), pp 96, 100–101.

18. *Analecta ex duobus vitis*, etc., in eds., G. Henschen, D. Papebroek, *Acta Sanctorum Maii* (Antwerp, 1685), 5, pp 277–284, 305–318; R.K. Emmerson, *Antichrist in the Middle Ages. A study of medieval apocalypticism, art and literature* (Manchester, 1981), pp 55–56; E. Delaruelle, *La piete populaire au Moyen Age* (Turin, 1975), pp 329–354.

19. W.A. Christian, Jr, *Local religion in sixteenth–century Spain* (Princeton, 1981), pp 54, 129.

20. F. Gonzaga, *De origine seraphicae religionis Franciscanae eiusque progressibus, de Regularis Observanciae* (Rome, 1587), [hereafter Gonzaga, *De origine*], p 864; J.R.H. Moorman, *Medieval Franciscan houses* (St Bonaventure, N.Y., 1983), [hereafter Moorman, *Franciscan houses*], pp 445–446.

21. Moorman, *Franciscan houses*, p 446; ed., J.M. Fonseca, L. Wadding, *Annales Minorum*, 15 vols (Quaracchi, 1931–1935), pp 15, 349.

22. Moorman, *Franciscan houses*, p 446.

23. D. de Colmenares, *Historia de la insigne ciudad de Segovia y compendio de las historias de Castilla*, 2nd edn (Segovia, 1970), 2, pp 131–132; Gonzaga, *De origine*, p 864; L. Cardeñoso, 'Convento de San Antonio de Clarisas de Segovia', *Archivo Ibero–Americano* [hereafter *AIA*], old series, 7 (1917), pp 5–26, 8 (1917), pp 321–349; J. Meseguer Fernández, 'Franciscanismo de Isabel la Católica', *AIA*, new series, 19 (1959), pp 153–195 at 154; Asenjo, *Segovia*, pp 555–556.

24. Asenjo, *Segovia*, pp 373–374; J.A. Ruiz Hernando, *Historia del urbanismo en la ciudad de Segovia del siglo XII at XIX*, 2 vols (Segovia, 1980), 1, pp 101–102.

25. *Fortalitium fidei*, etc., no author or date, published by Stephanus Gaeynard, no place.

26. *Sermones de excellentia nominis Iesu*, in Wadding, *Scriptores ordinis minorum* (Rome, 1806), p 10.

27. 'Secunda consideratio....Qualis debe esse predicata', *Fortalitium*, fol 5.

28. J.M. Iraola, 'La devoción a la Inmaculada en la provincia franciscana de la Concepción', *AIA*, new series, 18 (1958), pp 5–91 at 11–12; C.R. Fort, 'De los obispos españoles titulares de iglesias', *Hispania Sagrada*, 51 (1879), [hereafter Fort, 'Obispos'], p 288.

29. Fort, 'Obispos', p 288.

30. B. Pullan, *Rich and poor in Renaissance Venice. The social institutions of a Catholic state, to 1620* (Oxford, 1971), [hereafter Pullan, *Rich and poor*]

pp 431–432, 449–460; Edwards, *The Jews in Christian Europe, 1400–1700* (London, 1988), pp 82–83.

31. Compare the so–called laws of Ayllón (c.1412), in L. Suárez Fernández, *Judios espanoles en la Edad Media* (Madrid, 1980), pp 225–226.

32. Pullan, *Rich and poor*, pp 449–450.

33. D.H. Farmer, *The Oxford dictionary of saints* (Oxford, 1978), pp 20–21.

34. No author, 'Las reformas en los signlos XIV y XV', *AIA*, new series, 17 (1957), pp 339, 849.

35. *Pace* N. Round, *The greatest man uncrowned. A study of the fall of Don Alvaro de Luna* (London, 1986), pp 208–210.

36: C. Thompson, *The strife of tongues. Fray Luis de Leon and the Golden Age of Spain* (Cambridge, 1988), pp 151, 155, 161–164, 171.

THE CIVIL SERVANT AND MONASTIC REFORM: RICHARD FOX'S TRANSLATION OF THE BENEDICTINE RULE FOR WOMEN, 1517.

Barry Collett

In 1485, Henry Earl of Richmond was in France assembling his forces in preparation for crossing the channel to confront his enemy King Richard III. One of Henry's secretaries was a priest, Richard Fox, a Lincolnshire man of yeoman parentage, educated most probably at Oxford. He was then about 37 years of age. Little is known of Fox's background: he may have once been a schoolmaster, and probably he also had some practical experience in engineering and building, but by 1483 he was in Paris serving as administrator and diplomat to the Earl of Richmond who had urgent need of men like Fox, men who possessed 'diligence and speed'.[1]

Fox landed with the Earl and was present at the battle of Bosworth on 22 August 1485, and at the subsequent coronation of the victorious Richmond as King Henry VII. He rose rapidly in the royal service. In 1486 he was appointed a Privy Councillor and in February 1487 became Lord Privy Seal and also the Bishop of Exeter, at the same time as his colleague Morton became Archbishop of Canterbury and Lord Chancellor.[2] Fox's administrative and political talents matured during this post—war period: he had considerable flair as a mediator and diplomat, being able to use 'words like healing oil in wounds'.[3]

He was witty and learned, thorough in organization, and shrewd in the art of delegating authority.[4] Francis Bacon called him 'a grave counsellor for war on peace' who worked closely with Henry VII, 'as it were an instrument with the workman'.[5] In short, Fox was an able episcopal statesman in the medieval tradition.

The king's esteem for Fox was reflected in the wealth of his episcopal appointments. In 1492 he was translated from Exeter to the wealthier see of Bath and Wells, then in 1494 to Durham, and finally in 1501 he was given the extremely wealthy diocese of Winchester, where he remained until his death in 1527 and in whose cathedral he is buried.[6] Until his retirement in 1516 Fox was an absentee bishop, although he did take great care to see that his dioceses functioned smoothly in his absence whilst he was fully occupied at court.[7]

Thus, for 30 years from 1486, with his official duties as Lord Privy Seal and his unofficial duties as counsellor, Fox worked as a principal administrator, diplomat and adviser to Henry VII, and then to Henry VIII, until his retirement in May 1516.[8] Like most people in such positions of executive authority, he highly valued effort and persistency in getting done what has to be done. He himself always worked hard, from 5 a.m. to 6 p.m., six days a week with little time given to eating, more than 70 hours at work each week, often much more. 'You could wonder', said the Dean of Wells in 1506, 'what causes he has to do, and therefore we must abide his leisure'.[9]

But of more importance than the hours he logged and the number of tasks he worked at, is his sense of planning and determination in achieving goals. This attitude is illustrated by his advice to the members of Corpus Christi College that the College Statutes could only be fulfilled if they 'strive and labour for that object, shaking off all indolence'.[10] He also valued the habit of accurate analysis and appraisal of events, and his own assessment of situations was always cool and realistic. His executive experience had taught him that clear understanding was the only basis for effective action. Bacon described him as 'a vigilant man and secret', and also as 'a wise man, and one that could see through the present to the future'.[11] This quality of sound judgment, essential for someone in his position, is reflected in his choice of suffragen bishops and diocesan officials to whom he delegated authority during his absence. Invariably his choice was shrewd. There are many examples: Nicholas West his first vicar–general at Winchester became a successful diplomat and Bishop of Ely in 1515; also John Incent, another protegee of Fox was later vicar–general to Wolsey in diocese of Winchester, and became Dean of St Paul's in 1540. As Fox made clear in his letters, those to whom he delegated authority in his diocese were chosen for their ability — diligence, sound judgment, effective action, a sense of duty and also style and courtesy.

As Fox grew older, and particularly after his retirement in 1516, his letters reflect more deliberately upon the qualities to be desired in those who exercise authority. In many ways his ideas resemble those in the tradition of literature on the moral obligations of princes and others who exercised authority. But Fox's reflections were different in two respects. First, he did not abstract and set down his ideas in literary form. He was an executive, accustomed to confronting problems, making decisions and getting things done. His ideas are woven in amongst practical working instructions, statutes, and such like. This context often makes it difficult to sort out and define Fox's ideas, but on the other hand it gives his views considerable substance because they were embedded in concrete examples of action and behaviour. Second, Fox placed enormous emphasis upon clarity of thought rather than morality on the part of those who exercise authority: good effective government resulted not simply from moral choice, but more from a clear–eyed and rational understanding of particular situations followed by effective action. This applied both to the individual's personal affairs and, much more, to the exercising of authority within an organization.

Therefore, it is not surprising that Fox, a working bureaucrat from 1485 to 1516, encouraged education as a source of the desired knowledge and understanding necessary for essential management skills. As his career prospered he took an increasing interest in the educational potential of humanist studies. In 1490 and 1491 he had collaborated closely in diplomatic work with the Greek scholar William Selling, the Benedictine prior of Christ Church, Canterbury, and during the following years he became increasingly associated with other humanist scholars, such as his chaplain Richard Whitford who had studied in Italy.[12] Fox also became involved with Fisher's work in establishing the *studia humanitatis* at Cambridge, advised Lady Margaret on her educational bequests, and gave support to Erasmus, who dedicated a volume to him in 1506, so that by the first decade of the fifteenth century he was acknowledged as a strong supporter of humanist education.[13] At the same time he employed his literary skills for devotional purposes, publishing a book of meditations and his Salisbury Processional of 1508.[14]

One obvious reason for the Lord Privy Seal's interest in humanism was the need to train people in linguistic and other skills needed by administrators and diplomats, particularly in government service.[15] But Fox was looking for more than technical skills. He saw humane studies as a means of providing an education which trained minds in the art of understanding the world, and developed qualities of character and intellect which would give England a competent executive ruling class, to the benefit of government, Church and commonwealth.

In May 1516 Fox retired from the King's service and went to live in his diocese. For some years before his retirement he had been growing uneasy about the way his career in the service of the Crown had prevented the proper performance of his episcopal duties. On 23 April 1516 he wrote to Cardinal Wolsey, declining a request to come out of retirement and return to the royal service, saying that he was now 'occupied in my cure, whereby I may do some satisfaction for 28 years negligence ...(therefore) to serve (the world to) the damnation of my soul and many other souls whereof I have the cure, I am sure you would not desire'. The point must have been taken by Wolsey, for he himself, fourteen years later, expressed similar regrets in his famous lament on this deathbed at Leicester Abbey in 1530, that he had not 'served God as diligently as I have done the King...(with) worldly diligence and pains...not regarding my duty'.[16]

In Fox's case the sentiment was quite deep, for he was a genuinely devout man, who not only cared for his flock, but was also sensitive to his standing before God — on one occasion when he was harassed he wrote '...such matters trouble not a little my spirits. I fear that I shall not by reason thereof be in such quietness that I shall dare say mass this next v or vi days'.[17]

Now that he was retired from the King's service, Fox turned his energy upon his diocese and his educational interests. He was sixty–eight years old and still possessed great physical and mental power. As for education, his principal project, now well under way, was the new college of Corpus Christi about to be founded at Oxford in 1516, for the *studia humanitatis* in the three languages of Latin, Greek, and possibly Hebrew. However, at the same time Fox was also involved in other ways with both universities of England and with grammar schools. As for his diocese of Winchester, he threw himself into its administration with great energy. His register (five large volumes), and the records of his episcopal visitations of 1520 and 1527–8, and the records of the general proceedings of the consistorial court, all provide evidence of Fox's direct involvement after 1516 in both the diocese and the city. His first task was to get the diocese in order. He approached the task as would any competent executive, by first qathering information and then clarifying the issues.

He looked first at the clergy and the religious houses — his senior staff as it were. The parishes were troubled by the old problem of livings, especially wealthy livings, being held by priests who were permanently absent on government business or engaged in studies. Absentees were supposed to install and support a curate, but in fact these supply jobs carried such wretched salaries that the parishes were often served by inadequate priests, or had no priest at all: in these circumstances it was not only the cure of souls which suffered, for the buildings and ornaments were also neglected. In later years in the town of Winchester, Fox tried to rationalize the situation by uniting some of the poorer parishes, but in rural areas — with long distance and poor communications — this solution was not possible. In 1508, in an attempt to preserve property, Fox ordered records to be kept of damage or defects in church buildings. But he realized that the Church's problems could not be solved only by management procedures of this kind, and that there were underlying problems of poor education and indifference in parish clergy and the laity, which he would have to tackle.

There were also problems with the religious houses, the condition of which had become lax: by lax I mean that their members showed a lack of concern for piety or the devotional offices, as well as signs of casual cupidity, concupiscence and complacency. Amongst the male houses, Fox found a prior who enjoyed male and female 'suspicious company', and frequently travelled to Oxford upon frivolous pretexts. In several houses property was not safeguarded, inventories were neglected and many items of value disappeared. Monks frequently went out alone, visited public houses, went hunting, called upon female acquaintances, brought women visitors into their monastery, played games in the fields during the hours of service, kept pets in the dormitory, and held drinking parties in the evening. One abbot had a female penitent 'que publica peraget penitentiam in ecclesia parochiali', thus provoking comment and gossip in the town.

Fox's reaction was not one of outraged puritanism. He could be flexible and generous enough, especially towards ordinary carnal lapses, and severe denunciation was not his style. As one might expect from a man with his long political and diplomatic experience, he was able to see more deeply into the problems of the monasteries. They had once been centres of piety, learning and various other skills, but were now diminished and, in his diocese at least, possessed very little scholarship and certainly were not notable for their piety. These monastic inadequacies contrasted strongly with the new vigour being shown elsewhere by both laity and secular clergy in the Church, in universities, and in government administration. In short, Fox was faced with monasteries which were lacking in effectiveness and therefore losing something of their raison d'etre in contemporary society. His task was to restore their effective functioning.

This was also Fox's reaction to the condition of the female houses. The principal nunnery in the diocese of Winchester, Romsey Abbey, had a history of laxity which went back at least forty years. In 1478, its abbess had admitted to adultery and perjury (in this case meaning neglect), and resigned her abbacy, only to be re–elected by her nuns. During the remaining twenty–four years of her rule, she almost totally neglected the conduct of divine services, the finances, the fabric and ornaments of the building, the cuisine, and the behaviour of her nuns who were allowed to come and go as they pleased to taverns and 'other suspected places'. In 1492 Fox's predecessor had visited the abbey, but his instructions for reform were ignored by the abbess who said that she intended to rule her abbey 'as she had done before' — a point emphasized by her then bedding the hospital chaplain. She died in 1502, shortly after Fox became Bishop of Winchester, and her successor, Joyce Rowse, continued in the same way, presiding over a kind of hotel for women. Fox was informed of the situation and, after being given details, he sent instructions to the abbess that she must amend her behaviour: she was to remain sober, keep away from secular company, especially five named men — four of them priests — and cease eating and drinking 'to enormous excess' at parties in her chamber during the afternoons and evenings. But the abbess was not inclined to reformation, nor were her nuns. One of them, Anne Harvey, wore her splendid hair long, sang beautifully, kept company with priests, was loved by the Vicar of Romsey, and whenever she was within the abbey walls, spent time in 'obstinacy', 'contradictions and scandals'. However, Joyce Rowse resigned as abbess in 1515 and the nuns elected Anne Westbrooke, who improved discipline and standards of behaviour.[18]

This improvement came just as Fox retired from his political work in London and went to reside in Winchester in order to attend seriously to the affairs of the diocese. He took the advice of the Benedictine abbesses of Romsey,

Wherewell, and St Mary–within–Winchester, and the Cistercian prioress of Wintney on improving the quality of the religious life for women within the diocese.[19] In their opinion a basic weakness was that the *Regula Benedicti*, being used in its Latin form, was insufficiently understood by the nuns, despite commentaries and explanations being given in English. He was told that most nuns 'have no knowledge or understanding, but be utterly ignorant of Latin'. The daily readings of the Rule, which were intended to ensure that the nuns knew and understood it — both before and after profession — was therefore a pointless activity, without understanding, and there had developed within the nunneries some 'blindness and ignorance' of the Rule. Some sisters had said that they did not 'first know and understand' the Rule before they made their professions: he was told of at least one woman who had become a nun although 'she wyste not what she professed'. In other words, Fox found the nunneries endeavouring to function with many of their members uncertain of what they were supposed to be doing or how they were to go about it.

Fox's executive mentality found it unacceptable that the Rule — virtually the articles of association and the operating programme for the religious life — should not be clearly understood by all involved in its operation. Actions carried out without clear understanding were a waste of time if each nun herself did not know what she was about. 'The nuns' Fox wrote, 'do not only lose their time, but also run into the evident danger and peril of the perdition of their souls'. And he knew that, in addition to wasting time and placing individual souls in peril, ignorance and confusion threatened the vigour and quality of the community as a whole. Thus, when faced with the condition and problems of the nunneries in 1516, Fox immediately and succinctly applied the observation, drawn from his long career in politics and administration, that understanding is the essential prerequisite for action and achievement: in the preface he told the nuns that

> ...the reading of the thing that a person is bound to do or execute, except he understands it, is to the executing thereof no thing valuable.[20]

Fox gave the nuns an order of profession in English, probably his own translation.[21] However, the Rules was of much greater significance, and the abbesses and the prioress asked Fox to provide a version of the *Regula Benedicti* in English. He agreed to do so, translating it, as he said with characteristic vigour, into 'oure moders tonge, comune, playne, round englisshe, easy and redy to be understande'. They may also have advised him that the masculine form of the Rule was a barrier to nuns receiving it sympathetically, for when Fox translated from Latin to English he also converted the Rule's masculine terms and pronouns to their feminine equivalents — minchin or mynchin (nun), suster (sister), abbasse, and so on. He also adapted the Rule to modern times by inserting references to recent congregational forms of Benedictine organization, to papal authority in abbatial appointments, and to English conditions (by including ale and beer where the Rule mentions wine). He does not appear to have used any earlier translation of the Rule. His language was robust and his turn of phrase colourful. When he finished the translation, about Christmas 1516, he had several copies of the manuscript made, one for each of the convents and one sent to the London printer Richard Pynson, who published it on 26 January 1516/17, under the title *Here begynneth the Rule of seynt Benet*. The cost of printing and distribution was borne by Fox himself.[22]

The work is not a straightforward translation, but very free, extending the sparse Latin of the *Rule* with repetitions, illustrative phrases and vivid language with which to embellish the original text. Moreover, he inserted additional passages of his own in order to explain or elaborate on parts of the Rule. When the hard core of the *Regular Benedicti* is subtracted, as it were, from his text what remains is Fox's own contribution, consisting of free translations and interpolations: from these we are able to draw some conclusions about the piety of one of England's ablest and longest serving administrator politicians, and his perception of the monastic life in the later months of 1516 and early 1517 — on the eve of the Reformation — and his own attitudes towards these matters.

Although the emphases of translation and the interpolated material deal each with the topics of their own particular chapter of the Rule, it is nevertheless possible to discern common themes which were sufficiently repeated and emphasized to indicate what was uppermost in Fox's mind. First, he singled out what he saw to be problems or difficulties in the monasteries, that is, those things which inhibit communal life, retard improvement, lead to disorganization and loss of morale, and engender conflict, sourness and decay. Fox then concentrated upon the solutions to these problems, by emphasizing, expanding, and illustrating those elements within the Rule which could effectively rectify the weaknesses of the religious houses, particularly those in his diocese of Winchester in 1517.

He was quite clear about what was wrong with the monasteries. There were four problems: poor leadership; ignorance, uncertainty, and mis—understanding about the task in hand; aberrant and sinful behaviour arising out of pride; lack of diligence, lazy habits, and unstructured procedures.

He looked upon poor leadership as being particularly damaging to the corporate health and achievements of monastic life. It was a concern with which he had been familiar throughout his long political career. He had advised two kings in most senior appointments for thirty years, and it was in part due to his eye for executive qualities that Henry VII, in particular, had such an able and reliable team.[23] The quality that Fox had admired in Wolsey was the man's ability to know what to do and to get things done, both in details and on a large scale.[24] Similarly, in his own personal appointments, Fox looked for good leadership: his steward and his surveyor he had chosen for their being 'substantial, true men, and somewhat learned', capable of both dealing with tenants and protecting them, and on the other hand dealing with civic and other authorities and with other landowners.[25] He chose Robert Morwent, the first vice–President of Corpus Christi, for his executive skills.[26] Fox's appointment of suffragens and vicars–general for his diocese likewise showed a careful eye for leaders of quality: they included Richard Nykke, later Bishop of Norwich; Nicholas West, a diplomat, member of the King's Council in 1504, and in 1517 head of Wolsey's Commission on enclosures, John Dowman, and John Incent, later Dean of St Paul's. In a letter to Wolsey about Incent. Fox summed up the qualities needed for the proper exercise of authority: he 'has sufficient learning and experience' for the exercise of his office. He is also 'wise, discrete, sad [i.e. serious, steadfast] and circumspect in judgments,...he hathe also good will, diligence and boldness to do his office...he is very honest, virtuous, sad [serious, strong] and circumspect' and 'liberal hospitalitie keepeth'. As an official he is 'among the best'.[27] All Fox's staff were in this mould — disciplined, businesslike, and efficient.

Fox's experience had also taught him how failures of leadership are damaging to an organization. In the statutes of Corpus Christi College he listed the ways in which the president could fail as head of college — failure to give 'judgment, presence and diligence', or 'overmuch boldness and arbitrary behaviour', 'stubborn contempt or listless neglect'. He was also critical of the sub–prior of St Mary Overy whose familiarity with the younger monks made them contemptuous of his authority.[28]

Fox believed managerial qualities to be of such critical importance that when it came to the actual appointment of abbots and abbesses he carefully assessed the elected person and was quite prepared to use episcopal and royal powers to intervene in what he believed to be an unwise election. In 1493, whilst at Bath and Wells, he had annulled an election at Glastonbury, and with Royal licence nominated instead Richard Beere as the new abbot.[29] In 1515 he wrote to Wolsey, urging him to override the Canons of St Augustine's Bristol (in the diocese of Worcester, whose bishop was Silvestro de'Gigli) and telling him in some detail how to curb a destablizing faction within the house.[30] On the other hand he supported the election of an able abbess such as Avelena Cowdrey, elected Abbess of Wharwell in February 1518, 'pleasant to God, true to the King's grace, and profitable to the Monastery'.[31]

Consequently it is not surprising that, when Fox translated the Rule in the autumn of 1516, he paid careful attention to the question of leadership. His awareness of what makes for an improper exercise of authority and poor leadership is best seen in chapter 64, where he expanded the Rule's description of abbatial qualities from the original concise Latin into a stream of vivid tumbling English phrases:

> She shall not be full of hastiness, troubelous, nor of sour mood, or displayant countenance, she shall not be importune, or intolerable nor obstinate, nor self–willed, she shall not be entangled with jealousy, nor be too much suspicious, for such a person is never in quietness, nor never takes rest.[32]

Although Fox recognized the importance of the personality, he concentrated this emphases of translation and interpolations much more upon the actual manner in which authority is exercised. First, the abbess or prioress is left in no doubt of the fullness of her authority. In the preface Fox gave abbesses the standing of diocesans, describing them as 'oure right religious diocesans'. In chapter 2, entitled 'The qualities of an abbess', he ascribed to an abbess all the authority of an abbot, and actually went beyond the Rule to interpolate a phrase of his own, describing her authority as being from God 'whose royome (realm) and authority she hath and occupies'.[33]

Having assumed her full authority, the abbess should exercise it as a mother, showing two qualities which Fox likened to the 'two sides of a ladder' — virtue and learning.[34] The leader's virtue consists in guiding the community by understanding people and being both firm and gentle, which was a combination frequently apparent in Fox's own behaviour, both as a royal official and as a bishop.[35] Thus he inserted into chapter 2 this advice:

> She must show the sharp mind and authority of a mistress, that is to say she must sharply blame and roughly rebuke wilful, unruly, rude and combrous [hot tempered] persons, and such as be obedient, meek, patient and soft persons she must in loving manner exhort and desire them to increase daily more and more in their virtuousness from good to better.

What the abbess commands it to be 'like unto the sweetness and favour of mighty god', that is, authority exercised responsibly, generously, and with consideration for those subject to her.

The other side of the ladder was learning, which Fox considered equally necessary for leadership. Chapter 64 of the Rule requires the abbot to be learned in divine law. Fox's translation developed the Latin, bringing out the point that authority rests upon clear knowledge and understanding. When he referred to learning it is clear that he assumed a fair deal of scholarship in an abbess, and that there were in his diocese educated women able to fulfil these requirements, for:

> she must be well learned in the law of God, and her religion, and
> that she understand, and be that person that can show and teach
> the laws, rules and constitutions of the religion, with such histories
> of holy scripture and saints' lives as be most expedient for the
> congregation.

But Fox expected more of an efficient abbess than virtue and learning. He expected her to develop practical management skills — and his translation and interpolations reflect this expectation. First, the abbess should know how to delegate. Thus, in chapter 21, where the Rule deals with large houses where there was a need for abbatial power to be delegated to deans chosen for their virtue and wisdom, Fox added for emphasis...'[chosen for their] deserts and merits...[and] wise doctrine'. Similarly, where chapter 38 of the Rule has singers and readers appointed on the basis of their ability, Fox emphasized the point of choosing on the basis of the merit of the most able person 'that can best to the edifying of the house'. In other parts of the translation he developed his advice that authority can be delegated successfully only when shrewd appointments have been made according to merit. In chapter 2 the point is made that a sense of social rank exacerbates pride, and must therefore be excluded for the life of the convent. When he translated the passage, fox expanded the words of the Rule to emphasise the policy of delegating authority according to merit. At the same time he put the whole passage into vivid English:

> She that came of higher or noble lineage or of free kindred shall not
> be preferred in order of standing or in office before another of lower
> birth or of bond stock...for be she bond, be she free, be she of noble
> or ignoble blood and lineage All be one...

Similarly, he required the abbess to possess that executive talent which can lead people into hard work, both spiritual and physical, because hard work is important. As one might expect from a man who himself worked hard, idleness was perceived as an obstacle to accomplishments in one's chosen career. At several points in the translation he emphasized the need for steady patient effort at the 'craft of religious living'. In chapter 48 he described idleness not merely as an 'enemy of the soul', but as 'an utter and extreme enemy of the soul'. Nuns must work hard, not only at worship and studies, but also at their 'dayly hande laboure', and should it become necessary for the nuns themselves to do their own harvesting they should not

> take it heavily, nor be grieved therewith for then they be very true
> mynchins when they live with the labour of their own hands.

The abbess was also to have a sense of the practical needs of the members of the community. Fox insisted that 'a bakehouse' be added to the convent's facilities. He also added to the Rule his own stipulation that food was to be 'well dressed and seasoned', and bread was to be served with food, and the nuns were to be given 'not only of wine, but also of ale, beer, and all other drinks', and assessed the Rule's daily *hemina* of wine as 'nigh about...a pint in the English tongue'. Dinner was to be served 'after the English reckoning about an hour before the midday', and the nuns were to have knives to wear.[36] In this manner, using free translation and interpolations, Fox, the experienced man of affairs, made clear in his text that virtue and learning, together with practical management skills, were essential for the leader of a religious house.

However, he did not place responsibility for the community's well being upon the leadership alone: the qualities of learning and virtue, those 'two sides of the ladder', must be disseminated throughout the entire organization. Learning was essential in order to avoid the ignorance that leads to a poor understanding of one's work [or vocation], and how it may be carried out effectively. In the course of his long administrative and political career, Fox had developed an obsession with clear knowledge and understanding. In his negotiations with Wells Corporation in 1493 he refused to accept any answers which 'accord to no law or reason', or are 'neither clear, certain, nor reasonable'.[37] He had a sharp eye for words that obfuscate, such as the letter of James IV of Scotland, in which '...the words sound well, but what his mind is, it is uncertain...the mind of the King of Scots can not be known by this letter'.[38] He believed that ignorance and muddle were the chief causes of weaknesses amongst the clergy. Likewise, when he examined people charged with heresy at Farnsham in 1514, he seemed to consider them to be victims of ignorance and confusion, and treated them leniently.[39]

As a corollary he was convinced that education was necessary because it brought clear knowledge and understanding which in turn promised effective action in each person's sphere of work. In the statutes of Corpus Christi College [1516] he pointed out that, because the statutes are quote clear, 'no one can be so blear—eyed or dim sighted as to find them a stumbling block to be entangled by them': therefore 'each individual may readily support his own function'.[40] It was for this functional reason that Fox, whilst still serving as the king's chief executive officer, took such determined action to improve the education of the clergy at schools and universities. He admonished his diocesan clergy to study, and encouraged those who did so, dispensing from residence any who asked leave of absence for that purpose; he worked with the universities of Oxford and Cambridge and with individual colleges, and he founded schools and Corpus Christi.[41] He concerned himself also with the education of the laity, in part through his work with schools and universities, but also more directly through parish catechisms. In 1508 he directed that in certain parishes the laity be given classes, with careful guidance in English on the creed, the commandments, various prayers, and other material.

Consequently, when Fox came to visit the religious houses in the diocese of Winchester, he brought with him strong views on education and its part in promoting clear understanding and functional efficiency. He found it intolerable that any nun should waste her time, not knowing what she was about because 'she wyste not what she professed', for there could not be effective action and achievement of the 'thing that a person is bound to do or execute, except he understands it'. He was determined to alter the situation in which nuns could live in the convent in 'blindness and ignorance' of the Rule, and the first step in their education was therefore to translate the Rule into 'cure monders tonge, comune, playne, round englisshe, easy and redy to be understande'.

Fox clearly assumed that the nuns were as literate as monks and able to read at least English, for in translating the chapters on learning he made no accommodation for the nuns being women, as he did in some other chapters. On the contrary, in chapter 48, where the Rule requires that private reading not disturb others [ut alium non inquietet], Fox actually elaborates his translation, adding the words 'let her read softly by herself'. Nor does he exempt the nuns from the Sunday and Lenten private reading required in the same chapter. Similarly, as his preface shows, he accepted that the professed nuns could both read and expound the Bible and the Fathers as required in chapter 38 of the Rule, actually extending this task to 'exposition...of the most famous doctors and best learned in holy scriptures and most catholic fathers', that is, presumably including more modern commentators in his phrase 'the most famous doctors'.

Fox also brought to this translation his conviction, earlier expressed in his statutes for Corpus Christi, that effective learning requires enjoyment and enthusiasm. The Rule touches upon this matter in chapter 4;56 where the Latin says simply lectiones sanctas libenter audire, but Fox's vigorous translation for the nuns was:

> hear with a merry heart and glad mind holy doctrines, sermons, exhortations, lectur[es], and scriptures.

It was the responsibility of the older nuns to engender and encourage such enthusiasm for learning in their younger colleagues. It is typical of Fox's pragmatic approach that he expanded the simple precept in chapter 4:69, 'love your youngers' [juniores diligere], giving brief details of that affection and how it is to guide the young towards the practical goals of virtue and learning:

> ...love your youngers in the love of Christ, that is to say as nourishing them as fathers and mothers in piety, in erudition, by doctrine, in example of holiness by directing them when they be out of the way, and in plentiousness of consolation by comforting them when they be feeble.

The first problem of the monastic life that Fox had perceived was poor leadership, the second was ignorance. The third problem was the corrupting effect of pride upon behaviour and judgment. Once again, his view was grounded in long experience. In 1493, in the course of protracted business with the Corporation of Wells, he had noted that some confusion and disorder in the negotiations stemmed from 'wilfulness and haultnesse'.[42] Again, in 1506 there had been some conflict at Magdalen College, and the problem came to Fox as College Visitor: his decision in the matter, communicated in a letter written at 5 a.m. on Christmas Eve 1506, noted that the trouble had arisen because one group's unreasonable interpretation of the statutes 'cometh of pride and wilfulness which would be repressed, else it shall return to the dishonour and hurt of the place'.[43]

Fox's experience of the effects of pride in worldly affairs is reflected in the way he treated the Rule's own warnings on the dangers of pride, translating the Latin into vigorous English and inserting his own words. Chapter 4:34 of the Rule gives terse advice to avoid pride [non esse superbum], but Fox expanded the phrase into an emphatic and colourful paragraph:

...be not proud, neither in your mind or heart, bear not yourself
above another, nor despise none other, nor be...opinionative.

His interpolations into chapter 4:43 reminded nuns not to be proud of their
virtue, for goodness is a gift of God and 'not of yourself, nor of your merits, nor
deserving'. Fox inserted other glosses derived from his experience of the way
pride creates emotional turbulence as people are 'troubled, vexed, grieved or
made angry' [chapter 3]. In this context he emphasized the Rule's prohibition of
private property. The brief Latin phrase of chapter 33, condemning pride of
possession [*neguissimo vitio deprehensus*] was translated vividly as:

> And if any mynchin be espyed to delight of to have pleasure in this
> most wicked vice...

Since private property engenders pride in the possessor, envy in others and is
therefore destructive of harmony within the community, it is to be prohibited.

The fourth problem in religious houses was lack of diligence, that is,
careful, structured orderly effort. Fox's entire career was marked by his own
thorough attention to detail and application in order to achieve a purpose and by
the diligence he expected of others. In 1497, whilst he was Bishop of Durham, he
prepared Norham Castle against siege by the Scots, personally paying meticulous
attention to the smallest details and considering every contingency.[44] Similar
effort is evident in 1513, when he had the task of procuring supplies for the
invasion of France — which, incidentally, Fox opposed. Also, he was
conscientious in the arrangements for the administration of his dioceses during
his absence, punctual with his correspondence, and orderly in his routine. In
turn, he was appreciative of intelligent diligence in others: he praised a carpenter
for being 'right cunning and diligent', and a port overseer who 'neither lacks
diligence nor shall lack diligence'.[45] Perseverance was the quality that got things
done, not only in practical affairs but also in education: thus, not only the
executive, the overseer, or the carpenter, but also heads and fellows of colleges
were to be diligent and orderly in their scholarly pursuit of knowledge and
understanding.[46]

Similarly, the nuns required diligence in the pursuit of piety. The
religious life, with its goals of learning and virtue, was to be lived in an orderly
and workmanlike way. Fox drove the point home by the insertion of his own
introduction into the beginning of chapter 4:

> Like as all worldly artificers have material instruments apt for the
> accomplishment of their worldly works, in likewise there be
> instruments spiritual for the craft of religious living...directed,
> composed and ordered...

These were the words of a man who was a systematic and hardworking politician
and administrator, and also, when time permitted, was skilled in work as a
builder, architect and civil engineer. In this and other passages we see Fox's
work ethic applied to the labours and achievements of religious houses.

Fox distinguished between two kinds of virtue to be sought by nuns — and
indeed by all Christians. The first was an inward virtue, personal, intense, and
characteristic of European piety of the late fifteenth century. The second kind of
virtue was that which appertains to the well—being and efficient functioning of
the monastery or any other organization. Inward virtue required self—discipline

to bring human emotions, especially pride, and its troublesome manifestations under control. Whenever Fox added his own gloss to the Rule it was to remind the nuns of their priorities (not to worship 'yourself [or] any other earthly creature'), their duties (not 'withdrawing service owed to God'), and keeping themselves in good condition (not to harm their souls and to be at peace with themselves so that they may effectively do good).[47]

Deficiencies of inward virtue were to be overcome through self examination of personal sins. The Rule prescribes that this be done *cum lacrimis vel gemitu* [chapter 4:58], but Fox expanded the phrase to the much more thorough 'with weeping tears, or at the least with moaning, sobbing and sorrowing for the doing of them.' I suspect that Fox emphasized self-examination in this way the better to strip away self-deception and recognize things as they really are: the clear-eyed perception of reality was a recurring theme in what Fox did and wrote throughout his career. This theme is similar to that of *Praise of Folly*, published in 1509 by Erasmus, with whom Fox had some contact. Just as Erasmus satirized human follies which feed upon self-deception, nourish destructive pride, and vitiate relationships, so Fox emphasized the need for clear honesty in chapter 4:25, where the Rule's simple *pacem falsam non dare* was expanded vividly:

> ...use no simulation, no dissimulation, nor give no Judas kiss, but when you make any peace or lovedaye [concord], or else reconcile yourself with any person...then you do it was well and truly in heart and deed as in word and outward countenance.

Again, in chapter 4:28 he urged the nuns:

> When you speak, you speak the truth all way both with heart and mouth.

There is an engaging streak of commonsense in Fox's advice. It is the considered observation of a shrewd and experienced politician — that one must try to be clear-eyed, accurate, and straightforward about oneself and others, and, in the case, about God.

But this kind of work is achieved only with much labour. In chapter 4:1, on loving God with all one's mind, Fox added to the test 'that is to say, applying all your studies, wits, and delectations only to him'. Nevertheless, despite his emphasis on effort, Fox was a long way from preaching mere muscular Christianity: there is depth of insight in his advice, mentioned earlier, that one must first of all be at peace with oneself, into chapter 4:50, on putting aside evil thoughts 'by fixing your thoughts and remembrances upon Christ and his passion, merit and benefit'. His insertion of these words suggest a familiarity with the notion of the *beneficio di cristo*, the Pauline totality of grace, which was such a strong feature of contemporary, especially Italian, Benedictine spirituality (which, I believe, had an influence in England as yet unrecognized).[48]

When the nun sees her spiritual condition with clarity, and then works with thoroughness at 'the craft of religious living...directed, composed and ordered', she is carried along by the Spirit and her life is renewed, and she comes at length to a rich and burning love of God. This condition was described by Fox in a remarkably vivid translation of the conclusion of chapter 7, on humility:

> ...all these degrees of humility ascended and climbed, a mynchyn at
> once shall come to that brennynge [burning] love of God, the which
> love, once established and made perfect in her, driveth out all fear,
> by the which she shall begin to keep of custom, and in manner
> naturally, without labour and pain, all manner of virtuous things,
> which she kept not for the fear of the bitter pains of hell but for the
> love of Christ and for the same custom and delectation of virtue,
> which things almighty God shall then vouchsafe to show in this
> servant purified and made clean of vices through the grace of the
> holy ghost.

Thus, by perseverance, practice makes perfect, and the skills of virtue, becoming habitual, are carried along by the Spirit to create a new personality. This king of piety was common enough at the time, but what is unusual in this case is the way Fox approached it, applying to the religious life the mentality of an experienced executive in politics and administration.

In tandem with his approach to inward virtue, was Fox's understanding of the outward virtues needed for operating successfully within an organization. These outward virtues, so vital for corporate functioning, consist of courtesy and good works.

The habit of courtesy enables the religious house, like any other organization, to operate smoothly and efficiently, and is tied in with knowledge and understanding of the business of the house. A nun without courtesy 'lacks understanding' (the English has a quite different emphasis from the Latin *improbus* in chapter 23), and 'if she be rude and sturdy [refractory] without shame or fear of God', then her behaviour disrupts the community. For the sake of courtesy, in one's pride has to be curbed, and enemies prayed for – though in chapter 4:70 Fox adds rather primly 'that is to say for their reformation and salvation'. There is a similarly realistic touch to his gloss on the injunction of chapter 13 to forgive enemies lest thorns of contention spring up: Fox expanded the *scandalorum spinas* of the Rule, translating it as 'dissensions and debates, malices, greves [grievances] and grudges the which be wont often times to spring', thus emphasizing the damage done by personal quarrels to the functioning of the corporate body. In chapter 4:48 his discretion and experience in politics and diplomacy emerge in another piece of advice on the practical virtue of courtesy, which he added to the translation:

> ...be well ware at every hour...that at no time you fail or offend
> recklessly or negligently be deed, word or thought, but that you
> ever premeditate and discuss before what you shall do, say or
> intend.

The concept of 'courtesy' was prominent in Fox's understanding of personal and communal well–being. 'The honesty of good manners' is how he translated the *honestatem morum* of the Rule. As Rothenhausler and Fry point out, this Latin phrase, with its rich classical and patristic background, summarizes the mentality of the monastic life.[49] In his later years Fox was deeply affected by the humanist revival of classical and patristic thought, and he was therefore aware of the origins of the phrase, but for him *honestatem morum* also applied directly to contemporary religious life. Moreover, the 'honesty of good manners' was in accord with his worldly experience of the working skills required in politicians, administrators, diplomats and bishops, and was therefore required as much in society at large as in the religious life. His sense of the social importance of courtesy comes through in his translation of the passage:

> ...we may show ourself to have somewhat of the honesty of good manners, or else at the least some beginning of good conversation...to the very perfection of good living.

Thus, Fox's translation reveals his understanding of the monastic life in 1516. The individual member carried the personal responsibility of ascending a 'ladder', made up of learning and clear understanding on the one hand, and on the other hand the virtues of inward piety and outward courtesy. This responsibility implies a certain level of learning, or at least understanding, amongst the nuns and a high degree of involvement in the convent's organization — two elements that make for an egalitarian community. At the same time his experience of the world told him that the style and tone of leadership were critical for the well—being of the community, and that in all societies — whether their members were inadequate, or whether they were able, learned and virtuous — the exercise of authority called for special skills. Of course, Fox was not alone in pondering these issues, for it is obvious that Thomas More, his friend, who wrote *Utopia* in the same year, 1516, was concerned with the same questions of social behaviour, and reached much the same conclusions.

Fox's literary style also reflects his worldly experience. He discussed religion with common sense, employing examples that are concrete, often homely, and sometimes very vivid, such as his evocative description of early rising:

> That they be first up and ready toward the service of God shall make some soft and sober stirring with the sound of their mouths or of their feet, or knocking upon the bed's side to wake them that be sluggards.

Time after time, his English has a richness and a vivacity that bears comparison with Tyndale, Coverdale and Cranmer, who followed him. It was written to attract and stir the religious imagination of any person who read it, not just nuns. Sometimes his translation into 'oure moders tonge, comune, playne, round englisshe', especially the biblical passages, seems to anticipate the later translators, both in style and piety. Such was his translation of Psalm 69:

> Gracious God intend toward my succour, goode lorde, make speed to help me.

Here begynneth the Rule of seynt Benet is a valuable source of information about religious thought and practices in England during the early sixteenth century. It this paper I have sought to show how its author brought to bear on the organization of religious houses, also on theological understanding and pious practices, the attitudes he had forged out of his long experience in the secular world. Fox had no desire to inhibit the religious life; on the contrary he wished to reform and rejuvenate it. In order to do so he applied an approach and a set of criteria that he had drawn from the hard school of politics, administration and diplomacy. In short, he brought the mentality of a chief executive officer of one of the largest corporations in Europe, the English state, to matters of education, monastic reform and piety. Precisely the same hard—nosed attitudes were to be applied to the same area by Wolsey during the 1520s and Cromwell during the 1530s, but with results that Fox could not have foreseen.

NOTES

1. F. Bacon, *Henry VII*, in *The Works of Francis Bacon*, eds., J. Spedding, R.L. Ellis, D.D. Heath, 14 vols. (London, 1857–74), vol.6, pp 212, 184. In 1477 there was a Richard Fox, B.A., master of the grammar school at Stratford on Avon. It is very probable that during his exile in France Fox studied at Paris and there took a Bachelor's degree. By Feb. 1486, he had proceeded to a doctorate, probably a Doctor of Canon Law in the Faculty of Law at Paris; E.C. Batten, *The Life of Bishop Richard Fox* (London, 1889), p 4; T. Fowler, *The History of Corpus Christi College*, Oxf. Hist. Soc. 25, (Oxford, 1893), pp 1–3. Bacon says that Fox was 'a good surveyor of works' at the Westminster almshouses, Winchester cathedral and other places. He oversaw the extension of the great kitchen and great hall at Durham Castle, the fortifications of Norham Castle, and carried out the improvement of Calais harbour with sluices: P.S. Allen, *The Letters of Richard Fox, 1486–1527* (Oxford, 1929), no.57, 30 April 1517, pp 92–6. Very probably he designed the glass for the chapel of King's College, Cambridge: see Batten *Life*, pp 29–30, 43–44, 46, 62, 82–3., also T. Fowler, 'Richard Foxe', *D.N.B*, 7, (Oxford, 1921–2, reprint), pp 590–96.

2. Ed., W. Campbell, *Materials for a history of the reign of Henry VII*, 2 (London, 1877), pp 133, 158.

3. Bacon, *Works*, 6, p 200. From 1494 to 1501, as Bishop of Durham and temporal head of the County Palatine, Fox was responsible for diplomatic relations with the Scots and defence of the North against the Scots and border raiders. Batten, *Life*, pp 7–8, 16–17, says that Fox was largely responsible for the king's pacific policy towards his vanquished opponents after 1485.

4. Edward Hall, *Hall's Chronicle; containing the History of England etc.*, ed. H. Ellis (London, 1809), p 405. Hall died in 1547.

5. Bacon, *Works*, 6, p 241.

6. There were other rewards for Fox, which are listed in Campbell, *Materials...Henry VII*, vol. 1, pp 153–4 (Keeper of the Exchange, to issue letters of exchange for pilgrims and other travellers, held for ten years from 8 Nov. 1485, at a rent to the Crown of £30.6s.8d. p.a.); pp 303, 317 (Commissioner of King's Mines for 20 years from 21 Feb. 1486); pp 340, vol.2, p 359 (Notary of the Chancery, in survivorship, from 4 March 1486, but surrendered 30 October 1490).

7. *Letters & Papers Henry VIII*, 2,p 3831; ed., E.C. Batten, *The Register of Richard Fox...Bath and Wells* (London, 1889), where there are several passing references to the arrangements made by Fox for the care of his dioceses during his absences.

8. In 1510 the Venetian ambassador described Fox as England's 'alter rex', and the Spanish ambassador said that he held 'all business affairs' of state in his hands, *CSP Venetian*, 2, p 30; *CSP Spanish*, 2, p 40.

9. P.M. Howden described him as a man of 'tireless patience and inexhaustible energy', who carefully scrutinized both men and documents, always commended skill at all levels, was fair minded, not stern, and had few personal enemies: see ed., P.M. Howden, *The Register of Richard Fox, Lord Bishop of Durham, 1494–1501* (Durham, 1932). Fox refers to stopping work at 6 p.m. in a letter to Wolsey, 23 April 1516, '...lay apart all such business from vi of the clock in the evening', Allen, *Letters*, no. 52, p 84. In fact, when necessary Fox worked later, sometimes in bed. In 1524 he recalled the burdens of office, being 'daily and hourly occupied with great and weighty matters', *Letters*, no. 81, pp 139–41; also see

Batten, *Life*, p 73.

10.   G.R.M. Ward, *The Foundation Statutes for Corpus Christi College in the University of Oxford, AD 1517*, (London, 1843), p 218.

11.   Bacon, *Henry VII*, pp 49, 177.

12.   For Selling see A.B. Emden *A Biographical Register of the University of Oxford to AD 1500*, (Oxford, 1957) pp 1666–7; for Whitford, Emden, *B.R.U. Cambridge*, (Cambridge, 1963), pp 635–6.

13.   *Collected Works of Erasmus*, 2, (Toronto, 1975) ep.187, pp.102–3, Erasmus dedicated to Fox his translation of *Toxaris*, published with other translations in Paris, 1506. James McConica calls Fox 'an outstanding patron of early English humanism', *C.W.E.*, 3, p 220. Fox Fox's relations with Erasmus see Batten, *Life*, pp 105–8, and Allen, *Letters*, pp 33–5. There seems to have been mutual scholarly admiration between the two men rather than friendship.

14.   A critical edition of the processional is edited by W.G. Henderson, *Processionale ad usum insignis ac praeclarae ecclesiae Sarum* (Leeds, 1882). The book of meditations is the *Contemplacyon of Sinners*, written 'At the devoute & dylygent request' of Bishop Fox, and published in 1499. It contains quotations in Latin from the Bible, the Fathers and other authors, with meditations in English verse, the latter attributed to Fox. The work was reprinted in 1578.

15.   This topic has been treated fully by D. Hay, 'England and the Humanities in the fifteenth century', *Itinerarium Italicum. The Profile of the Italian Renaissance in the Mirror of its European Transformations*, Studies in Medieval and Reformation Thought, vol.XIV, eds., H.A. Oberman and T.A. Brady (Leiden, 1975), pp 305–66.

16.   Allen, *Letters*, no. 52, pp 82–4, 23 April 1516. Polydore Vergil implied that Fox was driven out of office by an ungrateful Wolsey, but Polydore was hostile to Wolsey, who had imprisoned him, *The Anglica Historia of Polydore Vergil, AD 1485–1537*, ed. and trans. D. Hay, Camden ser., 74 (London, 1950), pp 152–3, 194–8, 230. Fox's letter shows no such conflict with Wolsey, and his influence with the king remained strong. Also Fox's own strong desire to retire is apparent in his letters. Similarly, Nicholas Harpsfield's statement in *Historia Anglicana Ecclesiastica* (Douai, 1622), pp 643–4, that 'obrepens senectus' led Fox to resign is not supported by the evidence.

17.   Allen, *Letters*, no. 57, pp 92–6, the words appear on p 94.

18.   H.G.D. Liveing, *The Records of Romsey Abbey* (Winchester, 1906) pp 211–37. Fox also had problems with the male houses. In 1521 he wrote to Wolsey that he had found the monks 'so depraved, so licentious and corrupt' that he despaired of any reformation; (quoted p 227).

19.   Allen, *Letters*, no. 65, p 110.

20.   The quotations in this paragraph are taken from the preface to his translation, *Here begynneth the Rule of seynt Benet*. For the most part I have modernized Fox's spelling and grammar, though sometimes the original has been retained to give the flavour of his prose. Note the contemporary use of double negatives, and the lower case initial letters for God and other names.

21.   There is a copy of his order of profession in Cambridge University Library.

22.   It seems that his translation was also intended for use by monks because chapter 60 (which was not relevant to nuns) was nevertheless translated by Fox, partly to retain the integrity of the Rule, but also 'specyally for the instruction of some monks meynly lettered'. It is not clear which monasteries Fox had in mind.

23.   Bacon, *Henry VII*, p 233, says of the king's council 'as he chose well, so

he held them well'. Only one senior man was removed, Sir William Stanley, who was implicated in Warbeck's plot and executed in February, 1495: see R. Lockyer, *Henry VII* (London, 1972), pp 81–5. After Henry's death, Empson and Dudley were executed, in 1510, as scapegoats for the unpopularity of the high taxation harshly exacted during the late king's reign.

24. Allen, *Letters*, no. 67, pp 114–17, 2 Jan. (1519).
25. Allen, *Letters*, no. 19, pp 29–30; no. 66, p 113.
26. For the appointment of Morwent, 'a trained man of affairs', see Allen, *Letters*, no. 60, pp 103–4.
27. Allen, *Letters*, no. 85, pp.146–8, 17 November 1526: also see letter 86. For West see *BRUC*, p 629; *DNB*, 20, p 1246–49; for Incent see *BRUO*, p 999.
28. Ward, *Statutes*, (1843), pp 218–19. Such failings in leadership Fox designates 'perjury', that is, the breaking of a vow of solemn undertaking previously made. Thomas More uses the word in this sense in his confutation of Robert Barnes in 1532. Also note the phrase in Fox's register 'Nimia familiaritas parit contemptum' Reg. Winton., ii, ff 84d, quoted in Howden, *Register...Durham*, pp xliii–iv.
29. Ed., Batten, *Register...Bath and Wells*, pp 170–74.
30. Allen, *Letters*, no. 50, pp 79–80, 'If I were within the diocese of Worcester, I could...soon remedy the matter'. He suggested to Wolsey ways in which the election could be supervised by a court of by royal agents who could 'shut out three young fools not entitled to vote who want a voice in the election.' Alternatively, Wolsey should let the election go ahead, and 'if they do amiss, to reform it at the time of confirmation'.
31. Allen, *Letters*, no. 65, pp 110–11.
32. The Latin passage which Fox translated and expanded into his splendid English version runs as follows: *non sit turbulentus et anxius, non sit nimius et obstinatus, non sit zelotypus et nimis suspiciosus, quia numquam requiescit.*
33. It is interesting that Fox avoided any confusion between the full authority which pertains to an abbess, and the office of a priest. His clear belief that full authority, with its divine origin, could certainly be held by a woman did not imply that women could assume a priestly function. Almost certainly the question crossed his mind, for in the same chapter he made one small but significant alteration to the Rule: the phrase that should have been translated 'she occupies the place of Christ in the monastery', Fox rendered 'she occupies the place of almighty god in the monastery'. Presumably he wished to distance the abbess for the sacrificial role of Christ with which the priesthood has a particular relationship.
34. The ladder imagery is also used by Fox in the first chapter of the Statutes of Corpus Christi College, 'We give the name of virtue to the right side of the ladder and that of knowledge to the left, and between these two be steps, for either side hath rounds of its own, by which we may either soar on high or sink into the lowest depths', Ward, *Statutes*, ch.1.
35. The Venetian ambassador, Sebastiano Giustiniani, summed up Fox as a man of 'extreme authority and goodness', *CSP Venetian*, 2, p 277, 5 Jan. 1516. There is considerable evidence to support favourable assessments of Fox's character, especially Allen, *Letters*, nos. 33,34, pp 50–51; no. 66, pp 111–14; no. 87, pp 150–51. Also see p xiii for Allen's assessment of Fox as a man of goodwill, merciful, parific, and far–sighted.
36. In chapter 22 Fox translated in the feminine form the Rule's injunction

that 'nun's shall not sleep with their knife at side'. Chapter 41 specifies
dinner at the sixth hour, and chapter 40 gives the measure of wine. Fox's
warning about sobriety included 'not only wine, but also ale, beer and all
other drinks' — presumably he had in mind cider and mead.

37. Allen, *Letters*, no. 7, pp 14–15.
38. Allen, *Letters*, no. 45, pp 71–2, to Wolsey, 4 June 1513.
39. Only one heretic was burned under Fox's jurisdiction, Thomas Denys in
     July 1513: very probably Fox was away in France at the time. Batten,
     Life, p 94, says that the burning was 'alien to the temper and tone of
     Bishop Fox', but Howden *Register*, p li, is not so sure, though she does
     grudgingly admit Fox's merciful attitude to heresy.
40. Ward, *Statutes*, pp 230–1.
41. Richard Nykke, as Fox's vicar–general, dispensed William Benne, vicar of
     Wendon, from residence in order to study at Oxford, Batten,
     Register...Bath and Wells, pp 86–7,. For Benne's subsequent career see
     Biographical Register of the University of Oxford, p 168. On 18 June 1507,
     Thomas Yegg was given leave to study at Winchester College, Howden,
     Register, p 1. Fox was chancellor of Cambridge University 1499–1500,
     Master of Pembroke (absentee) from 1507 to 1518 or later. He advised
     Lady Margaret on her educational bequests and was her executor. He was
     connected with Fisher at St John's College, and with King's College,
     Cambridge. He was Visitor to New College and Magdalen, revised the
     statutes of Balliol in 1507; see H.E. Salter, [ed.], *The Oxford Deeds of
     Balliol College*, Ox. Hist. Soc., vol.64 [Oxford, 1913], pp 309–14. Fox
     founded Corpus Christi in 1516, Taunton School (on his manor) in 1522,
     and Grantham School, near his birthplace, in 1528.
42. Allen, *Letters*, no. 7, pp 14–15.
43. Allen, *Letters*, no. 23, pp 36–7.
44. For details of his preparations, and in particular his sound military
     judgment, see Allen, *Letters*, no. 9, p 17.
45. In Fox's letters his own style is very clear, first restating and defining the
     correspondent's principal points, then answering each point precisely. See,
     for example, Allen, *Letters*, no. 11, pp 19–20; no. 39, pp 60–61; no. 66,
     p 113; no. 81, pp 135–38.
46. See Statutes of Balliol (1507), also Corpus Christi (1516). For the
     appointment of Robert Morwent as Vice–President of Corpus, see Allen,
     Letters, no. 60, pp 103–4.
47. Chapters 4:2 – 4:4.
48. This insertion is tantalizing, as there are other passages in Fox's work
     which hint at a Benedictine influence, especially that of the Italian order
     of Santa Giustina of Padua. Perhaps there was some influence through
     John Colet and Fox's chaplain. The young Reginald Pole and his circle
     were at this time in close contact with the order in Italy; see B. Collett,
     Italian Benedictine Scholars and the Reformation (Oxford University
     Press, 1985), esp. pp 77–8, 111–12.
49. Ed., T.M. Fry, *RRB 1980. The Rule of St Benedict in Latin and English,
     with notes* (Minnesota, 1981), p 295.

THE SOCIETY OF JESUS IN THE WARS OF RELIGION

John Bossy

The first thing to say is that I should like this afternoon to make a contribution to the history, if not of the monastic, at least of the religious life. My subject is on the face of it a political subject, but I do not want to say more about the politics of it than will make comprehensible an episode in the history of 'religion'. It has some contemporary overtones, but I do not think it will be helpful to make too much of them: I shall be concerned with what actually happened at particular times and places in the late sixteenth century, and with what two excellent members of the Society of Jesus made of what actually happened in the context of the 'institute' of their Order.

In order to understand it and them, we need to know some things about the frame of mind of the Society, which at the time I am interested in was only some forty years old. We need to know that it differed from earlier forms of the religious life, and rather radically, by committing its members to a life of external activity with the purpose, not of the salvation of their own souls, but of assisting the salvation of others'; and that in the pursuit of this object it tended to cultivate an ideal of energetic action from which the competitive instinct, the doing something 'more' or 'greater' than others did, was never very far away. It also differed in embracing the doctrine of 'finding God in all things', which entailed a relatively novel attitude to traditional modes of prayer and also a relative disturbance of traditional boundaries between the sacred and the profane.[1] The doctrine applied in some degree to activity in politics, which for the purposes of this topic I shall define restrictively. I mean now by 'politics' the organization of, or collaboration in, civil or military action aimed at the overthrow of Protestant governments, or in Catholic governments thought to be in collusion with them. Considering how careful he was to lay down guidelines for the conduct of members of his Society in all sorts of fields, Ignatius Loyola had been markedly laconic on this subject. He had said that Jesuits ought not to take sides in hostilities between Christian, by which he meant Catholic, princes; he had made a general remark about not engaging in secular activities which seems to have been really about something else. On the other hand he had, rather to the surprise of some of his early followers, positively commended taking on the role of confessor to princes, on the grounds that more souls could be helped by converting them than by converting ordinary people.[2] He had also, of course, committed the Society to a vow of obedience to the pope, and there is nothing in the Jesuit institute which would entitle the Society or its members to resist an instruction from a pope on the grounds that it was political. In general I think it is clear that Ignatius had no objection, where he thought the general interest of Catholicism was at stake, to the sending of Jesuits on missions which an impartial observer would regard as political in the sense stated, or in other senses.

As to the Wars of Religion, I shall be concerned with happenings in or in connection with England and France during the 1580s. The governments of both countries were at the time the object of Catholic political hostilities: in the case of England, from the invasion schemes which closely followed the launching of the Elizabethan Catholic mission in the 1570s, and ended with the Armada of 1588; and in the case of France, from the forces of Catholic zeal which organized themselves into the Catholic League of 1585 and precipitated a civil war and the assassination of King Henri III in 1589. In both cases the inspiration for these hostilities has been attributed to the Jesuits. This was the position of Queen Elizabeth's government at the time, and in France it became a view widely held in official and learned circles after the accession of Henri IV.

The French version of this 'black legend', as one may call it, has undergone some transformations during the past century: it was vigorously opposed by the official historian of the French Jesuits, Henri Fouqueray, who produced quite a lot of evidence to show that the general of the Society, Claudio Aquaviva, was extremely hostile to the Catholic League, and disciplined Jesuits whom he thought too closely connected with it. It has recently been revived in a modified form by A. Lynn Martin, who has indicated that Aquaviva's protestations of hostility to Catholic politics were not always candid, and in particular that he concealed from King Henri III that several of his subjects in France were actively engaged in Catholic politics in respect of England. The most reliable authority at present, J.H.M. Salmon, takes the statesmanlike view that the Jesuits in France 'were by no means united in the Leaguer cause'.[3] In England the black legend remains healthy, and with reason, for there is some truth in it. Even its doughtiest opponent, Fr. Leo Hicks, conceded something to it, and it has been rather strengthened by Martin, from whose work it might be gathered that the Jesuit mission to England was, from a French point of view, a political enterprise from the start.[4] The exterior facts are not really in dispute; what I should like to do now is to offer a view of these exterior facts as they were digested into the religious experience of the Jesuits most concerned with them.

To get to the point at which I want to start, I shall remind you of two things. First: the distinct Jesuit mission to England, which reinforced an existing missionary operation, had been decided on a little reluctantly by the then general, Mercurian, in 1579[5]; two Jesuits, Robert Parsons and Edmund Campion, arrived secretly in England in the summer of 1580; in July 1581 Campion was arrested, and shortly afterwards Parsons escaped to France. Campion was executed for treason in December. Second: in the meantime, on 19 February 1581, Aquaviva had been elected to succeed Mercurian as general, and so began one of the longest (34 years) and possibly the most distinguished generalship the Society of Jesus has enjoyed.[6]

Three years ago I was in Rome, exploring the archives of the Society for evidence of the doings of English Jesuits in France during the 1580s. You may ask why I had not done this before, since I had completed a Ph. D. thesis on connections between France and the Elizabethan Catholics twenty–five years before that. The answer is that I was told at the time by the person to whom I carried a respectable letter of introduction that the archives would contain nothing of interest to me, and it was not until I read Martin's book that I realised that this might not be the case. It turned out to be very much not the case: I found, in no very recondite place, a set of letters from Parsons to Aquaviva which had escaped the notice of Martin and also of Fr. Hicks who had published Parson's correspondence for the period, and with one almost invisible exception had never been publicly quoted. Other letters from the same source had been published and used, but not these.[7] Together with letters in the opposite direction, which were in a different place and had been used by Hicks and Martin, they made up a remarkable corpus containing sixteen letters from Parsons and twenty–one from Aquaviva, written between August 1581 and August 1585. My purpose today is to inform you of its contents, and to convey such reflections upon it as have occurred to me so far: I think its implications will continue to reverberate for a long time to come. For inside knowledge or our present problem, we could not get nearer to the horse's mouth, since Aquaviva was the general of the Society at the time, and Parsons was the man in charge of the Jesuit mission to England. For convenience's sake, I shall view the correspondence, first from Parsons's angle, then from Aquaviva's.

As we see things from Parsons's end, the political dimension is hard to extricate from a variety of others.[8] The first matter was where and how he was to live, of what in the language of the Society was called his *mansio*. When he had escaped from England, via the Sussex coast, he had come to Rouen, and there he had been given houseroom by one of the more powerful clerical figures in the city, Michel de Monchy. De Monchy was a member of an important Norman noble family, a canon of the cathedral, Archdeacon of Rouen, and vicar–general of the non–resident archbishop, Cardinal Bourbon. The arrangement was made in secret, for good reason, and the secret was fairly successfully preserved as long as Parsons remained there. The question discussed between him and Aquaviva was whether he ought to be living more conventionally in a Jesuit house, and whether it was proper to keep his whereabouts secret. On both points Aquaviva deferred to Parsons's judgment, though he eventually concluded that he was keeping up this mode of life longer than was good for himself or for the Society.[9]

The issue was perhaps whether Parsons, though not actually in England, was still on the English mission or not, and there was good reason for Parsons to claim that he was. He was still in charge of such Jesuits as were still in England, and he was actively engaged during his time in Rouen in choosing and vetting new members to be sent over. When they got to him they were put through a period of searching examination, which some of them failed to pass: Parsons's judgment, as expressed in the correspondence, seems both secure and unconventional. He defended vigorously the choice of William Weston, a shy professor of Greek extracted from the Jesuit college at Seville, from the contempt of the French provincial; he agitated successfully for the despatch of Henry Garnet, who was being trained up to succeed Christopher Clavius as the mathematician/astronomer in the Roman College and would, I am sure, have had a memorable career in that profession. Weston was a success on the mission, Garnet a godsend. Once their mission was decided on, Parsons took responsibility for organizing their passage into England, which was an increasingly complicated and expensive business in face of the vigilance of the English authorities. His systems worked.[10] We do not hear much in the letters about what the missioners did, or were supposed to do, when they got to England, though it is clear that Parsons went over this exhaustively with them. I think this was partly a matter of security; partly a consequence of Parsons's excellent grip on the Jesuit principle that superiors should brief people properly on their missions, and then leave them to get on with them on their own; and partly because Aquaviva was at the time being fully apprised of the practicalities of the English mission by the principal lay coadjutor or Parsons and Campion in England, George Gilbert.[11]

Apart from this Parsons was also writing a great deal, as he had done in England, and he also set up a press in Rouen, run by competent people, to print his own writings and those of others. He had done this in England too: the Rouen press was almost equally clandestine, as were its methods of smuggling its products into England. Of his own writings at the time, the most important for continental purposes was his account of the persecution in England, *De Persecutione Anglicana*, and for English purposes his spiritual guidebook the *Book of Resolution*. The persecution book and the first part of the *Book of Resolution* were both printed at Rouen early in 1582, after which his work as a writer was interrupted.[12]

What is was interrupted by, Parsons wrote later, was a brusque interjection of political demands. We ought probably to take this description with a grain of salt. His instructions in England had permitted him to deal in political matters under conditions which emphasised security rather more than they did spiritual danger or undesirability. He had almost certainly taken advantage of the concession, notably in dealings with the Spanish ambassador, Bernardino de Mendoza, with whom he had continued to communicate from Rouen.[13] Besides, his relations with Archdeacon de Monchy were not politically innocent. De Monchy, I think both on his own initiative and as the vicar—general of Cardinal Bourbon, was the principal local figure in the semi—underground Catholic mafia which at the beginning of 1585 declared itself publicly as the Catholic League of Holy Union.[14] I do not know how Parsons had made contact with him, but the contact must have been made either before or immediately upon his arrival in Rouen, and one or more of Mendoza, Cardinal Bourbon, the Duke of Guise and Guise's principal lieutenant among the French Jesuits, Claude Matthieu, must have been involved in it. For political purposes Parsons was from the moment of his arrival in France a Leaguer *avant la lettre*. In contrast to his dealings with Mendoza, where his interpretation of his instructions seems over—liberal, these relationships could not I think have been avoided. He could not have done what he did without political protection; but there was a price to pay, and it is difficult to claim that he was not in a position to distinguish between what was political and what was not, when we find him in his early letters to Aquaviva committing political matters to cipher, which so far as I know he did not do even for confidential information concerning the mission.[15]

These shadowy connections were brought into the open in May 1582, when he was summoned to Paris to attend a meeting between the Duke of Guise, the Spanish ambassador, the papal nuncio, the representative of Mary Stuart in Paris, and William Allen, head of the English College at Reims and of the English mission so far as it was not composed of Jesuits. What they decided on was a scheme for the invasion of Scotland in support of Guise's friend the Duke of Lennox, who was temporarily in control of the country, and for a subsequent invasion of England from the north, which was intended to overthrow Elizabeth. Though Guise was to lead the enterprise, the Spaniards were to supply most of the troops, and the Pope most of the money. After the meeting, Parsons and the Scottish Jesuit William Crichton were despatched to Lisbon and to Rome to deal with King Philip and the Pope. In Lisbon Parsons found Philip, who was engaged in defending the Azores against an expedition supported by the French, none too keen on the idea, and anxious to put more of the burden on the Pope. On his way back Parsons fell severely ill in northern Spain, and did not get back to France until the following summer. Meanwhile the Duke of Lennox had been overthrown in Scotland, and in August 1583 another meeting was called in Paris, which decided that there should now be a two—pronged attack on England only, a force under Guise attacking Sussex and a Spanish force landing in the north—west. Although Philip was still unpersuaded, a network of informants was set up in England, under the supervision of Francis Throckmorton, and Parsons was sent on another mission, this time to Rome. He returned with a seemingly adequate promise of money and with bulls renewing the excommunication of Elizabeth and appointing Allen Bishop of Durham in preparation for the enterprise.[16] He seems to have persuaded Rome to act with unusual speed, for he cannot have been in Rome more than a couple of weeks: he left Paris at the end of August and was back by the middle of October. Although the scheme had the active support in London of Mendoza, and the silent acquiescence of the French ambassador, Castelnau, it was aborted by the arrest of Throckmorton towards the end of November, and no further scheme of the kind was attempted. In January 1584 Parsons and Allen attempted to keep Pope Gregory XIII to the idea, but his ministers had by then decided that the assassination of Elizabeth was cheaper than military intervention, and a few weeks later Parsons was in the Netherlands with a brief from both King Philip and Mary Stuart to explore the chances of an intervention in England by the Spanish commander there, the Duke of Parma.[17] Parma was then in the middle of a string of remarkable successes in the war against the Dutch rebels, which were fairly radically altering the balance of power in north—western Europe. Meanwhile Guise's interest in an expedition across the Channel faded with the illness and death, in June, of Henri III's brother and heir the Duke of Anjou, which obliged him to fix his attention on the impending civil war in France.

Parsons had now been engaged in political operations for two years, at a time when he was supposed to be running the Jesuit mission to England. It is true that after his return from Rome in October 1583 he went back to Rouen and resumed his interrupted missionary, logistical and literary labours, but it is not true that his political activities then came to an end.[18] Quite apart from his dealings with Parma, he continued to have plenty of a political kind on his plate in France. He had to pay increasing attention to a movement of opposition to his role which was gathering force both among English exiles and among his French colleagues in the Society. He became preoccupied with the future of the college at Reims and in the summer of 1585, when Allen appeared to be dying, organized a potential *coup d'etat* intended to keep it from falling into what he considered the wrong hands.[19] In the meantime he had printed, distributed in France and England, and perhaps written a scurrilous and highly successful political polemic against Elizabeth's favourite the Earl of Leicester generally known as *Leicester's Commonwealth*.[20] It is fair to say that all these operations had a fairly close relation to the destinies of the English mission; and during this time he became not only the person responsible for the Jesuits in England, but Allen's right—hand man for the running of the English mission as a whole. He did not, unlike some of his fellow—exiles, English and especially Scots, take any direct part in the enterprises of the Catholic League in France. But he was obliged to be on one side or the other, and there had never been any question which side he was on. If he had stayed in France after September 1585 he would have had to declare this allegiance more openly.

When we look at these matters from Aquaviva's side, the first thing we must grasp is the huge respect and admiration in which Parsons was held by his general. They had met in Rome, when Parsons had been putting together the package which would shortly result in the despatch of the English Jesuit mission; Aquaviva knew his way around the Curia, and helped him. He is credibly recorded as having wanted to to on the mission himself.[21] I think he regarded Parsons as a model of what a Jesuit ought to be, a sort of Francis Xavier updated for the 1580s; it is obvious from their correspondence that their relations were extremely intimate, and also that somewhat more than half of the warmth between them was contributed by Aquaviva. Parsons described one of his letters as 'dolcissima', which indeed it was.[22] We have to consider him, despite this formal superiority, as feeling towards Parsons in somewhat the position of a disciple or, if that is too strong, of an officer on the general staff in the presence of someone who had a history of brave conduct, tactical skill and organizational genius on the battlefield.

Nevertheless there were two points upon which Aquaviva felt obliged to bring considerations of high strategy to Parsons's attention. The first is very striking, and Aquaviva had insisted on it from the start, when Parsons had had to report to him Campion's arrest. It was that there was an obligation upon Jesuit missioners, in English conditions, to be careful, which Campion had not been. When at Rouen Parsons began to write Campion's life, Aquaviva repeatedly urged him to make sure that what he wrote was actually a *life*, that is, an account of a missionary career, and not an account of his martyrodom. Parsons wrote a great deal of the book, and he did not finish it, possibly because he had difficulty in knowing exactly what Aquaviva wanted him to do about Campion's death; Aquaviva was extremely disappointed. I think it took Parsons some time to realise what Aquaviva was getting at: he had just written his persecution book and I have little doubt that there was pressure from his French protectors to do more in the same vein, since it made good propaganda in France. In the end he made it his business to din into his missionaries the message that they were being sent to do a job and not to get martyred. They were not being sent to edify the Church in general but to bring help and comfort to souls in England: martyrdom, Aquaviva conceded in a letter to Allen, was more meritorious than a life of toil, but the salvation of the missionary's soul was not the purpose of his mission.[23] This seems to me to have been an admirable and properly Ignatian judgment: in persuading Parsons of its propriety Aquaviva justified the time and care he devoted to their correspondence. I suspect that the cautious and fruitful career of Henry Garnet in England was a consequence of the interchange, and also the missionary narratives of Weston and John Gerard, whose freshness and durability seem to reflect Aquaviva's wishes.

The other issue was the political one, and we are now in a position to realise what a minefield this was. In general Aquaviva construed Ignatius's scattered remarks on the subject as constituting a ban on Jesuit political activity. Since this had not been the previous policy of the Society, or indeed of Ignatius, he had problems in enforcing his interpretation. The decision was, in his mind, particularly relevant to France, where he took the long-sighted view that the future of the Society depended upon amicable relations with the French crown; but it was practically impossible to separate the English case from the French.[24]

It seems clear that his first intervention in the matter was to remove from the instructions of Jesuits going to England the previous qualification to the ban on political dealings: this was done before the beginning of his correspondence with Parsons. It seems possible that the qualification had been made out of deference to the Duke of Guise, and Aquaviva's removal of it must have been connected with his unwillingness to sanction a mission to Scotland, which had almost entirely political objectives.[25] Parsons must have detected a change in the wind, but it does not appear to have influenced his own conduct for some time. Either he thought he was still working under his own instructions, which included the qualification, or else he regarded the instructions as no longer valid after he had left England for France. When his patrons required his attendance at the meeting in Paris, and still more when they sent him to Portugal to recruit Philip II to the enterprise, he was fairly nervous about explaining what had happened to Aquaviva.[26] We do not have Aquaviva's reply, but it seems that he went along with Parsons's employment as a political agent: he had indeed little choice. But he cannot have liked it much, and when he had had time to reflect offered a judgment which indicated the difficulty of his position. In a letter written the following June he appears to say that, since such enterprises were being planned by the Catholic powers, including the Pope, the vow of obedience to the Pope inhibited Jesuits from opposing them: but it was not their business to participate in or to run them, presumably unless there was a specific and personal instruction from the Pope to do so.[27]

By this date, when Parsons had got back to France after his convalescence in Spain, Aquaviva had evidently decided that he wanted to get Parsons out of his entanglement, and that the best way to do this was to use some gentle persuasion to get him to come to Rome:

> 'It has occurred to me', he wrote on 11 August 1583, 'that perhaps it would be a good idea for you to make a journey to Rome; which would not only bring us and your people (meaning either the English in general or the English in Rome) much consolation, but also perhaps be of some help to the *negotia* themselves.'

The last phrase has been taken by Martin as an accommodation to the English enterprise and an authority for Parson's participation in it, and this is obviously for Parson's participation in it, and this is obviously correct in principle. But it seems a misjudgment of his part to take it as an instance of what he considers Aquaviva's feeble and disingenuous handling of the matter.[28] In a cautious and crabwise way, he was actually rebuking Parsons, and I am satisfied that his plan to get Parsons to Rome was a way of extracting him from his dealings on behalf of the invasion scheme, even at the risk of extending his absence from the task of running the Jesuit mission in England.

He must have got quite a shock when his letter crossed with one from Parsons saying that he was indeed coming to Rome, and *instanter*, but coming on the business of the enterprise.[29] As we saw, he was bearing a revived set of instructions from Guise about the second invasion plan, which concerned England alone and entailed, among other things, the reissue of the Bull of Excommunication against Elizabeth. Parsons must have seen Aquaviva on his brief and busy visit. We do not know what transpired between them, but Parsons certainly persuaded Aquaviva to let him stay in France for the time being, which amounted to a permission to continue his dealings for the invasion: presumably, the Pope was Parsons's trump card.[30] There is no sign at all that he reduced his involvement after his return to Paris; on the contrary, the evidence (from the Spanish side) is that he was agitating more vigorously on behalf of the enterprise than the Spaniards thought realistic, and despite the arrest of Throckmorton and the consequent exposure of the scheme he continued in this vein until the spring of 1584.[31]

During this time Aquaviva appears to have suspended his efforts to get Parsons out of politics, and to have contented himself with trying to get him back so far as possible to strictly missionary operations, and also (which was not altogether compatible) to persuade him to abandon his cover and return, at least for a time, to a stable life in a Jesuit community. Hence we find Parsons, after his trip to the Duke of Parma in the spring, writing a welcome letter from the French professed house at St Louis in Paris, where he was living with his *socius* Ralph Emerson:

> 'Here we are enjoying great peace and quiet; it seems to me a paradise.' True, he was having difficulties with enemies among English *emigres* in Paris; 'but all such things seem trivial compared to that sweetness which, after so long disuse, I receive from the embrace of my fathers and brothers. Assuming, that is, that I shall be permitted to remain in it for a while, which it is up

to your Paternity to decide.'

He added that Guise, perhaps to defuse the disputes among his English followers in Paris, was anxious for him to go to Scotland, which he was very unwilling to do.[32]

Aquaviva had them made some kind of impression on Parsons, but at this time his compliance was perhaps more apparent than real. The French professed house was under the rectorship of his friend Claude Matthieu, who was a tireless promoter of Catholic politics in France, Scotland and England, and was full of Jesuits of a like mind. In Paris it was the centre of the zealous party among the Jesuits in France, as the Collège de Clermont was of the royalists. I doubt if the tranquillity of the house went very deep. Parsons stayed there for some months, delegating to Emerson the work which could only be done in Rouen: Emerson piloted Weston over to England in September.[33] His own return to Rouen, which occurred shortly afterwards, seems to have an unpremeditated consequence of another activity of this time, the publication and distribution of two substantial political writings: Allen's *Defence of Catholics* against Lord Burghley's apologia for the Elizabethan government, *The Execution of Justice in England*, and *Leicester's Commonwealth*.[34] The latter first appears in the Jesuit correspondence in a complaint written by the French provincial Pigenat to Aquaviva on 25 November 1584. It had already caused a huge stir: Leicester himself took it extremely ill, and was alleged in retaliation to have sent a gang of people over to Paris to assassinate the author. This was the reason Parsons gave for going back into hiding in his safe house in Rouen, and though he may have had a hankering to get back to it anyway I see no strong reason for doubting him.[35]

Since a French version of *Leicester's Commonwealth* was brought out — with a 'villainous addition', so the English ambassador said — early in 1585,[36] it seems rather likely that in venturing into such a new and dangerous field Parsons was acting under some kind of instruction from Guise. Now that Guise had withdrawn from the English enterprise, Englishmen in France could now best serve him by anti–English propaganda which would damage Henri III by damaging his ally Queen Elizabeth. Hence the extremely hostile reaction of the provincial Pigenat. But Aquaviva cannot in any case have appreciated Parsons's involvement, and he took advantage of the assassination scare to revive in a less tentative form the suggestion that Parsons leave France and come to Rome. He made it in a letter of 29 November 1584, and repeated it on 9 January, when he also told Pigenat to take a hand. Considering the extreme sensitivity with which he had handled Parsons for the past three years and more, it is fairly clear that this time the suggestion was actually an instruction, and Parsons took it as such.

His reply, a long letter written from Rouen on 12 February 1585, is on any score the most interesting item in the correspondence. In the light of the traditional notion of Parsons as a primarily political figure, which this paper will so far probably not have done much to dispel, it contains a few surprises. It is worth recording at length, since nobody appears to have quoted it in print before.[38]

Parsons began by saying that he had talked about the idea of leaving France to Allen, whom had been very hostile to it on the grounds that he could not run the mission without him; but he had finally decided that he would come as soon as he had got three things out of the way. The first two involved his dealings with Parma, which had been put personally into his hands both by

Philip and by Mary. He said he did not think that anything would come of them, but reasonably thought it would not do to drop them on the spur of the moment. His third reason, which he said was more important to him, was not political. He wanted to finish his *Book of Resolution*, from which he said he had been 'very peremptorily summoned' by the politicians in 1582. This, he said, would take him three or four months, by which time he would have extracted himself from his political obligations, so he would be free to come away in the summer. He also said he was afraid of new Anglo–French alliance against Parma and Guise, which would lead to a crack–down on his friends in France and possibly to the arrival of English troops in Normandy. Although the tone of his remarks about political engagements was unenthusiastic, we might think that he was saying what Aquaviva wanted to hear, of playing for time. Objectively speaking, he was still as deep in politics as ever.

If these are our suspicions, I think they will probably not survive a reading of the rest of the letter. He now said that he would like to make a proposal which he had been turning over in his mind for the past year:

> 'Since for some years now I have been involved in these great distractions, I should like, according to the constitutions of the Society, to be allowed to make my third year of novitiate (tertianship) so as to recollect myself... For I feel myself extremely debilitated by these daily dealings with the world, and even though I were never more keen to perform them, the importunity of these affairs (*negotiorum*) does not allow me to find any satisfaction in them. The passions of my nature (*passions animi*) have greatly grown and strengthened, and unless I get time to attend carefully and undistracted to *this* business I do not see how I shall be able to subjugate them.'

> So, when he comes to Rome he would like to go into the novice–house at Sant'Andrea 'so that I can strengthen myself (*perhaps* confirm my vocation) in that place where first I received the spirit of the Society'. He hopes that Aquaviva would not want him to do a job concerned with England, at least for the time being. 'I therefore beg that I may shut myself up inside the walls of Sant' Andrea for at least eight or ten months, and that there I may for once lay down the burden of these affairs and begin to take a look at myself. I confess to your Paternity that when I had the advantage of the place (as a novice) I did not realise the benefits of it; but now that I have learned from the lack of them I do not doubt that I shall get more profit from it in a month than I did in the whole year I spent there.'

Many years ago Philip Hughes drew attention to two of Parsons's letters dating from a little earlier, where he seemed to show regret on his and Allen's part for their period of political activity: the more explicit was written to Mary in September or October 1584. Here he wrote that, considering the opposition they had aroused by it and the lack of achievement, they 'had resolved... to leave cogitation of such matters, and to follow only our spiritual course, whereon all dependeth though in longer time'. He took the 'lets and hindrances' which had occurred as evidence that in the strategy of divine providence 'it was not yet time to relieve us temporarily'.[39] It is true that here Parsons expressed more discouragement than regret, and that he went on to say that they had been cheered up by the arrival of an emissary from Spain and to suggest that Mary might stir up Parma's resolution by offering to marry him. The idea that Parma might take up the English enterprise where Guise had left it was still at this point the active issue which in the following February it appears to have ceased to be. But if Hughes pre–dated Parsons's conversion somewhat, his judgment will now seem to be in the right direction, and besides the letter to Aquaviva I can produce something from our new source to confirm it. Some seven weeks after he wrote to Aquaviva, he being then at Mézières on the way from Reims to the Duke of Parma, he wrote to his friend the rector of the English College in Rome, Alfonso Agazzari (who passed it on to Aquaviva, as he was meant to). Agazzari had transmitted Aquaviva's anxiety about the rising feeling among English lay exiles against Allen and Parsons, and invited Parsons to make his peace with those like Thomas Morgan and Charles Paget in Paris who were agitating against them. Parsons's reply, which was not actually very conciliatory, consisted of two points. First he said that he knew that it was his duty to feel fraternally towards them, and cited St Paul to the effect that all the labours in the world were of no avail without charity. He said that he remembered them daily at his mass. Then he said that there was no longer any reason for friction between them, since he and Allen had given up politics.

> 'There was a time when Allen and I had some business to conduct
> with them (that is, in the invasion scheme of 1583). Now that time
> has passed, along with the occasion of the business, and so now we
> attend solely to our own functions, and they to theirs, without
> getting mixed up with one another. That will be good, I hope, for
> both parties'.[40]

There was still a fair amount of business for Parsons to get through in the north: in particular he had to cope with the crisis in the English College at Reims, which he did with a strong and distinctly political hand.[41] In spite of this interruption he managed to keep his word to Aquaviva more or less, and arrived in Rome, with Allen, early in November 1585. It appears that he did get some of the peace and quiet he had asked for, for it was reported in the spring that he had gone to make the Spiritual Exercises in Sant'Andrea.[42] His correspondence with Aquaviva now of course came to an end, and the story of their relationship is plunged back into darkness.

I do not feel equipped at the moment to place this correspondence and its outcome in their full historical setting. They were very closely affected by Aquaviva's concern for the Jesuit provinces In France in their divided and unhappy condition. It would take too long to give a proper account of this here; Lynn Martin has described it fairly fully in *Henri III and the Jesuit Politicians*, though one would not quite gather from the book that Aquaviva was driven at one point to face the idea that he might have to abandon the English mission altogether.[43] The question would arise whether the issue between himself and Parsons was not between politics and no politics, but between one kind of politics and another. But that is not a question for this afternoon. We have for the moment quite enough to think about in trying to extract from the correspondence what it has to say about the history of Jesuit spiritual doctrine and practice.

We need first to think about what Parsons's letter of 12 February 1585 has to tell us about his own experience as a Jesuit. There are obvious points to be picked up. He had not, he said, profited much by his novitiate in 1575–1576. I take this to mean that, having joined the Society in a spirit of commitment to heroic enterprise, he was too impatient to get on with them to appreciate the merits of a year spent washing dishes and investigating his soul. I imagine that

William Good, with whom he had done the Spiritual Exercises in Louvain after his withdrawal from Oxford, had been an influence in this direction.[44] We may diagnose a rather simply activist understanding of the Jesuit institute. In writing to Aquaviva about his *Book of Resolution*, which contained the memorable affirmation that 'the things a man hath to believe are much fewer than the things he hath to do', he confessed his lack of learning in spiritual matters; we might well see him as an instance of what an older Jesuit, Oliver Mannaerts, diagnosed in a younger one, Pedro de Ribadeneira — an over–esteem for 'magnanimity' in the Society which might encourage individual and collective self–glorification.[45]

I do not know whether this would count as one of the 'passions' Parsons described as getting out of hand. Whatever they were, he attributed them to a lack of *otium* or leisure in his life, and while this was certainly something to do with his own nature, he would seem to have been faithfully following the 'spirit' of the Society as expounded by Ignatius and communicated by Jerome Nadal, who was Ignatius's most authoritative interpreter during the 1570s. Nadal had said that there was 'no such thing as *otium* in the Society'.[46] In following the principle to its utmost Parsons would appear to have sacrificed community life, continuous prayer and (except for his correspondence with Aquaviva) regular spiritual advice. One result of this had presumably been to bring about the illnesses which had dogged him during 1582, though he was generally thought to have the constitution of an ox.[47] I wonder whether we ought to interpret his climactic letter of 12 February 1585 as evidence of some sort of incipient nervous breakdown as well; I find something nightmarish about his conviction that his passions were becoming too strong for him, though this may be excessive. We now have in any case material for a less adventurous commentary than A.L. Rowse's diagnosis of a complex of social inferiority, or Garrett Mattingly's of a pre–Celtic racial stereotype:[48] it would be a reasonable inference from the rest of his life to suppose that two of the passions in question were a passion for organizing things and a difficulty in tolerating or forgetting opposition. The first might have concealed a guilty longing for power. This was the charge of his enemies, and Parsons referred to it in such a way as to concede that there might be something in it: he said that the real issue between them was 'a matter of judgment and opinion which is secret and private to myself and pertains to my status (*sc.* as a priest or religious)'.[49] The second, and much better supported by the evidence, would indicate ungovernable feelings of enmity, mainly directed towards those who deplored his rise to prominence in the counsels of the Catholic powers and did their best to undermine it. From his letter to Agazzari it is clear that this is what Aquaviva supposed; it is also clear to me, from his creative interpretation of St Paul, that he had had sufficient leisure to recognise this problem as not simply a matter for his own soul but one for the Society at large. There was indeed a problem about the relationship between efficacious action and the practice of charity as traditionally understood.[50] In his own life I imagine that his repair to Sant'Andrea did something to resolve his problem and to restore his command of himself: the passions in question, so far as we can judge what they were, did not indeed miraculously disappear, but they no doubt became less of a nightmare to him.

On Aquaviva's side I think that for the time being there are four things to be said, which I shall state simply.

First   On the evidence of this correspondence, Martin's particular criticism of Aquaviva, that at the time in question he was saying one thing about Jesuit politics in respect of France and something else in respect of England, seems superficially justified but fundamentally unreasonable. He certainly handled Parsons gently, and it may be that he might have taken a stronger line at their unrecorded meeting in Rome in September 1583; but altogether the impression is not of weakness, but of cautious progress towards extracting a much admired subordinate from a situation for which Aquaviva was not responsible and of some aspects of which he disapproved. It is clear to me that he was quite aware of Martin's problem, and that he faced it with a sense of the implications which Martin hardly shows: that there was no way he could have taken stronger action short of abandoning the English Jesuit mission, and probably of wrecking the English mission as a whole.[51]

Second I am convinced of the depth and importance of the view which he continued to press on Parsons, that what was wanted in England was living missioners and not dead martyrs. He seems to have pressed it, in the end fairly successfully, on a correspondent who took a little time to see the point. I think this was a proper and in the circumstances rather courageous interpretation of the Jesuit institute, and distinctly beneficial to the English mission, for which he cared deeply. It is true that he probably had a political motive somewhere in his mind: that is, that under the strain of a continuing stream of executions in England the French monarchy was likely to collapse. But as far as I can see this consideration had no more that its due part in a judgment in which the needs and comfort of English Catholics were, as they should have been, the principal consideration.

Third I am not sure that the fundamental issue about Jesuit politics was, so far as the correspondence goes, really thrashed out between them. There seems to be an unexplored ambiguity about whether the distinction they were dealing with was between the temporal and the spiritual, or between the political and the non–political. Both of them seem to treat these distinctions as the same, which neither the Jesuit institute nor the situation of an underground church ought to have allowed them to do. Each of them seems to have been feeling his way towards some more satisfactory, though perhaps illusory, discrimination. Parsons got nearest to it when, in discussing Weston's and Campion's qualifications for the mission, he described them both as having little knowledge of 'the world'. I am not sure that he was exactly implying that Campion would have been a better missioner if he had been more 'worldly'; he judged, accurately, that Weston's unworldliness was not a disqualification.[52] But he did make sure that Weston was taken into England by his own *socius* Ralph Emerson, whose practical capabilities he praised as he ought to have done; and under Aquaviva's tutelage I think he may, despite his loyalty to his dead friend, have come to concede the point about Campion. It was no doubt unthinkable for two distinguished religious, even it Jesuits, to turn worldliness into a virtue; but this was surely what Aquaviva was asking for in his English missionaries, and rightly.

From these large prospects we may turn with some disappointment to Parsons's (and Allen's) final surrender to a traditional separation of the temporal and the spiritual, and their earnest undertaking that henceforth they would stick to their spiritual last.[53] I think they were letting themselves off, and perhaps letting Aquaviva off, too easily.

Finally I should be extremely surprised if his intercourse with Parsons had not a fairly considerable impact on one of Aquaviva's main contributions to the inner development of the Society of Jesus. I mean the rehabilitation in the Society of a comparatively traditional notion of prayer, as against what might have been thought the Ignatian view that prayer was not something different from work.   This he affirmed in his circular letter to the Society *On the Renovation of the Spirit*, written in the middle of his exchanges with Parsons in 1583 and subsequently adapted by Parsons himself in a famous passage of his *Memorial for the Reformation of England*; and in his *Letter on Mental Prayer*, of 1590, which defended the practice of contemplative prayer among professed fathers of the Society.[54]   He seems, as in his doctrine about politics, to have been writing against a historic Jesuit consensus, and in this case against the view handed down as from the founder by Nadal that there was no room in the Society for *otium*.   It is none of my business to say which of them was right; but I think we can be fairly confident that one of the consequences of our most absorbing correspondence was to help to persuade Aquaviva that there was a limit to the amount of *negotium* which was tolerable even for a Jesuit so gifted at various kinds of it as Robert Parsons.

NOTES

1. Much the best guide is now Thomas H. Clancy, *An Introduction to Jesuit Life* (St Louis, Mo., 1976) [hereafter Clancy, *Introduction*; for a more historical view, H.O. Evennett, *The Spirit of the Counter–Reformation* (Cambridge, 1968).

2. P. de Chastonay, *Les Constitutions de l'ordre des Jesuites* (Paris, 1941), pp 149, 188–191.

3. H. Fouqueray, *Histoire de la Compagnie de Jesus en France*, ii (Paris, 1913), pp 120–181; A. Lynn Martin, *Henry III and the Jesuit Politicians* (Geneva, 1973) [hereafter Martin, *Henry III*], chaps iv, vii–xv; J.H.M. Salmon, *Society in Crisis* (London, 1975), p 237.

4. Ed., Leo Hicks, *Letters and Memorials of Father Robert Persons, S.J.*, i (to 1588) (Catholic Record Society, vol. xxxix, 1942) [hereafter Hicks, *Persons Letters*], introduction, pp lii–lxi; Martin, *Henry III*, pp 63–74.

5. Clancy, *Introduction*, p 139.

6. The exterior facts of Aquaviva is generalship are recounted in William V. Bangert, *A History of the Society of Jesus* (St. Louis, Mo., 1972), pp 97–176, interior matters in J. de Guibert, *The Jesuits: their Spiritual Doctrine and Practice* (St. Louis, Mo., 1972 edn) [hereafter De Guibert, *Doctrine*], pp 230–281.

7. The source is Archivum Romanum Societatis Iesu, Fondo Gesuitico 651 (Epistolae Selectae ex Anglia).   This contains files of letters from Englishmen, arranged alphabetically by author; the one containing Parsons's letters is numbered 640.   The source was first reported in C. Devlin, *The Life of Robert Southwell* (London, 1956), pp viii, 350 f, as 'found in Rome very recently', and the file of Southwell's letters was there used; P. Caraman used those of Garnet in *Henry Garnet and the Gunpowder Plot* (London, 1964); and P. Renold others, mainly of William Allen, in her edition of *Letters of William Allen and Richard Barret* (Catholic Record Society, vol. lviii, 1967) Miss Renold gave references to those of Parsons ibid., pp 148n. 2, 156n. 2, 171n. 1; for the exception, see below, n.19.

    The other sources I have used from the same archive, mainly of Aquaviva's letters to Parsons, are the volumes Francia 1/i, and Gallia 44 and 91.   I refer to them as described, and to the main source as Fondo Gesuitico 651.   I should like to record my gratitude to Fr. Edmond Lamalle, S.J., the then archivist, for the extreme kindness and generosity which he showed me when I was working in the archive, and for permission to quote.

8.   The narrative is best followed in Hicks, *Parsons Letters*, pp xxxix–lxxii.

9.   Aquaviva to Parsons, 17–ii, 19–iii, 5–xii–1582, ll–viii–1583 (Francia 1/i, ff. 121v, 130v, 144v, 170v).

10.   Parsons to Aquaviva, 29–v, 10–vii, 20–viii–1584 (Fondo Gesuitico 651), 15–ix–1584 (Hicks, *Persons Letters*, p 241); Aquaviva to Parsons, 22–x–1584 (Francia 1/i, f. 204v).

11.   Gilbert's account is in Hicks, *Persons Letters*, pp 321–340; Aquaviva said he spent a lot of time listening to Gilbert on the subject: to Parsons, 17–ii–1582 (Francia 1/i, f. 121v).

12.   Hicks, *Persons Letters*, pp lii–xlv; Parsons to Aquaviva, ll–iv–1582 (Fondo Gesuitico 651). The English version of *De Persecutions Angicanna* is reproduced in ed., D.M. Rogers, *English Recusant Literature*, vol. 125 (Menston, Yorks., 1973); at the title–page records, it was produced over the French version by Matthieu de Launay. In his letter to Aquaviva Parsons did not mention the French version, which was admittedly printed in Paris.

13.   The evidence is given by Philip Hughes, *The Reformation in England*, iii (London, 1954) [hereafter Hughes, *Reformation* iii], pp 317–321.

14.   See my Ph. D. thesis, 'Elizabethan Catholicism: the Link with France' (Cambridge, 1961), pp 78–91; and P. Benedict, *Rouen during the wars of Religion* (Cambridge, 1981), index under name. There is a lot about de Monchy's relations with the Jesuits, which were intimate, in Aquaviva's correspondence; in 1584 Parsons wrote recommending him for the bishopric of Verdun: to Aquaviva, 10–vii–1584 (Fondo Gesuitico 651).

15.   As in Parsons to Aquaviva, ll–iv–1582 (Fondo Gesuitico 651), where he sent him a better cipher, which he had presumably got from the Spanish ambassador in Paris, Tassis.

16.   Hicks, *Persons Letters*, pp lii–lxii, and 356–355, for the texts.

17.   Parsons to Mary, 10–?x–1584 (Hicks, *Persons Letters*, pp 246–252); to Aquaviva, 12–ii–1585 (Fondo Gesuitico 651).

18.   As might be supposed from Hicks, *Persons Letters*, p lxi: 'His mission to Rome may be said to have terminated his activity as political negotiator.'

19.   Parsons to Agazzari, 12–viii–1585 (Fondo Gesuitico 651); Richard Barret to Agazzari, 8 & 22–viii–1585 (Renold, *Letters of Allen and Barret* (above, n. 7), pp 168, 172–175). Miss Renold gave an abstract of Parsons's letter ibid. p 171, n. 1.

20.   Its proper title was *The Copy of a letter written by a Master of Art of Cambridge*, and it was seemingly printed at Rouen about June 1584: see the edition of D.C. Peck, *Leicester's Commonwealth* (Athens, Ohio, 1985), pp 5–7. Peck has a careful discussion of the authorship, and accepts with qualifications the probable attribution made by Hicks to Charles Arundell: L. Hicks, 'The Growth of a Myth: Fr. Robert Persons, S.J., and *Leicester's Commonwealth*', *Studies* (Dublin), xlvi (1957), 91–105. Peter Holmes, *Resistance and Compromise: the Political Thought of the Elizabethan Catholics* (Cambridge, 1982), which is in general very reliable, continues to attribute it to Parsons without qualification (pp 129–134).

21.   Clancy, *Introduction*, p 139 (from Parsons).

22.   Aquaviva to Parsons, 19–iii–1582 (Francia 1/i, f. 130v); Parsons to Aquaviva, 3–v–1582 (Fondo Gesuitico 651).

23.   Aquaviva to Parsons, 14–x–1581, 17–ii, 19–iii–1582, ?3–vii–1584 (Francia 1/i, ff. 109r, 121v, 130v, 197v); to William Allen, 14–x–1581 (Catholic Record Society, vol. ix (1911), p.80). The manuscript of Parsons's Life of Campion is at Stonyhurst College, Collectanea P, and has never been publicly printed. But it has been extensively used since

Richard Simpson, *Edmund Campion* (2 edn, London, 1896); Simpson (p 506), says that the Life ends about November 1580).

24. Martin, *Henry III*, pp 98 f; Clancy, *Introduction*, p 138.

25. Hicks, *Parsons Letters*, p 318, n. 19; Martin, *Henry III* p 69; cf. Aquaviva to Parsons, 19–iii–1582 (Francia l/i, f. 130v): James in trouble, 'sed nos aliam opem ferre non possumus quam precibus'.

26. Parsons to Aquaviva, 3–v–1582 (Fondo Gesuitico 651): 'molte difficultà mi se offerivano in abbracciar questo viaggio, ma bisogna pigliarlo...'

27. Aquaviva to Parsons, 5–vi–1583 (Gallia 44, f. 9r). He says that he is forwarding his comments on the 'principum negotium' by William Crichton. I am sorry that my reading of this letter depends on short notes from a difficult draft, and is somewhat conjectural.

28. Aquaviva to Parsons, ll–viii–1583 (Francia l/i, f. 170v); Martin, *Henry III*, pp 107, 113.

29. Parsons to Aquaviva, 22–viii–1583 (Fondo Gesuitico 651).

30. Aquaviva to Matthieu, 20–x–1584 (Francia l/i, f. 224r).

31. Tassis to Philip II, 15–xi–1583 (*Calendar of State Papers, Spanish, 1580–1586* (ed., M.A.S. Hume, London, 1896), p.507); Hicks, *Persons Letters*, pp 193–195; above, n. 17.

32. Parsons to Aquaviva, 29–v–1584 (Fondo Gesuitico 651).

33. Parsons to Aquaviva, 20–viii, 15–ix–1584 (Fondo Gesuitico 651; Hicks, *Parsons Letters*, p 241). He was back in Rouen by the end of September (Ibid. pp.lxviii, 245).

34. Parsons to Aquaviva, 20–viii–1584: Emerson just back from Rouen, where he has sent into England '800 delli nuovi libri in Inglese'. Since Parsons said he hopes soon to send a Latin version, the ostensible reference is to the *Defence of Catholics* only, and I think this is compatible with the plural; but I should be surprised if *Leicester's Commonwealth* had not gone too. Cf. above, n. 20; Holmes, *Resistance and Compromise*, pp 129–135, argues that the publication of these two books opened a new and aggressive period in Elizabethan Catholic political writing.

35. Pigenat to Aquaviva, 25–xi–1584 (Gallia 91, f. 309); Aquaviva to Parsons, 29–xi–1584 (Francia l/i, f. 207r; Hicks, *Persons Letters*, p 260 n, cf. p. lxviii). Parsons first mentioned *Leicester's Commonwealth* in a propaganda letter written to Agazzari, 13–xii–1584 (Fondo Gesuitico 651), when he said that it was selling like hot cakes.

36. Stafford to Walsingham, 30–iii/9–iv–1585 (*Calendar of State Papers, Foreign, 1584–1585* (ed. S.C. Lomas, London, 1916 p 386); Peck prints a contemporary English translation of the 'addition' in his edition of *Leicester's Commonwealth*, pp 228–248.

37. Aquaviva to Pigenat, and to Parsons, 9–i–1585 (Francia l/i, ff. 209v, 210v).

38. Parsons to Aquaviva, 12–ii–1585 (Fondo Gesuitico 651); cf. Parsons to Mary, 15–ii–1585 (Hicks, *Persons Letters*, pp 269–270), where his statement that he was 'commanded by obedience to retire my self into Lorraine for a time' shows him fulfilling his promise to Aquaviva to extract himself from the business.

39. Hughes, *Reformation* iii, p 329; Parsons to Mary, i.e. 10–?x–1584 (Hicks, *Persons Letters*, p 246).

40. Parsons to Agazzari, 3–iv–1585 Fondo Gesuitico 651.

41. Above, n. 19.

42. Soloman Aldred to Walsingham, 27–iii/6–iv–1586 (*Calendar of State Papers, Domestic: Addenda 1580–1625* (ed., M.A.E. Green, London, 1872), p 170). On the history of the tertianship, see De Guibert, *Doctrine*, p 236.

43.   Martin, *Henry III*, *passim*; Aquaviva to William Allen, 15–vii–1584 (Catholic Record to Society, vol. ix, p 96).

44.   Hicks, *Persons Letters*, p 5, n. 1, and the long letter to Good in Sweden, March 1579, ibid. pp 5–28.

45.   Parsons to Aquaviva, 12–ii–1585 (Fondo Gesuitico 651); J. Bossy, *The English Catholic Community, 1570–1850* (London, 1975), p 17; Clancy, *Introduction*, pp 110–116.

46.   Clancy, *Introduction*, p 110.

47.   The brief description of his long period of illness at Bilbao at the end of 1582 (Hicks, *Persons Letters*, pp 171–2) may suggest that it was mental ('malenconico') as well as physical.

48.   A.L. Rowse, *The England of Elizabeth* (London, 1950), pp 462–463; G. Mattingly, *The Defeat of the Spanish Armada* (London, 1962 edn), pp 80–81. I should add that both these pen–portraits contain a good deal of insight.

49.   Parsons to Agazzari, 3–iv–1585 (Fondo Gesuitico 651); cf. J. Bossy, 'The Character of Elizabethan Catholicism', in ed., T. Aston, *Crisis in Europe, 1560–1660* (London, 1965), pp 238 f.

50.   Clancy, *Introduction*, pp 113–114; it was surely unconventional, though no doubt appropriate, for Parsons to quote 1 Corinthians 13.II 2–3 to the effect that all the labours in the world were no good without charity.

51.   Martin, *Henry III*, pp 101, 113–114, 218; cf De Guibert, *Doctrine*, p 230, for Aquaviva's 'gentleness without weakness', which I think he showed in this case; above, n. 43.

52.   Parsons to Aquaviva, 20–viii–1584 (Fondo Gesuitico 651).

53.   Above, nn. 39, 40.

54.   De Guibert, *Doctrine*, pp 237–242; Bossy, *English Catholic Community*, p 17.

COMMUNITY SOLIDARITY AMONG YORKSHIRE RELIGIOUS
AFTER THE DISSOLUTION

Claire Cross

The Marian restoration constitutes a melancholy chapter in the later Professor Knowles' magisterial study of *The Religious Orders in England*. With the assistance of her cousin, Cardinal Pole, Mary Tudor brought back Benedictines to Westminster Abbey, Carthusians to Sheen, Dominican Friars to St. Bartholomew's, Smithfield and Observant Franciscans to Greenwich and re-established two orders for women, Bridgettines at Syon and Dominicanesses at Dartford, but singularly failed to inspire the laity to emulate her example of returning former monastic properties to the church. Between them these six houses contained around a hundred monks, friars and nuns, 'not a great number', Dom David Knowles observed, 'out of the fifteeen hundred or so ex-religious who must still have been living up and down the country'. He then proceeded to deliver a measured but characteristically severe judgement.

> No doubt we should remember that the monasteries and friaries had been alienated or destroyed, and that both spiritual and economic motives had driven most of the male religious to find occupation in clerical posts, withdrawal from which would have needed a very lively sense of vocation. Doubtless, also, ten or twenty years of quiet under a Catholic sovereign would have seen an increase in the number of houses and an intake of young recruits. Nevertheless, a general conclusion seems to impose itself; while twenty years of religious turmoil and secularization had not extinguished the sense of vocation in a few individuals, the conception of the religious life as an occupation for a young man in the neighbourhood of a monastery had gone for ever, and the appearance of anything like a widespread desire for the monastic life as a vocation would never be seen in England until a fresh epoch of fervour had dawned.

In the final analysis the monks, nuns and friars dispossessed by Henry VIII had not risen to the challenges offered to them in the reign of Mary. They had been tested in the fires of adversity and found wanting.[1]

Perhaps sub specie eternitatis subsequent events in sixteenth century Catholic history justified such a censure. Nevertheless, to an outsider it seems rather harsh, and in particular tends to belittle the aspirations and efforts of individual former monks, friars and nuns. However much after Mary's accession they may have wished to resume their monastic obedience and they could only do so formally if lay proprietors restored their buildings and some of their lands. The reign of Mary proved to be very short, and this never happened, but at the time they could not have forseen this outcome and in Yorkshire at least there emerged among some of the former religious a hope, perhaps an expectation of a more widespread revival or monasticism. The wills of former monks, friars and nuns, not previously systematically exploited, supply incontrovertible evidence in the north of England of nostalgia for the religious life, and among some bolder souls a desire for its re-institution.

In 1535 Yorkshire exemplified in a relatively small compass the different stages of the spread of monasticism throughout England in the high and later Middle Ages. Within the county there were five Benedictine houses, no less than eight Cistercian abbeys, eleven Augustinian priories, four Gilbertine priories, two Charterhouses, three small Premonstratensian priories and single establishments of both Cluniacs and Grandimontines. Early in the thirteenth century the friars had colonised the region and three hundred years later the Dominicans, Franciscans and Carmelities all still maintained five urban convents, the Austins three and the Trinitarian friars of Knaresborough one. In addition the Benedictine and Cistercian nuns had twenty—three mainly small priories between them. At the dissolution there must have been well over a thousand monks, friars and nuns in the county, that is around a ninth of all those in England at the time. So it may not be inappropriate to regard the Yorkshire religious as a microcosm of the whole nation and see their reaction to the abolition of monasticism as more typical of the religious in general than has previously been allowed.[2]

In the north as in the south of England the Carthusians gave the most unequivocal witness of the importance both for them and for the church in general of the continuation of the monastic life. Only six monks besides the prior remained in the Hull Charterhouse when Ralph Malevory surrendered it to the crown in December 1539. One monk, Robert Fuyster, perhaps influenced by the uncertainties of the previous months, had already obtained a transfer to Mount Grace. Of the seven still in Hull in 1539 three succeeded in persevering as Carthusians. William Remington, who received a gold angel and a bequest of books in the will of the last prior, died at the Perth Charterhouse, his name being entered in the obit list of 1560. Although little evidence survives about his career after his departure from Hull, John Bennet eventually made his way to the Charterhouse of Roermond where he died in 1580. Having served for some years as a curate at Grafton in Lincolnshire, Thomas Synderton joined the re—founded Charterhouse of Sheen and then, after Elizabeth's accession, moved with the community to Bruges: at his death in 1580 he had lived fifty years 'laudabiliter' in the order.[3]

Mount Grace furnished an even more impressive testimony to its commitment to monasticism. When royal commissioners were visiting monasteries in 1536 to extract from the monks individually a recognition of the royal supremacy the prior, John Wilson, with several of his brethren, proved very reluctant to comply. Richard Marshall fled into Scotland to avoid taking the oath. Robert Fuyster from Hull, Geoffrey Hodgeson and Thomas Leighton intitally refused to swear, though they eventually conformed. John Wilson together with Robert Fletcher, John Saunderson, Leonard Hall and Robert Marshall all rejoined the Sheen Charterhouse. Wilson, Marshall and Fletcher died there in Mary's reign, but Saunderson and Hall both went into exile in Bruges after the restoration of Protestantism, Hall living on in the Bruges Charterhouse till 1575. Roger Thomson, only a novice at Mount Grace in 1538, became vicar of Ampleforth after the dissolution but for him, also, the call of the religious life triumphed in the end. Deprived of his Yorkshire benefice for refusing the royal supremacy, in 1561 he appeared on a list of obdurate Yorkshire recusants as 'late a superstitious monk of Mount Grace and unlearned'. Some time after this he took refuge on the continent and rose to be first vicar and then in 1581 prior of Sheen Anglorum where he died in October 1582. Perhaps William Bee, who never lived to see the refoundation of Sheen, gave the most eloquent affirmation of the sense of community clearly shared by all these monks. After his expulsion from the priory he had moved north, and when he came to make his will on 27 March 1551 he referred to himself rather touchingly as 'clerk and some time a professed brother of the monastery of Mount Grace, and now abiding at Newcastle upon Tyne.' He had kept in contact with a considerable number of his brethren. Leonard Hall seems to have been his companion in Newcastle since Bee asked him to make a dirige and communion with note for him on the day of his burial. He bestowed upon Robert Marshall a black tippet lined with worsted and a hood and four and three quarter yards of tawney worsted to use as he had previously explained. Hall also received his cloak, his tawney tippet and all his books at Newcastle and Wakfield while he bequeathed to 'the father of Mount Grace, presumably the last prior, John Wilson, two pairs of silver spectacles and 12d to every one of my professed brethren of Mount Grace'. His total goods amounted to a mere £7 2s.10d.[4]

Although none of the other orders once established in the county showed as much eagerness to persist in the religious life as the Carthusians some from far less austere houses also nourished hopes that their communities might again be restored. A small group of Benedictines from Monk Bretton Priory perhaps came nearest for a time to re–creating some sort of community existence in Yorkshire. After he had surrendered the monastery in November 1538 the last prior, William Browne, acquired a house in Worsborough where he lived with Thomas Frobisher, his sub–prior, and two other former Monk Bretton monks. Thomas Wilkinson and Richard Hinchcliff. Between them these four priests re–assembled a hundred and fifty books from their former monastic library. Frobisher died early in 1557 and in June in the same year Browne drew up his will. In addition to providing 12d. 'to every one of my brethren being at my burial' he gave 40s. each to seven of his former colleagues, Sir Robert Scoley, Sir John Pickard, Sir Thomas Wilkinson, Sir William White, Sir Richard Hinchcliff, Sir John Henryson and Sir William Adcoke, and forgave the debts of two more, Sir William Lund and Sir Thomas Wilson. He lastly ordained that if it should ever come to pass 'by any manner of means that the late dissolved monastery of Monk Bretton' should be 'erected and inhabited with religious persons' that his executors should then immediately restore his house and two closes in Worsborough, all his vestments, books and household utensils. One of Browne's supervisors, Robert Scoley, outlined the rest of this little band of former Monk Bretton monks. Still in receipt of his pension he surfaced, aged seventy–eight, in an ecclesiastical court case of 1575 when he revealed that he had been a member of the community for twenty years before the dissolution. In the will, which he made as vicar of Brodsworth on 10 January 1579, he bequeathed all his books, very probably the remnants of Monk Bretton library, to his godson, Robert Helm, on condition that he continued in his resolution to become a priest.[5]

Some Cistercians from Kirkstall, like the Monk Bretton Benedictines, also went to considerable lengths to try to protect their library. On his deathbed in August 1558 Edward Heptonstall alias Pomfret, then a priest in Leeds, gave the parish church a vestment of silver and damask and a book called *Sermones Discipuli* before consigning to the schoolboy son of John Heptonstall all the books in a chest at the foot of his bed and all other books in his custody which had once belonged to Kirkstall Abbey with the proviso that his executors should look after the books carefully and return them to the abbey 'if it go up in their times'. Several former Kirkstall monks had in fact congregated in the Leeds area. Richard Elles, 'priest of Leeds', remembered another Kirkstall monk, Sir Anthony Jackson, of Horsforth, chaplain, when he died in 1550, leaving him his best gown, his horse, a vestment and an altar cloth. In a tithe case brought by the vicar of Leeds in 1545 Jackson, then aged fifty, gave evidence that he had been a monk of Kirkstall for thirty–one years, and had acted as bursar for ten or twelve years before the abbey's surrender. He was the godfather of yet another former member of the house, Thomas Pepper of Adel, who appointed Jackson one of his supervisors when he died in 1553 and gave him and his mother jointly a lease of a parcel of land in Cubrig. In his turn Pepper had kept in touch with two other members of the Kirkstall community, Leonard Wynderer to whom he left a jacket and William Lupton who received bedding and a gown. Since most monasteries seem to have recruited their members from a fairly restricted area in the vicinity of the house it is not surprising that for one or even two decades after the dissolution former monks should have been maintaining links with each other but certainly at Monk Breton and probably at Kirkstall these associations seem to have been more than merely casual. At least some of the former members of the community seem to have been consciously looking forward to a time when their abbeys might be reinstated.[6]

At Bolton Abbey, also, one monk died anticipating the return of monasticism in Yorkshire. After the secularisation of his house George Richmond may have served as a curate in Skipton since the vicar there owed him wages at the time of his death. Referring to himself as a priest and late canon of Bolton when he made his will in November 1554, he requested burial in the parish church of Long Preston. In addition to giving a gold ring to another Bolton canon, Sir Thomas Castell, he poignantly bequeathed his chalice and two vestments 'to the monastery of Bolton whensoever it shall please God that it shall be restored'.[7]

For the former monks who survived until Mary came to the throne such forward planning would not have seemed impractical. With the queen at that very time refounding monasteries in the south, only the obstinacy of the proprietors of church lands prevented the reappearance of monasticism in the north. Had one of the new owners of ecclesiastical property shown the same willingness to make restitution of their buildings and at least part of their former endowments, there can be little doubt that priests such as George Richmond, William Browne or Edward Heptonstall would have been more that ready to resume their former lives. Elizabeth's accession must have put an end to all such expectations. On the dissolution of the monasteries newly erected by Mary northerners could no longer retain any realistic hope of a revival of monasticism in Yorkshire. Yet even as Elizabeth with the passage of years strengthened her hold on the crown, one or two former monks still anticipated a Catholic restoration, even if this had now to be through armed rebellion or the aid of a foreign power. In 1568 the Court of High Commission considered a charge against Edward Sandall, once also a monk of Kirkstall, of publicly bragging that he longed for the day when the heretics then in authority would receive their just deserts. Adding insult to injury on another occasion he had rebuked his York hostess, who had commented approvingly on a Protestant sermon, for turning 'with every wind'. The failure of the rebellion of the Earls, when the mass had been temporarily brought back in Durham cathedral, and much later of the Spanish Armada, curbed such open speculation. Nevertheless conservatives in the later sixteenth century still looked to the future. Some years ago the late Professor Wormald drew attention to certain gentlemen sympathetic to the old religion who in the Elizabethan period took particular pains to acquire former monastic libraries. One such was John Nettleton, a Catholic of Hutton Cranswick in the East Riding. In 1581 the vicar of Driffield, Robert Baker, appointed this John Nettleton together with Edward Nettleton of his neighbouring parish of Emswell a trustee of his collection of more than a hundred and fifty medieval books until one or more of Barker's natural kin were of an age to understand them. Barker could possibly have inherited his books for his namesake and predecessor in the vicarage of Driffield who can probably be identified with the last prior of Byland: if this conjecture is correct, then as late as 1581 a cleric was attempting to preserve a part of Byland monastic library.[8]

Whereas, understandably, not much evidence remains concerning attempts to continue a form of monastic life in Yorkshire after the dissolution, the wills of former religious yield a very great deal more information about their concern to maintain some association with their erstwhile brethren. At St Mary's, York, for example, Thomas Ketland who had briefly become vicar of Alne, requested Thomas Clint, a former fellow monk, to say a trental of masses for his soul at his death in 1540, gave 6s.8d. each to two other St Mary's monks, Guy Kelsey and Thomas Burwood, and provided 8d. a piece 'to those that was of our monastery'. His fellow monk, Richard Barwick, when he came to die two years later at his family home in Escrick left 12d. each to those of his 'brethren of the house of religion' who might attend his funeral. Richard Wood, another former member of the house, in 1544 appointed one of his monastic brothers, John Thompton, one of his executors to dispose of the residue of his estate for the health of his soul. In 1555 Thompson, then sixty years old, made a deposition in an ecclesiastical court case over Hornsea Quay, recalling events which had taken place thirty years earlier when Whalley had been abbot of St Mary's.[9]

Former Cistercian monks proved just as diligent as the Benedictines in keeping open contacts with their colleagues in religion. John Pynder alias Malton composed his will in January 1539, no more than a month after the surrender of his house. After presenting Thornton church with a white vestment, a corporax, altar cloths and a mass book, which must surely have come from Rievaulx, he left most of his belongings to a niece and other relations, but paid 10s. to a former member of the community, Roger Watson, to sing a trental of masses for his soul and gave another colleague, Thomas Jackson, a worsted hat in addition to bequeathing to 'every one of my brether late of the monastery of Revalles xiid.' on condition 'that every one of them say or cause to be said iii masses for the health of my soul.' Since he died within weeks of the loss of the abbey Pynder not surprisingly had his former brethren uppermost in mind, but subsequently other former Rievaulx monks chose to recall priests who had participated with them in the opus dei years, even decades, after their common life had come to an end. In 1549 Robert Smith alias Stainthorpe, ordained acolyte from Rievaulx Abbey almost fifty years previously, asked to be buried in Helmsley churchyard, providing 2d. for every house in Rievaulx village and 12d. 'to every one of my brether being of live' and nominated his 'brother', the former Rievaulx monk. Thomas Jackson, one of his executors. Roger Watson, who eventually settled in Farlington in the parish of Sherrif Hutton, in his will in 1555 bequeathed 2d. 'to every of my brethren that was in Ryvall the day of our suppression and be on live' in addition to bestowing small remembrances upon the former prioress of Marrick and her 'sister', Dame Anna, and on Dame Barbara Bromley, once a nun of Basedale. He also revealed that Sir William Bradley, yet another former Rievaulx monk, then incumbent of Whenby, owed him 16s. for the services Watson had performed for him in his parish church. After the surrender of their abbey these former monks, who had secured ecclesiastical employment in the vicinity of Rievaulx, seem to have been operating a sort of self–help scheme.[10]

Less information has emerged concerning the Cistercians from Byland or Fountains, but at least among the group of former Fountains monks who subsequently found employment in Ripon a similar sense of solidarity existed. In 1557 Christopher Jenkinson, who had gone on to serve a chantry for a time in Ripon, mentioned four former Fountains monks in his will, bestowing 10s. a head upon William Donwell and Marmaduke Jenkinson and 6s. 8d. each upon Thomas

Greenwood and Richard Norress. When Thomas Metcalf drew up his will in 1558 he still thought fit to refer to himself as 'late monk of the late dissolved monastery of Byland in the parish of Kilburn' before proceeding to leave his former abbot, Sir Alanbrig, his best spoon.[11]

Members of large and rich monasteries like St Mary's, Fountains and Rievaulx with property throughout the north of England and beyond may well have found it more difficult to stay in contact with their brethren than those of smaller houses for the simple reason that at the dissolution, while they still could, abbots and convents had instituted their own members to benefices appropriated to their monasteries. This, to cite but one example, took a succession of St Mary's monks to the living of Hargham in Norfolk. Consequently if often proved easier for the former inhabitants of more modest houses with less far flung possessions to keep in touch with their colleagues. Three Yorkshire Augustinian priories in particular seem to have retained a sense of community for several decades. Thomas Waredrop, or Wardroper, from Newbrugh sought burial in Coxwold, the village adjacent to his priory, when he made his will in 1546. He bequeathed the church a surplice and two psalters, set aside money for an honest dinner for every priest and parish clerk and his former neighbours within the site of Newbrugh, in addition to giving William Barker a bonnet, William Gray a velvet cap, William Edward two cloth tippets and a pair of wooden beads, William Johnson, whom he also appointed one of his executors, clothes and other goods and 10s. to pray for him, and John Flint a sarcenet tippet, a silver spoon and an angel noble. All these priests had been canons of Newbrugh at the dissolution. When William Johnson died a year later he recalled no less than eight former members of the priory, William Edward, John Flynt, Richard Lolly, Robert Tennand, Richard Dunning, Roland Foster, William Gray and William Barker. At Guisborough, Richard Starre in 1546 witnessed the will of Richard Lasingby, a fellow canon, and ten years later was asked by John Clarkson, another former canon, to sing for his soul in Guisborough church and to dispose of the residue of his library for which he received 2s.6d. a short rachet, his next best kerchief and various service books. When Starre appeared in a tithe case in 1553 he said he was fifty—four years old, he had known the priory since he was twelve and that he had been a canon there from the age of twenty—two. The former prior of Kirkham, John Kildwicke, rather like Prior Browne of Monk Bretton, seems to have taken the initiative in maintaining contact with certain members of his community, when he died in 1552 leaving gold angels to five former canons, James Parkinson, Williams Beckfield, Edmund Newton, Anthony Watson and Richard Morwinge, Parkinson also being given a short gown for witnessing the will.[12]

This sort of communal feeling might have been anticipated from houses whose members had taken vows of stability, but even among the peripatetic friars evidence of group solidarity exists. By the sixteenth century the membership of Yorkshire convents had become less mobile than in the past and it may be this period have been possible for some friars to have remained in one house throughout their lives, even though others certainly spent some years at one of the two universities before moving back to the north. Irrespective of whether they had been largely based in Yorkshire or had lived in several southern convents, some friars quite clearly identified themselves with one northern friary. This was particularly the case with William Vavasour. A junior member of the Vavasour family of Copmanthorpe, a village a few miles outside York, he was ordained from the York convent acolyte and subdeacon in 1484 and deacon in 1487. He moved from the city first to the Franciscan convent at Stamford where he became priest in 1488 and then to Oxford where he incepted as doctor of

Divinity in 1500. Although he later rose to be warden of the Oxford convent he seems always to have placed the north first among his priorities, and eventually returned as warden of the friary in York. After the dissolution he stayed on in the city in the parish of St Mary, Bishophill Junior where he asked to be buried in 1544. In addition to commissioning a trental of masses for his soul in St Mary's church he left 10s. to Thomas Johnson, a former member of his convent, in return for prayers while another York Franciscan, Robert More, received the substantial sum of £9.6s.8d. to celebrate for two years at St Peter's altar where Vavasour wished his body to be buried. He named a third member of the convent, Ralph Clayton, as one of his executors to whom he bequeathed the residue of his very impressive library of more than eight score printed and manuscript books.[13]

A similar sense of local allegiance can be discerned among the York Austin friars. George Bellerby, who may always have served in York after the surrender of his friary obtained the rectory of the very poor York church of St Wilfrid which he held for two years from 1544. When he composed his will in 1546 after bestowing a corporax of cloth of gold and two portases upon his parish church he left virtually all his meagre goods, valued at only 49s.9d. to his two natural brothers John and Thomas Bellergy, but called upon a former member of his York friary, Peter Glenton, to witness his will.[14]

Of much more social consequence than Bellergy was Brian Godson, prior of the York Dominicans in 1538. He, too, had been ordained as subdeacon, deacon and priest in York in 1505 and 1506 but, unlike Bellerby, had studied at a university, in his case Oxford. After the dissolution of his house he acquired a chantry in St Mary, Bishophill Junior. He may have orginated from Newton on Ouse just outside York where he asked to be buried and where his brother was still living in 1541. He included among his bequests a silver spoon for Dame Isabel Warde, late prioress of Clementhorpe nunnery, and divided a suit of purple vestments lined with silk between the former York Dominican, William Bradfurth, and Edward Smythe, previously canon of St Andrew's, York. While all these friars took some pains to retain links with their former brethren, none, to judge from their wills, showed the same devotion to their former way of life as Robert Hill, the last prior of the Beverley Dominicans. Made acolyte in York in 1513, deacon in 1516 and priest in 1517 he may never have left the Beverley convent. After the surrender of his house he found employment in the town as a chantry priest in the chapel of Trinity Maisondieu, reported as being fifty years old in 1548, of honest conversation and learned. On his death bed in 1558 he requested burial within St Mary's, Beverley, for which privilege he gave the church 20s. and two of his best vestments. In addition to a considerable bequest of £5 to the Beverley poor, bedding to the Trinity maisondieu and quarters of coal to all the bedehouses in the town, he made provision for 40s. to be delivered to Friar Richard Hargrave of the newly restored Black Friars convent in St Bartholomew's in London to dispose 'for the use of the religion for the health of my soul' with a further 20s. to Friar Richard on the understanding that the prior and convent would offer an obit and trental of masses for his salvation. He remembered several priests in his will including Thomas Bradfurth, then parish priest of Walkington, who had an old angel to say a trental and who may well have been the former Dominican from York.[15]

Several other former religious besides Brian Godson showed concern for dispossessed nuns when they came to die. Although there were twenty-three nunneries in the county at the time of the dissolution there had never been remotely as many female religious as male, and by the early sixteenth century most houses only had the resources to support about half a dozen nuns. Female monasticism might, therefore, have been expected to have been at a low ebb in the diocese but members of several houses still exhibited signs of community feeling after their ejection. In contrast with the monks and friars who could still serve as secular priests, former nuns, in most cases provided with grossly inadequate pensions, had no role at all in the post Reformation church. Understandably, despite the Henrician prohibition, some nuns married, some, though not all, probably from economic necessity. Yet others among the two hundred and fifty or so Yorkshire nuns still tried to retain a vestige of their former way of life. In May 1541 Katherine Nandike, the former prioress, remembered all eight of the sisters who had been professed with her at Wykeham with gifts of 6s.8d. with a pounced mislin basin and 5s. in gold to Mistress Isabel Percy, and furniture, bedding and £3.6s.8d. for her god daughter and former nun, Katherine Gale. Katherine Foster, until 1536 prioress of Sinningthwaite, who had retired to Tadcaster, made one of her sisters, Alice Shefield, one of her executors in addition to giving her a gown. In 1546 Alice Thomlinson of Keyingham, once a member of the Nunkeeling community, bestowed a sanguine gown, bedding and linen upon Joan Bowman, and a violet gown and other clothes upon Dorothy Wilberfoss, who had both been with her in the convent. Margery Conyers, once a nun of Marrick, singled out for particular attention in 1547 two of her sisters in religion, Jane and Elizabeth. Dame Joan Harkey mentioned four other erstwhile members of the Ellerton convent in her will, Dame Alice Thomson, Dame Cecily Swale, Dame Agnes Aslaby and Dame Elizabeth Parker, though she only had the means to give them 12d. a piece. In 1551 Elizabeth Lord made bequests of 6s.8d. each to her former sisters at Wilberfoss Priory, Agnes Barton, Alice Thornton, Joan Andrew and Margery Brown. Elizabeth Thorne, once a nun of Swine, lived in Hull with another sister from the same convent, Elizabeth Patricke, leaving her the house and appointing her as her executor on her death in 1557. The last prioress of Kirklees, Joan Kippax, may have retired in the company of four of her nuns to Mirfield, where she died in 1562. As late as 1566 Christiana Burgh, the last prioress of Nunkeeling, still kept in contact with two of her former sisters in religion, Isabel Beyn and Alice Sidgewick.[16]

The testimentary evidence shows that many Yorkshire religious looked back with nostalgia to their community way of life. It also demonstrates that some of the former nuns, some of the former monks and a few of the former friars lived together with other members of their order after the dissolution. Perhaps these arrangements were purely domestic. The last surviving monk of the restored Westminster Abbey, when questioned at the turn of the sixteenth century, recalled far more about the monks' diet than he did concerning their performance of the divine office, retailing to Father Baker 'that they rose at midnight, that they did eat flesh, that at refection in the refectory they sat face to face on both sides the table being four to every mess as they do in the Inns of Court; that at supper they had so in common between every four, first a dish of cold slice powdered beef, and next after a shoulder of mutton, roasted ...'. But if a monk of the time could take as read a spiritual discipline which, even if in an attenuated form, he must have been observing, so it is perhaps not straining credulity too far to suggest that, despite the silence of the sources, at least some of these Yorkshire households after the dissolution may also have been maintaining some sort of corporate spiritual life. The Yorkshire Carthusians apart, who chose exile in order to continue in their profession, none of the other Yorkshire religious led particularly heroic lives after the Reformation, but, from the odd glimpses which their wills afford, their witness to the vitality of late medieval monasticism in the north of England may have been a little less feeble than Dom David Knowles supposed.[17]

NOTES

1. D. Knowles, *The Religious Orders in England*, III, (Cambridge, 1961), p 440.

2. G.W.O. Woodward, *The Dissolution of the Monasteries*, (London, 1966), p 139.

3. C.B. Rowntree, 'Studies in Carthusian History in later Medieval England', York D.Phil thesis 1981, pp 1280, 529, 536, 491; B[orthwick] I[nstitute], York Prob Reg 13 pt. II f 720v (Malevory); G.A.J. Hodgett, *The State of the Ex–Religious... in the Diocese of Norwich, 1547–1574*. Lincoln Record Society, LIII, 1959, p 94.

4. *Letters and Papers of Henry VIII*, VIII, no. 1038; *L & P Hen VIII*, XI, no. 75; *L & P Hen VIII*, XIV, pt. II nos.749, 750; *L & P Hen VIII*, XV no. 125; *L & P Hen VIII*, XXI, pt. I, no. 1084; Rowntree thesis, pp 192, 486, 490, 510, 521, 537; J. Raine, ed., *Wills and Inventories*, I, Surtees Society II, 1835, pp 134–6 (Bee).

5. B I Prob Reg 15 pt. III ff 151r–152r (Browne); Archbp Reg 31 ff 80v–81r (Scoley).

6. B I Prob Reg 15 pt. III f 59v (Heptonstall); Prob Reg II pt. II f 607v (Elles); CP G 866/2; Archbp Reg 29 ff 107v–108v (Pepper).

7. B I Prob Reg 14 ff 118r–119r (Castell).

8. J.C.H. Aveling, *Catholic Recusancy in the City of York, 1558–1791*, Catholic Record Society, 1970, pp 166–7; 168; F. Wormald and C.E. Wright, *The English Library before 1700*, (London, 1958), pp 157–8; H. Aveling, *Post Reformation Catholicism in East Yorkshire*, East Yorkshire Local History Society, 1960, p 31; C. Cross, 'A Medieval Yorkshire Library', *Northern History*, forthcoming.

9. B I Archbp Reg 29 ff 73v–74r (Ketland); Prob Reg II f 640r (Barwike);Y[ork] M[inster] L[ibrary] D & C Prob Reg 3 f 3r (Wood); B I CP H 5168.

10. B I Prob Reg II pt. I f 347v (Pynder); Archbp Reg 25 f 110v; Prob Reg 13 py. II ff 578v–579r (Smyth); Prob Reg 14 ff 179v–180v (Watson).

11. B I Prob Reg 15 pt. III f 55v (Jenkinson); Prob Reg 15 pt. II f 334v (Metcalf).

12. B I Prob Reg 13 pt. I f 138v (Wardrop); Prob Reg 13 pt. I f 312v (Johson); Prob Reg 13 pt. I f 190v (Lasynby); Prob Reg 13 pt. II ff 846r–v (Kyllwycke); Prob Reg 15 pt. I ff 242v–243r (Clarkson); J.S. Purvis, ed., *Select XVI Century Causes in Tithe*, Yorkshire Archaeological Society, Record Series CXIV, 1949, p 41.

13. V I Archbp Reg 28 ff 390r, 394r, 409r; D & C Original Wills 1544/5 (Vavasour); Y M L D & C Prob Reg 5 ff 6r–7r (Vavasour); A.B. Emden, *A Biographical Dictionary of the University of Oxford to 150*, (Oxford, 1959), III, p 1843.

14. B I Archbp Reg 26 ff 104v, 124r, 125r; Archbp Reg 29 f 99v; Chancery Wils 1547 (Bellerby).

15. Y M L D & C Prob Reg 2 ff 196v, 198v–199r (Godson); B I Archbp Reg 26 f 124r; Archbp Reg 27 ff 174r, 177v; Prob Reg 15 pt. III ff 103v–104r (Hill); A.B. Emden, *A Biographical Register of the University of Oxford, 1501–1540*, (Oxford, 1974), p 236; ed., W. Page, *The Certificates of the Commissioners appointed to survey the Chantries in the County of York*, Surtees Society XCII, 1895, p 536.

16. B I Prob Reg II pt. II ff 559v–560v (Nandike); f 715v (Foster); Prob Reg 13 pt. I ff 270r–v (Thomlinson); ff 335v–336r (Conyers); Prob Reg 13 pt. II ff 705r–v (Lord); Prob Reg 15 pt. I f 357v (Thorne); Leeds Record Office RD/AP1/43/19; ed., J. Raine *Richmond Wills*, Surtees Society

XXVI, 1853, pp 143–4 (Harkey); Leeds R O RD/AP1/8/140; Raine, *Richmond Wills*, pp 191–193 (Burghe); S.J. Chadwick, 'Kirklees Priory', *Yorkshire Archaelogical Journal*, XVI, 1902, p 322 (Kippax).

17.   Knowles, *Religious Orders*, III. p 431.

THE FATE OF MONASTIC CHURCHES IN CUMBRIA : A CONSIDERATION OF THE POSITION AT LAW

John Horden

On the 5th of April, 1537, Roger Pyle, Abbot of Furness, signed a document, in the present of the Earl of Sussex, which ostensibly transferred the abbey and all its possessions, by way of surrender, to the king.[1] The surface language of this deed betokens the penitent, the spontaneous, above all, the voluntary as motivating its execution. Most historians, however, elicit from it, and from what is known about the circumstances which marked its production, artificiality, calculation and the sense of a fear on his part, that if the document had not been executed, then its signatory would have been, instead. Pyle had been summoned peremptorily from his abbey across the Sands (of Morecambe Bay) to attend the King's commissioners at Whalley. The difficult journey of almost seventy miles length had been accomplished in little over a day. He was immediately subjected to interrogation upon his arrival in the early evening, after having followed a route which had passed by the priory of Cartmel, outside which the corpses of some of its erstwhile occupants were hanging; as, outside the gates of his own House, was the body of John Paslew, the late abbot of Whalley, as that destination was reached. Whether or not these incidents were part of a deliberately engineered piece of psychological warfare waged by the commissioners or not, it does not require any very strained construction of the historical evidence to assume a growing unease, which may have developed into unrelieved terror, as the beleaguered abbot assessed his situation. The commissioners were not slow to indicate to him their awareness of things said and transacted in the abbey over the preceding few months, the essential accuracy of which must have confirmed beyond doubt that there was an informer in the midst of the community, as indeed there was. Even disregarding the press of national events, the abbey had experienced a good deal of internal turmoil and dissension over the decade before the Whalley episode.[2]

The abbot soon found himself accepting the truth of allegations of 'misorder and evil lives, both unto God and our prince, of the bretheren of the said monastery', if he did not, indeed, actually take the initiative in confessing them. In any event, a supposed confession was woven into the fabric of the deed of surrender (on the assumption, that is, that it was not simply interpolated into a copy of a document already brought in to being) and confirmed all that the suppressors of the already doomed smaller houses had been claiming of *them*, in terms of sinful conduct and incompetent management. The surrender itself was absolute in terms and expressed in the formulary language of a fairly normal conveyance (not surprisingly, since, almost certainly, it was drafted by Sir Anthony Fitzherbert, one of the commissioners and, of course, one of the leading lawyers of his day) though, having said that, there is also a simplicity and informality about some of the phrases which suggest that it was not a carefully constructed and long—preconceived document. Roger Pyle had, however, been a comtemporary of Cromwell's at the Inns of Court, and may, thus, have been capable of drafting the document himself. In any event, the words used ought not simply to be dismissed as so much legal verbiage. If seen merely as common—place legal formulary, it is worth noting that deviation from the norm is detectable; and the fact that legal regularity was being essayed, though falteringly, has its own historical significance. Abbot Pyle gave up, 'all such interest and title as I have had, have, or may have, of and in the said monastery

of Furness, &c., and in the lands, rents, possessions, revenues, services, &c., both
spiritual and temporal.... belonging or in any way appertaining to the said
monastery and every part and parcel thereof, in as large and ample manner and
form as every I had or ought to have had, of and in the same or any part or
parcel thereof by any manner of means, title, interest, gift, grant, or otherwise,
permitting and binding myself by these presents that from henceforth, I shall at
all times and in all places, whensoever I shall be called upon, be ready and glad
to confirm, ratify and establish this my deed, purpose, mind and intent, as shall
be desired by the learned council of the King's Highness, which cometh freely of
myself and without any enforcement, in consideration of the evil disposition of
the bretheren of the said monastery, aforesaid.' None of the words used is
supererogatory, from a legal point of view.

There are many aspects of the situation in which the unfortunate Pyle
found himself, and of this document to which his dilemma gave rise, which are of
interest and worth pursuing, but in this paper, there will only be opportunity to
give brief consideration to two of them, namely the legal and the territorial. As
far as the first is concerned, interest will be entered on the legal status of the
document of surrender, and of the legal problems to which it gave rise. In
territorial terms, reflection will be upon how the Abbey of Furness, in particular
its church building, fared in relation to its neighbours within the confines of what
is now the county of Cumbria. As a connection between the two strands, there
will be a brief assessment of whether the different fates, which befell the churches
considered, were in any way resultant from the different position at law of the
houses to which they had belonged.

There can be little doubt that enough was known of the situation at
Furness for the commissioners to proceed by way of attainder against the abbot,[3]
but Sussex was apprehensive about the possibility of obtaining absolutely
conclusive evidence against him, and so, by a simple expedient amounting almost
to genius, as he subsequently reported to the King, 'I, the said earl, devising
with myself, if one way would not serve, how and by what other means, the said
monks might be rid from the said abbey, and consequently how the same might
be at your gracious pleasure.... determined to essay him as of myself, whether he
would be contented to surrender, give and grant, unto your heirs and assigns the
said monastery.' The supposed voluntariness of the surrender has to be judged
against that authoritative (in the circumstances, unimpeachable)
contemporaneous statement; even a lawyer, bound by practice to have virtually
exclusive regard to the deed and its internal construction, is entitled so far to
explore external circumstances as to weigh the effect of coercion or duress on the
validity of an otherwise unexceptionable document. The mid–fifteenth century
may well have been more robust in its attitude to coercion, and the legal doctrine
of 'Duress' less sophisticated than now it is, but it is very doubtful whether a
court of that period seised of a matter involving any deed executed in
circumstances such as have already been described, but without the authority of
the King's commission, would have felt able to ignore the effect of those
circumstances on the validity of that document.

Another matter of significance, in the circumstances of the supposed
surrender, so far as a lawyer is concerned, is the capacity of the parties to the
transaction. In this regard, it is interesting to note that the abbot signed the
document, indeed apparently wrote it in extenso,[4] but this clearly could not be in
his private capacity, because he personally had no interest in the property to be
conferred. On the other hand, he did not purport to convey as agent for the body
corporate, the abbot and brethren of the Abbey of St Mary, Furness.[5] And if

Sussex himself had not taken the point, it seems clear that Fitzherbert had done so, for as soon as the abbot's signature had been procured, three knights were despatched to Furness 'to take into their hands the rule and governance of the said house to the use of your highness, and to see that the monks and servants of the same be kept in due order and nothing to be embezzled.' The abbot's document was being seen less as the definitive and authoritative record of a transaction necessary to provide for the transfer of the abbey, than as a crucial preliminary to a surrender to which the whole Chapter was privy, as Sussex reported to the King, explaining that Fitzherbert, 'liked the same very well, saying, that the thought it was the most convenient way that could be to conduct that monastery to your grace's hands, and that now they may be ousted.' There was no assumption that the deed itself had already done the trick and, indeed, Fitzherbert seems to have put his mind to drawing up a new deed addressed to the monks as a body,[6] so that Sussex could present it to them for signature within a few days. Interestingly, Ayliffe,[7] writing at the beginning of the eighteenth century would not have seen any great difficulty in the abbot alone transferring at least the greater part of the abbey's property to another before the Statute of Marlebridge, because 'the property of the goods and estate of the abbey was in the abbot during his life, but after his death, it was then in the House; and this was the reason, that, at common law, if such goods were taken away in the abbot's life–time, his successors could not have an action of trespass: for by the taking, the property was divested. But this was remedied' (by the statute). Thereafter, it would seem, the abbot's capacity to alienate would have been considerably circumscribed. Ayliffe gives further indication of this.[8] 'The abbot, or chief head of abbies, being together with the monks of the House, a convent, made a corporation; and was not by the common law, further charged with his predecessor's acts, than for such things as were for the use of the House, or such acts as were done under the Common Seal thereof .... But the abbot was only capable of taking a feoffment; for it could not be made to him and his convent: since they were reckoned dead persons in law.'

On Monday, April 9th., the commissioners, together with the abbot, arrived at Furness, read the prepared document to the monks in the chapter–house and secured their acceptance of the terms contained in the deed. The latter ratified the abbot's surrender unconditionally, under the convent seal, by means of Fitzherbert's new formal deed—in fact, of the thirty three bretheren, thirty signed, including the abbot and the prior, two were in prison at Lancaster, and only one seems to have demurred—through in so doing they were acceding to the transfer of property variously estimated[9] to have been worth £800 to £1200 per annum, free of charge, and accepted virtually nothing in return, for they were not granted pensions. The majority of them were given 40s, and three 'being sick and impotent' were given £3. It is hardly surprising that, within months, the monks were complaining that they had submitted only be reason of 'a politic compulsion'. Later consideration will be given in this paper to the fate which befell the abbey church, but, for the time being, it is necessary to pursue the various legal problems to which the abbot's supposed voluntary surrender, and its ratification by the plenary chapter, give rise.

The pattern once established by the Furness procedure, commissioners throughout the whole country, following an announcement made by Cromwell that dissolution of monastic houses ought only to occur with the full consent of the inmates arrived at by the exercise of their free wills, took the surrender of 158 monasteries, over the following three years. This compares with the 215 smaller houses and 103 nunneries suppressed under the Act of 1536, and the 12 monasteries suppressed between 1537 and 1539, as a result of attainder.[10]

Clearly, had the expedient of voluntary surrender not been hit upon, something like 170 houses would necessarily have had to be dissolved by attainder, or, alternatively, the Act for the Dissolution of the Greater Monasteries would have had to be promulgated in 1537 instead of 1539, and its content would have been materially different from that which it actually contained.

The Act of 1539 is, indeed, an interesting piece of rationalization. It states in the preamble (which lawyers regard as a non—operative part of any document, simply being there to establish the situation which gave rise to the need for the enactment, or whatever is in question) that since February 4th of that year, the heads of diverse religious houses had voluntarily surrendered their establishments and other possessions into the hands of the King, of their own free and voluntary minds, good wills and assents, without constraint, coaction, or compulsion of any manner of person or persons. The operative part of the statute provided that 'the King, his heirs and successors for ever shall have, hold, possess and enjoy all that had been surrendered since the mentioned date, and everything of the same nature to be dissolved thereafter'. The retroactive part of the enactment was clearly thought to be necessary; and so it was, because nothing in the statute of 1536 had allowed for the confiscation of the greater monasteries and it was not even certain that the King was entitled to receive in possession the lands and other property surrendered by consent. And the fact that the consents were more notional than real must have been a sensitive point, even for the hard—nosed Cromwell. It made assurance doubly sure to ratify by statutory authority, than which there is now, and arguably was then, no more absolute legal provision, transfers whose actual validity, however effective the legal expression of it, was open to doubt. There is also the narrower legal concern of precisely what interest the heads and the chapters of the religious houses were free to convey, even allowing that they did so in a genuinely voluntary manner.[11] It must be recalled that the precursor of all the induced surrenders had probably been drawn up by none less than Sir Anthony Fitzherbert, the chief judge and lawyer of the age. He seems to have had no qualms that a simple gift of all the possessions of an abbey could be properly effected without special Act of Parliament or any kind of escheat or particular inquisition, and that this could be done by the present members of a religious corporate body.[12] Had the latter the right and the capacity to alienate the whole property of the foundation? The answer to that question would depend on three interdependent legal factors. First, consideration would have to be given to the institution's own governing statutes, the foundation charters and other original and subsequent deeds of grant. As a matter of form, but probably of actual intent, at least anciently, these deeds would, invariably, have been expressed as granting whatever was in issue in perpetuity to the institution; and the abbot and chapter constituted a corporate body, with all that that would imply in respect of perpetual succession, even then. Perhaps even more pertinently, the grants would invariably have been of the fee simple and thus formally expressed as being absolute and in perpetuity. A characteristic final clause would be on the lines of, 'Hanc autum praedictam terram cum omnibus pertinentiis ego et haeredes et successores mei warrantizabimus praefatis monachis contra omnes homines in perpetuum.' Sometimes the absolute and perpetual character of the gift would be expressed in the recital at the beginning of the deed ... 'I have given and conceded in free, unconditional and perpetual alms to God...' as in the case of Cartmel. Secondly, it would have been necessary to look to the general provisions of Canon Law, whole chapters of which were given over to religious houses, their property and governance and the jurisdiction, often visitational, to which they were subject. Finally, one might almost have said, residually, there would have been the secular law, the Common Law as dispensed by the King's

Courts. I have just referred to the Canon Law as one relevant determinant of the legality of the voluntary conveyances, but, in fact, by 1537 this would be something of an anachronism, at least so far as its comprising a discrete and primary source of law is concerned.[13] The reason for this is to be found in the then recent legislation establishing the Royal Supremacy and the break with Rome.

The Act for the Submission of the Clergy and Restraint of Appeals[14,15] had provided for the appointment by the King of a commission of thirty two persons to whom were given power (exercisable only with the Royal Assent[16]) to examine the canons, constitutions, and ordinances, both provincial and synodal, in other words, the existing Canon Law contained in the Corpus Juris Canonici, together with the provincial constitutions. They were given power to abolish those of which they disapproved and to allow to stand those with which they were in general agreement. They were given no power to draw up new canons. It would seem the position at that point was that the canon law was, theoretically, in abeyance; but a saving provision in the Act for the Submission of the Clergy had the effect of preserving in force some of the canons, on the terms specified by the statute.

In fact, however, no action was taken under the Act or, indeed, under a similar Act passed in 1535 (27 Henry VIII, c 15) but in 1543, yet another Act was to be passed (35 Henry VIII, C.16) which conferred new power on the King to appoint thirty two commissioners. On this occasion, they were given power to make new canons.[17] There is no evidence extant that such a commission was ever, in fact, appointed. A new code was prepared by someone unidentified, but apparently working closely with Cromwell, between the passing of the Act and the death of Henry VIII. It was provided by the Act, as by a subsequent one of Edward's reign, also never effectively implemented, that the canons in the code compiled by the commissioners were to be the only ones 'taken, reputed, practised, and put in use for the Ecclesiastical Laws'. In reality, since the commissioners were never actually appointed, such laws were not promulgated. The Act for the Submission of the Clergy had, however, provided that, should the attempt to produce a new code in place of the Canon Law contained in the Corpus and the provincial constitutions be nugatory, then, the canons, constitutions, ordinances and synodals provincial being already made, or which should in future be made, 'which be not contrariant or repugnant to the law, statutes and customs of this realm, nor to the damage or hurt of the King's prerogative' were to continue in force till the commission had done its work. The Act of 1543 made the same provision with the addition of 'other Ecclesiastical Laws or Jurisdictions Spiritual, as be yet accustomed and used here in the Church of England.' The words 'accustomed and used' are of great significance, because they reflect a change in status of the Canon Law, brought about by the adoption of a theory about the Canon Law, which had been development in France by the end of the fourteenth century[18] and given an airing in this country by Henry Standish, provincial of the Greyfriars, in 1518.[19] Its official adoption came in the Act of 1534 which forbade papal dispensations and the payment of Peter's Pence (25 Henry VIII, c.21). The theory in question postulated that 'the realm of England had been, and was, free from subjection to any laws but those devised, made, and ordained within it; and the laws of any foreign prince, potentate, or prelate (e.g. the papal codes) were only laws of the realm if the people had taken them at their free liberty, by their own consent and amongst them, and had bound themselves by long usage and custom to their observance'.[20] (It will doubtless have been noted that this principle fitted very congruently with the 'imperial' notion canvassed by Henry and Cromwell in the early 1530's, when working their way to establishing definitively the Royal Supremacy). In any event, the consequence of the legislation's having been promulgated was to establish that the chapters in the Corpus Juris Canonici which were not contrary to the laws, statutes and customs of the realm, or harmful to the royal prerogative, were to continue as the law of the Church until the new code appears, not because they were the work of the popes, hitherto largely unquestioningly regarded as the Church's sovereign law–givers, but simply because they had been long observed in England and had acquired through this long observance the authority not of written or original statutory law, but of customary law. After 1543, they could be described as customs recognised by statute. Since the tenor of the Act is declaratory and its premises retroactive in character, it would seem that whatever the status of canon law in 1537, it was deemed to have been then customary and effective, subject to the statutory savings, in 1547. Commentators on English ecclesiastical law in the seventeenth and early eighteenth century took it to be the case, in the absence of any definitive pronouncement on the issue, that chapters of the papal codes ceased de jure to be the law, when the phenomena to which they attached de facto ceased to obtain. The civilian lawyer, Ayliffe,[21] writing a century later would seem to establish that the dissolution of the religious houses meant that, thereupon, the appropriate chapters of the Corpus, a considerable section, passed out of the use but, apparently, not before. It would seem, therefore, that at the time Furness was surrendered, so much of the code as was relevant to the greater houses, and not repugnant to the general law of the realm or to the King's prerogative, was still valid as customary law. Which may be no more than simply to confirm that not only was the King free to do, in fact, just as he chose, but also that he could properly claim that ecclesiastical law, the secular law of the land and, in most cases, the visitational jurisdictions and the constitutions of the Houses themselves, all permitted of the surrenders and of his receiving the property thus conveyed. There is one possible flaw in the legal claim, however, consideration of which will lead on to a short assessment of the second issue with which this paper is concerned.

Before the break with Rome, the church courts exercised the Ordinary[22] and the Visitational jurisdiction of the bishops, jurisdictions delegated to judges of those courts in turn from, and, therefore, subject to, the bishops themselves, the archbishops and beyond that, the Pope. These jurisdictions were not destroyed by the anti–clerical legislation; on the contrary, the King was recognised as the ultimate source of jurisdiction, in lieu of the Pope. The jurisdictions were exercisable, inter alia, over ecclesiastical property, real and personal. The assumption of visitational jurisdiction, not its destruction, was one of the key elements in the policy of suppression, indeed, a condition precedent of its effective implementation. The Act of Supremacy of 1534 forbade visitation of exempt English monasteries, that is those subject only to international and not purely indigenous visitations. Professor Scarisbrick[23] has pointed out that this step had the effect of 'nationalising' the English monastic system, thus paving the way for royal, instead of papal visitation to be superimposed upon the existing metropolitical and episcopal visitational jurisdictions.[24] Created Vicegerent of Spirituals,[25] soon after this legislation, Cromwell was able to operate the existing powerful machine, to which he attached the process of ecclesiastical census, as a formidable information gathering exercise, followed by the most draconian of controls permitted by the system—namely suppression.[26] It was the scale of the remedy to perceived wrongs, the extent and thoroughness of the inquisitions by which they were detected, and the innovative national and non–clerical overall base of jurisdiction which made the Cromwellian processes so unique, but the system at large which enabled the work to be done was that already in place as it had been for centuries; and it should not be overlooked that the chief agents by which the system was made to work so effectively were all canon lawyers. They, in the end were better placed than anyone to divine which parts of the system in which they had been trained could be made amenable to the emerging new order, and which could not.

Fundamental to the jurisdictional concept of property in church buildings, as opposed to other ecclesiastical real property, was the notion of consecration.[27] Land (by which is meant the ground surface, all adhering to it, above it to the uttermost heavens, and all below it to the very centre of the earth) is, and was, real property at law. Land, therefore, included all that was permanently affixed to the ground, and especially buildings. Once consecrated, a church building was, and still is taken to be land returned, conveyed, as it were, back to God, the creator of the earth, from whom it had originally derived, in perpetuity. Church buildings were, thus, land, but they differed from other buildings in that their consecration gave them a special status—for consecration was not merely a matter of religious but also of legal significance, because it had the effect of bringing the thing consecrated within the jurisdiction of the Ordinary. Since the promulgation of a constitution of Otho[28] it had been necessary for all cathedral, conventual and parochial churches to be consecrated, those then in existence to be dealt with within two years, and those subsequently to be built to be so treated, automatically. It would be possible thereafter to assume that all churches had been consecrated by reason of the operation of the maxim 'omnia paesumuntur rite esse acta.' Strictly speaking this process should be described, as it anciently was, as one of 'dedication', but since this latter term now has a technical and different meaning in church law, it is necessary to use the generally, though mistakenly, accepted term. Consecration had the effect of setting aside in perpetuity from all common and profane uses, the building dedicated to God and his worship, and of accepting the building thus committed on His behalf. This posed for the lawyer the difficult problem of tenure, for who was the earthly holder of the fee simple? Clearly, God needed a representative or agent for this purpose. At the time when there was only one ecclesia, the bishop was seen as the appropriate person to stand in this stead, not least as he held the cure of souls attached to that ecclesia. As in so much else, once the principle was established, it was transferred by the delegation to those at lower levels of the hierarchy, subject to the residual superintendence of the delegator—hence, the possession of reciprocal rights and duties of the Deans and Abbots and their Chapters, parochial incumbents, and others. The point which requires to be made about consecration, however, is that as a result of the legislation of the early fifteen thirties to which reference has already extensively been made, Henry became Supreme Head of the Church of, and in, England, and Cromwell his Vicar–General (actually exercising the jurisdiction in spiritualities – including that over consecrated buildings – on behalf of the former). The Head of the Church and his senior delegate were at law the representatives of God, charged, inter alia, with protecting what was set aside to be peculiarly His. And even if this specific legal obligation had not existed, a case could be made that the confiscation of the churches was ultra vires the King (or, the King in Parliament) since he held them only in a representative, and not an absolute capacity, as God's principal agent in that behalf. Cromwell, as agent of God's most immediate agent (despite the maxim, 'delegatus non potest delegare' – or, more accurately, in illustration of it) could have no greater power or authority than he from whom his own derived.

The Act in Restraint of Appeals had, in its preamble, declared the realm to be an empire governed by one head and monarch, and that his subjects were subject to two jurisdictions, spiritual and temporal, both subordinate to the King who had 'entire power...to render and yield justice and final determination to all manner of folk....without restraint or provocation to any foreign princes or potentates.' This statute may have thrown off jurisdictional subjection in spiritual matters to Rome, but it "did not represent an acceptance of an Ecclesia Anglicana restored to a primitive independence.[29] It simply affirmed a dependent, not an autonomous, jurisdiction over which the King was now unequivocally claiming, not only for himself but for his predecessors complete ascendancy, save that his powers were to be exercised in conformity with the laws of the Kingdom, the arbiters of which process were Parliament and the royal courts. The Act of Supremacy of 1534, declaratory in form, omitted the reserving clause urged by the clergy, 'so far as the law of Christ allows'. As Sir David Keir[30] put it, 'The Church lay within the uncovenanted mercy of her Supreme Head'. And yet, as Defender of the Faith and Supreme Head of the Church, and not withstanding his penchant for presenting as a matter of the highest principle whatever most conduced to his own convenience, Henry took very seriously the roles which Divine Providence had fixed on him. He was, after all, Supreme Head of Church by divine ordination, not by Act of Parliament. As Elton[31] has expressed it, 'The supremacy was personal, vested in the King by no earthly authority, and exercised by him without reference to any earthly authority'. The personal regulation of his action by Christ in God, as part of the 'jus divinum', Henry would have allowed, no doubt; but to be restricted by 'Christ's laws', which Cromwell would have seen as a term of art for 'papally created Canon Law' was precisely not possible, since Headship of the Church on earth bestowed with it the right to determine and promulgate what the ecclesiastical law should be. It is all the more surprising that as Christ's general — and in the matter of church buildings — specific trustee and representative, chief defender of what was legally and theologically peculiarly God's, he should have countenanced the destruction of any single edifice given over to the worship of God. God alone, not Parliament, and not any foreign potentate, did Henry acknowledge to be over him. The potency of financial need, in conjunction with raw pragmatism as squarers of tender conscience, is starkly revealed by the default of a consecrated monarch in allowing the wholesale destruction of consecrated buildings.

This brings us to a short consideration of the fate of Furness and the other principal religious houses in its region. In fact, Calder was the first of the abbeys in the area to be closed down, in February, 1536, as part of the routine, statutory suppression of the smaller houses. Seaton, Conishead and Cartmel followed in the same year; as a result of attainder, in the case of the latter, which, ironically, should have obtained respite from suppression as a smaller house, after a reassessment of its true income. Armathwaite was suppressed in the same year as Furness; to be followed by Holm Cultram (whose fate will be examined in greater detail later), Wetheral (all the site of which 'with the church, steeple, churchyard and all other lands and possessions' was subsequently granted to the Dean and Chapter of Carlisle) and St Bees (which passed into a number of private hands) in 1538. Lanercost went down in 1539, thought its nave was respited, as having been used by the local parishioners as their place of worship. The church itself was originally expected from the post—dissolution grant to the Dacre family, but this was provision was reversed by an additional grant to that family in the time of Edward VI. In 1777, Nicholson and Burn[32] were writing that, 'the conventual church has been large, and somewhat magnificent. A small part of it is now only used by the parishioners: the rest is in ruins'. Carlisle, and Shap followed in 1540. The latter is an interesting case, in that, as one of the smaller houses, it ought to have gone down at least four years before. It is generally supposed that its usefulness as a hostelry in that remote part of the world saved it.

The first thing to remark, in regard to this brief general survey, is that most of the religious houses in what is now Cumbria were small and poor, with the consequence that they were caught by the terms of the Act of 1536. This exposed them to the statutory dissolution provided by the Act 'for the honour of this realm that the possessions of such small religious houses .... should be used and converted to better uses' to effect which purpose 'the King and his heirs for ever should have and enjoy', inter alia, such monasteries, &c. The statute goes on to include under separate heading, 'all the sites and circuits of every such religious houses and all and singular the manors, granges, meases, lands, tenements &c.&c. churches, chapels'. It would appear, as a matter of construction, that conventual and abbey churches were being regarded first and foremost as monastic buildings, no different from the secular buildings with which they were in physical proximity, and not the same as the parochial church buildings, attached to rectories appropriated by the religious houses, though the latter undoubtedly constituted property of the foundations. I have not been able to identify any single such parish church in the area under consideration which was destroyed, as a consequence of the dissolutions. Indeed, monastic churches which had some sort of parochial use were often preserved wholly or in part, on that account alone, as will shortly be illustrated.

It has already been explained that, no less than the parochial churches conventual ones were, or could as a matter of law be presumed to be, consecrated buildings. From an early time, it was, as it still is, the case that, once consecrated, a church may not be consecrated again; nor can it be deconsecrated, though circumstances may secularize it, de facto. When a church has fallen in to ruin and decay or has been entirely or almost entirely destroyed by fire, or has been profaned, it may be 'reconsecrated', however (though a more accurate description of the process would be that of 'consecration de novo'. In 1634, for example, the ruinous quire of the former Cistercian Abbey of Abbey Dore was reconsecrated on Palm Sunday by the Bishop of St David's, under a commission from the Bishop of Hereford; and in 1637, when Laud was Archbishop of Canterbury, there was brought to his notice the case of a chapel also in the diocese of Hereford, which once belonged to the Priory of St John of Jerusalem and had been from the time of its dissolution desecrated by being applied to secular and profane purposes. It had been used for a stall for cattle and as a hay–loft, yet because the walls were entire, a reconciliation and not a reconsecration was deemed proper.[33] It is difficult to elicit any certain legal attitude to the Dissolution, from these two cases. The apprehended need for reconsecration in the former may be accounted for simply by reference to the extreme of ruination which had beset the quire, but could be explained by reference to the irreligious and profane activities carried on by the inmates of the Abbey before, and justifying its dissolution. There is some suggestion in the writings of seventeenth and eighteenth century jurists that the behaviour of the monks may be viewed as having profaned the buildings which they occupied and used, Ayliffe, e.g. refers to monasteries as 'nurseries of licentious people'.[34] Such a theory extrapolated to all the suppressed religious houses would justify their physical destruction even by the criteria of the old Canon Law, on account of their de facto secularisation by profanation. Against that, the fact that there was no perceived need to 'reconsecrate' the Priory Chapel, despite its ruinous condition, clearly does not allow for any 'blanket coverage' theory of 'secularization through profanity of monastic church buildings' at the time of their suppression and dissolution.

The way in which some abbey churches were saved from destruction is illustrated by the case of Holm Cultram. In 1538, the parishioners petitioned Cromwell to allow the church to remain standing, whatever happened to the other abbey buildings (none of which had, at that time, been destroyed): 'Your orators and beedesmen, beynge eighteen hundred houselyng people ... (beg) ... for the preservation and standynge of the church of Holm Coltrane ... which is not onlye unto us our parish churche, and little enough to receive all us ... but also a great aid, succour and defence for us against our neighbours the Scots'.

In the case of the tower, the respite was of comparatively short duration, though its destruction owed nothing directly to the Dissolution. A Memorandum in the church register[35] tells the story. 'The steeple of the church, being of the height of 19 fathoms, suddenly fell down to the ground, upon the 1st. day of January in the year 1600, about three o'clock in the afternoon, and by the fall thereof brought down a great part of the chancel, both timber, lead, and walls; and after the said fall, the same continued in a very ruinous condition for the space of two years; during which time, there was much lead, wood and stone carried away.' The church was rebuilt in part, and refurbished, but in 1604, when, on 18th. April, 'one Christopher Harden, carrying a live coal and a candle into the roof of the church, to search for an iron chisel which his brother had left there and the wind being exceeding strong and boisterous, it chanced that the coal blew out of his hand into a jackdaw's nest, which was within the roof of the church, and forthwith kindled the same, which set the roof on fire and within less than three hours it consumed and burned both the body of the chancel, and the whole church, except the south side of the low church, which was saved by means of a stone vault'. So much for the monastic church of Holm Cultram.[36]

Furness itself was soon torn down, though not levelled. The roofs and ceilings seem to have attracted the interest of those charged with the demolition. A letter to Cromwell from Robert Southwell, the Receiver of the Court of Augmentations, dated 3rd. July, 1537, indicates the thoroughness with which the task of destroying the building and appropriating its most valuable elements was undertaken. He explains that, 'the leade is all moltene and case in sowys wyth the Kynges marke fyxyde thereto and put in a suer house ac cordynge to his graces commandment, there can be no better leade as sayne the plomers...I humbly thanke yr. lordshippe for teachinge me to melte the Assys wherein we ffounde grett profett we shulde els therein have offendyde the Kynge be Ignorance and not for want of will to serve.' Later, in passing, he mentions ... 'after the Church and stepill being close dissolvede being now in good towardes therein ... Mr. Holcroft has been very diligent here for whiche he was put in only trust to pluck down the church'.[37]

Commentators in the last century generally seem to have assumed that the Priory Church of Cartmel was largely ruinous by 1600; Christopher Haigh and J.C. Dickinson have shown that this was not so.[38] The great problem for the four and twenty men, as their Minute Book reveals, and one which continued well in to the seventeenth century, was the condition of the roofs. Repeated church leys and a very generous benefaction by Mr. Preston, the owner of the Priory estates, eventually allowed the problem to be solved in the 1620's. This paper has been in the nature of a 'bal d'esprit'. It is hoped that it may have done enough to draw attention, once again, to the fact that the actual fate of the monastery churches was in any way commensurate with the ostensible justification for their individual dissolutions. Furness was a 'greater' abbey, and so should not have gone down in 1537, by the tenets of statute or, arguably, by the then operating 'customary' canon law. Its inmates had only peripherally, and without absolute proof, been implicated in the Pilgrimage of Grace; they surrendered their abbey quiescently, but they received no pensions and their great buildings, including the church, were pulled down, almost to the ground in parts, within a very short time. Cartmel, on the other hand, was heavily implicated in the Northern Rising; it had been formally listed for suppression as a smaller foundation but had received, at least temporary, respite as it was reassessed, but it went down, as attainted, notwithstanding which, its church was allowed to remain standing because, unusually, its chancel and choir (and not its nave) had been used as parish church by the local people. In the end, chance, expedience and the residual effects of the old legal orthodoxy seem to have contributed in significant proportions to determining how Cromwell's shrewdly—conceived and remorselessly —executed policy of monastic destruction actually worked out in respect of the specific cases of the great church buildings which had been at their heart.

NOTES

Since this papers was written, there has appeared J.H. Bettey's fascinating study, 'Suppression of the Monasteries of the West Country', Gloucester, 1989. The way in which conventual church buildings in that area were treated follows a pattern as illogical as that which this paper has suggested to obtain in Cumbria.

1. See, T.J. Beck, *Annales Furnesiensis: History and Antiquities of the Abbey of Furness*, (London, 1844), (hereafter, Beck): F.A. Gasquet, *Henry the Eighth and the English Monasteries,* (London, 1906) [hereafter, Gasquet] p 275: J. Youings, The Dissolution of the Monasteries, London, 1971 [hereafter, Youings], p 64, and F. Barnes, *Barrow and District: an illustrated History*, 2nd. Ed., (Barrow, 1960), pp 49–5.
2. Gasquet, op. cit., p 274: Youings, op. cit., p 63.
3. Gasquet op. cit., p 274.
4. Beck, op. cit., p 350.
5. Beck, op. cit., pp 347, 355–367; Youings, op. cit., p 64.
6. Youings, op. cit., p 64.
7. Ayliffe, *Parergon Juris Canonici Anglicani; or a Commentary By Way of Supplement not the Canons and Constitutions of the Church of England, Not only from the Books of the Canon and Civil Law, but likewise from the Statutes and Canon Law of this Realm,* (London, 1726), p 9 [hereafter, Ayliffe].
8. Ayliffe, op. cit., p 12.
9. S.M. Harrison, *The Pilgrimage of Grace in the Lake Countries, 1536–1537*, Royal Historical Society Studies in History Series,(London, 1961); C. Haigh, *The Last Days of the Lancashire Monasteries and the Pilgrimage of Grace,* Chetham Society, 3rd. Series,(Manchester, 1968), p 7; Youings, op. cit., p 64; Gasquet, op. cit., p 277.
10. T.S. Fletcher, *The Reformation in Northern England,* (London, 1925), p 65, quoting Gairdner, *The English Church in the Sixteenth Century,* (London, 1912).
11. Ayliffe, op. cit., p 9.
12. Youings, op. cit., pp 60–63.
13. C. Garbett, (Chairman), *The Canon Law of the Church of England, a Report of the Archbishop's Commission on Canon Law,* (London, 1947), p 45.
14. Garbett, op. cit., p 46.
15. G. Nicholson, '*The Act of Appeals and the English Reformation in Law and Government under the Tudors*', eds.,Cross, Loades and Scarisbrick,

(Cambridge, 1988), pp 19–20.

16.   Ayliffe, op. cit., p 23.

17.   Garbett, op. cit., p 46.

18.   T.A. Lacey, *A Handbook of Church Law*, (London), p 30., and cf. J.V. Ballard, *The Past and Present of Canon Law in the Church of England*, (Standing Orders of the Church of England), pp 3, 5, 13 and also H.S. Box, *The Principles of Canon Law*, (Oxford, 1949).

19.   Garbett, op. cit., p 46.

20.   Garbett, op. cit., p 46.

21.   Ayliffe, op. cit., p 23.

22.   R. Burn, *Ecclesiastical Law* 5th Ed., Vol. III, (London, 1788), p 22.

23.   J.J. Scarisbrick, *Henry VIII*, (London, 1968), p 294, n.1.; p 324, n.2.

24.   See, e.g., Cheney, *Episcopal Visitation of Monasteries in the Thirteenth Century*, (Manchester, 1931).

25.   G.H. Cook, *Letters to Cromwell and others on the Suppression of the Monasteries*, (London, 1965).

26.   R. Burn, op. cit., Vol. II, pp 487–491.

27.   A. Phillips (Ed.), *Ecclesiastical Law,* General Synod Edition, (London, 1975), pp 1054–5.

28.   Phillips, op. cit., p 1055, and see, F.W. Muncey, *A History of the Consecration of Churches and Churchyards*, (Cambridge, 1930).

29.   D.L. Keir, *The Constitutional History of Modern Britain, 1485–1951*, 5th. Ed., (London, 1953).

30.   Keir, op. cit., p.

31.   G.R. Elton, *The Tutor Constitution: Documents and Commentary*, (Cambridge, 1972), p 333.

32.   J. Nicolson and R. Burn, *The History and Antiquities of the Counties of Westmorland and Cumberland*, Vol. I., (London, 1777), p 179.

33.   F.W. Muncey, op. cit., p 96., and see, also, G. Kightly, *A. Traveller's Guide to Places of Worship*, (London, 1986), p 8.

34.   Ayliffe, op. cit., p 8.

35.   Nicolson and Burn, op. cit., p 179.

36.   Grainger and Collingwood, *Register and Records of Holm Cultram*, C. & W.A.A.S., Rec. Ser..Vol. VII, (Kendal, 1929), pp 156–9.

37.   Beck, op. cit., p 350. And for a good, well–illustrated history of the buildings of Furness before the Dissolution, see W.H. St John Hope, *The Abbey of St Mary in Furness, Lancashire*, C. & W.A.A.S., Vol. 16. (1900) pp 221–303.

38.   J.C. Dickinson, *This Land of Cartmel*, 1981; C. Huigh, *The Last Days of the Lancashire Monasteries and the Pilgrimes of Grace*, Anethem Society, 3rd. Series, 7, (Manchester, 1969).

WOMEN OF THE 'ENGLISH CATHOLIC COMMUNITY' : NUNS AND PUPILS AT THE BAR CONVENT, YORK, 1680–1790

Susan O'Brien

In 1759 fourteen–year–old Susannah and May Caley, twin daughters of William and Elizabeth Caley of Grimoldby Grange, Lincolnshire, were sent to the Bar Convent boarding–school at Micklegate, York. At intervals over the next fifteen years each of their seven sisters attended the school. By the time the younger girls reached school age, the Bar must have seemed an inevitable part of their destiny, its routines and requirements well–known to all the family. Their aunt, Mary Caley, had gone before them in 1718 and by the end of the century family loyalty and tradition meant that four more Caley girls and a number of their cousins from other landowning families in Holderness and Lincolnshire were at the school. Most girls' boarding–schools came and went with rapidity in the eighteenth century, but the Bar had a continuous and stable tradition from its foundation in 1686 through the eighteenth and nineteenth centuries.[1] Its longevity and stability derived from the fact that it was run by a religious community supported by the élite of the Catholic community. This paper will try to show that the school and the life of the religious community were inseparable aspects of the Bar Convent in the eighteenth century, and that both played a part in the continuing formation of the English Catholic community.[2]

I

From the time of Elizabethan Church settlement and throughout the seventeenth century, women played crucial roles in the maintenance of English Catholicism, and contemporaries were well aware that this was so. Once Roman Catholicism had been proscribed, its adherents were forced to practise their faith privately in the home instead of in public buildings. The faith had to be taught to children by parents and to servants by their mistresses and masters. If the sacraments were to be available young men had to be sufficiently inspirited to wish to become priests, at best an uncomfortable and unprofitable occupation. Women were essential to all this.[3] Moreover, when male members of the Catholic élite felt forced to apostasise to save family lands from financial penalties, women could often avoid being even nominally 'protestantised'.[4] Although it has been demonstrated conclusively that by the eighteenth–century Catholics were — relatively speaking — tolerated, this did not mean that they could openly flaunt their religion.[5] Moreover, before repeal of the penal code in the 1790s they had few institutional props, and the Catholic gentry was correct in believing that the continuing loyalty and piety of their class was vital to English Catholicism.[6] The Bar Convent's part within this culture was the spiritual and devotional training of young women who would, in their turn, ensure the survival of Catholicism in England.

The nuns of the Institute of the Blessed Virgin Mary, whose convent the Bar was, were particularly well matched to this task.[7] Founded on the continent, at St Omer in 1609, the Institute had strong Yorkshire connections. Not only was its founder, Mary Ward, from the Ripon area, but among her first seven companions were her own sister and cousin and at least two others who were related to each other and, more distantly, to her.[8] Throughout the seventeenth century many of the Institute's senior members came from a group of kith and kin Yorkshire gentrywomen. This was one reason why its leaders were

approached in the 1660s by a group of northern gentry, led by Sir Thomas
Gascoigne of Barnbow Hall, and asked to undertake the risk of opening a convent
and school in Yorkshire. The presence of a convent in York can be partly
understood in terms of the Institute's provenance, but for any religious order to
have a convent in England at all in this period, requires further explanation.
Mary Ward had modelled her Institute on the Society of Jesus, taking the Jesuit
Constitutions as its basis.[9] Just as Ignatius had broken with the traditions of the
religious life for men, so Mary Ward, by taking the Jesuit Constitutions, insisting
on the same degree of mobility and flexibility for women, *and* female leadership
under a Chief Superior, had challenged the ecclesiastical and social norms for
women. Her nuns, who were nick–named 'Jesuitesses' and 'galloping girls' by
their critics, were not bound by cloister, the rule of the choir, or traditional
religious habit. The aim of the Institute, apart from the personal sanctification
of its members, was to 'promote the greater glory of God and, *in any place*,
further the propagation of our Holy Mother, the Catholic Church'.[10] In keeping
with her evangelical and reformation spirit, Mary Ward's particular concern was
for England and she committed the Institute to undertake missionary activity
there.[11]

   As founder and first Chief Superior, Mary Ward directed the Institute
herself between 1609 and 1645. She saw it as making a special contribution to the
life of the Church through the mental and spiritual development of women, and
she recognised the importance of a home–centred reformation in non–Catholic
countries. Her nuns were prepared for a life as teachers, catechisers and spiritual
directors. Where necessary the novices received a higher education and were
encouraged by the example of Mary Ward to sustain their intellectual
development beyond their first training. Once professed they taught in schools
for girls of all social ranks and gave direction to women in their homes. During
Mary Ward's lifetime the Institute's approach to teaching was professional and
the range of subjects taught in their élite schools included Latin, Greek, modern
European languages, mathematics and astronomy.[12] Far from being deterred by
these high expectations, young women were attracted to join Mary Ward and by
1631 some 300 women had entered the Institute, including many from England.[13]
Between them they ran houses and schools in seven countries where they were
known as the English Ladies. Such success was short–lived. A concerted
opposition to these 'Jesuitesses' was organised by powerful laymen and clerics,
including English Jesuits, and in 1631 Pope Urban VIII was persuaded to issue a
Bull of Suppression of the Institute. The Institute was disbanded but through
the persistence of Mary Ward, who had the personal support of Pope Urban, it
was re–formed anew on a more modest scale. John Bossy has described the
rejection of Mary Ward's Institute by English Catholics as a failure of nerve, a
desire to play safe rather than to push on by using the Institute as a key
instrument of expansion and reformation.[14] The spokesmen for English
Catholicism in the 1620s were not prepared to share the initiative for the English
mission with an organisation of women, did so only on a small scale, at its own
risk and through the support of individual Catholic gentry.

   From 1615 to 1650 some members undertook missionary work in England.
Mary Ward herself made missions to England on several occasions and returned
permanently in 1639.[15] In 1669, nearly twenty–five years after Mary Ward's
death one of her last companions, Frances Bedingfield, came to England from
Germany and established a school at Hammersmith. A few years later another
handful of sisters opened a school at Dolebank near York, but in 1679 at the time
of the Popish Plot the existence of the school and convent was exposed and
several nuns and their supporters imprisoned. Members of the Institute hung on

in England and the accession of James II in 1685 provided an opening which was seized by Frances Bedingfield. In 1686 she used some money endowed by Sir Thomas Gascoigne to purchase a house at Micklegate Bar, York, and started the convent and school.

II

For over a hundred years, until the government welcomed priests and nuns as refugees from the French Revolution, the Bar and its sister–house at Hammersmith, London, were the only two convents in Britain. Founded, supported, and patronised in the main by north of England Catholics, the Bar Convent's primary function was educational, but it was more than simply a school. Strategically situated in York it became a clearing–house for news, an active centre within a Catholic network. It was a place where people met at high days and holy days, came to borrow money and to meet old friends. Its chapel was a public (though covert) place of worship until 1828, and here priests were occasionally ordained and hundreds of people regularly baptised and confirmed. Relics and religious artefacts were left with the nuns for safekeeping in a place where they could also be venerated. From loans to novenas, the functions of the Bar in the eighteenth century cannot be disentangled from the family ties between the convent and the northern Catholic community. The key to understanding the Bar and the relative autonomy of the nuns in this period, is the familial, gentry–dominated world of eighteenth–century English Catholicism.

Little is known about the convent or school before 1710 when the first extant register begins.[16] At that point there were 43 girls in the school which remained about the same size until the 1720s and then experienced a virtual halving of its intake. Nothing about the internal affairs of the convent suggest why this downward trend should have happened and demographic changes alone may be sufficient explanation. Recovery was slow but steady up to 1760, after which the school experienced a rapid increase in size which was sustained through to 1820.

Fig. 1. 10–yearly averages of pupils starting school

1700s	11.0 [estimate]
1710s	11.4
1720s	6.1
1730s	6.1
1740s	7.4*
1750s	8.3
1760s	11.4
1770s	15.8
1780s	13.7
1790s	20.0

* the names and precise distribution of 39 pupils between 1749 and 1753 are missing and the calculation has been based on an even distribution of the 39.

The total school population grew from about 30 in the 1720s to just below 50 in the 1760s with most pupils staying for at least two years, during which time they did not return home for holidays.

Alongside their boarding–school the nuns ran a separate day–school for local Catholic girls from artisan and small shop–keeping families.[17] The few surviving indications suggest that it might have been about the same size as the boarding–school by the later decades, for in 1773 twenty–one girls from the day school were confirmed along with nineteen boarders, and in 1785 twenty day–pupils and twenty–four boarders.[18] The numbers of pupils who went through the schools in the eighteenth century, over 800 in the boarding–school and perhaps as many again in the day–school, means that the Bar Convent's educational role was relatively significant within the Catholic community. By comparison, the school run by the famous and fashionable English Blue Nuns in Paris, was tiny, taking only 155 girls — many of them French — between 1732 and its closure in 1792.[19]

Social status rather than geographical location was the real divide between the day and boarding–school. The boarding–school was usually referred to as the young ladies' school while the day–school was sometimes known, rather misleadingly, as the poor school. Before the 1770s, the lesser gentry of Yorkshire, Lancashire, Lincolnshire, County Durham and Northumberland, such as the Caleys and their relatives the Robinsons and Knights, were the mainstay of the boarding–school. It was less socially exclusive than its continental counterparts, presumably because it was not as expensive to send a girl to York, but possibly also because its location prevented it from developing the pretensions which could so easily accrue from being near the French court at Versailles, or the prince–bishop of Liege, or the aristocratic English Catholic emigres who clustered in several continental cities.[20] Between the 1730s and 1760s for example, the occasional aristocrat such as the Honourables Anne Fairfax, Mary Howard, and Elizabeth Vavasour learned their lessons alongside the two daughters of Thomas and Mary Keregan, actors and managers of York's first theatre, Ann and Mary Reynoldson whose father was in the upholstery and undertaking trade, and the daughters of Catholic professionals such as George Russell, writing–master, and Charles Atkinson, surgeon. What most of these girls had in common, apart from their Catholicism, was their northern origins — North defined here as Yorkshire, Lincolnshire, Lancashire, County Durham, Northumberland and Scotland.

Once the school began to expand more rapidly, the relative importance of its traditional catchment area declined. From the 1760s the school began to attract pupils from London, the south–east, proportionately more from Lancashire, and, in the 1770s, a few from plantation and trading families in India and the West Indies. The most likely explanation for the increase lies in the decline of the former Mary Ward convent in Hammersmith and the closing of its school in 1781.[21] At the same time there was a general increase in the school–age population, in which Catholics shared to a lesser degree. As a result, a number of families who had previously never used the York school began to do so.

Although the school was gradually diversifying its base between the 1760s and 1790, its close relationship to a northern, and more specifically a north–eastern, clientele was still fundamental. There is evidence that the school was valued by parents not so much as an intellectual hot–house, but more as a peculiarly enriched seed–bed for raising virtuous and pious Catholic women and that the serious devotional life practised at the Bar was sustained by some of these young women in later life.[22] The religious influence of the nuns can be seen

Susan O'Brien 271

Fig. 2. Regional distribution of boarding—school pupils

	1710s	1720s	1730s	1740s	1750s	1760s	1770s	1780s
Yorkshire & S Durham	50	24	24	17	36	30	36	28
Lancashire	14	12	9	10	12	24	28	36
Lincoln—shire	16	8	6	5	6	8	14	2
N.Durham & Northumber—land	14	5	9	17	10	16	14	9
Scotland	1	0	0	4	0	7	14*	8
London	4	1	1	1	1	7	13	26
Rest of England	5	7	5	5	5	15	16	13
Ireland	0	0	2	0	2	0	2	3
Europe	0	0	2	0	2	0	1	1
Elsewhere	0	1	0	6	0	2	12	3
Not known	7	3	3	1	3	5	8	8
Total	111	61	61	66	77	114	158	137
% from north of those known	91.3	84.0	82.0	81.5	86.0	77.9	70.6	64.3

* increase accounted for by the patronage of the Gordon family.

most readily in the fact that one in ten of their boarding-school pupils between 1710 and 1790 themselves became nuns.[23] Not all their former pupils would have been so fully committed and not all of them went on to marry Catholics and raise Catholic families, but it is worth noting Hugh Aveling's conclusion, derived from detailed genealogical researches in York, that 'family continuity in Catholicism ... from the eighteenth into the nineteenth century seems to have been preserved mostly through the female line in mixed marriages'.[24]   His evidence was for exactly those social classes whose daughters were sent to one or other of the schools.

If the school was valued by parents for the reliability of the spiritual, doctrinal, and devotional teaching given by the nuns it is not clear whether they expected or valued a scholarly education and chose the Bar accordingly. In the schools established during her lifetime, Mary Ward had advocated and implemented the normal liberal arts education taught in boys' schools, with greater emphasis on modern languages and less on logic but a firm insistence on the importance of Latin.[25] To what extent had the Institute's educational policy and practice changed since her death? The direct evidence about what was taught at York at various times is scanty, leaving us to infer from indirect evidence. Before the 1790s the nuns continued to revere Mary Ward and it seems clear that they had copies of her writings in their library. Moreover, the channels for oral tradition were strong. Frances Bedingfield, the first York superior, had joined Mary Ward in Rome in 1632 and had later been her companion in England between 1639 and 1645. She was in turn succeeded by her great-niece, Dorothy, who was superior between 1699 and 1734. Although little is known about the earliest community members at York, three of them were Thwing sisters from a local York family related to the Wards. At least one of the sisters, Helen, and probably all three, had been educated at the school established by the English members in Paris in the 1650s. Several other nuns in York before 1720 were sent over for short periods from other Institute houses in Germany.[26] All this points to a knowledge of their own history which might have been sufficient to override the discontinuities of organization and place. Equally important, given that the nuns were the teachers, it suggests that they had sufficient learning themselves to be able to continue with at least some of the curriculum prescribed by Mary Ward.

The majority of the nuns who entered before 1790 had been pupils either at the Bar or at one of the Institute's schools on the continent. Of the 26 women who were professed as teaching nuns between 1700 and 1790, 16 had been educated by the Institute, a further 4 had been to school on the continent, and for 3 there is no information.[27] Eleanor Clifton, for example, who entered in 1720 straight from the school, would have been taught by Cecilia Cornwallis who was the Bar's most scholarly sister, learned in Hebrew, Greek, astronomy, philosophy and mathematics as well as Latin and several European languages.[28] How much of this she taught to Eleaner Clifton and the three other nuns who entered whilst she was still alive is not known. The nun's library included a few Greek and Hebrew texts, including a Hebrew grammar, but the dominant language of the eighteenth-century library, and one suspects of the school, was French. French was taught at the Bar before it became the fashion more generally and most of the nuns seem to have been fluent. The fact that they used French as the medium of correspondence with their German Chief Superior suggests that German had lapsed in the community by the later eighteenth century.[29] Latin, however, continued to be taught. Mary Dalton, for example, one of the nuns who had attended the school, entered the novitiate in 1761 at the age of eighteen and taught French and Latin. She later became mistress of novices and held this position until she died in 1803.[30]

Set alongside the rare references to the academic curriculum and pedagogical seriousness of the school is evidence that the pupils spend time on the decorative arts.[31] This too was part of the tradition of the Institute which had included music, painting and embroidery in its curriculum in Mary Ward's lifetime. The Bar taught italic handwriting, and needlework of all sorts must have occupied a good deal of time. Needlework was taught as an art but the girls were also responsible for the more humdrum tasks of making and maintaining their own wardrobes and their six—monthly bills were dominated by items for sewing.[32] Dancing, which was taught by masters, was taken by most of the pupils at an additional charge of two guineas a half year. By the 1780s some of the pupils were also taking additional music and drawing lessons but they were not an essential part of the diet at the Bar Convent in the eighteenth century.

The evidence indicates that the nuns offered a curriculum which was *sui generis*. In so far as it retained elements of the liberal arts curriculum of the early seventeenth century, it was actually more intellectually challenging than the education then provided generally for girls. On the other hand, the nuns do not seem to have kept pace with the intellectual developments of their own age. Apart from some extension into the teaching of history, they seem not to have expanded the curriculum until after 1790. Indeed, it is difficult to see how they could have done so given the self—perpetuating nature of the convent's recruitment and the lack of fresh literature in the library. Their reading had depth only in such Catholic spiritual literature as St Thomas a Kempis, St Augustine, St Francis de Sales and St Teresa of Avila. By comparison with the contemporary libraries of the Jesuits and Benedictines, the Bar library is small and narrowly focused.[33] Even so, the very presence of a well cared—for library suggests that the female mind was taken seriously at the Bar and it should be remembered that a library entirely owned by a group of women for their own use was a rare phenomenon. The books are well—worn, many of the Latin grammars and other texts have pencilled margin notes dating from the eighteenth century, and the bindings of two texts have been painstakingly mended with old kid gloves. Perhaps it is not unreasonable to take as indicative of the nuns' attitude towards female education the views of Elizabeth Coyney who had been a Bar pupil from 1770 to 1776 and later became Mistress of the school. The annals record that 'She made no secret of her preference for those who possessed minds, and she used often to say that she could not endure to see women with childrens' heads upon their shoulders'.[34]

Beyond their teaching in the schools the nuns also gave religious instruction to children and adults, preparing them for first communion and confirmation, and instructing converts. George Hill, a local tradesman, remembered them with affection. In 1814 he wrote to the convent to subscribe £20 for their day school in gratitude for the education of his two sisters. Jane Charge had been their teacher and 'under the same Gentlemaid the present writer had the happiness to secure his early religious instruction'.[35] In the case of adults some of the religious instruction given by the nuns seems to have been more in the nature of spiritual direction. Anne Maxwell, for example, who was Mistress of the day—school for ten years and then Mistress of the boarding—school was visited by people from 'far away as well as near, all of whom derived great benefit from her advice and decisions'.[36] The evidence indicates that the convent had a number of religious functions apart from its strictly educational work. Its specific influence is not easy to calculate for there are few appropriate yardsticks by which to make a reliable measurement. Hugh Aveling's *York*

Catholic Recusants gives the impression that the majority of York's Catholics, about 650 in the mid 1760s, were poor, and that they had little to do with the Bar Convent and vice versa. Yet his general interpretation of the Bar nuns as inward–looking conflicts with the evidence he presents of the importance of female lineage in sustaining Catholicism in York, and in the final paragraph of his conclusion he seems to feel that the Bar must have played some larger part – 'the influence of the Bar on the poor of the city through their Day School and chaplains was very obscure, but it existed'.[37] There was certainly more contact between the convent and the poor than he believes, much of it through the apothecary porch and home nursing. It would not be surprising if health care proved to be the most effective means of 'inspiriting' poorer Catholics, and perhaps of evangelisation since medicines and treatment were given 'without religious distinction'.[38] When Mother Eleanor Clifton (IBVM 1720–1789) was Infirmarian, for example, she apparently 'was one of those most employed in nursing the Poor in their own homes'. The annals give one particular case where Mother Clifton and lay sister Fanny Audas went together to nurse 'a poor woman, a middle–aged widow, who was in her death'. As the woman was dying the nuns promised her that they would care for her young daughter. 'The poor girl was adopted, taken care of and educated in the Day School and ranked as one of the household until she could earn her board'.[39] To judge from the spirit and tone of these accounts it was a normal part of the community's life to attend the sick at home and give religious instruction – what the annalist described as 'administering to their every want in sickness and at death'.[40] The evidence is at least consistent in depicting a convent active among the local community and, unlike the enclosed English communities abroad, not solely occupied with the Catholic élite.

A much clearer case *can* be made about the strong spiritual relationship between the convent, the gentry families of the region and York's small group of middle–class Catholics. The convent chapel was a 'public' place of worship and its popularity with the better–off seems to have increased despite the alternative offered by the secular priests at the Blake Street mission throughout the eighteenth century.[41] During the 1760s Mother Anne Aspinal set up a public subscription list to help the nuns finance the construction of a new and enlarged chapel in the convent. The £750 raised came from the Yorkshire gentry, York citizen Catholics, and the parents of past and present pupils.[42] The new chapel remained concealed from the eyes of outsiders but inside provided a substantial, fashionably designed and well–constructed place of worship. To realise her dreams of a 'worthy' chapel Mother Aspinal procured a wooden model from Rome and employed the architect Thomas Atkinson, who had recently designed the facade of Bishopthorpe Palace. Once completed in 1769, the chapel was open to the public and it is easy to understand why many preferred it – with its gold and white stucco work, religious pictures and silver altarware – to the rudimentary mission chapels of the period, even though they had no control over it.[43] Here, the Catholic laity could take part in a well–developed and lively devotional life consisting of daily mass, access to a confessor, retreats, frequent sermons and the opportunity to venerate the convent's collection of relics.[44] A rosary confraternity, promoted by the Dominican fathers in the north of England, had been heavily supported by the nuns as early as 1728. By the 1750s the superior sponsored local men and women for membership, as well as pupils from the two schools, and had incorporated the Rosary Sunday ceremony into the convent's religious calendar.[45]

The level of religious activity at the Bar meant that it was possible for pious Catholics to build their life around the convent community, and it is hardly surprising that women featured prominently amongst those who did. A Catholic enclave developed around Micklegate, and one which was almost entirely female. In 1767, for example, the List of Papists for Trinity Parish, Micklegate recorded a total of 128 Catholics, the largest for any parish in York, of whom only 23 were male. There were 16 men and 38 women in addition to the nuns, their servants, and the pupils. Since 28 of the women have no occupation listed and 10 of them were listed as servants it seems fair to conclude that they were women of independent means with their maidservants. By comparison, the returns for the parish of St Michael le Belfry, the other large Catholic enclave, showed 36 men and 54 women of whom 26 had occupations listed, including that of mantua maker, washerwomen, milliner and aleseller.[46] The women in Micklegate can only be accounted for as independent widows and unmarried women who either rented houses or rooms in Micklegate so as to be near the nuns. The few who can be identified from their initials on the list, such as Lady Haggerstone and her house—guest Lady Winifred Constable, and Dame Judith Tancred and her daughter Mary, fall into this category.[47] For those living further away there was the possibility of being linked to the Bar and to former teachers and school—friends through the spiritual confraternities and prayers.[48] The bonds between former pupils and nuns are reflected in the many gifts of china and furniture, altar—silver, religious pictures and vestments donated by women, whose subscriptions accounted for £337 of the total £750 raised for the new chapel.[49]

The religious and social attractions of the Bar Convent were mutually reinforcing for its friends. The convent's location in fashionable York and the concentration of relatively wealthy Catholics in this part of the city guaranteed that it had a steady flow of visitors. The celebrations for Superior Anne Aspinal's golden jubilee as a nun in 1777 not only included a week of breakfasts, dinners and dancing for the pupils and local Catholic élite, but were continued through the following month by a series of visitors. On October 5th 1777, for example, the procuratress recorded in her memorandum book that Mr and Mrs Haggerstone 'breakfasted with Madam [Anne Aspinal]. Two Misses and Lady Ann Sortmarsh drank tea here, tea made a second time for Mr G Atkinson and daughter'. Two days later 'three friars came at recreation'.[50] According to the Institute's Rule, approved in 1703, such comings and goings should have been kept to a minimum.[51] The practices at the Bar in the eighteenth century, however, seem to have been singularly adapted to suit the English situation and the needs of the social group who supported the convent. By maintaining channels for communication and exchange, the nuns at York acted more in keeping with Mary Ward's original conception for the English mission. Mary Ward had shown an acute awareness of the potential usefulness of her social position in England and, as we have already seen, the Bar nuns did likewise. To help them in their works of charity and social discourse they even had private purses and discretion over the use of an allowance – a practice without parallel in the records of any other religious congregation of women, not only in this period but in the following century.[52] In the context the comment made in convent annals, written in the 1860s as the collective memory of the then members, is as revealing about the mid—nineteenth century as the mid—eighteenth: 'The manners and customs of the nuns in those days, their free intercourse with seculars, entertaining and drinking with them, added much to this extraordinary friendly feeling...the house was a sort of "bond of union" among the Catholics...'.[53]

The people who said their rosaries and supped tea with the nuns were sometimes linked further into the life of the convent through business transactions. Edward Haggerston, for example, who 'breakfasted with Madam' in 1777, had female relatives at the school throughout the century, and one member of the family resident in Micklegate after 1764, had borrowed £500 at 4% interest in 1759.[54] He was not alone among Yorkshire and Northumberland Catholics in looking to the nuns for a loan or mortgage. According to Geoffrey Bawdon, who has studied the Bar's financial history in the middle eighteenth century, loans and mortgages played a crucial part in the finances of the convent and almost all this business was transacted with the Catholic gentry. By the 1760s the convent had over £7000 a year out on loan.[55] Formal business arrangements were made for these transactions, which were essential to protect the convent's finances and the nuns' dowries which formed the bulk of their capital. In Bawdon's view the nuns 'showed financial acumen and a determination to make their money work'.[56] Their capital, which consisted largely of the inherited wealth of a small number of the nuns, worked for them in two senses: it generated further income and increased their usefulness to the Catholic community.

All of these activities — teaching, religious instruction, medical care and nursing the dying, financial transactions, along with frequent hostess duties — were undertaken by a relatively small group of nuns. By comparison with English convents on the continent, the York community was small. Whereas the Franciscans at Bruges professed 97 women between 1690 and 1790, and the Poor Clares at Rouen 111, the Bar professed only 33.[57] Although all the orders experienced a fall—off in postulants during in the second half of the eighteenth century, Superior Anne Aspinal believed that the Bar had particular recruitment problems. 'We so rarely see persons willing to embrace our manner of living', she wrote to her Chief Superior in Munich. 'When they see the labour and fatigue attending our manner of living, they dare not undertake it'.[58] There is no reason to doubt her diagnosis. The growing demands of the school meant that even the most elderly nuns continued to work. In addition to all their school—teaching, catechising and nursing work, and the constant sewing required to provide clothes and bedlined for their large household, the community made its own beer and bread, kept cows and pigs, worked a kitchen garden which at various times provided them with asparagus, raspberries, strawberries, apricots, and cultivated herb garden to supply the kitchen and the apothecary shop.[59]

Some potential novices may have been discouraged by the constraints on the religious life in England. The nuns had to judge just how much leeway could be made in order to function despite the penal code, and how much to respond when toleration levels were affected by local and national tensions. Their convents at Hammersmith and York were just beyond the most densely populated parts of their respective cities, but they were none the less immediately adjacent to large urban populations. Even though York was a relatively favourable environment for an illegal convent, the nuns took care not to offend the authorities or arouse popular anti—Catholic sentiment.[60] Each nun wore her own adaptation of widow's dress, rather than a more obviously recognisable religious habit.[61] She kept her own name with the courtesy title of Mrs or Madam and even in the privacy of the community, religious names were not used.[62] Other visible and outward signs of religious life such as holy pictures, crucifixes, and statutes were not displayed in the parlour, garden or corridors of the convent and most were confined to the chapel and workrooms. It was, therefore, an unusual young women who felt called to live out her religious vocation at the Bar Convent. Instead of acquiring the protection and status given to nuns in Catholic countries, she had to forego most of the privileges of a religious and to appear as something of an oddity to the world at large — a cultivated and socially superior women who lived as a widow with other supposed widows, and taught school. While we do not know how young women made their decision, or what influence parents may have had, a striking testimony to the Bar Convent's minority appeal is the low proportion of its pupils who chose to enter these. Any convent with a school might reasonable expect that most of those with a religious vocation would simply stay on. One in 10 of the 800 pupils at the school between 1710 and 1790 became nuns, showing that the Bar was producing its fair share of vocations, but only one in 80 entered there.[63] On the other hand, it seems to have had no difficulty in recruiting and retaining an adequate number of lay sisters. For lower-class women the possibility of entering a convent in England, or even locally, had the attractions of low travelling expenses, no language problems, and general familiarity. Given the role of lay sisters, which included being provisioners and portresses, the latter was important. The Bar's lay sisters, most of whom were from York and had attended the convent day-school, would have been very familiar with the local markets and traders.[64]

III

Enough has been said to indicate the kind of life led by the nuns in this period but their sense of history, tradition, and autonomy needs to be emphasised because it was characteristic of the period before 1790 but no after. Again, it is instructive to note the way in which the community of the 1860s perceived their forebears of the 1760s. The Victorian convent historian wrote: 'She [Ann Aspinal] was peculiarly gifted by God with a managing spirit. His tender mercies were conspicuous in blessing this house at that period with women of masculine minds, for we must recollect that the Bishop was not then, as now, the immediate Superior of the House'.[65] The degree of self-direction and independence experienced by any convent has always been subject to contemporary ideas about women and the Church's translation of these ideas into Rule, Constitutions, and Customs. On the other hand, the religious and spiritual needs of a particular group of people have not infrequently led them to deviate from gender norms and Rome could not always determine what would happen at grass-roots level. The situation of Catholics in England provided the context for the Institute's nuns to develop in York as they did, and their own traditions and history provided them with a particular set of responses. In the absence of the normal apparatus of the Catholic Church — parishes and parish priests, dioceses and bishop — the nuns had more say in their own lives and that of the Catholic community. The community was too small for rigid hierarchies, and many of these women had known one another from girlhood. Clerical interference or direction was unlikely. In this period the nuns looked directly to their Chief Superior in Munich when guidance was needed, and their chaplain and the Vicar Apostolic for England recognised her authority.[66] The York Superior was responsible for the day-to-day running of the school and convent and although one feels that their chaplains must have been influential, it was in spiritual rather than administrative matters.[67] The direct and close relationship which the nuns had with their clientele and the convent's success in providing for that clientele did much to enhance their autonomy.

Because of their understanding of Mary Ward's aims and intentions, the Bar Convent nuns were able to act on the spirit which underlay their Rule, rather than be bound absolutely by its provisions. In the Institute there was a high level of awareness of Mary Ward as a female pioneer. Before she died her nuns on the continent had commissioned a group of artists to paint her life history, themselves supplying narrative and vignettes to the painters. The result was a pictorial biography consisting of fifty large oil paintings, some painted before 1645 but most dating from the latter half of the seventeenth century — a striking testimony to the regard in which her spiritual daughters held her.[68] 'We are all children of this glorious mother', one of the Austrian superiors wrote to York in 1711, 'and therefore will rather lose our lives than let ourselves be drawn or separated from the Corpus that cost her so much labour and suffrance'.[69] The York nuns sustained Mary Ward's legacy even longer then the convents on the continent and remained happily ignorant of Pope Benedict XIV's pronouncements against her in 1749.[70] Each year they made a pilgrimage to her grave at Osbaldwick, where a number of the earliest York members were also buried. These women were part of the social nexus which had been hers, and the world of Yorkshire Catholic gentry was sufficiently small for that to have meaning a hundred years after her death.

Christopher Haigh, in his review of Bossy's *English Catholic Community* asked where the evidence was of the formation of 'community':

> Bossy does not tell us how far the separation extended beyond ecclesiastical issues to education, marriages, friendships, testamentary bequests: I suspect the answer is 'Not very far', since there was never a distinctly Catholic social nexus.[71]

The existence and survival of the Bar Convent indicates a self–conscious separatism among the solid gentry and yeoman Catholic families of the north–east which did not need to be totally exclusive to have a reality. As we have seen, their faith did affect the decision–making of these Catholic families in the realm of education, and from this stemmed a particular pattern of friendships. The nuns of the Bar Convent were part of a 'distinctively Catholic social nexus' and through the socialization of young Catholic women played a role in community formation.

NOTES

I am grateful to Sr. Gregory IBVM, Archivist at the Bar Convent for her patient help and encouragement, to Sr. Agatha IBVM for her hospitality, and to Sr. Lavinia Byrne IBVM. This work was undertaken with the assistance of the Nuffield Foundation.

1. The boarding and day–schools merged in 1919 to become a Direct Grant Grammar School, although a few weekly boarders were taken up until 1983. There was a school on this site, run by the nuns, until 1986.
2. J. Bossy, *The English Catholic Community 1570–1850* (London, 1975). References here are to the 1979 edition.
3. This point is particularly well made by Marie B. Rowlands, 'Recusant Women 1560–1640', in Mary Prior ed., *Women in English Society 1500–1800* (London, 1985).
4. J. Bossy, *English Catholic Community*, (1979 ed.), p 154–5.
5. Both J.C.H. Aveling and J. Bossy have argued this in their works. See, for example, J.C.H. Aveling, *The Handle and the Axe: The Catholic recusants in England from reformation to emancipation* (London, 1976) and *Catholic Recusancy in York 1558–1791*, Catholic Record Society Publications, Monograph Series Vol. 2. (St. Albans, Hertfordshire, 1970).
6. J. Bossy, *English Catholic Community*, p 181 (1979 ed.).
7. The original name, apart from English Ladies, was Institute of Mary, changed in the eighteenth century to Institute of the Blessed Virgin Mary

to ensure no ambiguity about the 'Mary' referred to in its title.

8.   See, M.C.E. Chambers IBVM, *The Life of Mary Ward* ed., H.J. Coleridge, (London, 1882) 2 Vols., Vol. I, pp 231–263 and Vol. II, p 325 and materials on the early members in the IBVM Archive, St. Mary's Convent, 47 Fitjohn's Avenue, London NW3 6PG.

9.   See, I. Wetter IBVM, 'Mary Ward's Apostolic Vision', *The Way* supplement 17 (Autumn 1972): pp 69–91. Other secondary works include: Lavinia Byrne IBVM, *Mary Ward: A pilgrim finds her way* (Dublin, 1884); Ida G. Coudenhouve, *Mary Ward* trans. E. Codd (London, 1938); Mary Oliver IBVM, *Mary Ward 1585–1645* (London, 1959); M. Emmanuel Orchard IBVM, *Till God Will: Mary Ward through her writings* (London, 1985); 'Mary Ward: Journey into Freedom – Essays in honour of the fourth centenary of her birth', *The Way* Supplement No. 53 (Summer 1985). Translations of many of the manuscript sources used in the biographies of Mary Ward are located in the IBVM Archive, St Mary's Convent, London.

10. Translation of the 1616 *Ratio Instituti* in Chambers *Life of Mary Ward* Vol. I, p 377.

11. Chambers, *Life of Mary Ward*, I, pp 208–9 and II, p 21–22.

12. *The Sower* (Jan–Feb 1929), pp 7–10 and references. Chambers, *Life of Mary Ward*, e.g., Vol. II p 531.

13. Prior, 'Recusant Women', p 170 and Chambers, *Life of Mary Ward*, II p 97.

14. Bossy, *English Catholic Community*, p 281.

15. Chambers, *Life of Mary Ward*, I pp 209–30; 304–6; 326–43; 402–446; II pp 21–48; 457–506.

16. Bar Convent Archives [hereafter Bar] Vol. 41 'Names of the Pensioners from the Year 1710'. An incomplete register was printed as an Appendix to ed., H.J. Coleridge, *St Mary's Convent Micklegate Bar 1686–1887*, (London, 1887), pp 389–416. Vol. 41 is a copy probably made in the 1860s or 1870s. It has been cross–checked for accuracy wherever possible and used as the source for all the calculations and interpretation made in this essay.

17. No register survives for the day–school. Several former pupils became lay sisters at the convent and their origins have been checked in Aveling, *Catholic Recusancy in York*. Two other sources provided insights into the day–school's membership: Bar, 5A 2 Confirmation Catalogue from 1773–1843 and Catholic Record Society, *Miscellanea*, Vol. IX (London, 1914) 'Two Rosary Confraternity Lists at Bornham and the North of England'.

18. Bar, 5A 2 Confirmation Catalogue.

19. Compiled from eds., J. Gillow and R. Trappes–Lomax, *The Diary of the 'Blue Nuns' or Order of the Immaculate Conception of Our Lady at Paris, 1658–1810* Catholic Record Society Vol. VIII (London, 1910).

20. The English convents on the continent are described in Peter Guilday, *The English Catholic Refugees on the Continent 1558–1795* (London, 1914).

21. D. Evinson, *Pope's Corner: An historical survey of the Roman Catholic institutions in the London Borough of Hammersmith and Fulham* (London, 1980), pp 3–15. The Bar Convent Archives have a copy of the Hammersmith register 'Pensioners and Members' which has been in the custody of St Scholastica's Abbey, Teignmouth.

22. On the value to parents see Edward Bedingfield's Jubilee Ode 1771, extracts of which are printed in Coleridge, *St Mary's Convent*, pp 214–5. On the devotional life practised by those in association with the Bar see

Aveling, *Catholic Recusancy in York* pp 130–31.

23. Calculated from Bar, Vol. 41 'Names of the Pensioners from the Year 1710' and Vol. 42 'A list of young ladies who entered religious communities.'

24. Aveling, *Catholic Recusancy in York*, p 145.

25. Mary Ward repeatedly encouraged and exhorted women to learn languages, including Latin: 'I would have Cecilia and Catherine to begin out of hand to learn the rudiments of Latin...what time can be otherwise found besides their prayers, let it be bestowed on their Latin.' Quoted in *The Sower* (Jan–Feb 1929), p 9; 'Let Kate perfect her Latin with all possible care, without loss of health, also to write Italian.' 'All such as are capable [of learning Latin] invite them to it, and for such as desire to be of ours, no talent is so much to be regarded in them as the Latin tongue.' Quoted in Bryne, *Mary Ward*, pp 29–30.

26. Bar, 3F 1. 'Annals of St Mary's Convent of the Institute of the IBVM, Micklegate Bar, York; preceded by a brief account of the Institute in Germany; compiled from authentic records and venerable traditions by a member of the community ... 1867'.

27. Bar, Vol. 14 'Records of the Nuns'; Vol. 17 'Some account of the first members of the Blessed Virgin Mary'; Vol. 19 'Nuns of the Institute of Mary at York 1677–1825' and 4A 12.

28. See Evinson, *Pope's Corner*, p 9.

29. Bar, 6B MS Letters 1–7.

30. Bar, Annals 3F.14 Chapter 40.

31. Bar, Account Books A/C B 'Copies of the young ladies bills.'

32. E.g., Bar, A/C B. 1. March 1761–1773.

33. The library is still housed at the Bar Convent Museum and the Archive includes a card–index catalogue which includes any information which can date a book's arrival in the library.

34. Coleridge, *St Mary's Convent*, p 310 quoting from Bar, Annals 3.F.

35. Bar, 5A 6. Letter from Geo. Hill to Mrs. Coyney, 2 March 1814.

36. Bar, Annals 3 F 1/7 Chapter 21.

37. Aveling, *Catholic Recussancy in York*, p 162.

38. Bar, Annals 3 F 1/8 Chapter 25.

39. Bar, Annals 3F 1/6 Chapter 20.

40. *Ibid.*

41. See, Aveling, *Catholic Recusancy in York*, Appendix V and passim.

42. Bar, 3 D10 'A Memorandum of all those who were so charitable as to contribute to the building of our House 1765.'

43. For example the chapel at nearby Egton bridge, a fervent Catholic enclave. The present church has a permanently mounted display showing the construction and environment of the eighteen century mission chapel which preceded it.

44. Bar, 4 K 'Relics' and Vol. 39 'Benefactions made to the community'.

45. Catholic Record Society, *Miscellanea*, Vol. IX (1914). 'Two Rosary Confraternity Lists at Bornhem and the North of England.'

46. The 1767 'List of Papists or Reputed Papists in the Diocese of York' is reprinted in Aveling, *Catholic Recusancy in York*, pp 279–187.

47. Identification has been made from collaborative evidence such as: Bar, 3 B/4 'Anecdotes of the Bar from the Year 1735' otherwise known as the Procuratress' Book. Aveling has tracked down some of these women in *Catholic Recusancy in York*.

48. See Aveling, *Catholic Recusancy in York*, p 131–2 and Annals 3 F.

49. Bar, 3 D10 and Vol. 39.

50. Bar, 3 B/4.

51. Bar, Vol. 22 'Rules of ye Superior of every House' e.g. para. 84.
52. Bar, Annals 3 F 1/4 Chapter 40. The discontinuance of private purses around 1800 was a 'reform' undertaken by the convent chaplain, Fr. Allain who 'laboured strenuously for the good ... He encouraged and much promoted more enclosure, discouraging going out that was not necessary ... by the wish of the community, to whom he proposed it, he applied for the Bishop's approbation for the "private purses" to be discontinued, and it was done.' Other references to the discretionary money held by the nuns: Annals 3 F 1/5 Chapter 17.
53. Bar, Annals 35 F 1/7 Chapter 21.
54. G. Bawdon, 'The Bar Convent York. Its finances and role in the Catholic community', p 15. [unpublished York University undergraduate thesis, 1984] Typescript in the Bar Convent Archives.
55. Bawdon, pp 1–17.
56. Bawdon, p 27.
57. Calculated from the profession lists in Catholic Record Society, Vol. XXIV (London, 1922) 'The English Franciscan Nuns 1619–1821' and Ann H.C. Forster ed., 'The Chronicles of the English Poor Clares of Rouen Part 2' *Recusant History*, Vol. 18, no 2. (October 1986): pp 165–179.
58. Bar, Annals 3 F 1/8 Chapter 23.
59. The best insight into the daily life of the convent in the eighteenth century is given in Bar, 3 B/4 — 'Anecdotes of the Bar'. Bar, Vol. 22 'The Rules of ye Superior' gives the rule for the Infirmarian and the Apothecary.
60. Although there were a number of periods of anti–Catholic tension and activism when the convent was threatened, it is worth emphasising the extend to which the nuns were allowed to exist in peace. There was always an ambiguity about whether they were actually nuns, but the authorities knew of their activities and their absenteeism from the established church, for which they were fined. The nuns, for their part, were always careful not to offend. See, for example, Bar, Annals 3 F 7 Chapter 22.
61. Authenticated portraits of Anne Aspinal and Cecilia Cornwallis hang in the Bar Convent Museum. Procuratress Mary Davis regularly noted the conversion of the nuns gowns, of various shades, into bed covers and quilts. Bar, 3 B/4.
62. Religious names were not taken in the community until 1810.
63. See note 23. above.
64. See note 17. above.
65. Bar, Annals 3 F 1/11 Chapter 33. The changes in the Bar's ethos and organisation are striking and the author is undertaking further research into the Bar during the nineteenth century.
66. Ushaw College Archives, Ushaw Collection of MSS. Letters from Edward Dicconson, Vicar Apostolic and Peter Maire, Chaplain at the Bar. 12 November 1747. The issue was the removal and replacement of Superior Esther Coyners, a sensitive issue requiring higher authority. In this instance the Vicar Apostolic and Chaplain note that they were commissioned to act by 'Mrs Hawserin', [Francesca von Hauser] Chief Superior of the Institute and that they do so under her authority.
67. The evidence of a high degree of activity and initiative by the chaplains in the first half of the nineteenth century contrasts markedly with the few references to the chaplain in the eighteenth century records.
68. The original 'Painted Life' hangs in the Institute's provincial house in Augsburg and there is a copy in the Bar Convent Museum. The 'Life'

has never been the subject of a detailed published scholarly analysis and there are some doubts about when and where it was painted. For an introduction see John P. Marmion, 'Some Notes on the "Painted Life" of Mary Ward', *Recusant History*, Vol. 18, No. 3 (1987): pp 318–322 and L. Byrne, *Mary Ward*, passim.

69.   Chambers, *Life of Mary Ward*, p 545.
70.   The crucial point here is that until the mid 1790s the York nuns were unaware of Pope Benedict XIV's Bull Quamvis Justo which, in sanctioning the position, authority and rights of female superiors in women's congregations, had forbidden the Institute to recognise Mary Ward as founder, but as 'first member' only.
71.   Christopher Haigh, 'The Fall of a Church or the rise of a Sect? Post–Reformation Catholicism in England', a review essay in *The Historical Journal*, Vol. 21, No. 1 (1978): pp 181–186.

TWO EIGHTEENTH CENTURY VIEWS OF MONASTICISM
JOSEPH BINGHAM AND EDWARD GIBBON

Leslie W. Barnard

This paper studies the accounts of monasticism given by two eminent eighteenth—century scholars, Joseph Bingham and Edward Gibbon. The first was the leading Patristic scholar of his age and wrote during the first decades of the century; the latter, the great historian of the Roman Empire, wrote later during its final decades. Gibbon's account of early Christian monasticism is a brilliant *tour de force* born of eighteenth—century rationalism — for him the monks were 'non—men', a useless group who had darkened the face of the Christian world, an uncivilised and irrational irruption into the natural order of things. Bingham's approach, on the other hand, was purely historical. He wished to discover what the early Fathers actually said about monasticism without passing moral judgments on the material he was recording. I shall deal firstly with Bingham.

I

Joseph Bingham (1668–1723) was born in 1668 at Wakefield and was educated at the Queen Elizabeth Grammar School, then at the height of its influence.[1] In 1684 Bingham entered University College, Oxford[2] where his zeal for persevering study found ample fulfillment in the study of the Church Fathers in their original languages. His ability was soon recognised by his election in 1689 to a Fellowship when one of his first pupils was John Potter, later to become Bishop of Oxford and Archbishop of Canterbury. Bingham's Oxford career now seemed set fair; however he became embroiled in the Trinitarian controversy which was then agitating the University. Following a University sermon on the Patristic notions of *ousia, persona* and *substantia* in October 1695 he was delated to the Vice—Chancellor for heresy and the upshot was that he was forced to resign his fellowship and withdraw from the University. The celebrated Dr Radcliffe heard of his plight and presented him to the benefice of Headbourne Worthy, a mile outside Winchester, which was to be the scene of Bingham's literary and historical studies for the next quarter of a century. He began his work on the antiquities of the Christian Church, *Origines Ecclesiasticae*,[3] in 1702 and was grateful for the use of the valuable Patristic library bequeathed to the Dean and Chapter of Winchester by Bishop Morley.[4] Modest, gentle and unworldly Bingham pursued his studies with unwearied perseverance through illness and straitened circumstances — his sole income being his living valued at £100. In 1712 he was collated to the rectory of Havant and this removed to some degree his immediate poverty although in 1720, with so many others, Bingham lost all his profits from his work in the bursting of the South Sea Bubble. The *Origines*, was finished in 1722 and Bingham died on 17 August 1723 before he could complete a second edition and a popular abridgement as a supplement. The *Origines* is characterized by immense erudition, a reasonableness of approach and a sureness of judgement which is largely free from a controversial spirit. The eminent Roman historian, the late A.H.M. Jones, described it as 'the most useful and comprehensive work which I know on the organisation and discipline of the Church',[5] a remarkable tribute to a work more than two—and—a—half centuries old.

Bingham's account of early Christian monasticism is found in Book 7 of the *Origines*,[6] He remarks that while there were always ascetics in the Church there were not always monks. Every Christian who made profession of a strict and austere life was dignified with the name of ascetic — a name which was borrowed from the ancient philosophers. So Origen refers to those who abstain from flesh in order to discipline the body; such abstinence the Apostolic Canons call ἄσκησις, the exercise of an ascetic life. Those, too, who spent their time largely in prayer were thought to deserve the name of ascetics — so Cyril of Jerusalem styles Anna, the prophetess, who departed not from the Temple, as ἀσκήτρια εὐδαβεστάτη, the religious ascetic. The exercise of charity to an extraordinary degree, as when men gave up their estates to the service of God and the poor, also was termed asceticism. So Jerome calls Pierius a wonderful ascetic because he embraced voluntary poverty and lived an austere, philosophic life. Widows and virgins, according to Bingham, were also reckoned among the ascetics, as can be seen from Origen who alludes to the name when he says that the numbers of those who exercised themselves in perpetual virginity among the Christians was great in comparison to the few who did it among the Gentiles.[7] So in the time of Justinian the civil law word *ascetriae* signified the widows and virgins of the Church. Lastly all who underwent extreme forms of hardship for the promotion of piety and religion were called ascetics. So the *Synopsis Scripturae* styles Lucian the Martyr as μέγαν ἀσκητὴν, the great ascetic, because of the hardships he endured in prison, being forced to lie on sharp potsherds for twelve days, with his feet and hands bound in stocks so that he could not move, and denied food. Rather than pollute himself with food sacrificed to idols he chose to die of famine, according to his *Acta Martyrium*. Sometimes the primitive ascetics were called by other names: so Eusebius and Epiphanius calls them σπουδαῖοι, persons eminent for their sanctity and diligence in fasting, prayer and almsgiving. Clement of Alexandria styles them ἐκλεκτῶν ἐκλεκτότεροι, the elect of the elect — while all Christians were called the elect, the ascetics were the more eminent of these. Having established the difference between ascetics and monks (a distinction which, while obvious to us, was not widely understood in his day) Bingham proceeds to discuss the rise of monasticism in some detail. Until *c* 250 there were no monks, only ascetics in the Church; from that time until the reign of Constantine monachism was largely confined to anchorites living in cells in the desert. However when Pachomius erected monasteries in Egypt other countries followed his example and so the monastic life came to full maturity in the Church. Bingham shows that several kinds of monks were distinguished by different ways of life. He sketches in detail the anchorites, coenobites, sarabites and stylites. He shows that monks were originally laymen although the clerical and lay monastic life was sometimes conjoined. One of his most interesting sections concerns the ancient laws relating to the monastic life.[8] He shows that no solemn vow or profession was required of the early monks, although the power of the abbot was considerable in exercising discipline. Monastic life was a matter of choice and monks could return to secular life, if they so wished. Married monks were not obliged to dissolve their marriages or put away their spouses.

One of the most significant aspects of Bingham's work is the information he provides about curious practices, some of which is hard to come by elsewhere. Not all monks lived up to their calling: Bingham instances the case of the *Remboth*,[9] noted by Jerome, who were monks who lived in small groups of two or three, under no rule or government. They lived, not in the desert, but in cities and castles, turning religion to commercial gain. Whatever they sold of their own handwork, was at a higher price than any others. They were turbulent and contentious, making even fasting a matter of strife. Everything about them was affected — loose sleeves, wide stockings, coarse clothes, often sighing, making frequent visits to virgins and always bitterly hostile to the clergy. At Feast days they indulged in riot and excess. Jerome brands them as the pests of the Church, while Cassian, who also knew about them, designates them *Sarabaitae*.

One of Bingham's more interesting sections is on the *Stylitae* or *Pillarists*,[10] monks who lived perpetually on a pillar or column. The case of St Simeon Stylites who lived in the mid–fifth century is well known. Even the Egyptian monks, who had sent anathematizing letters against him, came to understand and communicate with the Syrian saint. Bingham points out that the severity of this way of life made few converts. Evagrius mentions another Simeon who lived sixty–eight years on a pillar and who is commonly called Simeon Stylites Junior. Surius, in his Catalogue of Saints, has the life of Alipius, a certain bishop of Adrianopolis, who renounced his see to live on a stone pillar for seventy years. Alipius had two choirs of virgins and one of monks attending him, with whom he sang psalms and hymns alternately day and night. Bingham clearly regards this as a legend and notes, with acerbity, that 'we scarce meet with any other of this way in ancient history'.

Bingham had a keen eye for the more unusual manifestations of monasticism. In the regions of Syria and Mesopotamia Sozomen, he notes, refers to monks called βοσκοί or *Grazers*. These men lived in the same way as flocks and herds upon the mountains, never dwelling in houses or eating bread or flesh or drinking. They spent their time in the worship of God until feeding time when each went out with knife in hand to get food from the herbs of the field – their only diet.[11] Then there were the long–haired brethren, the *cromoto fratres* known to Jerome and Augustine.[12] Certain of these walked in chains, had long hair and goats' beards, wore black coats and went barefoot in winter Such affectations in habit and dress were frowned on, and monks were to were simple clothes and short hair as is prescribed by certain *Canons* of Councils.

Voluntary poverty was a *sine qua non* of the monastic life but not all monks could live up to this. Bingham gives the remarkable story of one of the monks of Nitria in Egypt who was punished for hoarding up a hundred shillings as his own property which he had saved out of his daily labour. At his death, when this was discovered, a council of monks had to decide what to do with the money – incredible as it may see five thousand monks met for the consultation. Some said it should be given to the poor, others to the Church, yet others that it should be given to the monk's parents. Macarius, Pambo and Isidore and others of those called Fathers among them decreed that the money should be buried with the dead monk in his grave with the words 'Thy money perish with thee'.[13]

Bingham largely confines his *Origines* to the patristic period of the Church. However his profound knowledge extended to English Church History as may be seen from his remarkable account of the Council of Becanfeld. Bingham refers to the presence of abbots or fathers at Councils of the Church where they were often allowed to sit and vote as presbyters – so at the Council of Constantinople in 448 twenty three archimandrites subscribed with thirty bishops to the condemnation of Eutyches. However England seems to have led the way in women's liberation for at the Council of Becanfeld in Kent held in A.D. 694 abbesses, as well as abbots, subscribed to the decrees and did so before both presbyters and temporal lords, according to the Saxon Chronicle. According to Bingham this is the first time that this had happened in the records of the ancient Church.[14]

It should not be thought that Bingham was a mere scribe, a compiler of curious and out–of–the–way information. He was the foremost student of Christian antiquity of his day and his appeal, in his account of monasticism and elsewhere, was always to the evidence of ancient writers, not the opinions of later authors as to what those writers said or meant. His concern was purely historical, to recover what the early Church believed and did and to free the study of Christian antiquity, once and for all, from the shackles of the scholastic method. Likewise he was not interested how his early eighteenth–century contemporaries viewed monasticism. In this no greater contrast exists than between his approach and that of Edward Gibbon to which I now turn.

II

Gibbon wrote his monumental *The History of the Decline and Fall of the Roman Empire*[15] in the years 1776–1788. In his closing pages he states that the theme of his work has been to describe 'the triumph of barbarism and religion'.[16] Gibbon believed that an inseparable connection existed between the decline of the Empire and the growth and triumph of the Church. The Fall of Rome was due, in his view, not primarily to the assault of the barbarians but to the Catholic Church which had undermined, and eventually destroyed, the religion of Rome. The role of Christianity was essentially that of a disruptive force which had destroyed the social fabric of society and early monasticism was, in Gibbon's view, an extreme example of such disruption.

It is in chapter 37[17] of the *Decline and Fall* that Gibbon deals most fully with the monks, monastic life and organisation. He begins by berating the early ascetics 'who obeyed and abused the rigid precepts of the Gospel, were inspired by the savage enthusiasm which represents man as a criminal and God as a tyrant'.[18] He has a particular animus against the Egyptians whom he associated with violent passions – 'Egypt, the fruitful parent of superstition, afforded the first example of the monastic life'.[19] This began with Antony, 'an illiterate youth ... who deserted his family and native home, and executed his monastic penance with original and intrepid fanaticism'.[20] Gibbon however acknowledges Anthony's discretion and dignity when he appeared at Alexandria to support the doctrine of Athanasius whom Gibbon greatly admired for his forceful leadership and who was one of his few Christian heroes.[21] But Pachomian monasticism, which spread rapidly with large numbers of men and women adopting his Rule, only excited Gibbon's ironic humour:

> The Egyptians, who gloried in this marvellous revolution, were disposed to hope, and to believe, that the number of the monks was equal to the remainder of the people; and posterity might repeat the saying, which had formerly been applied to sacred animals of the same country, that, in Egypt, it was less difficult to find a god than a man.[22]

Monastic development in Asia Minor, which centred on the cities, was more congenial to Gibbon. However in his view the fame of Basil of Caesarea, its founder was associated with 'an ambition scarcely to be satisfied by the archbishopric of Caesarea'.[23] Basil's retirement to Pontus was to a savage interruption in his life. In Gibbon's opinion monasticism throughout the Christian world 'diffused ... a doubtful ray of science and superstition',[24] particularly was this so of the Celtic variety found on Iona. Monks everywhere were unhappy exiles from social life, impelled by the dark and implacable genius of superstition. Gibbon ridicules the belief that the monks were the best qualified for the spiritual direction of the Christian movement for ambition soon discovered the secret road which led to the possession of wealth and honours:

> They insinuated themselves into noble and opulent families; and the
> specious arts of flattery and seduction were employed to secure those
> proselytes who might bestow wealth or dignity on the monastic
> profession. The indignant father bewailed the loss, perhaps of an only
> son; the credulous maid was betrayed by vanity to violate the laws of
> nature; and the matron aspired to imaginary perfection, by
> renouncing the virtues of domestic life.[25]

The vast increase of numbers of obscure and abject plebeians in the monasteries
'gained in the cloisters much more than they had sacrificed in the world'.[26]
Legions of men were buried in religious sanctuaries and while this may have
relieved the despair of individuals it, in Gibbon's view, impaired the strength and
fortitude of the Roman Empire. The feeble dykes, behind which the Emperors
attempted to support the obligation of public and private life, were swept away
by a torrent of superstition.[27]

Gibbon was not unaware how monasticism in the early Christian period
differed from that of his own day. Monastic profession in the early Church was
supposed to be voluntary and in theory monks were at liberty to quit their
monasteries and resume the character of men and citizens, if they so wished.
However within the Egyptian monastries this was not easy as 'a blind submission
to the commands of the abbot, however absurd, or even criminal, they might
seem, was the ruling principle, the first virtue of the Egyptian monks'.[28] A
monk could be ordered to move an enormous stone; to water a barren staff which
had been planted in the ground until, after three years, it vegetated and
blossomed like a tree; to walk in a fiery furnace. Several saints, or madmen, had
been immortalized in the accounts of their thoughtless obedience. In a footnote
Gibbon refers to the Rule of Columbanus, prevalent in the West, which inflicted
one hundred lashes for very slight offences. Before the age of Charlemagne
abbots had been known to mutilate monks by gouging out their eyes, a
punishment much less cruel than the tremendous *vade in pace*, the subterranean
dungeon, which was afterwards invented. Gibbon cites the admirable discourse
of the learned Mabillon 'who on this occasion, seems to be inspired by the genius
of humanity. For such an effort I can forgive his defence of the holy tear of
Vendôme'.[29] Throughout the early Christian world fanaticism reigned and
nowhere more than in the East:

> The Peace of the Eastern Church was invaded by a swarm of fanatics,
> incapable of fear, or reason, or humanity; and the Imperial troops
> acknowledged, without shame, that they were much less apprehensive
> of an encounter with the barbarians.[30]

Gibbon had a profound dislike for the monastic way of life, particularly
that of the anchorites:

> They wrapped their heads in a cowl, to escape the sight of profane
> objects; their legs and their feet were naked, except in the extreme
> cold of winter; and their slow and feeble steps were supported by a
> long staff. The aspect of a genuine anchorite was horrid and
> disgusting; every sensation that is offensive to man was thought
> acceptable to God; and the angelic rule of Tabeene condemned the
> salutary custom of bathing the limbs in water and anointing them
> with oil.[31]

Pleasure and guilt were synonymous terms in the language of the monks and rigid fasts and an abstemious diet were thought to preserve the soul from the impure desires of the flesh. Gibbon had no great admiration for the studies of the early monks although he does acknowledge that later monasticism preserved the monuments of Greek and Latin culture by the assiduous copying of manuscripts. The wealth of the monasteries, which accrued over the centuries, drew Gibbon's ire. The pride of wealth led to corruption and he quotes with approval Zosimus' observation that for the benefit of the poor. the Christian monks had reduced a greater part of mankind to a state of beggary. In a footnote Gibbon quotes the answer of the monk Pambo to a certain Melania, who wished to specify the value of her gift to him: 'Do you offer it to me, or to God? If to God, He who suspends the mountains in a balance need not be informed of the weight of your plate'.[32]

Gibbon was particularly hard on the solitude of the early monks whose lives were occupied in penance, undisturbed by the various occupations which fill the time, and exercise the faculties, of reasonable, active, social beings. Conversation with strangers was regarded as dangerous and a monk was thought to be meritorious if he afflicted a tender sister or an aged parent by the obstinate refusal of a word or look. Pior, an Egyptian monk, did allow his sister to see him but he shut his eyes during the whole visit.[33] Monks passed their lives without personal attachments — even at meals their cowls made them largely invisible to each other. Gibbon again returns to the subject of monastic study for the monks had, in his view, insufficient education for liberal studies,'industry must be faint and languid which is not exerted by the sense of personal interest'.[34] Racked by despair and disease the unhappy monks were sometimes only relieved by madness or death. In the sixth century a hospital at Jerusalem was founded solely for the care of mentally deranged monks.

Gibbon regarded cenobitism as preferable to anchoritism for the latter reduced men to the state of a brute scarcely distinguished from the animals. S. Simeon Stylites, who lived on top of a column in Syria for some thirty years, is 'immortalized by the singular invention of an aerial penance'.[35] Gibbon regards him as mad fanatic for his voluntary martyrdom gradually destroyed the sensibility of his mind, body and lively affection for the rest of mankind.

> A cruel unfeeling temper has distinguished the monks of every age and country; their stern indifference, which is seldom mollified by personal friendship, is inflamed by religious hatred; and their merciless zeal has strenuously administered the holy office of the Inquisition.[36]

Gibbon is not surprised by the fact that the supposed monastic saints, such as Simeon, were adored by the crowds who fell prostrate before their shrines and avidly believed the miracles which their relics were alleged to perform. He held that the extravagant tales associated with the lives and actions of the monks had seriously affected the reason, faith and morals of the Christians. Their credulity had debased the faculties of the mind and had corrupted the evidence of history. All the manly virtues had been oppressed by the servile and pusillanimous reign of the monks.[37]

It was not only in chapter 37 but throughout the *Decline and Fall* that Gibbon's antagonism to monasticism appears. He consistently describes the monks by such terms as 'swarms', 'legions', 'myriads', 'army', 'multitudes', 'millions'. The five hundred Nitrian monks in Cyril of Alexandria's time are described as 'wild beasts of the desert'.[38] Their bigoted and cold—blooded murder of Hypatia, vividly recorded by Gibbon, was a fiendish act.[39] Enthusiasm and superstition were among the major faults of Christianity and, for Gibbon, the monks manifested these to a supreme degree.[40] He is always on the look out for opportunities to flay the monks. So in his chapter on Mahomet he remarks that the Muslim picture of paradise 'has provoked the indignation, perhaps the envy, of the monks'.[41]

III

That Gibbon's account of monasticism is biased is self–evident to the reader. By picking on what was bad and ignoble, and ignoring the good, Gibbon vitiated one of the primary aims of historical study. In a letter to his step–mother written two years before his death Gibbon sums up his life: 'Although I have long been a spectator of the great world, by unambitious temper has been content with the occupations and rewards of study'.[42] Gibbon's sense of detachment, his eighteenth–century hatred of enthusiasm, his scepticism and empiricism, failed him in his study of monasticism. He could not penetrate the essence of monastic spirituality but was merely a spectator of the bizarre which he recorded to such devasting effect. For Gibbon to be effective movements and institutions had to be firmly based in reality and in human contact. Once this was cut, as in monasticism, vanity, cruelty, fanaticism was released which easily got out of the control of social norms. Gibbon believed that the monks had torn this web of reality by destroying the knife edge between superstition and social restraints. The monk had ceased to be a man firmly rooted in reality and his culture was that of 'non–men'. This is seen supremely in Byzantium which he regarded as a monk–ridden society illustrating the final divorce between civilisation and the Church. It is however worth noting that Gibbon hated, not Christianity itself, but monks, priests and the Church as an institution. Detached from both the Catholic and Protestant views of the early Church Gibbon wished to keep religion in its place, the place which it held before the advent of the Jewish and Christian zealots. The savage irruption seen in monasticism had for him, destroyed the fabric of social life.

Gibbon's tendentious *tour de force* reflected not only his own rationalism and scepticism but that of his age. It was a detached, outside view of the eighteenth–century Enlightenment unable to penetrate a monastic spirituality which was centred on a conviction of sin, the Cross and Resurrection and which was firmly based on the Bible. Gibbon could not understand that many monks, notwithstanding certain bizarre practices so congenial to his scepticism, were genuinely seeking union with God.

Joseph Bingham's approach, on the other hand, was purely historical and concerned only to record accurately what the Fathers had said about the monks and the monastic movement with little evaluation. Although possessing a keen eye for the vagaries of human nature Bingham's work is however overall sympathetic. From his sermons,[43] and his somewhat straitened personal circumstances, we know that asceticism was not foreign to his nature. Bingham and Gibbon[44] thus reflect contrasting eighteenth–century attitudes towards the past and their works can still be read with profit today.

NOTES

1.   M.H. Peacock, *History of the Free Grammar School of Queen Elizabeth at Wakefield* (Wakefield, 1892). For University College, Oxford's judgement on the school see the testimony of its Master, Arthur Charlett, who in

1718 presented books inscribed *Bibliothecae Publicae Scholar celeberrimae de Wakefield* and others in 1719 *Scholae eximiae de Wakefield*; Peacock, *ibid.*, p 129.

2.   W. Carr, *University College* (London, 1902). Bingham was made deacon by Bishop Hough on 20 December 1691 and priest on 12 March 1692/3 both in Magdalen College chapel; MS Oxf. dioc. paper, ch. 106, fols. 137, 144.

3.   The best edition is that of descendant R. Bingham, *Works* (Oxford, 1855). Vols. 1–8 contain the *Origines*, Vol. 9, *The Scholastic History of Baptim by laymen* and a *Dissertation on the Eighth Nicene Canon.* Vol. 10 has *The French Church's Apology for the Church of England* and *Sermons on the Trinity, the Divinity of Christ inter alia.* The *Origines*, completed in 1722, was translated into latin and published by J.H. Grischovius of Halle in 1824–1729. An abridgement into German was published anonymously at Augsburg in 1788–1796.

4.   Bingham pays an eloquent tribute to Morley in *Works* 1, pp xlv–xlvi, lxxxv.

5.   Bibliography to *The Later Roman Empire* (Oxford, 1964).

6.   *Works* 2, pp 318–397.

7.   *Ibid.*, p 321.

8.   *Ibid.*, pp 352–395.

9.   *Ibid.*, p 330.

10.   *Ibid.*, pp 331–333.

11.   *Ibid.*, p 344.

12.   *Ibid.*, p 359.

13.   *Ibid.*, pp 365–366.

14.   *Ibid.*, pp 373–374.

15.   All quotations are taken from the edition of J.B. Bury (London, 1909).

16.   Vol. 7, pp 320–321.

17.   Vol. 4, pp 62–81.

18.   Vol. 4, p 62.

19.   Vol. 4, p 64.

20.   Vol. 4, p 64.

21.   L.W. Barnard, 'Edward Gibbon on Athanasius' in ed., R.C. Gregg, *Arianism, Historical and Theological Reassessments* (Philadephia, 1985), pp 361–370.

22.   Vol. 4, p 65.

23.   Vol. 4, p 66.

24.   Vol. 4, p 67.

25.   Vol. 4, pp 68–69.

26.   Vol. 4, p 69.

27.   Vol. 4, p 69, n. 21. It is imporant, in studying Gibbon, always to read his footnotes. Sometimes these qualify what he has written in his text.

28.   Vol 4, p 71.

29.   Vol. 4, p 71, n. 37.

30.   Vol. 4, p 71. Cf. the Cappadocian monks involved in the banishment of Chrysostom.

31.   Vol. 4, p 72.

32.   Vol. 4, p 75, n. 55.

33.   Vol. 4, p 76, n. 59.

34.   Vol. 4, p 77.

35.   Vol. 4, p 79.

36.   Vol. 4, p 80.

37.   Vol. 4, p 81.

38.   Vol 5, p 116. Cyril is Gibbon's arch–tyrant.

39.   Vol. 5, p 117.
40.   Vol. 5, p 120.
41.   Vol. 5, p 374.
42.   Ed., J.E. Norton, *The Letters of Edward Gibbon* (London, 1956), III, p 266, quoted in eds., G.W. Baversock, J. Clive, S.R. Graubard, *Edward Gibbon and the Decline and Fall of the Roman Empire* (Cambridge, Mass., 1977), p 13.
43.   *Works* 10.
44.   Gibbon has read Bingham's *Origines*. In vol. 4, p 62, n 1, Gibbon states 'the cautious Protestant, who distrusts any Popish guides, may consult the seventh book of Bingham's Christian Antiquities'.

FOUNDERS AND FOLLOWERS:
LEADERSHIP IN ANGLICAN RELIGIOUS COMMUNITIES

Brian Taylor

In the study of ecclesiastical history of all periods, the division between fact and fantasy is often blurred. If I say that in my own parish, there is within peacock cry of the rectory a Redemptorist monastery, with novices, giving obedience to Archbishop Lefebvre, and that above the church, on the old road down from the Hog's Back, the cemetery chapel a few steps from Lewis Carroll's grave has been taken on a long lease by a congregation of the True Orthodox Church of Greece, a denomination so small in this country that the recent resignation of its priest left the whole of Great Britain without one — then you will understand that I sometimes wonder which side of the looking glass is which. One of the most valuable commentators on some aspects of church life in the late nineteenth and early twentieth centuries was Compton Mackenzie, and it makes little difference whether his novels or the octaves of his autobiography are read. And Malford Abbey in Surrey or Alton Abbey in Hampshire, Clere Abbey on the Berkshire Downs or the Retreat at Milton Abbas in Dorset — there is little to distinguish one from the other.

The sesquicentenary of Keble's assize sermon occasioned much writing. In one short but perceptive essay Francis Sutcliffe suggests that one of the weaknesses of the Anglican women's communities is found in the fact that there are so many of them, all with their own idiosyncracies and customs.[1] This cannot be contradicted. Many societies soon come to an end for lack of novices. Others have struggled to survive. An example is the Community of St Katharine of Alexandria, founded in 1879. It now has three sisters, one of whom is in residential care elsewhere. In their convent at Parmoor, King Zog's wartime home, they been joined by the only surviving sister of the Community of the Good Shepherd, founded in 1909, though she is Benedictine and they are Augustinian. I wish to suggest that another reason for lack of growth in both men's and women's societies is to be found in the background of those who have led the revival of the religious life in the Church of England.

Behind much that happened was the powerful figure of *ho megas*, Dr Pusey (Eton and Christ Church). In fact, no Pusey blood flowed in his veins. They were Bouveries, religious refugees from Belgium. His father, the son of Viscount Folkestone, the grandson of Baron Romney, and the great–grandson of Sir Cloudesley Shovell, changed his name for inheritance reasons. Pusey's mother was the daughter of the earl of Harborough.

The Senior existing Anglican men's community is the Society of St John the Evangelist (1865), but there were attempts before that. E. Steere, (University College School, University College London and the Inner Temple) the son of a barrister, used a legacy to acquire the chapel of the ancient hospital of St James at Tamworth, and set up the Brotherhood of St James in 1855. He soon found that his companions suffered from romantic illusions, and it lasted only a few months. Later Steere became bishop in Central Africa. I shall not say much about J.L. Lyne, Father Ignatius (St Paul's School, Ayscoughfee Hall Spalding and Trinity College Glenalmond). He was connected through his mother with the barons de Tabley, and founded his bizarre Benedictine community at Claydon, Suffolk, in 1863.

When we come to the Cowley Fathers, we reach stability. The father founder, R.M. Benson (educated at home, then at Christ Church) was of royal descent. His father was a man of property, but his mother was a Meux, of the brewing family, one of whom had married a descendant of Edward III. Several men had been hoping that a mission brotherhood could be established, and they found in Benson their natural leader. At a meeting in Soho in February 1865 were gathered A.P. Forbes (Edinburgh Academy, University of Glasgow, Haileybury and Brasenose) son of Baron Medwyn and descended from Nova Scotia baronets, and already bishop of Brechin since 1847 after a few months as vicar of Pusey's church, St Saviour's Leeds; C.C. Grafton, whose parents were from military and legal backgrounds (Boston Latin School, Phillips–Andover Academy and Harvard Law School); G.F.S. Lane–Fox (Eton and Christ Church) collaterally descended from the earl of Lanesborough and Baron Bingley; S.W. O'Neill (Mr Snow's school at Barnstaple and Emmanuel); and C.L. Wood (Eton and Christ Church) son of a baronet later to become Viscount Halifax, and through his mother, the daughter of Earl Grey of Howick, connected with the duke of St Alban's, the marquess of Bristol, the earls of Carlisle, Durham, Home and Minto, and with other peers of inferior rank. With them was their host, R. Tuke (King's College London) a gentleman of private means, who was to found his own Order of St Joseph in 1886, and then become a Roman Catholic. Pusey had taken Grafton to Benson, and as they met, Grafton said portentously, 'I have come from America. Where is the man who longs to form a religious community in England? I want to find him'.[2] Of those who met, only Benson, Grafton and O'Neill persevered, and made their profession on 27 December 1866.[3] O'Neill, who became a notable missionary in India, was the son of a missionary of the London Society for Promoting Christianity Amongst the Jews, who had worked in Warsaw and Hamburg, who died when his son was young. O'Neill was ordained while a master at Eton, and was a curate for Carter at Clewer and Butler at Wantage, before joining Benson. Following Benson, the superiors general have been R.L. Page (St John's Cambridge), G.S., Maxwell (Oriel), H.P. Bull (Hereford Cathedral School and Brasenose), W.B. O'Brien (Worcester), F.B. Dalby (Malvern and Keble), G.C. Triffitt (Moulton Grammar School and University College Nottingham) and F.D.G. Campbell (Winchester and Exeter).

In the history of the Oxford Mission, published as recently as 1979, the first members of the Brotherhood of the Epiphany (1880) are described as 'a strong team; all were the best products of the public schools and the universities'.[4] The first four priests were E.F. Willis, the first superior (Uppingham and Balliol), E.F. Brown, the fourth superior (Charterhouse and Trinity Oxford), W. Hornby (Marlborough and Brasenose) and M.F. Argles (Harrow and Balliol). The second superior, C.W. Townsend, went up to Keble from what was described as 'a school in York', but he left and became a Jesuit. The other superiors have been H. Whitehead (Sherborne and Trinity Oxford), T.E.T. Shore (Westminster and Magdalen), A.R. Macbeth (Emmanuel School and Keble) and P. Thorman (St Edward's School and Sidney Sussex). From 1985 to 1988 there was an Indian superior, V. Yardi (Bishop's College Calcutta), but another missionary followed him, T. Mathieson (Rugby and Sidney Sussex).

Three of Charles Gore's great–grandfathers were earls (Arran, Bessborough and Westmoreland); the fourth was a baronet descended from the parliamentarian, king Pym. Gore (Harrow and Balliol) was joined by five others when he founded the Community of the Resurrection in 1892: M.C. Bickersteth (Eton and New College), J. Carter (Upper Canada College, Trinity College Toronto and Exeter), W.H. Frere, the second superior (Charterhouse and the seventh generation, father to son, at Trinity Cambridge), G. Longridge, the third superior (Eton and Brasenose) and J.O. Nash (King William College and Hertford). Other superiors have been E.K. Talbot (Winchester and Christ Church), son of the bishop of Winchester, with Earl Talbot and Baron Wharncliffe among his great–grandfathers and Baron Lyttelton as a grandfather, B. Horner (Nottingham High School and Hatfield Durham), R.E. Raynes (St Paul's and Pembroke Oxford), J.D. Graham (Trinity Cambridge), W.F. Bishop (Malvern and Keble), E. Simmons (Leeds) and G.R. Berry (University of New Zealand).

The Society of the Sacred Mission (1894) has had a rather different story, following the convictions of its founder, H.H. Kelly (Manchester Grammar School, Woolwich and Queen's). His founding companion, H.W. Woodward, and also the third director, J.C. White, were both ordained in Africa after some years as lay missionaries of the Universities' Mission to Central Africa. The second director was D. Jenks (King's College School and Pembroke Cambridge), and White was followed by R.H. Tribe (London, also with medical qualifications) and S.F.B. Bedale (Weymouth College and Exeter). The remaining directors, L.P. Hume, F.W.G. Wilkins, D.J.D. McKee and C.D.E. Wheat all received their further education in the society's colleges, and the last three took degrees after ordination and profession (Wilkins at Bristol, McKee at Western Australia, and Wheat at Nottingham and Sheffield), and that accorded with the founder's views on university education, as set out in *An Idea in the Working*.[5] In 1989, however, Wheat has been succeeded by T.W.G. Brown, a graduate of the University of Queensland be–joining the society. The Society of the Divine Compassion (1894) began with J.G. Adderley (Eton and Christ Church) who was superior but never professed, H.E. Hardy (Clifton and Keble) and H. Chappel (Marlborough and Exeter). B.F. Carlyle (Blundell's and St. Bartholomew's Hospital) must be regarded as the founder of the Anglican Benedictines (1896), though they prefer to look back to the first modern abbot of Pershore, W.G.C. Prideaux (Geneva, Leipzig and Clare). G.J.F. Stokes (Rugby and Sidney Sussex) restored their fortunes more recently.

There were several tributaries to the great stream that is now the Society of St Francis. The Brotherhood of St Francis of Assisi at Hilfield (1921) began to take real shape when R.D. Downes, Brother Douglas (Dulwich and Corpus Christi, Oxford) became the leader in 1922. The Brotherhood of the Love of Christ (1934) grew from the Christa Seva Sangha (1922) in India, founded by J.C. Winslow (Eton and Balliol). One of the members of the Sanga was W.S.A. Robertson, Father Algy (Westminster and Queens'), who returned to England and formed the brotherhood at St Ives in Huntingdonshire. The union of the two brotherhoods to make the Society of St Francis was decided in 1936, and Downes became the first minister in 1937. He has been succeeded by D. Wynne–Owen, Brother David (Friars' School Bangor and St Chad's Durham), H.G. Pearson, Brother Geoffrey (Christ's) and R.L. Fisher, Brother Michael (Clapham Central School).

Two more recent societies are the Community of the Servants of the Will of God (1938) founded by R.C.S. Gofton–Salmond (Marlborough and Keble), and the Community of the Glorious Ascension (1960), with its founding twins P.J. Ball and M.T. Ball (Lancing and Queens').

Apart from those of noble birth (and we need not pay much attention to Aelred Carlyle's claims to descent from the earl of Mar), most of the founders and superiors have been sons of county, service or professional families, or of prosperous businessmen. There have been exceptions. Fr Triffitt was the son of a Holbeach saddler and shopkeeper. Fr Kelly's great–grandfather was an Irish labourer, and Brother Douglas was from a humble Yorkshire family. The Society of St Paul (1889), which became the Order of St Paul in 1894, was founded by the son of an American master mariner. C.P. Hopkins (Trinity College of Music, after study at Heidelburg) managed to keep the common touch, in the work for sailors, and this has continued at Alton since the community settled there in 1895. It is now part of the Order of St Benedict. G. Potter (King's College London), the founder of the Brotherhood of the Holy Cross (1924), which like the Society of the Divine Compassion did not quite manage to be absorbed into the Society of St Francis, was also from a poor family, a railway clerk's son. Nonetheless, as Pusey wrote in 1853, after remarking that many of the clergy were sons of tradesmen, a 'good and religious education, after a few years, will leave no traces of this distinction of birth'.[6]   The air of gentlemanliness prevailed. Fr Pridham (Worcester), who was professed in 1901, used to recall the decanter of port put out at midmorning for visitors at Cowley. This atmosphere lingered on in the huge mission houses maintained by the Cowley Fathers at Panch Howd, Pune until 1967, and by the Oxford Mission in Vivekananda Road, Calcutta until 1969.

When we turn to the women's communities, information is more elusive, and there is frequently a reticence which it is not delicate to penetrate. Here it is possible to mention only a random selection. The founding mothers of the earlier sisterhoods were mostly educated at home. Usually there was also a founding father — and also a founding father's wife. Those wives were patient women, accepting the need for their husbands to spend long hours with the mothers superior, arranging the details of the daily lives of the sisters. Occasionally these wives became closely associated with the communities, as when Mrs Butler of Wantage became the first of the exterior sisters of the Community of St Mary the Virgin. Mrs Pusey died in 1839, two years before Marian Rebecca Hughes made her act of dedication on 6 June 1841. Miss Hughes was the daughter of a clergyman (Magdalen), and hers were the first religious vows in the Church of England in modern times, but it was eight years before she was able to found her community, the Society of the Holy and Undivided Trinity (1849), with Pusey as warden.

The first community was Pusey's Sisterhood of the Holy Cross (1845) in Regent's Park, following the confidential circular letter composed by Gladstone and signed by several peers and other influential men.[7]   The first three sisters included Jane Ellacombe, daughter of a priest (Oriel), and Sarah Anne Terrot, daughter of the bishop of Edinburgh (Carlisle Grammar School and Trinity Cambridge). Emma Langston, the superior, had been a governess. The other society with which Pusey was most associated was the Church of England Sisterhood of Mercy of Devonport and Plymouth (1848), founded by Priscilla Lydia Sellon, daughter of a naval officer who had an estate in Monmouthshire. She grew up as Miss Smith until 1847, when her father took the name of Sellon on inheriting a family fortune. This community was united with the Park Village sisterhood in 1856 to form the Society of the Most Holy Trinity, with Mother Lydia as superior — or lady abbess as she became in 1857. Her early successors as superior were Elizabeth Bertha Turnbull, from a Scottish border family, whose father was chamberlain of the city of Edinburgh, and Georgina Louise Napier, daughter of Baron Napier or Merchistoun.

If Mrs Pusey had lived longer, and if the marriage had become less tense and anxious, Pusey's influence on the communities might well have been less sombre and oppressive. Perhaps the sisterhoods at Wantage and Clewer, and their growth and vigour, owed something to Bishop Wilberforce for excluding Pusey from both of them.

The Community of St Mary the Virgin (1848) was the creation of the vicar of Wantage, W.J. Butler (Westminster and Trinity Cambridge), and its survival and growth were secured by his firm guidance. The first superior, Elizabeth Crawford Lockhart, came from a clerical family, and her brother, W. Lockhart, one of Newman's companions at Littlemore, was the first of the Tractarians to be received into the Roman Catholic Church, in 1843. Elizabeth Lockhart followed her brother in 1850, and soon the other original sister took the same step. Butler was left with Harriet Day, a farmer's daughter, and Charlotte Gilbert, the daughter of a labourer. They rose to unexpected responsibility, and Mother Harriet was superior for thirty—one years. In the meanwhile, Elizabeth Lockhart founded the Roman Catholic Missionary Franciscan Sisters of the Immaculate Conception, in 1857.

At Clewer there was a strong partnership between the rector, T.T. Carter (Eton and Christ Church) and Mrs Monsell, who came to help at the house of mercy, and stayed to become the founding mother of the Community of St John Baptist (1851). She was an O'Brien of county Clare, the daughter of a baronet, descended from the first Baron Inchiquin, and from the high king Brian Boroimhe, and she was clothed as a novice just four months after her husband's death.

Two friends went to visit the Park Village sisterhood, and were drawn to the religious life — but they did not find their vocation there, or together, for both started new communities. Harriet Brownlow Byron, from a wealthy Surrey family, founded the Society of All Saints, the Sisters of the Poor (1851), under the guidance of the vicar of All Saints' Margaret Street, W. Upton Richards (Bodmin School and Exeter). Etheldreda Anne Benett served her novitiate with the All Saints sisters, but then founded the Society of the Sisters of Bethany (1866). Her father (Merton, Wadham and Lincoln's Inn) was descended from one of the oldest Wiltshire families, claiming kinship with Archbishop Chichele.

The Society of St Margaret (1855) was planned in detail by J.M. Neale (Sherborne and Trinity Cambridge). The first sister, who became the first mother, Ann Gream, was the daughter of a clergyman (St Edmund Hall). The best—known of all the East Grinstead sisters was Mother Kate of Haggerston, Katherine Anne Egerton Warburton, from an ancient Cheshire Family, and descended from Henry III.

The Community of the Holy Name began as the St Peter's Mission Sisterhood in Vauxhall in 1865, and was created by the vicar, G.W. Herbert (Eton and Exeter). He was the son of a prosperous builder, and his wife was the daughter of a London silversmith — not aristocratic, but they made their way socially. One daughter married a clergyman, D.R. Pelly (Harrow and Emmanuel), the grandson of a baronet; another married D.M. Milne—Watson (Merchiston Castle, Edinburgh, Balliol and Marburg), an industrialist who became a baronet; and another became the comtesse de Preux. The first superior was Charlotte Broadley, the widow of a clergyman (Exeter, Trinity Cambridge, but finally M.A. Lambeth); but the real mother foundress was Frances Mary Seymour, the grandaughter of Lord Saltoun, and the widow of a grandson of the duke of Somerset.

The Sisters of the Church (1870) were founded by Emily Ayckbowm, whose father (Trinity College Dublin) was a clergyman of German descent. She had the guidance of the vicar of St Augustine's Kilburn, R.C. Kirkpatrick (Trinity College Dublin), who was descended from King David I of Scotland.

The Community of the Epiphany was founded in 1883 by G.H. Wilkinson (Durham School, Brasenose and Oriel), Bishop of Truro and later of St Andrew's. The Wilkinsons were landowning gentlefolk of Durham and Northumberland. He chose as the first mother Julian Warrender, who had done parish work with him in London. She was the daughter of a baronet and her mother was a daughter of the earl of Lauderdale.

The Society of the Precious Blood (1905) began with the profession of one sister, Millicent Taylor, daughter of an Indian Army general. She had been prepared for two years by her parish priest, A.T.B. Pinchard (Shrewsbury School, London College of Divinity and University College Durham).

There have been exceptions. One of them was Mary Sylvia Frances Cope, Mother Margaret, the foundress of the Order of the Holy Paraclete (1915), and the confidential friend of Archbishop Garbett. She was the daughter of a Great Western Railway clerk, later station master at Wolverhampton, and was educated at Dudley High School, King Edward's School Birmingham and Cherwell Hall, Oxford. Another was Grace Emily Costin, the foundress of the Franciscan Servants of Jesus and Mary (1935) as Mother Teresa, and known also as Two Gun Annie. She had few advantages of family or education, but wide experience of life, including patrol duty in the Women's Police Service. Nonetheless, what was written of Edith Langridge (Queen's College Harley Street and Lady Margaret Hall), the daughter of a prosperous business man and the mother foundress of the Oxford Mission Sisterhood of the Epiphany (1902) could have been written of many. 'She had the advantage of being born into one of those large, well—off, leisured and cultured Victorian families which are now things of the past'.[8]

Another distinction found in some communities was between choir and lay sisters, copied from Roman Catholic practice. In the Society of St Margaret, for example, this lasted until 1934, with a separate and longer lay novitiate. In my congregation I have had two old ladies, both of whom were once at East Grinstead. One was a professed lay sister, the daughter of a London and South Western Railway painter at Guildford station. The other was a choir novice, and she was a Durant of Tong. They owned the castle there at the time when Little Nell and her grandfather lived in one of the ruinous dwellings in the churchyard. A detailed study of the family background of membership of sample Anglican communities on the lines of the investigations of Dr Susan O'Brien into Roman Catholic sisterhoods[9] would be illuminating. More generally, Dr Peter Williams and several other contributors to the modern section of the summer conference of the Ecclesiastical History Society in 1989, often found it necessary to distinguish between the work of ladies and of women.

The pattern that can be seen in not surprising, and perhaps it was inevitable. The upper and middle classes were bred and educated to be leaders, and leadership remained in their hands; but they were not typical of the membership of the church. The valuable contribution that the religious communities make is often acknowledged. The 'Lima Text', from an ecumenical point of view, says, 'Men and women in the communities of religious orders fulfil a service which is of particular importance for the life of the Church'.[10]

Nonetheless, in the Church of England the movement has never become truly popular. In 1986 there were 1349 Anglican religious in England, including novices, 264 men and 1085 women, just .087 per cent of the Easter communicants.[11] We can do more than speculate whether that figure would have been higher if there had been a more noticeably proletarian element in the leadership of the communities. Even the former secretary of the Advisory Council for Religious Communities admitted, 'there is still much of the atmosphere of an English public school in a lot of communities'[12] — but perhaps lately, there are signs of a broadening of the base.

NOTES

1. C.F.H. Sutcliffe, 'Orders for Tomorrow' in *Tracts for Our Times* (London, 1983), pp 56–61.
2. Quoted in R.C. Smith, *The Cowley Fathers in America, the early years* (nd), p 4.
3. Grafton, who left the society in 1883, and became bishop of Fond du Lac in 1889, was described by J.D. Wade in the *Dictionary of American Biography* as 'distinguished in appearance and manner, suave in his contacts, consciously, if never complacently, as true a medieval Prince of the Church as Wisconsin ways could warrant'.
4. *A Hundred Years in Bengal* (Delhi, 1979), p 8.
5. H.H. Kelly, *An Idea in the Working* (4 ed. Kelham, 1967), pp 74–86.
6. Quoted from *Report and Evidence upon the Recommendations of Her Majesty's Commissioners for inquiring into the State of the University of Oxford* in P. Butler ed, *Pusey Rediscovered* (London, 1983), p 331.
7. The letter with its signatures is printed in H.P. Liddon, *Life of Edward Bouverie Pusey* (3 ed. London, 1895) vol 3, pp 18–21.
8. G. Madge, *Mother Edith O.M.S.E.* (Beaconsfield, 1964), p 9.
9. S. O'Brien, '*Tera Incognita*: the Nun in Nineteenth–Century England' in *Past & Present* no 121, pp 110–140.
10. *Baptism, Eucharist and Ministry* (Geneva, 1982), p 27.
11. *Church Statistics* for 1986 (London, 1987), p 21, with additional information provided by the Statistics Department of the Central Board of Finance of the Church of England, August 1989.
12. A. Harrison, *Bound for Life* (Oxford, 1983), p 38.

THE ENGLISH BENEDICTINES:
THE SEARCH FOR A MONASTIC IDENTITY
1880 — 1920

Dom Aidan Bellenger

A cricket match at Downside is, in most ways, much like one anywhere else in England, but there is a difference. When the Angelus bell sounds from the tower of the abbey church, all matches on the First Eleven Square come to a stop. The players stand to attention, look towards the church and say the Angelus. Visiting teams are sometimes taken off—guard by this practice and some have even suspected it as a clever ploy by the home team to wrongfoot the opposition. The tradition could also be seen as an image of the English Benedictine Congregation as it is generally perceived — a monastery, a house of prayer, at the heart of a boarding school organised on English 'public school' lines with the majority of the resident *conventus* involved on the one hand in the *opus Dei* of the choir and on the other in the administration of the school. In the modern Congregation such a model exists even if, at many of the contemporary abbeys, a significant proportion of the community is involved in 'missionary' (that is, parish work) outside the monastery. In the first three hundred years of its revival, however, such a model would have seemed inconceivable to most of the members of the Congregation. This paper will look at the monastic reform movement sometimes known as 'the Downside movement' which wrought a fundamental change in the character of the English Congregation. This reform was centred at the monastery of Downside in the four decades following 1880. The English Benedictine Congregation (henceforth EBC) was an early seventeenth century attempt to revive the medieval congregation which had perished with the Reformation. Some 'continuity' was provided by an aged monk of Marian Westminster, Dom Sigebert Buckley, but the founding fathers of the EBC were less influenced by the loose confederation of independent houses which constituted the Medieval Congregation than by the reformed congregations of Italy and Spain which emphasized congregational as opposed to abbatial authority. The 1619 Constitutions of the EBC placed central authority in the hands of a General Chapter which met every four years. As time went on the Chapter had a tendency to drift from oligarchy towards gerontocracy because many of those who had a right to attend Chapter were elected or appointed for life. Day—to—day government was provided in a parallel system with the missioners in England under the authority of two provincials (of Canterbury and York) in North and South and the conventuals resident in the monasteries under their superiors, priors without full authority. The majority of the ordained monks were on the Mission. All monks — like their secular counterparts at the time — were bound to take the Missionary Oath which was a solemn undertaking to work on the English Mission when called upon to do so. The President of the Congregation, who was the central executive figure, was elected by General Chapter.[1]

The four most resilient communities of men in the Congregation (which also included monasteries of women) were those of St Gregory, Douai (1607), St Laurence, Dieuonlard (1608), St Edmund's, Paris (1615) and Lambspring, in what is now lower Satony (1644), the last being the only abbey in the Congregation. Monks of St Gregory's are often called Gregorians, those of St Laurence's Laurentians and those of St Edmund's Edmundians and I will use these designations throughout the paper. St Gregory's was the first EBC community to be properly established and in its first generation — as in the other houses — monastic observance within the *conventus* was very strict. A school was established at St Gregory's at an early date (perhaps by 1610) and, although never large by modern standards, it provided an important source of vocations for the community and gave the community an influence within the English Catholic community.[2] Most of the Gregorian *conventus* was occupied working on the English mission where the Benedictines had important centres in both town and country. During the course of the eighteenth century, Bath became the greatest of the Benedictine missions[3] and it was twelve miles from Bath, south along the Fosse Way, that the community settled in 1814 at Downside House in the village of Stratton–on–the–Fosse following a decade of disruption which included departure from France during the Revolution and a period of nearly twenty years as temporary refugees at Acton Burnell in Shropshire. The school continued and developed, especially in the late Victorian period, and the complex of monastic and school buildings grew in scale and style.

The Congregation, too, adjusted to life in England and a common novitiate and house of studies was established in 1859 at Belmont, Hereford, where the conventual church served until 1920 as a cathedral priory for the Welsh diocese of Newport and Menevia. Here for the first time the EBC had a monastic centre which resembled monasteries in other countries and Congregations but its life was still atypical of the Congregation and 'unmonastic' to the degree that while having a strongly observant liturgical and conventual life, it took young monks away from their own monasteries for all the years of their formation. It was a congregational rather than a conventual concept. If anything, in the expansive evangelical atmosphere of Victorian Catholicism, the monasteries increasingly appeared as staging posts and the Benedictines became even more mission–minded not only in England where many fine parish churches were built but also undertaking work overseas. Imperial expansion in the country was reflected among the Benedictines and their work — especially that of the Downside community — in Australia was instrumental in providing the foundations for much of the now well–established structure of the Australian Catholic Church. To many it seemed that the 'provisional' arrangements of 1619 — 'provisional' because they legislated for 'an underground church' that was no more — were as good for the late nineteenth century as they were for the early seventeenth century. There are still some in the Congregation today who would favour the earlier arrangements or at least emphasize the importance of the parishes, and 'the mission father' is still an important figure in many communities. Monastic *familiae*, notoriously, have long if sometimes selective memories, but in 1880, the fourteen–hundredth anniversary of St Benedict's birth, the forces of change were grouping and putting their memories back not to the seventeenth century but to the origins of the monastic *ordo* in late antiquity.

In Rome, Leo XIII was attempting, in the face of the *kulturkampf* of Bismarckian Germany and the anti–clericalism of Third Republic France, to withstand the secular challenge. Reform movements within religious orders were given papal blessing and active support. The 'primitive observance' of the Rule of St Benedict was emerging as a model of monastic reform. Benedictine reform was developing across the continent. The Pope was aware of the anomaly of the English Benedictines and 1880 was a year for going back to roots. The discrepancy between the Benedictine ideal as expressed in the Rule (and by the various continental commentators) and the way of life of the English Black Monks was not only noted in Rome. English bishops like Manning of Westminster (no lover of the religious orders, especially the older ones), Clifford of Clifton (in whose diocese Downside was situated) and the two Benedictines, Brown of Newport and Menevia and Ullathorne of Birmingham (both Gregorians) made it clear that the Benedictine charisms of life in community and public liturgical prayer were being obscured among the English Benedictines where many monks were living alone and where spiritual life was concentrated not on the *opus Dei* but on personal, mental prayer. Ullathorne's gesture in inviting the Beuronese monks to establish a community at Erdington in his diocese indicated Ullathorne's monastic position. In Victorian England, he considered Benedictines should live in great abbeys or, at least, in community as they had in Medieval Catholic England. Ullathorne was convinced that community life was the essential Benedictine characteristic and in 1875 he made this explicit in an address on the festival of the Saints of the Benedictine order. 'And a great voice is heard speaking in accents like these: Well have you done in the past: return, return, as occasion serves, return to community life'.[4] The Beuronese ideal appealed to Ullathorne. Beuron, the inspiration of the two Wolter brothers, had become an abbey in 1868 and its influence was to spread far beyond its German homeland. In 1880 its first abbot, Maurus Wolter (1825–90) published his *Praecipua ordinis monastici elementa* which presented an elaborate but well–presented 840 page introduction to monastic principles. This book, like Beuron itself, emphasized the importance of life abbacies and the autonomy of each house with the mother abbey, setting the pattern of observance for the whole congregation. Erdington, founded in 1876, became an abbey in 1899 and survived (uneasily after 1914 as a predominantly German community) until 1919. Ullathorne's reputation may have been high at Beuron but his name was not held in such great esteem by some among the EBC mission fathers who disliked his plea for a return to a more obviously 'Benedictine' life. Those at Downside who favoured reform looked on him as a hero and as a link with the past. The life of the resident conventuals at St Gregory's, Douai, with its full choral office and monastic round in a (relatively) spacious choir and cloister was now looked back to 'reformers' as a golden or, at least, a silver age.

Ullathorne's open declaration for reform was typical of the outspoken character of the man but it was probably manoeuvres in Rome which led to action. Prelatical mutterings, especially from Cardinal Howard, Bishop Clifford (encouraged by his cousin Dom Jerome Vaughan) and Monsignor Weld (of whom more later), were heard in the highest circles. Clifford and Weld, it would appear, were crucial in persuading Leo XIII that an Apostolic Visitation was the only way to circumvent the 'immobilisme' of the EBC oligarchy. This 'immobilisme' could be perhaps summarised in the attitude of Dom Austin Bury, the Laurentian Provincial of the North. He confessed that the only effect of his monastic training on his subsequent life was to weaken his health. Later, Bury, a theologian of distinction, was to say that 'he would as soon vote for his damnation as for the "family" scheme',[5] the idea of autonomous houses. It was views such as these that persuaded the Roman officials to act in the way they did. The Apostolic Constitution *Romanos Pontifices* (1881), which called on the religious orders in England to bring their missionary way of life into line with their respective rules, was backed up by the decree *Inclyta* which announced an apostolic visitation of the EBC.

The visitation of 1881, which signalled the beginning of a pamphlet war in the Congregation, was conducted by the Claustral Prior of Montecassino Father Boniface Krug (1838–1909), a German–born monk who had made his profession at St Vincent's Pennsylvania in 1860, and marked in the words of the official EBC annalist, Abbot Basil Whelan, 'definite turning point in the fortunes and policy of the English Benedictines'.[6] At Downside, Krug was 'received with joy' by those who wanted the monasteries to become autonomous communities with abbatial rank.[7] The conversation between Fathers Cuthbert Butler and Edmund Ford at Downside, quoted in part by David Knowles in his memoir of Butler,[8] and quoted in full here, suggests something of the surprise and the expectation which the Visitation elicited. Here is Butler speaking in the first person:

> 'So a Visitor is coming'. These are the words Dom Ford addressed to me as we met on the spiral winding stairs in the monastery about 10 o'clock on the morning of Saturday, June 11th 1881. I did not understand the remark, and said in a puzzled way: 'Who? Anybody special?'. 'An Apostolic Visitor', he replied: 'it is in "The Tablet"'. 'Indeed', said I, 'what is he coming for?' 'Oh, to look up the Congregation and see how we are getting on, and if any changes are wanted'. 'Well', said I deliberately, 'I am very glad: it is not before it was wanted'. As I said this I looked him straight in the face, and I saw clearly that such was his opinion also.
>
> The following week he and I were Reader and Server in the Refectory, and so met at second table for dinner, and we talked freely of the state of the Congregation and our hopes and fears; and before long I was satisfied that Dom Ford's views substantially agreed with mine, and that like me, he was on for a root and branch reform inside and out.[9]

In general, the *conventus* at Downside also favoured a radical change in the order of things, while Ampleforth and Douai were against it, and Belmont was divided. On the mission, the fathers were against change (as perhaps could only be expected) but, according to Krug, the Province of the South was more 'monastically' inclined and two missioners, Dom Ephrem Guy (Gregorian) and Dom Laurence Shepherd (Laurentian), were said to be full of monastic spirit.[10]

The Visitation Report was published on 9 July 1882. It concluded that there should not be a full-scale dismantling of the missionary structure but that the monasteries should be raised to abbatial rank and that Downside and Fort Augustus established in 1874 (which was to leave the Congregation and become, it was hoped, the mother house of a revived Scots Congregation) should have their own novitiates. At this time, too, some thought that it might be opportune to make Downside an arch-abbey on the model of Beuron, but this plan was not given official backing. Downside's reforming influence was not to be institutionalized. The fruit of the Visitation was the rescript 'Cliftonien' (6 July 1883), which called on the Congregation to prepare new Constitutions.

The sixty-sixth General Chapter of the EBC met in November 1883 and elected a new President, Father Anselm O'Gorman, to replace President Placid Burchall who had held the office for thirty years, but O'Gorman did not bring a wind of change. Present O'Gorman saw to it that the Constitutional committee was packed with what can only be called 'reactionaries'. It was at this stage that the Downside movement entered its second phase. Downside took on the initiative of 'reform' under its newly elected prior, Dom Edmund Ford, who drew up an eight point plan which could be described as the *Magna Carta* of the reform party.[11] This document is undated but was probably published soon after Ford took over from the ailing Prior Gasquet in 1885. The plan of reform suggested the following:

1.   That the Monastery be made an Abbey.

2.   That it have its own novitiate, and the control of the studies of its own subjects.

3.   That the term of the Superior's office be considerably lengthened, e.g. to 10 or 12 years.

4.   That the houses be empowered to found residences (subject to the provisions of 'Romanos Pontifices') which shall be immediately dependent on the Monasteries.

5.   That the R.R. President's power of translation be limited in the sense of the Constitutions of 1617, and of the General Chapter of 1621, i.e. that a religious be not removed from his Monastery without the consent of his Superior, nor against the expressed wish of the majority of the Community, unless the monk himself is willing to go.

6.   That the missionary oath be no longer taken.

7.   That the missionary work fall under the ordinary obedience to the conventual Superior; provided that the work is done from houses in which the ordinary characteristics of Benedictine life obtain, viz. a community of ten or twelve, vita perfecta communis, (and in agreement with) such organisation and *general* laws as are laid down in our Constitutions for our Monasteries.

      In order, however, to provide for the service of our smaller missions, let it be open to anyone after his 30th year, to volunteer to serve such missions, by which the religious will place himself at the disposal of the conventual Superior in the same way as he is now at the disposal of the R.R. President.

8.   That any professed Gregorian may accept the dispensation from his missionary oath, and come under the above arrangements; and that all professed hereafter take their vows according to this arrangement.

      Cuthbert Butler summarised the 'objects' specifically in view during this 'second phase of the Downside Movement' under three headings:

1.   The assertion of the principle that the Congregation is not essentially missionary, but in the full sense a normal Benedictine Congregation, like any others; which has received a commission to carry out missionary work and for that purpose is empowered to dispense individual monks from the obligations of claustral life.

2.   The securing of the fundamental Benedictine conception that a monk may spend his life in his monastery and an enlarging of the ideas current as to the kinds of work suitable for our own monks, so that biblical and historical studies and other traditional forms of Benedictine work should be recognised as being lawful and suitable objects of the life work of any of our monks suited for it.

3.   The raising of the monasteries from the abject estate in which they lay, and the winning for them that power of controlling their own destinies,

and that autonomy which is the birthright of a Benedictine monastery, that they might take their due place in the Order and in English Catholic life.[12]

These plans were, in time, to become the accepted approach to Benedictinism in the EBC. The fight for their implementation was, however, to be long and bloody. To many in the Congregation, the Downside reformers were a youthful and presumptuous clique. The reforms adopted in 1888 were strangely muted, something which cannot be said of the debates at the General Chapters of 1888 and 1889 which were full of sound and fury. Dom Clement Fowler, a non–reformer, became Prior of Downside and to many the work of a decade seemed wasted. At Downside, Fowler's arrival caused a flurry. Appeals were sent to Rome, letters circulated. Many hard things were said. The 'monastic' party was not only dispirited but soon, under Prior Fowler, disbanded. Ex–Priors Ford and Murphy, Fathers Meinrad Fulton and Gilbert Dolan, all 'reformers', were exiled (as they would have seen it) to the mission. But in the wider church things were moving in the reformers' direction. In 1888, Leo XIII revived the Collegio Sant'Anselmo in Rome as an international college for young monks from all over the world. This college soon came under Beuronese influence which became greater in 1893 with the appointment – a controversial move towards Centralism in many Abbots' view – of an Abbot Primate to oversee the Benedictine Confederation to attempt to regularise the lives of its monks. Leo XIII similarly reformed the Cistercians, Premonstatensian and the Franciscans. It was becoming apparent, by the Chapter of 1888, that Rome wanted more than a half–hearted response to its request for reform. The bull 'Religiosus Ordo' (1890) called for the abolition of the provinces, the division of the missions by monastery, and the drawing up of new constitutions which reflected these changed. In the short–term, 'Religiosus Ordo' brought more bickering. The division of missions and funds was a controversial and difficult task. Downside, in particular, was going through a retrograde period in which calls for stricter observance on the 'reform' side were countered by cries for a 'fairer' distribution of missions on the 'reactionaries' side. In the long term 'Religiosus Ordo' revealed to those that had eyes to see it that the 'old' Congregation was dead and that the 'reformers' had won.

The draft of 1893 for new constitutions was considered as unsatisfactory by the Abbot Primate and in the spring of 1894 President O'Neill, an Edmundian like O'Gorman, whom he had succeeded as President in 1888 announced his intention of compiling a revised form of the Constitutions. This revision still did not come up to Roman standards. It was not until 1900, following the setting up of a commission to draw up new constitutions by the bull 'Diu Quidem' (June 1899), that new Constitutions were finally introduced.

It is apparent from this brief history of the events leading to 'Diu Quidem' that Downside was at the centre of debate and controversy throughout the period. It was there that the reform had its prime movers. Why Downside? In his unpublished memoir of the Downside Movement, Cuthbert Butler provides a number of answers to this question which I think are worth quoting fully. The first person in the following extracts is Cuthbert Butler:

1.   I believe it is the case that there had been at St Gregory's a succession of men who were dissatisfied with the state of affairs in the Congregation. Among those whom I have heard mentioned as having wished for better things were DD. Barber (Prior 1818–30), Hodgson, Blount, A. Bulbeck, B. Bulbeck, de Paiva, and G.

Kendal, who died in 1879. Thus the sacred fire had been handed on from old St Gregory's at Douai, and a tradition of discontent had smouldered on at Downside, which every now and then burst forth into a flame, resulting in the malcontents being sent on the Mission as 'dangerous men'. In 1880, there were half a dozen such men at Downside.

2.   I think that a great influence in inspiring and developing monastic ideas must be attributed to the then new monastic buildings. John Stuart Mill says: 'Nothing contributes more to nourish elevation of sentiments in a people, than the large and free character of their habitations. The Middle Age architecture, the baronial hall, and the spacious and lofty rooms, so unlike the mean and cramped externals of English middle class life, gave the sentiment of a larger and a freer existence' (Autobiography, p 55). The grand monastery embodied an ideal, and inspired us with a desire to live up to our buildings. This influence I felt on my return to Downside; but I never fully realised it until I visited Ampleforth in 1891, where 'the mean and cramped' domestic style of the old house used as the monastery, with its debased renaissance ornaments, made me feel how much we owe at Downside to our monastic buildings.

3.   In the year 1880 was celebrated the Centenary of St Benedict, which event occasioned no small stir throughout the Order. A number of books were published, and sermons and addresses delivered, and attention was naturally much directed to other Congregation and countries. This widened our horizon, suggested ideals and methods and led to thought.

4.   The monastery at Fort Augustus was opened in the same year by the English Congregation; and all understood that it was intended to a certain extent to be a new departure. Those at Downside did not wish to be left behind by the new monastery.

5.   There was, moreover, a widespread feeling that the monasteries were sacrificed to the missions. They were sadly undermanned, a mere handful of young men being left, so overworked that monastic life, ecclesiastical studies, and even the efficient carrying on of the School were well nigh out of the question. Many felt that this state of things ought to be put a stop to, and the monasteries duly manned both as regards numbers and age.

6.   Unwonted energy had been put into the pusillus grex by the fact that those of the other way of thinking — those, that is, who held strong missionary views — had just become very aggressive. At the Chapter of 1873, Fr Bury had been chosen Provincial of York (i.e. Superior of the Missions and missioners of the North); he was a man of extraordinary ability and learning, of strong will and a great determination of character, and from his youth upwards had been noted for holding missionary views in their extremist form. Fr Snow, a Gregorian, also able and clear–headed, became his right hand man; and these two soon gathered a following around them and for a couple of years became the dominant power

in the Congregation, the President, Abbot Burchall, being mostly guided by their advice. Rumours were afloat that they talked openly of getting the monasteries put under the Provincials, and of other measures that would soon have eradicated the monastic element of the Congregation, or would at least have made it entirely subservient to the missionary. Thus the cry of 'the monasteries in danger' was raised, and those monastically inclined were compelled to make a protest and strike a blow for their principles.

7.   The fears of these latter were especially aroused by events that took place at Ampleforth in the spring of 1880. There is no need to enter into this episode. Suffice it to say that the prior resigned, and the President, acting on Fr Bury's advice, succeeded in getting authority from Rome to appoint a new prior, in spite of the protests of the Community. Whatever was thought at Downside about the disputes at Ampleforth, this high–handed proceeding was regarded as the beginning of the threatened attack on the monasteries, and so caused no small consternation, and made the monastic party close up their ranks.[13]

Who were the monastic party? As late as Christmas 1888, President O'Neill isolated 'twelve mischievous young men' as the reforming party. In fact, there were fourteen. All were Gregorians. Not all were so young. Cuthbert Butler lists them by initial and sometimes by office. I will list them in the same order as Butler but naming names. The fourteen 'mischievous young men' were Edmund Ford, Bernard Murphy, Aidan Gasquet, Wilfrid Corney, Gilbert Dolan, Joseph Colgan, Cuthbert Butler, Osmund Knight, Wilfrid New, Meinrad Fulton, Conrad Banckaert, Aelred Kindersley, Ethelbert Horne and Stephen Rawlinson. There were also 'a handful' of Gregorian missioners who were in sympathy: Bernard Bulbeck, Anthony Bulbeck, Ephrem Guy and Dunstan Breen, as well as 'one or two Gregorian juniors not in residence at Downside'. But the 'fourteen' are the men who 'were out in '88'.[14]   I do not propose to discuss the contribution of all these Gregorian monks but I will say something about four of them: Gilbert Dolan, Aidan Gasquet, Edmund Ford and Cuthbert Butler. I will conclude this part of the paper by saying a little about three men who don't figure on the 'mischievous' list – Mgr Weld, Dom Laurence Shepherd and Dom Jerome Vaughan – but who nevertheless played an important, if indirect, part in the 'movement'.

First among the reformers perhaps, it is appropriate to place Gilbert Dolan. At Downside as a young monk he acted as monastic librarian and archivist, positions which suited him well, especially at the time that he became one of the chief inspirations behind the building of the new church and monastery. The completed buildings owed much to his preliminary sketches and ideas. From 1884 until his death in 1914, he worked outside the monastery: at Liverpool, Warrington, Woolton and Dulwich, before his appointment in 1894 as chaplain to Stanbrook. In 1899, he went to Ealing where he remained in charge of the mission until 1907. In 1908, after a brief spell at Redditch, he went to Little Malvern where he stayed until his death. Throughout his varied monastic career, he remained a keen student. He wrote, studied and collected books and was a notable benefactor of the monastic library at Downside.[15] According to Butler, Dolan was:

The first of us to get hold of sound principles on Benedictine life and government. He was the only one among us who had read monastic history or had visited monasteries of other Congregations. He was the first among us to cultivate historical and archaeological tastes and studies of the type identical with the Benedictine name; he was very intimate with Dom Shepherd. Dom Dolan thus had ideas very much in advance of the rest of us, and he lost no opportunity of spreading the light. Shortly after my arrival at Downside I spoke to him about putting some books in the library, and remarked that Prior Gasquet advised me to put my name in them, that I might take my name out when I went on the Mission. 'Tush', said Dom Dolan, 'that is all going to be changed; no more going on the Mission unless you want to'. I replied that I certainly hoped such would be the case, and added that I often hoped I might become one of the professors at Belmont, to escape the Mission. 'Oh', interposed Dom Dolan, 'we must do away with Belmont. These common houses are quite unsound for Benedictines. It is the tradition of the Order to have the novices in their own monastery'.

At another time he called my attention to a paragraph in the paper, to the effect that the 'quadriennial demoralisation' preceding the election of the President of the United States had begun. 'That is just the case with us', he said, 'we get thoroughly demoralised before every General Chapter. The quadriennial system is bad and quite opposed to Benedictine traditions; we are the only ones that have it; we must get life–superiors. Fancy a family meeting every four years to elect a Father for the quadriennium!'. These and similar statements staggred and even shocked me at first; but the seed thus broadcast struck root, and by the end of the year I came to see that Dom Dolan's principles were right, and our polity was unique.[16]

Dolan's obituarist in *The Downside Review*, Dom Roger Huddleston, said of him that he was 'too big, too magnificent in his ideals to worry very much about practical details'.[17]

Gasquet, too, had magnificent ideals and whatever his merits as a historian, and these have been often harshly judged, it was the future cardinal who first put the ideals into personal practice. Gasquet was, like Dolan, a native of London (where he was born in 1846), and an old boy of Downside. He was professed in 1867 and was Prior of Downside from 1878–1885. He was involved in more–or–less full–time historical work after 1885 and in 1900 became Abbot President of the EBC.[18] In Butler's memoirs, he is described during his period as prior (an office in which he succeeded Dom Bernard Murphy, whose imagination and drive created the physical environment of Downside and who did so much to foster the reform mentality) as:

keenly alive to the shortcomings of the system then in vogue, and did not conceal his desire for great changes. He more than anyone else embodied the spirit of St Gregory's in its many–sided phases; he was the most representative Downside man of the day. He had not then very clear views — none of us had; principles were a gradual growth; he was often inconsistent; but his heart was in the right place. The day before my solemn profession I went to confession to him, he exhorted me to pray while prostrate on the pall, when it is piously believed all prayers are heard, that Almighty God would bring about a revival of monastic life and observance in the Congregation.[19]

It was after his breakdown in health that Gasquet's real contribution to the movement came. He took to the life of the monk—scholar and he became a respected member of the London historical scene. Coulton had not as yet sharpened his knives. Enemies were closer to home. Conservative elements in the Congregation had attempted to nip his historical work in the bud. His first historical interest was the dissolution of the monasteries under Henry VIII and the truth or falsehood of the charges against the monks, 'still believed on all hands'.

> After he had made some progress at his work, and his book on Henry VIII and the English monasteries was planned, and well advanced in execution, he received from President O'Gorman orders to go on the mission as his health was sufficiently restored, and the sort of work he was engaged on could be allowed only to an invalid. He represented to the President the importance of clearing the reputation of the monks of Henry VIII's reign, and of vindicating their good name. 'No; no life—work but missionary work was legitimate for an English Benedictine'. Fr G's studies were of course known to a wide circle of Cath(olic)s and others, and among others, to Cardinal Manning, an old family friend and connection by marriage to Fr Gasquet's brother. So Fr G went to say good—bye to him, and tell him he had to go to Acton Burnell — I think it was. Cardinal Manning had been keenly interested in Fr G's investigations, and deeply impressed as to their value, and importance, for religion in England. He said nothing, but wrote to Rome, and got the Pope to send instructions to the President that Fr G. should not be moved from his present sphere of work. The President obeyed but with a regret expressed in (a) letter to Fr G... Thus the inauguration of serious historical work in the Congregation was in spite of the superiors, by the personal act of Leo XIII, at Cardinal Manning's instance.[20]

This academic work of Gasquet, always backed up by he genuine scholarship of Edmund Bishop, ushered in the arcadian period so beautifully evoked in the opening chapter of Dom Adrian Morey's memoir of Dom David Knowles published in 1979.[21] The scholarship of Gasquet was both an instrument in working for a more monastic outlook in the Congregation, and a sign, especially with his appointment as cardinal in 1914, the centenary year of the arrival of St Gregory's at Downside, of its rapid accomplishment.

The most active and influential member of the reforming party was, at least in its early state, however, undoubtedly Hugh Edmund Ford who was to become the first Abbot of Downside in 1900.[22] Ford was a native of Bristol (where he was born in 1851) and an Old Gregorian. Like all the leading protagonists of the reform, he had done his novitiate at Belmont. He made his profession in 1870 and was ordained priest in 1877. During his years of training, his health, never robust, was particularly poor, and he spent much of his time outside the monastery. This was used in evidence against him when he preached on stricter observance. Ford was a man of charm and great qualities of leadership, which he was able to use in his first difficult term as superior after 1885. He managed to attract and keep disciples. There was no doubt that he was on the side of change and that he was the kind of man who could turn ideas into action. Butler thought that he was just the right man for the job:

> I saw him to be a man of extraordinary ability, with a clear head, cool judgement, great determination and much tact in dealing with men and pushing his views. His opponents and even some of those who approved of his policy thought him a schemer who would deliberately work for a crisis in order to run his views. He was much distrusted in many quarters; but I became very attached to him and used warmly to defend him. Before I had been three months at Downside I made up my mind that he was *the man* to carry changes in the Congregation.[23]

The changes which were carried in 'Diu quidem' were pushed forward with tenacity by Prior Ford especially in the difficult years between 1894 and 1899 when the war seemed almost over but the outcome of the final battle was as yet unsettled. Butler continued:

> He urged now, as he had done all along from the beginning, that the government and the monasteries of the Congregation should be in conformity with what was the universal practice among Benedictines. He maintained that the English Benedictines had for many decades lived under a *lex particularis*, especially framed to meet the abnormal circumstances which had long ceased to operate. The continuance of such a system was unreasonable and illogical. But human nature is notoriously conservative, and conscientious men, acting on principle, are not easy to move.[24]

Ford, despite making enemies, caused many men to move.

Edward Cuthbert Butler (1858–1934) was a scholar, and he provided Ford with the intellectual ammunition which he required for the fight. Butler, Irish by birth, Gregorian by education, Belmont by novitiate, came to a 'monastic' view early in his career.[25]   He was much impressed, at the time of Prior Krug's visitation, by the visitor's monastic principles 'which coincided substantially with those of Dom Guéranger and Abbot Wolter's *Elementa*'.[26] Again, I turn to Butler's account:

> His advocacy of his own views was a serious indiscretion on Prior Krug's part; the cry was soon raised that he was going beyond his powers and was indoctrinating the young men. This and the frequent visitations paid to certain Bishops and prominent laymen, well-known to be much opposed to the state of things in the Congregation, greatly aggravated the enmity felt towards the Visitation by the bulk of the Congregation, and raised quite a storm of indignation. But this is anticipating. Fr Krug and I got on very well together, and were both much pleased with our conference. He asked me, like the rest, to put down on paper the sum of what I had said, and expressed his conviction that things would soon be put on a sound basis for us. I still have the rough draft of the paper I gave him; and I think it will be of interest to put down here the heads of what I suggested in 1881, as it will show how little I have had to change my views during the course of the Movement.

I advocated (A) that a definition of our monastic contemplative character should be given; that it should be made clear that the monasteries are supposita i.e. sui juris et undique, not seminaries for the missions or staffs of professors for the schools.

1. That missions and missioners should be put under the monastic superiors.

2. That the monasteries should be erected into Abbeys, and the Abbots eventually be chosen for life.

3. That as soon as the monasteries were ready for it, they should each have their own novitiate.

4. That General Chapter should be reformed, so as to lessen the missionary and strengthen the house element.

5. That the individual monks should be given some kind of fixity of tenure in the monastery; so that they might look forward, during good behaviour, to remaining in their monastery if they felt that such was their vocation.

6. The reorganisation of the studies.

7. An improvement in the discipline of the monasteries.

8. The appointment of a Rector to work the School.

9. A change in the Vacation system.

10. The erection of Missionary Priories and better discipline in the Missions.

Except for a few natural developments it will be seen that this programme is substantially the one that has been kept to throughout. I fancy half a dozen or so of those at St Gregory's in 1881 made suggestions practically identical with mine; as for the rest of the Community, some would have gone in for some parts of it, and others for others — some more, some less. But speaking broadly, I believe it is true to say that at that time Downside went solid for reform.[27]

Indeed, in Butler's view perhaps the Congregation itself, at least implicitly, was 'solid for reform'. He concluded in his *Notes on the Origin and Early Development of the Restored Benedictine Congregation, 1600–1661* that the move towards reform was not a break with the past but a rediscovery of it:

From what has been brought forward in the preceding pages it is clear that the movement towards a monastic revival in the English Benedictine congregation is in no way revolutionary or subversive of the institute. Though custom and prescription can do much, they cannot change the essence of the congregation, which must be the same now as it was in 1633. Those if its members, therefore, who, while desiring that it may retain its missionary character, desire too that, in view of the altered politico–religious condition of England, it may enter more fully into the spirit of the monastic Rule of St Benedict, so that alongside of the missionary element there may be an equally strong and recognised monastic element; aim at nothing else than the application to present circumstances of the principles and methods that prevailed among the first two generations of the Restored English Benedictine Congregation.[28]

Throughout his presentation of the monastic case, he emphasised the essentially monastic character of the EBC.[29] He saw this monastic character as being only fully enshrined in the Benedictine 'family' idea and as being much facilitated by fuller monastic studies, and was the leading theorist of the movement, the man who more than any other expressed its highest aspirations.

As a young monk, Butler had been impressed by the monastic spirit advocated at retreat conferences and in conversation by Monsignor Weld. I have referred in passing once or twice to the pamphlet war which the reform movement prompted. Monsignor Weld was the author of a pamphlet, *The English Benedictines* (1882), which includes some of the more out–spoken attacks on the old Congregation. Weld maintained that there was a good spirit within the Congregation but he was prepared to criticise abuse with a force which seemed to combine the rhetoric of Reformation debate with the shock–horror tactics of the Victorian 'penny dreadful'.[30]

Monsignor Francis Weld was a member of the well–known Dorset Catholic family. Born in 1819, he was at Downside in the school from 1831–1836. He went to Rome for his theological studies and was ordained priest in March 1842. He was appointed a Domestic Prelate by Gregory XVI and later promoted Protonotary Apostolic. He ministered first in the West Country (he was chaplain at Lanheerne Convent from 1844–48) and later in the Westminster diocese where, from 1855 to 1896, he was missionary rector at Isleworth. He was a material benefactor to his old school and a consistent advocate of reform. His activities in Rome and the success of his propaganda were crucial ingredients in the success of the movement.[31]

Lest it be thought that the movement reflected only a Downside inclination, the pioneer work of Dom Laurence Shepherd of Ampleforth must not be forgotten. Laurence Shepherd (1926–1885) was the greatest English advocate of the French monastic ideal associated with Dom Prosper Gueranger (whose Année Liturgique he translated) and Solesmes. At Stanbrook, the women's monastery near Worcester, where he was chaplain from 1863–85, he was able to give practical expression to his ideals.[32] Father Shepherd gave the community retreat at Downside in the Lent of 1882. In the extract that follows, 'Fr S' is Dom Laurence Shepherd, 'Fr B' is Dom Austin Bury, in the first instance, and after that Dom Augustine Baker, 'Fr R' is Dom Wilfred Raynal, 'D.G.' is Abbot Guéranger, 'S.S.' is *Sancta Sophia*:

> As a young monk he (Dom Shepherd) and Fr B had been sent to Italy, the former to study asceticism and monasticism in the Italian monasteries, the latter to study theology. It is curious that they became the two most extreme men in the Congregation at opposite poles. Fr S visited Solesmes in the early days and became a close friend of D.G., and for many years he spent his summer holiday at Solesmes and became saturated through and through with D.G.'s spirit and views of the monastic life. This was what he

set before us at the Retreat. It had a great effect on many of us, certainly it had on me, permanently modifying many of the ideas I had previously held on Benedictine life ...

Fr S showed that in some matters of first moment (S.S's.) teaching is not in accord with the best Benedictine traditions. We had of course been taught to value and love the chanting of the Office, and it had been clearly put before us, especially by Fr R, the first duty of monks; but Fr B puts the duty of mental prayer above the Office as the higher prayer and real means of attaining to the spiritual life, and he would even turn the Office into a sort of mental prayer. When Fr S put before us the fine doctrine (*sic*), especially did he emphasise the fine doctrine of the Preface Général to the An(née) Lit(urgique), in my judgement by far the best piece of all Guér(anger)'s writings I have ever seen; according to this teaching he urged upon us the view that the choral celebration of the Office is not only our great and first corporate duty and public act of Divine worship as a Benedictine Community — this of course we held; but also as individual monks it is our chief means of personal sanctification and of progress in the spiritual life. We had, many of us, more or less, been brought up on Fr B, who attached greater value to the exercise of interior or mental prayer, and certainly tended to depreciate the Office, and to look for progress in spirituality only, or mainly, from interior prayer. Another point insisted on by Fr S was the place held in Benedictine life by higher ecclesiastical studies — the Bible, the Liturgy, the Fathers, the Councils, the Commentators, the theologians, the canonists, the Church historians. 'If I went round your cells', he said, 'and found on the table of one a volume of your own Saint Gregory and on another Cassian, on another a volume of the Boll(andist)s, or of Cornelius a Lap(ide), or Thomassinus, and so on: I should say that here is a Community which in spite of the busy life it leads, has its heart steadfastly fixed on the Benedictine life'. After more than 20 years I remember the words well, for this making of ecclesiastical studies an integral part of Benedictine life not only was altogether congenial to my own bent, but it removed a difference I had always felt in Fr Baker's teaching: he barely tolerates such studies — indeed there is no place for them in his system — though in his life he cultivated them. I had felt that on his ideal of a Benedictine vocation there was no place for a Mab(illon) or even a Venerable Bede — and yet they were nearly ideal Benedictine monks; and that if Fr B's views had always prevailed, the history of the Order would have been different from what it was. So I realised once for all that Fr B must here again be given up. On one side of the life, his teaching was still good and applicable, but as a complete philosophy of Benedictine life he had to be abandoned.

Fr S. spoke freely and strongly on the controversies and struggles going on in the Congregation, and one of the Conferences was a veritable call to arms: — though a minority, we hold together and fight till we have won the victory. On some points Fr S went beyond anything that has ever been contended for in Downside. Not only did he advocate the complete abandonment of extra claustral work, but also the closing of the School. But in spite of

these points wherein no one followed him, the Retreat made a great
impression: nearly all were pleased, and the extremists were
delighted.[33]

While 'the extremists' were delighted in Father Laurence's discourses,
another monk, a Gregorian by profession, was attempting at Fort Augustus to
implement a fully observant Benedictine monasticism.   This was Dom Jerome
Vaughan (1841–1896), the fourth son of Colonel and Eliza Vaughan and the
brother of Cardinal Herbert Vaughan and Archbishop Roger Bede Vaughan.   He
was educated at Downside and did his novitiate and studies at Belmont, being
professed in 1861.   In 1863, on grounds of ill–health, he was sent to Monte
Cassino where he made his solemn profession as a monk of Downside.   After
finishing his studies in Italy, he spent six months at Solesmes.   He was ordained
priest in 1867.   He worked at Belmont for several years as professor of Sacred
Scripture and Junior Master.   He had great skills, notably as a fund–raiser, but
he also suffered from a scrupulous and histrionic temperament that was
characteristic of his family.   An episode from his time at the Common Novitiate
illustrates this point.   'Those who lived with him at this time will remember how
at the end of a retreat which he gave to the community, he fell on his knees and
begged the pardon of his hearers for his mistakes and unfitness to preach to
them'.[34]   He left Belmont in 1875 and devoted his energies to the founding of a
monastery at Fort Augustus.   It was a difficult and often painful birth, and after
eight years, Dom Jerome left its management to others which included a period
of Beuronese management.   But at Fort Augustus, Dom Jerome had attempted
to build for the first time in the English Congregation a truly monastic setting
for conventual life.   His was a difficult and controversial character but he had
something of the visionary about him and vision was something that was lacking
among the English Black monks.

In 1899 *Diu Quidem*, as we have seen, represented the victory of the
reforming movement within the Congregation, and before I turn to look at the
second half of the movement, lest I appear too parochial, I would like to mention
three other influences which were moving in the same reforming direction as the
movement at Downside.   I will, on account of time, look at them briefly but I
think it would be a mistake not to mention them.

First, then, is the establishment in England of monasteries of a reformed
character outside the EBC.   Erdington has been referred to already.   It was not
the first.   The Cistercians, in their Trappist form, had established as early as the
1790's a fully observant monastic house – an abbey indeed – at Lulworth[35] in
Dorset and their abbey at Mount Saint Bernard in Leicestershire had a truly
'monastic' setting in the buildings of 1844 which A.W.N. Pugin provided them.
In 1848 Mount St Bernard became any abbey.[36]   In 1856 Father Wilfrid Alcock,
an old boy of Ampleforth and a monk of the Subiaco Province of the Cassinese
Congregation arrived at Ramsgate, at the invitation of Bishop Grant of
Southwark, and soon a monastery (erected in 1861) was completed alongside
Pugin's small and beautiful church (which had been built in 1847).   This
monastery – which became an abbey in 1896 – was conducted along Primitive
Observance lines although its troubled early history somewhat its influence and a
number of its monks made their way into the EBC where they were not
conspicuous leaders of reform.[37]   In 1895, at the height of the monastic
controversy, the monks of Solesmes established a house in the buildings erected
in 1880 as a burial place for the Emperor Napoleon III by the Emperor Eugénie
at Farnborough in Hampshire.   This monastery, which was to close in 1946 (the
present Farnborough Abbey in the same buildings is a community of the Subiaco

Congregation) established a great reputation as a centre of scholarship and liturgy.[38]   Perhaps the most important of these monasteries was Buckfast in Devon established in 1882 by the reformed monastery of La Pierre—qui—Vire in France.   Here, on the site of an old Cistercian house, the monks began to rebuild their new monastery and church on the foundations of the old.   'In all the externals of religion the present community desire to renew the broken links in the chain of old English monastic life, and in church furniture, vestments and ritual, to follow the old models, and to really be what their neighbours deem them to be, "the old monks come back again"'.[39]

Second, alongside the parallel growth of Benedictine communities within the Catholic community was the development of the Catholic Revival in the Church of England.   Several monastic foundations were made and some, especially those for women, were notably successful.   At the time that 'the Downside Movement' was stirring, a community was founded by Benjamin Fearnley Carlyle (afterwards Father Aelred) in 1896 on the Isle of Dogs which attempted to establish a Benedictine life in the church.   This community settled on Caldey Island in 1906 and was received into the Catholic Church in 1913.[40] By the last decade of the nineteenth century, many converts — or, more importantly those who came from convert backgrounds (that is with one or both parents being converts to Catholicism) — were entering the Downside *conventus*[41] and this brought, I feel sure, a change of atmosphere from the predominance of 'old Catholic families' (so often Lancastrian) whose close—knit cousinage had perhaps put off the earlier Oxford Converts.[42]   These men from a 'convert' background brought with them much of their Anglo—Catholic devotion to godly order and good taste.   Such an influence should not be entirely neglected in any study of the reform movement in the EBC, especially in its latter stages.

Third, and related to good taste and godly order, is the question of the Gothic Revival in architecture.   The churches constructed by the EBC monks in the nineteenth century were, as far as I know, entirely in the Gothic taste.[43] This reflected an Englishness of outlook — as opposed perhaps to the consciously Italianate buildings of the Oratorians and the ambiguous stylistic stance of the Jesuits.[44]   It reflected, too, a return to the past and if not to St Benedict, who might have felt ill—at—ease in a great Gothic church, at least to the grand claustral buildings of the High Middle Ages, the age *par excellence* of the monasteries.   This revival is nowhere more clearly seen than in the unexecuted designs made by A.W.N. Pugin for Downside in the 1840's.[45]   The moulding force of environment and of buildings is not something that should easily be set aside.

By 1900 much had been achieved in the Congregation.   The major houses had become autonomous abbeys.   Independent novitiates were being re—established.   Monastic studies were being recognizably Benedictines but to some the remaining source of parochial obligations of the Congregation were a barrier to the full observance of the monastic life.   On 13 April 1920, some twenty years after the election of Dom Edmund Ford as first Abbot of Downside, Dom Leander Ramsay,   then Novice Master at Downside, in a letter to Cuthbert Butler summarized what had become the central issue in the minds of those (like Butler and Ramsay) who believed that the momentum of 'the Downside Movement' needed to be continued:

> At the beginning of his Rule S. Benedict tells us that he is legislating for cenobites, and it is plain that in its characteristic features the Rule is inapplicable apart from the conditions of cenobite life.   Thus conventual life lies at the heart of the Rule,

and the desire for such a life — and fitness for it — should be a principal test of vocation to our Order.

On the other hand the conditions which have existed hitherto in the English Congregation make permanent conventual life practically unattainable for those professed in our body.

It follows that unless our large extra–conventual obligations are removed, we cannot offer to prospective subjects any well–grounded hope of stability in the mode of life presupposed by the Rule and therefore those who appear to have a true Benedictine vocation cannot rightly be advised to join us.

All the novices now under my care believe that they have a call to 'the pursuit of holiness' under the conditions of common life and common prayer prescribed by the Rule, and, in my opinion there is good ground for thinking that their belief is well–founded.[46]

The guarantee of a full conventual life for all aspirants to St Gregory's combined with a reduction of 'external', principally missionary, calls on the community's manpower were at the centre of debate in the first twenty years of the present century at Downside. Abbot Cuthbert Butler steered the community for much of this period but in the four great debates on the missions which took place in the Conventual Chapters of 1910, 1919 and 1921, he did not always have an easy ride — as I have suggested elsewhere[47] — and in 1922, he resigned as abbot as a 'final witness to the ideas and beliefs of a lifetime'.[48] But, however disappointed Butler may have been in the completion of reform, the character of the Downside *Conventus* was changing very much in line with the ideas of the monastic party. The exterior character of the life at Downside reflected the change. The abbacies of Ford and Butler witnessed the climax of the great building programme which had begun in earnest in the 1870's. The new abbey church, without doubt then and probably still now, the most splendid of modern English monastic churches, was an expression in stone of the Downside movement.[49] Here was the heart of a great praying community. The opening ceremonies of 1905 included a series of special sermons which 'still recall the first freshness of Downside's advance into the future'.[50] When Pevsner saw the Downside complex, he was reminded of Pugin's dream of a Catholic Gothic England came to life. There is, undoubtedly, a triumphalism in the buildings, a bold assertion of the Second Spring but, it seems to me, that the buildings were not intended (except in a very secondary sense) as revivalist. Gothic was the chosen architectural medium but it has a freshness about it which is unusual in a Neo–Gothic church. The building in its development reflects the changes in the community. There is a movement from imitation to innovation, from continentalism (Pevsner talks of the almost Spanish effusiveness of the transept) to Englishness, from parish church to monastic architecture.[51] The transeptal altar with its exuberant throne for the monstrance would not be out of place in a big Lancastrian Catholic parish church while the nave is almost Cistercian in its purity. The uncompleted West End was a reminder, however, that the future was uncertain and would bring its own challenges. The ensemble of architectural styles reflected a mixed community united in a common pursuit and looking forward, for the most part, to a conventually–based future.

Once the new choir was put into service, liturgy and music could be brought up to standard. The ceremonies at the opening of 1905 were glimpses of things to come. They included 'the blessing performed by the Abbot in procession round the church, with chanting and sprinkling with holy—water both without and within; the singing of *Urbs Jerusalem* to its old Sarum melody; and at five o'clock the carrying of the Blessed Sacrament to its new shrine while *Salve Festa Dies* was sung. Finally Compline was recited by the monks in their new choir, and this was followed by what has become a customary usage at St Gregory's, the signing of the antiphon of Our Lady in her own chapel'.[52]

Many of the things in the 'customary usage' of Downside date from these twenty years. A daily sung conventual mass was introduced as an experiment in 1914.[53] Two years later, in 1916, Dom Bruno Hicks asked the Council for permission to use blue vestments on the Feasts of Our Lady.[54] This custom, often seen as a continuous tradition dating from the Spanish origins of the Congregation, was one of the many innovations made by Dom Bruno (1878–1954), who acted as bursar and master of ceremonies. He was particularly involved in the refurbishment of the vestments to bring them up to the highest monastic standards. In this, he was ably assisted by Dom Anselm Rutherford (1886–1952), a convert, later Headmaster of Downside (1934–1940) and Prior of Worth and Downside. The Hicks/Rutherford style of vestment has survived to this day. Many would think that this full Gothic—style vestment has 'always' been in use at Downside. We should beware the word 'always'. Time out of mind is sometimes the day before yesterday.

Cuthbert Butler was a great advocate of monastic theory and particularly of the study of the monastic past. The short—lived historical house of studies in London and Benet House, Cambridge, of which Butler was first head, brought Downside into the wider academic world of the capital and the ancient universities. The expanding monastic library at Downside provided the wherewithal for professional scholarship. Downside had about it almost a Maurist air which, at least in the opinion of some, it has never quite lost. 'Probably, indeed, the literary output of Gregorians, at Downside or elsewhere, for the decade 1900–10, exceeded in quantity that of any ten years before or since'.[55] This scholarship had a strong missionary aspect to it. The study and interpretation of monastic history, in particular, was intended to back up the reform movement. *Benedictine Monachism* was first published in 1919. These 'Studies in Benedictine Life and Rule' expressed with great clarity and at considerable length Butler's idea of a monastery. It was propaganda masked as history but good history nevertheless. I will not attempt here to look in detail at the monastic view of *Benedictine Monachism*, but it is interesting, however, that Butler's outstanding remark that 'our contribution to the New Era unfolding itself before us will be proportionate to our fidelity to the basic and permanent principles of our Rule',[56] is so close in spirit to the famous purple passage which concludes the final volume of David Knowles' *Religious Orders*,[57] and that he states clearly that external works — mission or parish — are far less important than the spiritual life. 'The real use of a monastic house', he writes, 'lies not in its activities and usefulness' but in its role as 'a reservoir of religion' and its monks men primarily absorbed in 'the pursuit of regligion'.[58]

Butler's 'still centre' view of the monastic quest is too easily forgotten in all the talk about missions and schools. Nevertheless, before returning to the 'still centre', Butler travels through some controversial by—ways. A significant if not prolix part of *Benedictine Monachism* is dedicated to the place of education, that is, the teaching of young lay students, in the Benedictine world picture. Butler, as in all his Benedictine studies, looks beyond the EBC and sees the training of the young as an integral part of the Benedictine apostolate in both the past and the present:

> In modern times, since the Reformation and the Wars of Religion, the external schools have again become common in Benedictine monasteries. Though it is not well known, the Maurists had a number of excellent secular colleges. At the present day, secondary education, whether in boarding schools or in day schools, has come to be perhaps the commonest and best recognised form of Benedictine external work, most of the Black Monk congregations laying themselves out for it. At the reconstitution of the Hungarian Congregation in 1802, the Government made it a condition that the monks should chiefly devote themselves to secondary education; they have six colleges with 2000 pupils. The Austrian monasteries have twelve large colleges with nearly 3000 pupils. The Swiss Congregation has four colleges with 800 pupils, and the Bavarian twelve with 2100. In all these congregations the education is under the full control of the State. In the five schools of the English Congregation are 700 pupils; in those of the Cassinese are 400; and all the American monasteries have schools with a total of 3000 pupils. All told, large and small, there were in 1914 more than a hundred schools attached to the Benedictine monasteries, with an aggregate of over 15,000 pupils.[59]

If it was good enough for the Maurists, he might have said it is good enough for the EBC. During Butler's abbacy, the school at Downside expanded in numbers and modernised its system of education.

Downside school had a long tradition behind it when in 1902 Dom Leander Ramsay was appointed Headmaster. It is easy to look back on the pre—Ramsay school with disdain, but as Dom Adrian Morey has reminded us 'by contemporary standards, the teaching was not perhaps so poor'.[60] Most English schools were underdeveloped before the present century and Downside was typical of many other old—established schools in needing modernisation. This had been spotted by Mgr Lord Petre (1847–93) in the 1870's. His exotic educational theories were much ahead of his time an his benefactions to Downside School gave it a head start in the race for educational efficiency.[61] However good or bad the school was, it still tended to cling to its continental Jesuit—style constitution and its uneconomically small numbers. Ramsay replaced the old prefectorial system and 'line' government by a strong centralised headmastership and a house system. In September 1902, the school numbered 115 boys. By 1908 there were 150. By 1912 there were almost 200 and by 1918, the last year of Dom Leander's term of office, there were 212.[62]

Ramsay's name has come up several times already in this paper and in many ways he was the heir and executor of the Butler tradition. Born in London in 1863, he was educated at King's College School, London, Exeter College, Oxford, and Peterborough Theological College. He became an Anglican clergyman and he found his chief ministry in theological colleges, first at St Augustine's College, Canterbury, and then at Wells where he was Vice—Principal from 1893–95. He was Butler's only convert and entered the Downside novitiate straight from Wells. He was Headmaster of Downside from 1902–18, Novice Master from 1919–22, and Abbot from 1922 until his death in 1929, the first of the three convert clergymen to be Abbots of Downside (the others being John Chapman and Christopher Butler). What he brought to his work as headmaster was a detachment from the Gregorian past, a sound knowledge of modern educational ideas, and a profound pastoral sense.

> Always he looked upon his work at Downside as an Apostolate,
> labouring in hope and trust that those, whose minds and characters
> he strove to form, would carry through life, with the memory of
> their school—days, a courage and a grasp of Christian principle
> which should be absolute, unwavering and indefatigable.[63]

The First World War, in which so many of Ramsay's boys were to fall, cast its shadow on his regime, but in general the Ramsay years were years of great progress. Games and examinations were brought in line with other 'public schools'. Rugby Football began its triumphant progress. Scholarship to Oxford and (particularly) Cambridge were won. 'Indeed it is no exaggeration to say that the results achieved and the standard reached roused the Catholic Schools of England to emulation, and thus helped to bring them as a body to a state of efficiency which they had never before attained'.[64] Dom Leander was very much the father figure in the school and this might explain why, according to Dom Sigebert Trafford, his secretary and successor as Headmaster, he was reluctant to introduce a house system.[65] It is difficult to have too many fathers in a household. Once introduced, however, the system of monk housemasters seemed not only to work, even if some of the early housemasters were little more than companions for the boys, but also to be a system closely in line with the idea of a reformed conventual monastery. The housemasters could be seen as deans within the family of the school in so many ways parallel to the monastery. Cardinal Hume, talking about his time as housemaster at Ampleforth wrote:

> I was, as the father of this little community, teaching its members
> to live the Christian life and be members of a community. I was
> there as their priest, as if presiding over a small parish.[66]

No better system of integrating the community life of the monastery into the monastic school than the monk—housemaster regime has yet been devised. Dom Leander Ramsay's death brought to an end the great period of continuous reform at Downside. Dom David Knowles, the perfect Downside schoolboy and young monk, was an obvious successor at the next election, but his defection from the monastic mainstream, following his own attempt at reform which aimed at moving Downside from its Cluniac to its Cistercian phase, left the field open to others.

It is difficult, at the end of such as impressionistic survey of the reform movement within the EBC, to make a concluding statement. The EBC and Downside continue and develop, and any final word on the question of the impact of the reform is not quite appropriate. A living religious community is an organic growth which is not easily broken into component parts or periods. Moreover, its aspirations and ideals are only truly realized eschatalogically. Continuous reform, daily conversion, is at the heart of every monastic quest. Nevertheless, some trends emerge which are characteristic of the years 1880—1920 in the EBC and which might be of wider application.

First, as I hope I have hinted (but not expanded), the transformation (and that is not too strong a word) of the EBC in the years before and after 1900 was part of a wider attempt within the Church to come to terms with the meaning of monastic life in an increasingly secularist and anti—clerical world. The magnificent foolishness of the complete monastic observance can be seen as an effective antidote to a secular world which dismisses Christian values.

Monasticism, in its reformed model, is an expression of the possibility of a fully–led Christian life, a necessary witness in a world which increasingly sought temporal answers to the ultimate questions posed by eternity. Moreover, in the eyes of the Church, the monasteries by their prayers and by their scholarship could provide specialised troops for 'the Pope's Divisions'. The English Benedictines, for all their Englishness, were part of a wider Church and their reform part of a wider monastic reform.

But, secondly, the particular character of the monastic reform in England owed much to the personalities and the interactions of individual leaders of reform. Charismatic leaders are as necessary a part of any reform movement as hierarchical leadership. At Downside, Ford and Butler in particular were the men for the time. They provided the necessary ingredient of vision which transforms a religious movement into a religious ideal. The emphasis I have placed on individuals is, I think, justified not only by the evidence but also by the fact that within the monastic tradition the place of the abbot, the father, the prophet of the community is always central. Vision and prophecy are not abstractions but individual gifts. Those who follow the monastic path must never forget this.

Thirdly, and lastly, the search for reform is an essential and continuing part of the search for God which is at the heart of the monk's life. The title of this paper is 'the search for a monastic identity' and this could be applied just as pertinently to all periods of monastic history. What is a monk? What is monasticism? What is the nature of the monastic community? Fundamental questions. Such questions were at the root of the monastic reform movement at Downside and within the EBC. They are the basic questions to which all monks and nuns address themselves every day of their lives.

NOTES

This paper is based in part on two addresses to the English Benedictine History Symposium which have been published as 'The Downside 'Stirs': Personalities, Principles, Documentation', *EBC History Symposium* 6 (1986), pp 11–66 and 'Vingt ans après: Downside from Ford to Knowles', *EBC History Symposium* 7 (1987), pp 2–27. The first of these has an extensive bibliography.

1.   For the history and development of the revived EBC see D.Lunn, *The English Benedictines 1540–1688* (London, 1980).
2.   See H.N. Birt, *Downside* (London, 1902) for a general survey of Downside History.
3.   See J.A. Williams, *Bath and Rome: The Living Link* (Bath, 1963) for the Benedictine mission in Bath.
4.   W.B. Ullathorne, *Ecclesiastical Discourses* (London, 1876), p 320.
5.   Downside Abbey Archives (henceforth DAA), Downside Movement Collection, 'Recollections of Abbot Burge' (Extraordinary General Chapter of 1889), p 5.
6.   B. Whelan, *The Annals of the English Benedictines 1850–1900* (Privately Printed, 1932), Volume 2, p 6. I have relied heavily on Whelan for the historical account.
7.   *Ibid.*, p 18.
8.   Much of David Knowles account of the moment is based on the contemporary report of Cuthbert Butler. In Box B of Dom Cuthbert Butler's papers (DAA, 1435), there are two typescript accounts of the

Downside Movement.   In referring to them I will use the criteria
established by Knowles.   'The one', he writes, 'by far the shorter, was
begun 1 October 1891, and apparently written in entirety at least within
six months; it carries the story only so far as the summer of 1881. It is
lively, in tone. I refer to this as MS. A. The second, five or six times as
long, was also apparently written all at one time; it was completed on 18
February 1905. It presupposes the earlier narrative (which it occasionally
supplements) as far as the summer of 1881, and then carries the story
down to the election of Abbot Ford in 1900. It is somewhat more soberly
written, and marginal notes show that it had been carefully read by
Edmund bishop and others. I refer to it as MS. B.' (M.D. Knowles,
'Abbot Butler: a Memoir', in his *The Historian and Character*
(Cambridge 1963), p 266n.

9.   MS. A, p 22.
10.   B. Whelan, *Annals*, pp 22–3.
11.   *Ibid.*, pp 57–8.
12.   MS. B, p 43.
13.   MS. A, pp 13–16.
14.   MS. B, pp 77–8.
15.   Obituary of Gilbert Dolan, *Downside Review* 33 (1914), pp 252–4.
16.   MS. A, pp 19–20.
17.   *Downside Review* 33 (1914), p 253.
18.   For a brief biographical and archival introduction to Cardinal Gasquet,
        see D. Bellenger, 'Cardinal Gasquet's Papers at Downside', *Catholic
        Archives* 4 (1984), pp 40–47. A new biography is needed to replace S.
        Leslie, Cardinal Gasquet (London, 1953) which is too episodic.
19.   MS. A, p 17.
20.   MS. B, p 39.
21.   A. Morey, *David Knowles, a memoir* (London, 1979).
22.   Ford is the subject of a rather hagiographical biography by one of his
        abbatial successors, Dom Bruno Hicks (Fifth Abbot of Downside), *Hugh
        Edmund Ford* (London, 1947).
23.   MS. A, p 21.
24.   *Ibid.*
25.   See R. Yeo and L. Maidlow Davis, 'Abbot Cuthbert Butler, 1858–1934',
        Studia Anselmiana 84 (1982), p 92.
26.   MS. A, p 27.
27.   *Ibid.*, pp 28–9.
28.   C. Butler, '*Notes on ... English Benedictine Congregation*' (Privately
        Printed, 1887), p 60.
29.   Cuthbert Butler's annotated and marked copy of 'Religiosus Ordo'
        (DAA, Butler Papers, Constitutional Controversy) reveals the strength of
        Butler's belief.
30.   See, for example, pp 24–5.
31.   Biographical details from *Downside Review* 17 (1898), pp 291–2.
32.   E. Edwards and M. Truran, 'Dom James Laurence Shepherd', *EBC
        History Symposium* 5 (1985), pp 37–59.
33.   MS. B, pp 17–19.
34.   *Downside Review* 15 (1896), p 293.
35.   See D.A. Bellenger, 'A Standing Miracle': La Trappe at Lulworth
        1794–1817, *Studies in Church History* 22 (1985), pp 343–350.
36.   For a modern survey of the Cistercian spirit and history see L.J. Lekai,
        The Cistercians: Ideals and Realities (Kent State, 1977).
37.   For Ramsgate see D. Parry, *Monastic Century* (Tenbury Wells, 1965).
        Dom Anselm O'Gorman (1833–1901), President General 1883–88 and

1896–99 was among those who transferred his stability from the Cassinese to the English. There were four at Downside, John Stutter (1842–1922), Dunstan Sweeney (1845–1929) and the two O'Hare brothers, Julian (1842–1921) and Richard (1844–1906). All four spent most of their monastic lives on the missions and were not among the 'reforming party'.

38.   For a brief history of Farnborough see D. Higham 'Farnborough Abbey. A Monastic Centenary', *South Western Catholic History* 6 (1988), pp 13–16. Dom Leander Hogg of Farnborough is presently (1989) engaged on a fuller study.

39.   St George Mivart, 'A Devonshire Relic', *Merry England* 2 (1884), p 401. See also E. Graf, *Anscar Vonier: Abbot of Buckfast* (London, 1957).

40.   See P.F. Anson, *The Benedictines of Caldey* (London, 1940), and R.M. ollar, 'Archbishop Davidson, Bishop Gore and Abbot Carlyle: Benedictine monks in the Anglican Church', *Studies in Church History* 22 (1985), pp 377–96.

41.   A thorough examination of the convert ancestry of the Downside community has yet to be made, but it is significant perhaps that Abbot Ford had a convert father and Abbot Cuthbert Butler a convert grandfather.

42.   See J.C.H. Aveling, 'The Eighteenth–Century English Benedictines', in ed., E. Duffy *Challoner and his Church* (London, 1981), p 161.

43.   See R.M. O'Donnell, 'Benedictine Building in the Nineteenth Century', *EBC History Symposium* 3 (1983), pp 38–48.

44.   See B. Little, *Catholic Churches since 1623* (London, 1966) for the development of Catholic architecture in the nineteenth century.

45.   R.M. O'Donnell, 'Pugin's designs for Downside Abbey', *The Burlington Magazine*, April 1981, pp 230–33.

46.   D.A.A. (Monastic Controversy) 1404. Ramsay to Butler, 13 April 1920.

47.   D.A. Bellenger, 'Vingt ans après: Downside from Ford to Knowles', *EBS History Symposium* 7 (1987), pp 3–12.

48.   *Ibid.*, p 12.

49.   See A. James, *The Story of Downside Abbey Church* (Downside 1961).

50.   *Ibid.*, p 55. The three sermons were by Bishop Hedley on 'The Monastic Choir', Cardinal Gasquet on 'The Makers of St Gregory's' and Bishop Burton on 'Light after Dark'.

51.   N. Pevsner, *North Somerset and Bristol* (Harmondsworth, 1958), pp 182–3.

52.   James, *Downside Abbey Church*, p 55.

53.   D.A.A. Council Book, 24 November 1914.

54.   *Ibid.*, 7 February 1916.

55.   D. Knowles, *The Historian and Character* (Cambridge, 1963), p 305.

56.   C. Butler, *Benedictine Monachism* (London, Second Edition, 1924), p 383.

57.   D. Knowles, *The Religious Orders in England* 3 (Cambridge, 1959), p 468.

58.   Butler, *Benedictine Monachism*, p 383.

59.   *Ibid.*, p 326.

60.   Morey, *David Knowles*, p 7.

61.   See S. Foster, 'Mgr Lord Petre and Downside', *South Western Catholic History* 2 (1984), pp 8–11.

62.   *Downside Review* 47 (1929), p 10.

63.   *Ibid.*, p 121.

64.   *Ibid.*, p 112.

65.   D.A.A., Memoirs of Abbot Trafford, p 23.

66.   B. Hume, 'Searching for God', quoted in ed., T.Castle, *Basil Hume* (London, 1986), pp 48–9.

APPENDIX

IN COMMENDATION OF A MONASTIC EMDEN: PROSOPOGRAPHIC SOURCE MATERIAL FOR ENGLISH MEDIEVAL BENEDICTINE HISTORY

Joan Greatrex

Medieval historians and scholars in general have long been grateful to Dr A.B. Emden for his biographical registers of the universities of Oxford and Cambridge to A.D. 1500, with their several supplements which include a volume bringing the Oxford data to 1540.[1] This was an impressive undertaking, an invaluable reference tool that we now take for granted. Absorbed in our own research niches, where our problems have often been alleviated if not resolved as a result of his endeavours, we may perhaps be pardoned for our failure to marvel that his example has not been followed in other areas. In fact, he went on to produce a survey and list of the English Dominicans;[2] but apart from the much earlier directory of Westminster monks by Canon Pearce (1916) and the rather confusing compilation of the medieval lists of the monks of Christ Church, Canterbury, by W.G. Searle (1902),[3] there appears to be little enthusiasm to take up Emden's mantle. However, there have been a few scholars working quietly away along similar lines whose work has not been published. For example, the late Seiriol Evans, a former Dean of Gloucester, who most generously shared with me his register of Ely monks, and Bishop John Moorman who completed a register of the English Franciscans before his death.[4]

Some fifteen years ago, when embarking on the research for my forthcoming comparative study of the English monastic cathedrals in the later middle ages, I decided to work simultaneously on the preparation of a register of all the monks of these monasteries from their foundation to their dissolution. Because of the vast abundance of source materials the study has been narrowed to the fourteenth century,[5] and because the register of Durham monks was found to be in preparation by Alan Piper, the latter project is now confined to the province of Canterbury. The monastic register which is here envisaged will, we hope include all nine monastic chapters, that is Durham in the northern province of York, and Bath, Canterbury, Coventry, Ely, Norwich, Rochester, Winchester and Worcester in the southern province. These nine chapters represent just over half of the seventeen later medieval dioceses;[6] and, as already noted, they are fertile ground for study because of the wealth of muniments, manuscripts and other records which have escaped the hands of the plunderer and the ravages of time. Other monastic establishments like Gloucester, Peterborough and Glastonbury suffered much less from both, while St Albans and Bury St Edmunds are perhaps the two most important abbeys whose records are plentiful and would surely prove fruitful sources for monastic personnel.[7]

The register now in preparation will provide a large enough sample to be used for comparative purposes since the priories, located in urban centres in north, south, east and west, drew most of their recruits from the surrounding regions as the use of toponymics in place of family names makes plain. At the same time it will comprise a small enough community, and one which is clearly defined by its Benedictine framework; to enable it to provide valuable source material as an aid to prosopographical analysis in the field of monastic studies.

The total number of monks involved will probably not be above 7,500, and of these about 5,700 have already been recorded, that is, approximately three quarters. (The Durham total, which Mr Piper considers to be complete, stands at 1400 and has been included in both figures.) The Canterbury profession and obituary lists, a little less complete than those of Durham, provide us with the names of well over a thousand monks between the conquest and the Dissolution, but there are a number of gaps which are gradually being filled by research in other records. References to the monks of all nine chapters are scattered throughout the monastic, episcopal and archiepiscopal registers, and are found on all of the extant obedientiary account rolls; these rolls number several thousand.

Among the particulars that occur most frequently are the admission and profession dates, the four ordination dates, the periods of university study, the order of seniority within the community and the date of death or departure. From this type of information we can often deduce fluctuations in the age of entry and sometimes the age at which monks were first sent away to university, as well as the average life span of the monks at different periods. Details of office—holding and other responsibilities within and outside the monastery are also plentiful, and these enable us to discern, for example, any pattern of administrative organization that may have evolved or, possibly, at a certain point of time been introduced. In addition we are given some insight into the personal character, attributes and skills of many monks. There were some who readily shared their pittance or pocket money by contributing to worthy causes such as building projects within the cloister, obedientiary offices struggling with a burden of debt, the purchase of land, or the provision of a new index to the manuscripts in the monastic library.[8] Others are distinguished by their musical interests and ability, their administrative and diplomatic skills, their learning, or their preaching talents, and a few by their restlessness and disobedience. Some of these last either migrated to another house or order[9] or, in a few cases, were allowed to serve as parish priests; and a small number who departed without leave were declared apostate and therefore excommunicate.[10]

In order to serve the dual function I have outlined above, the usefulness of this monastic register would be greatly enhanced if it were to be furnished with a number of subject indexes to permit ready access to different classes of information located under the names of individual monks. Subject headings such as Treasurers, Cellarers (and other obedientiary offices),. Books and Libraries, University Studies, Apostates, and so on would facilitate the compilation and collation of data for comparative and statistical purposes.

An appendix listing population statistics for each of the cathedral priories at fairly frequent intervals when these are available — and here the obedientiary accounts are an excellent and still rarely used source — would also provide valuable working data for further research on the model of Dr John Hatcher's study of fifteenth century morality rates based on evidence from the Canterbury chapter, and also those of Miss Barbara Harvey in conjunction with the Cambridge Group of the History of Population and Social Structure, based on Westminster and as yet unpublished. Together the latter have analysed patterns of life expectancy, fluctuations in age structure and morality ratios between 1390 and 1515.[11]

Preparatory work for this register has shown that Emden's records of university attendance of the monks of cathedral priories is by no means complete. At Norwich, for instance, over twenty new names have come to light as well as much additional information concerning those whom he has noted. As a result of extensive research in all of the manuscript sources I have found that the Norwich chapter has an unrivalled and almost unbroken year by year record of university attendance from 1290 to 1530; the proportion of monks selected for study was about one in seven, far better than the one in twenty required by the Benedictine General Chapter and an unexpected compeer for Canterbury with its ratio of one in eight.[12]   The standing of the other cathedral priories will be readily ascertainable by reference to the completed register.

A few biographic summaries will serve to illustrate the diversity of circumstances and the range of activities and accomplishments which have been and are being revealed, and also to remove any doubt that even a meagre store of factual evidence can begin to clothe names with some degree of personality; they are chosen from among the individual entries of those monks who may be described as the ordinary majority, that is those who did nothing remarkable enough to make the medieval headlines and who remain largely unnoticed to this day.[13]

First, Ralph Mascal of Winchester, son of John Mascal, *nativus* and reeve of the priory of Stockton, Wilts.   His manumission is not recorded, but he probably entered the community shortly before his ordination as acolyte in 1412. The father's manumission is dated 1417 and a corrody within the monastery was granted to him three years later, no doubt for his retirement.   The son went on to hold the important office of curtarian or cellarer and also that of infirmarer, and his monastic career spanned over thirty—five years.   Next, there is Ralph Basyng, another Winchester monk, who served the community for about half a century, about twenty years of which he spent in the office of hordarian.   The year 1375, when he obtained his master's degree at Oxford, is known only because the manorial account of Woolstone, another Winchester manor and conveniently close to Oxford, notes the expense of twelve capons sent to M, Ralph for the celebration.

A Norwich monk, by the name of Richard de Walsham, was discovered to have leprosy in 1456 while he was holding the office of prior of St Leonard's cell which lay on the outskirts of the city.   In the 1430s and 1440s he had served as master of the cellar and sacrist, and he seems to have been generous of spirit with small gifts of money to his brethren.   He had also been chosen by Bishop Brouns as a diocesan penitentiary and is known to have bequeathed at least one book to the monastic library.   Prior John Molt issued a charter allowing Walsham to continue to live at St Leonard's, but in isolation, and adequate supplies of food, clothing and other items were allocated to provide for all his needs.   Roger de Eston, also of Norwich, studied at Oxford between 1324 and 1327, and must have soon been recognised as skilled in diplomatic negotiations for the prior sent him on several missions both to the bishop and the king.   The sacrist's account for 1329 records the day to day travelling expenses of Eston's journey to Avignon via Paris and Nevers and also the money spent during the eleven week stay in the papal curia in order to press the chapter's suit against the archbishop of Canterbury over their rights regarding *sede vacante* jurisdiction.

Thomas Elys was professed at Christ Church Canterbury in 1367 and received minor and major orders during the following four years.   For the next four decades he lived a quiet but useful life serving as novice master and fourth prior, and later as third prior.   By 1395 he had moved up to seventeenth in order of seniority and the following year he was appointed one of the two anniversarians.

Robert de Sutton of Ely was put in charge of a succession of responsible offices there is the second half of the fourteenth century including those of sacrist, chamberlain and cellarer. His intellectual abilities are also revealed by his appointment as *instructor iuvenum* in the 1360s and as chancellor of the chapter in the 1380s, and he was chosen to preach in the presence of Archbishop Wittlesey's official who performed a visitation during the 1373 vacancy of the episcopal see.

Finally, at Worcester there occurs the only monk so far identified as a permanent *conversus* or lay brother. He was always referred to as 'brother John *conversus*' and as such was allotted his share of pittances, pocket money, clothing and other supplies during a twenty year period in the mid–fourteenth century. His training and talents appear to have been in the line of construction, and several of the entries suggest that he may have been a stone mason and possibly served the priory in the office of *magister operum* which at Worcester was dependent on the cellarer.

NOTES

1. *A Biographic Register of the University of Oxford to A.D. 1500* in three volumes (Oxford, 1957–1959) and *A Biographical Register of the University of Cambridge to A.D. 1500* (Cambridge, 1963).
2. *A Survey of Dominicans in England Based on the Ordination Lists and Episcopal Registers (1268 to 1538)*, (Rome, 1967).
3. E.H. Pearce, *The Monks of Westminster; Being a Register of the Brethren of the Convent from the time of the Confessor to the Dissolution, with Lists of the Obedientiaries*, (Cambridge, 1916), and W.G. Searle, 'Lists of the Deans, Priors and Monks of Christ Church Monastery' in *Christ Church Canterbury* (Cambridge Antiquarian Society Publications, Octavo Series XXXIV), 1902, pp 157–196.
4. I am indebted to Mr Alan Piper for the information about Bishop Moorman's work.
5. This decision was also based on the fact that Professor R.B. Dobson had planned a similar study, and generously agreed to limit his attention to the fifteenth and early sixteenth centuries.
6. Two of the seventeen bishops, viz., those of Bath and Wells and of Coventry and Lichfield, had to cope with both a monastic and a secular chapter.
7. Dr Antonia Gransden is working on the Bury records.
8. These examples have all been found on obedientiary accounts, references for which are in my files.
9. And some, of course, migrated *to* one of the cathedral priories *from* another religious house.
10. Professor Donald Logan of Emmanuel College, Boston, Massachusetts is currently preparing a study of apostate monks.
11. Miss Harvey's forthcoming volume based on her recent Ford lectures will no doubt incorporate these analyses.
12. These conclusions are to be found in 'Monk Students at Oxford and Cambridge: the Attendance Records and Achievements of Norwich Cathedral Chapter A.D. 1300–1530' — an article which I have recently completed and hope to publish in the near future.
13. See note 8 above.